# Trademark Acknowledgements

Wrox has endeavored to provide trademark information about all the companies and products mentioned in this book by the appropriate use of capitals. However, Wrox cannot guarantee the accuracy of this information.

# Credits

**Lead Author**
Bjarki Hólm

**Authors**
John Carnell
Jaeda Goodman
Ben Marcotte
Kevin Mukhar
Mauricio Naranjo
Mark Piermarini
Anand Raaj
Dr. P. G. Sarang
Sant Singh
Tomas Stubbs

**Technical Contributor**
Thomas Kyte

**Technical Architect**
Tony Davis

**Technical Editors**
John R. Chapman
Mankee Cheng
Nilesh Parmar
Mohammed Rfaquat

**Managing Editor**
Louay Fatoohi

**Author Agent**
Lorraine Clarke

**Project Administrator**
Claire Robinson

**Technical Reviewers**
Daryl Collins
Chris Crane
Michael Dean
Howard Freckleton
Jaeda Goodman
Ann Horton
Frank Hubeny
Thomas Kyte
Ramesh Mani
Ben Marcotte
Jon Millard
Dave Moore
Kevin Mukhar
Vincent Morris
Mark Piermarini
Phil Powers de George
Larry Rodrigues
Sue Spielman
Sakhr Youness

**Production Manager**
Liz Toy

**Production Coordinator**
Pip Wonson

**Production Assistant**
Dawn Chellingworth

**Cover Design**
Chris Morris

**Proofreader**
Fiver Löcker

# About the Authors

## Bjarki Hólm

For the past five years, Bjarki – the lead author on this book – has been working in software engineering at VYRE Corporation in Reykjavík, developing on-line design and content management systems. Currently, he is taking time off from work to pursue his studies of electrical engineering and occasional writing opportunities at Wrox.

This book combines Bjarki's two main areas of technical interest: Oracle and Java. He has considerable experience developing Java software in a three-tier model, using an Oracle backend and has recently embraced the advantages of using Java procedures inside the database, to increase both the performance and functionality of his applications. His hope is that you will too.

*I would like to dedicate my chapters to my fiancée Bryndís. Without her understanding, love and support, I would never have made it.*

Bjarki contributed Chapters 11 to 14, 16, 17 and Appendix C.

## John Carnell

John Carnell has had an obsession with computers since he was 12 years old working on his Commodore 64. This obsession never waned and he is currently working as a staff consultant with the Centare Group, a leading provider of e-software solutions. John's favorite topic of discussion, much to his wife's chagrin, is component-based, n-tier architectures. John has extensive experience with Microsoft, Oracle, and Java technologies. He lives in Waukesha, Wisconsin with his wife Janet and their two pups, Ginger and Ladybug.

John can be reached at john_carnell@yahoo.com.

*I would like to dedicate this to my godparents Judi and Jeff. Thanks for all of the love and support all these years. I hold you guys as close to my heart as my mother and father.*

John contributed Chapter 8.

# Jaeda Goodman

Jaeda Goodman is a Principal Software Engineer at Keane. After a degree in Philosophy and an MSc in Cognitive Science, she moved into the world of IT, focusing on Oracle data warehousing. For the last few years, she has been concentrating on Java technologies, and has started specializing in J2EE after having reluctantly abandoned her quest to become an InfoBus expert.

When she is not eulogizing to colleagues about the merits of the Apache Struts Framework and the mandatory omni-presence of Javadoc, she is usually either running ever-increasing distances, or trying to find new drinks that are better than both blue punch and smoothies. The two activities form a natural cycle.

> *Again, I would like to dedicate this to everyone, before and after Synchromatic, who has experienced the Synchromatic effect, but especially to Martin, who is a much better writer than he thinks.*

Jaeda contributed Appendix B.

# Ben Marcotte

Ben Marcotte received a BSc in Biology from the University of Oregon in 1994. In his progress from a research biologist to a computational biologist to a sysadmin to a web developer, many topics and technologies have held his interest, but presently Java, Oracle, XML, and PHP garner his attention. He is a fan of live theater and his hobbies include genealogy and enjoying Oregon's natural wonders through outdoor activities that include camping, hiking, and skiing.

Ben contributed Chapter 2.

# Kevin Mukhar

Kevin has dabbled in programming for many years, and has been a professional programmer for almost six years. For the last four years, he has worked primarily on providing web-based services using Java in a web server with an Oracle database as the backend.

> *I think that programming involves art as well as science. I get a kick out of writing a program that helps someone do their job better or easier; I get a thrill when tracking down and stamping out bugs; I think it's magic when programming turns ideas into software. And I want to share what I know with other programmers. That's why I'm grateful to the editors at Wrox for letting me contribute to this book. I hope that what we've written in this book will help you do your job a little bit better or easier.*
>
> *Finally, I dedicate my chapters to my wife, Anne, and my daughter.*

Kevin contributed Chapters 6 and 15.

# Mauricio Naranjo

Mauricio Naranjo is a software engineer from Colombia, South America. He currently works as a software architect at the Research & Development Division of Open Intl. Systems Corp. His main focus is on distributed computing, Internet technologies, OO techniques, and software architecture. For the last five years, he has been working with Java and Oracle for building B2B and B2C solutions. Besides designing and reviewing architectures, he is a regular speaker at local and international seminars. He enjoys learning about software engineering practices, new technologies, and finding an appropriate way to use them for solving real needs. He believes that the most difficult part is to design and architect solutions that work as simply as possible. Complex solutions are no more than lack of abstraction. Mauricio can be reached at mauricio_naranjo@hotmail.com or mnaranjo@open.com.

*This effort is dedicated to my family, Hermencia, Jose, Consuelo, and Fernando. Special thanks to Mark Kerzner (IOUG A-Live) and Tony Davis and the people of Wrox Press for giving me the opportunity to participate in this project. Also, I would like to thank all the people who supported me in this process of writing. In no particular order; Jaime Gaviria, Jorge Alvarez, Jorge Ramirez, David Lopez, Alex Cañizales, Luis Acosta, Gustavo Alvear, Sandra Perez, and my friends of the R&D team, Hernando Parrott, Edgardo Sierra, Francisco Chaves and DM. Finally, this is the combined result of all the people who have helped me in my whole life, the list is so long and there is not enough space, anyway you know who you are – thank you so much.*

Mauricio contributed Chapter 4.

# Mark Piermarini

Mark Piermarini has been working for Oracle for the past two years, focusing mainly on Java and Internet technologies. Prior to Oracle, he was with a large consulting company for a few years. This allowed him to work on document imaging and financial systems for state/local governments and universities.

He has considerable experience in programming languages such as assembly, C, and Smalltalk, but his current favorite is Java. Mark earned an undergraduate degree in Electrical Engineering and a minor in Computer Science from Virginia Polytechnic Institute and State University, respectively.

Mark's two brothers, Gregg and Matthew, also work in the computer industry as a VPN engineer and an extremely competent programmer, respectively.

*Thanks go to my entire family for their support.*

Mark contributed Chapter 9.

# Oracle 9i Java Programming
## *Solutions for Developers Using Java and PL/SQL*

Bjarki Hólm

John Carnell
Jaeda Goodman
Ben Marcotte
Kevin Mukhar
Mauricio Naranjo
Mark Piermarini
Anand Raaj
Dr. P. G. Sarang
Sant Singh
Tomas Stubbs

*Wrox Press Ltd.* ®

# Oracle 9i Java Programming
## *Solutions for Developers Using Java and PL/SQL*

wrox

Published by Wrox Press Ltd,
Arden House, 1102 Warwick Road, Acocks Green,
Birmingham, B27 6BH, UK
Printed in the United States
ISBN 1-861006-02-0

# Anand Raaj

Anand Raaj is a Principal Consultant with QED Solutions Inc., a Houston-based consulting firm specializing in Oracle and web technology. He graduated as a Mechanical Engineer from University of Madras (India), with a desire to do computer-related work in the field of engineering. His passion towards programming grew stronger, which made him switch to Computer Science after completing a formal post-graduate diploma in Computer Applications from College of Engineering, Anna University (India). He has nine years of experience in developing and implementing Oracle-based applications. He enjoys problem-solving and he is happy with what he is doing. He is an Oracle Certified Professional and he presents regularly at regional and national conferences (Oracle user groups). He is also a Sun Certified Java Programmer.

His interests include reading (motivational and spiritual), martial arts, traveling, photography, and bicycling. He lives in Houston, Texas with his loving wife Shubashini and an adorable new born daughter Raeshma.

> *I am grateful to God for his kindness and blessing in my life. I am greatly indebted to my parents, Dr. S. Rajemdran and R. SanthaKumari, for their support, motivation, and love. I have learned a lot from them and I owe everything to them. My heart and love go to my wife, also my best friend, without whom my life would not be complete.*

Anand contributed Chapter 3.

# Dr Sanjay Sarang

A contractor to Sun Microsystems, Dr. Sarang trains Sun's corporate clients on various courses from Sun's official curriculum. He also conducts the *Train The Trainers* program and *Instructor Authorization Tests* on behalf of Sun.

Dr. Sarang is a founder of ABCOM Information Systems Pvt. Ltd. who specialize in consulting and training on the latest technologies. With more than 20 years of industry experience, Dr. Sarang provides services in the area of architecting and designing solutions, and project-based training to many domestic and international clients. Dr. Sarang is a regular speaker in many international conferences on Java, J2EE, XML, and CORBA. He may be reached at sarang@abcom.com.

> *My special thanks to Chandan Parulkar and Raul Bhirud for providing valuable assistance in code development.*

Sanjay contributed Chapters 7 and 10.

# Sant Singh

Sant Singh is currently working with Cymbal Corporation, San Jose, California, USA as a system analyst. He has five years experience in client-server and Internet software development environment. He also has hands-on experience in the complete life cycle of project development; system analysis, design, development, testing, deployment, and end user training, with strong technical skills in Java, J2EE, EJB, JMS, Servlets, JSP, Swing, and Java Mail. His area of specialization is *Objected-Oriented Analysis and Design with Java*, and *Database Design and Development* with *Oracle and SQL Server*.

> *I would like to acknowledge Mr. Suraj Kumar of IBM-Enron and Mr. Lalan Kumar of Cymbal Corporation for their valuable suggestions in writing these chapters. I would like to dedicate this book to my parents.*

Sant contributed Appendix A.

# Tomas Stubbs

Tomas Stubbs has been developing and designing commercial software since 1989 and for most of that time, he has specialized in Oracle. He has a degree in Fine Art and came to IT via a torturous route, but is now a firm Java believer and has attained both Sun Programmer and Developer certification for the Java 2 platform. He currently works both as an independent contractor and as Technical Director for Firebrand Software Ltd., a software product development company, which he co-founded with three others. Tomas likes to fill his free time with various interests including playing flamenco guitar (since the age of 7), practicing yoga and kung fu, riding his motorbike as fast as he can, and traveling. He can be reached at tstubbs@firebrandsoftware.com or tstubbs@webnuts.co.uk.

> *Thanks to those friends who pulled out the stops to help me when I needed it, especially Tessa, Brian Vos, Mrushad Patel, Alastair Johnson and Steve Christall.*

Tomas contributed Chapters 1 and 5.

# Oracle 9i Java Programming

# Table of Contents

Table of Contents

Table of Contents

## Table of Contents

## Table of Contents

Table of Contents

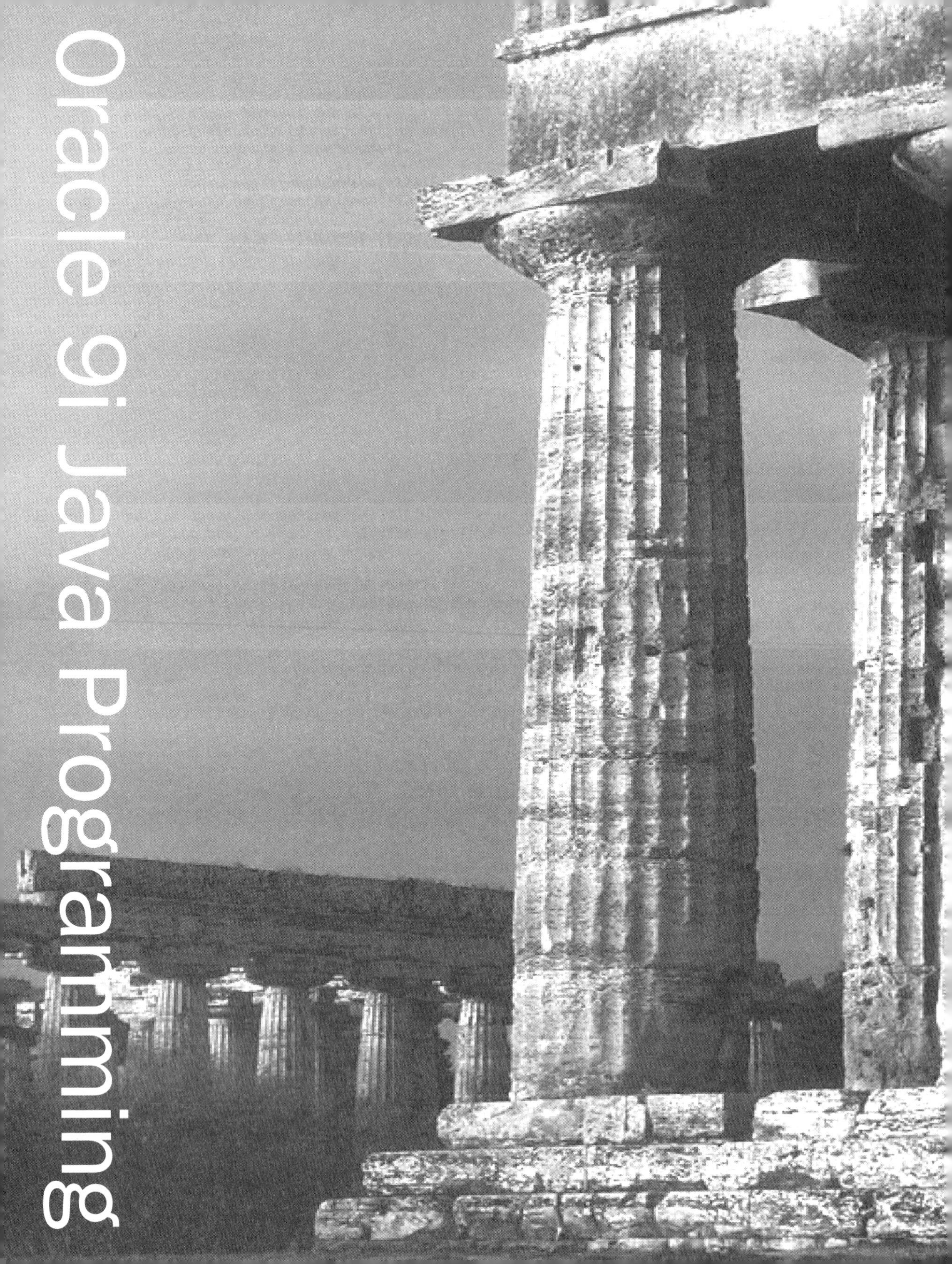
Oracle 9i Java Programming

# Introduction

The central theme of this book is the exploration of the practical uses for Java in the Oracle 9i database. Ever wanted to know how to compress your large objects in the database? How to have the database generate a chart or graph from a SQL query and e-mail it to your colleagues? How to write an FTP Java client that runs inside the database? All of these answers are in this book.

This book shows how to exploit the strengths of Java and to use them in conjunction with PL/SQL to build effective and elegant solutions in the Oracle database. It is certainly not advocated in this book that Java be used as a replacement for PL/SQL. In fact we prove (with benchmarks) that in many situations it simply makes more sense to use PL/SQL – and we recommend you do so.

However, Java provides versatile functionality that is simply not available using PL/SQL, and now you can exploit it right within the Oracle database. This ability opens up virtually endless possibilities. One of the great things about Java is the vast collection of utilities and extensions available to the language. Java language extensions are backed up by a whole community of Java users, which leads to rapid advancements and a widespread industry support for new technologies. If the code has been developed (and you trust it!) you can load it into the database and take advantage of it.

Hopefully this book will provide you with a few ideas for the practical use of Java in Oracle, and the incentive to think up some new ones of your own.

# From the Lead Author...

To be honest, I was skeptical when I first heard that Oracle 8i came with a fully functional Java Virtual Machine *inside* the database server. I couldn't see why you would want to run Java classes inside the database – Java Servlets and Enterprise Beans belong to the middle-tier and, in most cases, PL/SQL is best suited for SQL-oriented database logic. My basic opinion has changed little over the years but, nevertheless, I have come to embrace the use of Java stored procedures in the database. I now regard Oracle Java as a powerful tool for extending the functionality of traditional database applications, running within Oracle. I never use JDBC to do things I could more easily do in PL/SQL, just as I never deploy my Java web applications in the database. I do, however, use Java for things that are more efficient to code in the database but that cannot be accomplished with PL/SQL alone. Using Java stored procedures, I can now compress all my LOB objects to take up less space, use multicast sockets to automatically alert clients when data has changed, and to more work efficiently with files, to name but a few examples. This is the **true power** of Java in the database – to provide functionality not readily available in PL/SQL, in a simple and safe manner. After reading through this book, you will hopefully share this view.

# Who Should Use This Book?

This book is for experienced Oracle developers looking to understand the power and versatility that Java brings to database programming, and to exploit that in conjunction with PL/SQL. It will also be of interest to DBAs who need to know how Java is likely to be used inside the database and how this affects them, and to beginner/intermediate Java developers looking to apply their knowledge in the Oracle database. Knowledge of SQL, PL/SQL and Oracle architecture is assumed. Knowledge of the fundamentals of the Java programming language will help you progress quickly through the book. However, if you are relatively new to Java, then the explanations in the text should allow you to grasp all of the fundamental issues discussed, especially if you are migrating from another language, such as C.

# How this Book is Structured

Conceptually, the book breaks down into four distinct sections. We start with a introductory section covering the basics of Java. Subsequent chapters build on these foundations, challenging your Java skills as we add complexity to our Java programs and explore the integration of Java and Oracle. The second section looks at SQL, Java, and JDBC. In Section III we look at using Java in the database and in the final section we look at optimizing your code to get the most out of your database.

Following is a brief description of the chapter structure within each section. Every chapter in every section contains well-explained code examples – ones that you can actually run, as opposed to just code snippets – that will clearly demonstrate the issues being discussed.

## Section I: Basic Java for Oracle Developers

This section is essentially a concise Java tutorial, specifically tailored for the Oracle developer. This section, in conjunction with Appendix A, *Basic Java Syntax*, is intended to teach the fundamentals of object-oriented programming in Java, from the perspective of a developer with experience in the procedural world of PL/SQL.

❑ **Chapter 1, Getting Started**. This chapter introduces the Oracle 9i Java platform, covering the fundamentals of running Java code, both inside and outside the database.

❑ **Chapter 2, Java Classes and Objects**. This chapter introduces, with a working example, the fundamental concepts surrounding object-oriented programming in Java (classes, variables, methods, inheritance, interfaces and so on).

❑ **Chapter 3, Using Objects in PL/SQL and Java.** Building on the foundation provided in Chapter 2, here we aim to solidify your knowledge of Java concepts by relating them back to your understanding of how things work in PL/SQL. By way of a simple account maintenance example, we compare Java classes and PL/SQL packages and, more directly, Java classes and Oracle 9i object types, which incorporate OO functionality such as inheritance and polymorphism.

# Section II: SQL and Java

Section II of the book covers database access with JDBC and SQLJ and also shows how to elegantly and correctly handle potential errors in your Oracle Java applications.

❑ **Chapter 4, Connecting to Oracle with JDBC.** This chapter introduces the JDBC API, for connecting to relational databases through Java, and provides a definitive guide for connecting to Oracle through the JDBC thin, OCI and server-side internal drivers.

❑ **Chapter 5, Using JDBC.** This chapter delves deeper into the JDBC API, covering the interfaces that are most important to the Oracle developer, such as PreparedStatement, CallableStatement and ResultSet. The chapter focuses on writing high performance Oracle JDBC code via use of batch updates, multiple fetching and of well-designed code that avoids unnecessary parsing in the database.

❑ **Chapter 6, Handling Exceptions.** Easy to learn, difficult to master. This chapter stresses the importance of correctly catching and handling exceptions in your code, and takes a detailed look at the techniques available for doing so. This includes coverage of the OracleSQLException class.

❑ **Chapter 7, Oracle Extension Classes.** Here we look at some of the Oracle-specific classes provided for handling complex types, such as LOBs, CLOBs, BFILEs, and so on. For example, we show how to read a file from a directory folder and save it in the database.

❑ **Chapter 8, SQLJ Programming.** When working in the database, SQLJ can often provide an attractive alternative to the use of the JDBC API and is more intuitive for the Oracle developer – SQLJ is to Pro*C as JDBC is to OCI. Here, we discuss the standard in some detail and take a look at important new features in the Oracle 9i implementation.

# Section III: Using Java in the Database

This section is about practical problem solving in the database, with Java and PL/SQL – pure and simple.

❑ **Chapter 9, Using the Oracle JVM.** A detailed look at important aspects of creating, managing and debugging code in the Oracle JVM, covering details of the Java pool, the DBMS_JAVA package and the loadjava utility.

❑ **Chapter 10, Java Stored Procedures Basics.** This explains the fundamentals of creating, publishing and calling Java stored procedures and functions. We take a look at some simple but useful examples: an e-mail address validation procedure and a 'time translator'.

❑ **Chapter 11, Oracle Java Security.** Although the fundamental security concepts remain the same, certain differences exist between standard Java security and Oracle Java security, mostly due to the fact that the latter deals with code running within the boundaries of an already secure database. An understanding of this model is essential in order to safely run Java in the database. A practical bug tracking application is developed.

❑ **Chapter 12, Java Utilities.** We highlight some of the powerful utilities available with the Java language and then focus on two in particular: image generation and mail transport with JavaMail. Over the course of the chapter we develop an application whereby we can send e-mail, with custom image attachments, from the database. It incorporates use of a free, open-source image encoder in the database.

❑ **Chapter 13, Working with Operating System Resources.** In this chapter, we will discuss the capabilities of Java for working with resources of the database server operating system, such as files, sockets, host commands, and executables. We discuss the advantages of Java over C, in this regard. Again the chapter is highly practical - demonstrating, for example:

  ❑ How to uses multicast datagram sockets, used to broadcast a message to a large recipient group.

  ❑ How to implement a simple Java class that will run the Oracle SQL*Loader data import utility and load into the database data from text-based files in the file system.

❑ **Chapter 14, Using PL/SQL and Java Together.** There are many, many ways in which you could harness the strengths of Java and PL/SQL in the database to achieve an elegant solution. Here, we look at two specific examples:

  ❑ Use of both PL/SQL and Java to compress large documents stored in the database.

  ❑ An FTP Java client that runs inside the Oracle database, which makes use of PL/SQL for scheduling automatic transfer and processing of file content from a remote server.

# Section IV: Performance

Here we take a detailed look at performance issues. Having considered SQL tuning and Java application tuning separately, we take a detailed look behind the scenes of Java database access and try to illustrate how you should choose between Java and PL/SQL for database operations:

❑ **Chapter 15, Java Application Performance**. This chapter contains many useful performance monitoring and optimization techniques for your Oracle Java code, including use of Oracle's memstat utility and their native compiler (ncomp). Look out in particular for the concise and insightful example demonstrating the critical importance of optimizing the usage of String objects in your Java applications.

❑ **Chapter 16, SQL Tuning and Analyzing Queries.** Before you can even begin to make a judgment on whether your application SQL should be executed from Java to PL/SQL, your first job is **to fully optimize that SQL**. Useful scripts and packages for performance optimization are discussed here including the SQL_TRACE utility and how it can be used to analyze individual SQL statements.

❑   **Chapter 17, PL/SQL vs. Java: Benchmarking SQL Execution**. So, you've optimized your SQL as far as possible. Should you execute it from PL/SQL or Java? We present performance benchmarks for the execution of multiple SQL statements through the OCI and KPRB drivers and compare with that achieved when we group those statements in a PL/SQL procedure. The chapter also measures the cost of passing variables from the JVM to the Oracle SQL execution engine and compares it to the cost of passing variables from one PL/SQL procedure to another.

## Appendices

❑   **Appendix A, Basic Java Syntax**. This appendix covers the basic structure of a Java program, operators, keywords, datatypes and arrays from a PL/SQL programmer's perspective.

❑   **Appendix B, Useful Core Java Classes.** One of the most daunting aspects of learning Java is the incredible number of support classes that are available as a core part of the language. Here we cover those classes that will be most commonly used by an Oracle developer. For example, to understand CLOB handling, you need to know how Java deals with streams – and that is covered here.

❑   **Appendix C, The Logging API.** This appendix describes the Logging API that is used to log errors and exceptions in some examples in this book.

## Conventions

In order to help you understand and follow what is going on throughout this text, and to maintain consistency, we have used a number of different styles of text and layout. Here are some examples of these and what they mean:

When **important words** are introduced for the first time, they are displayed in a **bold** format to stand out from the page.

Words that appear on the screen in menus and windows, such as File or Open, are displayed in a similar style in which they would be viewed. URLs such as http://www.wrox.com are also displayed in this way.

Keys that you would press, such as *Ctrl-C* and *Enter*, are displayed in italics.

> **Important pieces of information come in boxes like this.**

> *Background is a style used to display information aside from the general discussion, such as advice, hints, and other sideline information.*

In this book, we have two main development environments in which we will be demonstrating code examples and snippets; Java and PL/SQL. As a result, we have different styles of formatting for each, although they do share some similar aspects, such as the following three styles to display code:

The first is used when we are referring to code within the main body of the text. In this case, we use a format called code in text. This applies to Java code, SQL queries, and PL/SQL commands.

```
The second is used when there are full pieces of code you can run, or when there
is code that is new or important to take in.
```

```
This type of formatting is used when there are snippets of code, or code that you
have seen before.
```

```
Sometimes, you may see some old bits of code, like this section here,
interspersed with a new section, where the code is highlighted in a gray box.
```

As well as the above conventions for presenting code throughout the book, we will also be showing command line Java inputs in the following way:

```
> java myClass
This is the output from the command.
```

The code background style is used for the showing the session, with the commands that should be typed in after the prompt highlighted in **bold**.

For PL/SQL programs, we will be showing SQL*Plus sessions like the following:

```
SQL> create or replace procedure StaticEmpProc(p_job in varchar2)
  2  as
  3    begin
  4      for x in (select ename from emp where job = p_job)
  5        loop
  6          dbms_output.put_line( x.ename );
  7        end loop;
  8    end;
  9  /

Procedure created.
```

In the above session output, we have shown the line numbers and the output in normal code foreground, together with the commands you need to type in **bold**.

# Customer Support

We always value hearing from our readers, and we want to know what you think about this book – what you liked, what you didn't like, and what you think we can do better next time. You can send us your comments, either by returning the reply card in the back of the book, or by e-mail to feedback@wrox.com. Please be sure to mention the book title in your message.

# How to Download the Sample Code for the Book

When you log on to the Wrox site at http://www.wrox.com/, simply locate the title through our Search facility or by using one of the title lists. Click on Download in the Code column, or on Download Code on the book's detail page.

The files that are available for download from our site have been archived using WinZip. When you have saved the attachments to a folder on your hard-drive, you need to extract the files using a de-compression program such as WinZip or PKUnzip. When you extract the files, the code is extracted into chapter folders. When you start the extraction process, ensure your software (WinZip, PKUnzip, and so on) is set to extract to Use Folder Names.

# Errata

We have made every effort to make sure that there are no errors in the text or in the code. However, no one is perfect and mistakes do occur. If you find an error in one of our books, like a spelling mistake or a faulty piece of code, we would be very grateful for feedback. By sending in errata you may save another reader hours of frustration, and of course, you will be helping us provide even higher quality information. Simply e-mail the information to support@wrox.com. Your information will be checked and if correct, posted to the errata page for that title, or used in subsequent editions of the book.

To find errata on the web site, log on to http://www.wrox.com/, and simply locate the title through our Advanced Search or title list. Click on the Book Errata link, which is below the cover graphic on the book's detail page.

# e-mail Support

If you wish to directly query a problem in the book page with an expert who knows the book in detail then e-mail support@wrox.com, with the title of the book and the last four numbers of the ISBN in the subject field of the e-mail. A typical e-mail should include the following things:

❑   The **name**, **last four digits of the ISBN**, and **page number** of the problem in the Subject field.

❑   Your **name**, **contact information**, and the **problem** in the body of the message.

We **won't** send you junk mail. We need the details to save your time and ours. When you send an e-mail message, it will go through the following chain of support:

❑   **Customer Support** – Your message is delivered to our customer support staff, who are the first people to read it. They have files on most frequently asked questions and will answer anything general about the book or the web site immediately.

❑   **Editorial** – Deeper queries are forwarded to the technical editor responsible for that book. They have experience with the programming language or particular product, and are able to answer detailed technical questions on the subject. Once an issue has been resolved, the editor can post the errata to the web site.

❑ **The Authors** – Finally, in the unlikely event that the editor cannot answer your problem, he or she will forward the request to the author. We do try to protect the author from any distractions to their writing; however, we are quite happy to forward specific requests to them. All Wrox authors help with the support on their books. They will e-mail the customer and the editor with their response, and again all readers should benefit.

The Wrox support process can only offer support on issues that are directly pertinent to the content of our published title. Support for questions that fall outside the scope of normal book support is provided via the community lists of our http://p2p.wrox.com/ forum.

# p2p.wrox.com

For author and peer discussion join the P2P mailing lists. Our unique system provides **programmer to programmer**™ contact on mailing lists, forums, and newsgroups, all **in addition** to our one-to-one e-mail support system. Be confident that your query is being examined by the many Wrox authors and other industry experts who are present on our mailing lists. At p2p.wrox.com you will find a number of different lists that will help you, not only while you read this book, but also as you develop your own applications.

To subscribe to a mailing list just follow this these steps:

**1.** Go to http://p2p.wrox.com/.

**2.** Choose the appropriate category from the left menu bar.

**3.** Click on the mailing list you wish to join.

**4.** Follow the instructions to subscribe and fill in your e-mail address and password.

**5.** Reply to the confirmation e-mail you receive.

**6.** Use the subscription manager to join more lists and set your e-mail preferences.

Oracle 9i Java Programming

# Getting Started

The first section in this chapter explains some of the set up that you may find useful in order for you to take advantage of the features of the object-oriented Java programming language. These are by no means the be all and end all of getting your test environment sorted out, it just makes life a little easier when working through examples in the book, and testing and developing your own applications.

After this first section, conscious that many of you may have had little experience of Java, we will explain a few of the key fundamental elements, which make up a Java platform and those that make up the Oracle Java Server platform in particular.

In this chapter we'll be trying to provide answers to the following questions:

- ❑ What is the Java platform?

- ❑ What is the Java Virtual Machine?

- ❑ What is the Oracle JVM and how can it be set up?

- ❑ How does Java inside the database differ from Java outside the database?

- ❑ How can I run Java programs inside the database?

## Setting Up

In this section of the chapter, we will be looking at the steps you need to take in order to run the examples encountered in this book and also at some functional scripts that will be useful to you in this process. One such script will be used to personalize your SQL*Plus prompt and another to create a batch file so that you do not need to hard-code environment variables on your system. These are not essential by all means, but it just means working through this book will be made much easier. However, let's start with the basic software requirements.

# Software Requirements

The first and most obvious piece of software you will need is an Oracle database. This can be either installed on your machine locally, or can be on a machine you can access remotely. Preferably, this will be an Oracle 9i database, but most of the examples will run fine on versions 8.1.6 and upwards of Oracle 8i. The current version at the writing of this book is 9.0.1.1.1.

If you are going to be accessing a remote database, then you will need to install the Oracle 9i Client on your machine. You will need to select the Runtime Installation. It requires around 486 MB of hard disk space. If you wish to use a local database, then we recommend you install Oracle 9i Personal Edition, which requires approximately 1.72 GB of space. These pieces of software, available under a restricted development-only license, can be downloaded from the Technet web site at http://technet.oracle.com, with the 9i database products located at http://technet.oracle.com/software/products/oracle9i/content.html. Bear in mind two things if you are looking to download the software from this site. First, you need to sign up for free membership, and secondly, the download files are hundreds of MB in size!!

The standard test platform for this book is Oracle 9i Enterprise Edition running on Windows 2000. For this reason, the examples show Windows/DOS-specific syntax. If you are using another platform you can expect there to be differences, but these should be confined to the specification of environment variables and path names. However, you should be familiar with how these are specified in your chosen platform and we trust that you will be just as able to follow the examples.

Throughout this book, we will be dealing with compilation of Java both inside and outside the Oracle database. This means that you will need to install a copy of Sun's Java 2 Software Development Kit Standard Edition also know as the J2SE SDK. At the time of writing, the current release is 1.3.1, but JDK 1.4 was at the Beta 3 stage of development. This software can be downloaded from the Sun web site at http://java.sun.com/j2se/. There are other versions of the Java 2 platform, which we will detail in *The Java API* section later in the chapter, but the Standard Edition is perfectly adequate.

It is important to note that although there is a newer version of the Java 2 platform available for mass consumption, the Oracle 9i Java Virtual Machine is only compliant with JDK 1.2.2. You should bear this in mind when compiling Java code that relies on features of a later version of the JDK. The code in question may well compile perfectly well outside of the database using the appropriate version of the JDK, but you are likely to encounter problems if you then attempt to load your classes into the database and run it in the Oracle JVM. Since it is quite common to have multiple virtual machines with different versions of the JDK installed on your machine, you may wish to install JDK 1.2.2 to ensure that your environments both inside and outside the database are equivalent.

In the *A Useful Batch File* section, we will see an easy way of how we can keep a track of what environment we are using in any session.

# Setting up a Test Schema

Many of the examples in this book draw on the EMP and DEPT tables, which come as part of the SCOTT schema. This schema is automatically created when you install Oracle 9i but since we will be utilizing these tables and the data within them a great deal throughout the book, we recommend that you create a test schema that mirrors the SCOTT schema. This way, you can avoid the side effects that may be caused by other users using the same data and schema. You may wish to do this even if working on a local database, in order to preserve the state of the original SCOTT schema.

For this book, we have created a new user, username, identified by password, on a test database called database:

```
> sqlplus username/password@database

SQL*Plus: Release 9.0.1.0.1 - Production on Tue Nov 20 16:09:04 2001

(c) Copyright 2001 Oracle Corporation.  All rights reserved.


Connected to:
Oracle9i Enterprise Edition Release 9.0.1.1.1 - Production
With the Partitioning option
JServer Release 9.0.1.1.1 - Production
```

To create the demonstration tables from the SCOTT schema in your test schema, you simply need to:

❑   cd [ORACLE_HOME]/sqlplus/demo

❑   run demobld.sql

when logged in as your test user.

The demobld.sql script will create and populate five tables for us. When it is complete, it exits SQL*Plus automatically, so don't be surprised when SQL*Plus disappears after running the script – it is supposed to do that.

Be aware that the standard demo tables do not have any referential integrity defined on them, so after you run demobld.sql, you may want to execute the following:

```
alter table emp add constraint emp_pk primary key(empno);
alter table dept add constraint dept_pk primary key(deptno);
alter table emp add constraint emp_fk_dept
                              foreign key(deptno) references dept;
alter table emp add constraint emp_fk_emp foreign key(mgr) references emp;
```

This finishes off the installation of the demonstration schema. If you would like to drop this schema at any time to clean up, you can simply execute [ORACLE_HOME]/sqlplus/demo/demodrop.sql. This will drop the five tables, and exit SQL*Plus.

Each chapter in this book is fairly self-contained. At the beginning of each chapter, we recommend that you drop your testing account, and recreate it. That is, each chapter starts with a clean schema – no objects.

# Customizing SQL*Plus

SQL*Plus allows us to set up a login.sql file, which is a script that is executed each and every time we start SQL*Plus initially. Further, it allows us to set an environment variable named SQLPATH so that it can find this startup script, no matter where it is located.

Here is an example `login.sql` file:

```
define _editor=vi

set serveroutput on size 1000000
call dbms_java.set_output(1000000);

set trimspool on
set long 5000
set linesize 100
set pagesize 9999

column plan_plus_exp format a80

column global_name new_value gname
set termout off
select lower(user) || '@' ||
decode(global_name, 'SKYDIVE', 'DATABASE', '9I',
'8i', global_name ) global_name from global_name;
set sqlprompt '&gname> '
set termout on
```

The meanings of the most important lines are as follows:

❏   `define editor=vi` – Set up the default editor SQL*Plus would use. You may set that to be your favorite text editor (not a word processor) such as Notepad or EMACs.

❏   `set serveroutput on size 1000000` – Enable DBMS_OUTPUT to be on by default (hence we don't have to type it in each and every time). Also set the default buffer size as large as possible.

❏   `call dbms_java.set_output(1000000);` – Redirects the Java System.out to your SQL*Plus session with a buffer matching the size of the DBMS_OUTPUT buffer.

❏   `set trimspool on` – When spooling text, lines will be blank-trimmed and not fixed width. If this is set off (the default), spooled lines will be as wide as your linesize setting.

❏   `set long 5000` – Sets the default number of bytes displayed when selecting LONG and CLOB columns.

❏   `set linesize 100` – Set the width of the lines displayed by SQL*Plus to be 100 characters.

❏   `set pagesize 9999` – Set the pagesize, which controls how frequently SQL*Plus prints out headings to a big number (we get one set of headings per page).

❏   `column plan_plus_exp format a80` – This sets the default width of the explain plan output we receive with AUTOTRACE. a80 generally is wide enough to hold the full plan.

The next bit in the `login.sql` sets up the SQL*PLUS prompt:

```
column global_name new_value gname
set termout off
select lower(user) || '@' ||
decode(global_name, 'SKYDIVE', 'DATABASE', '9I',
```

```
'8i', global_name ) global_name from global_name;
set sqlprompt '&gname> '
set termout on
```

The directive column global_name new_value gname tells SQL*Plus to take the last value it retrieves for any column named global_name, and place it into the substitution variable gname. We then SELECT the global_name out of the database (with a decode for some of the more common database instances on this particular machine, to give them familiar names), and concatenate this with the username logged in with. That makes my prompt look like this:

```
username@DATABASE.WROX>
```

so you know *who* you are logged in as and *where*.

Another very handy script to have in the same directory as your login.sql is this connect.sql script:

```
set termout off
connect &1
@login
set termout on
```

SQL*Plus will only execute the login.sql when it initially starts up. Generally, we want it to execute every time we connect. With the connect.sql script, all you have to do is:

```
username@DATABASE.WROX> @connect scott/tiger
scott@DATABASE.WROX>
```

instead of just connect scott/tiger. That way, your prompt is always set properly, as are all other settings such as serveroutput.

# A Useful Batch File

As we mentioned earlier in the *Software Requirements* section of this chapter, it is very likely that you will have more than one version of the Java runtime available for use on your machine. Apart from the fact that you want to be absolutely sure you are using the intended runtime, a simple way to switch between them would be very useful. Creating a batch file for this particular purpose is a good solution to this problem. Also, it means that you do not have to hard-code your PATH and CLASSPATH environment variables on your system.

Let's take a look at an example of the kind of batch file we can use for a Windows system:

```
set JAVA_HOME=C:\jdk1.3
set ORACLE_HOME=C:\oracle\ora90
set PATH=.;%PATH%;%JAVA_HOME%\bin;%ORACLE_HOME%\bin
set
CLASSPATH=.;%JAVA_HOME%;%JAVA_HOME%\lib;%JAVA_HOME%\lib\tools.jar;%ORACLE_HOME%\jd
bc\lib\classes12.zip;%ORACLE_HOME%\jdbc\lib\nls_charset12.zip;
```

The first two lines of the batch file, JAVA_HOME and ORACLE_HOME, simply point to the locations of the Java and Oracle installations respectively. In this case, Java is stored on the C drive in the jdk1.3 directory. Similarly, Oracle (whether the client or the actual database) is installed in the \oracle\ora90 directory on the C drive.

Next, we set the PATH variable, which tells your environment where to look for important executable files such as java.exe, javac.exe, and sqlldr.exe, amongst others. The CLASSPATH environment variable tells the command shell where to look for referenced classes to compile the Java code. This can be either a list of directories and/or ZIP or JAR files that contain the classes we require. In our example, the two Oracle packages containing the Oracle JDBC classes (classes12.zip) and National Language Support character sets (nls_classes12.zip) are included.

> Note that to set the PATH and CLASSPATH, we separate values with a semi-colon and we also use a period to tell the environment to look for appropriate executables and classes.

Now all you need to do is run this batch file when you open a fresh command window, and your environment will be fully set up for use. It is much easier to keep track of what locations will be searched for executables and classes, which runtimes are being used, and so on.

Throughout this book, we will be using this kind of set up to compile our code outside the database. Of course, compiling Java classes *inside* the database is a different matter, as we shall see later on in this chapter. In various chapters in the book, we will need to add more to our CLASSPATH in order to create and run more functional code. Examples of these include:

❑ The classes12.zip package that contains all the Oracle JDBC classes to connect to the database, which we have already seen in the example batch file

❑ The translator.zip and runtime.zip files in the %ORACLE_HOME%\sqlj\lib\ directory to translate and compile SQLJ-based code

> A JAR file is a special kind of ZIP file created with the jar command included in the Java installation. You can view the contents of a JAR file in much the same way you would a ZIP file, for instance, using the WinZip tool.

> Java 2 allows JAR files to simply be placed in the extensions directory for automatic inclusion in searches (the default location is %JAVA_HOME%/jre/lib/ext) instead of adding them to the CLASSPATH. This really amounts to the same thing for our purposes though.

# Java Architecture

Before we can explain what the Oracle Java Server platform is, it is useful to discuss the key elements of the Java architecture and to clarify the meaning of some of the key terms that crop up time and again.

## What is the Java Platform?

When you write Java programs, you produce Java source programs (.java files) and use the Java compiler to compile these to Java class files (.class files). These class files are the executables of Java. When you run your Java program, the classes produced are loaded and run within a Java runtime environment (JRE).

This JRE makes up the Java platform and comprises two parts. The first is the **Java Virtual Machine (JVM)** and the second is the Java Application Programmer Interface (API). The following diagram illustrates this:

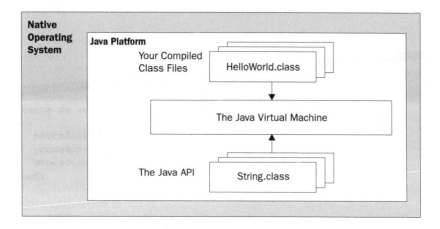

*You will also hear the Java platform referred to as the **Java 2 Platform**. Java 2 refers to Java releases 1.2 and onwards. It is given the name Java 2 because that release marked a major revision of the Java language. This is very pertinent to us since we need to be concerned with the version of Java that Oracle is running. We'll come back to this topic when we talk about the Oracle Java Server Platform later.*

The JVM is essentially a layer between the Java programs you write and the operating system. The platform-dependent details are handled in the JVM layer, which means you don't have to deal with them. That's why when you download a Java 2 platform from Sun's web site at http://java.sun.com/products you don't need to select the destination platform, such as Windows 2000 or Solaris. Your programs aren't really executables themselves – when you run the Java interpreter with the java command:

```
> java <class name>
```

Java reads your program class files and executes them for you.

## The Java API

As we have said earlier in the *Software Requirements* section, there is more than just one Java 2 Platform. Most people probably start using Java with the Standard Edition of the Java 2 platform, J2SE. If you haven't already, visit the Sun site at http://java.sun.com/products, you'll see some of the other Java 2 platforms available, such as the Micro Edition (J2ME) and the Enterprise Edition (J2EE). One you have gotten a foothold with the Standard Edition, the Enterprise Edition would be the next step up since it is this version for which Oracle is really providing an implementation for in the Oracle Java Server Platform.

The differences between these various platforms lie in the Java API that is included. For instance, the Standard Edition includes APIs for creating graphical forms (Swing) but does not include Enterprise APIs such as the Servlet and Enterprise JavaBeans APIs.

All Java 2 platforms must, however, include the core APIs. Essential classes like String and Object are not optional and are therefore included in the core APIs. Even Java 2 platforms designed to have a small footprint such as the Micro Edition, (J2ME is mainly used for handheld devices), which may exclude many of the other APIs of the Standard Edition must include the core classes.

## The Java Virtual Machine

Many people think of the JVM as the platform itself. This isn't the case – as we have said, the Java platform is the Java API *and* the JVM.

A JVM is a programmatic layer emulating a CPU. Your compiled Java class file(s) are made up of the **bytecodes** that are instructions to the JVM. The class file then runs *on* the JVM much as if it were a binary program for the virtual CPU. The JVM's job is to load your Java program classes and other classes involved in your program, and execute the bytecodes. In doing so, it will communicate with the underlying operating system as necessary. The JVM takes on the responsibility of platform-dependence so that your programs don't have to.

To compile Java source you use the javac command. javac is one of the tools provided as part of the Java SDK, and is located in the bin directory of your Java installation, for instance c:\jdk1.3\bin. The syntax for this command is as follows:

```
> javac <options> <source files>
```

The javac command produces class files corresponding in name to the class name(s) contained in the source file(s). For instance, a source file containing the source for a class called HelloWorld would be named HelloWorld.java. On compilation this would produce the class file HelloWorld.class.

The compiled class file is run by invoking the **Java interpreter**, java, which is also located in the bin directory of your JDK installation:

```
> java <options> <class name>
```

The following diagram illustrates this. (You can see a working example of this process in the *Java Outside The Database* section below):

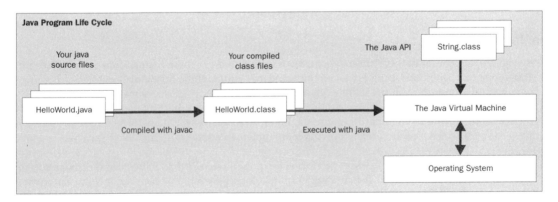

The JVM is often referred to as the Java interpreter. That's too simplistic for what it really does. In fact, the JVM can execute Java in a variety of ways. There are many JVMs around from different vendors, you don't have to use Sun's; some are free, some are not. Often, a JVM is geared for a particular purpose, for example, sheer execution speed in a number crunching environment or a slimmed down memory footprint in an embedded device.

JVMs don't have to just interpret bytecodes; JVM technology is rapidly advancing. You may have heard of Just In Time (JIT) or HotSpot compilers, these refer to compilers within the JVM itself that compile the bytecodes to *native code* (operating system machine instructions) as appropriate, so they will execute faster. This is made possible because it is only the *behavior* of the JVM which is mandated by Sun's specification, the details of *how* the behavior is achieved is left for the JVM vendor to implement. There is, therefore, considerable flexibility in the implementation details of any particular JVM and consequently, also considerable variation in their relative performance. Although JIT compilation is a standard feature of most JVMs, Oracle, in fact, uses an ahead-of-time compiler – discussed in Chapter 15.

> *The Java compiler is distinct from a compiler inside the JVM. When you produce your Java class file using the* java c *command, you are producing the bytecodes of the class file. The compiler, which may be incorporated into a JVM, takes those compiled bytecodes and further compiles them down to native code at run-time.*

# The Oracle Java Server Platform

The Oracle Java Server platform, also known as **JServer** in Oracle 8.1.7 and previous versions, or **9i JVM** in Oracle 9i, is an *enterprise-level* Java 2 platform. That is to say, it includes a JVM and an enterprise-level API. The Enterprise API (J2EE) is a set of APIs over and above the J2SE (Standard Edition) that are directed at the needs of the enterprise for distributed computing.

The Oracle JVM is a Java 2 JVM. In fact, Oracle versions 8.1.6 and above are Java 2-compliant, but the APIs for Java 1.1.8 are provided as well, for backwards-compatibility. Although Oracle version 8.1.5 is Java 1.1, Oracle did provide support for JDBC 2 features in that version by way of the oracle.jdbc2 package. The following table shows the Java versions supported by Oracle from 8.1.5:

| Oracle Version | Java SDK Version |
| --- | --- |
| 8.1.5 | 1.1 |
| 8.1.6 | 1.2 (Backwards compatible with 1.1.8) |
| 8.1.7 | 1.2 (Backwards compatible with 1.1.8) |
| 9.0.1 | 1.3 (Backwards compatible with 1.1.8) |

This is quite important to us as the Java 2 release (version 1.2 onwards) marked a substantial change and growth in the Java platform. Among the differences, there were fundamental changes in the security model, and particularly pertinent for database access, the introduction of JDBC version 2.0.

If your database version is Oracle 8.1.5, you will still be able to run Java. However, you will only have access to Java 2 features through Oracle's `oracle.jdbc2` package. It is not advisable to use the classes in that package any more since they must be changed to migrate to later Oracle versions – much better to begin with a real Java 2 version. This should be considered as a prerequisite for many of the examples in this book and you will be well advised to try to get access to a later Oracle version. For instance, Chapter 5, *Using JDBC* covers features almost exclusively only available in JDBC 2.0.

Conversely, if you have a Java 2-compliant database (Oracle 8.1.6 and onwards) you need a Java 2 SDK to develop with, otherwise you won't be able to develop using Java 2 features. This can be 1.2 or it could be later. If it is later, say 1.3 (still known as Java 2), you will be able to compile and run your programs in Oracle in most cases. Of course, to be absolutely sure no issues will occur it makes sense to develop with a Java 2 SDK to match the Oracle JVM, and we would advise you to stick with 1.2 until you have an Oracle version which supports a later version. If you are unsure about the compatibility of your code with SDK versions the changes between versions are documented at the Sun Microsystems web site. For instance, the changes introduced in Java 1.2 are documented at http://java.sun.com/products/jdk/1.2/compatibility.html.

As we have said, the Oracle Java Server platform is an enterprise platform and includes support for the standard J2EE APIs. Support for EJBs was introduced in 8.1.5 and version 8.1.7 incorporated a servlet engine so that servlets and Java Server Pages could be run directly in the database. However, with the emergence of the completely J2EE-compliant 9iAS Application Server, the database itself plays more of a supporting role in this respect. As such, we do not cover the J2EE components technologies in this book, instead concentrating on the development of **Java stored procedures**. We will briefly demonstrate their use in this chapter a little later when we are ready to verify that we can both create and execute Java in our database.

# Testing for a Java-Enabled Database

The Oracle JVM is installed by default with Oracle Typical or Minimal installs – you should select the JVM Option specifically during a Custom install.

To verify that you have a Java-enabled database, firstly check the messages you get when you start a SQL*Plus session. If Java is enabled you will see a JServer version message as follows:

```
SQL*Plus: Release 9.0.1.0.1 - Production on Wed Nov 21 11:00:53 2001

(c) Copyright 2001 Oracle Corporation.  All rights reserved.



Connected to:
Oracle9i Enterprise Edition Release 9.0.1.1.1 - Production
With the Partitioning option
JServer Release 9.0.1.1.1 - Production
```

If you believe your database is Java-enabled, skip ahead to the *Running Java Programs in The Database* section of this chapter, where we will show how to write and execute a simple Java class in the database.

# Installing The Oracle Java Server Platform

Manual installation of the Oracle Java Server Platform is a matter of running the supplied script. The script, in the file `initjvm.sql`, can be found in the `%ORACLE_HOME%/javavm/install` directory.

Initialization of a Java-enabled database is quite an intensive operation. To successfully run `initjvm.sql`, you have at least 30 MB free in the `SYSTEM` tablespace. In addition you should set the following database initialization parameters, which should then be left at these values for continuing Java development:

❑  `SHARED_POOL_SIZE` to 50MB

❑  `JAVA_POOL_SIZE` to 20MB

The script is going to need a lot of rollback space as well, which it uses to create additional rollback segments as required. You should ensure there is at least 90 MB of rollback space available and in order to run the script you must also log in as `SYS`. Unless you have the luxury of owning your own private Oracle instance, it is likely you will need to speak to your DBA to run the script. You will be very unpopular if you try to install Java into the database without their knowledge anyway!

The `initjvm.sql` script is self checking – if any problems are encountered along the way, the whole operation is backed out. If you do get problems, check the latest notes in the `%ORACLE_HOME%/javavm/readme` file that contains specific information for your platform. You can then adjust the necessary resources and re-run the script.

When successfully completed, in excess of 8,000 Java class objects are created, (the actual number is platform-dependent). They should all be valid as you can see from the following query, which you will need to submit when connected as `SYS`:

```
SQL> select count(*), status
  2    from user_objects
  3    where object_type = 'JAVA CLASS'
  4    group by status
  5    /

  COUNT(*) STATUS
---------- -------
      9872 VALID
```

In addition to creating the system Java classes. The script performs many other steps to enable Java on your database. These include:

❑  Creation of public synonyms for the system Java classes

❑  Creation of database roles that are used for specific Java operations

❑  Modification to the startup and shutdown database processes

❑  Configuration of the Oracle JVM

❑  Installation of SQLJ support

❑  Creation of the PL/SQL package `DBMS_JAVA` for managing Java in the database

For details on the important `DBMS_JAVA` PL/SQL package, refer to Chapter 9, *Using the Oracle JVM.*

**21**

# Running Java Programs in the Database

Section III of this book, *Using Java in the Database*, covers running Java programs within the database in detail. We introduce the subject here for three main reasons:

❏ To give you a brief taster of how to run Java inside the database

❏ To give you an appreciation of some of the differences between Java inside and outside the database as a primer for the detailed discussions to follow

❏ So you can actually see that it does really work – if you have had to perform a manual installation of the Oracle JVM you will certainly want to be encouraged at this point that you can indeed create and run Java inside the database

## Compiling Java Outside the Database

Before going on to show Java inside the database, let's first write and execute a simple program outside the database. We'll then take the same class and demonstrate the several ways it could arrive in the database, and how it is run once there.

No Java tutorial can be complete without the ubiquitous `Hello World` example. So, consider the following Java source file for the `HelloWorld` class, which is contained in a file called `HelloWorld.java`:

```
public class HelloWorld {

  public static void main(String[] args) {
    System.out.println("Hello World from Chapter 1!");
  }
}
```

To compile this class outside the database, you need to execute the `javac` command. You can enter the full path to the `javac` executable or you can include the Java `bin` directory in your environment `PATH` variable as we have shown in the *A Useful Batch File* section:

```
set JAVA_HOME=C:\jdk1.3
set PATH=.;%PATH%;%JAVA_HOME%\bin;%ORACLE_HOME%\bin
```

At the command prompt, you will need to run your batch file to set your environment and then do the following:

```
> javac HelloWorld.java
```

This produces a Java class file, `HelloWorld.class`, which is run with the `java` command:

```
> java HelloWorld
Hello World from Chapter 1!
```

When you run the `java` command on the command line, you are telling Java which class to run. In actual fact, you are telling Java which class with a `main()` method to run. It is special in that the java executable will look for it, invoke it, and pass the command line arguments to it. The signature of it, as we saw in the `HelloWorld` example above, is:

```
public static void main(String[] args)
```

Only a class that defines this method can be invoked directly with the `java` command as a Java application – that's the rule *outside* the database. Later on, we will see how a PL/SQL wrapper can be created to call a Java class from PL/SQL without this restriction.

The `System.out` and `System.err` Java streams are normally directed to the standard out and standard error for the operating system, this often means that output is fed straight back to us, as it was for the `HelloWorld` example when making the following call:

```
System.out.println("Hello World from Chapter 1!");
```

When running Java inside the database, `System.out` and `System.err` are defaulted to the current trace files. The location of these files is determined in the database configuration file (`init.ora` or equivalent). If you don't have access to them or know where they are, you will have to ask your DBA. To see output fed back to the screen in a SQL*Plus session we can use the `SERVEROUTPUT` SQL*Plus variable, and make a call to another DBMS_JAVA packaged function, `set_output`. This function has the following signature where `buffersize` matches the size of the buffer specified to the set `SERVEROUTPUT` command (default is 2,000 bytes):

```
PROCEDURE set_output (buffersize NUMBER)
```

For example, to set a buffer of 5,000 bytes and to have `System.out` redirected to your SQL*Plus session enter the following commands before running:

```
SQL> set serveroutput on size 5000
SQL> call dbms_java.set_output(5000);

Call completed.
```

# Getting Java into the Database

There are four ways you can get your Java classes into the database:

- ❑ Load a compiled Java class from outside
- ❑ Load a Java source from outside
- ❑ Load multiple Java source and/or class files from outside
- ❑ Write the source directly inside

To load either class files or source files from outside the database, we use the `loadjava` tool. This is provided by Oracle and is an executable script file found in your `%ORACLE_HOME%/bin` directory. The syntax for `loadjava` is as follows:

```
loadjava {-user | -u} username/password[@database]
  [-option_name -option_name ...] file_name file_name ...
```

`loadjava` has a number of options that can be specified, including:

- ❏ `-resolve` – This option tells `loadjava` to resolve all the references external to the loaded class. If you actually load a source Java file, this will involve compilation first. If this option is not specified, the class is not resolved (and for source files, not compiled) until it is run. You should always specify this option unless you have a good reason not to, since it avoids the unnecessary overhead of resolving the class at run-time and allows you to deal with any issues straightaway.

- ❏ `-resolver` – A resolver spec is a bit like the external CLASSPATH variable; it tells `loadjava` where to look for external references. For instance if you wanted the schemas SCOTT and PUBLIC to be searched, you would specify this option with ((* SCOTT) (* PUBLIC)). Note that you have to know which schemas to include, there is no wildcard * option for the schema name.

- ❏ `-verbose` – This option tells `loadjava` to output messages telling us what it's doing. We'll use this option for our examples so we can see what is happening.

- ❏ `-force` – This option forces the upload of a previously loaded file, which would otherwise fail. You are safe to use `-force` if you are reloading a new version of the same object, but not if, for example, you previously loaded the Java class and are now going to load the source of the same object. Since we will be doing exactly that in our examples, we won't use the `-force` option, but instead we'll drop the loaded objects using `loadjava`'s complimentary tool, `dropjava`. `dropjava` should always be used to drop objects loaded by `loadjava` because it causes all the associated references to be correctly removed.

## Loading Class Files From The File System

This is a relatively easy way to load a Java class to the database because the class has already been compiled so issues with compilation or debugging of errors have already been resolved by this point.

In order to demonstrate that we can run classes on the database regardless of whether they have a `main()` method or not, we'll make a small modification to our `HelloWorld` class first:

```java
public class HelloWorld2 {

  public static void main(String[] args) {
    System.out.println("Hello World from Chapter 1!");
  }

  public static void db_run() {
    System.out.println("Hello World from db_run method!");
  }
}
```

We have added a new static method, `db_run()`. First, we compile this new class as before using the `javac` command:

```
> javac HelloWorld2.java
```

If we run the changed class, you can see that the `java` command is not concerned with the new `db_run()` method – it just runs `main()` as normal:

```
> java HelloWorld2
Hello World from Chapter 1!
```

And we can load the compiled `HelloWorld2.class` to the database under the schema `USERNAME` as follows:

```
> loadjava -user username/password -resolve -verbose HelloWorld2.class
arguments: '-user' 'username/password' '-resolve' '-verbose'
                                       'HelloWorld2.class'
creating : class HelloWorld2
loading  : class HelloWorld2
resolving: class HelloWorld2
```

Notice the message output because we specified the `-verbose` option and that the class is resolved since that option was also specified.

If we now query the `USER_OBJECTS` view for the `USERNAME` schema we can see the newly loaded class file:

```
SQL> col name format a40
SQL> select dbms_java.longname(object_name) name,object_type type, status
  2    from user_objects
  3   where object_type like 'JAVA%'
  4  /

NAME                                      TYPE                STATUS
---------------------------------------   -----------------   -------
HelloWorld2                               JAVA CLASS          VALID
```

To show the difference, let's drop and reload the class. This time we'll omit the `-resolve` option:

```
> dropjava -user username/password -verbose HelloWorld2.class
dropping: class HelloWorld2
```

```
> loadjava -user username/passsword -verbose HelloWorld2.class
arguments: '-user' 'username'/'password' '-verbose' 'HelloWorld2.class'
creating : class HelloWorld2
loading  : class HelloWorld2
```

This time there are no messages to indicate that the class has been resolved, and if we re-query the `USER_OBJECTS` view, we can see that the class is marked as invalid. This means it will be resolved at run-time the first time it is run:

```
SQL> select dbms_java.longname(object_name) name,object_type type, status
  2    from user_objects
  3    where object_type like 'JAVA%'
  4    /
```

| NAME | TYPE | STATUS |
| --- | --- | --- |
| HelloWorld2 | JAVA CLASS | INVALID |

Even though the status of this class is INVALID, we can continue with our example and see what happens.

In order to invoke the db_run() method of this class within the database, we have to create a PL/SQL wrapper for it. The whole subject of running Java classes within the database and PL/SQL wrappers is covered in detail in Chapter 10, *Java Stored Procedure Basics*, so we won't go into detail about the PL/SQL wrapper – we'll just reveal enough to demonstrate our example.

```
SQL> create or replace procedure run_helloworld2
  2    as language java
  3    name 'HelloWorld2.db_run()';
  4    /

Procedure created.
```

Here we create a procedure called RUN_HELLOWORLD2. This is a PL/SQL procedure that simply wraps the loaded Java class method. Notice the specification of the Java class includes the static db_run() method. This is the method that will be run when the procedure is invoked. A wrapper must specify a static method but it can be any static method. In this way, it is quite feasible to have multiple entry points to a class, each being a static method with its own PL/SQL procedure wrapper.

> *A static method is one that is not associated with any one instance of the class. For this reason, they are also known as class methods. These will be covered in more detail in Chapter 2, Java Classes and Objects.*

Here's what happens when we run the wrapper procedure:

```
SQL> set serveroutput on size 5000
SQL> call dbms_java.set_output(5000);

Call completed.

SQL> execute run_helloworld2;
Hello World from db_run method!

PL/SQL procedure successfully completed.
```

Notice that we redirected the System.out calls to the SQL*Plus session using the call to the dbms_java.set_output procedure. This call has been implemented in the login.sql file discussed earlier on in the chapter. If you have used the suggested batch file method, then the call to this method would have already been made when you started your SQL*Plus session and your environment is already set up.

Having run the class, which was not resolved when loaded, the JVM had to resolve it at run-time. If we query USER_OBJECTS again, we can see that the class is now validated. The class will remain valid until some dependency it has changes, and forces it to be invalidated or it is itself changed. This takes advantage of Oracle's established object dependency mechanism.

```
SQL> select dbms_java.longname(object_name) name, object_type type, status
  2    from user_objects
  3    where object_type like 'JAVA%'
  4  /

NAME                                          TYPE                STATUS
--------------------------------------------- ------------------- -------
HelloWorld2                                   JAVA CLASS          VALID
```

## Loading Java Source Files to the Database

The second method for loading Java to the database is to load the Java source files themselves. This is essentially similar to loading the class file. However, this time, the source is kept in the database as an object in its own right. Again, the -resolve option to loadjava determines whether compilation is done at load or run-time, and as always, it is advisable to specify it.

Let's drop the HelloWorld2 class from the database and, this time, reload it from the source file. Again, we'll specify the -verbose option so you can see what goes on:

```
> dropjava -user username/password -verbose HelloWorld2.class
dropping: class HelloWorld2

> loadjava -user username/password -resolve -verbose HelloWorld2.java
arguments: '-user' 'username/password' '-resolve' '-verbose' 'HelloWorld2.java'
creating : source HelloWorld2
loading  : source HelloWorld2
creating : HelloWorld2
resolving: source HelloWorld2
```

The output is not so very different from loading the class file. However, when we view USER_OBJECTS, we see a new object created for the Java source:

```
SQL> select dbms_java.longname(object_name) name, object_type type, status
  2    from user_objects
  3    where object_type like 'JAVA%'
  4  /

NAME                                          TYPE                STATUS
--------------------------------------------- ------------------- -------
HelloWorld2                                   JAVA CLASS          VALID
HelloWorld2                                   JAVA SOURCE         VALID
```

and when we execute the PL/SQL wrapper:

```
SQL> execute run_helloworld2;
BEGIN run_helloworld2; END;

*
ERROR at line 1:
ORA-29549: class USERNAME.HelloWorld has changed, Java session state cleared
ORA-06512: at "USERNAME.RUN_HELLOWORLD2", line 0
ORA-06512: at line 1

SQL> set serveroutput on size 5000
SQL> call dbms_java.set_output(5000);

Call completed.

SQL> execute run_helloworld2;
Hello World from db_run method!

PL/SQL procedure successfully completed.
```

You can see that the first execution produces an error, this is because the dependency checking mechanism has detected that the class already has a state in the current session and that state had to be cleared when the referenced Java class changed as it did when it was dropped and reloaded from source. The second execution then succeeds because the database re-validated it when it was referenced automatically. We could get around this by reconnecting before attempting to run it.

## Loading Multiple Java Source/Class Files to the Database

Using the loadjava tool you can also specify a JAR or ZIP file to be loaded to the database. This file can contain Java source files and/or class files. Basically, the operations performed are identical to those described above for either loading the source or the class files individually, as that is exactly what loadjava does.

Loading a JAR or ZIP file is really just a convenient way to load multiple files at once. It is also an efficient way because files that have not been modified since they were last loaded are not re-loaded. (You can force them to be re-loaded if you want to by specifying the -force option of loadjava).

The syntax for using loadjava is just the same as before except you specify a JAR or ZIP file instead of an individual file:

```
> loadjava -user username/password -resolve AllMyJava.jar
```

## Writing Java Directly in the Database

Our last method for getting Java into the database is simply to write it directly through a SQL*Plus session. It is a very quick and easy way to get up and running with Java in the database. Since everything is done in the database, you need no JDK – or anything other than the database itself, in fact! One minor drawback of this method is that it doesn't integrate so nicely with editing in your IDE (if you use one). Before we rewrite this class directly into the database let's clear any references to the existing objects with dropjava:

```
> dropjava -user username/password -verbose HelloWorld2.java
dropping source  : HelloWorld2
```

Notice that we specify to drop the source file name explicitly – this is important. In order for all the internal references to be cleared up correctly the same name must be specified to drop the Java as was used to load it in the first place.

If we now query USER_OBJECTS, we can see HelloWorld2 has gone:

```
SQL> select dbms_java.longname(object_name) name, object_type type, status
  2    from user_objects
  3    where object_type like 'JAVA%'
  4  /

no rows selected
```

Now to write Java directly we create a Java source object as follows:

```
SQL> create or replace and compile java source named HelloWorld3
  2  as
  3  public class HelloWorld3 {
  4    public static void db_run() {
  5      System.out.println("Hello. Database only version!");
  6    }
  7  }
  8  /

Java created.
```

Notice we have specified the option that this object should be immediately compiled in the first line with the words and compile. Also, note that the main() method has gone altogether since we don't need it to make a call to this class.

If we query USER_OBJECTS again, we can see the new objects:

```
SQL> select dbms_java.longname(object_name) name, object_type type, status
  2    from user_objects
  3    where object_type like 'JAVA%'
  4  /

NAME                                              TYPE                STATUS
------------------------------------------------- ------------------- -------
HELLOWORLD3                                       JAVA SOURCE         VALID
HelloWorld3                                       JAVA CLASS          VALID
```

As you can see, the source object's name is now all in uppercase. This is to be expected since database objects are usually *case-insensitive*. The important object, the class object we are going to run, does have the correct case.

This time if we run the wrapper procedure (after reconnection to avoid the Java session state error), you can see the new version is executed:

```
SQL> create or replace procedure run_helloworld3
  2  as language java
  3  name 'HelloWorld3.db_run()';
  4  /

Procedure created.

SQL> execute run_helloworld3
Hello. Database only version!

PL/SQL procedure successfully completed.
```

Now when we want to drop the class from the database, we do it with the DROP JAVA SOURCE command. This also results in the class object's removal as you can see:

```
SQL> drop java source helloworld3;

Java dropped.

SQL> select dbms_java.longname(object_name) name, object_type type, status
  2    from user_objects
  3   where object_type like 'JAVA%'
  4  /

no rows selected
```

# Summary

In this chapter we have laid the groundwork for the chapters to come. The main goal of the chapter was to show you how to set up your database to enable Java and in the course of doing that we covered:

- ❏ The Java 2 platform – what this means
- ❏ The Java API
- ❏ The Java Virtual Machine
- ❏ How Java programs are run outside the database
- ❏ The Oracle JVM and how to install it
- ❏ The Oracle Java Server platform
- ❏ The main methods for loading Java programs to the database
- ❏ Running Java programs in the database

We have kept the latter two fairly brief because they are covered in depth later in the book. However, they have served as a primer and to prove the installation if you had to go through the process of manual installation of the Oracle JVM.

Oracle 9i Java Programming

# Java Classes and Objects

In the traditional n-tier model for application development, Java resides in the business logic layer and PL/SQL in the data layer. Oracle, however, is busy ripping up the rulebook and the optimal distribution of your application logic is now less clear-cut. The addition to Oracle 9i objects of object-oriented (OO) features such as inheritance and polymorphism pushes PL/SQL into the business tier. The advent of Java in the database, along with support for the JDBC and SQLJ interfaces, pushes Java towards the data tier.

Despite the fact that Oracle developers will be familiar with object types, and that Oracle 9i adds OO features to PL/SQL, it is still a relatively under-exploited feature. It is fair to say that, as Oracle developers, we come from a **procedural programming** world that is driven by the concepts of structured analysis and design, which is different from the **object-oriented** (OO) world of Java. The underlying paradigm is different between Java and PL/SQL, but once the underlying model is understood, the rest is syntax and environment details.

The basic syntax of Java is not, on the whole, all that conceptually different from many of the other popular programming languages available today.

*Appendix A presents a comparison of basic syntax and control structures for PL/SQL and Java.*

At that level, it doesn't appear to accomplish any major goals that absolutely cannot be accomplished in other languages. So why has Java become so popular, why has Oracle incorporated the language directly into their database server, and why would you want to use it in the database? At a practical level, it is the goal of this book to answer that last question.

However, before we do this, it is worth exploring the fundamental OO concepts in a little detail because of the many reasons that Java has gained in popularity, undoubtedly one of the more important ones is that it is a very good example of a language that makes effective use of the concepts of object-oriented programming methodologies. These methodologies, many of which we will see shortly, are of great value as our projects become bigger and more complex, especially when multiple developers will be collaborating. After seeing just a little of the basic syntax of the Java, a programmer could accomplish a fairly linear translation into Java of their existing project, previously written in some traditional non-object-oriented language such as C, FORTRAN, or COBOL. They could analyze old procedural code line-by-line and find functionally equivalent code in Java to accomplish the same thing. But, what would be gained by doing this? Simply because something is written in Java, it doesn't make it better. To benefit from using Java you need to accomplish sound software engineering objectives, such as:

- **Code Reuse** – If I create a solution today, will I be able to use it to solve a different problem tomorrow?

- **Encapsulation** – Can my black box present an accessible interface to the outside world, while still protecting my internal implementation from external twiddling?

- **Modularity** – Are functional components partitioned into black boxes or are their implementations scattered across the entire application?

- **Scalability** – Will my solution grow gracefully?

- **Maintainability** – How hard is it to track down where a problem is occurring and determine what components might be involved?

As you read through the topics in this chapter, keep in mind not only the nuts and bolts questions, such as 'How do I actually implement this technique?' but more importantly, 'How will this technique make my code better with regard to these software engineering objectives?'

So, keep these objectives in mind as we discuss:

- Creating and using Java classes and objects

- Inheritance in the Java language

- Packages in Java

- The `public`, `private`, and `protected` keywords

- Exceptions

# Making and Using Classes and Objects

Classes are the building blocks of any Java program. The typical definition of a **class** states that it is a template or a specification for the structure and behavior of objects of a given type or purpose. It describes a container for one or multiple variables and the **methods** (functions) that operate on them. Likewise the typical definition of an **object** is an instance of a given class. We can illustrate these abstract definitions with a real-word analogy. Imagine an architect's blueprint design for building a house. The blueprint itself obviously isn't a house, but it does describe a house. The blueprint doesn't build the house, but it provides necessary information to those who will. In Java, we can think of a class as being like a blueprint and an object as being analogous to a house. Whereas a blueprint gives a builder the information he or she needs to construct the building, a class gives the JVM the information it needs to construct an object. There can be, and there will be, many different kinds of classes that will be used to build many different kinds of objects, just as there are many different kinds of blueprints (for example, a skyscraper blueprint, a barn blueprint, a factory blueprint) that can be used to construct many different types of buildings.

It might also help database developers to think of classes as being analogous to the schema design for a given table and objects as being similar to the rows in that table. However, as we will see in this chapter, the behavior of both Java classes and objects will quickly grow beyond the bounds of that analogy in many ways. Or if, as database developers, you are interested in how Java objects compare to PL/SQL objects, don't worry we will be covering that in the next chapter.

Under this section on the Java classes and objects, we will be looking at the following:

- ❏ Instantiating objects
- ❏ Instance variables and static variables
- ❏ Constants
- ❏ Static methods and overloading methods

# Instantiating Objects

In Appendix A we demonstrate the use of the new keyword to create arrays and strings. When the new keyword was used to create an array, we emphasized its role in the allocation of memory space in which to store the contents of the array variable. If we have code like this:

```
int[] intArray = new int[3];
```

we will have an intArray variable that now has whatever resources it needs to be able to store three integers. When the new keyword was used with String variables, we saw how it could be used to initialize the value of a variable. As such, when we have code like this:

```
String str = new String("Java");
```

we can also expect that the str variable, in addition to having the resources it needs to store a String, has also somehow been initialized to have a string value of "Java". So, the new keyword causes two things to happen. It allocates the new object (or array) and it also triggers the initialization of the object. We refer to the building of an object from its blueprint as **instantiation** – the creation of an instance of a class.

Notice that we just said that the new keyword "triggers" the initialization of the object. It doesn't do the initialization itself, but it does start the process. The initialization is actually handled by what is called a **constructor**. Recall that a function that resides inside a class is called a **method**. A constructor is a special kind of method that is called by the new keyword to initialize the object. Constructors are easily identified in a class because the method has the same name as the name of the class. Therefore, the constructor for a class called House would also be named House. We don't invoke this method directly, however, as it gets called behind the scenes when you use the new keyword. Most of the time, we will only be accessing this method through the new keyword and not calling it directly ourselves (we will see an exception to this in the *Overloading Methods* section later in this chapter).

Since the purpose of constructors is primarily to quietly initialize the object, they have no return type. However, unlike other methods that have no return type, you should not use the void keyword. Technically speaking, the constructor does already have a return type. It is returning a reference to the current object, but this is handled automatically for us by Java. Attempting to define a return type will interfere with this process, so don't do it. Attempting to use the return keyword while inside a constructor will generate an error.

If you create a class without a constructor, a default constructor will be available in most cases. Until we learn about inheritance later in this chapter, we can pretend for the moment that the default constructor is just an empty method.

Let's see the use of a constructor in an example. The first file declares a `House` class that has a constructor method:

```
public class House {
  public House() {

    // This is the constructor for the House class
    // We will shortly see how to initialize variables in here

    // Normally, constructors should be quiet.  But to
    // prove we made it here, we print a message.
    System.out.println("I'm in the House constructor");
  }
}
```

In the second file, we create a little tester with a `main()` method that will instantiate two `House` objects. It is also an example of a class without a declared constructor. We'll explore shortly why we don't need one, but if some other class were to create an object instance of this class, the default constructor would be called.

```
public class HomeBuilder {
  public static void main(String arg[]) {

    // You can declare a variable and instantiate the object
    // on two different lines.
    House myHouse;
    myHouse = new House();

    // Or you can do the same thing but all in one line:
    House yourHouse = new House();
  }
}
```

Why do we need to create an object instead of just working with the class? There are significant differences in what we will be permitted to do to a class versus an object. Just as we can't move our furniture and knick-knacks into a blueprint – like we can with a house, we are limited in how we add or modify data to a class. Most of the time the changes we make to the values of variables, either directly or through a method that changes them, should be performed on objects and not classes. A special exception exists, which we will see shortly.

# Instance Variables

Objects have variables to store their data. This data may differ from object to object, even if the different objects have been instantiated from the same class. If you had a group of houses that were all built from the same blueprint they would still each have their own unique street address. These variables may be called **object variables** or **instance variables**. The values are retrieved using the notation `objectReference.variableName` from code outside the object's class or just `variableName` from code inside the object's class.

To see this in action, we'll make some changes to the classes from the previous example. We'll add a new instance variable called `streetAddress` to the House class:

```java
public class House {
  public String streetAddress;

  public House() {

    // We're inside the House class so we can refer to the
    // variable by its short name

    streetAddress = "No address defined yet";
  }
}
```

And here's our new `HomeBuilder` class.

```java
public class HomeBuilder {
  public static void main(String arg[]) {
    House myHouse = new House();

    // Let's print out the default value of streetAddress.
    // We're outside the House class, so we have to use the
    // long name.
    System.out.println(myHouse.streetAddress);

    // We can set the variable using the same notation
    myHouse.streetAddress = "123 Pine Street";

    // Lastly, we print out the new value
    System.out.println(myHouse.streetAddress);
  }
}
```

# Static Variables

Continuing with our blueprint analogy, a blueprint might have a variable that should have the same value for every house that might be built according to it. For example, the blueprint might describe a three-bedroom house, so presumably all buildings constructed according to the blueprint ought to be three bedroom houses. Classes, likewise, have variables that span all usages of the class. We call these **class variables** or **static variables**. We declare a variable as being a static variable by using the static keyword in the variable declaration. So, if we were to create a class called `ThreeBedroomHouse`, and we wanted to declare a variable called `numberOfBedrooms` to be a static variable, it would look something like this:

```java
public class ThreeBedroomHouse {
  public static int numberOfBedrooms = 3;
}
```

The `static` keyword in front of `int numberOfBedrooms` means that the value doesn't change from object instance to object instance. It remains the same no matter what object you access it from. Any variable without the `static` keyword in front may have different values from one object instance to another.

We can get the value of a static variable by using the notation `className.variableName`, or also by using `objectReference.variableName` if we have an instance of the class. We can use just `variableName` from code inside the class.

```
public class HomeBuilder {
  public static void main(String arg[]) {
    System.out.println(ThreeBedroomHouse.numberOfBedrooms);

    ThreeBedroomHouse myHouse = new ThreeBedroomHouse();
    System.out.println(myHouse.numberOfBedrooms);
  }
}
```

If we used the `myHouse` instance in the code above to change the value of the `numberOfBedrooms` variable to 4, for example, the value of `numberOfBedrooms` would appear to change to 4 in all of the other instances of `ThreeBedroomHouse` as well. That's because it's a property of the class and not the object, so every object of that class will see the change.

```
public class HomeBuilder {
  public static void main(String arg[]) {
    ThreeBedroomHouse myHouse = new ThreeBedroomHouse();
    ThreeBedroomHouse yourHouse = new ThreeBedroomHouse();

    System.out.println(ThreeBedroomHouse.numberOfBedrooms);
    System.out.println(myHouse.numberOfBedrooms);
    System.out.println(yourHouse.numberOfBedrooms);

    myHouse.numberOfBedrooms = 4;

    System.out.println(ThreeBedroomHouse.numberOfBedrooms);
    System.out.println(myHouse.numberOfBedrooms);
    System.out.println(yourHouse.numberOfBedrooms);
  }
}
```

# Constants

Since it would be rather silly to have a class called `ThreeBedroomHouse` with a `numberOfBedrooms` variable set to four, it would probably be a good idea to prevent that variable from being changed by any of the instances of the class. The keyword `final` can help us do exactly that. In combination with the `static` keyword it constitutes Java's way of declaring constants. If we changed the `numberOfBedrooms` declaration in the `ThreeBedroomHouse` class to the following:

```
public class ThreeBedroomHouse {
  public static final int numberOfBedrooms = 3;
}
```

then `numberOfBedrooms` would be a constant that could be accessed from any instance of `ThreeBedroomHouse`, but could not be changed by any of them.

Stylistically speaking, when we make a variable a constant, it is standard convention to change the capitalization of the variable name to uppercase, so the above line would more correctly be:

```
public class ThreeBedroomHouse {
  public static final int NUMBEROFBEDROOMS = 3;
}
```

For an example of a constant in a class that occurs in Java's core class library, see the class `java.lang.Math`, which has the constants `PI` and `E`.

## Considerations

So, why and when would you want to use static variables over instance variables? The first advantage is a saving in the amount of memory it takes to store your objects. If a variable has the same value in every object, why have a copy of the variable in every object? A static variable is stored only once. If you have thousands of instances, the savings could be enormous. Another use for static variables is to mimic some of the behavior of global variables in other languages. Since any change to a static variable (assuming it's not a `final` variable) made through one instance is visible in the other instances, the static variable can act as a mechanism for passing messages from one instance to another. The last advantage we'll mention is that when a variable is both static and final, and thus a constant, there are many things that most Java compilers can do with the variable during optimization since the occurrences of the variable can be safely replaced by the value of the variable.

> Unfortunately, there is also a major disadvantage to using static variables that is specific to using Java inside the Oracle database. The problem involves some rather advanced memory considerations and Oracle internals, which are beyond the scope of this chapter. However, this issue will be discussed in detail later in the book in the *Static Variables* section in Chapter 15.

# Instance Methods

Methods can be accessed via objects and sometimes via classes (in a manner similar to that described above for variables). Most often we use objects to invoke methods. We call these **object methods** or **instance methods**. We call the method using the notation `object.methodName()` from code outside the object's class or just `methodName()` from code inside the object's class. As an example, we'll add instance methods named `getStreetAddress()` and `setStreetAddress()` to our `ThreeBedroomHouse` class:

```
public class ThreeBedroomHouse {
  public String streetAddress = "No address defined yet";

  public String getStreetAddress() {
    return streetAddress;
  }
```

```
public void setStreetAddress(String newaddress) {

    // We're inside the ThreeBedroomHouse class so we can refer to
    // other methods of this class via their short name:
    System.out.println("Old address is " + getStreetAddress());

    streetAddress = newaddress;

    System.out.println("New address is " + getStreetAddress());
    }
}
```

And here is how we access the new methods using an instance of `ThreeBedroomHouse`:

```
public class HomeBuilder {
   public static void main(String arg[]) {
      ThreeBedroomHouse myHouse = new ThreeBedroomHouse();

      // We're outside the ThreeBedroomHouse class so we have to
      // refer to methods by their long name.
      myHouse.setStreetAddress("123 Pine Street");

      System.out.println(myHouse.getStreetAddress());
   }
}
```

# Static Methods

A method might be useful to a class even before an instance of an object is created. We call these **class methods** or **static methods**. For example, we might want a `getNumberOfBedrooms()` method. Presumably, we don't need an instance of a `ThreeBedroomHouse` to determine the number of bedrooms it should have. As such, we want to add `getNumberOfBedrooms()` as a static method to `ThreeBedroomHouse`. We do this by using the `static` keyword in the method declaration:

```
public class ThreeBedroomHouse {
   public static final int NUMBEROFBEDROOMS = 3;

   public static int getNumberOfBedrooms() {
      return NUMBEROFBEDROOMS;
   }
}
```

We can then call our new method using the notation `ClassName.methodName()` from code outside the class or just `methodName()` from code inside the class. We can also call it using `objectReference.methodName()`, if we have an instance of the class.

```
public class HomeBuilder {
   public static void main(String arg[]) {

      // Calling the static method via the class
      System.out.println(ThreeBedroomHouse.getNumberOfBedrooms());
```

```
        ThreeBedroomHouse myHouse = new ThreeBedroomHouse();

        // Calling the static method via an instance
        System.out.println(myHouse.getNumberOfBedrooms());
    }
}
```

## Restrictions on Static Methods

When we are creating a static method like getNumberOfBedrooms(), there is a major restriction on what other elements of the class we can access. A static method of a class can only access other static methods and static variables of the class. It cannot access any of the instance methods or variables of its class. On the other hand, instance methods are allowed to call either static or non-static methods and make use of static or non-static variables.

Consider the following uncompilable mixture of the last two examples:

```
public class ThreeBedroomHouse {
  public String streetAddress = "123 Pine Street";
  public static final int NUMBEROFBEDROOMS = 3;

  public static int getNumberOfBedrooms() {

    // This will not work!
    // The compiler will produce errors on these two lines
    System.out.println("A house with " + NUMBEROFBEDROOMS + " bedrooms at "
                       + getStreetAddress());
    System.out.println("A house with " + NUMBEROFBEDROOMS + " bedrooms at "
                       + streetAddress);

    return NUMBEROFBEDROOMS;
  }

  public String getStreetAddress() {

    // These two lines are OK
    System.out.println("A house with " + getNumberOfBedrooms()
                       + " bedrooms at " + streetAddress);
    System.out.println("A house with " + NUMBEROFBEDROOMS + " bedrooms at "
                       + streetAddress);

    return streetAddress;
  }
}
```

In this example, the static method getNumberOfBedrooms() would not be allowed to call the instance method getStreetAddress(), but getStreetAddress() can call getNumberOfBedrooms(). With regard to variables, getNumberOfBedrooms() would not be allowed to access the instance variable streetAddress, but it can access the static constant NUMBEROFBEDROOMS.

# Overloading Methods

Since Java is a strongly typed language, every argument of a method must have a defined data type. What if we needed the flexibility to call the same method but with different types of arguments? Also, you may have encountered other languages that allow a variable number of arguments to be passed to a function or method. There is no such allowance in Java. Every method has a fixed number of arguments. However, a technique exists called overloading that will allow some flexibility in dealing with both of these restrictions.

Method overloading occurs when you have two method definitions with the same method name, but with arguments that differ in type, in number, or both. At first, it may seem confusing to have multiple methods with the same name. Although we tend to the think of the name of a method as being its unique identifier, in Java it is a combination of the method name and the argument list that is used to tell them apart. Keep this in mind should you later get error messages reporting that the compiler can't find a particular method that you know is indeed defined. That message is often due to passing an argument of the wrong type, and what the compiler is saying is that it can't find a method with that method name that will accept that erroneous data type as an argument.

One of the most common uses of overloading is to provide multiple constructors for a class, so that different kinds of initialization parameters can be used and, as long as there is a matching constructor, an object will get instantiated.

```
public class House {
   public String streetAddress = "No address defined yet";
   public int numberOfBedrooms = 0;

   public House() {
     System.out.println("call to constructor with no arguments");
   }

   public House(String address) {
     streetAddress = address;

     System.out.println("call to constructor with 1 String argument");
   }

   public House(int bedrooms) {
     numberOfBedrooms = bedrooms;

     System.out.println("call to constructor with 1 int argument");
   }

   public House(String address, int bedrooms) {
     streetAddress = address;
     numberOfBedrooms = bedrooms;

     System.out.println("call to constructor with
                     1 String argument and 1 int argument");
   }
}
```

The following version of `HomeBuilder` ends up invoking each of the four constructors above, simply by passing different arguments to the constructor:

```
public class HomeBuilder {
  public static void main(String arg[]) {
    House myHouse;

    // This will call the first House constructor
    myHouse = new House();

    // This will call the second House constructor
    myHouse = new House("123 Pine Street");

    // This will call the third House constructor
    myHouse = new House(3);

    // This will call the fourth House constructor
    myHouse = new House("123 Pine Street", 3);
  }
}
```

```
> java HomeBuilder
call to constructor with no arguments
call to constructor with 1 String argument
call to constructor with 1 int argument
call to constructor with 1 String argument and 1 int argument
```

## Overloading and Return Types

One point about overloading that can be potentially confusing is that you can have multiple overloaded methods with the same name, but with different return types. However, two methods may not differ only in return type. They must always at least differ in argument number or type.

```
public class House {
  public int numberOfBedrooms = 3;

  public int getNumberOfBedrooms() {
    return numberOfBedrooms;
  }

  // Overloading getNumberOfBedrooms() with the following method
  // will NOT work. The compiler will complain about the method
  // already being defined:
  public String getNumberOfBedrooms() {
    return Integer.toString(numberOfBedrooms);
  }

  // Overloading getNumberOfBedrooms() with the following method
  // will work. It differs in return type and arguments
  public String getNumberOfBedrooms(String s) {
    return Integer.toString(numberOfBedrooms) + s;
  }
}
```

If you comment out the offending second method above, you can test it with the following `HomeBuilder` class:

```
public class HomeBuilder {
  public static void main(String arg[]) {
    House myHouse;

    myHouse = new House();

    // Call the method that returns an int
    System.out.println(myHouse.getNumberOfBedrooms());

    // Call the method that returns a String
    System.out.println(myHouse.getNumberOfBedrooms(" rooms"));
  }
}
```

# The this Reference

So, far it has been fairly simple to access the variables or methods of our own class. If we use the name of a variable or method without specifying a class or object using the dot notation (such as, using `variableName` instead of `objectReference.variableName`), it is assumed that the code is referring to a member that is present in the same class as the code, and most of the time that works perfectly. However, there are times when it's necessary to explicitly specify the object within which this code resides. Java provides us with a special variable that is available at all times whenever we're inside an instance method. It is called the `this` reference and it always refers to the current object within which the instance method is executing (never try to use `this` in a static method, it won't be defined there).

There are two common situations where the `this` reference is frequently used. The first is when there is going to be a local variable (often an argument) with the same name as an instance variable. In that case, we would refer to the local variable as `variableName` and the instance variable as `this.variableName`. As an example, the following code snippet is a very typical use of the `this` reference:

```
public void setStreetAddress(String streetAddress) {
  // Sets the streetAddress of the object to the streetAddress
  // that was passed to this method
  this.streetAddress = streetAddress;
}
```

The other common usage of the `this` reference is at times when you need to pass a reference of our current object as an argument to a method in another class. Suppose we added a `Room` class, and that when a new `Room` is instantiated, we want to store a reference to the `House` it is in:

```
public class Room {
  House house = null;

  public Room(House house) {
    // Here's an example of the first usage of the this reference
    this.house = house;
  }
}
```

Here's a simple `House` class that will create an instance of a `Room`, passing to it a reference to the current `House` object:

```
public class House {
   Room bedroom1;

   public void createRoom() {

      // Here's an example of the second usage of the this reference
      bedroom1 = new Room(this);
   }
}
```

There is another place where the `this` keyword might be used, but it's not technically as a reference like before. Inside of a constructor, we can use the `this()` syntax to refer to another constructor within our class. This can help us simplify a collection of overloaded constructors. A common technique for working with multiple constructors is to write one canonical constructor that takes the most complete set of arguments compared to the other constructors. The other constructors then call the canonical constructor, but fill in default values for the arguments that they're missing. Using this technique, we would rewrite our previous constructor overloading example like this:

```
public class House {
   public String streetAddress;
   public int numberOfBedrooms;

   // This is the canonical constructor.
   public House(String address, int bedrooms) {
      streetAddress = address;
      numberOfBedrooms = bedrooms;
   }

   // This constructor is missing the bedrooms argument so it fills
   // in a default value
   public House(String address) {
      this(address, 0);
   }

   // This constructor is missing the address argument so it fills
   // in a default value
   public House(int bedrooms) {
      this("No address defined yet", bedrooms);
   }

   // This constructor is missing the address and bedrooms arguments
   // so it fills in both with default values
   public House() {
      this("No address defined yet", 0);
   }
}
```

An important restriction on the use of `this()` is that the `this()` call must appear as the first line of a constructor. The reason for that restriction will be discussed later, in the sections on *Overriding Methods* and *The super Keyword*.

# Inheritance

One of the most powerful features common to many object-oriented languages, including Java, is that of **inheritance**. It is an approach where we designate a relationship between two classes, a **superclass** (sometimes called a **parent class**) and a **subclass** (sometimes called a **child class**), so that the subclass will inherit the methods and variables of the superclass. In essence, a variable or method that was declared for the superclass will act as if it was also declared for the subclass. In Java, we establish this relationship using the `extends` keyword – a subclass extends a superclass.

The topics of discussion in this section include:

- ❑ The breadth and depth of inheritance
- ❑ Overriding methods
- ❑ The `super` keyword
- ❑ Shadowing variables
- ❑ Abstract classes
- ❑ Interfaces

So, why is this feature so important? Consider the House examples above. When we created the `ThreeBedroomHouse` class, we had to recreate whatever members or variables the `House` class had in order to make them appear in the new class as well. Using inheritance, we could say that `ThreeBedroomHouse extends House` and then it would have the benefit of all the members of the `House` class, and could then build upon them with new methods and variables of its own.

```java
public class House {
    public String streetAddress = "No address defined yet";
    public int numberOfBedrooms;

    public int getNumberOfBedrooms() {
        return numberOfBedrooms;
    }

    public String getStreetAddress() {
        return streetAddress;
    }

    public void setStreetAddress(String newaddress) {
        streetAddress = newaddress;
    }
}
```

Here is an example of a class that extends `House`:

```java
public class TwoBedroomHouse extends House {
    public TwoBedroomHouse() {
        numberOfBedrooms = 2;
    }
}
```

```
public class ThreeBedroomHouse extends House {
  public ThreeBedroomHouse() {
    numberOfBedrooms = 3;
  }
}
```

Since the latter two classes extend House, they can both make use of its getNumberOfBedrooms() method:

```
public class HomeBuilder {
  public static void main(String arg[]) {
    TwoBedroomHouse myHouse = new TwoBedroomHouse();
    System.out.println(myHouse.getNumberOfBedrooms());

    ThreeBedroomHouse yourHouse = new ThreeBedroomHouse();
    System.out.println(yourHouse.getNumberOfBedrooms());
  }
}
```

Running HomeBuilder should display the following:

```
> java HomeBuilder
2
3
```

Due to this relationship, we can think of an instance of a ThreeBedroomHouse as also being an instance of a House. An instance of a TwoBedroomHouse is also an instance of a House. As such we could use a variable of type House to hold an instance of either of them.

```
public class HomeBuilder {
  public static void main(String arg[]) {
    House myHouse, yourHouse;
    myHouse = new TwoBedroomHouse();
    yourHouse = new ThreeBedroomHouse();
    System.out.println(myHouse.getNumberOfBedrooms());
    System.out.println(yourHouse.getNumberOfBedrooms());
  }
}
```

This would also hold true for an array of House objects. The elements of the array could be any mixture of TwoBedroomHouse and ThreeBedroomHouse instances.

```
public class HomeBuilder {
  public static void main(String arg[]) {
    House[] houses = new House[2];
    houses[0] = new TwoBedroomHouse();
    houses[1] = new ThreeBedroomHouse();
    System.out.println(houses[0].getNumberOfBedrooms());
    System.out.println(houses[1].getNumberOfBedrooms());
  }
}
```

There is a difference, however, between keeping an instance of a ThreeBedroomHouse in a variable of type House versus a variable of type ThreeBedroomHouse. Suppose we had defined a cleanThirdBedroom() method specific to the ThreeBedroomHouse class:

```
public class ThreeBedroomHouse extends House {
  public boolean thirdBedroomIsClean = false;

  public ThreeBedroomHouse() {
    numberOfBedrooms = 3;
  }

  public void cleanThirdBedroom() {
    thirdBedroomIsClean = true;
  }
}
```

We would only be able to call the cleanThirdBedroom() method by using a variable of type ThreeBedroomHouse or a subclass thereof. In the following example, we place an instance of a ThreeBedroomHouse, where this is an interface to the cleanThirdBedroom() method, into a variable of type House, where there is no interface for a cleanThirdBedroom() method. This will generate an error because, even though the contents of the variable have a declaration and a definition for the method, the variable is lacking the interface to allow the call to pass through. However, since the instance contained in the variable of type House is still a ThreeBedroomHouse, we can use casting to change it back into a variable of type ThreeBedroomHouse and then call the method:

```
public class HomeBuilder {
  public static void main(String arg[]) {
    ThreeBedroomHouse myHouse1 = new ThreeBedroomHouse();

    // This is legal.
    myHouse1.cleanThirdBedroom();

    House myHouse2 = new ThreeBedroomHouse();

    // This is not legal. It will generate an error
    // at compile time.
    myHouse2.cleanThirdBedroom();

    // But we could cast myHouse2 to a ThreeBedroomHouse:
    ThreeBedroomHouse myHouse3 = (ThreeBedroomHouse) myHouse2;

    // So this would be legal:
    myHouse3.cleanThirdBedroom();

    // Or we could do the casting above in one line
    // without using an extra variable
    ((ThreeBedroomHouse) myHouse2).cleanThirdBedroom();
  }
}
```

# Breadth versus Depth of Inheritance

It is permissible to further extend the ThreeBedroomHouse class with a new class:

```
public class ThreeBedroomTwoBathroomHouse extends ThreeBedroomHouse {
  int numberOfBathrooms;
  public ThreeBedroomTwoBathroomHouse() {
    numberOfBedrooms = 3;
    numberOfBathrooms = 2;
  }
}
```

Inheritance in Java can be as many levels deep as you want. In fact, due to some more of Java's behind-the-scenes activities, the inheritance of ThreeBedroomHouse was already three layers deep. In Java, all base classes (classes that don't explicitly extend another class, such as the House class above) actually do have a default class that they automatically extend: Object (actually, its full name is java.lang.Object and it resides in the core Java libraries). So, since all classes inherit either directly or indirectly from Object, then all objects in Java can be thought of as instances of Object and may make use of any of the methods that it provides, such as equals(Object obj) – a handy method for comparing this object to another.

Although inheritance can be as many layers deep as you want, it can only be one superclass wide. That is, a class can't extend more than one superclass at a time. The practice of extending more than one class is referred to as multiple inheritance, and it is allowed in some other object-oriented languages, but it is not allowed in Java. So, while it would be nice to be able to do the following, it will not work:

```
public class ThreeBedroomHouse extends House {
  public ThreeBedroomHouse() {
    numberOfBedrooms = 3;
  }
}
```

```
public class TwoBathroomHouse extends House {
  int numberOfBathrooms;
  public TwoBathroomHouse() {
    numberOfBathrooms = 2;
  }
}
```

```
// The following is not permitted.
public class ThreeBedroomTwoBathroomHouse
        extends ThreeBedroomHouse, TwoBathroomHouse {
}
```

If you would like to see a technique that finds different way to accomplish this, see the later section on *Interfaces*.

# Overriding Methods

What would happen if a subclass had a method with the same name and the same arguments as a method in the superclass? That technique is referred to as overriding (not to be confused with the concept of overloading that we saw previously), and it allows us to replace or refine a method from a superclass and adapt it to the needs of the subclass.

```java
public class House {
  public int numberOfBedrooms;

  public int getNumberOfBedrooms() {
    return numberOfBedrooms;
  }
}
```

```java
public class ThreeBedroomHouse extends House {
  public ThreeBedroomHouse() {
    numberOfBedrooms = 3;
  }

  // Taxes were too high on 3 bedrooms, so we
  // unscrupulously lie and say it's only got 2.
  public int getNumberOfBedrooms() {
    return 2;
  }
}
```

We can test it with the following class:

```java
public class HomeBuilder {
  public static void main(String arg[]) {
    ThreeBedroomHouse myHouse = new ThreeBedroomHouse();

    System.out.println(myHouse.numberOfBedrooms);
    System.out.println(myHouse.getNumberOfBedrooms());
  }
}
```

Which should produce:

```
> java HomeBuilder
3
2
```

This indicates that we still see the numberOfBedrooms variable from the superclass, but we now see the getNumberOfBedrooms() method from the subclass instead of the one in the superclass.

# The super Keyword

What if we needed to access the original `getNumberOfBedrooms()` method in the `House` class? There is a special reference, just like the `this` reference, called `super` that acts as a reference to the superclass of the current class. We'll add a method called `TestMethods()` to `ThreeBedroomHouse` so we can see `super` in action:

```java
public class ThreeBedroomHouse extends House {
  public ThreeBedroomHouse() {
    numberOfBedrooms = 3;
  }

  // Taxes were too high on 3 bedrooms, so we
  // unscrupulously lie and say it's only got 2.
  public int getNumberOfBedrooms() {
    return 2;
  }

  public void testMethods() {
    System.out.println(this.getNumberOfBedrooms());
    System.out.println(super.getNumberOfBedrooms());
  }
}
```

And then we'll test it with a simple `HomeBuilder`:

```java
public class HomeBuilder {
  public static void main(String arg[]) {
    ThreeBedroomHouse myHouse = new ThreeBedroomHouse();
    myHouse.testMethods();
  }
}
```

Which displays:

```
> java HomeBuilder
2
3
```

So, `this.getNumberOfBedrooms()` was calling the method in `ThreeBedroomHouse` and `super.getNumberOfBedrooms()` was calling the method in `House`.

As with many of the topics we've seen in this chapter, there is a restriction on the use of this mechanism. The `super` reference only works one layer deep – you cannot chain two or more supers together (such as `super.super.equals()`) to access anything from the superclass of your superclass or above.

## super and Constructors

We saw previously that the `this` keyword took two forms: one form without parentheses that acted like an ordinary object reference and a form with parentheses that acted like a special constructor. The `super` keyword also appears in both of these forms. We make use of its constructor form to call the constructor for the superclass from inside the constructor of the current class.

To demonstrate, let's go back and add a constructor to `House` that will help with setting the number of bedrooms:

```
public class House {
  public int numberOfBedrooms;

  public House(int numberOfBedrooms) {
    this.numberOfBedrooms = numberOfBedrooms;
  }

  public int getNumberOfBedrooms() {
    return numberOfBedrooms;
  }
}
```

Now, we can change the constructors in `TwoBedroomHouse` and `ThreeBedroomHouse` to make use of the new constructor in the superclass:

```
public class TwoBedroomHouse extends House {
  public TwoBedroomHouse() {
    super(2);
  }
}
```

```
public class ThreeBedroomHouse extends House {
  public ThreeBedroomHouse() {
    super(3);
  }
}
```

There are two very important details with regard to the use of `super()`. The first is that the `super()` call had to be the first line in the subclass' constructor. The compiler will yield an error if we attempt to use it on any other line. The reason for this relates to the second important detail – that even if we hadn't written a `super()` call in the subclass' constructor, the compiler would have automatically called `super()` anyway, but without any arguments. The explanation for all of this is that Java does what is called constructor chaining. It makes sure that all the constructors along the inheritance chain get a chance to perform whatever actions they deem necessary by calling `super()` whenever it's not explicitly called by our code.

In our example above, we sidestepped the default call to `super()` with no arguments by calling `super()` with one argument. In order for the compiler to notice that we took care of the `super()` call, the call needed to appear as the first line in the constructor. The following example demonstrates what happens when we do not make that call:

```
public class House {
  public House() {
    System.out.println("the House constructor was called");
  }
}

public class ThreeBedroomHouse extends House {
  public ThreeBedroomHouse() {
    System.out.println("the ThreeBedroomHouse constructor was called");
  }
}

public class HomeBuilder {
  public static void main(String arg[]) {
    ThreeBedroomHouse myHouse = new ThreeBedroomHouse();
  }
}
```

If we run `HomeBuilder`, we get:

```
> java HomeBuilder
the House constructor was called
the ThreeBedroomHouse constructor was called
```

So, even though we don't have a `super()` call in the `ThreeBedroomHouse` constructor, one was automatically added anyway.

We saw that we could momentarily avert the automatic `super()` call with no arguments by making our own `super()` call. The other way we could have prevented the `super()` call would have been to do a `this()` call as the first line of the constructor instead. Of course, this only applies when there is another constructor in the subclass. In turn, that second constructor would have to call `super()` explicitly, implicitly, or pass the buck onto yet another `this()` call. No matter how many `this()` calls we have, eventually some constructor is going to end up calling `super()` whether they want to or not. As such, each ancestor class is going to be given their chance at having their constructor called.

OK, one last example, this time in the form of a puzzle. Most of this example code is from two examples ago. One line has been commented out in `ThreeBedroomHouse`. The question is why do we get a compile-time error with this code?

```
public class House {
  public int numberOfBedrooms;

  public House(int numberOfBedrooms) {
    this.numberOfBedrooms = numberOfBedrooms;
  }

  public int getNumberOfBedrooms() {
    return numberOfBedrooms;
  }
}
```

```
public class ThreeBedroomHouse extends House {
  public ThreeBedroomHouse() {

    // super(3);
  }
}


public class HomeBuilder {
  public static void main(String arg[]) {
    ThreeBedroomHouse myHouse = new ThreeBedroomHouse();
  }
}
```

Attempting to compile this I get the following uninformative error:

```
> javac *.java
ThreeBedroomHouse.java:2: cannot resolve symbol
symbol  : constructor House ()
location: class House
  public ThreeBedroomHouse() {
               ^
1 error
```

Let's look at the code and see what happened. The `super(3)` call that was previously the first line of the `ThreeBedroomHouse` constructor has been commented out. Since there is no new `super()` call to replace it, the compiler will automatically insert one for us. However, the call that it inserts is `super()` with no arguments. So, the compiler goes looking for a constructor in the `House` class that also has no arguments. There is no such constructor so the compiler halts. Notice that in the error message the symbol it cannot resolve is `constructor House ()`, or in other words, a constructor with no arguments – just like the `super()` call would look for.

So, the mystery of the missing constructor is solved, right? Mostly, but there is one detail left. Take a look back at our example code in the *Overriding Methods* section:

```
public class House {
  public int numberOfBedrooms;

  public int getNumberOfBedrooms() {
    return numberOfBedrooms;
  }
}


public class ThreeBedroomHouse extends House {
  public ThreeBedroomHouse() {
    numberOfBedrooms = 3;
  }

  // Taxes were too high on 3 bedrooms, so we
```

```
    // unscrupulously lie and say it's only got 2.
    public int getNumberOfBedrooms() {
      return 2;
    }
  }
```

With your new knowledge of super() calls you should notice that the ThreeBedroomHouse constructor has no super() call, so the compiler will automatically add one in. But wait a minute, there's no constructor with zero arguments available in the House class. In fact, the House class has no constructors at all. What's going on here? Remember way back in the *Instantiating Objects* section toward the beginning of this chapter, where we said "If you create a class without a constructor, a default constructor will be available in most cases"? We can now be more specific. When you have a class with no constructors declared, Java inserts a default constructor that takes no arguments and has as its body only a single super() call. In other words, it provides a simple link in the constructor chain that will bridge the gap, and allow the super() calls to continue on up to the Object class.

# Shadowing Variables

If you can override methods, can you override variables? The answer is both yes and no. Yes in the sense that there can be variables in a subclass with the same names as variables in the superclass. But no in the sense that they don't do what you'd expect, based on our discussion of overridden methods. The variable in the subclass and the variable in the superclass end up acting like two separate variables that just happen to have the same name. That's why the technique is called shadowing variables instead of overriding them.

Unlike methods, the instance of the variable that you have access to depends on which class you access it from. A method in the superclass will see the variable in the superclass and a method in the subclass will see the variable in the subclass. For comparison, with overridden methods, you would get the method in the subclass no matter whether you accessed it from a variable of the superclass or subclass type (unless you used super to look it up). Inside the subclass you can choose between the two variables by using this.variableName or super.variableName, but from the superclass, you have no such option and you can only access the superclass version from there.

```
public class House {
  public int numberOfBedrooms = 0;

  public int getNumberOfBedrooms() {
    return numberOfBedrooms;
  }

}
```

```
public class ThreeBedroomHouse extends House {
  public int numberOfBedrooms = 3;

  public int getNumberOfBedrooms() {
    return numberOfBedrooms;
  }
}
```

```
  public void testShadowing() {
    System.out.println("");
    System.out.println("How it looks from inside ThreeBedroomHouse");
    System.out.println("");
    System.out.println("Using this:");
    System.out.println("By variable:" + this.numberOfBedrooms);
    System.out.println("By method:   " + this.getNumberOfBedrooms());

    System.out.println("Using super:");
    System.out.println("By variable:" + super.numberOfBedrooms);
    System.out.println("By method:   " + super.getNumberOfBedrooms());
  }
}


public class HomeBuilder {
  public static void main(String arg[]) {
    ThreeBedroomHouse myHouse = new ThreeBedroomHouse();

    System.out.println("How it looks from inside HomeBuilder");
    System.out.println("");

    System.out.println("Accessing the instance through a ThreeBedroomHouse
                reference:");

    System.out.println("By variable:" + myHouse.numberOfBedrooms);
    System.out.println("By method:   " + myHouse.getNumberOfBedrooms());

    System.out.println("Accessing the instance through a House reference:");
    House h = myHouse;
    System.out.println("By variable:" + h.numberOfBedrooms);
    System.out.println("By method:   " + h.getNumberOfBedrooms());

    myHouse.testShadowing();
  }
}
```

We get the following output:

```
> java HomeBuilder
How it looks from inside HomeBuilder

Accessing the instance through a ThreeBedroomHouse reference:
By variable:3
By method:   3
Accessing the instance through a House reference:
By variable:0
By method:   3

How it looks from inside ThreeBedroomHouse
```

```
Using this:
By variable:3
By method:   3
Using super:
By variable:0
By method:   0
```

This indicates that when we called getNumberOfBedrooms() through the House reference we got the version from ThreeBedroomHouse since that had overridden the one in House. However, when we queried the value of the numberOfBedrooms variable from the House reference, we see the superclass' instance of that variable. The this.numberOfBedrooms variable inside ThreeBedroomHouse saw the subclass' version of the variable, so the value of 3 that had been assigned in the subclass' variable declaration is printed.

# Abstract Classes

Sometimes when we're writing a superclass, we might come across a method that we know will be clearly defined in each of the subclasses, but it doesn't have a meaningful body to include with the method declaration in the superclass. While the technique of overriding provides a means for subclasses to supply their own definitions for the method, sometimes we need a mechanism that forces the subclasses to do so. Java provides such a mechanism and it is called an **abstract method**. An abstract method is a method that has a method declaration but no method definition (no body or implementation). Alternatively, the fully-defined methods that we have been dealing with so far are called **non-abstract methods** or **concrete methods**.

We designate that a method is abstract by using the **abstract** keyword in the method declaration. A class that contains at least one of these abstract methods is known as an **abstract class.** An abstract class must be labeled as such by placing the abstract keyword in its class declaration. An abstract class cannot be directly instantiated – another class must extend the abstract class and provide implementations for the abstract methods before an instance of the class can be created. If a class that extends an abstract class fails to implement all of the abstract methods, then the subclass is also an abstract class.

What would our familiar House example look like as an abstract class? To demonstrate this topic, we've added an abstract method cleanHouse() to the House class thus necessitating making it an abstract class. This method is then implemented in the TwoBedroomHouse and ThreeBedroomHouse classes.

```java
public abstract class House {

  public abstract void cleanHouse();
}
```

```java
public class TwoBedroomHouse extends House {
  boolean bedroom1clean = false;
  boolean bedroom2clean = false;

  public void cleanHouse() {
    bedroom1clean = true;
    bedroom2clean = true;
  }
}
```

```
public class ThreeBedroomHouse extends House {
   boolean masterBedroomClean = false;
   boolean kidsBedroomClean = false;
   boolean guestBedroomClean = false;

   public void cleanHouse() {
      masterBedroomClean = true;
      kidsBedroomClean = true;
      guestBedroomClean = true;
   }
}


public class HomeBuilder {
   public static void main(String arg[]) {
      ThreeBedroomHouse yourHouse = new ThreeBedroomHouse();
      TwoBedroomHouse myHouse = new TwoBedroomHouse();
      House otherHouse = new ThreeBedroomHouse();

      myHouse.cleanHouse();
      yourHouse.cleanHouse();
      otherHouse.cleanHouse();
   }
}
```

We can see that although TwoBedroomHouse and ThreeBedroomHouse have chosen to implement cleaning statuses differently, since they share a common cleanHouse() method declaration, the HomeBuilder class is able to invoke the class on either. Also notice that we can safely store an instance of ThreeBedroomHouse in a House variable and call the cleanHouse() method on it even though the method is not implemented in the House class.

# Interfaces

Java has another special construct known as an **interface**. In the last section, we learned how abstract classes have one or more abstract methods. An interface can also have abstract method declarations, but unlike an abstract class, an interface is limited to only having abstract declarations of methods and may not have any method definitions. Another difference is that all variables in an interface must be static final constants. Instead of a class extending an interface, it **implements** it. What's the difference between extending and implementing? There are no method definitions to inherit, so in order to implement an interface, a class must define all of the methods outlined in the interface before we can make new instances of the class. Otherwise, if the class does not define all the methods in the interface then the class will become an abstract class. Think of an interface as basically being a contract that a class promises to fulfill. In exchange for not inheriting method definitions, we gain a big advantage from interfaces: we can inherit from multiple interfaces at once if we want to.

Since our attempt to create a TwoBathroomHouse class was thwarted earlier, let's try it again, but as an interface this time:

```
public interface TwoBathroomHouse {
   static final int numberOfBathrooms = 2;

   public int getNumberOfBathrooms();
}
```

```
public class ThreeBedroomTwoBathroomHouse extends ThreeBedroomHouse
  implements TwoBathroomHouse {

  // We must define the following method as part of that
  // "contract" we agreed to when we implemented the interface
  public int getNumberOfBathrooms() {
    return numberOfBathrooms;
  }
}
```

Interfaces can extend other interfaces. While it may seem odd at first that a class implements an interface but an interface extends another interface, it actually does make sense. The sub-interface is not defining any of the methods from the super-interface, like a class does when it implements, but the sub-interface does add to the list of inheritable methods, which is more akin to what happens when a subclass extends a superclass.

# Packages

In Chapter 1, the concept of Java packages (not to be confused with Oracle packages) was briefly mentioned, but, so far, we haven't really discussed how to build them or use them. The basic premise is that you can bundle up multiple classes and interfaces together into a kind of collection referred to as a package, and that this act of bundling creates a special relationship between the items in this package. To declare a class or interface to be a member of a package, simply place the keyword package followed by the name of the package as the first line of code in the class or interface file. A package declaration line can only appear as the first line of the file (not counting comments) or else not appear at all. All classes that do not have a package declaration line are automatically placed into a default pseudo-package.

Why do we want to put classes and interfaces in packages anyway? One reason is to prevent name collisions between classes from different vendors or even developers. It is also the first step in controlling which external classes can access the classes in our package, and controlling what actions can be taken on them. Classes within a package have access to all the other classes or interfaces in that package, but classes or interfaces in a package can be protected from access from classes outside the package.

You may have noticed that in many of the code examples so far, the class declaration often starts with public class, which means that the class is publicly available to other classes both inside and outside the current package. We'll get into the other usages of the public keyword shortly, but let's consider for the moment what it would mean if a class was not publicly accessible – how would it ever get used? The answer is that a class that is not declared as public (that is, does not have the public keyword before its class declaration) is visible to other classes in its package, but not to classes outside the package.

For the following example, you will need to create a subdirectory named mypackage in your Java development directory (wherever you've been compiling .java files and that hopefully is already in your CLASSPATH). After you've created the directory, place the following code in a file named A.java in the mypackage subdirectory.

```
package mypackage;

// Notice that this class isn't declared public
class A {
  public void method1() {
    System.out.println("Made it to method1 in Class A");
  }
}
```

Now, place the next bit of code in a file named B.java in the mypackage subdirectory.

```
package mypackage;

// This class is declared public
public class B {
  public void method2() {
    System.out.println("Made it to method2 in Class B");

    // The class can access class A since they're in the
    // same package
    A a = new A();
    a.method1();
  }
}
```

Lastly, place this bit of code in a file named C.java. Class C is not in the package so it should reside one directory up from the mypackage directory, presumably in your previously mentioned Java development directory.

```
// This class does not declare a package - it's in the "default" package

public class C {
  public static void main(String arg[]) {

    // The following is legal
    mypackage.B b = new mypackage.B();
    b.method2();

    // The following is not legal - we can't access class A
    // from here
    // mypackage.A a = new mypackage.A();
    // a.method1();
  }
}
```

The following assumes that your environment has been set up properly. Please consult Chapter 1 for information on setting up your PATH and CLASSPATH variables.

Compile and run your new .java files:

```
> javac C.java mypackage\A.java mypackage\B.java
> java C
Made it to method2 in Class B
Made it to method1 in Class A
```

Notice that in class C, we had to refer to class B as mypackage.B (and class A would be referred to as mypackage.A if we could legally access it). That is because a package is a namespace that the classes are nested inside. By default, outside of a package, you have to refer to a class with its fully qualified name. Inside the package, you can refer to it via its short name. One way to make using a package easier is to use the keyword import to import a name or names from another package's namespace into the current one, so that those classes or interfaces can be referred to via their shorter names. So, we could rewrite class C like so: (to test, just save it to C.java, compile it and run it like before):

```
import mypackage.*;

public class C {
  public static void main(String arg[]) {
    B b = new B();
    b.method2();
  }
}
```

The .* at the end of the import statement above imports all of the class names from the mypackage package. What if we didn't want to import all of the names? For example, what would we do if there were another class named C inside mypackage? It would collide with our current definition. We can import individual classes into the current namespace by naming them explicitly in the import statement:

```
import mypackage.B;

public class C {
  public static void main(String arg[]) {
    B b = new B();
    b.method2();
  }
}
```

# Naming and Nesting Packages

A package can be nested inside of another package. Nested packages use dot notation for their names to indicate the levels of nesting. So, if we nested the package mypackage inside of a wrox package, the package declaration for mypackage would be changed to:

```
package wrox.mypackage;
```

You may have noticed this type of naming scheme for classes from the Java core class library. For example, the core Java class java.lang.String is a class named String inside of a package named lang inside of a package named java.

Nesting can be arbitrarily deep, so you can have a package inside a package inside a package, and so on. In fact, that technique is behind a standard industry naming scheme for Java packages. It is common practice to reverse your organization's Internet domain name and use that as the root of your package hierarchy. So, for example, for Java classes developed at wrox.com, the package names would start with com.wrox. There can be further nesting of packages underneath the domain portion of the package name, but the choice of a naming scheme for that portion of the name is left up to the discretion of each organization.

When you are dealing with Java classes outside the database as we have been here, the use of packages affects the filenames and the directory structure that you will use to store the .java files. Recall that we had to create a directory named mypackage in which to store some of our files. The name of the package in which a class appears is related to the directory that the source file will be expected to be found in. From our example code above, Java would look for the A and B classes in a subdirectory named mypackage. Where that subdirectory is specifically located depends on your CLASSPATH environment variable. If you try to use the mypackage.B class, then somewhere, in one of the directories listed in your CLASSPATH, there should be a mypackage directory with a B.java file inside of it.

Since packages can be nested inside one another, the directories that are used to store them are also nested. As an example, let's update our previous example to use a more conventional naming scheme for the package. In your Java development directory, create a directory called com. In the com directory, create a directory called wrox, and in that directory either create a new mypackage directory or move the old one in here. After you've created the directory tree, place the following code in a file named A.java in the com\wrox\mypackage subdirectory:

```
package com.wrox.mypackage;

class A {
  public void method1() {
    System.out.println("Made it to method1 in Class A");
  }
}
```

Now place the next bit of code in a file named B.java in the com\wrox\mypackage subdirectory:

```
package com.wrox.mypackage;

public class B {
  public void method2() {
    System.out.println("Made it to method2 in Class B");

    A a = new A();
    a.method1();
  }
}
```

Finally, place this bit of code in a file named C.java in the com\wrox subdirectory.

```
package com.wrox;

import com.wrox.mypackage.B;

public class C {
  public static void main(String arg[]) {
    B b = new B();
    b.method2();
  }
}
```

Now you need to navigate your way back up to your Java development directory and compile and run your new .java files like so:

```
> javac com\wrox\C.java com\wrox\mypackage\A.java com\wrox\mypackage\B.java
> java com.wrox.C
Made it to method2 in Class B
Made it to method1 in Class A
```

# The public, private, protected Keywords

The keyword public, which we just saw, along with the keywords private and protected, is part of a system that Java provides to help control access to methods and variables and so hopefully maintain the integrity of the internals of our classes and objects. Systems for controlling access and maintaining integrity are nothing new to the database world – we could put a constraint on a column of a table, perhaps stating that the value of a numeric field should always be between 1 and 100. Or, we could use GRANT statements to control who has access to a table and what they can do with it. Both methods work fine when the level of granularity we're dealing with is a row or a column or a table. But what if we need control at a more conceptual level? What if we want to prevent one object from fiddling with a value that another object was relying on? That's where public, private, and protected come in. In Java, if we label a variable, or even a method, as private, then we can only access it from the class that contains it. Conversely, labeling a variable or method as public, allows it to be accessed from external classes and objects.

```
public class House {
  private String streetAddress = "";

  public void setStreetAddress(String streetAddress) {

    // check streetAddress for our constraint
    if ((streetAddress.length() > 5) && (streetAddress.length() < 100)) {
      this.streetAddress = streetAddress;
    } else {
      System.err.println("Address needs to be between
                         5 and 100 characters long");
    }
  }

  public String getStreetAddress() {
    return streetAddress;
  }
}
```

```
public class HomeBuilder {
  public static void main(String arg[]) {
    House myHouse = new House();

    myHouse.setStreetAddress("123");
    myHouse.setStreetAddress("123 Pine Street");

    System.out.println(myHouse.getStreetAddress());
  }
}
```

Running `HomeBuilder` should produce:

```
> java HomeBuilder
Address needs to be between 5 and 100 characters long
123 Pine Street
```

To see the access restriction in action, try this version of `HomeBuilder`, which will attempt to write to the `streetAddress` variable directly:

```
public class HomeBuilder {
  public static void main(String arg[]) {
    House myHouse = new House();

    myHouse.streetAddress = "bad";
    System.out.println(myHouse.getStreetAddress());
  }
}
```

Trying to compile this code yields the following error:

```
HomeBuilder.java:7: streetAddress has private access in House
            myHouse.streetAddress = "bad";
                   ^
1 error
```

In these two examples we've effectively locked out other classes from changing the value of the `streetAddress` variable directly. Instead, they can access it through a pair of `public` methods dedicated to getting or setting its value. Why is this a good thing? From the point of view of encapsulation, we are attempting to hide some of the implementation details of the class so that the other classes don't have to be privy to the internal format in order to interact with this class. Consider the possibility of changing the implementation of the `streetAddress` variable. Perhaps at a later point it won't even be a variable stored in our class, and instead the value might be stored in and retrieved from the database, perhaps some form of a commit operation needs to occur when we set the value. The details of these changes need not be known to outside classes – as long as we provide the `getStreetAddress()` and `setStreetAddress()` methods and the arguments and return types remain the same, then any code that relies on these functions would not have to change if the internal implementation changed.

The `protected` keyword provides an intermediate level of visibility between `public` and `private`. When you declare a method or variable to be `private`, no other classes, including subclasses, can see it. On the other hand, when you declare a method or variable to be `protected`, it can be accessed by the subclasses while still being `protected` from access from external classes. It can also be accessed from other classes within the current package, whether or not they subclass the `protected` class.

When we don't use any of the `public`, `private`, or `protected` keywords, we get a level of visibility in between `protected` and `private`. This default level of access is sometimes called 'package' visibility. It only differs from `protected` in that subclasses will not be granted access if they are not in the same package. It only differs from `private` in that access is granted to other classes within the same package. If the class is not in a declared package, then all classes in the "default" package can access the method or variable. Since all classes that do not declare a package are considered to be in the 'default' package, this should be considered a pretty flimsy level of protection, which is simply remedied by placing your class in a package or by clamping down the level of visibility to `private`.

| Visible from: | private | 'package' (default) | protected | public |
| --- | --- | --- | --- | --- |
| Same Class | X | X | X | X |
| Same Package | | X | X | X |
| Subclass | | | X | X |
| Unrelated Class | | | | X |

# Exceptions

While many languages generate errors, few deal with them well. Java provides us with a means to handle errors and other less traumatic conditions in a graceful and systematic manner. It does so by introducing at the basic syntax level some flow control keywords including `try`, `catch`, and `finally` specifically targeted to this task. The basic model is that a line of code can "throw" (generate) an exception (a message that indicates an undesirable condition has arisen) that some later piece of code will need to `catch` (handle).

To make a block of code exception-savvy (which may be required when we make calls to methods that can throw certain exceptions), place the code in curly braces with a `try` keyword before to indicate that exceptions should be captured if thrown during the execution of that block of code. After the `try` block, there can be any number of `catch` clauses. If an exception occurs, the list of `catch` clauses is searched for one that claims it can handle an exception of the thrown type.

In Java, all exceptions are subclasses of the type `java.lang.Throwable` and fall into two categories, errors (instances of `java.lang.Error`) that usually indicate a fatal condition that should end execution of the program, and warning exceptions (instances of `java.lang.Exception`) that can be dealt with and then program execution can proceed. A `catch` clause will declare a variable of one of these types or of a subclass of one of these types. The first clause that has a compatible type to the current exception handles it. After the catch clauses is the `finally` clause – this is executed no matter what happens in the `try` block. Whether or not an exception is thrown, the `finally` block is guaranteed to execute, so it makes for a good place to clean up resources such as file handles, connections, and so on.

```
public class Tester {
  public static void main(String arg[]) {
    int numbers[] = {
      1, 2, 3
    };
    int last = 0;

    try {
      last = numbers[3];
    } catch (ArrayIndexOutOfBoundsException e) {
      System.err.println("You went beyond the end of the array");
    } finally {
      if (last == 0) {
        last = numbers[2];
      }
    }

    System.out.println(last);
  }
}
```

We will examine the topic of exceptions much more closely in Chapter 6, *Handling Exceptions*. In that chapter, we will look at the myriad of errors and exceptions that we might encounter while attempting to connect to the database through JDBC.

# Core Java Classes

By now you should a reasonable appreciation of the use of classes and objects in Java. And, in fact, a significant amount of all the Java code you will ever write will make heavy use of **existing** Java classes. If you want to do something relatively complex in your Java code, then there will usually be a **specialized API** available to you, with classes providing the functionality you need to help you achieve your goals. For example, if you want to write Java code that accesses a database, then you can use the JDBC API, implemented in the `java.sql.*` and `javax.sql.*` packages. Through a set of classes and interfaces, this provides you with the means to read, write, and manipulate data in a database, leaving you free to concentrate on the structure of the data you are dealing with (we will be covering all this in full detail in Section II of the book).

In essence, this means you only need worry about the SQL, and what you will do with the data once you have retrieved it. You do not have to write code that is capable of establishing a connection to the database, and then exposing the contents of that database to your program, since that has already been done for you.

However, you do not need to write specialized code to take advantage of existing Java classes. The Java Development Kit, or JDK, comes with hundreds of classes that serve to reduce the amount of code you need to write in order to accomplish everyday tasks. We will have already mentioned the `java.lang.String` class. This class eliminates the need for you to write your own function to test whether a string starts with a particular sequence of letters. You can use the `startsWith()` method of the `String` class instead. Note that this function is case-sensitive, so `there` is not the same as `There`.

```
public class StartsWithDemo {
  public static void main(String[] args) {
    String s = "There once was an ugly duckling";
    System.out.println("String starts with there: "
                          + s.startsWith("there"));
    System.out.println("String starts with There: "
                          + s.startsWith("There"));
  }
}
```

The output of this code is:

```
> java StartsWithDemo
String starts with there: false
String starts with There: true
```

When you start writing Java programs to complement your PL/SQL ones, you will probably initially want to concentrate on exploiting those areas of Java in which it is stronger than PL/SQL. This may well give you such a taste for the language and the power of object-oriented design that you go on to use Java much more heavily in the future. In Appendix B of this book we look at the supplied classes that you can pick up and use for instant benefit in your Oracle development, and that will crop up in this book:

❑ **Mathematical Operations**
As well as the primitive number types that Java provides, there are also a large number of supporting classes in the Java platform, such as `java.lang.Number` and `java.lang.Math`. These give you the ability to perform complex manipulation of numbers with much more grace and simplicity than is possible in PL/SQL.

❑ **Formatting Operations**
Java's support for context-sensitive formatting of data, including internationalization is exceptionally strong.

❑ **The Collections API**
The life's work of a database developer involves dealing with collections of data organized into result sets. Java provides a rich set of classes for treating collections in different ways, depending on whether they can best be handled as lists, sets, or even maps (data stored against keys, rather like primary keys on database tables). In fact, the set is too rich to be done much justice here, but it will at least be introduced.

❑ **Input and Output**
Classes contained in the `java.io.*` package working with I/O, or input and output, a fairly painless and easy task, whether you are dealing with network sockets, terminal input, or writing to and reading from files.

It is recommended that you use Appendix B as a reference source while using the book. For example, if you need a refresher on stream when you hit a section dealing with CLOBs and BLOBs (see Chapter 7) then you can refer to the *Input and Output* section of that appendix.

# Summary

In this chapter we discussed how to make and use Java classes and objects, as well as work with their variables, methods, and constructors. We learned how to overload methods, override methods and how to use the `this` and `super` keywords. We explored inheritance and extending classes, abstract classes and interfaces. We also discussed shadowed variables, packages, the `public`, `private`, and `protected` keywords, and exceptions.

In upcoming chapters we will be learning about more of the core Java classes and how Java is a useful tool for Oracle developers. For more information on the topics covered here, please refer to Sun's online Java API documentation at http://java.sun.com/.

Oracle 9i Java Programming

# Using Objects in PL/SQL and Java

Software projects are complex, and this complexity is handled by breaking the problem down into manageable pieces. In the procedural world, when we perform our process decomposition, each process and sub process in the hierarchy maps to a function or procedure. In the object-oriented world, it is different. The emphasis is on disintegrating a complex problem into objects rather than functions. These objects encapsulate both the data and the operations that can be performed on the data (whereas functions just represent operations).

Whereas the fundamentals, such as using programming constructs (if...then, loops), variable definitions and scope and passing parameters are very similar in any programming language (see Appendix A for a comparison between PL/SQL and Java, in this respect), the shift from thinking in functions and procedures to thinking in objects, is perhaps the biggest leap facing the Oracle developer wishing to use Java.

Thus in this chapter we attempt to bridge the gap somewhat, by taking a simple account example and analyzing its construction in both PL/SQL and Java. This will provide us with a means to build on the knowledge gained in the previous chapter and elucidate further some of the basic programming fundamentals in Java, in direct relation to what we already know: PL/SQL.

## Procedural Approach: the PL/SQL Account package

Our simple bank account maintenance program will provide two basic operations – the ability to deposit and to withdraw money. This can be done very easily and in a modular way using a database package in PL/SQL.

The procedure Deposit_Amount, which accepts a NUMBER parameter, will add the amount to the balance variable. The function Withdraw_Amount, which also accepts a NUMBER parameter, will deduct the amount from the balance, provided the remaining balance is not less than the minimum balance:

```
SQL> create or replace package Account
  2    as
  3        procedure Deposit_Amount(p_amount in number);
```

```
4       function Withdraw_Amount(p_amount in number)
5         return boolean;
6   end;
7   /
```

Package created.

The `Deposit_Amount` procedure and the `Withdraw_Amount` function are defined in the package specification so that the other procedures in the database have **public access** (in Java's parlance) to execute this procedure or function. Note, however, that in order to execute a procedure or function in this package from another schema, explicit `EXECUTE` permission has to be granted.

If we look in the package body below, the variables `min_balance` and `balance` are defined locally. In other words, these variables are **private** to the package and the only way they can be modified is through public procedures or functions defined in the package specification. So, in the example below, we cannot change the minimum balance for the account. If you need that capability, we either have to define the variable in the package specification or define a separate procedure that will set the minimum balance.

```
SQL> create or replace package body Account
2     as
3       min_balance     number := 25;
4       balance         number := 0;
5       procedure Deposit_Amount(p_amount in number)
6       is
7       begin
8         balance := balance + p_amount;
9       end Deposit_Amount;
10      function Withdraw_Amount(p_amount in number)
11      return boolean
12      is
13      begin
14  --  The remaining balance should not be less than minimum balance.
15        if balance - p_amount < min_balance
16        then
17          return false;
18        else
19          balance := balance - p_amount;
20          return true;
21        end if;
22      end Withdraw_Amount;
23    end account;
24  /
```

Package body created.

It is a good idea to use a separate procedure to set the minimum balance, since it promotes encapsulation and extensibility. How? With regard to the former, it means that if you want to alter that value, you have to go through the correct, defined business logic, security and auditing in order to do so. With regard to the latter – having a separate procedure makes it easier to add code to it to set the minimum balance based on a certain condition.

# OO Approach: the Account Java Class

To create the bank account object in Java, the class (blueprint) has to be defined first. Similarly to the PL/SQL `Account` package, the `Account` class has `depositAmt()` and `withdrawAmt()` methods to deposit and withdraw funds.

The attributes for this class are `balanceAmt`, `minBalance`, and `totalBalance`. If you notice, `balanceAmt` and `minBalance` are instance variables and the `totalBalance` is a class variable (defined as `static`). The `totalBalance` attribute is used to store the total balance amount for all the objects created using the `Account` class. That is why this attribute is defined as a class-level variable: it serves as a running total, and not as an instance variable. If it was defined as an instance variable, then a separate instance of that attribute would be created every time an object was created, which will not be useful in this case.

```
public class Account {
   public static double totalBalance = 0;
   protected double minBalance = 25;
   private double balanceAmt;

   public Account(double amt) {
      balanceAmt = amt;
      totalBalance += balanceAmt;
   }

   public void depositAmt(double amt) {
      balanceAmt += amt;
      totalBalance += balanceAmt;
   }

   public boolean withdrawAmt(double amt) {
      if ((balanceAmt - amt) < minBalance ) {
      return false;
      } else {
      balanceAmt -= amt;
      totalBalance -= balanceAmt;
      return true;
      }
   }
}
```

The `minBalance` is defined with an access type of `protected`, so that all the classes in the same package and the sub-classes in a different package can access that variable. This is explained further in the *Inheritance* section later in this chapter.

# Constructors In Java

The PL/SQL `Account` package and the `Account` class in Java have the same basic methods/procedures, with the exception of the special constructor method defined in the `Account` class:

```
public Account(double amt) {
   balanceAmt = amt;
   totalBalance = totalBalance + balanceAmt;
}
```

**73**

If you recall from the previous chapter, the constructor method gets called whenever an `Account` object is instantiated from the class using the `new` keyword. So, in this case, we can (and have to) set the balance amount when creating the `Account` object. Since the constructor method is executed automatically when the `Account` object is created, this is a good place to initialize the balance amount by passing a parameter. This enforces a business rule as well; you have to open an account with a balance amount. The constructor also has to set the class level variable `totalBalance` since it keeps track of total balance amount for all the objects.

The PL/SQL equivalent of a Java constructor is the initialization section in a package, which gets executed only once, the first time an object – a cursor, a variable, a procedure etc. – in the package is referenced. However, you cannot pass parameters to it or overload it as you can with a Java constructor.

```
create or replace package body Account
  as
    min_balance       number ;
    balance           number ;
-- rest of the code goes here
  begin  -- initialization section
    min_balance := 25;
    balance      := 0;
end account;
```

You can initialize a variable, if you know the value, when you are writing the package. Actually, the PL/SQL package `Account` initializes the initial balance to zero:

```
balance           NUMBER := 0;
```

If you do want to set the balance based on a parameter, a separate procedure, `Open`, must be created in the package to set the initial balance for the account. This will act like a constructor but it will not work in the same way as a constructor in Java, because it is the job of the programmer who calls this package to call this procedure first. Of course, you can write code to enforce this in the other procedures, but that adds unnecessary code, which can be done very easily using constructors in Java.

```
procedure Open(p_amount IN NUMBER)
is
begin
  balance         := p_amount;
end;
```

# Setting up Variables in Java and PL/SQL

There is nothing special in the way variables are defined in PL/SQL; we simply specify the variable name, data type and assign initial values, if necessary.

```
min_balance number := 25;
balance     number := 0;
```

However, we can obtain different behavior, depending on whether we define them in a standalone procedure or function or in a package specification or a package body. Any variable defined in a standalone stored procedure/function will be local and inaccessible from outside. The same effect is achieved in Java by defining local variables inside a method.

However, if we define a variable in a package body, it is available to all the procedures or functions in the package body but it cannot be accessed outside the package body. In Java-speak, we would say that they are private to the package body. Whereas, when we define them in a package specification, they can be accessed by other procedures and functions, so they are public in that sense. There is no intermediate state between the public access and private access in PL/SQL. You can, however, write procedures to set and get the values of a variable that is defined in the package body.

In Java, all the attributes have some kind of access modifier attached to them. If you recall, these are private, protected, public, or have default access, which puts the access level between private and protected. This feature is built into the language so that we make a conscious choice of how we want to define the attributes in Java.

```
public    static double totalBalance = 0;
protected double minBalance = 25;
private   double balanceAmt;
```

Another interesting and useful keyword used to define attributes in Java is `static`, which makes an attribute a class level variable instead of an instance level variable.

So far we have looked at defining variables (attributes) for a class but what about the temporary variables that we may need inside a method. This is similar to the local variables defined inside the PL/SQL procedures in a package.

```
public boolean withdrawAmt(double amt) {
  double diff;
  diff = balanceAmt -amt;
  if ( diff < minBalance ) {
    return false;
  } else {
    balanceAmt -= amt;
    return true;
  }
}
```

In the `withdrawAmt()` method, if we want to store the difference between the balance amount and the amount to be withdrawn in a temporary variable (`diff`) so that we can use it in the `if` statement, we can define a variable in the method for that purpose. This variable is local to that method and cannot be accessed outside just like a variable in a local procedure in PL/SQL.

Local variables in Java do not have any access modifier or `static` keyword associated with them, as it makes sense only to define an attribute that way and not a temporary variable. If you still insist, you will get an error during compilation. If you define a temporary variable with the same name as the attribute of the class, the local variable takes precedence over the attribute. However, you can use the `this` reference to refer to the attribute exclusively.

In the `Account` class, the `balanceAmt` was not defined with an initial value, but it will be automatically initialized to zero when the object is created. However, the local variables defined inside the methods have to be initialized explicitly before they are used in the method.

Interestingly, Java lets you define variables within a block of code and the scope of those variables is limited to that block. For example, you could define a variable `interest` (to calculate interest) in the `else` block of the `withdrawAmt` method. This variable gets created within this block and will not be available outside the `else` block. The block of code can be a `if...then...else`, loop statements or a simple anonymous block with open and close brackets.

```
public boolean withdrawAmt(double amt) {
  double diff;
  diff = balanceAmt -amt;
  if ( diff < minBalance ) {
    return false;
  } else {
    double interest;
    interest = diff * .04;
    balanceAmt -= amt;
    return true;
  }
}
```

In PL/SQL, this is similar to defining a cursor variable in the cursor `FOR` loop, the cursor variable will exist only within that loop. All other variables have to be defined only in the `DECLARE` section of the procedure/function and before defining the procedures/functions in a package body.

# Custom and Abstract Data Types

We know that a bank account is always tied to a customer. In order to establish that relationship in the package, a customer record type is defined in the specification. A procedure that will set the attributes of the `Customer` is also defined.

```
SQL> create or replace package account
  2  as
  3    type Customer_rec is record
  4    (full_name varchar2(100),
  5    address varchar2(200),
  6    phone_no varchar2(15) );
  7
  8    procedure new_customer
  9      (p_Cust Account.Customer_rec);
 10    end;
 11  /

Package created.
```

In the package body, the `new_customer` procedure will set the values for the attributes based on the `Customer` record passed as the parameter. The data type for the variable `Cust` is defined as `Account.Customer_rec`, which is of type `record`. This is a custom data type created based on the standard data types (it could be based on another custom type too) available in PL/SQL.

```
SQL> create or replace package body account
  2  as
  3    Cust      Account.Customer_rec;
  4    procedure new_customer
  5      (p_Cust IN Account.Customer_rec)
  6    is
  7    begin
  8      Cust.full_name := p_Cust.full_name;
  9      Cust.address   := p_Cust.address;
 10      Cust.phone_no  := p_Cust.phone_no;
 11    end new_customer;
 12
 13    function get_customer
 14    return Account.Customer_rec
 15    is
 16    begin
 17      return Cust;
 18    end get_customer;
 19  end;
 20  /

Package body created.
```

The `Customer_rec` data type has to be defined inside a procedure or a package, but if we want to use it across different procedures it should be defined in the package specification of a package. It could very well be in a separate package called `Customer`, but it cannot exist outside a package or a procedure. If you define it in a procedure it cannot be accessed outside that procedure, rendering it useless. The Oracle object type, available since Oracle 8, is the equivalent of a user-defined or an abstract data type, which will be discussed later in this chapter.

Here is the `Customer` class with its attributes and methods:

```
public class Customer{
  private String fullName;
  private String address;
  private String phoneNo;

  public Customer(String fname, String addr,  String phone) {
    fullName = fname;
    address  = addr;
    phoneNo  = phone;
  }

  public String getName() {
    return fullName;
  }
```

```
public void changeAddress(String addr) {
  address = addr;
}

public String getAddress() {
  return address;
}
}
```

In Java an abstract data type is a custom type that is not part of the standard data types provided by the language. The custom type in Java is another well-encapsulated class, with its own attributes and methods. Java has its own set of rich classes (types) that comes pre-defined with the language. We should try and use these classes as much as possible to avoid reinventing the wheel.

> **Please remember that abstract data types are different from abstract classes in Java. Abstract classes in Java are incomplete classes (at least one method with no definition) that require further specialization.**

In our `Account` example, a new private attribute (instance variable) of type `Customer` is defined. This attribute will be initialized inside the constructor, which is modified to accept a new parameter of type `Customer`.

```
public class Account{
  private    double   balanceAmt;
  protected static   double minBalance = 25.0;
  private    Customer cust;

  public Account( Customer pCust, double balance) {
    cust = pCust;
    balanceAmt = balance;
  }

  public Customer getCustomer() {
    return cust;
  }
}
```

The `Customer` class must exist before the `Account` class is compiled. The idea is that you are building an object and along the way you pick the right components, which already exist, for your object. This is called **aggregation** in the world of objects. Aggregation occurs when one object is composed of other objects. This is similar to building any object in the real world. For example, if you are building a plane you buy the pre-built engine and doors for your plane. Another interesting point to remember is that the engine can exist as an independent object without the plane. Similarly, the `Customer` class exists independently and it is used in the `Account` class as one of the attributes.

To summarize, both PL/SQL and Java support the idea of building a complex object using simple objects as building blocks. PL/SQL uses packages (in this example, later you will see that you can use object types as well) to do this and Java uses classes to accomplish the same.

# Passing Parameters and Returning Values

One of the essential ingredients of code reuse is the ability to pass parameters to a reusable program unit, which behaves differently based on the values being passed and sometimes returns a value too.

In PL/SQL when a value is passed the data type is specified along with a special keyword to indicate if the value is passed either IN (can be changed inside) or OUT (used to return values) or INOUT (combination of IN and OUT).

```
procedure Deposit_Amount(p_amount in number);
function Withdraw_Amount(p_amount in number)
  return boolean;
```

Methods in Java accept parameters along with the data types, just as in PL/SQL. The difference is if you are passing a primitive or standard data type parameter, you cannot use the parameter to pass and return values. So, when you pass the variable amt to the withdrawAmt() method then this value, even if it is changed inside the method, will not be changed in the calling class because only a copy of the amt is passed to the method. This is similar to passing a parameter with the IN keyword in PL/SQL.

```
public void depositAmt(double amt) {
public boolean withdrawAmt(double amt) {
  if ((balanceAmt - amt) < minBalance ) {
```

However, when you are passing an object as a parameter you can change the attributes of the passed object using its methods and it will be reflected in the calling class. This is because when you are passing an object, you are actually passing a reference (pointer to a memory location) to the actual object and not a copy of the object. If you use the changeAddress() method of the Customer class inside the Account class to change the Customer address it will be reflected outside the Account class as well.

```
public Account( Customer pCust, double balance) {
  cust       = pCust;
  balanceAmt = balance;
}
public changeCustomerAddr(String addr) {
  cust.changeAddress(addr);  // This will change the customer address
}            // outside this class
```

The changeCustomerAddr() method in the Account class will change the address of the customer and it will be reflected in the calling class. This is because the physical memory address of the Customer object (reference) is passed to the Account constructor. Now you can use that to actually change the attributes of that object using the changeAddress() method defined in the Customer class.

However, this will not work if you assign a new reference to the object reference variable cust. If you look in the doNotChangeAddr() method shown below, a new Customer object is created and assigned to cust. When this method is executed the object reference passed to the Account class is overwritten with the new reference. From now on, any changes made to the cust will not be reflected outside the Account class.

```
        public doNotChangeAddr(String addr) {
            cust = new Customer("Frank Wright", "3102 Madison Ave. TX 77042",
                                "713-221-3782");
            cust.changeAddress(addr);
        }    // This method will not change the address outside this class
```

Both Java and PL/SQL return values explicitly using the `return` keyword. PL/SQL classifies a program unit into a procedure or a function based on whether it returns a value or not, but Java does the same using the return data type in its method declaration. Basically, if you want a method to return a value you specify the return data type, if you don't then specify `void` in the method declaration.

# Calling Java From PL/SQL

Before you start writing Java programs inside or outside the database you might first run into a situation where you have to call a Java program from PL/SQL. Consider, for example, that you have some vendor applications written in Java and you want to use some of the functionality from those classes in your PL/SQL application, or when you want to leverage the benefits of Java in your application.

Let's take the bank example and create a wrapper class (`Bank`) with `static` methods to maintain the account. These methods act as wrapper methods so that they can be called from PL/SQL. If you are only going to run this program **outside** the database, you could just define the methods as instance methods. Keep in mind that you will definitely need the `main()` method, if you are going to run this program independently outside the database.

```
public class Bank {

  private static Account newAcct;

  public static void openAccount(double amt) {
    newAcct = new Account(amt);
  }

  public static void depositAmount(double amt) {
    newAcct.depositAmt(amt);
  }

  public static void withdrawAmount(double amt) {
    if (!newAcct.withdrawAmt(amt)) {
      System.out.println("\nLooks like you are bankrupt!!");
    }
  }

  public static void main(String args[]) {
    openAccount(200.0);
    withdrawAmount(822.5);
  }

}    // End of Bank class
```

Calling the `main()` method directly from a PL/SQL wrapper procedure would also do the trick, rather than calling the static methods individually from PL/SQL. It can be done either way, but you can call only a static Java method through a PL/SQL procedure. This is because static methods are associated with the class and not with the object, which means that you do not have to instantiate the object (this cannot be done in PL/SQL) to call the method.

Okay, how are we going to execute the Java code in the database? After loading the Java class using the `loadjava` utility, create a PL/SQL package, or a procedure, that calls the static Java methods in the Bank class.

```
SQL> create or replace package jbank
  2   as
  3     procedure open_account(p_amount in number);
  4     procedure deposit_amount(p_amount in number);
  5     procedure withdraw_amount(p_amount in number);
  6   end;
  7  /

Package created.
```

Each procedure in this package calls the individual Java method, which makes it look procedural and this way the Java methods can be blended into your PL/SQL programs to give you a heterogeneous mix.

The package specification for calling Java methods is no different from that used when calling PL/SQL procedures and functions. However, the package body syntax is somewhat different in that the procedures call the Java methods using the `ClassName.methodName` notation:

```
SQL> create or replace package body jbank
  2   as
  3     procedure open_account(p_amount in number)
  4     as language java
  5     name 'Bank.openAccount(double)';
  6     procedure deposit_amount(p_amount in number)
  7     as language java
  8     name 'Bank.depositAmount(double)';
  9     procedure withdraw_amount(p_amount in number)
 10     as language java
 11     name 'Bank.withdrawAmount(double)';
 12   end jbank;
 13  /

Package body created.
```

Since we are calling a Java program, the procedures in the package body acts as a wrapper that calls the corresponding Java method. The parameter passed to the procedure will be passed automatically to the Java method provided the number and datatype of the parameters match.

When passing parameters you also have to specify the complete package hierarchy for the non-primitive data types (`int`, `double`, `float` and so on) as well as for the return values. For example, if the Java method returns a Java `String` datatype to a matching PL/SQL `VARCHAR2` data type, you will have to specify it as `java.lang.String`:

```
        function open_account(p_amount in number)
        return varchar2
        as language java
        name 'Bank.openAccount(double) return java.lang.string';
```

If you recall from Chapter 1, we redirect the output from the default trace file to the SQL*PLUS text buffer by calling the `set_output` method in the `dbms_java` package (setting the buffer size to 10000 in the process):

```
SQL> set serveroutput on size 1000000
SQL> call dbms_java.set_output(1000000)
```

We then execute our methods as follows:

```
SQL> begin
  2     jbank.open_account(200);
  3     jbank.withdraw_amount(822.5);
  4  end;
  5  /

Your withdrawal amount was 822.5

Withdrawal cannot be > 200.0

PL/SQL procedure successfully completed.
```

# Comparing Java Classes and PL/SQL Packages

In this section we will discuss how Java and PL/SQL compare, while implementing object-oriented features like abstraction and encapsulation.

## Java Classes

Two of the most important object-oriented features, abstraction and encapsulation, are implemented using classes in Java. You will see later in this section that PL/SQL uses packages to implement these two features. Encapsulation binds operations and state to a particular object. It is closely linked to 'information hiding', and defines which parts of an object are hidden and which are visible.

One advantage of hiding implementation details is that the class may change, and provided the public interface remains the same then all programs using the class will be unaffected. This promotes reuse and reduces ripple effects when the code is changed.

In the `Customer` class defined above, `address` was defined as a `String`, but we know it's not practical to have one long string for an address:

```
public class Customer{
  private String address;
```

Building a simple `Address` class with the separate address lines, city and zip code as its attributes is a better idea to keep things organized. These attributes are `private` to this class – they can be accessed only through methods defined in the `Address` class. This gives tighter control over how these attributes are managed. For instance, if you decide to change the name of the attributes or type or add a new attribute, you can safely do so without invalidating any of the existing classes that are using this class.

```
public class Address {
  private String addrLine1;
  private String addrLine2;
  private String city;
  private String zip;

  public Address(String line1, String line2, String city, String zip) {
    addrLine1 = line1;
    addrLine2 = line2;
    this.city = city;
    this.zip = zip;
  }

  public String getZip() {
    return zip;
  }
}
```

Let's change the `Address` attribute in the `Customer` class from a `String` type to the new `Address` type. Interestingly, the Java compiler (just like the PL/SQL engine) automatically tries to compile the `Address` class when you compile the `Customer` class, if it was not already compiled. To see this in action, when you compile a Java program from the prompt use the `javac -verbose` option.

But if the `Address` class was compiled after making the change, the `Customer` class need not be compiled again (unlike PL/SQL).

```
public class Customer {
  private String fullName;
  public Address address;
  private String phoneNo;

  public Customer(String fname, Address addr, String phone) {
    fullName = fname;
    address = addr;
    phoneNo = phone;
  }

  // rest of the methods go here
}
```

You can access the `Address` methods through the `Customer` class, using the `address` attribute. For example, after instantiating a `Customer` object `cust`, you can use the `getZip()` method in the `Address` class to get the zip code. This cannot be done if the address attribute was defined as `private`.

```
cust.address.getZip()
```

If after going live with your `Address` class, you want to add a new attribute, such as a four-digit suffix code for the zip, this new attribute will be part of the complete zip code so the `getZip()` method has to be changed as well. You also want to rename the zip attribute to `postalCode`.

```
private String postalCode;
private String zip4;

public Address(String line1, String line2,
               String city,  String pCode, String zip){
    addrLine1  = line1;
    addrLine2  = line2;
    this.city  = city;
    postalCode = pcode;
    zip4       = zip;
}
public String getZip() {
    return postalCode + zip4;
}
```

Will any of these changes cause any problem in the `Customer` class or any other class that is using `Address`? Not at all. This is because the implementation detail was hidden from the outside world from the beginning.

# PL/SQL Packages

PL/SQL packages can also be used to implement abstraction and encapsulation. Whereas Java uses access modifiers to restrict access to its attributes, PL/SQL uses the concepts of a package specification and a package body. All procedures, functions and attributes that require `public` access are defined in the package specification. When we wish to hide implementation details, we define them in the body.

Let's say we want to maintain the address of the customer through a separate PL/SQL package that defines the `address` record type and also has a function to return the zip code. A separate procedure (`new_address`) that acts like a constructor is created to set the values of the address record:

```
SQL> create or replace package address
  2    as
  3    type Address_rec is record
  4      (Addr_line1   varchar2(100),
  5       Addr_line2   varchar2(200),
  6       City         varchar2(25),
  7       Zip          varchar2(20));
  8    procedure new_address(p_address address_rec);
  9    function get_zip_code return varchar2;
 10  end;
 11  /

Package created.
```

The record type (address_rec) and the procedure (new_addr) have to be defined in the package specification so that they can be used in the Account package for the Customer address. Here is the problem: when a new attribute is added to Address_rec, the package specification has to be recompiled and this will invalidate all procedures and functions that use this package (although they will try to recompile automatically, if possible, when they are executed the next time). If you put the Address_rec in the package body, to avoid compilation problems, then you cannot access it in the Account package. This is not a problem with the GET_ZIP_CODE function because the implementation is hidden in the package body.

```
SQL> create or replace package Account
  2  as
  3    type Customer_rec is record
  4      (full_name  varchar2(100),
  5       addressline     address.Address_rec,
  6       phone_no   varchar2(15));
  7    end;
  8  /

Package created.
```

There is another interesting similarity between the PL/SQL package and the interface in Java. That is, both the interface in Java and the package specification in PL/SQL specify the method or the procedure that will be implemented later. In Java, the class that implements the interface will implement the promised methods and in PL/SQL the package body will implement the procedures/functions.

One of the important differences between the PL/SQL package and a Java package is that when a procedure in a PL/SQL package is called it loads the whole package in memory, whereas in Java, the JVM loads the classes in a package only when it needs them.

# Comparing Java Methods and PL/SQL Procedures

In this section we will discuss how Java and PL/SQL implement procedures and functions.

## Java Methods

Java implements both the procedures and functions in PL/SQL, using methods. In general, methods in Java are basically the operations (behavior of the object) that are performed on the attributes (state of the object). This is because the attributes may not be visible to the class that is using it. Also, a method can be used to perform other programming tasks without altering the state of the object. A method can act like a PL/SQL procedure or a function by specifying the return data type in the method signature. If the return data type is void for a method then the method does not return any value:

```
public void depositAmt(double amt) {
public boolean withdrawAmt(double amt) {
```

So, the depositAmt() method can be considered as a procedure and withdrawAmt() as a function in PL/SQL.

```
procedure Deposit_Amount(p_amount in number);
function Withdraw_Amount(p_amount in number)
return boolean;
```

# PL/SQL Procedures

PL/SQL procedures and functions can exist independently as stored program units. To reiterate, PL/SQL is a procedural language, which is why you have procedures that exist independently and they don't have to necessarily be encapsulated inside a package. However, a Java method can only exist inside a class. An object can be created only using a class in Java and methods operate on the attributes (or perform other tasks internally) and they don't exist independently as standalone program units. This discipline is enforced by the language itself and not left to the programmer's discretion.

To access an instance method in a Java class you have to use the `objectName.methodName` notation and to access a class or static method use `className.methodName`. These notations are similar to using `Package_Name.Procedure_Name` in PL/SQL. However, a standalone-stored procedure in PL/SQL can be called directly without any prefix.

```
Acct.depositAmt(200)    // In Java
```

```
Acct.Deposit_Amount(200)   -- In PL/SQL
```

# Object-Oriented Features in PL/SQL and Java

So far we have seen a few of the similarities and differences between the way things are done in PL/SQL and the way they are done in Java, mainly from a programming language perspective. However, since Oracle 9i adds introduces OO features to PL/SQL, with object types that support inheritance and polymorphism, it makes sense to look at this too.

Is PL/SQL an object-oriented language? No it is not. Although OO features are available in PL/SQL, the language does not actually enforce their use, in the way that Java does. It is left to the developer's discretion to come up with a program design that behaves like an object-oriented program.

The following sections draw analogies between the object-oriented features in PL/SQL (using packages and object types) and in Java (using classes).

## Java Classes vs. Object Types

Our previous discussions have essentially focused on comparisons between PL/SQL packages and Java classes. However, there is probably a more direct correlation between Oracle **object types** and Java classes.

Object types in SQL were introduced in Oracle 8, but have been enhanced greatly in Oracle 9i, to include support for inheritance and full polymorphism. However, they still lack certain features that you would find with classes in Java such as, user-defined constructors, multiple inheritance (using interfaces), class level variables and variable initialization.

Object types have attributes and member procedures and functions. In a similar fashion to the way in which PL/SQL packages have a specification and a body, object types have a type and a type body. The sample code below (which will work in both PL/SQL 8 and PL/SQL 9i) shows how to build the `Account` object type in PL/SQL:

```
SQL> create or replace type account_typ
  2    as object (
  3      balance          number,
  4      min_balance      number,
  5      static function new_account (p_balance in number)
  6      return account_typ,
  7      member  procedure deposit_amount(p_amount in number),
  8      member  procedure withdraw_amount(p_amount in number)
  9    );
 10  /

Type created.
```

The attributes cannot be initialized with a default value when they are declared; you have to initialize them through a constructor.

Whereas in Java we can create a constructor for our class, we cannot define a constructor for an object type in PL/SQL. The object types have their own system defined default constructor, which accepts the values for all the attributes in the order they were defined. In the sample code below, you will notice that the constructor name is same as the type name (similar to Java) and the initial values for `balance` and `min_balance` (in that order) are passed as parameters. This is how the object type is instantiated in PL/SQL.

```
declare
    acct account_typ;
begin
    acct := account_typ(240,10); -- default constructor
end;
```

The default constructor is automatically created for every object type you create and it cannot be modified or overloaded with user-defined constructors. The problem with this is you cannot validate the opening balance (must be greater than the minimum balance) when the object type is created because you are not allowed to create your own constructor where this type of validation can be performed.

The sample code below shows how this validation can be done in Java using a user-defined constructor:

```
public class Account{

    public    double totalBalance = 0;
    protected double minBalance = 25;
    private   double balanceAmt;

    public Account(double amt) {
      if (!( amt < minBalance) ) {
        balanceAmt = amt;
        totalBalance += balanceAmt;
      }
    }
```

The workaround to this problem, in PL/SQL, is to define a STATIC FUNCTION that actually instantiates the object type and returns it to the calling program. In other words, this static function will act as a constructor for the object type. Now, you can also do a check inside this function to make sure the balance is not lower than a certain hard-coded value (you still cannot use the minimum balance because it is not yet defined):

```
SQL> create or replace type body account_typ
  2  as
  3    static function new_account(p_balance in number)
  4    return account_typ
  5    is
  6    begin
  7      return account_typ(p_balance, 25);
  8    end new_account;
  9    member procedure deposit_amount(p_amount in number)
 10    is
 11    begin
 12      balance := balance + p_amount;
 13    end;
 14    member procedure withdraw_amount(p_amount in number)
 15    is
 16    begin
 17      if (balance - p_amount) < min_balance
 18      then
 19        dbms_output.put_line('Looks like you are broke!!');
 20      else
 21        balance := balance - p_amount;
 22      end if;
 23    end;
 24  end;
 25
 26  /

Type body created.
```

The PL/SQL block shown below can be used to test the code using object types. If you notice, the new_account static function is used as a constructor to instantiate the object type.

```
declare
    acct account_typ;
begin
    acct := account_typ.new_account(240);
    dbms_output.put_line(' Customer balance is ' || acct.balance);

    acct.withdraw_amount(10);
    dbms_output.put_line(' Customer balance is ' || acct.balance);
end;
```

# Why Objects?

Now that you have seen the code for both PL/SQL and Java in action side-by-side, you may wonder why we have to use objects? Based on the examples above, you will realize that the programs written in PL/SQL and Java look very similar (actually, the intent is to show you that we can use PL/SQL packages to abstract and encapsulate). Some of you might say that it is pretty cool to write programs in Java and make it work inside Oracle database. That is true but it does not warrant the need for Java objects.

Let's say that the bank where you work bought an application similar to this one written in a third generation language (for example Pro*C) or PL/SQL, from a vendor with the basic modules. However, this does not satisfy your company's need, so the software is customized to the way your bank does business.

For example, the program that maintains the account is too generic and new programs are written using the vendor application for maintaining checking and savings account. Everything is fine and dandy, the new programs work very well with the vendor application, until you realize that the Calculate_Interest procedure will only calculate the interest based on a standard interest rate. While this is OK for checking accounts, for a savings account you want the interest to be calculated based tier levels (for example, if the balance amount is over $10,000 add 2 percent to the standard rate).

```
public class Account{
  public    static double totalBalance = 0;
  protected double minBalance = 25;
  private   double balanceAmt;
  protected double getBalance() {
    return balanceAmt;
  }

  public double calculateInterest(double intPct) {
    return getBalance() * intPct;
  }
// rest of the code goes here
}
```

Guess what, you cannot do this unless you can access the logic in your vendor package (for example through API calls). If you have the ability to change the package (and there are no standard APIs provided by the vendor application) you end up changing the code for that module on your own – which, by the way, happens frequently in almost every company that uses these types of vendor packages. This creates a maintenance nightmare as the vendor starts rolling out new patches every month or quarter and requires lot of time and effort to figure out which way is faster and easier; update the new patch with your changes or apply the changes from the patch to your code. This is especially true if the package is written in a third generation language like Pro*C and in some cases if the PL/SQL code is not well encapsulated using packages.

If this whole thing was done using objects, you could inherit this class into a subclass and simply *override* that particular method and replace it with custom code. This way if a new patch is rolled in, nothing happens to your code and it still works like a charm. This can be done in PL/SQL by creating a wrapper to the vendor API (if there is one!) but is a pain with a third generation language.

Here is something that you can do only using objects. Consider a generic class that accepts the **account object** as a parameter and returns the taxable interest for any bank account (checking or savings). To keep this class generic, the parameter's data type should not be defined as type checking or savings as this is too specific (that's why it is defined as account type) and will work for only that object (checking or savings).

```
public class Taxes {
  protected double interestPct = .02;

  public double TaxableInterest(Account acct) {
    return acct.calculateInterest(interestPct);
  }
}
```

At runtime, the parameter of type account is used to call the calculateInterest method of the corresponding account object. This is called **dynamic method dispatch** in Java. What happens during runtime is that when you pass a CheckingAccount object, the call to the calculateInterest method will call the CheckingAccount object's method and similarly if the object passed is SavingsAccount the interest calculation is done for that object. This is true even if you pass the Account object created from the base class. This is shown in the sample code below.

```
public class CalculateTaxes {

    double interest intrst;
    CheckingAccount c = new CheckingAccount(240);
    SavingsAccount  s = new SavingsAccount(1240);

    Taxes t = new Taxes();
    t.TaxableInterest(Account acct) {
    intrst = t.TaxableInterest(c); // interest for Checking
    intrst = t.TaxableInterest(c); // interest for Savings
    intrst = t.TaxableInterest(new Account(500));//interest for the baseclass
}
```

This means a developer can create generic Java programs based on the base class without having to worry about the overridden methods in the subclasses. One of the important points to remember here is that if you define a variable (or parameter) of parent class type, then you can only access the methods defined in that parent class (or the same methods in the subclass) and you cannot access other methods specific to the subclass.

Interestingly, this concept works even if your base class is an interface. This means you could design an application with classes and interfaces, which promises that the methods will be implemented later (may be at the client site), and write some generic classes based on the interfaces.

Objects encapsulate the methods and data in a natural way. Java also lets you think along those lines from the time you start designing an object, what attributes are needed for this object and what kind of operations need to be performed on the attributes of this object. Object encapsulation also makes maintaining the code easier because all the methods related to the object are in one place and there are no surprises during integrated testing.

# Inheritance Using Java

Two of the important object-oriented features are inheritance and polymorphism. Inheritance lets you create a new specialized class from a generic class. In our account maintenance example, the Account class is a generic class. Using that class we can create more specialized classes such as CheckingAccount, SavingsAccount, and MoneyMarket. Each of these new classes will inherit all the accessible methods and attributes from the base class.

Once inherited, these classes can either override or overload the base class methods with new methods to make the new class more specialized. The idea is to build a base class that will provide the common functionality for the subclasses and then add new methods unique for each subclass, which makes it different from the other subclasses.

The example below shows the subclass `SavingsAccount` inheriting from the superclass `Account`. The `SavingsAccount` class has its own constructors, which actually calls the parent constructor and another local method.

The `setMinBalance()` method is overloaded (not a new concept for PL/SQL developers!) to accept a parameter that will set the minimum balance. This way, the minimum balance can be changed depending on the type of the account or customer, if required.

The `calculateInterest()` method in this class overrides the base class method, to set the interest percent based on the outstanding balance and then return the interest amount. There are times when you would want to add some condition to the overridden method and use the rest of the logic from the superclass method, by calling the superclass method in the subclass. This technique allows you to add an extra condition to a method without tampering with the original code.

```java
public class SavingsAccount extends Account {

  public SavingsAccount(double balance) {
    super(balance);
    setMinBalance(50.0);
  }

  // This setMinBalance is an overloaded method in this class
  public void setMinBalance() {
    minBalance = 50.0;
  }

  public boolean setMinBalance(double minAmt) {
    if (minAmt < minBalance) {
      return false;
    } else {
      minBalance = minAmt;
      return true;
    }
  }

  // calculateInterest method is overridden in this class
  public double calculateInterest(double intPct) {
    double interestPct;

    if (getBalance() > 10000) {
      interestPct = intPct + .02;
    } else {
      interestPct = intPct + .01;
    }
    return getBalance() * interestPct;
  }
}
```

There is an interesting accessibility feature that needs to be pointed out here. If you look in the `setMinBalance()` method you will notice that the `minBalance` attribute, which is defined in the `Account` class, is being modified here. This is possible because of the way the `minBalance` attribute is defined in the `Account` class.

```
public class Account {
  private double balanceAmt;
  protected double minBalance = 25.0;
  private Customer cust;

  protected double getBalance() {
    return balanceAmt;
  }
}
```

If you recall, this particular attribute is defined as `protected`, which allows this attribute to be modified in its subclass and also in any other class within the same package. This could be accomplished by defining the `minBalance` variable as `public` as well. However, the problem with that is you are exposing the variable to the outside world and any class in any package can access the variable directly by referring it as `objectName.minBalance`. The `protected` modifier, however, will allow only the subclasses and the classes within the same package to modify the variable. This is true for the `getBalance()` method, which is also defined as `protected`, classes (that are not subclasses of `Account` class) from other packages cannot access this method.

# Inheritance Using Object Types in Oracle 9i

Object types were introduced in Oracle 8 without inheritance and full polymorphism. This gap is bridged in Oracle 9i with support for inheritance using the `UNDER` keyword, which is similar to `extends` in Java. Now, you can also override a member procedure or function using the `OVERRIDING` keyword (no special keyword is required in Java).

```
create or replace type account_typ
 as object (

  balance         number,
  min_balance     number,

-- member function
 calculate_interest(p_int_pct in number)
  return number,

-- Rest of the code goes here

) not final;
```

In Oracle9i, an object type can be inherited only if it is defined as `NOT FINAL`, by default an object type is `FINAL`. On the contrary, classes in Java can be inherited by default but if you don't want that class to be inherited, the class has to be defined as a `final` class.

```
public final class Account{
```

The object type, CHECKING_ACCT_TYP, below inherits from the base object ACCOUNT_TYP. This type overrides the WITHDRAW_AMOUNT member procedure and overloads the SET_MIN_BALANCE member procedure.

```
create or replace type savings_acct_typ
under account_typ (
   static function new_account(p_balance in number)
   return savings_acct_typ,
   overriding member function
   calculate_interest(p_int_pct in number)
   return number,
);
```

```
create or replace type body savings_acct_typ
as

   static function new_account(p_balance   in number)
   return savings_acct_typ
   is
   begin
     return savings_acct_typ(p_balance, 50);
   end new_account;

   overriding member function calculate_interest(p_int_pct in number)
   return number
   is
     interest_pct number;
   begin
     if balance > 10000
     then
       interest_pct :=  p_int_pct + .02;
     else
       interest_pct :=  p_int_pct + .01;
     end if;
     return balance * interest_pct;
   end calculate_interest;

end;
```

The object types in Oracle can be used to create Oracle tables (for data persistence) or collections. That is where it will be more useful than building objects in its true sense. However, you can map a Java object to an object type in the database that will come in very handy when you are working with the data stored in the database. You will see this in action in Chapter 7.

# Summary

Learning a new programming language and, generally, a new approach to programming is always a challenge. It is always easy to learn a new paradigm based on something that we already know and that's precisely why this chapter drew analogies between Java and PL/SQL. The first half of the chapter showed the way things are done in PL/SQL and in Java from a programming perspective, using a simple bank account program. The second half of the chapter compared the way PL/SQL implements the object-oriented features using the package and object types, with Java class. The concepts learned in this chapter and the previous one hopefully provided a useful foundation in OO concepts from which to progress through the rest of this book.

Oracle 9i Java Programming

# Connecting to Oracle through JDBC

The JDBC API is a specification for Java database connectivity. It consists of a set of classes and interfaces written in the Java programming language that documents a standard API for dealing with tabular and, generally, relational data. JDBC is the Java programmer's primary medium for sending and executing SQL statements in the Oracle database and for calling PL/SQL procedures.

*In Chapter 8, we will discuss SQLJ, an industry standard for embedding SQL directly in Java source code.*

Software vendors, such as Oracle, provide their own **JDBC drivers** to implement the API's interfaces and classes, to a greater or lesser degree, and to extend it. The JDBC specification is wide ranging and, in practice, most vendors are unlikely to implement the specification in its entirety. However, you can expect that the fundamentals of JDBC should be available in any implementation and this is certainly the case with Oracle. In addition it does provide many useful extensions to the specification.

*Use of proprietary extensions do limit the portability of the code to other database vendors but, in our case, this is not an important issue since our goal is to produce optimal Java code for working specifically with Oracle. In any case, the goal of complete portability is not really attainable anyway – certainly not without a very heavy investment in up front design.*

However, Oracle extensions to JDBC are the subject of Chapter 7. In this chapter we start at the beginning, covering the basic steps required to establish a connection to the Oracle database and an investigation of the JDBC drivers that Oracle provides for this process. Specifically, we will cover:

- ❑ **JDBC Fundamentals** – What JDBC is, an overview of the JDBC API, and what JDBC drivers are available

- ❑ **Oracle JDBC drivers** – Describing the JDBC drivers provided by Oracle and showing how they fit in the Oracle architecture

- ❑ **Using Oracle JDBC drivers** – Explaining how to configure the Oracle JDBC drivers and showing some working examples

After reading this chapter you will hopefully understand how to connect to the Oracle database using the various available drivers and will be in a better position to judge when use of a particular driver is appropriate.

# JDBC Fundamentals

The JDBC library of classes and interfaces are used within Java programs to open connections to particular databases, execute DML statements (and, if you wish, DDL), retrieve results back and invoke stored procedures and functions, as well as other regular database operations.

JDBC is an object-oriented, Java-based API for database access, and is intended to be a standard to which Java developers and database vendors can adhere. There is no implementation code in the methods of JDBC classes. Instead, a vendor-specific JDBC driver translates API calls into operations for that particular vendor's database. In theory, this means that the JDBC layer 'insulates' Java programmers from the particular characteristics of the database system being used, implying that you could port between different databases without having to re-engineer your JDBC code for each specific database. Indeed, this was a key tenet of the design of JDBC, true to Java's goal of being a 'write once, run anywhere' platform – and of course there is real value to the programmer in this 'loose coupling'. However, in practice, getting JDBC code to work well and **consistently** against multiple data sources requires very considerable effort and development. Every database (Oracle, SQLServer, DB2, mySQL, and so on) is different. Each is unique in the way it handles transactions, and in its locking and concurrency mechanisms. Data types are not completely standard across databases. Each database will offer unique, and often very valuable, object extensions and other DBMS-specific features. And so on. To write totally 'data source independent' JDBC code may require use of only the 'lowest common denominator' capabilities of your database. Since this is an Oracle book, we will, of course, make free use of the considerable functionality that is provided for us in order to produce the most effective Oracle Java programs.

## Exploring the JDBC API

One of the fundamental principles of JDBC's design was to make it practical to build JDBC drivers based on other database APIs. There is a very close mapping between the JDBC architecture and API, and their ODBC counterparts, fundamentally because they are all based on the same standard, the SQL X/Open Call Level Interface (more information can be found at: http://www.opengroup.org/); but JDBC is a lot easier to use. Because of their common ancestry, they share some important conceptual components (such as drivers and connections)

The core JDBC API, containing all the essential classes, interfaces (and exceptions) for accessing a database, is provided in the `java.sql` package, which forms part of Java's class library in the same manner as `java.io`, `java.util`, and so on. Thus, it is included in the current release of the JDK, Standard Edition. Also available is an extensions package, `javax.sql`, which adds functionality that is particularly required for enterprise applications.

The following diagram shows some of the key interfaces and classes in the `java.sql` package:

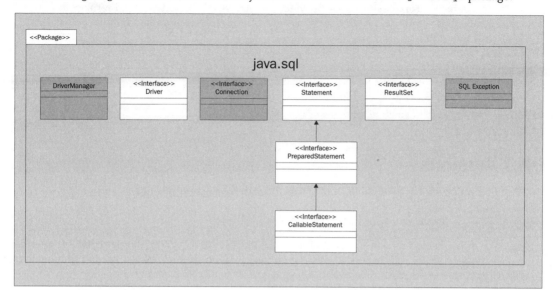

❑  `java.sql.DriverManager` – This class handles the JDBC drivers, it is used to register drivers and create JDBC connections.

❑  `java.sql.Driver` – this interface represents the JDBC driver and must be implemented by every driver vendor. The `oracle.jdbc.OracleDriver` is the class that implements the `Driver` interface in Oracle JDBC drivers. The `Driver` interface is only really used **directly** by people who need to write their own custom drivers. The `DriverManager` class will deal with the driver methods for us, behind the scenes.

❑  `java.sql.Connection` – this interface represents a database connection; it has methods to create SQL statements to perform regular SQL operations. SQL statements are always executed within the context of a `Connection`. Commit and rollback methods are provided for handling database transactions (these will be covered in more detail in the next chapter).

❑  `java.sql.Statement` – this interface provides methods for the execution of SQL statements in the context of a given database connection. The results of database queries are returned in `java.sql.ResultSet` objects. There are two important sub-interfaces of `java.sql.Statement`, and they are:

   ❑  `java.sql.PreparedStatement` – allows the execution of pre-parsed statements. This improves performance in all database operations; since the DBMS pre-compiles the SQL statement only once and then execute it multiple times. The use of prepared statements is a must for building high-performance real applications.

   ❑  `java.sql.CallableStatement` – allows execution of stored procedures, such as PL/SQL and Java Stored Procedures.

❑  `java.sql.ResultSet` – this interface contains and provides methods to access the rows found in a SQL query returned by the execution of a `Statement`. Depending on the type of `ResultSet` in use, we may also have methods for scrolling, modifying and manipulating the retrieved data.

❑    java.sql.SQLException – an exception that provides access to all the information related to database errors. Methods are provided to retrieve error messages and error codes provided by database vendors and to access the stack of errors. Exception handling is discussed in detail in Chapter 6.

For the scope of this chapter the classes and interfaces required to open a database connection will be the main focus. Specifically the DriverManager class and Connection interface will be explained. For practical purposes, the examples will include Statement and ResultSet objects to perform database queries and display the results found. The other interfaces will be reviewed in depth in the next chapter.

# JDBC Versions

Let's take a quick look at the evolution of JDBC through the version releases.

## JDBC 1.x

Originally distributed as an add-in, JDBC 1.x was soon integrated into the standard JDK. It provided the basic framework for data access, consisting primarily of the core interfaces listed in the previous section (DriverManager, Connection, Statement, ResultSet, and so on).

## JDBC 2.0

With this version, the current release, the API now comes in two parts:

❑    The JDBC 2.0 Core API, implemented in the java.sql package, which is included in the Java 2 SDK, Standard Edition

❑    The JDBC 2.0 Optional Package API, implemented in the javax.sql package, which is available separately from http://java.sun.com/products/jdbc/download.htm, or as part of the Java 2 SDK, Enterprise Edition

### The JDBC 2.0 Core API

The core API was changed little from the JDBC1.0 release. A few classes were added, but the major changes came in the form of enhancements to existing interfaces and classes and better performance. Using JDBC 2.0, you can access practically any data source possible. Your data can be stored in a fully relational database, a spreadsheet or even a flat file.

New functionality added in JDBC 2.0 included support for scrollable and updateable result set and batch updating (all of which are discussed in the next chapter). In addition, JDBC 2.0 extended support for new advanced data types to cover those in the SQL99 specification. We can now store, retrieve, and modify new SQL data types that are essentially objects (for example BLOB, CLOB, ARRAY). We cover this topic in Chapter 7.

The support and more details about exactly what these data types are can be found at the JDBC website at http://java.sun.com/j2se/1.3/docs/guide/jdbc/spec2/jdbc2.1.frame.html

### The JDBC 2.0 Optional Package API

This extension API adds functionality that is particularly required for enterprise applications, including support for `DataSource` objects, connection pooling, the Java Naming and Directory Interface (JNDI), and `RowSet` objects (which perform the same function as a `ResultSet`, but can be serialized for passing across a network). We will not cover the extension API in this book, instead concentrating on the fundamentals of the core API.

### The Oracle Extensions

The Oracle JDBC drivers provide additional functionality to the JDBC standard capabilities. The Oracle drivers provide extensions such as, Oracle specific data types (`VARRAY`s and nested tables) and support performance improvements by execution batching and row pre-fetching. The Oracle extensions are available for Java 2 JDK 1.2.x and comply with JDBC 2.0 and also with JDK 1.1 and the JDBC 1.2 standard. The Oracle extensions for JDK 1.2 are included in the following Java packages; `oracle.jdbc` and `oracle.sql`. We look at some of these extensions in detail: in Chapters 6 and 7.

## JDBC 3.0

At the time of this writing, the JDBC 3.0 specification was in final draft form. The JDBC API 3.0 is due to ship as part of J2SE (Java 2 Standard Edition) 1.4 which is planned for release in the fourth quarter of 2001. In this release, both the core API, found in the `java.sql.*` package, and the optional API, found in the `javax.sql.*` package will be included in the Standard Edition release.

The 3.0 package includes enhancements to support for transactions (it introduces the notion of a 'savepoint', which can be used to mark parts of a transaction so that the transaction can be rolled back to a given point) and SQL99 types. Backward compatibility with existing applications and drivers is provided to facilitate migration to JDBC 3.0 technology. To keep up to date with JDBC and the Java technology in general, make sure you visit the JavaSoft web site http://java.sun.com/products/jdbc/ and the Oracle web site http://technet.oracle.com/tech/java/sqlj_jdbc/content.html.

# How JDBC Works

As we discussed earlier, the JDBC architecture is based on a collection of Java interfaces and classes that together enable you to connect to data sources, to create and execute SQL statements, and to retrieve and modify data in a database. These operations are illustrated in the figure overleaf:

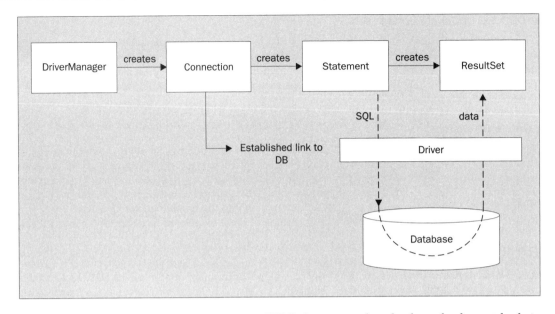

Each of the boxes in the illustration represents a JDBC class or interface that has a fundamental role in accessing a relational database. Although we will use `Statement` and `Resultset` objects in this chapter to execute SQL statements and retrieve the results, our focus is the process of establishing a connection to the Oracle database so we are largely concerned with the JDBC `DriverManager` class and the `Connection` interface, which are responsible for establishing connections to the database, and with the Oracle JDBC drivers through which we establish our connection and execute our SQL.

# JDBC Drivers

Databases usually have proprietary network protocols for communication between the client and the database. Every JDBC driver has the required code to connect and interact with a particular database. This code is database dependent and the database vendor, such as Oracle, usually provides these JDBC drivers.

Transparently to the Java programmer, the `DriverManager` class communicates with the database and performs the requested database operation and returns any requested data:

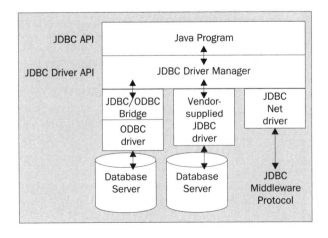

# Driver Types

The JDBC drivers are classified into four general categories into which the Oracle drivers fall:

| Driver Type | Description |
| --- | --- |
| Type 1 | These drivers provide access to a database bridging between JDBC and ODBC. They require additional software installed and configured in the client machine, such as ODBC drivers and supporting libraries for your database. An example of a type 1 driver is the Sun JDBC-ODBC Bridge Driver that allows a Java program to access a database through the use of an ODBC. This driver comes bundled with the JDK and is useful for practice and prototyping. Other than that, there are numerous reasons why use of this driver should be avoided (see http://java.sun.com/products/jdbc/faq.html). |
| Type 2 | These drivers perform native calls from Java to database access APIs that are built in other languages such as C or C++. The Oracle OCI Driver and the Oracle server-side internal driver are examples of Type 2 drivers. |
| Type 3 | This driver translates JDBC calls into a DBMS-independent net protocol, which is then translated to a DBMS protocol by a net server piece of middleware. For example, Oracle supplies Oracle Connection Manager (OCM), which is a middleware product through which thin driver requests can be redirected to the Oracle database. These drivers are suitable for Java Applets. |
| Type 4 | These drivers are 100% pure Java drivers. They establish a communication directly to the database using a standard Java Socket. The net-protocol being used depends on the database vendor, they do not require any client-side software, and neither do they perform any native calls to C or C++ libraries. They are portable across platforms. These drivers are also suitable for building Java applets. The Oracle thin and server-side thin drivers are examples of Type 4 drivers. |

In this book we will only consider those JDBC drivers supplied by Oracle. However, it is worth bearing in mind that third party vendors also supply drivers for the Oracle databases. There is a searchable database of all the JDBC drivers at http://industry.java.sun.com/products/jdbc/drivers.

# Oracle JDBC Drivers

Oracle provides four JDBC drivers that can be used for different scenarios. From a programming point of view there is no difference in the code. The DriverManager class is used to open new connections and the information it requires depends on the database driver being used. JDBC vendors provide all the information related to the driver. For instance, if a third-party JDBC driver for Oracle is used, the vendor should provide specific information needed to pass to the DriverManager class to establish a connection.

Oracle currently provides four JDBC drivers:

❑ Two client-side – **JDBC Thin** driver (type 2) and **JDBC OCI** driver (type 4)

❑ Two server-side – **Server-Side Thin** driver (type 4) and **Server-Side Internal** driver (type 2)

The following diagram shows the general architecture for the Oracle JDBC drivers:

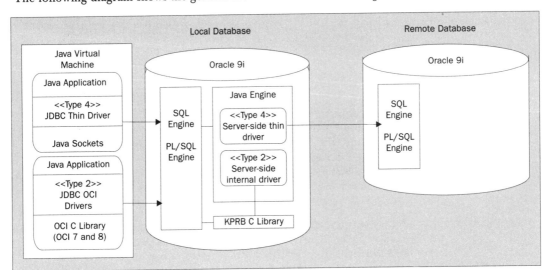

The Oracle JDBC thin and OCI drivers run outside of the database and are used for client-server applications including Java applets. They use different network mechanisms to open a connection to the database. The server-side thin driver and the internal driver, however, run inside the database and are **executed** within the context of the current database session. The internal driver allows Java programs, such as Java Stored Procedures, to access local database resources, such as data and stored procedures, without opening a physical connection. The server-side thin driver allows Java programs running inside the database to access an external Oracle database (remote database).

All the Oracle drivers provide basically the same functionality. They all support the JDBC 1.22 standard and the Oracle extensions for JDBC 2.0, the same APIs and syntax.

> **The server-side internal driver has only supported JDK 1.2 since release 8.1.7 of 8i. In previous releases, only JDK 1.1.x is supported. In Oracle 9i, the thin and OCI drivers support JDK 1.1.x and 1.2.x.**

The real difference between them is the way they connect to the database and how the data is transferred. For instance, the Oracle thin driver uses standard Java sockets over TCP/IP to connect to the database.

> *Java sockets are classes defined in the java.net package and implement a normal network socket. They are used to communicate with servers on the Internet or can be used if you wish to implement your own server.*

The OCI driver, on the other hand, uses Oracle Net8 in the client machine to communicate to the database. As a result, the thin driver can only connect to the database if the listener is configured to use TCP/IP, whereas the OCI driver is not restricted in this way – it can connect to a listener supporting different protocols.

The following sections will provide additional information about each driver provided by Oracle, how

## JDBC Thin Driver

The Oracle thin driver is a type 4 driver and, therefore, it is portable between platforms. It is used from the client-side (outside of the database). It uses standard Java Sockets to communicate directly with the database. It provides a lightweight implementation over TCP/IP that emulates TTC (Two-Task Common) and Net8. It is relevant to mention that it does not require any additional Oracle software installed on the client, such as the OCI (Oracle Call Interface).

> *The Net8 protocol and TTC are part of the stack communication between JDBC clients and the Oracle database. TTC is the Oracle implementation of the OSI presentation layer for exchanging data between the client and the Oracle database. Java TTC is the lightweight implementation of Oracle TTC. If necessary, this layer provides character set and data type conversion between the client and the server, which may be required when the client and the server are installed on different operating systems, for example.*

Since it does not require any additional software, the thin driver is suitable for client-server applications, as well as for Java applets. It can also be used in the middle-tier for building web applications that access Oracle databases and dynamically create web pages.

## JDBC OCI Driver

The JDBC OCI driver is a type 2 driver that uses the OCI (Oracle Call Interface) to communicate with the Oracle database. It performs native calls to the OCI libraries that are implemented in the C language. It requires the Oracle Net8 client to be installed in the client machine. This driver is not portable, in the sense that OCI libraries are operating system dependent (but the OCI libraries are available for a wide range of platforms). The OCI driver converts JDBC invocations to the Oracle Call Interface that are sent to the database through all the layers of the Net8 protocol.

The JDBC OCI driver is suitable for client-server applications and also applications that run in the middle-tier, such as web applications. Through the use of Net8 protocol, the JDBC OCI driver can achieve much higher throughput than other competing JDBC solutions, however it loses the portability of Java because it depends on the OCI libraries, Net8, and other necessary files installed on the client machine. It cannot be used for Java applets because the Oracle client cannot be installed on the web browser or downloaded from the Internet.

## Server Side Internal Driver

The Oracle server-side internal driver allows Java code deployed inside the Oracle database (such as a Java stored procedure or Enterprise JavaBean) to access, and perform local operations within the same database. Java programs running inside the database communicate directly with the SQL and PL/SQL engine by using the internal driver. It is tightly integrated with the Oracle database and the Java engine and runs as part of the same process of the database.

> *Enterprise JavaBeans (EJBs) are business components for the Java platform. They are intended to be deployed in the middle tier (for example, inside Oracle 9iAS), but can also be deployed inside the Oracle database and use the Oracle internal driver to process data. They are outside the scope of this book and will not be covered here. There are numerous Java texts that explain this topic. For coverage of EJBs in Oracle 8i, you might try Professional Oracle 8i Application Programming (Wrox Press, ISBN 1-861004-84-2) or Oracle 8i Java Component Programming with EJB, CORBA and JSP (Oracle Press, ISBN: 0072127376)*

The server-side internal driver is a type 2 driver. It is also referred to as the KPRB driver because it uses Java native methods to call entry points in the KPRB C libraries, which are part of the Oracle Server process. The internal driver uses the KPRB libraries to communicate directly with the Oracle internal SQL engine.

The main difference between this driver and the client-side drivers (thin and OCI) is that the internal driver runs within the default session in which the JVM was called. In other words, it provides optimized communication with SQL data and PL/SQL stored procedures. Java programs deployed in the database do not need to perform calls across the network. The database, the JVM, the KPRB C library, and the SQL engine all run within the same address space. There are no network round-trips involved. As a result, Java stored procedures that process data through he internal drivers will often run faster than the equivalent Java client code that uses Net8 to communicate with the database, as indicated by our benchmark results in Chapter 17.

## Server-Side Thin driver

The server-side thin driver is 100 percent pure Java (type 4 driver) and it provides the same functionality of the client-side thin driver. However, it is used by Java programs running inside the database that need to connect to external Oracle databases (remote databases).

Java programs installed in the local database that need to execute local PL/SQL stored procedures, or process local data and execute programs, must use the server-side internal driver. The intended use of the server-side thin driver is for situations where you accessing remote data only and are using Oracle instance where the Java is running, purely as an application server, rather than as a database. Here a database link would add overhead as everything would be a distributed transaction, a distributed query, even though all queries are against one single remote instance. We will not discuss this driver any further in this book.

# Choosing the Right Driver

If you are using an Oracle JDBC driver in your development then you obviously need to make sure you choose the correct driver for the job. Occasionally that choice is quite straightforward. If you are developing applets with Oracle then the JDBC thin driver is the only suitable choice. If you are developing data-intensive systems, then you can, if feasible, consider deploying your code in the database and using the server-side internal driver (or use PL/SQL!).

However, if you are developing Java code on the client in client-server applications or in the middle tier of a Web application, then you have a definite choice to make between use of the JDBC thin and OCI drivers. The following table summarizes some of the key features and differences between the two drivers:

| Feature Description | Oracle JDBC OCI Driver | Oracle JDBC Thin Driver |
|---|---|---|
| Support for Java Applets | No support, because it requires additional. Oracle software installed on the client-side. | Yes. It does not require pre-installation of any client-side software. The JDBC driver will be downloaded from the server onto the client. |

| Feature Description | Oracle JDBC OCI Driver | Oracle JDBC Thin Driver |
|---|---|---|
| SQL *Net version support | All adapters supported. Including IPC, named pipes, DEC-NET and TCP/IP. | Only TCP/IP networks supported. |
| PL/SQL stored procedures support | Yes, the execution of PL/SQL stored procedures and anonymous procedures are supported. | Yes, the execution of PL/SQL stored procedures and anonymous procedures are supported. |
| Data encryption and Advanced Networking Option. | Fully supported through the use of the Net8 Advanced Networking Option. | Not fully supported. The thin driver does not support third-party authentication (RADIUS, Kerberos or SecurID), neither it supports Oracle Advanced Security SSL implementation. |

For code running in the middle-tier, such as web applications, then the Oracle thin driver will provide maximum portability and will minimize software installation requirements. The OCI driver can be used but it requires the Oracle Net8 to be installed in the middle-ware host, which may not be possible. However, if you require support for a network protocol other than TCP/IP - or if you wish to implement third party security options, then you need to use the OCI driver.

Obviously performance is a big consideration. For example, the Oracle JDBC thin driver writes CLOBs 4000 bytes at a time. The OCI driver is not limited in this way so is faster when handling these data types (see Chapter 15). We perform benchmark tests on the OCI and KPRB drivers, with regard to SQL execution, in Chapter 17.

# Connecting to Oracle

In order to connect to Oracle, we must provide JDBC with sufficient details to identify the database to which we wish to connect. This information will also be used for setting up Net9. Following is the information we need about the Oracle database before we run the examples:

❑ HOST – The machine name or IP address in which your Oracle database is installed. If a local database is used, localhost can be used as the host name.

❑ PORT – The port defined for a valid database listener. The default port is 1521. Please check the listener PORT in the ORACLE_HOME\network\admin\listener.ora file.

❑ SERVICE_NAME – The service name is the new naming schema, implemented since Oracle 8i, to identify a database. It is a logical representation of a database. Prior to Oracle 8i, a SID (Service IDentifier) was used to identify the database name, and many Oracle developers still refer to it as such. The service name can be found in the SERVICE_NAMES parameter defined in your database initialization file init.ora. The init.ora file must be in the root directory of your database instance in a directory called: pfile.

❑ TNSENTRY – The TNSENTRY must be a valid entry in the `tnsnames.ora` file, found in the `ORACLE_HOME\network\admin` directory. It has all the information required to connect to the database you will use to run the examples. For systems with multiple Oracle homes, please check the `tnsnames.ora` file of your current Oracle home (from here it will be just referred as: ORACLE_HOME), because there will be more than one in your system. You can use the `Oracle Home Selector` utility to find out what is your current ORACLE_HOME; a shortcut can be found in the Oracle installation for Windows at Start-> Programs -> Oracle Installation Products -> Oracle Home Selector.

❑ Database username and password – In this book we use our own user, identified by `username/password` (see Chapter 1).

❑ DBA username and password – A user with DBA role will be required for the Oracle server-side thin driver.

In case a remote database is used, ask your DBA (Database Administrator) about the database connection parameters (HOST name or IP address, listener PORT and database SERVICE_NAME). Create an entry in the local `tnsnames.ora` file manually, or by using the Oracle Net Configuration Assistant, and verify the connection from SQL*Plus. The TNSNAMES entry will be used in the JDBC OCI driver and server-side internal driver examples.

# Oracle JDBC Connections

Armed with all of the relevant information with regard to our Oracle database, we are ready to create a connection from our Java program.

## Loading a Driver

First, we need to load our chosen JDBC driver and obtain a connection to the database. In order to do this, we use the JDBC `java.sql.DriverManager` class. The DriverManager class implements the `java.sql.Driver` interface.

> *The Driver interface is only really used directly by people who need to write their own custom drivers. The DriverManager class will deal with the Driver methods for us, behind the scenes.*

There are several ways in which to load a Driver class and register it with the DriverManager:

❑ Using the Class.forName() method

❑ Using the registerDriver() method of the DriverManager class

❑ Identifying the Driver class in the jdbc.drivers system property

We will focus on the first two methods here. A call to Class.forName() will cause the Java Virtual Machine to load the driver class. This method takes a String parameter that is the fully qualified class name of the driver class For an Oracle database, we use:

```
Class.forName("oracle.jdbc.OracleDriver");
```

The term "fully qualified class name" is just a fancy way to say "the package specification and the class name." In the example, `oracle.jdbc` is the package, and `OracleDriver` is the class name. Basically, we are loading the driver explicitly by calling the static `forName()` method in the `Class` class, and passing a `String` object, containing the driver class name, as an argument.

You should note that the `oracle.jdbc` package is new to Oracle 9i. If you are using an older version of the database or client, then you will need to reference the old package, `oracle.jdbc.driver`, as follows:

```
Class.forName("oracle.jdbc.driver.OracleDriver");
```

In fact, you can also use the above in 9i, since this package is still currently supported for compatibility purposes (although this may change in the future).

The `forName()` method can throw an exception of type `ClassNotFoundException` if the driver class cannot be found, and this must be caught. Therefore, a call to the function has to appear in a `try` block with an appropriate `catch` block:

```
public class OraConn {
  public static void main(String[] args) {

    // Load the driver
    try {

      // Load the driver class
      Class.forName("oracle.jdbc.OracleDriver ");

    ...JDBC connection code here...
    }
      catch (ClassNotFoundException cnfe) {
      System.err.println(cnfe);
    }
```

Each `Driver` class will typically create an instance of itself when it is loaded, and register that instance automatically by calling the `RegisterDriver` method of the `DriverManager` class. When this happens, the driver is added to the list of available drivers that is maintained by the `DriverManager` class. Some programmers prefer to force the issue by explicitly calling the `newInstance()` method on the class object:

```
Class.forName("oracle.jdbc.OracleDriver ").newInstance();
```

However, you should be aware that this would often create a second, superfluous object.

> *You don't need to create `DriverManager` objects (in fact you can't because the constructor is declared `private`), and all the methods in the `DriverManager` class are `static` so the operate on the whole class, not on specific instances.*

Be aware, that the `Class.forName()` instruction will not work with the Microsoft JVM. This situation could happen when a Java applet that uses the Oracle thin driver is executed on Internet Explorer using the Microsoft JVM.

**109**

A second method used to load a driver is to explicitly call the `registerDriver()` method of the `DriverManager` class:

```
DriverManager.registerDriver(new oracle.jdbc.OracleDriver ());
```

The final method is to set the `jdbc.drivers` system property by calling the `setProperty()` method for the `System` class, for example:

```
System.setProperty("jdbc.drivers", " oracle.jdbc.OracleDriver ");
```

The first argument is the key for the property to be set and the second argument is the value. This statement identifies the Oracle JDBC driver in the system property. If you want to specify multiple drivers in the system property value, you should separate the driver names within the string by colons.

# Establishing a Connection

An object of a class that implements the `Connection` interface – in other words, a `Connection` object – represents a connection to a specific data source. The `Connection` object essentially establishes a context in which you can create and execute SQL commands.

The `DriverManager` class provides three `static` methods for creating `Connection` objects. These are all overloaded versions of the `getConnection()` method. The simplest form of the `getConnection()` method looks as follows:

```
Connection OraConn = DriverManager.getConnection(sourceURL);
```

The argument, `sourceURL`, is a `String` object defining all of the parameters needed to establish a connection. From this information is built a JDBC URL (Uniform Resource Locator) that identifies and locates the database. Note that this is a `String` object specifying the URL, not an object of the `java.net.URL` class.

If the database requires username and password authentication we use the second overloaded form of the `getConnection` method:

```
Connection OraConn =
    DriverManager.getConnection(sourceURL, myUserName, myPassword);
```

The final overloaded version of the `getConnection()` method accepts a `Properties` object as shown below:

```
java.util.Properties info = new java.util.Properties();
info.put ("user", "username");
info.put ("password", "password");
Connection OraConn = DriverManager.getConnection( sourceURL, info );
```

The `Properties` object holds the information related to the connection in key value pairs; each key and its corresponding value in the property list is a String. The `user` is the key for the database user name; the `password` key stores the database user password.

# JDBC URLs

The JDBC URL will vary depending on the database and on the JDBC driver used. However, all JDBC URLs take the general form:

```
jdbc:<subprotocol>:<subname>
```

The scheme `jdbc:` indicates that the URL refers to a JDBC data source. The `<subprotocol>:` identifies which JDBC driver to use. The `<subname>` is the data source identifier, the format of which will be dictated by the JDBC driver.

## URL for the Oracle Thin Driver

The thin driver supports URLs in two basic formats. The first is as follows:

```
jdbc:oracle:thin:@HOST_NAME:PORT:SERVICE_NAME
```

The value of the `<subprotocol>` is `oracle:thin:`, indicating use of the JDBC thin driver. On my test system the URL looks as follows:

```
jdbc:oracle:thin:@openweb:1521:wroxdb
```

where, as described above, `openweb` is the name of the machine hosting the Oracle database, 1521 is the database listener port and `wroxdb` identifies the specific database to which we wish to connect.

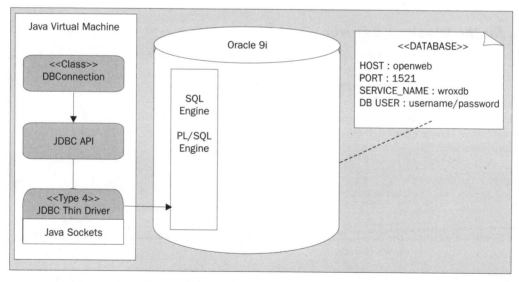

Thus the connection code may look like this:

```
String SourceURL = " jdbc:oracle:thin:@openweb:1521:wroxdb";
Connection OraConn = DriverManager.getConnection(SourceURL, username,
                                                 password);
```

**111**

The thin driver also supports URLs in the form of a keyword-value pair list – the same syntax supported by Net8:

```
// All this goes on one line.
String SourceURL = "jdbc:oracle:thin:@(DESCRIPTION = (ADDRESS_LIST =(ADDRESS =
(PROTOCOL = TCP)(HOST = openweb)(PORT = 1521)))(CONNECT_DATA = (SERVICE_NAME =
wroxdb)))";

Connection oraConn = DriverManager.getConnection(SourceURL, username,
                                                 password );
```

This format is very similar to that seen in the `tnsnames.ora` file:

```
# TNSNAMES.ORA Network Configuration File: ORACLE_HOME\network\admin\tnsnames.ora
#Generated by Oracle Configuration tools.

WROXDB =
  (DESCRIPTION =
    (ADDRESS_LIST =
      (ADDRESS = (PROTOCOL = TCP)(HOST = openweb)(PORT = 1521))
    )
    (CONNECT_DATA =
      (SERVICE_NAME = wroxdb)
    )
  )
```

## URL for the Oracle OCI Driver

The OCI driver uses the following syntax:

```
jdbc:oracle:oci8:@TNSENTRY
```

The parameter `oracle:oci8:` indicates that the Oracle OCI driver will be used. Since the OCI driver requires the Oracle client to be installed, we can directly reference a valid entry in the local `tnsnames.ora` file:

```
String SourceURL = "jdbc:oracle:oci8:@WROXDB";
Connection oraConn = DriverManager.getConnection( SourceURL, username,
                                                  password );
```

In the above example the name of the `TNSENTRY` is `WROXDB` (in accordance with the entry in the `tnsnames.ora` file shown above).

The JDBC OCI driver will look for it and extract all the information required for the connection, obtaining `openweb` as the name of the host, 1521 as the database listener port and `wroxdb` as the database to which we wish to connect.

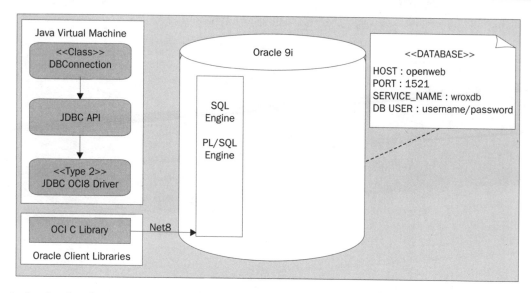

As for the thin driver, the OCI driver also supports keyword-value pair list syntax:

```
// All this goes in one line.
String SourceURL = "jdbc:oracle:oci8:@(DESCRIPTION = (ADDRESS_LIST =(ADDRESS =
(PROTOCOL = TCP)(HOST = openweb)(PORT = 1521)))(CONNECT_DATA = (SERVICE_NAME =
wroxdb)))";

Connection oraConn = DriverManager.getConnection( SourceURL, username,
                                                  password );
```

Additionally, the OCI supports an old Net Service syntax as the database URL:

```
// All this goes in one line.
String url =
"jdbc:oracle:oci8:@(description=(address=(host=openweb)(protocol=tcp)(port=1521))(
connect_data=(sid=wroxdb)))";

Connection con = DriverManager.getConnection( url, username, password );
```

# A Basic JDBC Application

Having established the definition of our JDBC URLs for the thin and OCI drivers, we will now create a Java program that establishes a connection with the Oracle Server, through either of these drivers, executes a Statement (query), retrieves the rows into a ResultSet and then displays the results in a command DOS prompt window.

The logical flow of the `DBConnection` class will be as follows:

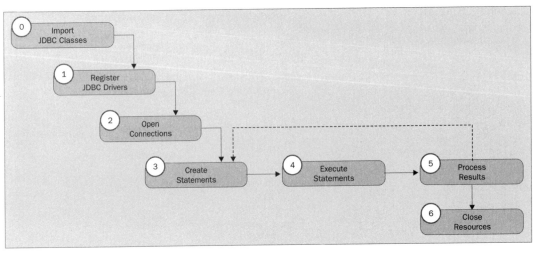

Our query will retrieve the name and the type of all the `user_objects` (such as tables, views, indexes and java classes), found in the current user's schema:

```
select object_name, object_type from user_objects
```

We will build up the code for the `DBConnection` Java class in logical stages.

The first step is to import the required JDBC classes. First we import the `DriverManager` class and the `Connection` interface needed to establish our connection, and also the `SQLException` class, which is required to catch any SQL exception:

```
import java.sql.DriverManager;
import java.sql.Connection;
import java.sql.SQLException;
```

The following classes are imported to execute the SQL query and to retrieve the results:

```
import java.sql.Statement;
import java.sql.ResultSet;
```

> Note that it is not strictly necessary to explicitly import each individual class and interface in the package. Instead, we can simply issue: `import java.sql.*`. Useing the wildcard, *, will not mean that you import all of the classes of the `java.sql` package – just the referenced ones in your Java class.

For ease of demonstration (and to avoid hard-coding the connection details), we are going to supply our JDBC URL, username and password from the command line. As we discussed earlier, these values are more often stored in a properties file:

```
public class DBConnection{
  public static void main( String args[] ){

    if ( args.length < 3 ){
      System.out.println( "Syntax: DBConnection [url] [username] [password]" );
      System.exit( -1 );  // Our program end here. Wrong number of parameters.
    }

    String url      = args[0];
    String username = args[1];
    String password = args[2];
    String sql = "select object_name, object_type from user_objects";
    String objName, objType;
```

Next, we register the Oracle JDBC driver, as described previously:

```
try{
  System.out.println( "Step 01. Registering JDBC Driver" );
  DriverManager.registerDriver(new oracle.jdbc.OracleDriver());
```

We then open a connection to the Oracle database by calling the getConnection() method of the DriverManager class. This method returns a Connection object that represents the actual connection to the database:

```
System.out.println( "Step 02. Establishing connection to: " + url);
Connection con = DriverManager.getConnection( url, username, password );
System.out.println( "        . Connected to Oracle!.");
```

We call the createStatement() method of our Connection object, which returns a Statement object that can be used to execute any SQL instruction valid for the database to which we are connected.

```
System.out.println( "Step 03. Creating SQL statement." );
Statement sta = con.createStatement( );
```

We then call the executeQuery() method of the Statement object, which is the standard way to execute valid SQL queries (if the query is not valid, a SQLException is thrown). This method returns a ResultSet object that contains all the data that matched the query:

```
System.out.println( "Step 04. Executing SQL statement.");
ResultSet query = sta.executeQuery( sql );
```

Next we must iterate through each row in our ResultSet and print the values of the object_name and object_type columns to the console. The ResultSet maintains a cursor that is initially positioned before the first row. The next() method of the ResultSet object is used to move the cursor one row. To display all the rows found in the query use the next() method within a while loop. After the last record the next() method returns null. The null causes the while to finish:

```
    System.out.println( "Step 05. Printing results.");
    while ( query.next() ){
        objName = query.getString( "object_name" );
        objType = query.getString( "object_type" );
        System.out.println( "            * " + objType + " " + objName );
    }
```

The getXXX() methods of the ResultSet are used to retrieve the data from the current row. The XXX represents the Java type that maps the SQL data type retrieved. In the DBConnection class the getString("column_name") method is used to retrieve a String that maps to a SQL VARCHAR2 column. The value specified as parameter must match the column_name in the SQL query. If the column name does not exist, a SQLException will be thrown.

*Alternatively we could have retrieved the data by specifying the column position in the current row, as follows:*

```
    objName = query.getString( 1 );
    objType = query.getString( 2 );
```

*This is a classic example of method overloading.*

It is very important that all the JDBC objects created are explicitly closed after they are not needed by your application. The ResultSet, Statement and Connection objects provide a close() method:

```
    System.out.println("Step 06. Closing JDBC objects.");
    query.close();   // Close ResultSet
    sta.close();     // Close Statement
    con.close();     // Close Connection
```

Finally, we handle any exceptions that might arise:

```
    }catch( SQLException e ){
      // This section will handle any errors
      System.out.println( "The following error occurred: " + e );
    }
  }
}
```

The above will give only very basic details regarding any errors that may have occurred. Full details concerning the handling of exceptions are given in Chapter 6.

By experience, if ResultSets or Statements are not closed, the system resources will be consumed until an exception is thrown. However, this is only likely to cause you a problem if you are opening numerous objects and never closing any of them. It does not mean that you must always immediately close a Statement as soon as the query is executed. If a SQL Statement is likely to be executed many times, then the Statement should be parsed once and then reused as many times as required. We should not be creating and parsing Statement objects every single time that SQL needs to be executed. We look at this topic in detail in Chapter 16.

# Running the DBConnection class

The full `DBConnection.java` source file, as described above, is available for download from the Wrox web site. Java sources files must be named identically to the Java class name because the compiler (`javac.exe`) is case-sensitive.

Include in your `PATH` environment variable the Java Compiler (`javac.exe`) and Java Interpreter (`java.exe`). These files are located in your the `JAVA_HOME\bin` directory. For example:

```
> set PATH=%PATH%;c:\jdk1.3\bin;
```

Note that we are not making permanent changes here, these setting will be valid for the current session only. Next we must include the `classes12.zip` file in our `CLASSPATH` environment variable. This file is located in the `ORACLE_HOME\jdbc\lib` directory. For example:

```
> set CLASSPATH=.;c:\oracle\ora90\jdbc\lib\classes12.zip;
```

The `classes12.zip` file bundles all the Oracle JDBC classes, including the JDBC Thin Driver library, for JDK version 1.2.x. Note that the above will overwrite any previous additions to the CLASSPATH variable for that session. If you actually want to add another library, then use:

```
> set CLASSPATH=%CLASSPATH%;.;c:\oracle\ora90\jdbc\lib\classes12.zip;
```

The above instruction defines the minimum content of the `CLASSPATH` variable to run the sample. In the `ORACLE_HOME\jdbc\lib` directory there are other files, such as `nls_charset12.zip` that contains all the files required for NLS character sets with the JDK 1.2.x, the `nls_charset11.zip` is for JDK 1.1. However these files will not be used in the examples, but must be included in the case that the Java application requires support for NLS.

If you wish to connect to a remote database using the thin driver and don't have an Oracle client installed then you will need to copy the `classes12.zip` file to a local directory and include it in your `CLASSPATH`. Remember the thin driver is portable, you can copy this file from a UNIX or Windows system. You can download various versions of the Oracle JDBC thin driver from http://technet.oracle.com/software/tech/java/sqlj_jdbc/content.html

Compile the `DBConnection` class from the directory where the `DBConnection.java` file was, as follows:

```
> javac DBConnection.java
```

## Connecting through the thin Driver

Execute the class from the command line, as follows:

```
> java DBConnection jdbc:oracle:thin:@openweb:1521:wroxdb username password

Step 01. Registering JDBC Driver
Step 02. Establishing connection to: jdbc:oracle:thin:@openweb:1521:wroxdb
  . Connected to Oracle!.
```

**117**

```
Step 03. Creating SQL statement.
Step 04. Executing SQL statement.
Step 05. Printing results.
          * TABLE BONUS
          * TABLE DEPT
          * TABLE EMP
          * INDEX PK_DEPT
          * INDEX PK_EMP
          * TABLE RECEIPT
          * TABLE SALGRADE
Step 06. Closing JDBC objects.
```

Of course, the output displayed will vary dramatically depending on the user. For instance, if you connect to the `system` database user many objects will be displayed.

### Connecting through the OCI Driver

When using the OCI driver, we must also include the dynamic link library `ocijdbc8.dll` in our `PATH`, which can found in the ORACLE_HOME\bin directory. For example:

```
> set PATH=.;c:\oracle\ora90\bin;c:\jdk1.3\bin;
> set CLASSPATH=.;c:\oracle\ora90\jdbc\lib\classes12.zip
```

Compile the code then execute the class from the command line, supplying the appropriate parameters:

```
> javac DBConnection.java
> java  DBConnection jdbc:oracle:oci8:@wroxdb username password
```

The output should be exactly as that shown above for the thin driver. If the `ocijdbc9.dll` library cannot be found by the JVM (`java.exe`), an `UnsatisfiedLinkError` exception will be displayed.

# Solution To Common Problems

While running the `DBConnection` class, the following exceptions might take place. All of the following errors were generated using the thin driver. Error messages may vary with different drivers. Only exceptions related to the connection process will be covered, due to the scope of this chapter.

# NoClassDefFoundError

The following error may occur if the required Oracle JDBC driver is not currently defined in the CLASSPATH:

```
> java DBConnection jdbc:oracle:thin@openweb:1521:wroxdb username password
Step 01. Registering Oracle Thin Driver
Exception in thread "main" java.lang.NoClassDefFoundError:
                        oracle/jdbc/driver/OracleDriver
at DBConnection.main(DBConnection.java, Compiled Code)
```

Make sure the `classes12.zip` file exists on your system and is correctly included in the CLASSPATH.

# Network Adapter could not establish connection

You may see the following error if the HOST or listener PORT of the database cannot be resolved by the JDBC driver:

```
> java DBConnection jdbc:oracle:thin@openweb:1521:wroxdb username password
Step 01. Registering Oracle Thin Driver
Step 02. Establishing connection to: jdbc:oracle:thin:@openweb:1521:wroxdb
The following error occurred: java.sql.SQLException: Io exception: The Network
Adapter could not establish the connection
```

Verify that they are both correct and properly included in the url variable. Also, check that your database listener is up and running (if you have a local database on Windows 2000, you can check the status of your Oracle services at: Start -> Settings -> Control Panel -> Administrative Tools -> Services).

# Io exception: connection refused

This might happen when the SERVICE_NAME is incorrectly defined in the url variable:

```
> java DBConnection jdbc:oracle:thin:@openweb:1521:woxdb username password
Step 01. Registering JDBC Driver
Step 02. Establishing connection to: jdbc:oracle:thin:@openweb:1521:woxdb
The following error occurred: java.sql.SQLException: Io exception: Connection
refused(DESCRIPTION=(TMP=)(VSNNUM=135294976)(ERR=12505)(ERROR_STACK=(ERROR=(CODE=1
2505)(EMFI=4))))
```

Correct the SERVICE_NAME entry. If this does not solve the problem, check that the database is up and running. If your listener is running but your database is down, you might see the following error:

```
> java DBConnection jdbc:oracle:thin:@openweb:1521:wroxdb username password
Step 01. Registering JDBC Driver
Step 02. Establishing connection to: jdbc:oracle:thin:@openweb:1521:wroxdb
The following error occurred: java.sql.SQLException: Io exception: Connection
refused(DESCRIPTION=(TMP=)(VSNNUM=150999297)(ERR=12500)(ERROR_STACK=(ERROR=(CODE=1
2500)(EMFI=4))(ERROR=(CODE=530)(EMFI=4))(ERROR=(BUF='32-bit Windows error: 2: No
such file or directory'))))
```

If your server crashes while you are connected to it you will see an Error: Connection reset by peer.

# Io exception: Invalid connection string format

This exception takes place when the database URL format is wrong:

```
> java DBConnection jdbc:oracle:thin:@openweb1521:wroxdb username password
Step 01. Registering JDBC Driver
Step 02. Establishing connection to: jdbc:oracle:thin:@openweb1521:wroxdb
The following error occurred: java.sql.SQLException: Io exception: Invalid
connection string format, a valid format is: "host:port:sid"
```

Please verify that your URL is of the correct format.

# Oracle 01017: invalid username/password

This one is pretty self-explanatory. The exception is thrown by the authentication mechanisms of your Oracle database:

```
> java DBConnection jdbc:oracle:thin:@openweb:1521:wroxdb username pssword
Step 01. Registering JDBC Driver
Step 02. Establishing connection to: jdbc:oracle:thin:@openweb:1521:wroxdb
The following error occurred: java.sql.SQLException: ORA-01017: invalid
username/password; logon denied
```

# The Server-Side Internal Driver

As discussed previously, the internal (or KPRB) driver allows Java code deployed inside the Oracle database to access and performs local operations with the same database.

# Using the KPRB Driver

There are several ways in which we can retrieve a Connection object when using the JDBC driver. The first way is to call the defaultConnection() method of the OracleDriver class:

```
Connection con = new oracle.jdbc.OracleDriver().defaultConnection();
```

As previously explained, the internal driver executes within the current database session; therefore, it does not create a new physical connection because you are already connected. Also, the KPRB driver does not need to be registered because this is automatically done by the database.

The alternative method of retrieving a Connection object is to use the DriverManager.getConnection() method, as we have for the client-side drivers.. The following database URLs can be passed to the getConnection() method to retrieve the connection:

```
String url = "jdbc:default:connection";
Connection con = DriverManager.getConnection(url);
```

or, alternatively:

```
String url = "jdbc:oracle:kprb:@";
Connection con = DriverManager.getConnection(url);
```

Note that the DriverManager does not require the username and password parameters. If they are specified then the DBConnection class will compile and run, but these parameters will not affect the connection. The internal driver will be using the current session of the connected user.

The following diagram shows the scenario:

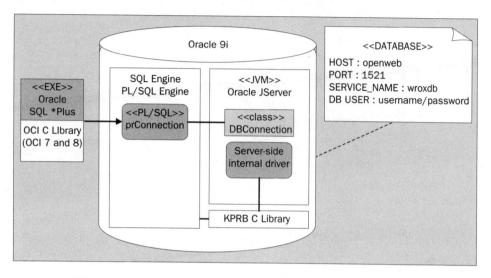

We will now modify our DBConnection class and deploy it into the database as a Java stored procedure. The JDBC internal driver will be used to obtain a default connection and execute the JDBC instructions.

# The DBConnectionInternal Class

The Java source file, DBConnectionInternal.java, is included in the code download and looks as follows:

```java
import java.sql.*;

public class DBConnection{
  public static void main( String args[] ){

    String sql = "select object_name, object_type from user_objects";
    String objName, objType;

    try{
      System.out.println("Step 01. Getting default connection.");
      Connection con = new oracle.jdbc.OracleDriver().defaultConnection();

    System.out.println( "Step 02. Creating SQL statement." );
    Statement sta = con.createStatement( );

    System.out.println( "Step 03. Executing SQL statement.");
    ResultSet query = sta.executeQuery( sql );

    System.out.println( "Step 04. Printing results.");
    while ( query.next() ){
```

```
      objName = query.getString( "object_name" );
      objType = query.getString( "object_type" );

      System.out.println( "          * " + objType + " " + objName );
   }
   System.out.println("Step 05. Closing JDBC objects.");
   query.close();    // Close ResultSet
   sta.close();    // Close Statement
   con.close();    // Close Connection

   }catch( SQLException e ){
   // This section will handle any errors that come about.
   System.out.println( "The following error occurred: " + e );
   }
  }
}
```

Save and compile the Java source file in the usual manner.

## Loading the Class

Load the DBConnectionInternal.class file into the database using the loadjava utility (as outlined in Chapter 1 and discussed in detail in Chapter 9):

```
> loadjava -user username/password@wroxdb DBConnectionInternal.class
            -resolve -verbose
initialization complete
loading  : DBConnectionInternal
creating : DBConnectionInternal
resolver :
resolving: DBConnectionInternal
```

The loadjava utility can use the thin driver or the OCI driver to upload classes into the database and uses the OCI driver by default, thus explaining our use of the username/password@TNSENTRY syntax. The -resolve parameter indicates that all the dependencies with other Java classes should be resolved. The -verbose parameter indicates to loadjava to display information in the standard output.

If we want the loadjava utility to load the class using the thin driver, the command would look as follows:

```
> loadjava -thin -user username/password@openweb:1521:wroxdb
            DBConnectionInternal.class -verbose -resolve
```

## Creating the PL/SQL Call Specification

Before we can call the main method in our loaded Java class, we must publish it to the Oracle data dictionary by creating a PL/SQL "wrapper":

```
create or replace procedure prConnection
As LANGUAGE JAVA
NAME 'DBConnectionInternal.main( java.lang.String[] )';
```

Save the PL/SQL specification as DBConnectionInternal.sql. Connect to SQL*Plus as the same user whose schema the Java class loaded and run the script to create the procedure. For example, if you saved the script in c:\OracleJava\Ch04:

```
SQL> start c:\OracleJava\Ch04\DBConnectionInternal.sql
  4 /
Procedure Created
```

Before you execute the prConnection procedure, it is convenient to enable the standard output for Java stored procedures, as follows:

```
SQL> set  serveroutput on size  10000;
SQL> exec dbms_java.set_output( 10000 );
```

If the standard output is not set, the Java stored procedure will run, but the results and/or exceptions will not be displayed in the screen. However this information is not lost, it is just sent to the session's current trace file, which can be found in the user_dump_dest directory, as a *.TRC file. Beware, when writing into the session's trace file, the initialization parameter MAX_DUMP_FILE_SIZE imposes a user-selectable size limit.

Finally, execute prConnection, thus calling our Java main method:

```
SQL> exec prConnection;
Step 01. Getting default connection.
Step 02. Creating SQL statement.
Step 03. Executing SQL statement.
Step 04. Printing results.
* TABLE BONUS
* TABLE CREATE$JAVA$LOB$TABLE
* JAVA CLASS DBConnectionInternal
...<etc>...
Step 05. Closing JDBC objects.
```

PL/SQL procedure successfully completed.

Again, the output displayed when the PL/SQL prConnection procedure is executed could be different because it depends on the objects installed in the database in use.

# Summary

In this chapter we covered all of the basic classes of JDBC API and concentrated on how to use the Oracle JDBC drivers for different scenarios. The following table summarizes the database URLs that can be used with every driver:

| Driver | Type | Database URL supported by `DriverManager.getConnection()` |
|---|---|---|
| Oracle thin driver (client-side) | 4 | `jdbc:oracle:`**`thin`**`:@`**`HOST_NAME`**`:`**`PORT`**`:`**`SERVICE_NAME`** |
| | | `jdbc:oracle:`**`thin`**`:@(DESCRIPTION = (ADDRESS_LIST = (ADDRESS = (PROTOCOL = TCP)(HOST = `**`YourHost`**`)(PORT = `**`YourListenerPort`**`))) (CONNECT_DATA = (SERVICE_NAME = `**`YourDatabase`**`) (SERVER=dedicated|shared)))` |
| Oracle OCI driver | 2 | `jdbc:oracle:`**`oci8`**`:@`**`TNSENTRY`** |
| | | `jdbc:oracle:`**`oci8`**`:@(DESCRIPTION = (ADDRESS_LIST =(ADDRESS = (PROTOCOL = TCP)(HOST = `**`YourHost`**`)(PORT = `**`YourListenerPort`**`))) (CONNECT_DATA = (SERVICE_NAME = `**`YourDatabase`**`) (SERVER=dedicated|shared)))` |
| Oracle server-side Internal driver | 4 | `jdbc:`**`default`**`:`**`connection`** |
| | | `jdbc:oracle:`**`kprb`**`:@` |
| Oracle server-side thin driver | 2 | `jdbc:oracle:thin:@`**`HOST`**`:`**`PORT`**`:`**`SERVICE_NAME`** |

Having introduced JDBC programming and the drivers provided by Oracle, the following chapters will delve deeper into some of the commonly used JDBC functionality that we have only touched on here, including use of statements, `CallableStatement` and `PreparedStatement`, handling transactions in JDBC, and writing high performance JDBC code.

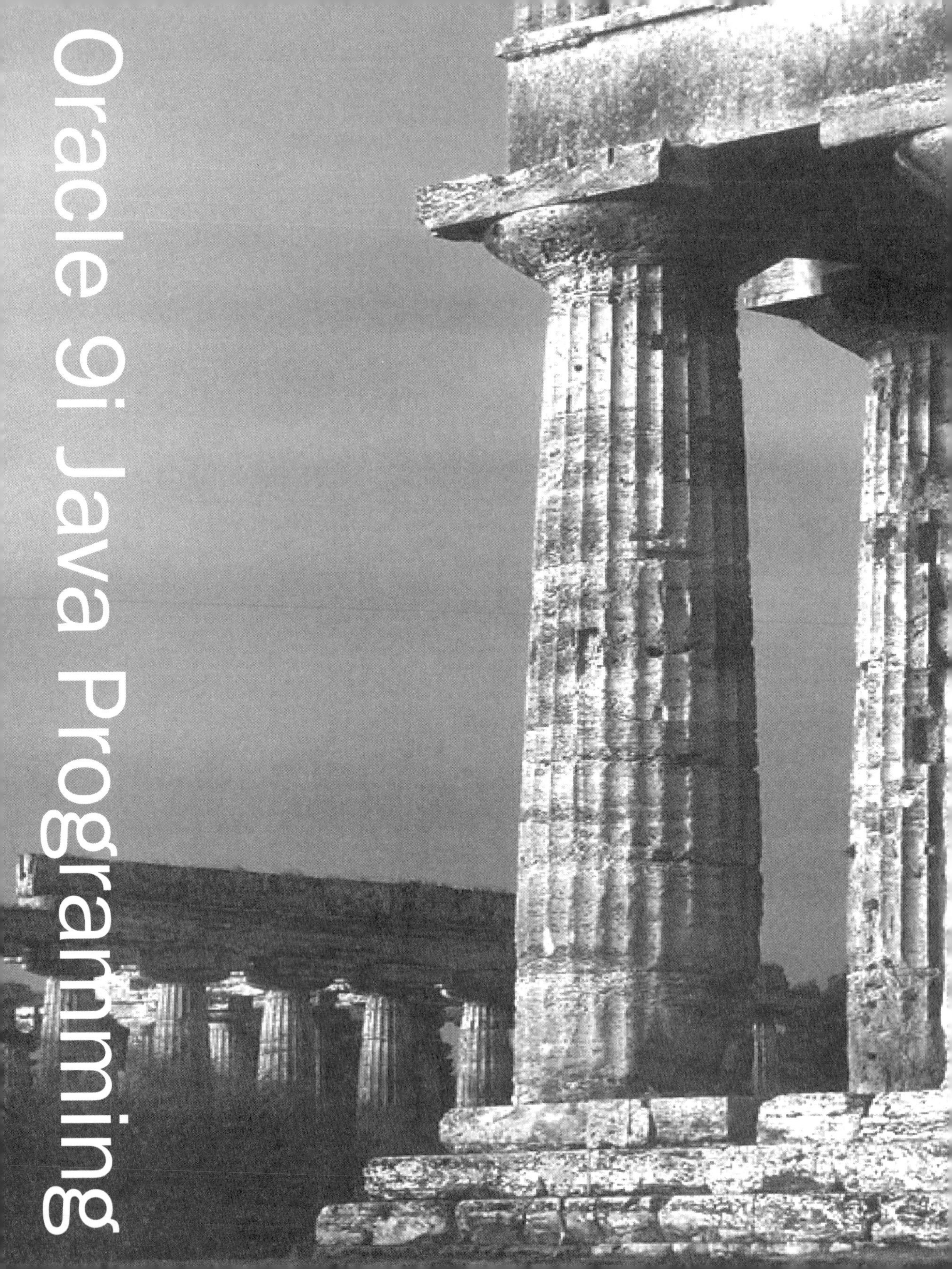
Oracle 9i Java Programming

# Using JDBC

The JDBC API is a big subject. You could fill a book this size just covering what's in it, let alone providing useful working examples. Since this may well be your first encounter with JDBC, the aim of this chapter is to give you a focused introduction to the fundamentals rather than a comprehensive dissection of the entire topic.

The JDBC API is a specification for Java database connectivity. Software vendors, such as Oracle, are free to produce their own drivers to implement the API's interfaces to a greater or lesser degree and to extend it. The specification is wide ranging and, in practice, most vendors are unlikely to implement the specification in its entirety. However, you can expect that the fundamentals of JDBC should be available in any implementation. Using proprietary extensions does limit the portability of the code to other database vendors, but in many cases this isn't really an important hindrance since, in practice, the holy grail of complete portability is often not attainable anyway.

In Oracle's case the fundamentals are all there as you would expect and we will be using them in this chapter. The Oracle drivers also provide functionally rich extensions to the capabilities of the original API. As you gain confidence with JDBC and want to try more advanced features, you will be well advised to consult Oracle's documentation to confirm the extent to which the software conforms to the specification. Delving further you will find that some features are not fully implemented or implemented in ways which may preclude their use. In addition, you will sometimes find a better solution to your problem is available in a proprietary extension.

In this chapter, we'll focus on the main interfaces you'll use again and again. These are the basic building blocks for writing JDBC programs. We'll also look at Oracle's extensions and why you might want to use them.

The main interfaces we'll be looking at are:

- ❑  `Connection`, which you will have already seen in depth in the previous chapter
- ❑  `Statement` and its sub-interfaces `PreparedStatement` and `CallableStatement`
- ❑  Oracle extensions, like `OraclePreparedStatement` and `OracleCallableStatement`
- ❑  `ResultSet` and `OracleResultSet`
- ❑  `MetaData` interfaces

We will also be introducing other topics along the way:

- ❑ **Transactions**
- ❑ **Array fetching** (a performance enhancing technique of fetching multiple rows in a single round trip from the database)
- ❑ **Batching updates** (another performance enhancing technique of holding updates to the database in a batch before sending them all together in a single round trip to the database)

As we progress through the chapter, we'll build up a sample application, wherever possible working each new topic into what has gone before so that you can see why it is relevant and what advantages it might produce.

# What Else is in the JDBC API?

When you're ready to look more widely at the JDBC API and want to find out more, a good place to start is the Sun documentation. The core JDBC API is basically everything you find under the `java.sql` package, and you can get its documentation at http://java.sun.com/j2se/1.3/docs/api/java/sql/package-summary.html. Another good source is the *JDBC Developers Guide and Reference* that comes with the Oracle documentation set.

There's also the JDBC Optional Package API, which contains useful extensions for building server-side applications using an open architecture. For instance, **DataSources** and **RowSets** and support for distributed transactions. A `DataSource` is a way of representing data sources in a generic way providing a common interface, whether your data source is a fully blown RDBMS like Oracle or just a simple flat file. A `RowSet` extends the capabilities of a `ResultSet`, allowing you to treat it as a JavaBeans component. If you installed the complete Java 2 SDK, Enterprise Edition you will have the optional package already, it's everything you find under the `javax.sql` package. Otherwise you can download it from http://java.sun.com/products/jdbc/. For more information on the JDBC Optional Package go to http://java.sun.com/products/jdbc/jdbc20.stdext.javadoc.

# A Tour of the Main JDBC Interfaces

Let's take a look at the fundamental interfaces we'll be covering in this chapter, so you have a clearer idea of how they interrelate. Later on, we will use them as building blocks to explore the other topics mentioned above.

## The Connection Interface

Everything starts with a `java.sql.Connection`. Before you can use any of the other interfaces you must use this one. We covered `Connection` in detail in Chapter 4, *Connecting To Oracle Through JDBC*; in this chapter we are also going to see how to use the `Connection` interface to control transactions within the Oracle database.

As you can see from the following diagram, there are methods in `Connection` to create objects implementing the `Statement` interfaces, (that is `Statement` and its sub-interfaces).

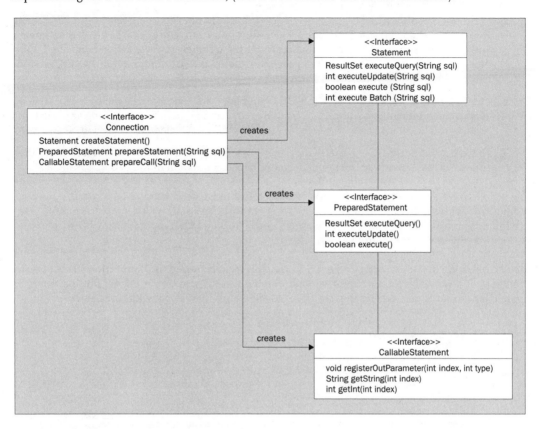

# The Statement Interface

The `java.sql.Statement` interface provides methods for executing SQL statements and retrieving the results. You get a `Statement` object by calling the `createStatement()` method of a valid `Connection` object:

```
Statement stmt = connection.createStatement();
```

When a `Statement` object is created, it provides a workspace for you to create a SQL query, execute that SQL in the database, and retrieve any results that are returned. A `Statement` can handle just about any SQL the database we connected to can handle, it can deal with DML (Data Manipulation Language, that is, SELECT, INSERT, UPDATE, DELETE), and DDL (Data Definition Language, like CREATE TABLE, ALTER TABLE and so on).

Once you have a valid `Statement` object, you can use it to execute SQL by calling one of its execute methods:

❏ `ResultSet executeQuery()` – Returns a single `ResultSet` object that encapsulates the results of the executed query.

❏ `int executeUpdate()` – to execute queries that do not return a `ResultSet`. For example, SQL DML statements or SQL DDL. The return value of `executeUpdate()` is an integer (referred to as the update count) that indicates the number of rows that were affected. For statements which do not act on rows such as CREATE SEQUENCE or DROP TABLE, the return value of `executeUpdate()` is always zero.

❏ `int [] executeBatch()` – In JDBC 2.0 (and later) we can assemble multiple SQL statements into a batch (using the `addBatch()` method), and submit them for processing as a batch to the database. The return value of executing each statement is an element in the `int` array.

❏ `boolean execute()` – a rarely used method to execute statements that return more than one result set, more than one update count, or a combination of the two.

We need to have a look at the `ResultSet` interface before we demonstrate the `executeQuery()` method and we'll do that in the next section. To begin with, let's start with a simpler example. We can use the `executeUpdate()` method to perform both DML and DDL operations. Let's write some DDL to create a table EMPLOYEES from a `Statement`.

Here's the listing for `CreateEmployees.java`. This class is passed the connection string as a single argument. It instantiates the Oracle driver and obtains a valid `Connection` from it using the connection string. It then creates the EMPLOYEES table and populates it with three rows:

```java
import java.sql.*;

//  Obtains a Connection to the database and create the Employees table.

public class CreateEmployees {

  /* All the work is done in the main method.
   * @param args The only argument is the connection string */
  public static void main(String[] args) throws Exception {
    Connection connection = null;
    try {
      // Load the driver
      Class.forName("oracle.jdbc.driver.OracleDriver");
    } catch (Exception e) {
      // Feedback the error and stop
      System.out.println("Could not load driver : " + e);
      System.exit(-1);
    }

    try {
      // DriverManager will return a Connection from the loaded driver
      // The connection string is passed as the only argument
      connection = DriverManager.getConnection(args[0]);
    } catch (Exception e) {
      // Feedback the error and stop
      System.out.println("Unable to connect : " + e);
      System.exit(-1);
```

```
    }

    try {
      // get a Statement from the connection
      Statement stmt = connection.createStatement();

      // create the Employees table with the Statement
      int res = stmt.executeUpdate("create table employees "
              + "(emp_id      number(10, 0) not null primary key"
              + ",first_name varchar2(100) not null"
              + ",surname    varchar2(100) not null)" );

      System.out.println("Created Employees table res = " + res);

      /* The int (res) returned from the call to executeUpdate() is 0.
         However, if we now populate three rows in the EMPLOYEES table
         with DML, the int returned will be 3. */

      res += stmt.executeUpdate("insert into employees "
              + "values (1, 'Freddie', 'Smith')");

      res += stmt.executeUpdate("insert into employees "
              + "values (2, 'Jack', 'Beanstalk')");

      res += stmt.executeUpdate("insert into employees "
              + "values (3, 'Hardy', 'Grafter')");

      System.out.println("Created 3 Employees res = " + res);

      stmt.close();
    } catch (SQLException e) {
      // Feedback the error and return an error code
      System.out.println("Unexpected sql error: " + e);
      System.exit(-1);
    } finally {
      // always close the open Connection
      connection.close();
    }
  }
}
```

We've wrapped the code in a try...catch...finally block. Both the calls to Connection
createStatement() and to Statement executeUpdate() (and, in fact, almost every JDBC
method call) can result in a SQLException being thrown, so we've caught that error and output a
suitable message whilst returning an error code to the caller. The finally block is there to make sure
the Connection object is closed and is executed regardless of whether the SQLException was
thrown or not. Actually, closing the Connection object also closes any Statements opened by that
Connection, so the code to close it explicitly after the call to executeUpdate() isn't strictly
necessary, but we prefer to include it for clarity anyway.

Now if we run this class you'll see that the number of rows returned is 3. (Notice we added a couple of output
messages to show the value of res after the DDL call to create the table and then after all the inserts):

```
> java CreateEmployees
            "jdbc:oracle:thin:username/password@localhost:1521:database"
Created Employees table res = 0
Created 3 Employees res = 3
```

Notice that the first and only argument is the complete connection string.

## Oracle Extensions: Statement Is An Interface

The JDBC interfaces form contracts by which implementations must abide. As in any Java interface, a class which implements it *must* provide an implementation for all the methods it defines. This applies to all the JDBC interfaces we're going to see, but we'll use `Statement` as an example. When you execute a statement such as this one:

```
Statement statement = connection.createStatement();
```

You get a reference to an object which implements the `Statement` interface, and you can use all the methods of that interface. We can demonstrate this more graphically if we try to create a `Statement` as though it were a class type:

```
Statement statement = new Statement(); //won't compile
```

This gives the compilation error message:

```
interface java.sql.Statement is an interface. It can't be instantiated.
```

Objects of classes that implement the `Statement` interface can only be obtained by calling the `createStatement()` method of a valid `Connection` object. The actual class you get depends on the implementation, for example, using the standard Oracle JDBC implementation as we are, the `Statement` object is an instance of the class `oracle.jdbc.driver.OracleStatement`.

The actual class type returned is only important when we wish to use extensions provided by the vendor. In our example above we only needed to use standard JDBC so it was enough to just use the interface. The client program didn't know it got an `OracleStatement` and didn't need to.

> *The implementing class type will be different depending on the vendor of the JDBC drivers you happen to be using. Don't take this as a guarantee that all the methods will work the same regardless of the vendor, some may only support certain features fully and you should check which these are against the vendor's documentation.*

If you want to use Oracle extensions, then you have to concern yourself with the actual class that is implementing the interface. In the above example we can use the Oracle extensions provided by `OracleStatement` only if we cast it to its true type. Before we can do that we must import the class to our program with this import statement, (actually imports aren't mandatory they're a convenience to make the code easier to deal with, without them we would have to always refer to the classes by their fully qualified package names):

```
import oracle.jdbc.driver.OracleStatement;
```

Now we can cast our `Statement` to an `OracleStatement` and use some method that we would not otherwise be able to use:

```
OracleStatement statement =
            (OracleStatement) connection.createStatement();
statement.setRowPrefetch(20);
```

We'll see what the method `setRowPrefetch()` does in the *Multiple Fetching* section later on. We'll also see a case where we have to cast a `CallableStatement` to an `OracleCallableStatement` when we look at an arrays example. However, before we get there, we still need to cover some more basic interfaces.

# The ResultSet Interface

The `Statement` interface method `executeQuery()` takes a `String` argument and returns a `java.sql.ResultSet`. The argument passed in should be a valid SQL query:

```
ResultSet results = stmt.executeQuery("select emp_id from employees");
```

You can build the query in any way you like, so for example, if you wanted to select just one particular employee, you might do the following:

```
int empId = 2; // probably get the id from somewhere else
ResultSet results = stmt.executeQuery("select * from employees "
                        + "where emp_id = " + empId);
```

A `ResultSet` is just a Java representation of a database **ref cursor** (a pointer to a database cursor). The cursor initially 'points' to a position immediately preceding the first row, and calling the `next()` method on the `ResultSet` object will move the cursor to the next position. A cursor remains valid (that is, open) until you either finish traversing all the rows or close it. It is also closed automatically when its parent `Statement` object is closed, and consequently when the `Connection` object is closed as well since that will result in the closure of the `Statement`.

> *It is possible to return a PL/SQL REF CURSOR to Java through JDBC. When you do this, the PL/SQL does not close the cursor at all, the cursor is closed by JDBC when the `ResultSet` is closed. We'll see this at work when we cover `CallableStatement` later.*

If the default `ResultSet` object is used then you will have a cursor that moves **forward only** (and also cannot be updated). Usually you will process rows from a result set in a loop, using the `next()` method:

```
ResultSet results = stmt.executeQuery("select * from employees");

while(results.next()){
// Process the row...
}
```

This method returns `true` if the move is to a valid row, and `false` if you fall off the end, so you can use it to control a `while` loop. This assumes the `ResultSet` object starts out in its default state with the cursor set to one before the first row. You can also use the `isLast()` or `isFirst()` methods to test whether you have reached the end or the beginning and `isBeforeFirst()` or `isAfterLast()` to detect that you are placed immediately before the first row or have already fallen off the end respectively.

Using the `ResultSet` reference, you can retrieve the value of any column for the current row (as specified by the cursor) by name or by position. You can also determine information about the columns such as the number of columns returned, or the data types of columns. The `ResultSet` interface declares the following basic methods for retrieving column data for the current row as Java types:

| | | | |
|---|---|---|---|
| getArray() | getByte() | getFloat() | getShort() |
| getAsciiStream() | getBytes() | getInt() | getString() |
| getBinaryStream() | getDate() | getLong() | getTime() |
| getBoolean() | getDouble() | getObject() | getTimestamp() |

We will see examples of several of these in this section, and we will also come back to arrays later on when we look at `CallableStatements`. Of the remaining methods, `getAsciiStream()` returns an object of type `InputStream` that you can use to read the data as a stream of ASCII characters. This is primarily for use with values of the SQL type LONGVARCHAR, which can be very long – strings that you would want to read piecemeal.

Most of the basic data access methods are very flexible in converting from SQL data types to Java data types. For instance if you use `getInt()` on a field of type CHAR, the method will attempt to parse the characters assuming they specify an integer. Equally, you can read numeric SQL types using the `getString()` method. `ResultSet` also includes more methods which allow you to access numbers as objects, for instance `getBigDecimal()` which we'll see soon, and still others for accessing so called SQL3 data types, such as arrays and **Large Objects** (LOBs).

There are overloaded versions of each of the methods that provide two ways of identifying the column containing the data. The column can be selected by passing the SQL column name as a `String` argument, or by passing an index value for the column of type `int`, where the first column has the index value 1. So for the following query:

```
ResultSet results = stmt.executeQuery(
                "select emp_id, surname from employees");
```

You can return the columns by name, (note that column names are not case sensitive so `Surname` is the same as `surname`):

```
while (results.next()) {
   int empId = results.getInt("emp_id");
   String surname = results.getString("surname");
}
```

or position:

```
while (results.next()) {
   int empId = results.getInt(1);
   String surname = results.getString(2);
}
```

Notice the use of get methods to obtain the column values in the form applicable to the data. So for EMP_ID, being an NUMBER integer, use getInt(), and for the VARCHAR2 column SURNAME use getString().

Here's an example of a class that obtains a Statement from the Connection as before and then returns a ResultSet from a query. It then iterates the rows of the result set and outputs the EMPLOYEE details:

```
import java.sql.*;

// Query the Employees table.

public class QueryEmployees {
  public static void main(String[] args) throws Exception {
    Connection connection = null;
    try {

      // Load the driver
      Class.forName("oracle.jdbc.driver.OracleDriver");

      connection = DriverManager.getConnection(args[0]);
    } catch (Exception e) {

      // Either could not load the class or connection error
      System.out.println("Unable to connect : " + e);
      System.exit(-1);
    }

    try {
      Statement stmt = connection.createStatement();

      // Query all the employees
      ResultSet results = stmt.executeQuery("select * from employees");

      // Output the results
      while (results.next()) {
        System.out.println("Employee id = " + results.getInt("emp_id")
                        + " " + results.getString("first_name") + " "
                        + results.getString("surname"));
      }

      // close open resources
      results.close();
      stmt.close();
    } catch (SQLException e) {
```

```
      // Feedback the error and return an error code
      System.out.println("Unexpected sql error: " + e);
      System.exit(-1);
    }
    finally {
      connection.close();
    }
  }
}
```

Running this class displays all the employees:

```
> java QueryEmployees
         "jdbc:oracle:thin:username/password@localhost:1521:database"
Employee id = 1 Freddie Smith
Employee id = 2 Jack Beanstalk
Employee id = 3 Hardy Grafter
```

## Handling Date And Date/Time Columns

The getDate(), getTime(), and getTimestamp() methods of ResultSet return objects of type Date, Time, and TimeStamp respectively. There's a potential pitfall to be aware of with dates though. Suppose we return the current SYSDATE in a ResultSet:

```
ResultSet results = stmt.executeQuery("select sysdate from dual");
```

If we use getDate() we don't get the time part and if we use getTime() we don't get the date part. The way to return both is to use getTimestamp(). In the following example, we use all three methods to show this is the case:

```
import java.sql.*;
import java.text.SimpleDateFormat;

// Query dates and date/times.

public class QueryDates {
  public static void main(String[] args) throws Exception {
    Connection connection = null;
    try {
      Class.forName("oracle.jdbc.driver.OracleDriver");
      connection = DriverManager.getConnection(args[0]);
    } catch (Exception e) {
      System.out.println("Unable to connect : " + e);
      System.exit(-1);
    }

    try {
      Statement stmt = connection.createStatement();
      ResultSet results = stmt.executeQuery("select sysdate from dual");
```

```
    // create a format to display the dates
    SimpleDateFormat dateFormat =
      new SimpleDateFormat("dd/MM/yyyy HH:mm:ss");
    while (results.next()) {
      System.out.println("date = "
                        + dateFormat.format(results.getDate(1)));
      System.out.println("time = "
                        + dateFormat.format(results.getTime(1)));
      System.out.println("timestamp = "
                        + dateFormat.format(results.getTimestamp(1)));
    }

    results.close();
    stmt.close();
  } catch (SQLException e) {
    System.out.println("Unexpected sql error: " + e);
    System.exit(-1);
  } finally {
    connection.close();
  }
}
}
```

Notice the use of the `SimpleDateFormat` object to format the results in the desired pattern. Although all three methods return subclasses of `java.util.Date`, they each override `toString()` in their own specific ways. By providing a format object we can choose to display them in any way we want. Here's the output from running the class:

```
> java QueryDates
        "jdbc:oracle:thin:username/password@localhost:1521:database"
date = 12/11/2001 00:00:00
time = 01/01/1970 17:05:32
timestamp = 12/11/2001 17:05:32
```

## Handling NULL Columns

There are pitfalls in dealing with nullable columns that we need to be aware of too. To demonstrate them we're going to need some new data. Let's say there's a table, NOTICES, which joins to EMPLOYEES:

If you're not familiar with using UML for entity relationships it's actually very similar to traditional ER diagramming. We can see optionality in the relationships where the multiplicity is 0 and if it is * or greater than 1 it's a many relationship. So the relationship called *deleted by* in the diagram could be expressed as a) An EMPLOYEE may have deleted zero or more NOTICES, or b) A NOTICE may be deleted by one EMPLOYEE.

Create the table in SQL*Plus with this statement:

```
SQL> create table notices
  2 (notice_id    number(10, 0) not null primary key
  3 ,emp_id_to    number(10, 0) not null references employees
  4 ,emp_id_from  number(10, 0) not null references employees
  5 ,emp_id_deleted  number(10, 0) references employees
  6 ,emp_deleted_note  varchar2(200)
  7 ,notice_read_date  date
  8 ,created_date  date not null
  9 ,description   varchar2(4000) not null);
```

To show what happens with NULL columns we just need to add one row to NOTICES. (The EMP_ID_DELETED and EMP_DELETED_NOTE columns are left out deliberately as they are the NULL columns):

```
SQL> insert into notices
  2 (notice_id, emp_id_to, emp_id_from, created_date, description)
  3 values (1, 1, 2, sysdate, 'A sample notice');
SQL> commit;
```

Let's select all the data from the NOTICES table with the following query:

```
ResultSet results = stmt.executeQuery("select * from notices");
```

And output the data in the row to demonstrate the issue:

```
while (results.next()) {
    System.out.println("notice id = " + results.getInt("notice_id"));
    System.out.println("description = "
                        + results.getString("description"));
    System.out.println("deletion note = "
                        + results.getString("emp_deleted_note"));
    System.out.println("deleted by  id = "
                        + results.getInt("emp_id_deleted"));
```

EMP_DELETED_NOTE has the value of NULL. This is not problematic because it is a VARCHAR2 column that translates to String in Java. Since String is an Object the ResultSet just returns null.

The next column shows the problem. Since EMP_ID_DELETED is an integer value we are naturally inclined to use the getInt() method to retrieve it. The problem is that the int data type cannot express null or "no value". The result of the getInt() method is 0. This isn't the value in the database but we have no way of knowing this from the value itself and must call the wasNull() method in the next line to determine that this was indeed the case.

```
        System.out.println("deleted by was null = " + results.wasNull());
```

Here we see the use of `wasNull()` to determine that the primitive value just read should not be taken at face value. The method returns `true` indicating that the `0` should really have been ignored.

There is an alternative. By using the `getObject()` method on the `NULL EMP_ID_DELETED` column we *do* see a `null` result. This is effectively the same as calling `getString()` on the `VARCHAR2` column as above, since an `Object` can express "no value" simply as no object, or `null`.

```
        System.out.println("deleted by as Object = "
                        + results.getObject("emp_id_deleted"));
        System.out.println("from = " + results.getObject("emp_id_from")
                        + " type = "
                        + results.getObject("emp_id_from").getClass());
```

The last statement shows that by calling the `getObject()` method on a column which does have a value the resultant `Object` is an instance of `java.math.BigDecimal`. The JDBC classes are clever enough to interpret which Java class to produce in a call to `getObject()`. In this example we could simply have used the `getBigDecimal()` method to get the result. Actually, we could have just used `getString()` on it as well, JDBC is also clever enough to convert the value to a `String` for us. This may be okay if all we're going to do is display the value, but it isn't efficient if we then need to do something with the numeric value since we will have to convert it back!

Here's the complete listing for the `QueryNulls` class:

```java
import java.sql.*;

// Query nullable columns

public class QueryNulls {
  public static void main(String[] args) throws Exception {
    Connection connection = null;
    try {
      Class.forName("oracle.jdbc.driver.OracleDriver");
      connection = DriverManager.getConnection(args[0]);
    } catch (Exception e) {
      System.out.println("Unable to connect : " + e);
      System.exit(-1);
    }

    try {
      Statement stmt = connection.createStatement();
      ResultSet results = stmt.executeQuery("select * from notices");

      while (results.next()) {
        System.out.println("notice id = " + results.getInt("notice_id"));
        System.out.println("description = "
                        + results.getString("description"));
        System.out.println("deletion note = "
                        + results.getString("emp_deleted_note"));
```

```
                System.out.println("deleted by  id = "
                                + results.getInt("emp_id_deleted"));
                System.out.println("deleted by was null = " + results.wasNull());
                System.out.println("deleted by as Object = "
                                + results.getObject("emp_id_deleted"));
                System.out.println("from = " + results.getObject("emp_id_from")
                                + " type = "
                                + results.getObject("emp_id_from").getClass());
            }

        results.close();
        stmt.close();
      } catch (SQLException e) {
        System.out.println("Unexpected sql error: " + e);
        System.exit(-1);
      }
      finally {
        connection.close();
      }
    }
  }
```

If we compile and run the class we see the following output:

```
> java QueryNulls
        "jdbc:oracle:thin:username/password@localhost:1521:database"
notice id = 1
description = A sample notice
deletion note = null
deleted by  id = 0
deleted by was null = true
deleted by as Object = null
from = 2 type = class java.math.BigDecimal
```

So what's the best method to use with NULL columns? Return a 0 with getInt() and have to call wasNull() to see if it was a null, or getBigDecimal() to get a null reference, or any other getObject() variation? The answer is there is no absolute answer. If you had to pass the value about as an object it would be better to get it as one, if you are doing simple math, a Java primitive is better since there is no overhead incurred in creating an object unnecessarily.

Object creation/destruction has a great impact on JVM performance, more so than compiled code execution speed. The latest adaptive optimizing compilers can execute Java at speeds at least as good as statically compiled C++ programs. This is quite an achievement for a dynamically linked language, but Object creation/destruction remains an area where Java lags behind.

## Metadata About Result Sets

Metadata is data about data and the ResultSetMetaData interface gives us information about the data being returned to us in a ResultSet.

Consider a statement like the following:

```
ResultSet results = stmt.executeQuery("select * from notices");
```

This statement allows maximum flexibility for future changes to the NOTICES table. If we add or remove columns from it the statement needs no changes. If we obtain the ResultSetMetaData from the ResultSet we can find out about the columns' attributes:

```
ResultSetMetaData rsmd = results.getMetaData();
```

So, to display the name and data type name of each of the columns in the ResultSet, we can write a simple loop (note it starts at 1, not 0 which is normal in Java), which iterates through each of the columns and calls the appropriate methods to get the information we require:

```
for (int i = 1; i <= rsmd.getColumnCount(); i++) {
  System.out.print("Column name=" + rsmd.getColumnName(i));
  System.out.print(" type=" + rsmd.getColumnTypeName (i));
  System.out.print(" java type=" + rsmd.getColumnType(i));
}
```

We output the Java type in two ways. The descriptive name will be a string such as NUMBER or DATE, the Java type returned as an int corresponds to one of the constant values in the java.sql.Types class. So you can make a test such as the following to return true or false.

```
if (rsmd.getColumnType(i) == java.sql.Types.DATE) ...
```

You should only use the java.sql.Types constant names to compare with the Java type of the column. That's what a constant is for, the actual value of the constant is immaterial. Here's the listing for the QueryMetaData class, in it we use the Java type to display a different message depending on whether the column is a Timestamp type or not:

```
import java.sql.*;

// Query metadata about columns

public class QueryMetaData {
  public static void main(String[] args) throws Exception {
    Connection connection = null;
    try {
      Class.forName("oracle.jdbc.driver.OracleDriver");
      connection = DriverManager.getConnection(args[0]);
    } catch (Exception e) {
      System.out.println("Unable to connect : " + e);
      System.exit(-1);
    }

    try {
      Statement stmt = connection.createStatement();
      ResultSet results = stmt.executeQuery("select * from notices");
```

```
        ResultSetMetaData rsmd = results.getMetaData();

        // Iterate through the columns, output a description for each one
        for (int i = 1; i <= rsmd.getColumnCount(); i++) {
          System.out.print("Column name=" + rsmd.getColumnName(i));
          System.out.print(" type=" + rsmd.getColumnTypeName(i));
          System.out.print(" java type=" + rsmd.getColumnType(i));
          if (rsmd.getColumnType(i) == java.sql.Types.TIMESTAMP) {
            System.out.println(" it's a Date/Time!");
          } else {
            System.out.println(" it's NOT a Date/Time.");
          }
        }

        results.close();
        stmt.close();
      } catch (SQLException e) {
        System.out.println("Unexpected sql error: " + e);
        System.exit(-1);
      } finally {
        connection.close();
      }
    }
  }
}
```

Here's what we get when we compile and run the class:

```
> java QueryMetaData
          jdbc:oracle:thin:username/password@localhost:1521:database"
Column name=NOTICE_ID type=NUMBER java type=2, it's NOT a Date/Time.
Column name=EMP_ID_TO type=NUMBER java type=2, it's NOT a Date/Time.
Column name=EMP_ID_FROM type=NUMBER java type=2, it's NOT a Date/Time.
Column name=EMP_ID_DELETED type=NUMBER java type=2, it's NOT a Date/Time.
Column name=EMP_DELETED_NOTE type=VARCHAR2 java type=12, it's NOT a Date/Time.
Column name=NOTICE_READ_DATE type=DATE java type=93, it's a Date/Time!
Column name=CREATED_DATE type=DATE java type=93, it's a Date/Time!
Column name=DESCRIPTION type=VARCHAR2 java type=12, it's NOT a Date/Time.
```

Using metadata makes more sense when you think of writing generic code: if we were to add a new column to the NOTICES table, we could do so without breaking this class and could then act on the Java type as necessary.

## Constraining Result Sets

A ResultSet can be constrained in a number of ways to control its behaviour. The methods to do this are sometimes available on both the ResultSet and on the Statement which created it. If you use the Statement methods, all ResultSets created by that Statement from that moment on will be constrained by the values you set. For example:

❑ `getMaxRows()` and `setMaxRows()` – allow us to retrieve and set the maximum number of rows in a `ResultSet`. These methods are only available from the `Statement`.

❑ `getFetchSize()` and `setFetchSize()` – the `setFetchSize()` method is a performance hint to the JDBC driver, suggesting the optimum number of rows that should be fetched from the database. This can yield a considerable performance benefit, but must be used carefully otherwise it could actually make matters worse. We'll see more on this later.

### Result Sets Which Can Be Updated and Scrolled

By default the `createStatement()` method of `Connection` returns a `Statement` which will return a result set that can only be iterated from beginning to end. However, a `ResultSet` can have more capabilities, it can be made **scrollable** (you can read through it backwards with the `previous()` method as well as forwards with `next()`) and **updatable**. To get a `ResultSet` that exhibits this behavior you must create your `Statement` with a variant of the `createStatement()` method:

```
Statement statement = connection.createStatement(
                ResultSet.TYPE_SCROLL_SENSITIVE,
                ResultSet.CONCUR_UPDATABLE);
```

`ResultSet`s created from this `Statement` will be both scrollable and updatable. Note that Oracle provides support for scrollable result sets in a client-side cache since the database does not support them internally. You need to bear this in mind if you have a very large result set because it will use a lot of memory, not to mention network bandwidth. There are other constants available to constrain the result set behavior although you'll probably find that you either need to set them as above, or you will just use the default which is actually `TYPE_SCROLL_INSENSITIVE` and `CONCUR_READ_ONLY`, that is, a result set which can neither be scrolled nor updated.

*Forwards is the only cursor movement possible with JDBC 1.0 drivers.*

Having created the `Statement` as above, we can now create a `ResultSet` which will allow updates. There is an Oracle limitation in that you cannot use the `SELECT *...` syntax for an updatable result set so we have to include the table alias. This is a workaround documented in the *JDBC Developer's Guide And Reference: Creating Scrollable or Updateable Result Sets*:

```
ResultSet results =
        stmt.executeQuery("select n.* from notices n");
```

Use the `updateXXX()` methods of `ResultSet` to update the value of the column according to its data type. Then the `updateRow()` method to actually update the database.

```
while (results.next()) {
    // update the deletion note
    results.updateString("emp_deleted_note",
            "marked for delete by batch process");
    results.updateRow();
```

To insert a new row, we have to navigate (scroll) using the `moveToInsertRow()` method which puts us into an empty row ready to accept new values:

**143**

```
results.moveToInsertRow();
```

The new values are inserted by calling the updateXXX() methods as before. Notice that we have to create a new Timestamp object to pass to the updateTimestamp() method. The constructor for Timestamp takes a long, so we have to create a new java.util.Date and use the getTime() method to return the current time as one:

```
Timestamp now = new Timestamp(new java.util.Date().getTime());
results.updateTimestamp("created_date", now);
```

Now we're ready to call insertRow() to actually insert it to the database. We then need to call the moveToCurrentRow() method to return us to where we were processing in the original set of results:

```
results.insertRow();
results.moveToCurrentRow();
```

Here's the complete listing. We've added an extra result set retrieval after the updates and some output messages so you can see that rows really have been updated/inserted:

```java
import java.sql.*;

// Return a ResultSet which can be updated.

public class UpdateableResults {
  public static void main(String[] args) throws Exception {
    Connection connection = null;
    try {
      Class.forName("oracle.jdbc.driver.OracleDriver");
      connection = DriverManager.getConnection(args[0]);
    } catch (Exception e) {
      System.out.println("Unable to connect : " + e);
      System.exit(-1);
    }

    try {
      Statement stmt =
        connection.createStatement(ResultSet.TYPE_SCROLL_SENSITIVE,
                                   ResultSet.CONCUR_UPDATABLE);

      // use an alias (Oracle workaround)
      ResultSet results = stmt.executeQuery("select n.* from notices n");
      while (results.next()) {

        // update the deletion note
        results.updateString("emp_deleted_note",
                             "marked for delete by batch process");
        results.updateRow();
        // create variables to insert new row
        int from = results.getInt("emp_id_from");
        int to = results.getInt("emp_id_to");
```

```
            Timestamp now = new Timestamp(new java.util.Date().getTime());

            // navigate to the 'insert' row
            results.moveToInsertRow();
            results.updateInt("notice_id", 2);
            results.updateInt("emp_id_to", to);
            results.updateInt("emp_id_from", from);
            results.updateTimestamp("created_date", now);
            results.updateString("description", "Row added by batch process");

            // insert it and move back to the current row
            results.insertRow();
            results.moveToCurrentRow();
          }

          results.close();

          results = stmt.executeQuery("select * from notices");
          while (results.next()) {
            System.out.println("notice id = " + results.getInt("notice_id"));
            System.out.println("description = "
                               + results.getString("description"));
            System.out.println("deletion note = "
                               + results.getString("emp_deleted_note"));
          }

          results.close();
          stmt.close();
        } catch (SQLException e) {
          System.out.println("Unexpected sql error: " + e);
          System.exit(-1);
        } finally {
          connection.close();
        }
      }
    }
```

Here's what we get when we compile and run the class:

```
> java UpdateableResults
        "jdbc:oracle:thin:username/password@localhost:1521:database"
notice id = 1
description = A sample notice
deletion note = marked for delete by batch process
notice id = 2
description = Row added by batch process
deletion note = null
```

It's difficult to show the power of updateable and scrollable result sets in the context of a program like this one, which just reads rows from the database and outputs messages. They come into their own when you have an interactive program, like a client-server form accessing the data. Then you can see that the ability to move backwards as well as forwards is vital. The fact that you can also update the rows in place is a boon in these situations since otherwise you are faced with having to construct and execute an appropriate UPDATE statement separately.

# The PreparedStatement Interface

As we have seen, the `PreparedStatement` interface inherits from `Statement`, and therefore adds to the functionality of `Statement`. In practice, we actually use `PreparedStatement` far more extensively because it offers performance benefits over and above the capabilities of `Statement`.

To illustrate, let's modify some code we looked at earlier. Imagine we wanted to iterate through all the possible values of `EMP_ID` to see if there was a current `EMPLOYEE` row. Assume `getLatestEmpId()` is a custom method which returns the last `EMP_ID` as an `int`:

```
Connection connection = DriverManager.getConnection(
    "jdbc:oracle:thin:username/password@localhost:1521:database");
Statement stmt = connection.createStatement();

for(int empId = 1; empId <= getLatestEmpId(); empId++) {
  ResultSet results = stmt.executeQuery("select * from employees "
                          + "where emp_id = " + empId);
}
```

Here the query string is rebuilt every time we iterate the loop and is different each time because the value of `empId` is incremented. Just as in SQL, each and every time the query is run it will be a brand new query and as such, will have to be parsed, qualified (names resolved), security checked, optimized, and so on. That's a very expensive operation. By using a `PreparedStatement` instead the situation improves dramatically.

A `PreparedStatement` allows us to use a SQL statement that contains input parameters. The value of these parameters are not specified when the SQL statement is created – they must be supplied by the application at query execution time. To recode the above example to use a `PreparedStatement`, we use the `prepareStatement()` method of `Connection`. This method takes the SQL query as its only parameter:

```
PreparedStatement pstmt =
  connection.prepareStatement("select * from employees "
                        + "where emp_id = ?");

for(int empId = 1; empId <= getLatestEmpId(); empId++) {
  ...
}
```

Notice that the query is now taken out of the loop and included in the construction of the `PreparedStatement`. When using `PreparedStatements` remember they only need to be created once, they are then reused.

> *`PreparedStatement` inherits from `Statement` and it provides overloaded versions of the "execute" methods, which don't take a SQL string as a parameter. This makes sense if you think about it. The whole point of the `PreparedStatement` is that it is parsed once on creation, to execute your query. You modify the values of the input parameters – not the SQL.*

The ? in the query string is used as a placeholder for each input parameter. These correspond to variables in the database known as **bind variables**. The query that uses bind variables will be compiled once and then the query plan is stored in a shared pool (the library cache), from which it can be retrieved and reused.

*The big difference between a `PreparedStatement` and a normal `Statement` is that the `PreparedStatement` contains SQL code that has already been compiled in the database.*

Now when we re-query the EMP table for each new value of `empId` this same plan is reused. We use `setXXX()` methods of `PreparedStatement` to set the values of the parameters each time before executing the query:

```
for(int empId = 1; empId <= getLatestEmpId(); empId++) {
    pstmt.setInt(1, empId);
    ResultSet results = pstmt.executeQuery();
}
```

Just as `ResultSet` has `getXXX()` methods to return values from the result set, `PreparedStatement` includes a corresponding `setXXX()` method for each Java type. The basic type methods are shown in the following table, and there are others for accessing object types and SQL3 data types. (Actually, we *have* to use a `PreparedStatement` for the SQL3 data types rather than a plain `Statement`, the reason is there is no way to build a query string incorporating, say an array, to pass to Oracle. We will see how to pass arrays to Oracle later in this chapter):

| | | | |
|---|---|---|---|
| setArray() | setByte() | setFloat() | setShort() |
| setAsciiStream() | setBytes() | setInt() | setString() |
| setBinaryStream() | setDate() | setLong() | setTime() |
| setBoolean() | setDouble() | setObject() | setTimestamp() |

For statements with multiple bind variable placeholders, note that they are consecutively indexed, starting with 1 for the first placeholder in the SQL string, so the above code sets the first input parameter to an int value of `empId`. If our `PreparedStatement` contained two values for EMP_ID like this:

```
connection.prepareStatement("select * from employees "
+ "where emp_id = ? "
+ "or emp_id = ?");
```

Then we'd have to set both values before executing the query, the second one would have the placeholder value of 2:

```
pstmt.setInt(1, empId);
pstmt.setInt(2, anotherEmpId);
ResultSet results = pstmt.executeQuery();
```

Here's a complete example for you to try. We'll use the looping `empId` example and keep iterating until we don't find an `EMPLOYEE` row. The point to stress here is that the `PreparedStatement` is constructed at the beginning of the whole process and stays open and available the whole time even though we may use it any number of times to obtain result sets. There's no need to close or reopen it – that would just negate the benefit of having it in the first place.

```java
import java.sql.*;

// Query the Employees table one by one using a PreparedStatement.

public class BindQueryEmployees {
  public static void main(String[] args) throws Exception {
    Connection connection = null;
    try {
      Class.forName("oracle.jdbc.driver.OracleDriver");
      connection = DriverManager.getConnection(args[0]);
    } catch (Exception e) {
      System.out.println("Unable to connect : " + e);
      System.exit(-1);
    }

    try {
      PreparedStatement pstmt = connection.prepareStatement(
                      "select * from employees "
                    + "where emp_id = ?");

      for(int empId = 1; ; empId++) // loop forever (exit with break) {
        pstmt.setInt(1, empId);
        ResultSet results = pstmt.executeQuery();

        // Either there is one row or finish
        if (results.next()) {
          System.out.println("Found an employee with EMP_ID = "
                            + empId
                            + " Surname = "
                            + results.getString("surname"));
        } else {
          break;
        }
        results.close();
      }

      pstmt.close();
    } catch (SQLException e) {
      System.out.println("Unexpected sql error: " + e);
      System.exit(-1);
    } finally {
      connection.close();
    }
  }
}
```

Running the class produces the expected results, a line for each employee. (Of course the logic is a bit flawed, if there were any breaks in the sequence of EMP_IDs in the EMPLOYEES table, the processing would stop, but it serves to illustrate the example):

```
> java BindQueryEmployees
            "jdbc:oracle:thin:username/password@localhost:1521:database"
Found an employee with EMP_ID = 1 Surname = Smith
Found an employee with EMP_ID = 2 Surname = Beanstalk
Found an employee with EMP_ID = 3 Surname = Grafter
```

> The difference between using **PreparedStatement** with bind variables and the plain **Statement** method in terms of performance and scalability is huge. Your application should always incorporate the use of bind variables where applicable – it is how Oracle is expecting you to program.

# The CallableStatement Interface

CallableStatement is a sub-interface of PreparedStatement so has all the capabilities of both PreparedStatement and its super-interface Statement. It allows us to call PL/SQL code on the database, either anonymous blocks or stored (optionally packaged) procedures and functions and so adds the capability to accept output parameters from them.

Here's the syntax for calling a block of PL/SQL which accepts an integer number of days which it adds to SYSDATE (the current date) returning the result as a date:

```
CallableStatement callPlsql = connection.prepareCall(
        "{ call begin ? := SYSDATE + ?; end }");
```

The PL/SQL code is passed as a string and the whole statement must be enclosed in curly braces. The syntax is similar to that for a PreparedStatement in that it uses placeholders for variables. In this example the second placeholder is an input parameter so its value is set in the normal way as for a PreparedStatement:

```
callPlsql.setInt(2, 500);
```

The first parameter is an output parameter and we need to use the CallableStatement method registerOutParameter() to tell the driver what kind of variable is going to be returned from the call:

```
callPlsql.registerOutParameter(1, Types.DATE);
```

> Note that placeholders are still consecutively indexed, starting from 1 in the order they appear in the string, regardless of whether they represent input or output parameters. So in the above example the return value holds the index position 1, the first input parameter 2.

The first argument to `registerOutParameter()` is the index of the placeholder for the bind variable, the second is the data type to return. This is one of the supported types from the `java.sql.Types` class, which has constants defined for any data type you might conceivably need using standard JDBC. Oracle also provides support for SQL3 data types, such as arrays defined in the `oracle.jdbc.driver.OracleTypes` class. To use arrays we must pass a type name with the out parameter and there is an overloaded version of the method to do this (we'll do this in a moment). There is also another overloaded version of `registerOutParameter()` in which you can specify the scale of a numeric value being returned.

Now we're ready to run the PL/SQL using the `PreparedStatement execute()` method.

```
callPlsql.execute();
Date result = callPlsql.getDate(1);
```

To return the date variable to a Java variable, call the appropriate `CallableStatement getXXX()` method that matches the data type with the index to the placeholder. These `getXXX()` methods are very similar to those in the `ResultSet` interface, which we covered earlier.

Here's the complete listing for the example:

```
import java.sql.*;

// Call an anonymous PL/SQL block to show use of a CallableStatement.

public class CallPlsql {
  public static void main(String[] args) throws Exception {
    Connection connection = null;
    try {
      Class.forName("oracle.jdbc.driver.OracleDriver");
      connection = DriverManager.getConnection(args[0]);
    } catch (Exception e) {
      System.out.println("Unable to connect : " + e);
      System.exit(-1);
    }

    try {
      CallableStatement callPlsql = connection.prepareCall(
              "{ call begin ? := SYSDATE + ?; end }");

      // register the out parameter
      callPlsql.registerOutParameter(1, Types.DATE);

      // set the input parameter to 500 days from today
      callPlsql.setInt(2, 500);

      // execute the plsql and return the result
      callPlsql.execute();
      Date result = callPlsql.getDate(1);

      System.out.println("500 days from now is " + result);
```

```
            callPlsql.close();
        } catch (SQLException e) {
            System.out.println("Unexpected sql error: " + e);
            System.exit(-1);
        } finally {
            connection.close();
        }
    }
}
```

We've added an output message so we can see if it works when we run it:

```
> java CallPlsql
        "jdbc:oracle:thin:username/password@localhost:1521:database"
500 days from now is 2003-03-29
```

## Calling Stored Procedures/Functions

This is real power. In many applications, the database isn't just viewed as persistent data storage – it actually forms an important part of the business application layer. PL/SQL is a powerful tool for programming, just because we *can* use Java to do everything doesn't mean we must or should. It that light the ability to call stored procedures/functions opens up the available options greatly.

Calling stored procedures/functions is essentially very similar to calling an anonymous PL/SQL block. The syntax differs slightly between them though. Here's how you would call an example procedure that takes three parameters:

```
CallableStatement callProcedure = connection.prepareCall(
        "{ call my_procedure(?, ?, ?) }");
```

Syntactically, there's no distinction here between input and output parameters. You need to make that distinction yourself by either calling setXXX() for input or registerOutParameter() for output. On the other hand, for calling a function there is a syntactic difference. The return value appears as a placeholder at the beginning in the form:

```
CallableStatement callFunction = connection.prepareCall(
        "{ ? = call my_function(?, ?) }");
```

In all other respects it is exactly the same as calling a database procedure.
We've seen examples of passing the basic PL/SQL types both to and from the database to JDBC. Calling database procedures and functions means we can now very easily pass more complex types. The most basic of these is probably the array so we'll continue now by working out a couple of array examples so you can see how to pass them to the database and how to get them back.

## Passing Arrays To/From Oracle

When looking at arrays we have to get Oracle specific, so what we're really talking about here is converting between standard Java array types and PL/SQL collections. We have to get Oracle specific because Oracle only supports passing of arrays as **user-defined types**.

Under JDBC 2.0, if you want to get a reference to a database type of array, which is a User Defined Type, you must create a custom mapping for it. The basic method is to identify the array to the JDBC driver as an Oracle type. The way we do this only differs depending on whether we're passing an array as input or as output. The driver will then be able to look up the array's elements' types and convert them to/from the correct Java type.

### Getting An Array From The Database

This is the simpler case. To do it we need to use a database type, so let's create one that will hold employee surnames. Then we'll build an example where a database function returns all surnames as an array to our Java class:

```
SQL> create type array_of_surname as table of varchar2(100);
  2  /
```

Here's the database function. All it does is read all the EMPLOYEES rows and adds the surname of each in order to the output array:

```
SQL> create or replace function get_all_surnames
  2  return array_of_surname
  3  is
  4
  5    -- a cursor to select all employee surnames
  6    cursor c_employees
  7    is
  8    select surname
  9    from    employees
 10    order by surname;
 11
 12    -- a return variable of the surname array type
 13    l_surname_array array_of_surname := array_of_surname();
 14
 15    -- a subscript to the return array
 16    l_sub            NUMBER := 0;
 17
 18  begin
 19    -- create an output row for each row in the results
 20    FOR r_employees IN c_employees
 21    loop
 22
 23      l_surname_array.EXTEND;
 24      l_sub := l_sub + 1;
 25
 26      l_surname_array(l_sub) := r_employees.surname;
 27    end loop;
 28
 29    -- return the filled array
 30    return l_surname_array;
 31
 32  end get_all_surnames;
 33  /
```

If you're reading an array from the database you must supply the name of the User Defined Type in the database for the array using the overloaded `CallableStatement registerOutParameter()` method which takes a type name:

```
CallableStatement callFunction = connection.prepareCall(
            "{ ? = call get_all_surnames() }");
```

```
callFunction.registerOutParameter(
        1, OracleTypes.ARRAY, "ARRAY_OF_SURNAME");
```

There's only one placeholder for this function call because it doesn't take any parameters, it just returns the array variable. Notice the use of the constant from the class `OracleTypes`, we have to import that separately beforehand with the following statement:

```
import oracle.jdbc.driver.OracleTypes;
```

After executing the call, we return the out parameter as a `java.sql.Array`.

```
callFunction.execute();
```

```
Array outputArray = callFunction.getArray(1);
```

This isn't yet a Java array type, to decompose this down to a Java array you have to call the `getArray()` method of the `java.sql.Array`.

```
String[] surnames = (String[]) outputArray.getArray();
```

Each of the elements of the array is now mapped to a Java type following the rules for data type mapping. That's why surnames is defined here as a `String[]`, if it was some other complex type we'd have to cast it to an `Object[]` and deal with each `Object` occurrence according to its complex type. (The discussion of complex `Object` types is beyond the scope of this chapter).

Here's the complete listing:

```
import java.sql.*;
import oracle.jdbc.driver.OracleTypes;

// Call a database function to return an array of surnames

public class GetSurnamesArray {
  public static void main(String[] args) throws Exception {
    Connection connection = null;
    try {
      Class.forName("oracle.jdbc.driver.OracleDriver");
      connection = DriverManager.getConnection(args[0]);
    } catch (Exception e) {
      System.out.println("Unable to connect : " + e);
      System.exit(-1);
```

**153**

```
      }

      try {
        CallableStatement callFunction = connection.prepareCall(
                "{ ? = call get_all_surnames() }");

        // register the out parameter
        callFunction.registerOutParameter(
              1, OracleTypes.ARRAY, "ARRAY_OF_SURNAME");

        // execute the function and return the result
        callFunction.execute();
        Array outputArray = callFunction.getArray(1);
        String[] surnames = (String[]) outputArray.getArray();

        // output each surname
        for (int i = 0; i < surnames.length; i++)
          System.out.println("Surname #" + i + " is " + surnames[i]);

        callFunction.close();
      } catch (SQLException e) {
        System.out.println("Unexpected sql error: " + e);
        System.exit(-1);
      } finally {
        connection.close();
      }
    }
  }
```

As usual, we've included output messages to show that it worked:

```
> java GetSurnamesArray
         "jdbc:oracle:thin:username/password@localhost:1521:database"
Surname #0 is Beanstalk
Surname #1 is Grafter
Surname #2 is Smith
```

### Passing An Array To The Database

This is a bit more complicated because we have to do a bit more up front in the Java. We're going to build another example that calls a database function and this time it will pass an array of EMP_IDs to it. The function's job is then to insert a row into the NOTICES table for each EMP_ID.

We'll also return a query of the inserted rows as a return value from the function. This has to be done by returning a PL/SQL REF CURSOR variable, which will be materialized by JDBC as a ResultSet. That's really useful, and nice that we already know quite a bit about ResultSets
First we need another database type to hold the EMP_IDs:

```
SQL> create type array_of_emp_id as table of number(10, 0);
  2  /
```

To make life easier, we'll create a database sequence to use for the primary key to NOTICES. We'll start it at 3 since we've already created two rows in previous examples:

```
SQL> create sequence notice_seq start with 3;
```

And we need a database function to insert the rows and return the result set. We'll create this one as a packaged function, mainly so we can define a CURSOR REF type to return the result set. Note that the database cursor is not closed in the PL/SQL – we have to read its contents from our Java class. It will be closed for us when the ResultSet which materializes it is closed:

```
SQL> create or replace package test_arrays
  2  as
  3    -- create a weak ref cursor to type the return variable
  4    type t_ref_cursor IS ref cursor;
  5
  6    -- create the function which takes the array type as input
  7    -- and returns the cursor variable
  8    function insert_notices(i_employee_ids in array_of_emp_id)
  9    return t_ref_cursor;
 10
 11  end test_arrays;
 12  /

SQL> create or replace package body test_arrays
  2  as
  3
  4    function insert_notices(i_employee_ids in array_of_emp_id)
  5    return t_ref_cursor
  6    is
  7
  8      -- index to the array
  9      l_sub             number(5);
 10
 11      -- cursor to return the newly inserted rows
 12      l_cursor          t_ref_cursor;
 13
 14      -- other variables
 15      l_last_notice_id  notices.notice_id%TYPE;
 16      l_emp_id              employees.emp_id%TYPE;
 17
 18    begin
 19      -- trap empty array
 20      if i_employee_ids is null
 21      or not i_employee_ids.EXISTS(i_employee_ids.FIRST)
 22      then
 23        raise_application_error(-20000, 'No employee ids passed');
 24      end if;
 25
 26      -- store the last notice_id to filter the new rows returned
 27      -- at the end
 28      select MAX(notice_id)
```

```
29        into    l_last_notice_id
30        from    notices;
31
32        -- iterate the array inserting a notice for each element
33        l_sub := i_employee_ids.FIRST;
34
35        loop
36          exit when not i_employee_ids.EXISTS(l_sub);
37
38          -- insert a notice to/from this employee
39          l_emp_id := i_employee_ids(l_sub);
40
41          insert into notices
42          (notice_id
43          ,emp_id_to
44          ,emp_id_from
45          ,created_date
46          ,description)
47          VALUES
48          (notice_seq.NEXTVAL
49          ,l_emp_id
50          ,l_emp_id
51          ,SYSDATE
52          ,'Notice added by database function');
53
54          l_sub := i_employee_ids.NEXT(l_sub);
55        end loop;
56
57        -- return a result set containing the inserted rows
58        if l_cursor%ISOPEN
59        then
60            close l_cursor;
61        end if;
62
63        open l_cursor for
64        select * from notices where notice_id > l_last_notice_id;
65
66        return l_cursor;
67
68      exception
69        -- propagate any error to the caller
70        when others then
71          raise;
72
73      end insert_notices;
74
75    end test_arrays;
76  /
```

Meanwhile, back with the Java, we have to import some more Oracle specific classes:

```
import oracle.sql.ARRAY;
import oracle.sql.ArrayDescriptor;
```

An `oracle.sql.ArrayDescriptor` is the object which maps the database User Defined Type to an instance of `oracle.sql.ARRAY`. You create the `ArrayDescriptor` with the User Defined Type name and then you can create your `ARRAY` object using that `ArrayDescriptor` and whatever the source of the array data is. Both of these operations need a valid `Connection` object:

```
ArrayDescriptor inputArrayDescriptor =
    ArrayDescriptor.createDescriptor("ARRAY_OF_EMP_ID", connection);

BigDecimal[] empIds = getAllEmpIds(connection);

ARRAY empArray = new ARRAY(inputArrayDescriptor, connection, empIds);
```

We're using numeric `EMP_IDs` so we could use an array of `int`s but it'll be easier to create if we use an array of `java.math.BigDecimal`. The `getAllEmpIds(connection)` method is a custom method which reads all the `EMPLOYEES` rows from the database and creates a `BigDecimal[]` with them. (See the complete listing below for the code).

`CallableStatement` has no method to return a result set, but `OracleCallableStatement` does. This is the class we actually get from our call to `prepareCall()` so all we have to do is cast it:

```
OracleCallableStatement callFunction = (OracleCallableStatement)
    connection.prepareCall(
        "{? = call test_arrays.insert_notices(?) }");
```

The `oracle.sql.ARRAY` which implements `java.sql.Array` can now be passed to the `CallableStatement` in the second placeholder position using the `setArray()` method:

```
callFunction.setArray(2, empArray);
```

As far as the result set returned from the function goes, we'll need to register the output parameter as another `OracleTypes` constant, `CURSOR`:

```
callFunction.registerOutParameter(1, OracleTypes.CURSOR);
```

Now when we call the `OracleCallableStatement` method `getCursor()`, we are returned a `ResultSet` which we can deal with in the normal way:

```
ResultSet results = callFunction.getCursor(1);
```

Here's the complete listing:

```java
import java.sql.*;
import java.math.BigDecimal;
import java.util.ArrayList;
import oracle.jdbc.driver.OracleCallableStatement;
import oracle.jdbc.driver.OracleTypes;
import oracle.sql.ARRAY;
import oracle.sql.ArrayDescriptor;

/* Call a database function to insert a notice for each employee in
   an input array and to return the inserted notices as a result set. */
public class InsertNoticesFromArray {
  public static void main(String[] args) throws Exception {
    Connection connection = null;
    try {
      Class.forName("oracle.jdbc.driver.OracleDriver");
      connection = DriverManager.getConnection(args[0]);
    } catch (Exception e) {
      System.out.println("Unable to connect : " + e);
      System.exit(-1);
    }

    try {
      OracleCallableStatement callFunction = (OracleCallableStatement)
          connection.prepareCall(
                "{ ? = call test_arrays.insert_notices(?) }");

      // create the ArrayDescriptor to indentify the Oracle type
      ArrayDescriptor inputArrayDescriptor =
          ArrayDescriptor.createDescriptor("ARRAY_OF_EMP_ID", connection);

      // create an oracle.sql.ARRAY from the empIds and the descriptor
      BigDecimal[] empIds = getAllEmpIds(connection);
      ARRAY empArray = new ARRAY(inputArrayDescriptor, connection, empIds);

      // register an out parameter as a result set
      callFunction.registerOutParameter(1, OracleTypes.CURSOR);

      // set the input array
      callFunction.setArray(2, empArray);

      // execute the function and return the result
      callFunction.execute();
      ResultSet results = callFunction.getCursor(1);

      // output each notice
      while (results.next())
      {
        System.out.println("notice id = "
                + results.getInt("notice_id"));
        System.out.println("description = "
```

```
                        + results.getString("description"));
      }

      results.close();
      callFunction.close();
    } catch (SQLException e) {
      System.out.println("Unexpected sql error: " + e);
      System.exit(-1);
    } finally {
      connection.close();
    }
  }

  /**
   * This method looks up all the EMP_IDs from EMPLOYEES
   * and returns them as a BigDecimal array.
   * @param connection The valid Connection
   * @return The array of empIds
   * @exception SQLException Any unexpected sql error
   */
  private static BigDecimal[] getAllEmpIds(Connection connection)
    throws SQLException {
    Statement stmt = connection.createStatement();
    ResultSet results = stmt.executeQuery("select emp_id from employees");

    // create an ArrayList to add the emp_ids to
    ArrayList empIdList = new ArrayList();

    while (results.next())
      empIdList.add(results.getBigDecimal(1));

    // create an array to pass the values to Oracle
    BigDecimal[] empIds = new BigDecimal[empIdList.size()];
    empIdList.toArray(empIds);

    results.close();
    stmt.close();

    // return the array
    return empIds;
  }
}
```

When we compile and run this class you can see that the rows have been inserted because they are returned back in the result set:

```
> java InsertNoticesFromArray
          "jdbc:oracle:thin:username/password@localhost:1521:database"
notice id = 3
description = Notice added by database function
notice id = 4
description = Notice added by database function
notice id = 5
description = Notice added by database function
```

## Other Metadata Interfaces

There are two more metadata interfaces, (we already saw the ResultSetMetaData interface earlier). The first of these is DatabaseMetaData and the second is new in JDBC 3.0, ParameterMetaData.

## The DatabaseMetaData Interface

The DatabaseMetaData interface provides many methods (well over a hundred) that give you information about the database itself. This is of limited value to us in the context of this chapter because we know we're dealing with an Oracle database, we'll know what version it is and we probably already know a lot about its limitations.

If you were writing features into your application that might only be supported on certain databases or database versions, this interface provides a means by which you can find out about the database you are running against programmatically. For instance, you could use getDatabaseProductVersion() to determine the version of the database and disable an unsupported feature. Perhaps you might need to find out about support for certain operations and there are many methods prefixed with support that return boolean, such as supportsFullOuterJoins() or supportsGroupBy() for these purposes. This gives you a bit of a flavor for the level you might need to use this class for.

Let's just build a very simple example so you can see how easy it is to use this interface. In it we'll get a DatabaseMetaData instance from our Connection and use it to determine the maximum length that a column name can have with the getMaxColumnNameLength() method.

Here's the listing:

```
import java.sql.*;

// * Use DatabaseMetaData to get the maximum length for a column name

public class GetMaximumColumnName {
  public static void main(String[] args) throws Exception {
    Connection connection = null;
    try {
      Class.forName("oracle.jdbc.driver.OracleDriver");
      connection = DriverManager.getConnection(args[0]);
    } catch (Exception e) {
      System.out.println("Unable to connect : " + e);
      System.exit(-1);
    }

    try {
      DatabaseMetaData dbmd = connection.getMetaData();
      System.out.println("The max length for a column name is "
                    + dbmd.getMaxColumnNameLength());
    } catch (SQLException e) {
      System.out.println("Unexpected sql error: " + e);
      System.exit(-1);
    } finally {
      connection.close();
    }
  }
}
```

When we compile and run this class you can see what you probably already knew, the max length allowed for a column name in Oracle is 30:

```
> java GetMaximumColumnName
        "jdbc:oracle:thin:username/password@localhost:1521:database"
The max length for a column name is 30
```

### The ParameterMetaData Interface

The `ParameterMetaData` interface is new in JDBC 3.0. It provides methods to get information about the parameters passed to a `PreparedStatement`.

There are several methods available, some of the most useful ones include:

❑ `getParameterClassName()` which returns the fully-qualified name of the Java class whose instances should be passed to the method `PreparedStatement.setObject()` for a parameter.

❑ `getParameterType()` which returns a parameter's SQL type.

❑ `getParameterTypeName()` which returns a parameter's database-specific type name.

# Multiple Fetching

We've now seen the main JDBC interfaces. However, there are still some JDBC and Oracle extended features that we need to cover in this chapter. The first subject we will address is a performance enhancing feature – multiple fetching.

We've already focused on the importance of performance enhancement when we discussed the benefits of using a `PreparedStatement`. The main benefit of using bind variables and a `PreparedStatement` is that it is more efficient and makes our code faster to execute. This is a topic we have to return to again and again. JDBC is a programmatic layer that acts on the database across a network. For this reason, it carries a network overhead and a database access overhead. There are many techniques we can use to reduce these overheads both using standard JDBC and using Oracle's own extensions.

> *Actually, if you run your JDBC program inside the Oracle database JServer engine using the server-side internal drivers there is no network layer, so no network overhead.*

Multiple fetching is the ability to adjust the number of rows fetched from the database for a query operation so that they are fetched in groups rather than individually and there are two methods available to us. One is standard JDBC and the other is an Oracle extension. The reason there are two is that standard JDBC only introduced it with version 2.0, Oracle already had its implementation before that. We'll have to consider each in isolation because they don't mix.

Before we can build any examples we need to add some more data – it's not possible to show the effects of performance techniques on very small amounts of data so we will add some more to the NOTICES table. Ten thousand rows should do the trick!

The content of the NOTICES is unimportant, here's the PL/SQL we'll use to create the extra rows:

```
sql> begin
  2    for i in 1..10000
  3    loop
  4      insert into notices (notice_id, emp_id_to, emp_id_from,
                                created_date, description)
  5        values (notice_seq.nextval, 1, 1, sysdate,
                                'just added to create more numbers');

  6
  7    end loop;
  8    commit;
  9  end;
 10  /
```

# Standard JDBC Multiple Fetching

The Statement interface defines a pair of get/set methods for fetch size, getFetchSize() and setFetchSize(). The default for fetch size is implementation specific, but should be ignored anyway unless you set it explicitly (by setting it to 0 you can return it to the default). Actually, using setFetchSize() is only a hint to the JDBC driver to fetch a particular number of rows. Again it depends on the implementation as to whether it has any effect. Using the Oracle drivers it does, as we can show.

Incidentally, you can set the fetch size against either the Statement or the returned ResultSet before you begin fetching. The effect is the same. Naturally setting it against the Statement will then mean all subsequent ResultSets have the same setting unless explicitly reset.

Our example is quite straightforward. We'll query the NOTICES table several times with the following PreparedStatement:

```
PreparedStatement stmt = connection.prepareStatement(
    "select notice_id, description from notices");
```

Each time we execute the query we'll output a message to explain what the setting of the fetch size is and call a custom method showStats() to output timings, (see the full listing below for the code in showStats()):

```
System.out.println("#1 JDBC fetch default = " + stmt.getFetchSize());
ResultSet rs = stmt.executeQuery();
showStats(rs);
```

In between each execution of the query, we'll set the fetch size to another value:

```
stmt.setFetchSize(10);
```

We'll use several values so we can then compare the results. The values we'll use are the default value, then 10, 1, 0 and 15.

Here's the full listing:

```java
import java.sql.*;

// Use standard JDBC multiple fetching

public class JDBCMultipleFetching {
  public static void main(String[] args) throws Exception {
    Connection connection = null;
    try {
      Class.forName("oracle.jdbc.driver.OracleDriver");
      connection = DriverManager.getConnection(args[0]);
    } catch (Exception e) {
      System.out.println("Unable to connect : " + e);
      System.exit(-1);
    }

    try {
      PreparedStatement stmt = connection.prepareStatement(
          "select notice_id, description from notices");

      System.out.println("#1 JDBC fetch default = " + stmt.getFetchSize());
      ResultSet rs = stmt.executeQuery();
      showStats(rs);

      stmt.setFetchSize(10);
      System.out.println("#2 JDBC fetch = " + stmt.getFetchSize());
      rs = stmt.executeQuery();
      showStats(rs);

      stmt.setFetchSize(1);
      System.out.println("#3 JDBC fetch = " + stmt.getFetchSize());
      rs = stmt.executeQuery();
      showStats(rs);

      stmt.setFetchSize(0);
      System.out.println("#4 JDBC fetch = " + stmt.getFetchSize());
      rs = stmt.executeQuery();
      showStats(rs);

      stmt.setFetchSize(15);
      System.out.println("#5 JDBC fetch = " + stmt.getFetchSize());
      rs = stmt.executeQuery();
      showStats(rs);

      stmt.close();
    } catch (SQLException e) {
      System.out.println("Unexpected sql error: " + e);
      System.exit(-1);
    } finally {
      connection.close();
    }
```

```
  }

  /**
   * This method takes the results from a query and outputs the time it
   * takes to execute
   * @param results - The ResultSet from the query
   * @exception SQLException - Any unexpected error
   */
  private static void showStats(ResultSet results)
    throws SQLException {
    // start time
    long start = System.currentTimeMillis();
    int i;
    String str;
    while (results.next()) {
      i = results.getInt(1);
      str = results.getString(2);
    }

    // end time
    long end = System.currentTimeMillis();

    System.out.println("Took " + (end - start) + " milliseconds");

    results.close();
  }
}
```

Now when we run it we can compare the relative execution times:

```
> java JDBCMultipleFetching
         "jdbc:oracle:thin:username/password@localhost:1521:database"
#1 JDBC fetch default = 10
Took 1031 milliseconds
#2 JDBC fetch = 10
Took 972 milliseconds
#3 JDBC fetch = 1
Took 8442 milliseconds
#4 JDBC fetch = 10
Took 981 milliseconds
#5 JDBC fetch = 15
Took 731 milliseconds
```

Several of the times show similar results coming in at about the 1000 milliseconds mark. The best time by a comfortable margin was when the fetch size was set to 15, so this might spur us on to try some larger times. Setting the size to 1 was a disaster, though, taking over eleven times as long as the fastest time.

The more perceptive amongst you will have noticed that the fourth setting was actually 0. So how come it shows as 10? As we said before, setting fetch size to 0 indicates to the driver to use the default, which in this case is 10.

Let's see how Oracle's multiple fetching method compares.

# Oracle Multiple Fetching

The Oracle terminology for its own version of multiple fetching is **row prefetching**, and the
OracleStatement class (which is what we actually get from the Oracle JDBC driver), provides the
methods getRowPreFetch() and setRowPreFetch(), for setting the prefetch size. The default prefetch
size is 10, so in theory we should get reasonable performance without even touching the prefetch size.

We'll build another example along the same lines as the standard JDBC multiple fetching example, but
this time we'll use Oracle row prefetching.  To use it we have to cast our PreparedStatement:

```
OraclePreparedStatement stmt = (OraclePreparedStatement)
        connection.prepareStatement(
            "select notice_id, description from notices");
```

And call the Oracle prefetch method:

```
stmt.setRowPrefetch(10);
```

The complete listing is otherwise very similar except that the values we'll use are the default value, then
10, 1, 15 and 25. We left out 0 this time because it's not a valid setting for a prefetch size and would
just throw an error (we made up for it by including 25 though):

```
import java.sql.*;
import oracle.jdbc.driver.OraclePreparedStatement;

//  Use Oracle multiple row prefetching

public class OracleMultipleFetching {
  public static void main(String[] args) throws Exception {
    Connection connection = null;
    try {
      Class.forName("oracle.jdbc.driver.OracleDriver");
      connection = DriverManager.getConnection(args[0]);
    } catch (Exception e) {
      System.out.println("Unable to connect : " + e);
      System.exit(-1);
    }

    try {
      OraclePreparedStatement stmt = (OraclePreparedStatement)
            connection.prepareStatement(
                "select notice_id, description from notices");

      System.out.println("#1 Oracle row default pre-fetch = "
                    + stmt.getRowPrefetch());
      ResultSet rs = stmt.executeQuery( );
      showStats(rs);

      stmt.setRowPrefetch(10);
```

```
        System.out.println("#2 Oracle row pre-fetch = " +
                             stmt.getRowPrefetch());
      rs = stmt.executeQuery( );
      showStats(rs);

      stmt.setRowPrefetch(1);
      System.out.println("#3 Oracle row pre-fetch = " +
                             stmt.getRowPrefetch());
      rs = stmt.executeQuery( );
      showStats(rs);

      stmt.setRowPrefetch(15);
      System.out.println("#4 Oracle row pre-fetch = " +
                             stmt.getRowPrefetch());
      rs = stmt.executeQuery( );
      showStats(rs);

      stmt.setRowPrefetch(25);
      System.out.println("#5 Oracle row pre-fetch = " +
                             stmt.getRowPrefetch());
      rs = stmt.executeQuery( );
      showStats(rs);

      stmt.close();
    } catch (SQLException e) {
      System.out.println("Unexpected sql error: " + e);
      System.exit(-1);
    } finally {
      connection.close();
    }
  }

  private static void showStats(ResultSet results)
    throws SQLException {
    // start time
    long start = System.currentTimeMillis();
    int i;
    String str;
    while (results.next()) {
      i = results.getInt(1);
      str = results.getString(2);
    }

    // end time
    long end = System.currentTimeMillis();

    System.out.println("Took " + (end - start) + " milliseconds");

    results.close();
  }
}
```

Now when we run it we can compare the relative execution times again:

```
> java OracleMultipleFetching
            "jdbc:oracle:thin:username/password@localhost:1521:database"
#1 Oracle row default pre-fetch = 10
Took 1042 milliseconds
#2 Oracle row pre-fetch = 10
Took 911 milliseconds
#3 Oracle row pre-fetch = 1
Took 1101 milliseconds
#4 Oracle row pre-fetch = 15
Took 892 milliseconds
#5 Oracle row pre-fetch = 25
Took 881 milliseconds
```

All the results are much closer. The most notable difference is that setting prefetch size to 1 didn't impair the performance that much, certainly not compared to doing it the JDBC standard way.

# What did we Learn About Multiple Fetching?

We've seen two methods for setting multiple fetching sizes, one standard JDBC, one Oracle. They didn't produce the same results, but they did both offer considerable savings *for the most part*. There's another important point to make here, not all the possible settings were good ones, we also saw that by inappropriate setting performance can even be negatively impacted.

You should not take the figures that occurred in these small samples as an indication of whether one method is better than the other nor which settings are going to be best for your application, that's not really the point here. These examples queried a smallish sample of data on our own machine/network/database.

Your data and your installation will be completely different and a lot of external factors come into the equation, particularly concerning the database's own internal structures. Like the state and number of the rollback segments, and redo logs. The numbers of concurrent users, especially if they're performing updates will have a massive affect on the results as well.

The real point is to demonstrate that by building a test case relevant to our specific needs we can systematically test the methods available to us. We should do this in a way that gives us enough information to know how to proceed for our real world needs.

# Defining Column Types

The Oracle extension OracleStatement also provides us with another technique to speed things up a bit, defining column types. We'll mention it so you know it's there, but compared with other techniques like multiple fetching and update batching (we'll see that later) the benefits aren't nearly as impressive.

When standard JDBC performs a query, it first uses a round trip to the database to determine the types that it should use for the columns of the result set. Then, when JDBC receives data from the query, it converts the data, as necessary, as it populates the result set. By defining the column types you are telling the driver about the types of the columns in the query about to be executed and the extra round trip to the database isn't needed.

To use this feature we must tell the driver about the columns before we begin fetching any data, so in the example above (Oracle multiple fetching) we'd add the code immediately after the call to the Connection prepareStatement():

```
OraclePreparedStatement stmt = (OraclePreparedStatement)
    connection.prepareStatement(
        "select notice_id, description from notices");
```

```
stmt.defineColumnType(1, Types.INTEGER);
stmt.defineColumnType(2, Types.VARCHAR, 4000);
```

We've told the driver that the first column is an integer and that the second is a character column which could have a value of anything up to 4,000 characters and that's really all you need to do.

We found that the saving of the extra round trip was about one hundredth of a second on our particular setup. Whether you go as far as to define your statements' column types depends on how important that extra saving is to you. Sometimes every possible saving is so vital you won't be able to ignore it. Of course, saving one round trip in a statement which has to make twenty or so round trips isn't saving a massive amount, but contrast this with the case where one trip is saved where only two round trips would have been needed, that's a 50% saving.

# Transactions

Up to now all our examples have used the default transaction model provided in JDBC, which is that every change is committed automatically as it completes. This is fine in some simple cases as we have seen, but in the real world that has to be the minority. Normally a process does not consist of just a single update to the database, there will be other actions going on, perhaps other database updates. If one fails they should all fail, so the developer needs to retain transactional control.

*There are also some other circumstances where you must retain transactional control, for instance, when you write to a database column as a data stream. An insert/update from a data stream will potentially involve many individual writes to the database, to have each write commit before the whole is complete would be totally wrong.*

In JDBC the transaction is controlled by the Connection. The default mode is for commits to occur automatically but we can set this easily enough using the setAutoCommit() method:

```
Connection connection = DriverManager.getConnection(
    "jdbc:oracle:thin:username/password@localhost:1521:database");
```

```
connection.setAutoCommit(false);
```

From this time on commits do not occur automatically (until the mode is reset), so we have to commit changes ourselves with the commit() method:

```
connection.commit();
```

We also have the option to rollback changes when things don't go as planned. This might happen in a catch exception block:

```
catch (SQLException e) {
  connection.rollback();
    System.out.println("Unexpected sql error: " + e);
}
```

It is good practice to always ensure that your transactions are either committed when they complete successfully or are rolled back if they fail. If no commit is explicitly executed on the Connection, the updates will automatically be rolled back when the Connection is closed. It is dangerous to rely on this though, particularly if you get your Connections from a pool where they are reused, because any future commit issued on the same Connection will commit the changes still pending.

For our example, let's say we want to change our data model a bit. All employees should now belong to a department. We'll go through all the employees and add each one to a default department, but when we do so we want to let the employee know this has happened by adding a row to the NOTICES table. All being well we'll finish up committing the update and the insert as a single transaction. If there is any problem we want neither operation to succeed.

First let's create the new DEPARTMENTS table and add a row to it:

```
SQL> create table departments
  2  (dept_id   number(10, 0) not null primary key
  3  ,dept_name varchar2(100) not null)
  4  /

SQL> insert into Departments (dept_id, dept_name)
  2  values (1, 'Default Department');
SQL> commit;
```

Now we must add the foreign key column to the EMPLOYEES table:

```
SQL> alter table employees
  2  add (dept_id number(10, 0) null references departments);
```

And we're ready to go. After setting the Connection mode to not commit automatically, we need a PreparedStatement to do the inserts into the NOTICES table. We'll only have two placeholders – the to and from EMP_IDs, We'll set these so the NOTICE comes from the employee it pertains to:

```
PreparedStatement insertPstmt = connection.prepareStatement(
            "insert into notices (notice_id, emp_id_to, "
        + "emp_id_from, created_date, description) "
        + "values (notice_seq.nextval, ?, ?, sysdate, "
        + "'You have been added to the default department')");
```

We need to update the EMPLOYEE rows too. The simplest way to do that is to update them through the ResultSet, so we'll set the Statement's properties on creation. Updates occurring through a ResultSet are still governed by the Connection commit mode so they will also be part of the transaction:

```
Statement stmt = connection.createStatement(
                    ResultSet.TYPE_SCROLL_SENSITIVE,
                    ResultSet.CONCUR_UPDATABLE);
```

Because we're acting on all the employees and we're going to stop in the event of failure, the code needs to be re-entrant. By that we mean, if we succeed in updating the details for one employee we don't want to have to do it again if we re-run the code. The following query ensures only those not assigned to a department already are processed:

```
ResultSet employees = stmt.executeQuery(
                "select e.* from employees e "
            + "where e.dept_id is null");
```

Here's the whole listing:

```
import java.sql.*;

public class UpdateEmployeesInTransaction {
  public static void main(String[] args) throws Exception {
    Connection connection = null;
    try {
      Class.forName("oracle.jdbc.driver.OracleDriver");
      connection = DriverManager.getConnection(args[0]);
    } catch (Exception e) {
      System.out.println("Unable to connect : " + e);
      System.exit(-1);
    }

    try {
      connection.setAutoCommit(false);

      PreparedStatement insertPstmt = connection.prepareStatement(
                    "insert into notices (notice_id, emp_id_to, "
                + "emp_id_from, created_date, description) "
                + "values (notice_seq.nextval, ?, ?, sysdate, "
                + "'You have been added to the default department')");

      Statement stmt = connection.createStatement(
                    ResultSet.TYPE_SCROLL_SENSITIVE,
                    ResultSet.CONCUR_UPDATABLE);

      ResultSet employees = stmt.executeQuery(
                    "select e.* from employees e "
                + "where e.dept_id is null");

      while (employees.next()) {
        // our transaction begins here
        int empId = employees.getInt("emp_id");

        System.out.println("Processing emp_id = " + empId);
```

```
                // update the dept_id
                employees.updateInt("dept_id", 1);
                employees.updateRow();

                System.out.println("Department updated");

                // add a notice to that effect
                insertPstmt.setInt(1, empId);
                insertPstmt.setInt(2, empId);
                insertPstmt.execute();

                // and commit the whole transaction
                connection.commit();

                System.out.println("Notice added and all changes committed");
            }

            employees.close();
            insertPstmt.close();
            stmt.close();
        } catch (SQLException e) {
            connection.rollback();
            System.out.println("Unexpected sql error changes rolled back: " + e);
            System.exit(-1);
        } finally {
            connection.close();
        }
    }
}
```

Before we run it, we'll show you what happens when the program fails with some SQL error. We know from the data already inserted into the NOTICES table that the last value of the sequence used for the primary key was 10005, and we also know that there are three EMPLOYEE rows. To force an error we'll insert the following rogue row into NOTICES with a primary key of 10008. This should result in only the first two EMPLOYEE rows being completed successfully. The third should fail with a primary key error when the insert to NOTICES is attempted:

```
SQL> insert into notices
  2  (notice_id, emp_id_to, emp_id_from, created_date, description)
  3  values (10008, 1, 2, sysdate, 'A rogue notice')
  4  /
SQL> commit;
```

Here's what happens when we run it:

```
> java UpdateEmployeesInTransaction
          "jdbc:oracle:thin:username/password@localhost:1521:database"
Processing emp_id = 1
Department updated
Notice added and all changes committed
Processing emp_id = 2
Department updated
Notice added and all changes committed
Processing emp_id = 3
Department updated
Unexpected sql error changes rolled back: java.sql.SQLException: ORA-00001: unique
constraint (USERNAME.SYS_C001612) violated
```

The code failed at the appropriate point. However, because the code is re-entrant, the EMPLOYEE should be reprocessed successfully when the program is re-run.

```
> java UpdateEmployeesInTransaction
          "jdbc:oracle:thin:username/password@localhost:1521:database"
Processing emp_id = 3
Department updated
Notice added and all changes committed
```

If you look at the results from the first run, you can see that EMP_ID 3 had its DEPT_ID updated but then the changes were rolled back because of the error. If they hadn't been the EMPLOYEE row would have been excluded from the re-run. This shows us a) that the successfully processed rows were actually committed in the first run and b) that unsuccessful transactions are being rolled back successfully.

## Global Transactions

This example showed how to control a transaction on a single Connection to a database. This is known as a *local* transaction. By contrast a *global* transaction is one that spans multiple Connections to differing database instances, in other words, a *distributed* transaction.

Global transactions are out of the scope of this chapter but the interested reader will find that Oracle JDBC drivers do provide support for them and we refer you to Oracle's own documentation, particularly the *Oracle9i JDBC Developer's Guide and Reference*.

# More Go-Faster Code: Update Batching

Update batching is the name given for the feature by which multiple updates (insert, update, delete) through a Statement object can be executed all together instead of one at a time. Its purpose is to enhance performance. Essentially, it is the complement of multiple fetching which deals with querying data from the database rather than making updates to it.

As with multiple fetching there are two ways of doing this, the standard JDBC 2.0 way and the Oracle specific way and similarly to multiple fetching the two methods cannot be mixed. Again, the reason there are two ways is because Oracle implemented its own method in advance of the JDBC 2.0 release when the standard way was introduced.

We need a lot of rows to show update batching working. Fortunately, our NOTICES table has over 10,000 rows that we inserted for the examples on multiple fetching. In the forthcoming examples we'll update these 10,000 rows one at a time in a loop but with varying batch sizes and we'll do this several times within each example, rolling the changes back each time. To enable rolling back we have to tell the Connection object not to commit automatically and then we can roll back as desired with:

```
connection.rollback();
```

This allows us to re-run the updates the several times required to show how it all works. The update doesn't have to be clever, we just want to be able to execute it once for every row, so a PreparedStatement updating a single row at a time is fine:

```
PreparedStatement updatePstmt = connection.prepareStatement(
        "update notices "
    +   "set notice_read_date = SYSDATE "
    +   "where notice_id = ?");
```

We do have to be careful about what we deduce from the results though, it's not as straightforward as it might seem. Please take note of the sub-section *What Did We Learn About Update Batching?* at the end of this section once you've finished reading through the examples.

# Standard JDBC Update Batching

Let's start with the standard JDBC update batching, which is provided for Statement and its subclasses. If you are using the Oracle drivers you'll find that only PreparedStatement gives any performance improvement and Oracle's own documentation states that it does not implement true batching for generic Statements and CallableStatements (see *JDBC Developer's Guide And Reference, Update Batching*).

The way the standard JDBC method works is whenever you have an update to make, instead of making a call to the PreparedStatement executeUpdate() method you add it to a batch with a call to addBatch():

```
PreparedStatement updatePstmt = connection.prepareStatement(..);
...
updateStmt.addBatch();
```

When we want to execute the whole batch we call executeBatch() to have all the statements sent to the database for execution at once.

```
int[] updates = updateStmt.executeBatch();
```

executeBatch() returns an array of int which will be the update counts for each of the statements in the batch. Once executeBatch() has been called the batch is empty and we can just start adding more statements to it again until we're ready to execute again. The control of when the batch is executed is up to the developer, so we have to maintain a count of how many updates we've processed and execute the batch when we hit the limit.

This makes things a little bit untidy at best and even potentially error prone. Let's start building our example so you can see what we mean.

We're going to put the batch updates into a custom method for the purpose (it's much easier that way, otherwise there would be a lot of repetition). The batchUpdateResults() method will take the result set from the query of all the NOTICES, the PreparedStatement for the update and a batch size as parameters, it will execute the batch for us and time the whole update so it can output a message telling us how it went.

Firstly, we need to maintain a count of statements executed. We have to control the execution of the statements in the batch by detecting how many have been added:

```
int statementCount = 0;

while(rs.next()) {
    ...
    updateStmt.addBatch();

    if (statementCount++ >= batchSize) {
        // initialize the statementCount
        statementCount = 0;
```

When the limit is reached we know we want to execute the batch and call the executeBatch() method:

```
int[] updates = updateStmt.executeBatch();
```

We want to know how many rows were actually affected by all the statements in the batch, so we have to write a loop to go through the array returned and add them to another count:

```
for (int i = 0; i < updates.length; i++)
    updateCount += updates[i];
```

You might think we've finished now, but this is where an error could easily creep in. If we now exit the loop we don't know if there are pending updates still in a batch. That's because we only executed the batch when it reached a size threshold. If for instance the threshold was 10, and we added nine statements since the last executeBatch() call, those nine statements are still pending. So we have to repeat ourselves outside the loop to make sure we get everything. (These statements would be sent on the next call to executeBatch(), but that's not likely to be what was intended. If you were to call executeUpdate() on the Statement while there were pending updates you'd get a SQLException, and worse still, if you close the Statement or commit, they are not processed!):

```
int[] updates = updateStmt.executeBatch();
for (int i = 0; i < updates.length; i++)
    updateCount += updates[i];
```

Now we've got our method to do the batch updates. The main method can call it multiple times as necessary and then roll back changes so we can run it again with another batch size:

```
batchUpdateResults(selectPstmt.executeQuery(), updatePstmt, 10);
connection.rollback();
```

As a comparison, we'll be doing a first run without any batching. We'll use another custom method to do it, updateResultsNoBatching(), but it essentially just executes each statement one at a time directly to the database and keeps a count of the rows processed. At the end it outputs its results just like the batching method does.

Here's the complete listing:

```java
import java.sql.*;

// Update notices in batches to show the standard JDBC method

public class JDBCUpdateBatching {
  public static void main(String[] args) throws Exception {
    Connection connection = null;
    try {
      Class.forName("oracle.jdbc.driver.OracleDriver");
      connection = DriverManager.getConnection(args[0]);
    } catch (Exception e) {
      System.out.println("Unable to connect : " + e);
      System.exit(-1);
    }

    try {
      connection.setAutoCommit(false);

      PreparedStatement updatePstmt = connection.prepareStatement(
                "update notices "
          + "set notice_read_date = SYSDATE "
          + "where notice_id = ?");

      PreparedStatement selectPstmt = connection.prepareStatement(
                "select notice_id from notices");

      System.out.println("#1, no batching...");
      updateResultsNoBatching(selectPstmt.executeQuery(), updatePstmt);
      connection.rollback();

      System.out.println(
              "#2, standard JDBC update batching - per 1000 rows...");
      batchUpdateResults(selectPstmt.executeQuery(), updatePstmt, 1000);
      connection.rollback();

      System.out.println(
              "#3, standard JDBC update batching - per 10 rows...");
      batchUpdateResults(selectPstmt.executeQuery(), updatePstmt, 10);
```

```
        connection.rollback();

        // Output to standard output
        System.out.println(
                "#4, standard JDBC update batching - per 50 rows...");
        batchUpdateResults(selectPstmt.executeQuery(), updatePstmt, 50);
        connection.rollback();

        selectPstmt.close();
        updatePstmt.close();
    } catch (SQLException e) {
        connection.rollback();
        System.out.println("Unexpected sql error changes rolled back: " + e);
        System.exit(-1);
    } finally {
        connection.close();
    }
}


/**
 * Update the rows from the ResultSet supplied without batching
 * @param rs The ResultSet from the query
 * @param updateStmt The prepared update statement
 * @exception SQLException Any unexpected SQL error
 */
private static void updateResultsNoBatching(
                    ResultSet rs, PreparedStatement updateStmt)
    throws SQLException {
    java.util.Date start = new java.util.Date();
    int updateCount = 0;

    while(rs.next()) {
        int noticeId = rs.getInt("notice_id");
        updateStmt.setInt(1, noticeId);

        updateCount += updateStmt.executeUpdate();
    }

    java.util.Date end = new java.util.Date();

    System.out.println("Total number of rows updated = "
                    + updateCount
                    + " and took "
                    + (end.getTime() - start.getTime())
                    + " milliseconds\n");

    rs.close();
}

/**
 * Update the rows from the ResultSet supplied in a single batch
 * @param rs The ResultSet from the query
```

```
 * @param updateStmt The prepared update statement
 * @param batchSize The size to allow the batch to grow before executing
 * @exception SQLException Any unexpected SQL error
 */
private static void batchUpdateResults(
      ResultSet rs, PreparedStatement updateStmt, int batchSize)
   throws SQLException {
   java.util.Date start = new java.util.Date();
   int updateCount = 0;

   // maintain a count of the number of statements in the current batch
   int statementCount = 0;

   while(rs.next()) {
     int noticeId = rs.getInt("notice_id");
     updateStmt.setInt(1, noticeId);

     // issue the update to the batch
     updateStmt.addBatch();

     // when reaches batchSize execute the batch
     if (statementCount++ >= batchSize) {
       statementCount = 0;

       int[] updates = updateStmt.executeBatch();
       for (int i = 0; i < updates.length; i++)
         updateCount += updates[i];
     }
   }

   // In case any statements remain un-executed call executeBatch()
   int[] updates = updateStmt.executeBatch();
   for (int i = 0; i < updates.length; i++)
     updateCount += updates[i];

   java.util.Date end = new java.util.Date();

   System.out.println("Total number of rows updated = "
                  + updateCount
                  + " in batches of upto "
                  + batchSize
                  + " and took "
                  + (end.getTime() - start.getTime())
                  + " milliseconds\n");

   rs.close();
  }
}
```

You'll notice we've added a few output messages so you can see how it went. Here's what happens when we run it:

```
> java JDBCUpdateBatching
        "jdbc:oracle:thin:username/password@localhost:1521:database"
#1, no batching...
Total number of rows updated = 10008 and took 21400 milliseconds

#2, standard JDBC update batching - per 1000 rows...
Total number of rows updated = -20016 in batches of upto 1000 and took 3976
milliseconds

#3, standard JDBC update batching - per 10 rows...
Total number of rows updated = -20016 in batches of upto 10 and took 7691
milliseconds

#4, standard JDBC update batching - per 50 rows...
Total number of rows updated = -20016 in batches of upto 50 and took 4927
milliseconds
```

There's no doubt here that batching the updates was a much better option that not doing so. But don't be too quick to make a deduction about the results, as we said before, please take note of the subsection *What did we Learn About Update Batching?* at the end of this section once you've finished reading through the examples.

Before moving on, you'll have noticed that the total rows updated in the results show −20016 for each of the batched updates. We said earlier that the number of rows affected were returned in the array of ints from the call to executeBatch(), this is actually driver implementation dependent. If the call is successful, but the number of rows affected is not available, a value of −2 is returned. This explains why we have exactly a negative of double the number of rows, indicating success for all updates.

Incidentally, if any of the executions in a batch fails the SQLException subclass BatchUpdateException is thrown. What happens to the pending updates in the batch when this exception occurs is implementation dependant. The JDBC specification permits it to continue executing the remaining updates in the batch or to fail at that point, (in Oracle's case you'll get a failure). Where this is the case, the update counts can be obtained from the getUpdateCounts() method of BatchUpdateException, and the particular statement(s) which failed will have a value of −3. If you do get a failure, be aware that some statements may have changed the database – these may get committed by accident later so you should roll them back unless you want that to happen.

# Oracle Update Batching

Oracle update batching achieves much the same ends, but the method is different, and more elegant, although it is only implemented for OraclePreparedStatements.

Oracle's method centres around a batch value and this is the size of the batch that should be sent. An OraclePreparedStatement actually always has a batch value, but the default value is 1 so every statement is immediately sent to the database. The batch value is modified by a call to setExecuteBatch():

```
PreparedStatement updatePstmt = connection.prepareStatement(..);
...
updateStmt.setExecuteBatch(20);
```

Having set the batch size you continue to call `executeUpdate()` in the normal way (as though you were not batching):

```
updateCount += updateStmt.executeUpdate();
```

The driver keeps hold of the statement until the number of them reaches the set batch value then they are all sent. The `int` returned from the `executeUpdate()` statement is 0 unless it happens to be the call which causes the batch to be sent to the database. In that case it's the total of all the rows updated for all statements in the batch.

If at any time you need to have the pending statements sent to the database you just call `sendBatch()` which also returns the number of updates which took place as a result. (We need that information for our example):

```
updateCount += updateStmt.sendBatch();
```

Watch out for commits though: if you commit while there are pending statements in a batch they are sent for processing before the commit. We'd say this is what you want to happen and is intuitive, but it might not be what you *expect* to happen as it contrasts with the behavior of standard JDBC batching which will ignore pending updates.

In effect you can almost dispense with the need to call the `sendBatch()` method for pending updates if you are committing the changes anyway. The inverse of this means that if an error occurs somewhere, you should clear the batch so that a future commit doesn't try to process the rows.

To show Oracle's update batching working we only need to make some very minor changes to the previous example using standard JDBC batching. These include changes to output messages and calls to the `batchUpdateResults()` method, (it now has to take an `OraclePreparedStatement` as input). But the biggest change is simplification of that method, whereas before it had all that clunky looping and counting code, we've now replaced all that with the Oracle batching methods. Here's the new code for the method:

```
private static void batchUpdateResults(
    ResultSet rs, OraclePreparedStatement updateStmt, int batchSize)
  throws SQLException {
  java.util.Date start = new java.util.Date();
  int updateCount = 0;

  // maintain a count of the number of statements in the current batch
  int statementCount = 0;

  // set the batch size
  updateStmt.setExecuteBatch(batchSize);

  while(rs.next()) {
    int noticeId = rs.getInt("notice_id");
    updateStmt.setInt(1, noticeId);

    // issue the update to the batch
```

```
        updateCount += updateStmt.executeUpdate();
    }

    // In case any statements remain un-executed call sendBatch()
    updateCount += updateStmt.sendBatch();

    java.util.Date end = new java.util.Date();

    System.out.println("Total number of rows updated = "
                    + updateCount
                    + " in batches of upto "
                    + batchSize
                    + " and took "
                    + (end.getTime() - start.getTime())
                    + " milliseconds\n");

    rs.close();
  }
```

```
> java OracleUpdateBatching
          "jdbc:oracle:thin:username/password@localhost:1521:database"
#1, no batching...
Total number of rows updated = 10008 and took 16704 milliseconds

#2, Oracle update batching - per 1000 rows...
Total number of rows updated = 10008 in batches of upto 1000 and took 5368
milliseconds

#3, Oracle update batching - per 10 rows...
Total number of rows updated = 10008 in batches of upto 10 and took 5618
milliseconds

#4, Oracle update batching - per 50 rows...
Total number of rows updated = 10008 in batches of upto 50 and took 5407
milliseconds
```

As with the standard JDBC update batching example, there's no doubt here that batching the updates was a much better option that not doing so. You'll also notice that this method does yield the exact counts for all the updates that took place.

Incidentally, we tried some wild batch sizes here. In your testing you might want to start with small batches. Oracle actually recommends an optimal batch size of between 5 and 30 in its documentation and even warns that larger sizes might have a negative effect. (See *JDBC Developer's Guide And Reference, Update Batching*)

# What did we Learn About Update Batching?

Everything we said about being careful about interpreting the results of the examples in the *What Did We Learn About Multiple Fetching?* section above is also true here. If anything, here it's even more difficult because we're dealing with updates to the database.

To reiterate, the real point is to demonstrate that by building a test case relevant to our specific needs we can systematically test the methods available to us. What we've demonstrated here is just a method to enable you to see how you can proceed in testing your own applications.

# Designing for Performance

One of the main goals of designing a scalable database application is to limit the number of times Oracle has to parse your SQL statements. Such parsing is divided into two steps:

❑ **Soft parse** occurs each time a statements is issued against the database. Soft parsing is the process of taking a statement, verifying that the user that issues it has permission to access the objects it references, calculating the internal hash value for the statement, and finally looking for a similar compiled statement in the shared library cache. If the statement is not found compiled in the library cache, a hard parse occurs.

❑ **Hard parse** is the process of compiling a SQL statement and storing it in the library cache.

For more information on parsing, consult Chapter 16, *SQL Tuning and Analyzing Queries.*

Although hard parsing is much more expensive than soft parsing, both phases do count considerably in the total execution time for a statement. We can reduce hard parsing by using bind variables, since that allows us to identify similar statements, which differ only in the literal values, as a single statement. For example, instead of having two different statements, as shown here:

```
select * from emp where ename = 'JOHN';
select * from emp where ename = 'SCOTT';
```

we can have a single statement with bind variables:

```
select * from emp where ename = :bv1;
```

To use bind variables in our Java stored procedures, we use the `PreparedStatement` interface instead of `Statement` when issuing SQL statements. When using SQLJ, bind variables are automatically used when Java variables are substituted instead of literals.

Reducing soft parses, however, is not so straightforward. If you are familiar with PL/SQL, you may aware that statements in PL/SQL procedures are cached at a session level. That is, if you have executed a given statement earlier in the same session – even from another procedure or function – the PL/SQL engine will look that statement up from the cache, and avoid soft parsing it all over again. When using Java for database access, this is not automatically done for us. However, with a bit of clever thinking, we can design our procedures so that statements are cached at the session level. In the next couple of sections, we will discuss a couple of methods of doing that.

# Sharing Statements

To share statements at the session level, as is done in PL/SQL; we need to declare our statements globally for each class, rather than for each method. However, unlike connections, statements need to be closed eventually in Java, lest we affect the memory and performance of the database. When it comes to closing shared statements, there are two methods available, depending on whether you are conscious of when it is appropriate to close, or not.

## Explicit Statement Closure

When you are aware of the duration of your transactions, and have means of explicitly closing your statements, you can declare your database objects as static variables within a class, and use a static method to close them, as illustrated in the sample class below:

```java
import java.sql.*;

public class Explicit {

  // Class variables.
  private static Implicit instance;
  private static Connection conn;
  private static PreparedStatement pstmt;

  public static void doSomething() throws SQLException {
    if (conn == null || pstmt == null) {
      // Initialize objects.
    }
    // Do something...
  }

  public static void close() throws SQLException {
    if (pstmt != null) {
      pstmt.close();
    }
  }
}
```

As you can see from this example, we do not explicitly initialize the connection and statement objects until we need to use them. You should always do this when using shared statements – because otherwise you might take up resources that are never used. To use this class, you might create call specs as shown below:

```
create or replace procedure do_something
as language java
name 'Explicit.doSomething()';
/

create or replace procedure close
as language java
name 'Explicit.close()';
/
```

Using these procedures, you can call DO_SOMETHING() as many times as you like – just remember to call CLOSE() at the end.

## *Implicit Closure*

More often than not, we do not have control over the lifetime of our Java procedures. We want to share statements globally, yet close them eventually. Using our "explicit" design from the previous section, the statements would never get closed, and resources would be lost.

A better approach is to use the Singleton design pattern by creating a static wrapper around a reference to a single instance of the class. A *Singleton* is a design pattern that constrains a class to a single unique instance to which clients can reference by calling a static method. Further discussion on the Singleton pattern can be found in various design books, such as *Design Patterns* by Eric Gamma, Richard Helm, Ralph Johnson and John Vlisseides. ISBN 0-20163-361-2, published by Addison- Wesley

By constraining our classes to a single instance, we can then make sure that each gets closed in the end, by extending the finalize() method of the Object class, which all classes in Java inherit. In Java, objects are automatically garbage collected when no longer referenced, as you may already know. When an object is garbage collected, the garbage collector invokes its finalize() method. By default, this method does nothing. But if you implement it for your own classes, and for example add a clause that closes your statements, you can make sure that all resources are shut down when the session ends (since the garbage collector will be run before that happens).

For example, look at the following example. The Implicit class is a Singleton. Clients are not able to initialize new Implicit objects, since its constructor has private visibility.

```java
import java.sql.*;

public class Implicit {

  // Class variable.
  private static Implicit instance;

  // Instance variables.
  private Connection conn;
  private PreparedStatement pstmt;

  // Private constructor.
  private Implicit() {}

  public static void doSomething() throws SQLException {
    if (instance == null) {
      instance = new Implicit();
    }
    instance.localDoSomething();
  }

  private void localDoSomething() throws SQLException {
    if (conn == null || pstmt == null) {
      // Initialize objects.
    }
    // Do something...
  }
```

```
protected void finalize() throws Throwable {
  if (pstmt != null) {
    pstmt.close();
  }
}
}
```

As you can see, we now store the `PreparedStatement` and `Connection` objects as instance variables. However, since we only have a single, static instance of `Implicit`, these are in effect shared through the session. The `doSomething()` method now relays its call to the private non-static method, `localDoSomething()`. As before, we only initialize the database objects when needed.

Finally, note how we define our `finalize()` method – as protected. This is not at our whim – all `finalize()` methods must be declared that way. For more information on `finalize()`, you can consult http://www.ecs.umass.edu/ece/wireless/people/emmanuel/java/java/javaOO/finalize.html.

# Summary

In this chapter we've looked at some of the major elements available in Oracle JDBC. Hopefully, you'll have gained a flavor, at least, for what is possible and an interest to use the technology and explore it further. There's a lot we haven't had space to cover, but we have seen the fundamentals at work, both in standard JDBC form and some of the extended functionality provided by Oracle.

We've seen extensive examples of the following, all of which you should now be confident to try in your own programs:

❑   Use of `Statement`, including important methods extended to its subinterfaces and how this differs from them.

❑   Use of `ResultSet` and `OracleResultSet`, how to use the `getXXX()` methods to return values to your Java program and how to handle `null`s.

❑   Use of `PreparedStatement` and `OraclePreparedStatement`, how to use the `setXXX()` methods to set bind variables.

❑   Performance features of `Statement` and `OracleStatement`, and `OraclePreparedStatement`. Multiple fetching and batch updating both standard JDBC and Oracle specific methods. Also other Oracle specific performance features such as defining column types.

❑   Use of transactions for modifications to data in the database.

❑   What metadata is, and how to make use of it.

❑   Use of `CallableStatement` and `OracleCallableStatement`, to pass parameters in and how to get values back from the database. We've seen how to pass the basic PL/SQL types and also others such as PL/SQL tables and REF CURSORS.

Oracle 9i Java Programming

# Handling Exceptions

As we briefly discussed in Chapter 2, *Java Classes and Objects*, Java exceptions are objects that can be used to deal with errors. **Programmer errors** include problems such as incorrectly implementing an algorithm or failing to check for invalid parameters such as a divisor of zero. **User errors** include entering invalid data – entering an alphanumeric string when only digits are allowed, or entering a filename for a file that does not exist. In today's distributed computing environment, errors can arise from not just the user's system, but from systems across the network. **System errors** can arise from a lack of resources such as memory or file descriptors or a failure in a remote server.

Regardless of the cause of errors, Java provides specific mechanisms for dealing with them. Since Java is an object-oriented language, errors in Java programs are represented as objects. These objects are known generically as **exceptions**. One reason for calling them exceptions is that they represent exceptional situations in the program. Exceptions represent errors in a program, or abnormal conditions in a JVM, or failures throughout a local or networked system. Java has language keywords for declaring and handling exceptions, at points in the code where we expect that they could occur. When an error does occur, an exception is created and **thrown**. Code that deals with the error **catches** the exception (Java has keywords for these actions too). By properly throwing and handling exceptions, your code can be more robust and be better able to recover from errors.

In this chapter we will:

- ❑ Cover the basics of exceptions you may come across
- ❑ Look at exception classes forming part of the JDBC API
- ❑ Examine Oracle's exception classes and how to use them
- ❑ List various techniques for dealing with exceptions.

# Exception Fundamentals

In this part of the chapter, we will look at exception objects and how the objects are divided into three categories. Specifically, we will:

- ❏ Examine the base class of all exceptions, `Throwable`, and its primary subclasses

- ❏ Show how to throw and catch exceptions using `try...catch...finally` blocks or `throws` clauses

- ❏ Look at what to do with unhandled exceptions

The `Throwable` class is the base class of all exceptions in the Java language. This class defines almost all the methods used by exception objects (later in this chapter we'll look at additional methods added by some of the subclasses). The figure to the right shows a UML class diagram for `Throwable` and three of its primary subclasses.

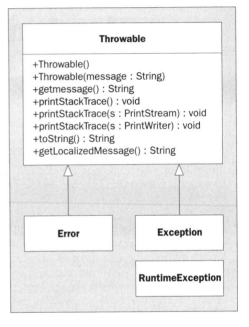

In this chapter we will use the `printStackTrace()` method. This method provides information about the current chain of methods that was being executed when the exception occured. It provides valuable debugging information about the programmer errors and other exceptions that need to be fixed or handled in your code. You can find detailed explanations for all the methods in the Java API documentation.

## Unchecked and Checked Exceptions

The Java environment divides exceptions into two categories; **unchecked** exceptions and **checked** exceptions. Unchecked exceptions are so called because your code is *not required* to handle or declare unchecked exceptions, and the compiler does not check that you do so. On the other hand, your code *must* handle or declare checked exceptions, and the compiler does check your code to enforce this.

# The Exception Subclasses

The three primary subclasses of Throwable are Error, Exception, and RuntimeException (as a subclass of Exception, RuntimeException is also a subclass of Throwable). Error and its subclasses generally represent abnormal situations from which the program cannot recover. Exception and its subclasses are errors from which the program can recover. Finally, some exceptions are further categorized as runtime exceptions. Runtime exceptions are generally caused by a programmer error.

The RuntimeException class and its subclasses represent unchecked exceptions. The class Exception and its subclasses (except, of course, RuntimeException) represent checked exceptions.

## Error

A Java error, according to the Java documentation for the Error class, is a class

> ... that indicates serious problems that a reasonable application should not try to catch. Most such errors are abnormal conditions.

Errors are unchecked. Your code does not need to declare that it can throw an error, nor do you need to handle errors. This is because errors usually indicate unrecoverable problems in the JVM or in your program. For this reason, your code will rarely need to handle an error. What are some error conditions? One common error condition is an OutOfMemoryError, which means the JVM has no more memory it can allocate for objects. Another error occurs when a class file cannot be found by the JVM. This error is a NoClassDefFoundError. With a class file missing, the program cannot continue to execute and must terminate. There are other error conditions, and you can learn what they are from the Javadoc for java.lang.Error at http://java.sun.com/j2se/1.3/docs/api/index.html.

## RuntimeException

Runtime exceptions usually result from programmer errors, and thus, are exceptions that can be prevented by proper coding. For example, accessing an array element that does not exist is a runtime exception:

```
String[] s = new String[5];
String aString = s[6];   // causes ArrayIndexOutOfBoundsException
```

If you have an array, you can prevent an ArrayIndexOutOfBoundsException by checking the array size before trying to access an element of the array. If you obtain an object reference from some method that can return a null, and then try to use that reference, you can get a NullPointerException.

```
ResultSet rset = statement.executeQuery("select col1 from my_table");
String s = rset.getString(1);   // assume col1 is Null
int l = s.length();             // NullPointerException because s is null
```

You can prevent a NullPointerException by checking the reference before using it. You can learn about other possible run-time exceptions by consulting the Java API documentation.

## Exception

That leaves us with the Exception class and its subclasses (excluding RuntimeException and its subclasses). These exceptions are checked exceptions and usually result from situations that are outside the direct control of the programmer. For example, if your program tries to connect to a server, and the server is down or unavailable, this can result in any of a number of IOExceptions such as a SocketException or a RemoteException. Although you have to deal with the problem, your program is still able to continue executing. Whether or not the server is available is outside the control of your program. As we have seen in earlier chapters, if you are trying to access and query a database and there is an error in the database, your code will have to handle an SQLException. SQLException is another subclass of Exception, and is thus a checked exception.

# Handling Exceptions

The Java language defines five keywords for exception handling:

❑   throw – A keyword used to throw an exception

❑   try – A keyword that starts a block of code that might throw an exception

❑   catch – A keyword that starts a block of code to handle an exception

❑   finally – A keyword that starts a block of code that will always execute after a try or catch block is complete

❑   throws – A keyword used to declare that a method could throw an exception

In the next few sections we'll investigate how these keywords are used in code.

### throw

You use the throw keyword to throw an exception. You can only throw an object that is a subclass of Throwable. Thus, since String is not a subclass of Throwable, you can't do the following:

```
throw new String();    // not allowed, String is not a subclass of Throwable
```

However, SQLException is a subclass of Throwable, so you can do this:

```
throw new ArrayIndexOutOfBoundsException();
```

The line of code above may look a little strange, but it is perfectly legal. The code is creating and throwing an exception in the same line. The compiler sees this code and creates byte code that first creates the exception object, and then throws the object.

### try...catch...finally

When you want or need to handle an exception, you do so with try...catch...finally blocks. The try block contains the code that might throw an exception. This block can contain one or more Java statements. So, a try block might look like this:

```
try {
  // ...Java statement
  // ...Java method call
  // ...Java statement
}
```

If any of the statements or method calls throws an exception, execution is immediately terminated, and the control is passed to an exception handler, or `catch` block. Each `try` block can have one or more `catch` blocks. The JVM looks for a `catch` block that can handle the exception thrown. A `catch` block looks like this:

```
catch (exception_type variable) {
  // ...code to handle the exception
}
```

The structure of a `catch` clause is similar to that of a method declaration. The `catch` keyword is followed by a parameter list. This list indicates the class of the exception handled by the block and the identifier that can be used to access the exception object. A `catch` block can handle a given exception if the exception is of the same type as the type declared in the `catch` clause, or is a subtype of the declared type. For example, the following `catch` clause can handle a `java.io.IOException`, and all the subclasses of `IOException`:

```
catch (IOException e)
```

When an exception is thrown, control is passed to the first `catch` block whose declared exception type matches the thrown exception type. None of the other `catch` blocks will be invoked. Thus, when you use multiple `catch` blocks, you must structure them from the most specific exception to the least specific exception. Suppose you had code to open and read a file. The code will handle all the `IOExceptions` that occur during this process, but you want to perform special handling for a `FileNotFoundException`. You would structure your `catch` blocks like this:

```
catch (FileNotFoundException e) {
  // ...code to handle the file not found
} catch (IOException e) {
  // ...code to generically handle other IOExceptions
} catch (Exception e) {
  // ...code to handle any other exception
}
```

The first block handles a `FileNotFoundException` (a subclass of `IOException`); the second block handles an `IOException` (a subclass of `Exception`); the third block handles any other exception. If you put the catch (Exception e) block first, then that block would handle all exceptions (since all exceptions are subclasses of `Exception`), and neither of the other handlers could ever be executed. The compiler will see this problem and report the error with a message such as

```
catch not reached.
```

*The actual message may vary depending on your compiler.*

If no `catch` block in the current scope can handle the thrown exception, then control passes to the `finally` block (see below) if one exists, and then immediately exits the current method. The thread of execution then passes back to the calling method. The JVM searches for a matching `catch` in the calling method. If none is found, the JVM will continue moving up the chain of method calls until it finds a handler for the exception, or until it reaches the first method in the method chain. If no handler for the exception is found, your program will terminate with an uncaught exception.

The last block is the `finally` block. When it is included, the `finally` block includes code that is always executed after either the `try` block or a `catch` block completes. It will look like this:

```
finally {
   // ...cleanup code
}
```

The `finally` block is usually used to release some resource that was obtained in the `try` block. For example, a common construct in JDBC code is the following:

```
try {
   // get a database connection and execute some SQL
} catch (Exception e) {
   // deal with exceptions that occur
} finally {
   // close the connection and any other resources
}
```

In the `try` block, the code gets a database connection and other database resources. It then uses these resources to perform some inserts, updates, deletes, or queries. Regardless of whether the `try` block completes successfully, or an exception is thrown and the `catch` block executes, the connection and other resources need to be closed or released. The resources are released in the `finally` block because the Java language guarantees that the `finally` block will always be executed before control leaves the method. In fact, when you are closing a connection in a `finally` block, you will often see a construct known as a **nested** `try...catch` block. The `close()` method of `Connection` can throw a `SQLException`. If you did not want that exception to be thrown out of the method, you would need to put the method call into its own `try...catch` block because when you are in the `finally` block, you are no longer inside an enclosing `catch` block. Nested `try...catch` blocks can be inside a `catch` block or even a `try` block. The nested `try...catch` will look something like this:

```
finally {
   try {
      conn.close();
   } catch (SQLException e) {
   }
}
```

It is also possible to have a `try` block without a `catch` block, but only if you use a `finally` block. That is, every `try` must be followed by a `catch`, or a `finally`, or both.

```
try {
   // Java statements
} finally {
   // cleanup
}
```

You would use this construct when you need to ensure that code in the `finally` block is executed, but the exception is allowed to propagate to the calling method.

### throws

The `throws` keyword is used in a method declaration to indicate which exceptions the method does not handle. In other words, if any checked exception is thrown from your method, your method must declare that it throws the exception. The `throws` keyword appears after the parameter list but before the opening brace of the method.

```
public void updateEmp()
   throws SQLException {
      ...
}
```

If the exception will throw multiple exceptions, each exception type is separated by a comma in the `throws` clause:

```
public void updateEmp()
   throws SQLException, FileNotFoundException
```

Also, as with the `catch` blocks, if you have a number of exceptions that are all subclasses of the same base class, you can declare that the method throws the base class rather than listing each subclass.

```
// assume this method throws EOFException, FileLockInterruptionException,
// and FileNotFoundException, since these are all IOExceptions,
// we can do this
public void someMethod()
   throws IOException
```

Whether you declare all subclasses, or declare just the superclass will depend on the application. Sometimes the caller will just need to know whether the operation succeeded or failed, so declaring just the superclass is acceptable. Other times, the caller may need to take different actions based on the precise error, so you will declare subclasses.

> **Every checked exception that occurs in a method must be declared or handled. If the method throws an unchecked exception, that exception must be declared in the method declaration.**

# Unhandled Exceptions and PL/SQL

All of the examples above have a hidden assumption that we are dealing with Java classes calling methods of other classes. What happens when we call a Java stored procedure from PL/SQL? In this situation, the exception is passed to the PL/SQL caller as an ORA-29532 error. Regardless of the underlying Java exception, all uncaught exceptions become ORA-29532 errors. The error also includes additional information that specifies the underlying Java error. For example, if you try to access an array element with an illegal index, you'll get an error message similar to this:

```
SQL> exec print_array_element(-1);
java.lang.ArrayIndexOutOfBoundsException
at ArrayDemo.printElement(ArrayDemo:15)
BEGIN print_array_element(-1); END;

*
ERROR at line 1:
ORA-29532: Java call terminated by uncaught Java exception:
java.lang.ArrayIndexOutOfBoundsException
```

If you are a PL/SQL developer calling Java stored procedures in the database, you must be prepared to handle an ORA-29532 error raised by the stored procedure. As a developer of Java stored procedures, you need to ensure that callers of your stored procedure know what kind of exception can be raised by the procedure.

### Creating Your Own Exception Class

The exception classes can be inherited just like almost any other Java class. (The anomaly to this rule is classes that use the keyword final in their class declaration. These classes *cannot* be subclassed.) So, if none of the built-in Java exception classes properly indicate the problem in your code, you can create your own exception class by extending Exception. Suppose you have an application that does a credit card authorization. You could create a number of exceptions that indicate a problem with authorizing or charging the credit card. For example, you could create an InvalidCardNumberException to indicate the card number did not have the correct number of digits, or had an invalid digit combination. When you create your own exception class, you will usually only need to provide the constructors; everything else you need is provided by the base class Throwable. So, the InvalidCardNumberException class would look like this:

```
public class InvalidCardNumberException extends Exception {
  InvalidCardNumberException() {}
  InvalidCardNumberException(String message) { super(message); }
}
```

# JDBC Exceptions

The JDBC API provides two specific classes that allow you to deal with database errors. Most of the rest of this chapter will be spent looking at the SQLException class since you will almost always be using this class when handling database exceptions. Then, we will take a brief look at the SQLWarning class.

# SQLException

Errors that occur in the database or while interacting with the database are represented by one of two exception classes: SQLException and SQLWarning. SQLException is a subclass of Exception, and thus is a checked exception, and SQLWarning is a subclass of SQLException. This relationship is illustrated in the class diagram below.

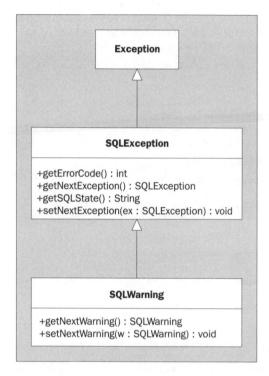

The `SQLException` class implements four new methods in addition to the methods it inherits from `Throwable`. The class provides the `getNextException()` and `setNextException()` methods that allow the programmer to deal with a chain of exceptions which occurs during a database transaction. We look at this in the following *Exception Chaining* section. The other two methods, `getErrorCode()` and `getSQLState()` give the programmer access to specific error information from the database. These are discussed in the *Error Codes and SQL State*, following *Exception Chaining*.

## Exception Chaining

At times, the `SQLException` caught by an exception handler is just one of several `SQLExceptions` that have been thrown by the current thread of execution. For example, suppose in the process of updating a table, a trigger is executed, but the trigger fails. This causes the table update to fail. What exception should the database driver throw; an exception that says the trigger failed, or an exception that says the table update failed? By allowing `SQLExceptions` to be **chained**, the database can signal both errors. Chained exceptions are just a singly linked list. The first `SQLException` in the chain contains a reference to the next `SQLException` in the chain, and so on, until the last reference in the chain is null. This is illustrated in the diagram below:

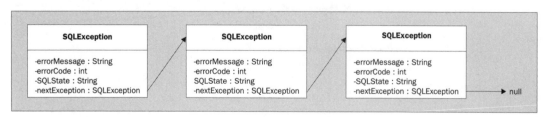

Very few exceptions in Oracle are chained. For that reason, the example in this section shows how to create your own chain of exceptions, and then shows how to handle each exception in the chain:

```
SQL> create or replace and compile java source named "ChainedExceptionDemo"
  2  as
  3  import java.sql.*;
  4
  5  public class ChainedExceptionDemo {
  6    public static void doit() {
  7      ChainedExceptionDemo ced = new ChainedExceptionDemo();
  8      try {
  9        ced.updateEmp();
 10      } catch (SQLException e) {
 11        while (e != null) {
 12          System.out.println(e.getMessage());
 13          e = e.getNextException();
 14        }
 15      }
 16    }
 17
 18    public void updateEmp() throws SQLException {
 19      Connection conn = null;
 20      Statement stmt = null;
 21
 22      try {
 23        String url = "jdbc:default:connection:";
 24        conn = DriverManager.getConnection(url);
 25        String sql = "update emp set deptno=50 where empno=7934";
 26        stmt = conn.createStatement();
 27        stmt.executeUpdate(sql);
 28      } catch (SQLException e) {
 29        conn.rollback();
 30        SQLException sqle = new SQLException("Could not update table");
 31        sqle.setNextException(e);
 32        throw sqle;
 33      } finally {
 34        stmt.close();
 35        conn.close();
 36      }
 37    }
 38  }
 39  /

Java created.
```

We then create a procedure call specification to execute the class:

```
SQL> create or replace procedure chain_demo
  2  as
  3  language java
  4  name 'ChainedExceptionDemo.doit()';
  5  /

Procedure created.
```

Now that we are ready to execute the procedure, we set the server environment to send output to the SQL console, and call the procedure:

```
SQL> set serveroutput on
SQL> call dbms_java.set_output(2000);

Call completed.
```

*We will call the two PL/SQL statements above for nearly every code example in this chapter. You can avoid the need to type these by putting them into your* login.sql *file.*

```
SQL> exec chain_demo;
Could not update table.
ORA-02291: integrity constraint (USERNAME.FK_DEPTNO) violated - parent key
not found


PL/SQL procedure successfully completed.
```

Looking at the output, you can see two messages. The first error message:

```
Could not update table.
```

is the error message from the first exception in the chain. The next message:

```
ORA-02291: integrity constraint (USERNAME.FK_DEPTNO) violated - parent key
not found
```

is the error message from the second exception in the chain.

The JDBC code in the ChainedExceptionDemo class causes an integrity violation in the database. As a result of the error, the database driver throws a SQLException. This exception is immediately caught in the updateEmp() method. The exception handler in the updateEmp() method then constructs a new SQLException with the message:

```
Could not update table.
```

It then chains the original exception to the new exception with a call to setNextException(). After chaining the exceptions, the handler throws the new exception. Before leaving the method, the finally block executes. Notice that because the updateEmp() method declares that it can throw a SQLException, we do not need a try...catch block around the close() method calls.

The control of execution passes back to the doit() method, where the JVM looks for an exception handler for the SQLException. It does indeed find one, and so control passes into the handler in the doit() method. Inside this handler, the error message for the exception is printed, and then a call is made to getNextException(). If getNextException() returns a non-null reference, the code loops back to the error message print statement. This continues until the chain of exceptions is exhausted.

As I mentioned at the start of the example, you will find that exception chaining is rarely used by Oracle. Almost all Oracle errors will result in a single exception instance. What you may find more useful are the methods in the next section, which return the Oracle error codes and X/Open SQL state codes.

## Error Codes and SQL State

The other two methods added by SQLException allow you to get database-specific information about the error that occurred. Those methods and their descriptions are:

❑ SQLException.getErrorCode() – Returns an integer that is the vendor's (Oracle's) error code.

❑ SQLException.getSQLState() – Returns a String containing a code that describes the error. These codes are known as **state codes**. The X/Open SQL standard specifies the codes and their meanings.

*Complete details about SQL state codes and how they map to Oracle error numbers can be found in the Oracle documentation. One place for that information is in* Chapter 9 *of the* Pro*C/C++ Precompiler Programmer's Guide. You can find that document at* technet.oracle.com *or with the database documentation.*

Let's look at a simple example that displays the Oracle error code and the SQL state for an exception thrown when we violate a constraint on a table. As we've done in other example in this chapter, we will attempt to update the USERNAME.EMP table by setting the deptno field to a non-existent department:

```
SQL> create or replace and compile java source named "ErrorCodeDemo"
  2  as
  3  import java.sql.*;
  4
  5  public class ErrorCodeDemo {
  6    public static void doit() throws SQLException {
  7      Connection conn = null;
  8      Statement stmt = null;
  9
 10      try {
 11        String url = "jdbc:default:connection:";
 12        conn = DriverManager.getConnection(url);
 13        String sql = "update emp set deptno=50 where empno=7934";
 14        stmt = conn.createStatement();
 15        stmt.executeUpdate(sql);
 16      } catch (SQLException ex) {
 17        System.out.println("Message: " + ex.getMessage());
 18        System.out.println("Error code: " + ex.getErrorCode());
 19        System.out.println("SQL state: " + ex.getSQLState());
 20        throw ex;
 21      } finally {
 22        stmt.close();
 23        conn.close();
 24      }
 25    }
 26  }
 27  /

Java created.
```

Next, we create a simple call specification with which to call the Java code:

```
SQL> create or replace procedure pdemo
  2  as
  3  language java
  4  name 'ErrorCodeDemo.doit()';
  5  /

Procedure created.
```

Then we set the environment to display messages to the console and call the class.

```
SQL> set serveroutput on
SQL> call dbms_java.set_output(2000);

Call completed.

SQL> exec pdemo;
Message: ORA-02291: integrity constraint (USERNAME.FK_DEPTNO) violated -
parent key not found

Error code: 2291
SQL state: 23000

    .
    .
    .
```

After printing the same error message that we have seen before, the code prints the Oracle error code (2291) and the SQL state code (23000). The Oracle error code 2291 (ORA-02291) and the SQL state code 23000 both mean that an integrity constraint was violated. Whether you are looking at the Oracle error code or the SQL state code, you can easily determine what the code means by examining the message from the SQLException.

As before, an SQLException is thrown when we attempt to update the table. However, in this example we are more interested in getting error code information from the exception. Inside the catch block, we call the getMessage(), getErrorCode() and getSQLState() methods. Respectively, these methods return a short text message about the exception, the Oracle error code for the exception, and the SQL state code for the exception. As can be seen from the error message, ORA-02291 is the Oracle error code for integrity constraint violation. As you might expect, the SQL state code 23000 also indicates that an integrity constraint was violated.

Unfortunately, the SQLException does not provide an easy means to know which integrity constraint was violated. This information is available, however, as you can see it is embedded inside the error message. What we would like is a way to get that information without parsing the error message string. We can do that through an Oracle specific exception class, the OracleSQLException.

## OracleSQLException

Oracle provides a subclass of SQLException that can provide additional information about the exception to the Java programmer. This class is oracle.jdbc.driver.OracleSQLException. The OracleSQLException object can hold parameters that provide information about the error that occurred. This information is obtained through the two methods of the OracleSQLException class. These methods are:

❑ int getNumParameters() – Returns the number of additional parameters contained by the OracleSQLException.

❑ Object[] getParameters() – Returns an array consisting of the parameters. Each element in the array is a String object or an Integer object.

The information provided by the parameters is dependent upon the exception that occurred. In the Oracle documentation, there is an example that attempts to delete a non-existent table; the OracleSQLException thrown for this error contains one parameter – the string NO_SUCH_TABLE. Other errors will contain different parameters as we will see in the following example.

We will look at the extra parameters in an OracleSQLException when we once again violate a constraint on a table. We will take the ErrorCode demo from above and modify it to print out the parameter information. This class will be very similar to the ErrorCodeDemo class above; we will change the class name, add a catch block for an OracleSQLException, and print out the parameter information in the new catch block in addition to the message, error code, and SQL state:

```
SQL> create or replace and compile java source named "ParameterDemo"
  2  as
  3  import java.sql.*;
  4  import oracle.jdbc.driver.OracleSQLException;
  5
  6  public class ParameterDemo {
  7    public static void doit() throws SQLException {
  8      Connection conn = null;
  9      Statement stmt = null;
 10      try {
 11        String url = "jdbc:default:connection:";
 12        conn = DriverManager.getConnection(url);
 13        String sql = "update emp set deptno=50 where empno=7934";
 14        stmt = conn.createStatement();
 15        stmt.executeUpdate(sql);
 16      } catch (OracleSQLException ex) {
 17        System.out.println("Message: " + ex.getMessage());
 18        System.out.println("Error code: " + ex.getErrorCode());
 19        System.out.println("SQL state: " + ex.getSQLState());
 20        int numparams = ex.getNumParameters();
 21        if (numparams == 0) {
 22          System.out.println("No parameters");
 23        } else {
 24          Object[] params = ex.getParameters();
 25          for (int i = 0; i < params.length; i++) {
 26            System.out.println("Param " + i + ": "
 27                            + params[i].toString());
 28          }
 29        }
 30        ex.printStackTrace();
 31      } catch (SQLException ex) {
 32        ex.printStackTrace();
 33      } finally {
 34        stmt.close();
 35        conn.close();
```

```
36        }
37    }
38  }
39  /

Java created.
```

Next, we create a procedure that can be used to execute the class:

```
SQL> create or replace procedure pdemo2
  2  as
  3  language java
  4  name 'ParameterDemo.doit()';
  5  /

Procedure created.
```

Now we are ready to execute the class and see what information we get out of the exception. First, set the environment so that program output is displayed on the console:

```
SQL> set serveroutput on
SQL> call dbms_java.set_output(2000);

Call completed.
```

and then call the procedure:

```
SQL> exec pdemo2;
Message: ORA-02291: integrity constraint (USERNAME.FK_DEPTNO) violated - parent
key not found

Error code: 2291
SQL state: 23000
Param 0: USERNAME
Param 1: FK_DEPTNO
oracle.jdbc.driver.OracleSQLException: ORA-02291: integrity constraint
(USERNAME.FK_DEPTNO) violated - parent key not found

at oracle.jdbc.kprb.KprbDBAccess.check_error(KprbDBAccess.java)
at oracle.jdbc.kprb.KprbDBAccess.executeFetch(KprbDBAccess.java)
at oracle.jdbc.kprb.KprbDBAccess.parseExecuteFetch(KprbDBAccess.java)
at oracle.jdbc.driver.OracleStatement.executeNonQuery(OracleStatement.java)
at oracle.jdbc.driver.OracleStatement.doExecuteOther(OracleStatement.java)
at oracle.jdbc.driver.OracleStatement.doExecuteWithTimeout(OracleStatement.java)
at oracle.jdbc.driver.OracleStatement.executeUpdate(OracleStatement.java)
at ParameterDemo.doit(ParameterDemo:13)

PL/SQL procedure successfully completed.
```

As in the previous example, the error message, error code, and SQL state are printed out in the catch block. In addition, we can see that even though we caught an SQLException in ErrorCodeDemo, the exception object is really of type OracleSQLException, the type caught in this code.

> **Recall that an exception handler will catch all exceptions of the indicated type, and exceptions that are subclasses of that type. Thus, in ErrorCodeDemo, catch (SQLException) will also catch OracleSQLExceptions.**

The OracleSQLException provided two additional pieces of information about the exception; the strings USERNAME and FK_DEPTNO. The final bit of code executed in the catch block was to print the **stack trace**. The stack trace is a list of every method call that led to the method in which the exception was thrown. We will look at it in more detail near the end of this chapter.

When the code attempts to update the table, an OracleSQLException is thrown. This exception contains the error code 2291, which is the Oracle error code for integrity constraint violation and the state code 23000 which is the state code for integrity constraint violation. The OracleSQLException also contains two parameters related to the exception. The first parameter is the schema name in which the constraint is defined, and the second parameter is the name of the constraint:

```
Param 0: USERNAME
Param 1: FK_DEPTNO
```

These parameters are obtained by calling the getParameters() method of OracleSQLException. This method returns an Object array where each element of the array is a parameter. According to Oracle documentation, this array can consist of a mix of String and Integer objects. The Integer objects hold any numeric parameters; the String objects hold all other parameters. The code loops through and calls the toString() method of each element in the array.

Usually, the SQLException message, error code, and state will provide enough information to specify the cause of the error. What these methods do provide is an easy way to extract the pertinent details from the exception. Suppose that you needed to do additional processing for certain exceptions, such as the integrity violation exception we have used in several examples in this chapter. With an SQLException, you can easily get the Oracle error code that tells you that there is an integrity violation. However, to get the information about the schema or constraint name, you would need to parse the exception message or stack trace. While not being technically difficult, parsing the error message does involve more code that searches the string, and extracts the needed information. With OracleSQLException you can get that information with less effort.

# SQLWarning

There are times when a problem occurs in the database that is not fatal to the operation being performed. In these cases, JDBC provides the SQLWarning class to provide information about a non-fatal error in the database. When programming with Java and Oracle however, you will have little call to use the SQLWarning. The only time you may need to be aware of warnings is when performing operations on scrollable result sets. (Scrollable result sets are result sets that allow both forwards, backwards, and random movement through the rows. See Chapter 5, *Using JDBC* for more information.) In this section we briefly examine the use of SQLWarning and highlight the warning results from a scrollable result set.

SQLWarning is a subclass of SQLException, but unlike Exception, it will never be thrown by JDBC code. Rather, it is silently chained to the object that was executing when the error that caused the warning occurred. The JDBC objects that can produce SQL warnings are Connection, Statement, PreparedStatement, CallableStatement, and ResultSet. If there is a warning, you can get it with a call to the getWarnings() method. Each of the previously mentioned objects implements or inherits the getWarnings() method.

Since SQLWarning is a subclass of SQLException, it inherits all the methods of Throwable, and all the methods of SQLException. Specifically, if you have an SQLWarning object, you can call the getMessage(), getErrorCode(), and getSQLState() methods just as we have seen in examples earlier in this chapter. In addition, SQLWarnings can be chained similarly to SQLException. SQLWarning implements a setNextWarning(SQLWarning) method to chain an SQLWarning to another; and it implements a getNextWarning() method to get a chained warning.

So, code that needed to access a SQLWarning would look very similar to some of the code we have looked at previously in this chapter. Here is a snippet from the ParameterDemo class above, modified to get and display SQLWarning information:

```
11      String url = "jdbc:default:connection:";
12      Connection conn = DriverManager.getConnection(url);
13      String sql = "update emp set deptno=50 where empno=7934";
14      Statement stmt = conn.createStatement();
15      stmt.executeUpdate(sql);
        // check for warnings...
        SQLWarning sqlw = stmt.getWarnings();
        while (w != null) {
           System.out.println(w.getErrorMessage());
           System.out.println(w.getErrorCode());
           System.out.println(w.getSQLState ());
           w = w.getNextWarning();
        }
```

The only differences between this code and the SQLException code is that we have to explicitly retrieve the warning object (rather than catching an exception) and the chained warnings are obtained through the method getNextWarning(). Also, in the snippet above, the SQLWarning, if any, was retrieved from the Statement object. We can also check for warnings from the Connection:

```
12      Connection conn = DriverManager.getConnection(url);
        SQLWarning sqlw = conn.getWarnings();
        // handle warning
```

or from a ResultSet:

```
        ResultSet rset = stmt.executeQuery(sql);
        SQLWarning sqlw = rset.getWarnings();
        //handle warning
```

However, you will probably never have occasion to use this class while programming Java with the Oracle database. Oracle handles most errors with the SQLException class. Oracle's Java documentation states

*... the Oracle JDBC drivers generally do not support* `SQLWarning`. *(An exception to this, scrollable result set operations do generate SQL warnings, but the* `SQLWarning` *instance is created on the client, not in the database.)*

# Now That You've Caught One...

Now that you've caught an exception, what exactly can you do with it? This is a question without a good answer, because the answer is heavily dependent upon your application and environment. The examples in this chapter did not do much except to print information and then re-throw the exception. What I will attempt to do here is provide some brief general guidelines on what to do or not do with exception handlers.

During development, I recommend that you put a call to `printStackTrace()` in every exception handler. The `ParameterDemo` example above called `printStackTrace()` in its exception handler. Here is the stack trace from above again:

```
oracle.jdbc.driver.OracleSQLException: ORA-02291: integrity constraint
(USERNAME.FK_DEPTNO) violated - parent key not found

at oracle.jdbc.kprb.KprbDBAccess.check_error(KprbDBAccess.java)
at oracle.jdbc.kprb.KprbDBAccess.executeFetch(KprbDBAccess.java)
at oracle.jdbc.kprb.KprbDBAccess.parseExecuteFetch(KprbDBAccess.java)
at oracle.jdbc.driver.OracleStatement.executeNonQuery(OracleStatement.java)
at oracle.jdbc.driver.OracleStatement.doExecuteOther(OracleStatement.java)
at oracle.jdbc.driver.OracleStatement.doExecuteWithTimeout(OracleStatement.java)
at oracle.jdbc.driver.OracleStatement.executeUpdate(OracleStatement.java)
at ParameterDemo.doit(ParameterDemo:13)
```

The first method in the chain is at the bottom of the stack trace. It shows that the first method was the `ParameterDemo.doit()` method. The `doit()` method called the `executeUpdate()` method, shown in the next line up in the stack trace. This continues up to the method in which the exception was thrown, `check_error()`. If you look at the stack trace, you will see that for the `ParameterDemo` code, the stack trace indicates which line in the method was executing when the exception occurred. Line numbers are not provided for the Oracle JDBC classes because the classes have been natively compiled and no longer contain source line information. This also occurs with a JVM that uses a just-in-time compiler. See Chapter 15, *Java Application Performance* for more information on just-in-time compilation and Oracle native compilation.

If you are writing Java stored procedures, you should *always* declare the exception and either catch it and re-throw it, or not catch it at all. If you catch the exception and hide it by not re-throwing it, the caller will not know that any problems occurred.

> **Always declare and allow exceptions to be thrown from Java stored procedures so that the exceptions are not hidden from the caller.**

If you are programming Java outside the database, or an application inside the database, you have more choices. You could, of course, ignore the exception entirely:

```
try {
  // some code that could throw an exception
} catch (Exception ignored) {
  //do nothing at all
}
```

There are some rare situations where this is acceptable. For example, the `FileInputStream` (an object used to read from a file) constructor can throw a `FileNotFoundException`; if you check that the file exists before you construct the `FileInputStream`, you could choose to ignore the `FileNotFoundException`. In general, though, if an exception could happen, you should either attempt to handle it at some point in your code, or propagate it back to the client. At the very least, you should be logging or printing some message about the exception. There have been several times when developers have asked me to help them figure out why their code was not working. I look at their code, which is riddled with empty `catch` blocks, and realize that it's no wonder they can't figure out what's going on. There could be exceptions occurring in half a dozen places, but because they are doing nothing in the `catch` blocks, there is no way to determine where the problem is.

So where should you handle an exception? At the place that makes sense. For example, a utility method that reads lines from a stream would not be the place to handle an `IOException`. Different classes that call the method may have different requirements. However, a method that gets called when the user selects **File -> Open** from a menu, creates a `FileInputStream`, and calls the utility method to read from the file, would probably be the place to deal with an `IOException`.

> If a method can intelligently handle an exception, then handle it there. Otherwise let it propagate.

An exception handler can also re-throw an exception. This is done the same way as throwing a new exception: the code uses the `throw` keyword followed by the exception reference. This was done several times in the examples earlier in this chapter. Here is part of the `ErrorCodeDemo` class:

```
16        } catch (SQLException ex) {
17            System.out.println("Message: " + ex.getMessage());
18            System.out.println("Error code: " + ex.getErrorCode());
19            System.out.println("SQL state: " + ex.getSQLState());
20            throw ex;
21        } finally {
```

After printing out various messages using the variable ex, the exception was re-thrown. You will often do this when you want to allow the exception to propagate back to the caller, but you need to do a rollback or some other clean up before the method exits. However, one thing you do not need to do is this:

```
try {
  // some code that throws an exception
} catch (Exception e) {
  throw e;
}
```

If the exception handler does nothing but re-throw the exception caught, then eliminate the `try...catch` block entirely.

Finally, avoid separate `try...catch` blocks for every single line of code. One of the purposes of exception handling is to avoid error checking every single line of code. Find some block of code that represents a unit of work and put your `try...catch` block around that code. For example, each of the examples in this chapter used this code:

```
try {
   String url = "jdbc:default:connection:";
   conn = DriverManager.getConnection(url);
   String sql = "update emp set deptno=50 where empno=7934";
   stmt = conn.createStatement();
   stmt.executeUpdate(sql);
}
```

The methods `getConnection()`, `createStatement()`, and `executeUpdate()` can each throw a `SQLException`. Rather than having three separate `try...catch` blocks for each statement, I used a single `try...catch` block. For the purposes of the examples, the five statements together constitute a unit of work that could be handled together, not segregated into separate blocks. Although I expected the exception on the call to `executeUpdate()`, the demonstration would have worked just as well regardless of which line of code threw the exception. This will not always be the case, however. In a real application or stored procedure, you may want to put the `getConnection()` call into a separate `try...catch` from the `executeUpdate()`. You may want to handle a failed connection very differently from a failed update. The point is to make a reasoned decision about which code can be put into the same `try` block.

At the opposite end of the spectrum, you should avoid `try...catch` blocks that encompass hundreds of lines of code. Again, find the block of code that logically goes together and put your `try...catch` around that code. Or, as we did above, let the exception be thrown from the method, and put the `try...catch` around the method call.

# Summary

Many introductory Java texts provide very little information about exceptions. Maybe a page or two about how to set up a `try...catch` block, maybe a few paragraphs on how to throw an exception or declare that an exception is thrown from a method. Even in this chapter, there are some topics we have left untouched. However, I think I've presented enough information to help you make your Java code more resistant to errors and better able to handle and recover from errors.

We looked at the hierarchy of exception classes, including the `Error`, `Exception`, and `RuntimeException` classes. Errors are generally exceptions that your program cannot recover from; whereas `Exception` and its subclasses are exceptions that your program should be able to handle gracefully. The meaning of *handle gracefully* will depend on the environment and the application. A Java stored procedure should always handle an exception by letting it propagate back to the caller. On the other hand, a Java application might handle an exception by displaying a dialog box to the user and allowing the user a chance to fix the problem.

If you need to catch and handle an exception, you would put a `try...catch` block into your code. Java code uses `try` blocks to enclose code that could throw an exception and `catch` blocks to catch a thrown exception. An exception causes the thread of execution to immediately halt, so we use `finally` blocks to guarantee the execution of code that must be run regardless of whether or not an exception was thrown or handled.

`RuntimeException` and its subclasses are known as unchecked exceptions; all other subclasses of `Exception` are checked exceptions. If we don't handle checked exceptions inside a method, the method must declare that it throws those checked exceptions it does not handle.

JDBC provides specific exception subclasses to represent errors in database programs. These classes are the `SQLException` and `SQLWarning` classes. Since these two classes represent all possible database errors, they must also carry additional information about the specific database error that occurred. That information is obtained through methods defined by these classes.

One of the last topics we looked at was an Oracle specific subclass of `SQLException`. This JDBC extension class provided additional information about the database errors we created. As part of its JDBC implementation, Oracle provides other extensions to JDBC. We'll look at those extensions in Chapter 7, *Oracle Extension Classes*.

# Oracle 9i Java Programming

# Oracle Extension Classes

Oracle provides several extensions to the JDBC standard by incorporating several new Java classes. These classes allow you to access and manipulate Oracle data types directly by providing lots of flexibility in data manipulations and performance improvements. These classes are defined in the following Java packages:

- ❑  `oracle.sql` – Defines classes for Oracle type extensions
- ❑  `oracle.jdbc.driver` – Defines classes for database access and updates in Oracle type formats
- ❑  `oracle.jdbc.pool` – Support for JDBC 2.0 features

The `oracle.sql` package provides support for the additional data types of Oracle such as `CLOB`, `BLOB`, and so on, while the `oracle.jdbc.driver` package provides support for data manipulation of all these data types through Java.

Additionally, Oracle now supports the JDBC 2.0 standard. The JDBC 2.0 API has many new added features such as database connection pooling, creating and registering data sources with JNDI based directory servers, and so on. Oracle provides support for these features by providing additional Java classes in `oracle.jdbc.pool` package.

In this chapter, we will study the various classes provided in these three packages, and their use in Java programs. We shall first discuss the benefits of using these extensions to the JDBC API, followed by an overview of the `oracle.sql` and `oracle.jdbc.driver` packages. Then, we will be looking in detail at the following extensions, together with example applications:

- ❑  The `STRUCT` and `ARRAY` data types
- ❑  The `CustomDatum` and `CustomDatumFactory` classes
- ❑  The `oracle.sql.REF` class
- ❑  The `BLOB` and `CLOB` classes
- ❑  The `oracle.sql.BFILE` class
- ❑  The `oracle.sql.CHAR` class

❑   The `oracle.sql.DATE` class

❑   The `oracle.sql.NUMBER` class

# Benefits of JDBC Extensions

JDBC extensions provide several benefits to a Java programmer. The new classes allow direct access to Oracle data types and manipulation of data in the native format. They also allow the programmer to access the Oracle data objects and supports, thus eliminating the need for conversion between Oracle SQL types and Java data types. Thus we eliminate any potential risk of loss of precision during conversion and increase the efficiency of data retrieval and storage. Thus, all the intermediate calculations in your programs may be done in native data formats. The result of the manipulation may later be converted into a Java data type by using the `java.sql` package.

Oracle 8i supports the use of structured data. For example, one can create a user-defined type containing a few attributes and store an object of this data type in a single column of the database table. The extension classes allow you complete control in manipulating such structured objects. These classes provide the following features:

❑   Mapping between the Oracle `object` data type and a Java class

❑   Mapping of object attributes from types defined in `oracle.sql` package to appropriate Java types

The mapping of the Oracle data objects may be done to either the provided `STRUCT` class or to a custom Java class. A custom Java class can be strongly type-checked and may be generated easily using the JPublisher utility.

The extension classes support the fully qualified schema names for Oracle data objects. Thus, if your schema named `USERNAME` contains an object called `Customer`, it may be referred by its fully qualified name, in other words, `USERNAME.Customer`. If the object belongs to the current schema, the schema name may be omitted. If the object name is complex (containing a dot) it must be quoted. For example, if you have an object called `Customer.Address` in the `USERNAME` schema, its fully qualified name is `USERNAME.'Customer.Address'`. The fully qualified schema names allow you to refer to the objects belonging to other schemas through your Java clients programs.

We will now study the JDBC packages defined in Oracle.

# Oracle JDBC Packages

To support the various features described in the preceding section, Oracle has introduced two Java packages containing several Java classes:

❑   `oracle.sql`

❑   `oracle.jdbc.driver`

There is one additional package called `oracle.jdbc2` used for supporting JDK 1.1.x. We will not cover the classes in this package, as these are mostly similar to the classes from other two packages. We will concentrate only on the mentioned two packages that directly support the Java 2 platform.

# The oracle.sql package

The oracle.sql package provides the wrapper classes for Oracle SQL data types. For SQL structured types such as objects and arrays, the wrapper classes provide conversion methods. All the classes in this package extend oracle.sql.Datum class. This superclass provides the common functionality required by all the subtypes. The various data type classes available in oracle.sql package and their mappings to the corresponding Oracle data types are listed here:

| Java Class | Oracle SQL type |
| --- | --- |
| oracle.sql.STRUCT | STRUCT (objects) |
| oracle.sql.REF | REF (object references) |
| oracle.sql.ARRAY | VARRAY or nested table (collections) |
| oracle.sql.BLOB | BLOB (binary large objects) |
| oracle.sql.CLOB | CLOB (character large objects) |
| oracle.sql.BFILE | BFILE (external files) |
| oracle.sql.CHAR | CHAR, VARCHAR2 |
| oracle.sql.DATE | DATE |
| oracle.sql.NUMBER | NUMBER |
| oracle.sql.RAW | RAW |
| oracle.sql.ROWID | ROWID (row identifiers) |

In addition to the above data type classes, the oracle.sql package defines the following support classes and interfaces:

| Java Class or Interface | Purpose |
| --- | --- |
| oracle.sql.ArrayDescriptor | Used for constructing oracle.sql.ARRAY objects |
| oracle.sql.StructDescriptor | Used for constructing oracle.sql.STRUCT objects |
| oracle.sql.CustomDatum <br> oracle.sql.CustomDatumFactory | Java classes that provide Oracle object support implement these interfaces |

# The oracle.jdbc.driver package

The oracle.jdbc.driver package defines several classes required for database access. The classes defined in this package are listed overleaf:

| Java Class or Interface | Purpose |
| --- | --- |
| OracleCallableStatement | Used for calling stored procedures |
| OracleConnection | Represents a connection to the database |
| OracleDatabaseMetaData | Represents the schema information of the database |
| OracleDriver | Used for calling stored procedures |
| OracleLog | Used for maintaining database log |
| OraclePreparedStatement | Used for SQL prepared (pre-compiled) statements |
| OracleResultSet | Represents the result set returned by the SQL query |
| OracleResultSetMetaData | Represents the meta data information of the result set |
| OracleStatement | Used for constructing SQL statements |
| OracleTypes | Defines various Oracle data types |
| StructMetaData | Represents the meta data information of the Oracle STRUCT object |

We will study some of the more important and useful classes in depth and understand their use in practical applications though several programming examples. For a more detailed look at the various classes of both oracle.sql and oracle.jdbc.driver packages, consult the Oracle JDBC *Developer's Guide and Reference*, which can be found as part of the Oracle documentation or at this URL: http://download-eu.oracle.com/otndoc/oracle9i/901_doc/java.901/a90211/toc.htm.

# The STRUCT and ARRAY Data Types

In this section we will discuss the STRUCT and ARRAY data types, and their use by illustration through programming examples. We will be using following classes in our application:

❑ oracle.sql.STRUCT

❑ oracle.sql.StructDescriptor

❑ oracle.sql.ARRAY

❑ oracle.sql.ArrayDescriptor

Each of these classes and methods used is described below. The purpose of each class and its few methods are described below.

### oracle.sql.STRUCT

Oracle allows you to store objects of composite data structures in the database. For example, you can define a structure for an employee record containing various fields such as name, ID, social security number, department, and so on. The objects of this type can be inserted in a single column of the database. The oracle.sql.STRUCT class allows easy insertion and retrieval of such structured objects. The object may be mapped to a generic JDBC type or a custom Java class.

The STRUCT class provides a wrapper on the Oracle STRUCT data type. This is a value class; once an object of this class is constructed, the user should not change its contents, in other words, it is immutable. The class provides several methods, including:

| Method | Purpose |
| --- | --- |
| public Object[] getAttributes()<br>    throws SQLException | Returns the structure attributes in an object array. |
| public OracleConnection getConnection() | Returns a reference to the current connection. |
| public String getSQLTypeName()<br>    throws SQLException | Returns a fully qualified name of the Oracle STRUCT data type that it represents. |

### oracle.sql.StructDescriptor

This class is used as the descriptor of Oracle's SQL structured object. Its main responsibility lies in understanding how to convert between various representations of a structure. Its methods include:

| Method | Purpose |
| --- | --- |
| public static StructDescriptor<br>    createDescriptor(<br>      String name,<br>      Connection conn) | Looks up the database for the name specified and returns the characteristics of this array as a StructDescriptor object. This is a static method. The con specifies the connection to the database. |
| public int getLength()<br>    throws SQLException | The number of fields in the current structured object. |
| public ResultSetMetaData<br>    getMetaData()<br>    throws SQLException | Returns the meta data information of the current object as a ResultSetMetaData object. This may be used for introspecting the structure. |
| public String getName()<br>    throws SQLException | Returns fully qualified type name of the structured data type that this object represents. |

### oracle.sql.ARRAY

Oracle allows you to store an array of elements in a single column of the database. For example, you can create an array of integers representing the marks scored by a student in various subjects. The object of this array type can be represented as a single column in the database table, in other words, the database stores this data type as a single column. The oracle.sql.ARRAY class allows the manipulation of such arrays. The ARRAY class represents the Oracle ARRAY data type. A few of the more important methods are mentioned overleaf:

| Method | Purpose |
|--------|---------|
| `public int getBaseType()`<br>  `throws SQLException` | Returns the type of element the array holds. |
| `public ResultSet getResultSet()`<br>  `throws SQLException` | Returns a result set containing the elements of the array designated by the current `Array` object. The result set contains two columns. The first column specifies the index into the array and the second column specifies the element value. |
| `public String getSQLTypeName()`<br>  `throws SQLException` | Returns the fully qualified SQL type name of the structured type that the current object represents. |
| `public Object getArray()`<br>  `throws SQLException` | Returns the contents of the SQL array designated by the current object as a Java array. |

### *oracle.sql.ArrayDescriptor*

This class represents the structure of Oracle's ARRAY data type. Some of its methods include:

| Method | Purpose |
|--------|---------|
| `public static ArrayDescriptor`<br>  `createDescriptor(String name,`<br>                 `Connection`<br>`conn)`<br>  `throws SQLException` | Looks up the database for the specified name and returns the characteristics of this array as an `ArrayDescriptor` object. This is a static method. The `con` specifies the connection to the database. |
| `public int getBaseType()`<br>  `throws SQLException` | Returns array element's type code. |
| `public String getName()`<br>  `throws SQLException` | Returns the name supplied when `ArrayDescriptor` was constructed. |

# Using the STRUCT Class

To illustrate the use of STRUCT and ARRAY classes in a Java application, first we will create a table containing a column of type STRUCT and then write a Java application to manipulate data in this table. The STRUCT object will hold an array of numbers. We will use Oracle's ARRAY class to access the elements of this array.

To understand how to use the STRUCT class through Java code, let's first create a table in the Oracle database containing a column having STRUCT object type, and insert few records in it:

```
SQL> create or replace type marks_type
  2     as varray(6) of number(5);
  3  /

Type created.
```

```
SQL> create or replace type student_info_type
  2     as object(student_ID number(5),
  3                 student_name varchar2(30),
  4                 student_marks marks_type
  5  );
  6  /

Type created.

SQL> create table student_table (
  2     student student_info_type
  3  );

Table created.

SQL> insert into student_table values(
  2  student_info_type(521, 'Smith', marks_type(87,98,89,78,94,86))
  3  );

1 row created.

SQL> commit;

Commit complete.
```

We create a new type called MARKS_TYPE as an array of numbers. This data type will be used for storing the marks obtained by a student in the various subjects. We create another data type called STUDENT_INFO_TYPE that consists of three fields; the student ID, the student name, and the MARKS_TYPE that holds the marks obtained by the student in various subjects. Finally, a table called STUDENT_TABLE is created to hold the records of various students in the class. The table consists of one single column of type STUDENT_INFO_TYPE. The SQL INSERT statement inserts a single record in the database. We will write Java code to retrieve this record and print it to the user console.

## Inserting and Retrieving STRUCT Data Types

Next, we will write a Java client program that inserts a record in the STUDENT_TABLE table and later retrieves all the records from the table. The program will print the records on the user console, demonstrating the retrieval and output of the oracle.sql.STRUCT type. Here is the code for the class, named TestSTRUCT:

```java
import java.sql.*;
import oracle.sql.*;
import oracle.jdbc.driver.*;
import java.math.*;

public class TestSTRUCT {
  public static void main(String args[]) {
    try {

      // load the jdbc driver
      Class.forName("oracle.jdbc.driver.OracleDriver");
```

```
// make a connection
Connection conn =
  DriverManager.getConnection("jdbc:oracle:oci8:@DATABASE",
                              "username", "password");

// create a statement
Statement stmt = conn.createStatement();

Object ObjArr[] = new Object[3];
Object MarksArr[] = {
  new java.math.BigDecimal(65), new java.math.BigDecimal(87),
  new java.math.BigDecimal(89), new java.math.BigDecimal(90),
  new java.math.BigDecimal(98), new java.math.BigDecimal(98)
};

ObjArr[0] = new java.math.BigDecimal(574);
ObjArr[1] = new String("Ford");
ObjArr[2] = new ARRAY(new ArrayDescriptor("USERNAME.MARKS_TYPE", conn),
                      conn, MarksArr);

// create new object of type oracle.sql.STRUCT
STRUCT struct =
  new STRUCT(new StructDescriptor("USERNAME.STUDENT_INFO_TYPE", conn),
             conn, ObjArr);

// prepare oracle.jdbc.driver.OraclePreparedStatement to
// insert the object into table
oracle.jdbc.driver.OraclePreparedStatement ps =
  (oracle.jdbc.driver.OraclePreparedStatement)
    conn.prepareStatement("insert into student_table values(?)");

// set the oracle.sql.STRUCT object to the first column
ps.setOracleObject(1, struct);

// execute the OraclePreparedStatement
ps.executeUpdate();

// create resultset from STUDENT_TABLE table
oracle.jdbc.driver.OracleResultSet rs =
  (oracle.jdbc.driver.OracleResultSet)
    stmt.executeQuery("select * from student_table");

// advance to first row
if (!rs.next()) {
  System.out.println("NO Records");
  System.exit(0);
}

// print the type name
struct = (oracle.sql.STRUCT) rs.getObject("student");
System.out.println("Type name: " + struct.getSQLTypeName() + "\n");
while (true) {
  System.out.println("-----------------------------------------------");
  Object Attributes[] = struct.getAttributes();
  System.out.println("Student ID: "
                     + (String) Attributes[0].toString());
  System.out.println("Student Name: "
                     + (String) Attributes[1].toString());
```

```
        BigDecimal[] items =
          (BigDecimal[]) ((oracle.sql.ARRAY) Attributes[2]).getArray();
        System.out.print("Marks : ");
        for (int i = 0; i < items.length; i++) {
          System.out.print(((BigDecimal) items[i]).intValue() + "  ");
        }
        System.out.println("\n");
        if (!rs.next()) {
          break;
        }
        struct = (oracle.sql.STRUCT) rs.getObject("student");
      }
      System.out.println("------------------------------------------------");
      rs.close();
      stmt.close();
      conn.close();
    } catch (Exception e) {
      e.printStackTrace();
    }
  }
}
```

When you compile and run this code, you should see the following output:

```
> java TestSTRUCT
Type name: USERNAME.STUDENT_INFO_TYPE

------------------------------------------------
Student ID: 521
Student Name: Smith
Marks : 87  98  89  78  94  86

------------------------------------------------
Student ID: 574
Student Name: Ford
Marks : 65  87  89  90  98  98

------------------------------------------------
```

This shows that our example application has indeed inserted another row into the STUDENT_TABLE table, and then retrieved the entire contents of it.

Note that if you receive an error like this:

```
> java TestSTRUCT
java.sql.SQLException: Non supported character set: oracle-character-set-178
  at oracle.gss.util.NLSError.throwSQLException(NLSError.java:46)
  at
oracle.sql.CharacterSetUnknown.failCharsetUnknown(CharacterSetFactoryThin.java:171
)
  at oracle.sql.CharacterSetUnknown.convert(CharacterSetFactoryThin.java:1
35)
```

```
    at oracle.sql.CHAR.<init>(CHAR.java:133)
    at oracle.sql.CHAR.<init>(CHAR.java:157)
    at oracle.jdbc.oracore.OracleTypeCHAR.toDatum(OracleTypeCHAR.java:145)
    at oracle.sql.StructDescriptor.toOracleArray(StructDescriptor.java:438)
    at oracle.sql.StructDescriptor.toArray(StructDescriptor.java:839)
    at oracle.sql.STRUCT.<init>(STRUCT.java:121)
    at TestSTRUCT.main(TestSTRUCT.java:35)
```

then it means that the character set required cannot be found. What you need to do is to make sure that the `nls_charset12.zip` file found in `$ORACLE_HOME\jdbc\lib`, is added to your classpath. The character set is found in this file.

Let's now take a look at how it works.

## The Mechanics

The console-based application first loads the Oracle JDBC driver and makes a connection to the database:

```
// load the jdbc driver
Class.forName("oracle.jdbc.driver.OracleDriver");

// make a connection
Connection conn =
  DriverManager.getConnection("jdbc:oracle:oci8:@DATABASE",
                              "username", "password");
```

Once a connection is successfully established, the program constructs a record of type `student_info_type` and inserts it in the table. To construct the record, we need to create an instance of `oracle.sql.STRUCT` class. This is done using the following constructor:

```
// create new object of type oracle.sql.STRUCT
STRUCT struct =
  new STRUCT(new StructDescriptor("USERNAME.STUDENT_INFO_TYPE", conn),
             conn, ObjArr);
```

The first parameter to the constructor is an instance of the `StructDescriptor` class. The `StructDescriptor` class requires the pre-defined data type `student_info_type` as the first parameter, and the connection object as the second parameter.

The second parameter to the `StructDescriptor` constructor is the connection object and the third parameter is of type `ObjArr` where each element of the array will hold the corresponding field value of the structure. Thus, we need to construct this array of field value objects before we call the above constructor. The field value array is declared using the following statement:

```
Object ObjArr[] = new Object[3];
```

Note that we allocate an array of three objects, since our structure has three fields. The first two fields of the array are initialized using the following statements:

```
ObjArr[0] = new java.math.BigDecimal(574);
ObjArr[1] = new String("Ford");
```

The third parameter is initialized thus:

```
ObjArr[2] = new ARRAY(new ArrayDescriptor("USERNAME.MARKS_TYPE", conn),
                      conn, MarksArr);
```

We construct an `oracle.sql.ARRAY` object in the above statement. The first parameter to the constructor is an instance of the `ArrayDescriptor` class. The `ArrayDescriptor` class constructor takes the Oracle pre-defined data type as the first parameter and the connection object as the second parameter. The third parameter is an array specifying the values for the individual elements of the `ARRAY`:

```
Object MarksArr[] = {
  new java.math.BigDecimal(65), new java.math.BigDecimal(87),
  new java.math.BigDecimal(89), new java.math.BigDecimal(90),
  new java.math.BigDecimal(98), new java.math.BigDecimal(98)
};
```

This completes our `STRUCT` creation process. Likewise, to insert a record of type `STRUCT` in the database, you will need to create an instance of `STRUCT` class and initialize all the required fields as shown above.

We now create a `PreparedStatement` object for inserting the record in the database table:

```
// prepare oracle.jdbc.driver.OraclePreparedStatement to
// insert the object into table
oracle.jdbc.driver.OraclePreparedStatement ps =
  (oracle.jdbc.driver.OraclePreparedStatement)
    conn.prepareStatement("insert into student_table values(?)");
```

The prepared statement requires one parameter, and is set by calling the `setOracleObject()` method on the `PreparedStatement` object:

```
// set the oracle.sql.STRUCT object to the first column
ps.setOracleObject(1, struct);
```

The first parameter to the method specifies the parameter number and the second parameter is the previously constructed `struct` object.

The record is inserted into the table by calling the `executeUpdate()` method:

```
// execute the OraclePreparedStatement
ps.executeUpdate();
```

In the previous section, we inserted a record in the `STUDENT_TABLE` table. We will now write code to retrieve all the records from the table and print it on the user console. The program creates a `Statement` object and uses a SQL `SELECT` statement to create a result set as shown below:

```
// create a statement
Statement stmt = conn.createStatement();
    .
    .
    .
// create resultset from STUDENT_TABLE table
oracle.jdbc.driver.OracleResultSet rs =
  (oracle.jdbc.driver.OracleResultSet)
    stmt.executeQuery("select * from student_table");
```

Note that we typecast the result set to the `OracleResultSet` type. The cursor is set to the first record by calling the `next()` method on the result set object. This is contained within an `if` block to check that there are some records in the table:

```
if (!rs.next()) {
  System.out.println("NO Records");
  System.exit(0);
}
```

From the result set, we obtain the data for the column having name `student` by calling the `getObject()` method on the result set.

```
struct = (oracle.sql.STRUCT) rs.getObject("student");
```

The result set contains only one column. We could have retrieved the column value by specifying the column number in the `getObject()` method. The `getObject()` method returns the Java data type `Object` and must be typecast to the `STRUCT` type.

The program prints the SQL type name for the structured data by calling `getSQLTypeName()` method on the retrieved `STRUCT` object:

```
System.out.println("Type name: " + struct.getSQLTypeName() + "\n");
```

The program now iterates through all the records using a `while` loop and prints the fields of each `STRUCT` object retrieved:

```
while (true) {
    .
    .
    .
  }
  System.out.println("\n");
  if (!rs.next()) {
    break;
  }
  struct = (oracle.sql.STRUCT) rs.getObject("student");
}
```

For each STRUCT object, the attributes are retrieved by calling the getAttributes() method:

```
Object Attributes[] = struct.getAttributes();
```

This returns an array of objects holding the values of the various fields of the structure. The first two fields are printed on the user console by using the following statements:

```
System.out.println("Student ID: "
                    + (String) Attributes[0].toString());
System.out.println("Student Name: "
                    + (String) Attributes[1].toString());
```

The third field, of type Array, is retrieved by calling the getArray() method, as shown below:

```
BigDecimal[] items =
   (BigDecimal[]) ((oracle.sql.ARRAY) Attributes[2]).getArray();
```

This returns an array of BigDecimal type objects. Each element of this array is printed:

```
System.out.print("Marks : ");
for (int i = 0; i < items.length; i++) {
   System.out.print(((BigDecimal) items[i]).intValue() + "   ");
}
```

Finally, we close all our resources, namely our result set, statement and connection objects, and catch any exceptions that might have been raised:

```
      rs.close();
      stmt.close();
      conn.close();
   } catch (Exception e) {
      e.printStackTrace();
   }
  }
 }
```

# The CustomDatum Interface

An Oracle structure may be mapped to a Custom Java class. By doing so, you will be able to provide validations on the individual fields of the structure while initializing its various fields. For this, Oracle has defined CustomDatum and CustomDatumFactory interfaces. In this section, we will create a Java class to map the student structure defined in the last program. We will create an object of this class and insert the record in the STUDENT_TABLE table. We will also develop code to read the table using the newly created class and print all the records in the table.

First of all, here is the code for the Student class:

```java
import java.math.BigDecimal;
import java.sql.SQLException;
import oracle.jdbc.driver.OracleConnection;
import oracle.sql.*;

public class Student implements CustomDatum, CustomDatumFactory {

  // fields
  public BigDecimal StudentID;
  public String StudentName;
  public ARRAY Marks;

  static final Student StudentFactory = new Student(null, null, null);

  public static CustomDatumFactory getFactory() {
    return StudentFactory;
  }

  public Student() {}

  // constructor
  public Student(BigDecimal StudentID, String StudentName, ARRAY Marks) {
    this.StudentID = StudentID;
    this.StudentName = StudentName;
    this.Marks = Marks;
  }

  // CustomDatum interface
  public Datum toDatum(OracleConnection conn) throws SQLException {
    StructDescriptor sd =
      StructDescriptor.createDescriptor("USERNAME.STUDENT_INFO_TYPE", conn);

    Object[] Attributes = {
      StudentID, StudentName, Marks
    };
    return new STRUCT(sd, conn, Attributes);
  }

  // CustomDatumFactory interface
  public CustomDatum create(Datum d, int sqlType) throws SQLException {
    if (d == null) {
      return null;
    }
    Object[] Attributes = ((STRUCT) d).getAttributes();
    return new Student((BigDecimal) Attributes[0], (String) Attributes[1],
                       (ARRAY) Attributes[2]);
  }
}
```

And now we have the code for a console-based application that uses the above Student class to insert a Student record in the table, and then retrieve and print all the records it finds in the STUDENT_TABLE table. This class is called TestCustomClassStudent:

```java
import java.sql.*;
import oracle.jdbc.driver.*;
import oracle.sql.*;
import java.math.BigDecimal;

public class TestCustomClassStudent {
  public static void main(String args[]) throws Exception {

    // connection
    DriverManager.registerDriver(new oracle.jdbc.driver.OracleDriver());
    OracleConnection conn = (OracleConnection)
      DriverManager.getConnection("jdbc:oracle:oci8:@DATABASE",
                                  "username", "password");

    Object objArr[] = {
      new java.math.BigDecimal(65), new java.math.BigDecimal(87),
      new java.math.BigDecimal(89), new java.math.BigDecimal(90),
      new java.math.BigDecimal(98), new java.math.BigDecimal(98)
    };

    ARRAY Marks = new ARRAY(new ArrayDescriptor("MARKS_TYPE", conn), conn,
                            objArr);

    // create a CustomDatum object
    Student StudentObj = new Student(new BigDecimal("635"), "Mike", Marks);

    // insert the CustomDatum object
    PreparedStatement pstmt =
      conn.prepareStatement("insert into student_table values (?)");

    pstmt.setObject(1, StudentObj, OracleTypes.STRUCT);
    pstmt.executeQuery();
    pstmt.close();

    // select records
    Statement stmt = conn.createStatement();
    OracleResultSet rs =
      (OracleResultSet) stmt.executeQuery("select * from student_table");

    while (rs.next()) {
      System.out.println("-------------------------------------------------");
      StudentObj = (Student) rs.getCustomDatum(1, Student.getFactory());
      System.out.println("Student ID: " + StudentObj.StudentID);
      System.out.println("Student Name: " + StudentObj.StudentName);
      BigDecimal[] StudentMarks =
        (BigDecimal[]) StudentObj.Marks.getArray();
      System.out.print("Marks :");
      for (int i = 0; i < StudentMarks.length; i++) {
        System.out.print(((BigDecimal) StudentMarks[i]).floatValue()
                         + "  ");
      }
      System.out.println("\n");
    }
```

**223**

```
        System.out.println("--------------------------------------------------");
        rs.close();
        stmt.close();

        if (conn != null) {
          conn.close();
        }
      }
    }
```

Compiling and running this code should yield the following:

```
> java TestCustomClassStudent
--------------------------------------------------
Student ID: 521
Student Name: Smith
Marks :87.0  98.0  89.0  78.0  94.0  86.0


--------------------------------------------------
Student ID: 574
Student Name: Ford
Marks :65.0  87.0  89.0  90.0  98.0  98.0


--------------------------------------------------
Student ID: 635
Student Name: Mike
Marks :65.0  87.0  89.0  90.0  98.0  98.0


--------------------------------------------------
```

## How It Works

Now we are going to focus on how the entire application involving the two classes work, starting with the Student class.

Firstly, the Student class implements CustomDatum and CustomDatumFactory interfaces:

```
public class Student implements CustomDatum, CustomDatumFactory {
```

The class defines an object of type Student called StudentFactory using the following declaration:

```
static final Student StudentFactory = new Student(null, null, null);
```

The object is initialized to an instance of the Student object. The Student object itself is constructed by calling its constructor that takes three parameters. The constructor is defined later. All the three fields are set to null in this case. The Student variable is declared as a constant using the final keyword and it is declared with a static modifier so that it may be accessed without creating an instance of the class. This variable is required by the getFactory() method defined below. A call to the getFactory() method itself is required while retrieving Student records. This is shown later.

```
public static CustomDatumFactory getFactory() {
  return StudentFactory;
}
```

The getFactory() method simply returns the Student object initialized above.

We now write the constructor for the Student class, which takes three parameters:

```
// constructor
public Student(BigDecimal StudentID, String StudentName, ARRAY Marks) {
  this.StudentID = StudentID;
  this.StudentName = StudentName;
  this.Marks = Marks;
}
```

This is where you can provide validations on the individual fields. Although the above constructor does not do any validations, the desired validations can be easily added by any Java programmer. This is the major advantage of using CustomDatum interface to represent Oracle STRUCT object.

Next, we need to implement the toDatum() method of the CustomDatum interface. The implementation is shown here:

```
// CustomDatum interface
public Datum toDatum(OracleConnection conn) throws SQLException {
  StructDescriptor sd =
    StructDescriptor.createDescriptor("USERNAME.STUDENT_INFO_TYPE", conn);

  Object[] Attributes = {
    StudentID, StudentName, Marks
  };
  return new STRUCT(sd, conn, Attributes);
}
```

The toDatum() method transforms the data into the oracle.sql.* representation. The method constructs a descriptor using the createDescriptor() method that takes the SQL data type (structure type) as the first parameter, and the connection object as the second parameter. The Attributes array specifies the three fields of the structure. Finally, a new STRUCT object is created by calling its constructor. The STRUCT object is returned to the caller.

We need to implement one more method of CustomDatumFactory interface. The method is called create() and its definition is shown below:

```
// CustomDatumFactory interface
public CustomDatum create(Datum d, int sqlType) throws SQLException {
  if (d == null) {
    return null;
  }
  Object[] Attributes = ((STRUCT) d).getAttributes();
  return new Student((BigDecimal) Attributes[0], (String) Attributes[1],
                     (ARRAY) Attributes[2]);
}
```

The create() method retrieves the structure attributes by calling the getAttributes() method. A Student object is then constructed using these attribute values and returned to the caller.

Most of the code for the TestCustomClassStudent class is similar to the application we looked at earlier for the STRUCT class and is thus not going to be explained again here. Only the important lines where the code is different will be exposed here.

The following program statement creates a Student object. In the earlier example application, we constructed a STRUCT object on which custom validations were not possible:

```
// create a CustomDatum object
Student StudentObj = new Student(new BigDecimal("635"), "Mike", Marks);
```

After constructing the object, it can be added to the database using the following code segment:

```
// insert the CustomDatum object
PreparedStatement pstmt =
  conn.prepareStatement("insert into student_table values (?)");

pstmt.setObject(1, StudentObj, OracleTypes.STRUCT);
pstmt.executeQuery();
pstmt.close();
```

Note that we now pass the constructed Student object in the parameter to the setObject method.

The Student records can be retrieved by executing the appropriate SQL SELECT statement, similar to our earlier application. Once a result set is constructed, the Student record is retrieved from the first column of the result set:

```
StudentObj = (Student) rs.getCustomDatum(1, Student.getFactory());
```

The second parameter to the getCustomDatum() method requires a Student object having null fields. This is where we use the getFactory() static method defined in the Student class. The method returns a Student object. The members of the Student class can then be printed:

```
System.out.println("Student ID: " + StudentObj.StudentID);
System.out.println("Student Name: " + StudentObj.StudentName);
```

# The oracle.sql.REF class

This is a generic class that supports Oracle object references. An object reference is a pointer to an Oracle object type. This class has methods to retrieve and pass object references. The reference data type may be used for accessing Oracle cursors. A few of the class' methods are given opposite:

| Method | Purpose |
|---|---|
| `public String getBaseTypeName()`<br>  `throws SQLException` | Gets the fully qualified SQL structured type name of the item referenced. |
| `public STRUCT getSTRUCT()`<br>  `throws SQLException` | Returns the structure of the referenced object as `oracle.sql.STRUCT`. |
| `public StructDescriptor`<br>  `getDescriptor()`<br>    `throws SQLException` | Returns the type descriptor of the `STRUCT` type that the referenced object points to, as `StructDescriptor`. |
| `public Object getValue()`<br>  `throws SQLException` | Gets the referenced object. |
| `public void setValue(Object value)`<br>  `throws SQLException` | Sets the `REF` value. |

To demonstrate the use of this class, we will develop a small application to illustrate the use of the REF class.

First, we will create a type, then create a database table for storing order details of our customers, and finally insert a couple of rows:

```
SQL> create or replace type item_array_type as varray(20) of number(5);
  2  /

Type created.

SQL> create or replace type order_details_type
  2      as object(order_ID number(5),
  3              customer_ID number(5),
  4              customer_name varchar2(30),
  5              list_of_items item_array_type,
  6              date_of_order date);
  7  /

Type created.

SQL> create table orders of order_details_type;

Table created.

SQL> insert into orders values(
  2  101, 521, 'Smith',item_array_type(432,446,6545,7654,4434),
  3  '8-NOV-2001');

1 row created.

SQL> insert into orders values(
  2  102, 589, 'Mike',item_array_type(656,6545,446,4434),
  3  '11-NOV-2001');

1 row created.

SQL> commit;

Commit complete.
```

**227**

The SQL code first creates a type called `item_array_type` as an array of numbers. Next, it creates another type called `order_details_type` as an Oracle object containing order ID, customer ID, customer name, list of ordered items, and order date as fields. A table is then created to store records of this `order_details_type`. Finally, two records are inserted in the table by calling SQL `INSERT` statements.

# Getting REF Object Values

We will now write a Java console-based application to access the records from the `ORDERS` table we have just created. Here is the full listing of the `TestREF` class:

```
import java.sql.*;
import java.math.BigDecimal;
import oracle.sql.*;
import oracle.jdbc.driver.*;

public class TestREF {
  public static void main(String args[]) throws Exception {

    // register the Oracle JDBC driver
    DriverManager.registerDriver(new oracle.jdbc.driver.OracleDriver());
    Connection conn = DriverManager.getConnection(
                "jdbc:oracle:oci8:@DATABASE", "username", "password");

    // create a Statement
    Statement stmt = conn.createStatement();

    ResultSet rs = stmt.executeQuery(
      "select ref (order_details_type) from orders order_details_type");
    REF ref;
    while (rs.next()) {

      // retrieve the ref object
      ref = (REF) rs.getObject(1);

      // retrieve the object value that the ref points to in the
      // object table
      STRUCT order = (STRUCT) ref.getValue();
      Object Attributes[] = order.getAttributes();
      System.out.println("--------------------------------------");
      System.out.println("Order ID: "
                      + ((BigDecimal) Attributes[0]).intValue());
      System.out.println("Customer ID: "
                      + ((BigDecimal) Attributes[1]).intValue());
      System.out.println("Customer Name: " + (String) Attributes[2]);
      BigDecimal[] items =
        (BigDecimal[]) ((oracle.sql.ARRAY) Attributes[3]).getArray();
      System.out.println("Items :");
      for (int i = 0; i < items.length; i++) {
        System.out.println("\t" + ((BigDecimal) items[i]).intValue());
      }
      System.out.println("Date of Order: "
                      + (java.sql.Timestamp) Attributes[4]);
```

```
      }
      System.out.println("----------------------------------------");
      rs.close();
      stmt.close();
      conn.close();
   }
}
```

Compiling and running the code gives the following output:

```
> java TestREF
----------------------------------------
Order ID: 101
Customer ID: 521
Customer Name: Smith
Items :
        432
        446
        6545
        7654
        4434
Date of Order: 2001-11-08 00:00:00.0
----------------------------------------
Order ID: 102
Customer ID: 589
Customer Name: Mike
Items :
        656
        6545
        446
        4434
Date of Order: 2001-11-11 00:00:00.0
----------------------------------------
```

First, the program makes a database connection using code similar to the earlier examples. It then creates a `Statement` object and creates a result set by executing the SQL statement as shown in the code below:

```
// create a Statement
Statement stmt = conn.createStatement();

ResultSet rs = stmt.executeQuery(
  "select ref (order_details_type) from orders order_details_type");
```

From the result set, we will retrieve the Oracle object in each row of it by using the following code segment:

```
REF ref;
while (rs.next()) {

  // retrieve the ref object
  ref = (REF) rs.getObject(1);
```

The getObject() method retrieves the first column and assigns it to Oracle REF type. We call the getValue() method on the REF object to recover the structure represented by the Oracle object:

```
STRUCT order = (STRUCT) ref.getValue();
```

Alternatively, you may call the getSTRUCT() method on the REF object to retrieve the structure object. Note that the REF variable simply points to an object reference. The type of object must be known to you to retrieve the object members.

Once a structure object is obtained, you can retrieve its attributes by calling its getAttributes() method:

```
Object Attributes[] = order.getAttributes();
```

After retrieving the structure attributes, the attribute values can be printed on the user console using code similar to what we have already seen.

# The BLOB and CLOB Classes

The Oracle BLOB data type allows you to store a binary large object in a database column. The oracle.sql.BLOB class allows you to manipulate such BLOB objects through your Java program code.

The Oracle data type BLOB represents a large unstructured binary data item. The BLOB class represents the Oracle BLOB data type. Some of the methods of the BLOB class are as follows:

| Method | Purpose |
|---|---|
| public OutputStream<br>  getBinaryOutputStream()<br>    throws SQLException | Returns the output stream for writing data to the BLOB. |
| public byte[] getBytes(long pos,<br>                        int<br>length)<br>  throws SQLException | Returns the BLOB contents from the position specified by pos parameter and the number of bytes equal to the length parameter. |
| public int putBytes(long pos,<br>                     byte bytes[])<br>  throws SQLException | Puts data from the bytes array to the BLOB at the position specified by the pos parameter. |

The Oracle data type CLOB represents a large fixed-width character data item. The CLOB class supports the Oracle CLOB data type. The CLOB data type in Oracle represents a character-based large object. This is similar to the BLOB data type except that the data now represents characters rather than binary data. The oracle.sql.CLOB class allows the manipulation of such data through Java program code. To illustrate the use of the CLOB class, we will create a table containing the CLOB data type, insert a record into it and develop Java code that retrieves this record. Here are some of the methods available in this class:

| Method | Purpose |
|--------|---------|
| `public InputStream getAsciiStream()`<br>  `throws SQLException` | Returns the CLOB value as a stream of ASCII bytes. |
| `public Reader getCharacterStream()`<br>  `throws SQLException` | Returns the CLOB contents as a Unicode stream. |
| `public int getChars(long pos,`<br>              `int length,`<br>              `char buffer[])`<br>  `throws SQLException` | Returns the copy of the substring of the CLOB in buffer. The pos parameter specifies the first character of the substring to be extracted and length specifies the number of characters to be copied. |
| `public String getSubString(long pos,`<br>              `int length)`<br>  `throws SQLException` | Returns a copy of the specified substring. pos indicates the starting position and length indicates the length of the substring. |
| `public int putString(long pos,`<br>              `String str)`<br>  `throws SQLException` | Writes a Java string str at the position specified by pos in the CLOB. |

To illustrate the use of the BLOB and CLOB classes in program code, we will first create a database table having columns of BLOB and CLOB data. The table contains three fields, indicating the employee ID, the employee picture, and the resume of the person. The picture will be stored as a BLOB and the resume will be stored as a CLOB. The program will ask for the external files and load them into the database. Later, we will retrieve these fields from the database and store them to the external files.

The following SQL code creates a table called LOB_TEST, which has three columns. The first one is of type number, the second one is of type BLOB, and the third one is of type CLOB.

```
SQL> create table lob_test (
  2    id number(6),
  3    image blob, resume clob
  4  )
  5  /

Table created.
```

# Manipulating BLOBs and CLOBs

To illustrate using BLOB and CLOB data types, we will look at an application that reads in an ID, loads in a file to be stored as a BLOB and a file to be stored as a CLOB, and then saves them in the appropriate column in our LOB_TEST table.

**231**

The full listing for the `BlobClobAppl` class is as follows:

```java
import java.io.*;
import java.sql.*;
import oracle.jdbc.driver.*;
import oracle.sql.*;

public class BlobClobAppl {
  public static void main(String args[]) {

    String fileName1 = null;
    String fileName2 = null;
    int id = 0;
    try {

      // initailize BufferedReader to read from standard input
      BufferedReader br =
        new BufferedReader(new InputStreamReader(System.in));

      System.out.println("Load the BLOB & CLOB fields from external file");
      System.out.println("-------------------------------------");
      System.out.print("Enter id : ");
      id = Integer.parseInt(br.readLine());
      System.out.print("Enter File Name for BLOB : ");
      fileName1 = br.readLine();
      System.out.print("Enter File Name for CLOB : ");
      fileName2 = br.readLine();
      if (load(id, fileName1, fileName2) == -1) {
        System.out.println("Error in loading files");
      } else {
        System.out.println("Successful...");
      }

      System.out.println("");

      System.out.println("Save the BLOB & CLOB fields to external file");
      System.out.println("-----------------------------------");
      System.out.print("Enter id : ");
      id = Integer.parseInt(br.readLine());
      System.out.print("Enter File Name for BLOB : ");
      fileName1 = br.readLine();
      System.out.print("Enter File Name for CLOB : ");
      fileName2 = br.readLine();

      // call save() to store the contents of BLOB field to external file
      if (save(id, fileName1, fileName2) == -1) {
        System.out.println("Error in copying to files");
      } else {
        System.out.println("Successful...");
      }
    } catch (Exception e) {
      e.printStackTrace();
    }
  }

  // this method stores contents of the BLOB & CLOB fields to external files
  private static int save(int id, String fileName1, String fileName2) {
    int retCode = 0;
```

```
try {

    // load OracleDriver class
    Class.forName("oracle.jdbc.driver.OracleDriver");

    // get connection with the database using oci8 drivers
    Connection conn = DriverManager.getConnection(
                    "jdbc:oracle:oci8:@DATABASE", "uesrname", "password");

    // set autocommit off
    conn.setAutoCommit(false);

    String sql = "select image, resume from lob_test where id = ?";

    // create OraclePreparedStatement on connenction with the
    // sql given above
    OraclePreparedStatement ops =
      (OraclePreparedStatement) conn.prepareStatement(sql);

    ops.setInt(1, id);

    // execute the query
    OracleResultSet ors = (OracleResultSet) ops.executeQuery();

    // traverse through all selected records
    while (ors.next()) {

        // get the BLOB object from result
        BLOB blob = ors.getBLOB(1);

        // get InputStream on BLOB to read data
        InputStream is = blob.getBinaryStream();

        // create the FileOutputStream to write data in BLOB field
        FileOutputStream os = new FileOutputStream(fileName1);

        // get the buffer size of BLOB to read data
        int size = blob.getBufferSize();
        byte buffer1[] = new byte[size];

        // variable to count no. of bytes written
        long wcount = 0;
        int length;

        // read the data from BLOB field and store it to external file
        while ((length = is.read(buffer1, 0, size)) != -1) {
            wcount += length;
            os.write(buffer1, 0, length);
        }
        System.out.println(wcount + " bytes written to file");

        // get the CLOB object from result
        CLOB clob = ors.getCLOB(2);

        // get Reader on CLOB to read data
        Reader rd = clob.getCharacterStream();
```

```
      // create the BufferedWriter to write data in CLOB field
      BufferedWriter wr = new BufferedWriter(new OutputStreamWriter(
                         new FileOutputStream(fileName2)));

      // get the buffer size of CLOB to read data
      size = clob.getBufferSize();
      char buffer2[] = new char[size];
      wcount = 0;

      // read the data from CLOB field and store it to external file
      while ((length = rd.read(buffer2, 0, size)) != -1) {
        wcount += length;
        wr.write(buffer2, 0, length);
      }
      System.out.println(wcount + " bytes written to file");

      // close all input and output streams
      is.close();
      os.close();
      rd.close();
      wr.close();

    }

    // close OracleResultSet and OraclePreparedStatement
    ors.close();
    ops.close();
  } catch (Exception e) {

    // return -1 if there was an exception
    retCode = -1;
    e.printStackTrace();
  } finally {
    return retCode;
  }
}

// this method is used to load the contents BLOB field with external file
private static int load(int id, String fileName1, String fileName2) {
  int retCode = 0;

  try {

    // load OracleDriver class
    Class.forName("oracle.jdbc.driver.OracleDriver");

    // get connction with the database using oci8 drivers
    Connection conn = DriverManager.getConnection(
                "jdbc:oracle:oci8:@DATABASE", "username", "password");

    // set autocommit off
    conn.setAutoCommit(false);

    // create FileInputStream to read data
    FileInputStream is = new FileInputStream(fileName1);

    // PL/SQL code for INSERT and UPDATE statement
    String sql1 = "begin " + "  insert into lob_test(id, image) "
```

```
                  + "  values (?,empty_blob()) "
                  + "  return image into ?; " + "end;";
// create OracleCallableStatement using above code
OracleCallableStatement ocs1 =
  (OracleCallableStatement) conn.prepareCall(sql1);

// register in and out parameters
ocs1.setInt(1, id);
ocs1.registerOutParameter(2, OracleTypes.BLOB);

// execute the PL/SQL code
ocs1.executeUpdate();
BLOB blob = ocs1.getBLOB(2);

// create OutputStream to write data in BLOB field
OutputStream os = blob.getBinaryOutputStream();

// get Buffer size
int size = blob.getBufferSize();
byte buffer1[] = new byte[size];
int length;

// variable to count no. of bytes written
long wcount = 0;

// copy contents of the external file to BLOB field
while ((length = is.read(buffer1, 0, size)) != -1) {
  wcount += length;
  os.write(buffer1, 0, length);
}
System.out.println(wcount + " bytes written to BLOB field");

BufferedReader br =
  new BufferedReader(new InputStreamReader(
                     new FileInputStream(fileName2)));
String sql2 = "begin "
             + "  update lob_test set resume = empty_clob() "
             + "  where id = ? " + "  return resume into ?; "
             + "end;";

OracleCallableStatement ocs2 =
  (OracleCallableStatement) conn.prepareCall(sql2);
ocs2.setInt(1, id);
ocs2.registerOutParameter(2, OracleTypes.CLOB);
ocs2.executeUpdate();
CLOB clob = ocs2.getCLOB(2);

// create Writer to write data in CLOB field
Writer wr = clob.getCharacterOutputStream();
size = clob.getBufferSize();
char buffer2[] = new char[size];
wcount = 0;

// copy contents of the external file to CLOB field
while ((length = br.read(buffer2, 0, size)) != -1) {
  wcount += length;
  wr.write(buffer2, 0, length);
```

```
    }
    System.out.println(wcount + " bytes written to CLOB field");

    // close all open connections and streams
    is.close();
    os.close();
    br.close();
    wr.close();
    ocs1.close();
    ocs2.close();
    conn.commit();

} catch (Exception e) {

    // return -1 if an Exception is generated
    retCode = -1;
    e.printStackTrace();
} finally {
    return retCode;
}
    }
}
```

When you compile and run the script, you will be prompted for the ID and file names for the BLOB and CLOB to load. Then, in a similar style, you are prompted for the ID and file names to save the BLOB and CLOB to. You should see output similar to the following:

```
> java BlobClobAppl
Load the BLOB & CLOB fields from external file
------------------------------------
Enter id : 9
Enter File Name for BLOB : c:\image.jpg
Enter File Name for CLOB : c:\resume.doc
14966 bytes written to BLOB field
31744 bytes written to CLOB field
Successful...

Save the BLOB & CLOB fields to external file
----------------------------------
Enter id : 9
Enter File Name for BLOB : c:\image_bkup.jpg
Enter File Name for CLOB : c:\resume_bkup.jpg
14966 bytes written to file
31744 bytes written to file
Successful...
```

## The Workings

The main method first opens a BufferedReader on the input stream (System.in) for reading from the keyboard:

```
BufferedReader br =
    new BufferedReader(new InputStreamReader(System.in));
```

The program requests the ID field from the user and converts it to an integer using the following code segment:

```
System.out.print("Enter id : ");
id = Integer.parseInt(br.readLine());
```

Next, we read in the name of the file to be stored as a BLOB:

```
System.out.print("Enter File Name for BLOB : ");
fileName1 = br.readLine();
```

Similarly, the name of the file to be stored as a CLOB is read in from the user:

```
System.out.print("Enter File Name for CLOB : ");
fileName2 = br.readLine();
```

The program then calls the load() method contained in an if block to store the data in the table:

```
if (load(id, fileName1, fileName2) == -1) {
  System.out.println("Error in loading files");
} else {
  System.out.println("Successful...");
}
```

The load() method first obtains a database connection by using the code similar to earlier examples. Then, a FileInputStream is opened on the first file name. This file contains binary data, so we need an InputStream class:

```
// create FileInputStream to read data
FileInputStream is = new FileInputStream(fileName1);
```

Then we create a SQL statement for inserting the BLOB into the database:

```
// PL/SQL code for INSERT and UPDATE statement
String sql1 = "begin " + "  insert into lob_test(id, image) "
            + "  values (?,empty_blob()) "
            + "  return image into ?; " + "end;";
```

A CallableStatement is created for running the above SQL. The first is set to the integer type and the second parameter is of type BLOB. The second parameter is an out parameter that returns the locator for the BLOB:

```
// create OracleCallableStatement using above code
OracleCallableStatement ocs1 =
  (OracleCallableStatement) conn.prepareCall(sql1);

// register in and out parameters
ocs1.setInt(1, id);
ocs1.registerOutParameter(2, OracleTypes.BLOB);
```

The statement is executed by calling the `executeUpdate()` method and the output parameter is retrieved by calling the `getBLOB()` method:

```
// execute the PL/SQL code
ocs1.executeUpdate();
BLOB blob = ocs1.getBLOB(2);
```

We will now create an output stream on the obtained BLOB object:

```
// create OutputStream to write data in BLOB field
OutputStream os = blob.getBinaryOutputStream();
```

We get the buffer size from the BLOB to allocate the buffer:

```
// get Buffer size
int size = blob.getBufferSize();
byte buffer1[] = new byte[size];
```

The contents of the input files are then written to the BLOB using the following `while` loop:

```
int length;

// variable to count no. of bytes written
long wcount = 0;

// copy contents of the external file to BLOB field
while ((length = is.read(buffer1, 0, size)) != -1) {
  wcount += length;
  os.write(buffer1, 0, length);
}
```

Writing the CLOB is similar to writing the BLOB, except that we use the `Reader` class instead of the `InputStream` class.

The code for reading CLOBs and BLOBs from the table and storing them in external files is similar to the code described above. We obtain the object locator for these data types as described above and use output streams to write to external files.

# The oracle.sql.BFILE Class

Oracle allows you to store references to binary files in your database by providing a data type called BFILE. The `oracle.sql.BFILE` class allows you to manipulate such data through Java program code. The BFILE class represents Oracle BFILE data type that points to the external file. The class defines several file handling methods. A few important methods are mentioned opposite:

| Method | Purpose |
|---|---|
| ```public boolean fileExists()```<br>```  throws SQLException``` | Indicates whether the file represented by the current BFILE object exists on the server's file system. |
| ```public InputStream getBinaryStream()```<br>```  throws SQLException``` | Used for retrieving the entire BFILE as a stream. |
| ```public void openFile()```<br>```  throws SQLException``` | Opens the file. |
| ```public byte[] getBytes(long pos,```<br>```                  int length)```<br>```  throws SQLException``` | Returns the file contents starting at position pos and number of bytes equal to length. |
| ```public String getName()```<br>```  throws SQLException``` | Returns the file name. |

To demonstrate the use of the BFILE class, we will develop a Java application that will display a few buttons in its parent frame window. Each button will have an icon, and the image icon will be read from the Oracle database and displayed on the button.

Like earlier cases, we will create a new database table having a column of type BFILE. We will insert a few records in the table and later develop Java code to retrieve these records.

The following is the SQL to create a table called PICTURE_TABLE in the database. It has two columns; the first is of string type and represents the file name, and the second is of type bfile, which stores a reference to the image of the icon to be displayed on the button:

```
SQL> create or replace directory PIC
  2  as
  3  'c:\Pictures';

Directory created.

SQL> create table picture_table (
  2     name varchar2(30),
  3     pic bfile
  4  );

Table created.

SQL> insert into picture_table values(
  2     'ADD', bfilename ('PIC', 'add.gif')
  3  );

1 row created.

SQL> insert into picture_table values(
  2     'CANCEL', bfilename ('PIC', 'cancel.gif')
  3  );
```

```
1 row created.

SQL> insert into picture_table values(
  2     'SEARCH', bfilename ('PIC', 'search.gif')
  3  );

1 row created.

SQL> commit;

Commit complete.
```

The above SQL inserts a few records into the database table. The second value in each record is of type BFILE. The constructor of BFILE takes the name of the directory as the first parameter and the name of the image file as the second parameter. The directory name is specified by creating an alias PIC that refers to the physical folder c:\Pictures. Note that the database stores only the *reference* to the file. Thus, if the file is physically moved or deleted, the reference would become invalid.

# Accessing BFILE Objects

Here is our test class named TestBFILE, which will retrieve and display BFILE objects from our PICTURE_TABLE table:

```java
import java.sql.*;
import java.sql.*;
import oracle.jdbc.driver.*;
import oracle.sql.*;
import javax.swing.*;
import java.awt.*;
import java.awt.event.*;
import java.io.*;

public class TestBFILE extends Frame {
  Frame frame;
  JButton button;
  public TestBFILE() {

    // initalize Frame object and set the layout
    frame = new Frame("BFILE Example");
    frame.setLayout(new FlowLayout());

    try {

      // load the driver
      Class.forName("oracle.jdbc.driver.OracleDriver");
      Connection con = DriverManager.getConnection(
              "jdbc:oracle:oci8:@DATABASE", "username", "password");
      Statement stmt = con.createStatement();
      ResultSet rset = stmt.executeQuery("select * from picture_table");

      while (rset.next()) {
        String Name = rset.getString("Name");
```

```
          // obtain the object of BFILE from each record in ResultSet
          BFILE bfile = ((OracleResultSet) rset).getBFILE("pic");

          // show the BFILE on the button
          showButton(con, bfile);
        }
        rset.close();
        stmt.close();
        con.close();
      } catch (Exception e) {
        e.printStackTrace();
      }

      // Window Closing event for the Frame
      frame.addWindowListener(new WindowAdapter() {
        public void windowClosing(WindowEvent we) {
          System.exit(0);
        }
      });
      frame.setSize(400, 400);
      frame.pack();
      frame.show();
    }

  private void showButton(Connection conn, BFILE bfile) throws Exception {

    // print the name of the file
    System.out.println("File Name: " + bfile.getName());
    System.out.println("File exists: " + bfile.fileExists());
    System.out.println("File open: " + bfile.isFileOpen());
    System.out.println("Opening File: ");

    // open the file
    bfile.openFile();
    System.out.println("File open: " + bfile.isFileOpen());

    // obtain the length of the file
    int length = (int) bfile.length();
    System.out.println("File length: " + length);
    InputStream instream = bfile.getBinaryStream();
    byte[] buffer = new byte[length];

    // read bytes from the InputStream and show on the Button as Icon
    instream.read(buffer);
    button = new JButton(new ImageIcon(buffer));
    frame.add(button);
    System.out.println();
    instream.close();
    bfile.closeFile();
  }

  public static void main(String args[]) {
    new TestBFILE();
  }
}
```

When you run the program, you will see the following output in it's own Java window:

We have also printed a few messages on the user console at run-time:

```
> java TestBFILE
File Name: add.gif
File exists: true
File open: false
Opening File:
File open: true
File length: 10483

File Name: cancel.gif
File exists: true
File open: false
Opening File:
File open: true
File length: 8969

File Name: search.gif
File exists: true
File open: false
Opening File:
File open: true
File length: 4842
```

Apart from similarities in obtaining a connection to the database, the result set is created by firing the SQL SELECT:

```
ResultSet rset = stmt.executeQuery("select * from picture_table");
```

The first column of the table that contains a name string for the icon is retrieved by calling the getString() method on the result set object:

```
String Name = rset.getString("Name");
```

The BFILE object is retrieved by calling the getBFILE() method:

```
BFILE bfile = ((OracleResultSet) rset).getBFILE("pic");
```

The program then calls the showButton() method that uses this BFILE object, retrieves the image information, and then displays the image icon on the button:

```
        showButton(con, bfile);
```

Let's now look at the showButton() code to study how the image object is created using the BFILE reference. The showButton() method calls the various methods on the BFILE object to print the information about the file. These methods were briefly described in the previous section:

```
        // print the name of the file
        System.out.println("File Name: " + bfile.getName());
        System.out.println("File exists: " + bfile.fileExists());
        System.out.println("File open: " + bfile.isFileOpen());
        System.out.println("Opening File: ");
```

After printing the file information on the user console, the program opens the file for reading by calling its openFile() method:

```
        // open the file
        bfile.openFile();
        System.out.println("File open: " + bfile.isFileOpen());
```

We determine the length of the file by calling the length() method on the BFILE object:

```
        // obtain the length of the file
        int length = (int) bfile.length();
        System.out.println("File length: " + length);
```

Next, we obtain the input stream on the BFILE object by calling the getBinaryStream() method. The program then creates a buffer for storing the file contents and reads the file into the buffer by calling the read() method on the obtained input stream object:

```
        InputStream instream = bfile.getBinaryStream();
        byte[] buffer = new byte[length];

        // read bytes from the InputStream and show on the Button as Icon
        instream.read(buffer);
```

A JButton object is then constructed. (JButton represents a button defined in the Swing library of the Java Development Kit.) The constructor takes one argument, which is an object of type ImageIcon. The ImageIcon constructor takes the previously constructed buffer as the argument. Note that the buffer contains the image information obtained through the BFILE object.

```
        button = new JButton(new ImageIcon(buffer));
```

The button is then added to the frame using the following program statement:

```
        frame.add(button);
```

# The oracle.sql.CHAR Class

Oracle allows you to create and store characters in your database using various character sets and the `oracle.sql.CHAR` class is the Oracle-specific representation of such characters. The data stored in `CHAR` objects is interpreted based on the current character set. The class provides several methods of type `xxxValue()` where `xxx` represents the data type. Each of these methods returns the object value in the specified Java data format.

A source file, `TestChar.java`, is available with the code download and demonstrates how to create a character string using one of the pre-defined character sets in Oracle, write this string to the database and later retrieve it and display it on the user console.

The important points in this code are as follows. The program creates a character set object by calling the `make()` method of the `CharacterSet` class. The input parameter to the method specifies the pre-defined character set to be used in the construction:

```
// obtain OracleID for oracle-character-set-31
int oracleId =
   CharacterSet.WE8ISO8859P1_CHARSET;   // this is character set 31

// make the character set
CharacterSet charset = CharacterSet.make(oracleId);
```

The program constructs a character string using the constructed character set object. The `oracle.sql.CHAR` class is used for constructing the string as shown below:

```
// create the object of type oracle.sql.CHAR
oracle.sql.CHAR tempChar = new oracle.sql.CHAR("Characters", charset);
```

A prepared statement is used for inserting the constructed character array in the database. The following segment creates a prepared statement, sets the parameter value, and inserts the record in the database:

```
// prepare an OraclePreparedStatement
// for inserting the oracle.sql.CHAR type object into table
oracle.jdbc.driver.OraclePreparedStatement ps =
   (oracle.jdbc.driver.OraclePreparedStatement)
      conn.prepareStatement("insert into char_test values(?)");

ps.setCHAR(1, tempChar);
ps.executeUpdate();
```

We retrieve the inserted record and display it on the user console as follows:

```
// retrieve the ResultSet from the table
oracle.jdbc.driver.OracleResultSet rs =
   (oracle.jdbc.driver.OracleResultSet) stmt.executeQuery(
                                "select * from char_test");
```

Once a result set is constructed, the execution of the getCHAR() method on the result set will retrieve the stored character array:

```
// retrieve the oracle.sql.CHAR object from ResultSet
tempChar = rs.getCHAR(1);
```

The retrieved string can be displayed on the user console, by simply calling the toString() method of the CHAR class:

```
System.out.println(tempChar.toString());
```

The name of the character set used for creating the string is obtained by calling the getCharacterSet() method of the CHAR class:

```
System.out.println(tempChar.getCharacterSet());
```

Running the code will produce the following output, illustrating the fact that the application has inserted and retrieved the character array stored as a CHAR:

```
> java TestCHAR
Characters retrieved from ResultSet
-----------------------------------
Characters
oracle-character-set-871
```

# The oracle.sql.DATE class

The Oracle DATE type allows you to store date and time objects in the database. The oracle.sql.DATE class allows you to manipulate such data through your Java program.

The basic use of the oracle.sql.DATE class is rather straightforward. The sample source code is provided in the code download (TestDate.java). To insert a record containing a DATE type from Java, we can construct an object of DATE class and then use it as a parameter in a prepared statement:

```
String strDate = "1979-11-17 12:23:60";

// create object of oracle.sql.DATE
oracle.sql.DATE Birthdate = new oracle.sql.DATE(strDate);

// create OraclePreparedStatement to insert oracle.sql.DATE
// object into table
oracle.jdbc.driver.OraclePreparedStatement ps =
    (oracle.jdbc.driver.OraclePreparedStatement)
        conn.prepareStatement("insert into Birthday values(?,?)");
ps.setString(1, "Smith");
ps.setDATE(2, Birthdate);
ps.executeUpdate();
```

The program constructs a DATE object by calling its constructor, which accepts the date in the string format. The prepared statement accepts two parameters, the string name and the date containing a birth date. The setDate() method sets the parameter to the date object.

We retrieve the records:

```
// retrieve ResultSet from table
oracle.jdbc.driver.OracleResultSet rs =
    (oracle.jdbc.driver.OracleResultSet)
        stmt.executeQuery("Select * from birthday");
```

The DATE field is retrieved from the result set by calling the getDATE() method on the result set. The date is then printed on the user console by calling the stringValue() method on the DATE object:

```
// retrieve object of DATE from ResultSet
Birthdate = rs.getDATE("birthdate");
System.out.println(Name + ":\t" + Birthdate.stringValue());
```

# The oracle.sql.NUMBER Class

Converting between SQL and Java numeric types is a potential source of problems. All the numeric data types of SQL can be mapped to any Java numeric data types and vice-versa. But there may be precision loss, if the receiving data type is not large enough to hold the value. If you have a SQL smallint type in the database, it may be tempting to map that to the java.lang.short class. However, consider the following:

```
SQL> set serveroutput on
SQL> declare
  2  x smallint;
  3  begin
  4  x := 12345678901234567890123456789890;
  5  dbms_output.put_line( to_char(x) );
  6  end;
  7  /
1234567890123456789012345678901234567890

PL/SQL procedure successfully completed.
```

You cannot look at the type smallint and make a supposition about the values in it. This smallint is not going to fit into a Java Short. This is a common source of the ORA-00932: inconsistent datatypes error. In fact, you should probably consider not using the native short, int, and float Java types as they do not support the concept of nullability and have no indicator variables.

A safe way to circumvent such potential problems is to use the oracle.sql.NUMBER class. We can create an object of type oracle.sql.NUMBER in our Java code as follows:

```
oracle.sql.NUMBER tempNum = new oracle.sql.NUMBER(40);
```

The NUMBER data type is retrieved from a result set by calling the getNUMBER() method. The stringValue() method converts the NUMBER to the string value:

```
// retrieve the oracle.sql.NUMBER object from ResultSet
tempNum = rs.getNUMBER(1);
System.out.println(tempNum.stringValue());
```

To see this in action, run the TestNumber.java source file, available in the code download for this chapter.

# Summary

In this chapter, we studied the various extensions to the JDBC API provided by Oracle. Oracle supports several additional data types to those defined in the JDBC API. These additional data types are supported by introducing new Java packages, such as oracle.sql and oracle.jdbc.driver. The oracle.sql package defines various classes that operate on the Oracle specific data types. The oracle.jdbc.driver package defines various classes that provide support for accessing the database using enhanced functionality. We studied several classes in these packages followed by many programming examples illustrating the use of these classes.

# SQLJ Programming

Java is a powerful programming language that can be used to write a wide variety of applications. As we have already seen, Java provides an API called **JDBC** (Java Database Connectivity), which is a sophisticated and flexible set of calls for manipulating and retrieving data from a relational database. JDBC is completely vendor-independent. Java code written to use one particular database, such as Oracle, can easily be ported to use another database, such as Microsoft SQL*Server, with minimal or no amount of code rework.

JDBC is very powerful, but it does not offer an intuitive for syntax writing relational-database applications. JDBC is a low-level API similar to Oracle's C-based OCI, the Oracle Call Interface. The developer needs to know more Java than SQL to successfully write an application using JDBC. Even a simple task like retrieving a set of rows from a single database table requires a significant amount of code.

What is needed is some way to allow the database-oriented developer to write their Java-based database code in a manner that is natural and easy to understand. Ideally, the developer should be able to **embed** their SQL statements directly inside of the Java source code without the use of a low-level database API like JDBC.

The concept of embedding SQL code is not a new one. One of Oracle's earliest development tools was their PRO* line of language pre-compilers. Using a pre-compiler the developer could embed SQL statements directly into a program written in C, COBOL or FORTRAN. These SQL statements would be written with a special syntax. The source code would then be run through Oracle's pre-compiler software. The pre-compiler would parse the SQL code and translate it into source code that would invoke Oracle's OCI API.

Using Oracle's PRO* pre-compilers, a developer could write powerful database code without the need to understand or delve into low-level database APIs. When Java emerged as a development tool, it would seem natural that Oracle would extend their line of PRO* pre-compilers to include support for the JDBC API.

However, Oracle took a different approach. Rather, than writing a Java PRO* pre-compiler, Oracle and several other database vendors joined forces to create an industry-wide standard for embedding SQL code directly inside of Java source code. This standard, called **SQLJ**, enables database developers to:

❑   Write Java-based database code without resorting to low-level JDBC calls.

❑   Write Java-based database code that is portable to multiple database platforms. Oracle's PRO* pre-compilers are only usable with Oracle databases.

> **SQLJ is *not* an Oracle-based API. It is an *industry standard*. Most of the code examples in this book can easily be ported over to another SQLJ implementation.**

This chapter will introduce you to the power of SQLJ, so we will begin with a potted history of the standard and some background on the workings of it and the setting up required. Then, we will cover:

❑   An example of a simple SQLJ SELECT statement, invoking the SQLJ translator to convert and compile your SQLJ files into Java classes

❑   Write Java code that can retrieve and manipulate data from an Oracle database

❑   SQLJ declarations

❑   Using SQLJ to invoke Oracle stored procedures

❑   Using SQLJ to automatically generate Java classes and automate many common database manipulation tasks

❑   The new SQLJ features in Oracle 9i

# SQLJ – A Short History

SQLJ began life in April 1997 when Oracle, IBM, and Tandem (which is owned by Compaq) formed a consortium to explore the standardization of Java database access technologies. The JDBC API was already in use. However, these database vendors saw JDBC as being too low-level an API. They wanted a standard that would allow them to directly embed SQL code inside of Java source code.

Afraid that they would be left out, Informix, Sybase, and Sun quickly joined the consortium and pledged their support. The first reference implementation of the SQLJ standard was delivered in December of 1997. This reference implementation consisted of two parts:

❑   A SQLJ translator

❑   A SQLJ runtime library

The SQLJ translator took Java source code that contained embedded SQL written using the SQLJ syntax and converted it to Java. Remember, SQLJ behaves exactly like Oracle's PRO* pre-compilers. This means you cannot compile a SQLJ program until the SQLJ syntax has been translated into native Java source. Translated SQLJ code will contain JDBC and SQLJ API calls. Once the code has been translated it can be compiled into Java bytecode.

The SQLJ runtime library provides a buffer between the user and the underlying vendor's SQLJ implementation. This runtime library is 100 percent Java based, and contains standard APIs that help ensure binary portability across multiple SQLJ implementations.

In 1998, almost a year after the first SQLJ reference implementation was delivered by Oracle, the SQLJ consortium submitted the SQLJ standard to the American National Standards Institute (ANSI) for approval as a standard. SQLJ was accepted by the ANSI organization as a standard. The ANSI standard number for SQLJ is ANSI X3.135.

SQLJ is a standard and if you are careful in writing your applications to use the base SQLJ syntax, you can easily move your application code from one SQLJ implementation to another. However, the SQLJ standard does allow the individual vendors to add proprietary extensions that can limit portability of the code.

For purposes of this chapter, we will be using Oracle's SQLJ implementation. Keep this in mind if you try to use the examples with another SQLJ implementation. Any Java code that leverages Oracle specific SQLJ extensions will be highlighted.

# The SQLJ Translation Process

Before diving into code examples, let's take a conceptual look at the steps involved in writing a SQLJ application:

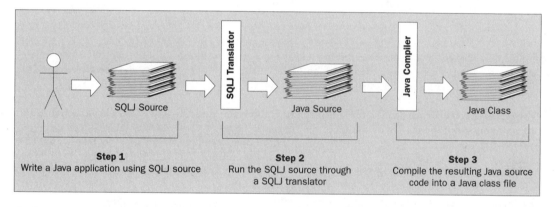

| Step 1 | Step 2 | Step 3 |
| Write a Java application using SQLJ source | Run the SQLJ source through a SQLJ translator | Compile the resulting Java source code into a Java class file |

In Step 1 of the diagram, an Oracle developer writes a Java-based application containing SQLJ-based code. This code is saved in a file with a `.sqlj` extension.

During Step 2, the translation process, the SQLJ translator is invoked to convert the SQLJ code into Java source code. The Oracle SQLJ translator will search the code for any SQLJ statements. When it finds a SQLJ statement it will perform the following steps:

❑   Validate that the SQLJ statement is syntactically correct

❑   Validate that the SQL code inside the SQLJ statements is correct

❑   Validate that the database objects being manipulated by the SQL code in the SQLJ statement are valid

❑   Translate that SQL code into syntactically correct Java statements

Step 3 of the process is to compile this resulting Java source file into a Java class file. The Java class file is now ready for use.

For the Oracle developers who have used Oracle's PRO* compilers (PRO*C, PRO*COBOL, PRO*FORTRAN), the translation process shown above should be very familiar. SQLJ is a pre-processor that converts easier-to-understand SQL code into Java equivalent code and then validates the embedded SQL code at compile-time rather than run-time.

# Preparing the Code Examples

For our code examples, we are going to use a simple set of tables that contain information about university students and the classes they are taking. The three tables in the database are as follows:

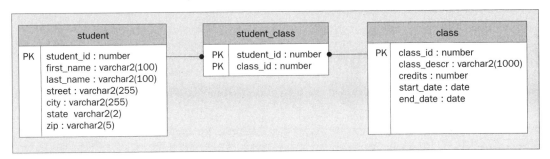

In this database, students can take multiple classes and many of these students can be in the same class at the same time. This shows a many-to-many relationship between students and the classes they take. The above three tables model this relationship.

The STUDENT table contains the basic information about the student. The CLASS table contains the information about the classes available to the students. The STUDENT_CLASS table acts as an intersecting table between the STUDENT and CLASS tables. It 'maps' which students take which classes. Multiple students can share the same classes because the multiple STUDENT_IDs in the STUDENT_CLASS table map to a single CLASS_ID in the CLASS table.

The script to create and populate the tables in this database, called training.sql, is found the code download that accompanies this book, available from http://www.wrox.com. What we would suggest is that you run this script when logged in as the new user you have created specifically for the code samples in this book. This is outlined in the *Setting Up* section at the start of this book.

> **All of the code in this chapter was tested with Oracle 8.1.7 and Oracle 9.0.1.1. Some of the code examples in the later sections rely on Oracle 9i-specific features. The code that will only run on Oracle 9i has been explicitly noted.**

# A Simple SELECT Statement

Let's start with a simple SQLJ application that retrieves a single line of data from the CLASS table in our test database. Once the data has been retrieved from the database, it will be printed to the console.

After reading this section and studying the example shown, you should be able to do the following:

❑ Understand the basic SQLJ syntax

❑ Demonstrate how to invoke the Oracle SQLJ compiler

❑ Discuss some of the different command-line arguments that can be set when the Oracle SQLJ compiler is invoked

The code for the example is shown below. It is saved in a file called SimpleSelect.sqlj. The example will retrieve a single row of data from the CLASS table and print the results of the query to the system console. The CLASS_ID for the application is passed in via a command line argument:

```java
package com.wrox.sqlj;

import oracle.sqlj.runtime.Oracle;
import java.sql.SQLException;

public class SimpleSelect {

  public static void main(String args[]) {
    try {
      try {

        // connect to Oracle database
        Oracle.connect("jdbc:oracle:oci8:@DATABASE", "username", "password");

        if ((args.length==0) || (args.length>1)) {
          String error = "This application needs a command line parameter";
          error +=       "containing the CLASS_ID being searched for.";
          error +=       "Please re-check your command line parameters and";
          error +=       "ensure that one command line parameter is";
          error +=       "being passed in and it is a numeric value.";
          throw new Exception(error);
        }

        // retrieve the CLASS_ID from the command line
        Integer requestedID = new Integer(args[0]);

        // initializing bind variables
        String classID = "";
        String classDescr = "TEST";
        String credits = "";
        String startDate = "";
        String endDate = "";

        // SQLJ statement used to generate the Java
        // code that retrieves data

        #sql { SELECT
                 class_id,
                 class_descr,
```

```
                credits,
                start_date,
                end_date
            INTO
                :classID,
                :classDescr,
                :credits,
                :startDate,
                :endDate
            FROM
                class
            WHERE
                class_id=:requestedID};

        // printing results
        System.out.println("Class Information");
        System.out.println("-----------------");
        System.out.println("Class id          : " + classID);
        System.out.println("Class Description : " + classDescr);
        System.out.println("Credits           : " + credits);
        System.out.println("Start Date        : " + startDate);
        System.out.println("End Date          : " + endDate);
    } catch (Exception e) {
        System.out.println(e.toString());
    } finally {
        Oracle.close();
    }
} catch (SQLException sqle) {
    System.out.println("Error closing my database connection in final: "
                        + sqle.toString());
}
}
}
```

# Translating the SimpleSelect Example

To translate the above code we are going to invoke the Oracle SQLJ transformer from a DOS command window. To simplify the transformation process, I have written a small DOS batch script called buildSQLJ.bat. This script sets the entire environment needed to run the Oracle SQLJ translator for the examples in this chapter. The buildSQLJ.bat batch file looks like:

```
@echo off

REM ################################################################
REM #
REM # buildSQLJ.bat - This script will set all of the environment variables
REM #                 for the SQLJ examples used in this chapter. The
REM #                 script will then invoke the Oracle SQLJ translator to
REM #                 translate and compile the user's SQLJ files.
REM #
REM #                 To invoke the SQLJ batch file, open a DOS command
REM #                 window and type the following at the DOS prompt:
```

```
REM #          > buildSQLJ.bat NAME OF THE SQLJ FILE TO TRANSLATE AND COMPILE
REM #
REM #              Here is an example:
REM #          > buildSQLJ.bat SimpleSelect.java
REM #
REM ####################################################################

REM # CLEARING MY CLASS PATH AND JAVA HOME
set CLASSPATH=
set JAVA_HOME=
set CODE_EXAMPLES=

REM # SETTING MY ORACLE HOME DIRECTORY
REM # You will have to point this to where your Oracle home is located.
set ORACLE_HOME=c:\Oracle\Ora90

REM # SETTING MY CLASSPATH VARIABLES
set CLASSPATH=%ORACLE_HOME%\sqlj\lib\translator.zip
set CLASSPATH=%CLASSPATH%;%ORACLE_HOME%\sqlj\lib\runtime.zip
set CLASSPATH=%CLASSPATH%;%ORACLE_HOME%\jdbc\lib\classes12.zip

REM # SETTING MY CODE EXAMPLE
REM # You will have to point to location of your compiled class files
set CODE_EXAMPLES=c:\classes
set CLASSPATH=%CLASSPATH%;%CODE_EXAMPLES%;.

REM # SETTING THE LOCATION OF WHERE MY JAVA BIN DIR. IS LOCATED -
REM # You will have to change this for your machine.
REM # The JDK is also available under %ORACLE_HOME%\Apache\jdk\bin
set JAVA_HOME=c:\jdk1.3\bin

REM # SETTING UP MY PATH TO INCLUDE MY JAVA_HOME
set PATH=%JAVA_HOME%;%PATH%

REM # SETTING FILENAME TO NAME OF THE FILE NAME PASSED IN FROM THE
REM # COMMAND LINE
set FILENAME=%1%

REM # INVOKING THE SQLJ TRANSLATOR
sqlj -compile=true -user=username/password -status -ser2class -warn -d=%CODE_EXAMP
LES% %FILENAME%
```

The majority of the batch script shown above is setting up the environment to properly translate and compile a SQLJ program. The most important line in the entire script is:

```
REM # INVOKING THE SQLJ TRANSLATOR
sqlj -compile=true -user=username/password -status -ser2class -warn -d=%CODE_EXAMP
LES% %FILENAME%
```

*Note that this line is in fact a single command, but due to the restraints of printing technologies, it is shown to be split into two lines.*

This line will invoke Oracle's SQLJ translator. The Oracle SQLJ translator is located in the `%ORACLE_HOME%\bin` directory, called `sqlj.exe`. The command line parameters used in the batch file perform the following action:

❏ `-compile-true` – Tells the SQLJ translator to compile the generated Java source code as soon as translation is complete

❏ `-user=username/password` – Tells the SQLJ translator to use login as the USERNAME user account and use that user's schema to validate the SQL code within the code.

❏ `-status` – Provide additional status information.

❏ `-ser2class` – Convert the serialized files generated by SQL to class files.

❏ `-d` – Defines the output directory where the compiled Java class files are to be placed.

To execute and compile the example, the following command needs to be issued in a DOS command window:

```
> buildSQLJ SimpleSelect.sqlj
```

If you see the following output in your DOS window, the Oracle SQLJ translator has successfully translated and compiled the `SimpleSelect.sqlj` file:

```
> buildSQLJ SimpleSelect.sqlj
[Translating]
[Reading file SimpleSelect]
[Translating file SimpleSelect]
[Compiling]
[Customizing]
[Converting serialized profile to class file]
[Compiling]
```

There are three JAR files of particular interest for translating and compiling our SQLJ code:

❏ `%ORACLE_HOME%\sqlj\lib\translator.zip` – Contains all of the class files needed to translate and compile your SQLJ applications.

❏ `%ORACLE_HOME%\sqlj\lib\runtime.zip` – Contains all of the class files needed by the SQLJ applications when they are translated and the compiled classes are run.

❏ `%ORACLE_HOME%\jdbc\lib\classes12.zip` – Contains all of the JDBC 2.0 classes. Be careful not to accidentally reference the `classes111.zip` file. This file contains all of the JDBC 1.0 class files. These will not run the code for our examples.

> **Oracle's SQLJ implementation still uses JDBC for the SQLJ translation process. Both the SQLJ translator and the source code generated by the translator use the JDBC API calls. Make sure you include the JDBC drivers in any of your CLASSPATH.**

# The SQLJ Translator Command Line Options

The SQLJ translator has a number of command line parameters that can be passed into it. Some of the more common options used with the SQLJ translator include:

| Option | Description |
| --- | --- |
| -d | Root class directory where all Java class files are put. |
| -user | Connect string of the Oracle database the SQLJ translator is going to connect to. If supplied, the translator will validate the code SQLJ executable statements against the structures they reference in the database. |
| -status | Provides additional detail as the translator is translating the file. |
| -compile | Compiles the translated Java code files after the translation. |
| -j | Passes a command line option to Java Virtual Machine running SQLJ. This option is used if you want to pass any additional information (for example, maximum heap size), to the JVM. |
| -version | Version of the SQLJ translator used. |
| -help | Lists all of the basic command line options for the SQLJ translator. |
| -classpath | Sets the classpath for the SQLJ compiler. You might need to set this if your SQLJ code is referencing classes or JAR files other than those that come with Oracle. |
| -ser2class | Converts all serialized Java resource files generated by the SQLJ translator (in other words, all files that have a *.ser extension) to Java class files. |
| -warn | Tells the SQLJ translator to issue warnings on any Oracle specific SQLJ code. |

# Outputs From the SQLJ Translation Process

When a SQLJ source file is run through the Oracle SQLJ translator, there are always at least three files generated as an output for the process. These files are:

- ❑ A Java source file containing your source code and the SQLJ statements translated into Java source code. This generated Java source file will always have the same name as the SQLJ source file.

- ❑ A Java source file with the extension _SJProfileKeys.java. This file contains source code that is specific to that particular implementation of the SQLJ translator. The _SJProfileKeys.java file is used to make your SQLJ code portable from one vendor implementation to the next. The idea here is to use the same SQLJ declarations inside your code, but each vendor can translate that code to their own specific database calls.

❑ SQLJ profile files with the extension _SJProfileX.ser. This file is a serialized Java resource file that contains meta data about the different database contexts within your SQLJ application.The topic of database contexts will be covered in the next several sections. For each different database context within your application you will have a _SJProfileX.ser file where X is the number, which gets incremented (starting with number 1).

Thus, for the SimpleSelect application shown in this section, the files generated by the SQLJ translation process would be named:

❑ SimpleSelect.java

❑ SimpleSelect_SJProfileKeys.java

❑ SimpleSelect_SJProfile1.ser

> **All SQLJ profiles end with a .ser extension. If there are no executable SQLJ source statements inside the source code, no SQLJ profile files will be generated.**

The outputs generated by the SQLJ translator can be affected by two parameters; -compile and -ser2class. The -compile option tells the SQLJ translator to compile all of the .java files generated during translation. The -ser2class option tells the SQLJ translator to convert all .ser files to java class files and then compile them. You are not required to use the -ser2class option when writing Java applications, but you will need it when writing Java applets that do not support serialized resource files.

# How It Works

To run the SimpleSelect application, issue the following commands in a DOS window:

```
> java com.wrox.sqlj.SimpleSelect 1
```

If the SimpleSelect application runs without error, the following output should appear in the DOS window:

```
> java com.wrox.sqlj.SimpleSelect 1
Class Information
-----------------
Class id          : 1
Class Description : Introduction to Western Literature
Credits           : 4
Start Date        : 2001-08-29 00:00:00.0
End Date          : 2001-12-15 00:00:00.0
```

The above example is a very simple illustration of using SQLJ to:

❑ Connect to our test database

❑  Retrieve a single row of data using a SQLJ executable statement

❑  Send data back from Java to SQLJ using expressions

## Making a Database Connection

The first line of code in our application makes a connection to the database:

```
// connect to Oracle database
Oracle.connect("jdbc:oracle:oci8:@DATABASE", "username", "password");
```

The Oracle class is a **helper class**. It contains two different types of methods for creating database connections with SQLJ applications. The first type of method is the connect() method. The Oracle.connect() method is a static method that creates a default connection that will be used by all of the SQLJ code in the SimpleSelect class. There are many different versions of the connect() method. The one chosen for this code example takes three parameters:

❑  The connection string for the Oracle database to which we are connecting

❑  The user ID

❑  The password for that user ID

The connect() method is used when you only need one Oracle database connection within your SQLJ application. When you use the connect() method, all of the SQL statements in your code share the same transaction context. This means that any uncommitted SQL code in your SQLJ application that inserts, updates, or deletes data will be committed or rolled back together. Keep this in mind if you need to independently commit or roll back one SQL statement from another.

> **SQLJ code by default has auto-commit turned off. JDBC by default has auto-commit turned on. The topic of SQLJ and database commits are covered later in the chapter.**

The second type of method used to create a connection to an Oracle database is called getConnection(). The getConnection() method is used when you need one of two things:

❑  Different transactions contexts in the SQLJ code within your SQLJ application.

❑  A database connection within your applications that connects to different Oracle databases.

We will be covering the getConnection() method in more detail later in the chapter.

## Our First SQLJ Statement

After the connection to the database method has been made, we are going to read the first command line argument parameter passed into the SimpleSelect application into an Integer object called requestedID:

```
// retrieve the CLASS_ID from the command line
Integer requestedID = new Integer(args[0]);
```

**259**

The `requestedID` object is used to hold the class ID for a record in the `CLASS` table. If a command line argument is not passed in when the `SimpleSelect` application is run from the DOS window, a `java.lang.ArrayIndexOutOfBoundsException` will be thrown.

After the `requestedId` variable has initialized, the `SimpleSelect` application initializes five objects:

```
// initializing bind variables
String classID = "";
String classDescr = "TEST";
String credits = "";
String startDate = "";
String endDate = "";
```

These variables will hold the results returned by the SQL query issued in our SQLJ statement.

After initializing the 'holder' variables, you will see your first SQLJ construct. All SQLJ constructs will always have the following syntax:

```
#sql {
  ...
  };
```

In SQLJ, there are two basic constructs:

❑ SQLJ executable statements

❑ SQLJ declarations

A SQLJ executable statement always contains SQL code you want your Java based application to execute. The valid SQL code that a SQLJ executable statement can perform includes:

❑ Statements that manipulate data in the database, Data Manipulation Language, or DML:

  ❑ SELECT
  ❑ INSERT
  ❑ UPDATE
  ❑ DELETE

❑ Statements that manipulate objects in the database, Data Definition Language, or DDL:

  ❑ CREATE
  ❑ DROP
  ❑ ALTER

❑ Statements for creating and invoking Oracle PL/SQL code:

  ❑ PL/SQL stored procedure calls
  ❑ PL/SQL blocks

The second SQLJ construct, the **SQLJ declaration**, allows you to use a Java wrapper to retrieve and manipulate the data being returned from your executable statement. This declaration will allow you work with the data returned via a straightforward Java class wrapper rather than low-level JDBC database APIs. We will be looking at SQLJ declarations in a later section.

The SQLJ executable statement used in the `SimpleSelect` application, shown below, retrieves a single record from the `CLASS` table:

```
// SQLJ statement used to generate the Java
// code that retrieves data

#sql { SELECT
          class_id,
          class_descr,
          credits,
          start_date,
          end_date
       INTO
         :classID,
         :classDescr,
         :credits,
         :startDate,
         :endDate
       FROM
         class
       WHERE
         class_id=:requestedID};
```

All of the items in the above SQLJ statement that start with a colon are called **host expressions**. There are six host expressions in the above SQLJ construct:

❑   `:classID`

❑   `:classDescr`

❑   `:credits`

❑   `:startDate`

❑   `:endDate`

❑   `:requestedID`

As we have already seen, all of the host expressions in the SQLJ statement shown have already been declared as Java variables earlier in the code.

Host expressions are Java statements or variables that can be used to move data back and forth from Java to SQLJ executable statements. Host expressions can also be used in SQLJ code with both a SQL query and stored procedure calls. SQLJ will follows the same rules as declaring parameter variables in a PL/SQL stored procedure, function, or package.

Host expressions can be of type:

❑   IN – A value is being passed into the SQLJ statement. An example of an IN host expression would be the `:requestedID` variable shown in the above code. A host expression that is an IN type is read-only. Its value cannot be modified by the SQL code or the stored procedure it is passed into.

❑ OUT – A value is passed from the SQLJ statement back to the Java application. An example of OUT host expressions are the values passed via the INTO piece of the above SELECT statement.

❑ INOUT – Host expressions that are declared of type INOUT can send and receive values from an SQLJ statement. They can be read and modified by SQLJ code without any restrictions.

It may seem unusual that the SQLJ code above does not show any host expressions with an IN, OUT, or INOUT designation. There are three reasons for this:

❑ All of the host expressions used as part of an INTO clause for a SELECT SQL statement are considered of type OUT.

❑ All host expressions that are part of the SET clause for an UPDATE SQL statement are considered of type IN.

❑ All host expressions that are used as part of the WHERE clause in an INSERT, UPDATE, or DELETE SQL statement are considered of type IN.

So, if we were to rewrite the above SQLJ statement to explicitly show the *type* of each host expression, our SELECT statement in the code would look like:

```
// SQLJ statement used to generate the Java
// code that retrieves data

#sql { SELECT
          class_id,
          class_descr,
          credits,
          start_date,
          end_date
       INTO
          :OUT(classID),
          :OUT(classDescr),
          :OUT(credits),
          :OUT(startDate),
          :OUT(endDate)
       FROM
          class
       WHERE
          class_id=:IN(requestedID)};
```

## Printing the Results

After the SQLJ statement shown earlier is executed, the classID, classDescr, credits, startDate, and endDate variables will hold the individual column values of the record retrieved from the database. The values retrieved from the database are printed out using the code below:

```
// printing results
System.out.println("Class Information");
System.out.println("----------------");
System.out.println("Class id            : " + classID);
System.out.println("Class Description : " + classDescr);
System.out.println("Credits             : " + credits);
System.out.println("Start Date          : " + startDate);
System.out.println("End Date            : " + endDate);
```

## Closing the Connection

The last step in the application is to close the database connection using the `Oracle.close()` method:

```
} finally {
  Oracle.close();
}
```

The `Oracle.close()` method tells the Oracle database that the application is done with the database connection, and that the database connection can be released back to the pool of connections available to process user requests.

The `Oracle.close()` method was placed inside of a `finally` block, because no matter what exception the program may have raised, we want the database connection to be cleanly closed. However, calling `Oracle.close()` itself can raise a SQLException. So, we surround the entire code block that is retrieving data with a `try...catch` statement, which will catch any SQLExceptions raised by calling `Oracle.close()`. This is why you see the code structured thus:

```
try {
  try {
    // do some work with SQLJ
  } catch (Exception e) {
    // catching and processing of any exceptions
  } finally {
    // closing Oracle connection
    Oracle.close();
  }
} catch (SQLException sqle) {
  System.out.println("Error closing my database connection in final: "
                     + sqle.toString());
}
```

> Always put your **Oracle.close()** calls in a **finally** block. This ensures that no matter what exceptions are raised, you are cleanly closing the connection. However, be prepared to catch the **SQLException** that can be raised by **Oracle.close()**.

Failure to call the `Oracle.close()` method can result in your applications holding onto database connections far longer then they need. This means your Oracle database will quickly run out of connections to hand out for other database requests.

> Always close your database connection when you are done with it.. Failure to explicitly close a database connection can quickly lead to Oracle running out of database connections to process user requests. This can be a particularly big problem in web-based application environment where database connections are scarce resources.

## More About Host Expressions

When using host expressions, remember the following items:

❑ A host expression variable must be already declared before being used in a SQLJ statement

❑ The type for the host expression variable must match the data type of the values being sent to and returned from SQLJ

Since we are using Oracle's SQLJ implementation, the Java variable used as a host expression must correspond to the Oracle data type that it is sending to or receiving data from. The table below shows some of the more common Java to Oracle data type mappings:

| Java Primitive Type | Java Wrapper Class | Oracle Data Type |
| --- | --- | --- |
| char | Java.lang.Char | CHAR |
| No equivalent | Java.lang.String | VARCHAR2 |
| byte | Java.lang.Byte | NUMBER |
| byte[] | No equivalent | LONGRAW |
| short | Java.lang.Short | NUMBER |
| int | Java.lang.Integer | NUMBER |
| long | Java.lang.Long | NUMBER |
| float | Java.lang.Float | NUMBER |
| double | Java.lang.Double | NUMBER |
| boolean | Java.lang.Boolean | NUMBER |
| No equivalent | Java.sql.Date | DATE |
| No equivalent | Java.sql.Time | DATE |
| No equivalent | Java.sql.Blob | BLOB |
| No equivalent | Java.sql.Clob | CLOB |

Oracle also provides Java wrapper classes for all of their database column types. These classes are usable with Oracle's SQLJ implementation, but are not portable to another SQLJ implementation. Some of the wrapper classes available from Oracle for use in both SQLJ and JDBC programming include:

| Java Wrapper Class | Description |
| --- | --- |
| oracle.sql.BLOB | Binary large object |
| oracle.sql.CLOB | Character-based large object |
| oracle.sql.BFILE | Read-only binary files |

| Java Wrapper Class | Description |
|---|---|
| `oracle.sql.ROWID` | Unique row number for an Oracle |
| `oracle.sql.NUMBER` | Oracle number data type |
| `oracle.sql.CHAR` | Oracle character data type |
| `oracle.sql.RAW` | Oracle long raw data type |

> Do not declare a host expression as a primitive data type if you are expecting to retrieve a null value from the database. Primitive data types cannot store a null database value and will raise a **SQLException**. Use an equivalent Java wrapper class if the value returned can hold a null value.

# SQLJ vs. JDBC

At this point you might be asking yourself why even bother with SQLJ. It is yet another new technology to learn and it looks like you could do all of your database work with JDBC. After all, you could have written the `SimpleSelect` application shown above using JDBC like this:

```
package com.wrox.sqlj;

import java.sql.*;

public class SimpleSelectJDBC {

  public static void main(String args[]) {
    try {

      // connect to Oracle database using JDBC
      Class.forName("oracle.jdbc.driver.OracleDriver");
      Connection con =
       DriverManager.getConnection("jdbc:oracle:oci8:@DATABASE", "username",
                                   "password");

      // build the SQL statement
      StringBuffer sql = new StringBuffer("");
      sql.append(" SELECT");
      sql.append("   class_id,");
      sql.append("   class_descr,");
      sql.append("   credits,");
      sql.append("   start_date,");
      sql.append("   end_date");
      sql.append(" FROM");
      sql.append("   class");
      sql.append(" WHERE");
      sql.append("   class_id = ?");
```

```
    // create a prepared statement to pass parameters into
    PreparedStatement ps = con.prepareStatement(sql.toString());
    ps.setString(1, args[0]);
    ResultSet classRS = ps.executeQuery();

    // print out results
    System.out.println("Class Information");
    System.out.println("-----------------");

    while (classRS.next()) {
      System.out.println("Class id:          "
                         + classRS.getString("class_id"));
      System.out.println("Class Description: "
                         + classRS.getString("class_descr"));
      System.out.println("Credits:           "
                         + classRS.getString("credits"));
      System.out.println("Start Date:        "
                         + classRS.getString("start_date"));
      System.out.println("End Date:          "
                         + classRS.getString("end_date"));
    }
    con.close();
  } catch (Exception e) {
    System.out.println(e.toString());
  }

  System.exit(0);
  }
}
```

*We are not going to walk through the JDBC code shown here. For further details on Oracle JDBC access, please refer to* Chapter 4, *Connecting to Oracle with JDBC and* Chapter 5, *Using JDBC.*

However, SQLJ offers four advantages over using JDBC:

❏   SQLJ will validate the syntax of your SQL code at translation-time. This means any errors in your SQL code will be caught before the application is executed. JDBC only takes a SQL statement as a string to be passed into its APIs. JDBC does not validate whether the SQL passed in this string is syntactically correct. Instead, it blindly executes the SQL command and blows up at run-time if there are errors with the SQL syntax.

❏   A SQLJ translator can not only validate whether the SQL statement is syntactically correct, but also whether the database structures (columns, tables, structures) and the SQL statements inside your Java code reference are valid. There are several things to keep in mind with the SQLJ translator:

　　❏   The Oracle SQLJ translator will check for type conflicts and the existence of a database object in a user's schema. It will not validate whether or not the user has the right to carry out a particular action (INSERT, UPDATE, DELETE, and so on) on a particular database object. It will catch things like your SQL code referencing a table column that does not exist in your database.

❑ The type checking done by the SQLJ translator is only done at compile-time. A DBA could alter database structures or database access permissions after your SQLJ code has been compiled and you could still get errors at run-time.

❑ SQLJ makes your code easier to read and understand because it allows you to clearly define database activity. SQLJ-based applications are easier to read and maintain than JDBC applications where the SQL code is buried amongst JDBC API calls.

❑ SQLJ, being a higher level API than JDBC, requires significantly less code to carry out a database related task. To perform even a simple SELECT statement in JDBC often requires several lines of code, where as in SQLJ, it requires only one line of code.

From the above bullet points you might think that SQLJ makes JDBC an obsolete technology. However, JDBC is still very useful. The SQLJ standard was designed for embedded, static SQL statements that never change their structure or physical form during run-time. This means that a SQLJ SQL statement cannot be altered at run-time based on conditions occurring within the application.

To handle dynamic SQL you have one of three options:

❑ You can write JDBC code that would build and execute SQL on the fly. Using JDBC requires knowledge of the JDBC API and defeats the purpose of SQLJ.

❑ You can mix JDBC and SQLJ calls together within one application. However, this topic is outside the scope of a beginning book and will not be covered in this text. If you are interested in JDBC and SQLJ interoperability, please refer to the SQLJ Developer's Guide and Reference, available as part of the database documentation or online at http://download-eu.oracle.com/otndoc/oracle9i/901_doc/java.901/a90212/toc.htm.

❑ You can leverage Oracle-specific extensions found in Oracle 9i's SQLJ implementation. These extensions allow the developer to dynamically build SQLJ statements, but they are not part of the ANSI SQLJ standard. Using this Oracle-specific feature can make porting your Java code to another SQLJ implementation difficult. Using Oracle 9i's dynamic SQLJ features is covered a little later.

Below is an example of using JDBC to dynamically build SQL statement on the fly. Let's rewrite the simple example above to dynamically append a WHERE clause:

```
package com.wrox.sqlj;

import java.sql.*;

public class SimpleSelectJDBC2 {

  public static void main(String args[]) {
    try {

      // connect to Oracle database using JDBC
      Class.forName("oracle.jdbc.driver.OracleDriver");
      Connection con =
        DriverManager.getConnection("jdbc:oracle:oci8:@DATABASE", "username",
                                    "password");
```

**267**

```java
// build the SQL statement
StringBuffer sql = new StringBuffer("");
sql.append(" SELECT");
sql.append("    class_id,");
sql.append("    class_descr,");
sql.append("    credits,");
sql.append("    start_date,");
sql.append("    end_date");
sql.append(" FROM");
sql.append("    class");

ResultSet classRS;

/* If the user does not pass in any arguments,
 * execute the SQL code. If the user does
 * pass in the class ID, append the
 * WHERE clause dynamically and then execute the
 * SQL statement. You could not do this with
 * SQLJ unless you use 9i extensions.
 */
if (args.length == 0) {
  Statement statement = con.createStatement();
  classRS = statement.executeQuery(sql.toString());
} else {
  sql.append(" WHERE");
  sql.append("    class_id = ?");

  PreparedStatement ps = con.prepareStatement(sql.toString());
  ps.setString(1, args[0]);
  classRS = ps.executeQuery();
}

while (classRS.next()) {
  System.out.println("Class id:              "
                     + classRS.getString("class_id"));
  System.out.println("Class Description: "
                     + classRS.getString("class_descr"));
  System.out.println("Credits:              "
                     + classRS.getString("credits"));
  System.out.println("Start Date:           "
                     + classRS.getString("start_date"));
  System.out.println("End Date:             "
                     + classRS.getString("end_date"));
}
con.close();
} catch (Exception e) {
System.out.println(e.toString());
}

System.exit(0);
  }
}
```

The SQLJ and JDBC database APIs each have the own their strengths and weaknesses. When using the technologies, it is important to understand this and know when to use the right database API for the job. Remember, the SQLJ standard only allows you to build static SQL statements. If you want to build dynamic SQL with SQLJ, you will need to use one of the three methods described earlier in this section.

# Manipulating Data with SQLJ

SQLJ can also be used to insert, update, and delete data from an Oracle database. To manipulate data using SQLJ you need to create a SQLJ executable statement that contains an SQL INSERT, UPDATE, or DELETE command.

Let's look at a simple program that loads the CLASS table with data from a comma-separated values (CSV) file. This program will parse the file and use SQLJ to insert one row at a time into the database.

This example will show more than just how to use an INSERT statement in SQLJ. It will also demonstrate:

❑   The default commit behavior for an SQLJ application

❑   How to change the default commit behavior of SQLJ

❑   How to explicitly tell SQLJ to commit and roll back data

## A Simple Insert Application

Here is the code for our application, named SimpleInsert.sqlj in the code download bundle:

```
package com.wrox.sqlj;

import oracle.sqlj.runtime.Oracle;
import java.sql.SQLException;
import java.io.*;
import java.util.*;

public class SimpleInsert {
  String csvFile =
    "c:/ Classes.txt";
  String dbName = "jdbc:oracle:oci8:@DATABASE";
  String userID = "username";
  String passwd = "password";

  // The parseFile() method will parse through a CSV file.
  // As it retrieves a line of data from the application, it will parse the
  // data into variables used as host expressions and then insert them into
  // the class table in the database.

  public void parseFile() throws SQLException{
    // declare the buffered reader that will read the CSV file
    BufferedReader in = null;
```

```
System.out.println("CLASS ID CLASS DESCR              CREDITS
                    START DATE    END DATE");
System.out.println("----------------------------------------
                    ------------------------");

try {
  Oracle.connect(dbName,userID,passwd);

  // create a buffered reader to read the CSV file
  in = new BufferedReader(new FileReader(csvFile));
  String holderString = "";

  while ((holderString = in.readLine())!= null) {
    // initialize string tokenizer with the string retrieved and a comma
    StringTokenizer st = new StringTokenizer(holderString,",");

    // populate the host expressions with data from the tokenizer
    String classID = st.nextToken();
    String classDescr = st.nextToken();
    String credits = st.nextToken();
    String startDate = st.nextToken();
    String endDate = st.nextToken();

    // print the results out to a screen
    StringBuffer results = new StringBuffer("");
    results.append(classID);
    results.append("       ");
    results.append(classDescr);
    results.append("      ");
    results.append(credits);
    results.append("        ");
    results.append(startDate);
    results.append("  ");
    results.append(endDate);
    System.out.println(results.toString());

    // inserting the SQL code
    #sql{
      INSERT INTO class(
        class_id,
        class_descr,
        credits,
        start_date,
        end_date
      )
      VALUES(
        :classID,
        :classDescr,
        :credits,
        :startDate,
        :endDate
```

```
        )};
      }

      // close the CSV File
      in.close();
    } catch (IOException ie) {
      System.out.println("There is a problem with the CSV file: "
                          + ie.toString());
    }
  }

  // this main statement will create an instance of the SimpleInsert class
  // and calls the parseFile() method
  public static void main(String args[]) {
    SimpleInsert simpleInsert = new SimpleInsert();

    try {
      try {
        simpleInsert.parseFile();

        // commit my data
        #sql{COMMIT};
      } catch(SQLException sqle) {
        System.out.println("Database or SQL error in the parseFile method: "
                            + sqle.toString());

        try {
          #sql{ROLLBACK};
        } catch(SQLException se) {
          System.out.println("Error rolling back: " + se.toString());
        }
      } finally {
        Oracle.close();
      }
    } catch(SQLException sqle) {
      System.out.println("Having trouble closing the Oracle.connection: "
                          + sqle.toString());
    }
  }
}
```

To translate and compile this application we will again run the `buildSQLJ.bat` file:

```
> buildSQLJ SimpleInsert.sqlj
```

After compiling the application, we can run it by typing the following command at the DOS command prompt:

```
> java com.wrox.sqlj.SimpleInsert
```

The corresponding `Classes.txt` is:

```
100,Introduction to Java,4,13-SEP-2001,10-DEC-2001
200,Introduction to SQLJ,3,13-SEP-2001,10-DEC-2001
100,OO Analysis and Design,3,13-SEP-2001,10-DEC-2001
400,Advanced Basket Weaving,3,13-SEP-2001,10-DEC-2001
500,Intermediate SQLJ,4,13-SEP-2001,10-DEC-2001
```

The output produced from the `SimpleInsert` application should look like this:

```
> java com.wrox.sqlj.SimpleInsert
CLASS ID CLASS DESCR              CREDITS START DATE   END DATE
-------------------------------------------------------------
100      Introduction to Java    4       13-SEP-2001  10-DEC-2001
200      Introduction to SQLJ    3       13-SEP-2001  10-DEC-2001
100      OO Analysis and Design  3       13-SEP-2001  10-DEC-2001
Database or SQL error in the parseFile method: java.sql.SQLException:
ORA-00001: unique constraint (USERNAME.SYS_C002825) violated
```

The errors you see above have been intentionally caused. The data file (`Classes.txt`) being read in by the application purposely has two lines with the same `class_id`:

```
100,Introduction to Java,4,13-SEP-2001,10-DEC-2001
200,Introduction to SQLJ,3,13-SEP-2001,10-DEC-2001
100,OO Analysis and Design,3,13-SEP-2001,10-DEC-2001
400,Advanced Basket Weaving,3,13-SEP-2001,10-DEC-2001
500,Intermediate SQLJ,4,13-SEP-2001,10-DEC-2001
```

These duplicate values cause a unique Oracle constraint exception to be thrown because the `CLASS_ID` field is the `CLASS` table's primary key. Let's now walk through the `SimpleInsert` application and take a look at how to use SQLJ to insert, rollback, or commit data.

## How It Works

The class data being inserted into the class table is done so on an all-or-nothing basis. If all of the data items being parsed from our CSV file are successfully inserted into the database, we will use SQLJ to issue a `COMMIT` statement to the database. If any SQL exceptions occur during the parsing process, all of the data will be rolled back.

This all-or-nothing method of committing the data is shown below in the `main()` method of the `SimpleInsert` application.

```java
public static void main(String args[]) {
  SimpleInsert simpleInsert = new SimpleInsert();

  try {
    try {
      simpleInsert.parseFile();

      // commit my data
```

```
        #sql{COMMIT};
    } catch(SQLException sqle) {
        System.out.println("Database or SQL error in the parseFile method: "
                            + sqle.toString());

        try {
          #sql{ROLLBACK};
        } catch(SQLException se) {
          System.out.println("Error rolling back: " + se.toString());
        }
    } finally {
      Oracle.close();
    }
  } catch(SQLException sqle) {
    System.out.println("Having trouble closing the Oracle.connection: "
                        + sqle.toString());
  }
}
```

The above code is declaring a variable of type `SimpleInsert`. This object is unimaginatively named `simpleInsert`. After the `simpleInsert` variable has been created, its `parseFile()` method is invoked.

The `parseFile()` method is responsible for opening the CSV file containing the class data to be loaded, retrieving line-by-line each record from this file, and then inserting that record into the CLASS table. If all of the inserts are successful, the data will be saved by issuing a:

```
#sql{COMMIT};
```

executable statement and the database connection will be closed by invoking the `Oracle.close()` method:

```
        try {
          simpleInsert.parseFile();

          // commit my data
          #sql{COMMIT};
```

A `#sql{COMMIT}` statement will make all changes to the database permanent, up to this point of the commit. If the `parseFile()` method, while trying to insert a record into the database, throws an `SQLException` exception, it will be caught in the `main()` method and all uncommitted changes made to the database will be rolled back using a `#sql{ROLLBACK}` statement:

```
        } catch(SQLException sqle) {
          System.out.println("Database or SQL error in the parseFile method: "
                              + sqle.toString());

          try {
            #sql{ROLLBACK};
          } catch(SQLException se) {
```

```
        System.out.println("Error rolling back: " + se.toString());
      }
    } finally {
      Oracle.close();
    }
```

We are catching one SQLException inside another. With the outer SQLException, called sqle, the error is printed out to the screen. Then, the code tries to roll back the statement and finally closes the database connection. The first SQLException might have been caused by bad data being inserted via our INSERT statement. However, the SQLException could have also been raised because the SimpleInsert application lost its connection to the Oracle database. Thus, issuing a #sql{ROLLBACK} could also throw another SQLException.

The second try...catch statement tries to roll back the uncommitted data inserts and close the database connection. If rollback fails, the exception is caught and an error message is written to the screen.

The last step in the SimpleInsert program is to close the Oracle connection we are using by calling Oracle.close() in the finally block.

Let's look at the parseFile() method. The first step in the parseFile() method is to declare a BufferedReader class called in. This variable will be used to open the CSV file and read line by line into the processing. In addition, as each line is retrieved from the CSV file and parsed, it will be printed to the screen. Thus, we also need to add a line to print out a header for the lines being printed out:

```
public void parseFile() throws SQLException{
    // declare the buffered reader that will read the CSV file
    BufferedReader in = null;

    System.out.println("CLASS ID CLASS DESCR            CREDITS
                    START DATE    END DATE");
    System.out.println("----------------------------------------
                    -----------------------");
```

After the preliminary work has been done, a connection to the test database is established via a call to Oracle.connect(), and the Classes.txt CSV file is opened:

```
    Oracle.connect(dbName,userID,passwd);

    // create a buffered reader to read the CSV file
    in = new BufferedReader(new FileReader(csvFile));
```

The dbName, userID, passwd, and csvFile variables have been assigned values in the first part of the SimpleInsert class. Once the database connection has been established we will use a while loop to cycle through each line in the Classes.txt file. Each retrieved line will be stored in the holderString variable and then in turn parsed into their individual component pieces using a StringTokenizer object called st. These individuals pieces are stored in the classID, classDescr, credits, startDate, and endDate variables:

```
while ((holderString = in.readLine())!= null) {
    // initialize string tokenizer with the string retrieved and a comma
    StringTokenizer st = new StringTokenizer(holderString,",");

    // populate the host expressions with data from the tokenizer
    String classID = st.nextToken();
    String classDescr = st.nextToken();
    String credits = st.nextToken();
    String startDate = st.nextToken();
    String endDate = st.nextToken();

    // print the results out to a screen
    StringBuffer results = new StringBuffer("");
    results.append(classID);
    results.append("        ");
    results.append(classDescr);
    results.append("      ");
    results.append(credits);
    results.append("        ");
    results.append(startDate);
    results.append("  ");
    results.append(endDate);
    System.out.println(results.toString());
```

After each of the individual class data elements are parsed from the line retrieved from the
Classes.txt file, you will use a SQLJ executable statement to insert the data into the class table:

```
// inserting the SQL code
#sql{
  INSERT INTO class(
    class_id,
    class_descr,
    credits,
    start_date,
    end_date
  )
  VALUES(
    :classID,
    :classDescr,
    :credits,
    :startDate,
    :endDate
  )};
}
```

If all of the lines in the Classes.txt file have been parsed and inserted into the CLASS table, the
close() method on the in variable will be called. This will close the handle the SimpleInsert
application is using to read the Classes.txt file:

```
// close the CSV File
in.close();
```

After all of this discussion, we have yet to see this code example work. To correct this code we need to edit the `Classes.txt` file and remove the duplicate class ID:

```
100,Introduction to Java,4,13-SEP-2001,10-DEC-2001
200,Introduction to SQLJ,3,13-SEP-2001,10-DEC-2001
300,OO Analysis and Design,3,13-SEP-2001,10-DEC-2001
400,Basket Weaving ,3,13-SEP-2001,10-DEC-2001
500,Intermediate SQLJ,4,13-SEP-2001,10-DEC-2001
```

Once the `Classes.txt` file has been updated, you can re-run the `SimpleInsert` example and you should see the following output:

```
> java com.wrox.sqlj.SimpleInsert
CLASS ID CLASS DESCR           CREDITS START DATE   END DATE
-------------------------------------------------------------
100      Introduction to Java  4       13-SEP-2001  10-DEC-2001
200      Introduction to SQLJ  3       13-SEP-2001  10-DEC-2001
300      OO Analysis and Design 3      13-SEP-2001  10-DEC-2001
400      Advanced Basket Weaving 3     13-SEP-2001  10-DEC-2001
500      Intermediate SQLJ     4       13-SEP-2001  10-DEC-2001
```

# A Few More Thoughts on Commits and Rollbacks

As you might have observed, Oracle's SQLJ database driver does not automatically commit to the database when a SQLJ `INSERT`, `UPDATE`, or `DELETE` executable statement is issued. Data manipulated by SQLJ will be saved to Oracle when one of the following actions occurs:

❑   The user explicitly issues a commit using a `#sql{COMMIT}` executable statement.

❑   The application ends without a commit being explicitly issued by the application.

❑   The database context in which the SQLJ `INSERT`, `UPDATE`, or `DELETE` statements occurred is successfully closed with a `close()` call. All outstanding transactions for that context that have not been committed to the Oracle database will do so.

How can you force your application to commit a transaction as soon as it occurs? Most of the time you do not want to do this. Setting up the database to perform a commit represents a significant amount of resources. A rollback segment must be allocated, the database must check to see if a lock needs to be applied and when the commit is issued, a physical write to the database has to take place.

Numerous, small commits are not efficient and can result in I/O performance problems in your application. However, this being said, there are specific times when you might want to commit a record as soon as has been inserted, modified, or deleted. An example of this might be a point in time financial transaction that must be committed immediately. You might not want that transaction to be committed in batch, because a rollback would cause that data to be lost.

> **In general, auto-committing database transactions is bad practice.**

There are two methods for forcing a commit on every SQL transaction issued in SQLJ. The first method involves issuing a #sql{COMMIT} call immediately following a SQLJ executable statement that modifies the database. For our previous example, we would move the #sql{COMMIT} call inside the while loop so that as each record INSERT takes place, a database COMMIT is issued:

```
while ((holderString = in.readLine())!= null) {
   .
   .
   .
   #sql{
     INSERT INTO class(
       class_id,
       class_descr,
       credits,
       start_date,
       end_date
     )
     VALUES(
       :classID,
       :classDescr,
       :credits,
       :startDate,
       :endDate
     )};
   #sql{COMMIT};
 }
```

While this method does work, it is a brute force method. Every SQL statement that you want to commit to the database immediately must be followed with a #sql{COMMIT} statement.

The second method to force a commit after every database change is to open the database connection and pass into the Oracle.connect() method an auto-commit flag set to true.

> This is a major difference between SQLJ and JDBC. SQLJ by default has the auto-commit turned off. JDBC has auto-commit turned on.

The Oracle.connect() method has 12 variations. Rather than using:

```
Oracle.connect(db connect string, username, password);
```

you would use:

```
Oracle.connect(db connect string, username, password, auto-commit flag);
```

While it is not required to pass in an auto-commit flag when opening a database connection, it is still good practice because it lets anyone looking at the code know what the commit behavior is for the database context.

> It is a good practice to always explicitly declare the auto-commit behavior for any SQLJ database contexts. Remember, sooner or later you will move onto to bigger and better things and the poor soul who has to take over your code will benefit from you explicitly spelling out what is occurring. It's better to be explicit in your code than have someone guess what is going on.

All code shown from this point on will pass in an `auto-commit` flag when creating a database context.

# SQLJ Declarations

In the previous example, we used SQLJ to insert records parsed from a CSV file. We did this using the default database context. Remember, by using a default database context all SQLJ executable statements that do not use a database context other than the default one will share the same transaction. By sharing the same transaction, any time a commit or rollback is issued for that transaction, all uncommitted data changes made by a SQLJ executable statements will either be written to the database or discarded.

A little earlier, we discussed the two basic constructs within SQLJ. The first construct, the SQLJ executable statement, is what we have seen in all of the earlier examples. Now we are going to change gears for a moment and look at the second type of SQLJ construct, the **SQLJ declaration**.

There are two different types of SQLJ declaration statements. These statements are:

❏ Connection contexts

❏ Iterators

**Connection contexts** allow developers to define multiple database connections inside one application. All of the examples shown so far have used the default connection context. Using SQLJ declarations, a developer can define their own connection context that is transactionally independent of other SQLJ code in the application. The second type of the SQLJ declaration, the **iterator**, allows the developer to create a wrapper class around the results returned from a query. This wrapper allows the developer to easily cycle through a query and pull the individual data elements out of it. Conceptually, a SQLJ iterator behaves in the same manner as a JDBC `Resultset`.

# Creating Multiple Connection Contexts

There can be times when you do not want database changes to share the default context. Examples of this might include when:

❏ You want to connect to the same database with multiple user accounts. Many applications, like Oracle Financials, will have the different pieces of the application segregated into different user accounts.

❏ You want to connect to multiple databases (be they Oracle or another vendors' database) within the same application. The default database context can only connect to one database schema at a time.

❑ You are writing multi-threaded code where database changes in one thread need to be completely independent of database changes in another thread. An example of this might be a data loading program that is going to perform a significant amount of inserts. Rather than performing inserts in a linear fashion, you might use database threads and independent database contexts to try to minimize the amount of time it will take to process the loads.

The next example, which we will call `ComplexInsert`, will update data in two different Oracle databases. This example will build on the `SimpleInsert` example shown previously. The code will build a simple data-loading program that will parse a `Classes.txt` file and insert the record into the `CLASS` table.

One of the challenges with a data loading programming is tracking what the application is doing and where the application is in parsing a file. This type of information is particularly useful when you have an extremely long running process and want to know where to restart if the application fails at some point.

The problem here is that you want your log information committed *independently* of the data being entered in the database. You do not want the data being parsed from the data file to be committed every time a log entry is made. You also do not want to lose uncommitted log information because a database exception forces a rollback in your code. In addition, with a long-running job you want to monitor the status of the application as it is running. You need to commit log data as it happens so that you can see what is going on in the application.

What is needed is for the log transaction to be independent of your data file transactions.

This can be done in a number of ways:

❑ The log transactions could be written out to a file in the operating system and then you do not have to worry about database transactions for the log. However, using the log file approach loses you the benefits of a database, mainly being able to sort and query large amounts of data quickly. This is extremely important when you are trying to diagnose why a long running, batch data load has failed.

❑ You can write asynchronous processing code using Oracle's `DBMS_PIPE` package to allow you to 'push' data from one process to another process that had its own transaction context. The second process would have its own transaction context and could commit independently of the first process.

❑ A `log()` method in the class you are working in can open a separate database context. The `log()` method can then insert a record into the log independent of the transactional activity in the rest of the application.

## Using Non-Default Database Contexts

Before looking at the `ComplexInsert` code we need to set up our `APP_AUDIT` table. To create this table, you will need to run the following Oracle DDL commands using SQL*Plus:

```
SQL> create table app_audit(
  2     app_id        VARCHAR2(30),
  3     class_descr   VARCHAR2(1000),
  4     date_created  DATE
```

```
    5 );

Table created.
```

With these steps behind you, lets look at the code for the `ComplexInsert` application:

```java
package com.wrox.sqlj;

import oracle.sqlj.runtime.Oracle;
import sqlj.runtime.ref.DefaultContext;
import java.sql.SQLException;
import java.io.*;
import java.util.*;

public class ComplexInsert {
  String csvFile =
    "c:/Classes.txt";
  String dbName = "jdbc:oracle:oci8:@DATABASE";
  String userID = "username";
  String passwd = "password";
  String appID = "COMPLEXINSERT";

  /* This method will log a message to the APP_AUDIT table. This method is
   * using a separate database context then the default context so log data
   * can be committed independently of the data in classes.txt.
   */
  public void logMsg(String auditMsg) {
    try {
      // connection Context for the log entry
      DefaultContext auditContext =
        Oracle.getConnection(dbName, userID, passwd, false);

      try {
        // inserting APP_AUDIT record into APP_AUDIT.CLASS_AUDIT
        #sql [auditContext] {
          INSERT INTO app_audit(
            app_id,
            class_descr,
            date_created
          )
          VALUES(
            :appID,
            :auditMsg,
            SYSDATE
          )};
        #sql [auditContext]    {COMMIT};
      } catch(Exception e) {
        System.out.println("An exception has occurred in the log method(): "
                           + e.toString());
      } finally {
        auditContext.close();
      }
```

```
    } catch(SQLException sqle) {
      System.out.println("Unable to close the audit database connection: "
                         + sqle.toString());
    }
}


/* The parseFile() method will parse through a CSV file.
 * As it retrieves a line of data from the application, it will parse the
 * data into variables used as host expressions and then insert them into
 * the class table in the database.
 */
public void  parseFile() {
  // declare the buffered reader that will read the CSV file
  BufferedReader in = null;

  try {
    // connect to the class context
    DefaultContext classContext =
      Oracle.getConnection(dbName, userID, passwd, false);

    try {
      // create a buffered reader to read csvFile
      in = new BufferedReader(new FileReader(csvFile));
      String holderString = "";

      int lineCount = 1;

      while ((holderString = in.readLine())!=null) {
        logMsg("Starting line #: " + lineCount);
        // initialize a string tokenizer with the string retrieved
        // and a comma.
        StringTokenizer st = new StringTokenizer(holderString,",");

        // populate host expressions with data from the tokenizer
        String classID = st.nextToken();
        String classDescr = st.nextToken();
        String credits = st.nextToken();
        String startDate = st.nextToken();
        String endDate = st.nextToken();

        logMsg("Tokenizing file data into individual pieces.");

        // insert class record into username.classes
        #sql [classContext] {
          INSERT INTO class(
            class_id,
            class_descr,
            credits,
            start_date,
            end_date
          )
          VALUES(
            :classID,
```

```
                    :classDescr,
                    :credits,
                    :startDate,
                    :endDate
               )};

          logMsg("Inserted entry into application");
          logMsg("Ending line #: " + lineCount);
          lineCount++;
        }
        #sql [classContext] {COMMIT};
        logMsg("All records committed.");

        /*Closing the CSV File*/
        in.close();
      } catch (IOException ie) {
        System.out.println("There is a problem with the CSV file: "
                           + ie.toString());
        #sql [classContext] {ROLLBACK};
      } catch(Exception e) {
        System.out.println("An exception was raised: " + e.toString());
        #sql [classContext] {ROLLBACK};
      } finally {
        classContext.close();
      }
    } catch(SQLException sqle) {
      System.out.println("Unable to close the classContext database connection: "
                         + sqle.toString());
    }
  }

  // This main statement creates an instance of the ComplextInsert class
  // and calls the parseFile() method.
  public static void main(String args[]) {
    ComplexInsert complexInsert = new ComplexInsert();

    // parsing the file
    complexInsert.parseFile();
  }
}
```

### How It Works

The ComplexInsert program looks very much like the SimpleInsert program shown earlier. However, this application is going to be using non-default SQLJ connection contexts to do the record inserts.

The application starts in the main() method. The main() method is creating an instance of the ComplexInsert class and calling the parseFile() method on the class:

```
ComplexInsert complexInsert = new ComplexInsert();

    // parsing the file
    complexInsert.parseFile();
    }
```

As before, the parseFile() method opens up the CSV file Classes.txt. It then establishes a specific, non-default connection to the database. This connection, called classContext, will be used to insert line items from the Classes.txt file into the database. It does this by declaring an object of type DefaultContext and using the Oracle.getConnection() method to create a DefaultContext instance:

```
    // connect to the class context
    DefaultContext classContext =
      Oracle.getConnection(dbName, userID, passwd, false);
```

The Oracle.getConnection() method behaves almost exactly like the Oracle.connect() method. The two methods each create a database context that can be used in the SQLJ application. However, the Oracle.connect() method creates a database context and stores that context as a static variable inside the Oracle class. When the SQLJ translator comes across a SQLJ statement that does not explicitly declare a database connection context, it will use the connection context stored by the Oracle.connect() method.

> **Remember, you must declare a default database context by calling the Oracle.connect() method before you try to use a SQLJ statement that uses the default context. Failure to do this will result in no connection being stored inside of the Oracle object.**

If it does not find a connection context stored inside the Oracle object it will throw an exception. The Oracle.getConnection() method creates a database connection context, but does not store a reference to it inside the Oracle object.

The parseFile() method will process each line in the Classes.txt file and then attempt to insert that retrieved record into the CLASS table. This time though, the SQLJ executable statement that is used to insert the record is different to the one seen in the SimpleInsert example. Let's takes a look:

```
        #sql [classContext] {
          INSERT INTO class(
            class_id,
            class_descr,
            credits,
            start_date,
            end_date
          )
```

```
                    VALUES(
                      :classID,
                      :classDescr,
                      :credits,
                      :startDate,
                      :endDate
                    )};
```

This time the SQLJ statement is passing the name of the student connect context created in the beginning of the `parseFile()` method into the SQLJ statement. Any SQLJ statement, be it an executable statement or a declaration, can define what connection context to use by using the following syntax:

```
#sql [name of the connection context] {};
```

When passing the connection context into a SQLJ statement, three things must be kept in mind:

❑   The connection context (in other words, the `DefaultContext` class) must be already declared before the SQLJ code can reference it. Writing the SQLJ statement and then creating the connection context will cause an error to be raised when the code is translated with the Oracle SQLJ translator.

❑   Before the connection context is used, it must have a valid reference to a `DefaultContext` object. This means that the connection context must hold a reference to a `DefaultContext` object returned by the `Oracle.getConnection()` method. Failure to do this will result in a run-time exception being thrown.

❑   The Java rules of scope apply to a connection context. A SQLJ statement cannot specify a `DefaultContext` object that it would like to use if the `DefaultContext` object is not in scope.

As the `parseFile()` method is processing, calls will be made to the `logMsg()` method. This method uses a separate database context to insert a single entry into the APP_AUDIT table. The `logMsg()` method will then immediately commit that record into the database:

```
public void logMsg(String auditMsg) {
  try {
    // connection Context for the log entry
    DefaultContext auditContext =
      Oracle.getConnection(dbName,userID,passwd, false);

    try {
      // inserting APP_AUDIT record into APP_AUDIT.CLASS_AUDIT
      #sql [auditContext] {
        INSERT INTO app_audit(
          app_id,
          class_descr,
          date_created
        )
        VALUES(
          :appID,
          :auditMsg,
```

```
              SYSDATE
          )};
        #sql [auditContext]   {COMMIT};
      } catch(Exception e) {
        System.out.println("An exception has occurred in the log method(): "
                          + e.toString());
      } finally {
        auditContext.close();
      }
    } catch(SQLException sqle) {
      System.out.println("Unable to close the audit database connection: "
                          + sqle.toString());
    }
  }
```

The first thing the logMsg() function does is to create a new database context called auditContext. The auditContext object will be used for all SQLJ relating to the insertion of an audit record:

```
DefaultContext auditContext =
    Oracle.getConnection(dbName, userID, passwd, false);
```

The SQLJ statements will then use the auditContext object to define what database context they are using. Like, the SQLJ INSERT statement in the parseFile() method, the SQLJ INSERT statement in the logMsg() method will pass in the database context it is going to use:

```
#sql [auditContext] {
  INSERT INTO app_audit(
    app_id,
    class_descr,
    date_created
  )
  VALUES(
    :appID,
    :auditMsg,
    SYSDATE
  )};
#sql [auditContext]   {COMMIT};
```

The SQLJ code above is using the auditContext as it is database connection context. When the code is run, you will see no output being generated by the application. However, if you examine the APP_AUDIT table, you will find a significant amount of work taking place. Issue the following SQL command in SQL*Plus and you would see the following:

```
SQL> select class_descr
  2     from app_audit;

CLASS_DESCR
-------------------------------------------------------------------------------
```

```
Starting line #: 1
Tokenizing file data into individual pieces.
Inserted entry into application
Ending line #: 1
Starting line #: 2
Tokenizing file data into individual pieces.
Inserted entry into application
Ending line #: 2
Starting line #: 3
Tokenizing file data into individual pieces.
Inserted entry into application
Ending line #: 3
Starting line #: 4
Tokenizing file data into individual pieces.
Inserted entry into application
Ending line #: 4
Starting line #: 5
Tokenizing file data into individual pieces.
Inserted entry into application
Ending line #: 5
All records committed.

25 rows selected.
```

In summary, by using non-default database contexts, we are able to independently control when and where certain SQL statements within an application are going to COMMIT or ROLLBACK. In the ComplexInsert application, we are using two separate database contexts to ensure that audit data is always committed the moment it is written, and data from the classes.txt data file is not committed until all records in the file have been read and inserted into the classes table.

This might be considered an overly simplistic example of non-default SQLJ database contexts. Other ways in which non-default SQLJ database contexts can be used include:

❑ A multi-threaded application where each thread can independently perform database transactions. In this case, each thread might be creating their own SQLJ database context to carry out their database work.

❑ An application that accesses multiple data schemas in Oracle. Some applications keep very tight control of their schemas and only let specific owner accounts for the schema have access to the database resources in it. In this case, an application might have to log in as different users in the same database in order to carry out this work. Oracle Financials is a perfect example where the application is partitioned into very specific user schemas and access to those schemas are usually tightly controlled via a single user account.

# Iterators

Out of all of the code examples shown so far, only one of them uses a SQL SELECT statement to query the database. Even then, that SELECT statement returns a single row. If you want to process the results of a query that contains multiple records, you need to use a SQLJ declaration called an **iterator**.

> **If you try to return more than one row into a SQLJ query that is only expecting one row, a run-time exception will be thrown.**

An iterator is a Java class generated for you by SQLJ. An iterator is in many ways analogous to a JDBC `ResultSet` or a PL/SQL cursor. You define the columns you are going to retrieve from the query and SQLJ will generate helper methods to scroll through the cursor and retrieve data. Let's look at one in action.

## Using an Iterator

The following is a small application to retrieve all of the student records in the STUDENT table and print the values retrieved back onto the screen. It uses an iterator to cycle through each of the records retrieved. Note that when you compile the code for this example, you will get an error about possible loss of precision on the STUDENT_ID field. Don't worry about it as there will be no loss of precision.

Here is the code for the `IteratorExample` class:

```
package com.wrox.sqlj;

import oracle.sqlj.runtime.Oracle;
import java.sql.SQLException;

public class IteratorExample {

  #sql public iterator StudentIterator(Integer  student_id,
                                        String   first_name,
                                        String   last_name,
                                        String   street,
                                        String   city,
                                        String   state,
                                        String   zip);
  public void retrieveStudents() {
    try {
      try {

        // make the database connection by using the default context
        Oracle.connect("jdbc:oracle:oci8:@DATABASE", "username",
                  "password", true);

        StudentIterator students = null;

        // retrieve the data into the students iterator
        #sql students = { SELECT
                    student_id,
                    first_name,
                    last_name,
                    street,
                    city,
                    state,
                    zip
                  FROM
```

```
                              student};

        // print out results
        System.out.println("ID FNAME   LNAME     STREET              CITY
                            STATE   ZIP");
        System.out.println("----------------------------------------------
                            ---------------------");

        // cycle through the returned results
        while (students.next()) {
          StringBuffer output = new
            StringBuffer(students.student_id().toString());
          output.append("  ");
          output.append(students.first_name());
          output.append("       ");
          output.append(students.last_name());
          output.append("     ");
          output.append(students.street());
          output.append("     ");
          output.append(students.city());
          output.append("     ");
          output.append(students.state());
          output.append("     ");
          output.append(students.zip());

          System.out.println(output.toString());
        }
        students.close();
      } catch(Exception e) {
        System.out.println(e.toString());
      } finally {
        Oracle.close();
      }
    } catch(SQLException sqle) {
      System.out.println("Code having a problem closing the Oracle connection: "
                         + sqle.toString());
    }
  }

  public static void main(String[] args) {
    IteratorExample iteratorExample = new IteratorExample();
    iteratorExample.retrieveStudents();
  }
}
```

To translate this code from SQLJ source to Java source, use the `buildSQLJ.bat` script shown earlier in the chapter. After the source has compiled, run it and you should see the following output:

```
> java com.wrox.sqlj.IteratorExample
ID FNAME  LNAME  STREET                  CITY          STATE   ZIP
------------------------------------------------------------------------
1  Mary   Jones  1502 Westchisre Avenue  Clintonville  WI      53188
2  Dan    Smith  1802 Miller Street      Clintonville  WI      53188
3  Ryan   Smith  1802 Miller Street      Clintonville  WI      53188
4  Dave   Doe    1008 Morre Street       Waukesha      WI      53088
```

### How It Works

The IteratorExample class starts by defining the SQLJ iterator that will be used to process the data retrieved from the query against the student database. A SQLJ iterator in its most basic form has the following syntax:

```
#sql <modifier> iterator classname(ParameterList)
```

The iterator for the IteratorExample class, StudentIterator, is defined as follows:

```
#sql public iterator StudentIterator(Integer  student_id,
                                     String   first_name,
                                     String   last_name,
                                     String   street,
                                     String   city,
                                     String   state,
                                     String   zip);
```

Just like a host expression, if a value you are going to retrieve into an iterator is going to be null, do not use a primitive java data type in the iterator declaration. Use the equivalent Java wrapper class.

The access modifier tag is used to indicate whether the SQLJ iterator is:

❑   public

❑   private

❑   No access modifier

SQLJ iterators are created as inner classes inside the Java class in which they are defined. Declaring an iterator as public means that other classes in the same package as the Java class that defines the iterator can access and use the iterator. Declaring the iterator as private will only allow the Java class that defines the iterator (also referred to as the outer class) to use the iterator. Declaring an iterator without a modifier will make the iterator 'friendly'. Friendly means that the iterator is accessible to any other class within the same Java package as the iterator.

After declaring the modifier for the iterator, you use the SQLJ key word iterator followed by the Java class name you would like to use for the iterator. This class name must follow all the rules for naming a Java class. In the example above, we have declared an iterator called StudentIterator:

```
#sql public iterator StudentIterator
```

SQLJ allows you to declare two different types of iterators:

❑   A named iterator

❑   A positional iterator

### Named Iterators

Named iterators are declared by explicitly providing the name of the column being returned and its corresponding Java data type. In the StudentIterator declared above, we are using a named iterator to hold the values returned from our SQL statement.

As you can see from the code, the StudentIterator is explicitly matching the data values and the column name of the SQL statement being used to return the data:

```
#sql students = { SELECT
                        student_id,
                        first_name,
                        last_name,
                        street,
                        city,
                        state,
                        zip
                  FROM
                        student};
```

There are three things to keep in mind with a named iterator:

❏   Since the name of each variable declared in the iterator must match the name of a column being returned in a SQL statement, the order of the variables in the iterator declaration does not matter. They can be in any order.

❏   You can us aliases to rename columns in your SQL statement, as long as the alias is used to declare that column in the iterator. The SQLJ translator is going to use the column declared in the iterator and verify that that name, be it a regular column name or a column alias, is available in the SELECT statement.

❏   Using a wildcard SELECT statement such as SELECT * FROM SQL commands can be used with a named iterator. However, all of the columns returned from the SELECT * must be named in the iterator and the variable names must match the name of the database column being returned.

> **Using a wildcard SELECT is bad practice. Often, you are going to retrieve more columns than you need to actually use *and* if you are accessing columns in your iterator positionally, your code can easily be broken by someone else adding a column to the database. Do not use wildcard selects. Be explicit.**

### Positional Iterators

Positional iterators do not explicitly define the name of the column being returned by the database in the iterator declaration. Instead, they only define the Java data type being returned from the SQL statement. The column names were left out. If we were to rewrite the StudentIterator as a positional iterator, it would look like this:

```
#sql public iterator StudentIterator(Integer,
                                     String,
                                     String,
                                     String,
                                     String,
                                     String,
                                     String);
```

The Java data type declared in the iterator must match the SQL data type being returned or the return type being retrieved from the database must be coercible to the type declared in the iterator.

### Retrieving the Data from SQLJ

After the iterator is declared, you can use it to hold the values returned from a SQLJ executable statement. To do this, you first need to declare the iterator as a Java variable. For the IteratorExample example, the StudentIterator SQLJ declaration is made at the top of the package and then later declared as a Java variable in the retrieveStudents() method:

```
StudentIterator students = null;
```

After the iterator has been declared, it can be used in combination with a SELECT SQLJ executable statement to hold the results of the query. The syntax for actually returning data into the iterator is:

```
#sql iterator_instance variable = {SELECT SQLJ Executable statement}
```

In the IteratorExample class, the students variable declared above holds the results of a SELECT statement from the student table:

```
// retrieve the data into the students iterator
#sql students = { SELECT
                     student_id,
                     first_name,
                     last_name,
                     street,
                     city,
                     state,
                     zip
                  FROM
                     student};
```

The syntax for retrieving data into the iterator is the same, regardless of whether a positional or named iterator is being used. After the data has been retrieved from the iterator we will walk through it using the students iterator's next() method and the helper method generated by the SQLJ translator:

```
while (students.next()) {
  StringBuffer output = new
    StringBuffer(students.student_id().toString());
  output.append("  ");
  output.append(students.first_name());
  output.append("        ");
  output.append(students.last_name());
```

```
output.append("      ");
output.append(students.street());
output.append("      ");
output.append(students.city());
output.append("      ");
output.append(students.state());
output.append("      ");
output.append(students.zip());

System.out.println(output.toString());
}
```

The above code example is using the StudentIterator's next() method to loop through each row returned from the database. The StudentIterator class is completely generated by the SQLJ translator so you do not need to know any of the coding details behind the next() method.

If you look closely, retrieving data from a SQLJ Iterator looks very similar to how you would navigate and retrieve data from a JDBC ResultSet. Like a ResultSet object, the iterator will contain the data retrieved from the SQL or stored procedure call. Also like the ResultSet, you loop through the Iterator using a while loop and retrieving data with a get() method.

To retrieve the actual column values from the query returned into the Students iterator, you are going to use helper methods that are generated based on the SQLJ iterator declaration shown earlier. These helper methods are going to have the same name as the Java variable names listed in the iterator. For the IteratorExample class you can see the helper method being used:

```
StringBuffer output = new
   StringBuffer(students.student_id().toString());
output.append("  ");
output.append(students.first_name());
output.append("      ");
output.append(students.last_name());
output.append("      ");
output.append(students.street());
output.append("      ");
output.append(students.city());
output.append("      ");
output.append(students.state());
output.append("      ");
output.append(students.zip());
```

It is important to note here that positional iterators will have different helper methods generated by the SQLJ translator for them. If we had written the StudentIterator as a positional iterator, then the SQLJ translator would have generated a method name called getColoumnPosition(), where column position would be the numeric position of the column in the iterator declaration.

The code for outputting the results of our query would have been rewritten as:

```
StringBuffer output = new
   StringBuffer(students.student_id().toString());
output.append("  ");
output.append(students.getCol2());   // first name
```

```
output.append("        ");
output.append(students.getCol3());   // last name
output.append("     ");
output.append(students.getCol4());   // street
output.append("     ");
output.append(students.getCol5());   // city
output.append("     ");
output.append(students.getCol6());   // state
output.append("     ");
output.append(students.getCol7());   // zip
```

After all of the data has been pulled from the iterator and printed out, we close both the iterator and the default connection by using their respective `close()` methods:

```
students.close();

Oracle.close();
```

## Last Thoughts on Iterators

The SQLJ iterator is a powerful tool for Oracle database development. Iterators allow developers to strongly type their SQL statements to help ensure the catching coding errors at compile-time rather than run-time. In addition, they wrap the query results in a Java class specifically tailored for retrieving those data elements defined in the iterator.

There are two things to keep in mind about SQLJ iterators:

❑ All of the iterator examples here have been using Java wrapper classes (in other words, `String`, `Double`, `Boolean`) in the iterator declaration. A primitive Java data type (in other words, `float`, `int`, `boolean`) can be used in an iterator declaration as long as the value being returned in the column is a non-null.

❑ Oracle will coerce the data type of the value being returned from the database to whatever the data type for an iterator element is if the data can be safely converted. For instance, if a `string` value in the database is being returned to a `float` object in the iterator, then as long as the value of the data returned could be safely converted to a `float`, the code will not generate an exception.

This section has only begun to discuss some of the power and flexibility of SQLJ iterators. The basics of the SQLJ iterator have been covered, but topics like the use of interfaces via the `implements` keyword or the use of the `with` keyword have not been covered in this chapter.

These topics are not necessary for beginning SQLJ iteration development. However, if you are interested in learning about these topics, you are encouraged to explore Oracle's *SQLJ Developer's Guide and Reference*. This document is a freely available from Oracle's web site at http://download-eu.oracle.com/otndoc/oracle9i/901_doc/index.htm.

# Using SQLJ to Invoke PL/SQL

SQLJ can be used for more than querying and manipulating Oracle data using SQL statements. SQLJ can also be used to invoke Oracle stored procedures. Invoking a stored procedure involves nothing more than declaring a SQLJ executable call and declaring the proper host expressions to pass data into and receive data out of the procedure. Let's look at how to use SQLJ and PL/SQL in two different scenarios:

❑ A basic PL/SQL stored procedure that does not return a value

❑ A PL/SQL stored function that returns a basic data type like a VARCHAR or BOOLEAN

## SQLJ and a Basic PL/SQL Stored Procedure

Let's start with a very basic PL/SQL stored procedure that inserts a record into the STUDENT table. Being a stored procedure and not a stored function, this PL/SQL will not return a value back to the application calling it. To compile it, you need to log into SQL*Plus and type the code in, or alternatively, run the insertStudent.sql script, which is part of the code download available from http://www.wrox.com:

```
SQL> create or replace procedure insertStudent (
  2     studentId    IN    INTEGER,
  3     firstName    IN    VARCHAR2,
  4     lastName     IN    VARCHAR2,
  5     street       IN    VARCHAR2,
  6     city         IN    VARCHAR2,
  7     state        IN    VARCHAR2,
  8     zip          IN    VARCHAR2
  9  ) as
 10  begin
 11    insert into student(
 12       student_id,
 13       first_name,
 14       last_name,
 15       street,
 16       city,
 17       state,
 18       zip
 19    )
 20    values (
 21       studentId,
 22       firstName,
 23       lastName,
 24       street,
 25       city,
 26       state,
 27       zip
 28    );
 29
 30    commit;
 31  end insertStudent;
 32  /

Procedure created.
```

After the `insertStudent` procedure is compiled in the database, we are ready to write a SQLJ application that can invoke a stored procedure. The PL/SQL stored procedure for this example will insert a row into the STUDENTS table. In real life, it is doubtful you would write a stored procedure to perform such a simple act.

> The stored procedures used is these examples should not be used as a model for writing Oracle stored procedures. They are designed to be learning tools to show how to use Oracle SQLJ to invoke a PL/SQL stored procedure. If you are interested in learning more about how to write stored procedures and good application design with stored procedures, I highly recommend you refer to Thomas Kyte's *Expert One on One Oracle* , ISBN 1-861004-82-6, published by *Wrox Press*.

## Using SQLJ to Call a Stored Procedure

The Java class below is named `SimpleStoredProc`:

```
package com.wrox.sqlj;

import oracle.sqlj.runtime.Oracle;
import java.sql.SQLException;

public class SimpleStoredProc {

  public static void main(String args[]) {
    try {
      try {
        Oracle.connect("jdbc:oracle:oci8:@DATABASE", "username",
                       "password", true);

        // initialize bind variables
        Integer studentID = new Integer(100);
        String studentFirstName = "John";
        String studentLastName = "Huenick";
        String studentStreet = "1342 WestLake Road";
        String studentCity = "Pewaukee";
        String studentState = "WI";
        String studentZip = "53188";

        #sql { CALL insertstudent(:IN(studentID),
                                  :IN(studentFirstName),
                                  :IN(studentLastName),
                                  :IN(studentStreet),
                                  :IN(studentCity),
                                  :IN(studentState),
                                  :IN(studentZip))};

        // reset bind variables
        Integer holderInt = new Integer(studentID.intValue());
        studentID = new Integer(0);
```

```
            studentFirstName = "";
            studentLastName = "";
            studentStreet = "";
            studentCity = "";
            studentState = "";
            studentZip = "";

            // retrieving the values the stored procedure just inserted
            #sql { SELECT
                        student_id,
                        first_name,
                        last_name,
                        street,
                        city,
                        state,
                        zip
                    INTO
                        :OUT(studentID),
                        :OUT(studentFirstName),
                        :OUT(studentLastName),
                        :OUT(studentStreet),
                        :OUT(studentCity),
                        :OUT(studentState),
                        :OUT(studentZip)
                    FROM
                        student
                    WHERE
                        student_id=:IN(holderInt)};

        // print out results out
        System.out.println("Student Information");
        System.out.println("--------------------");
        System.out.println("Student id:      " + studentID);
        System.out.println("First name:      " + studentFirstName);
        System.out.println("Last name: " + studentLastName);
        System.out.println("Street:          " + studentStreet);
        System.out.println("City:            " + studentCity);
        System.out.println("State:           " + studentState);
        System.out.println("Zip:             " + studentZip);
      } catch(Exception e) {
        System.out.println(e.toString());
      } finally {
        Oracle.close();
      }
    } catch(SQLException sqe) {
      System.out.println("Error closing the database connection: "
                        + sqe.toString());
    }
  }
}
```

Compile the above code using the `buildSQLJ.bat` script provided earlier in this chapter. Again, you will receive a warning of a possible loss of precision but this is nothing to worry about. You can run the `SimpleStoredProc` application by passing in the `STUDENT_ID` of a targeted student. You should see the following on the screen:

```
> java com.wrox.sqlj.SimpleStoredProc
Student Information
-------------------
Student id:     100
First name:     John
Last name:      Huenick
Street:         1342 WestLake Road
City:           Pewaukee
State:          WI
Zip:            53188
```

## How It Works

The `SimpleStoredProc` application calls the `insertStudent` PL/SQL stored procedure, and then retrieves the record inserted by the stored procedure. We are not going to examine all of the code because most of the material shown above has been covered in previous sections.

Invoking a PL/SQL stored procedure that does not return a value via SQLJ uses the following syntax:

```
#sql { CALL PL/SQL_stored_procedure_name ( parameter1,
                                           parameter2,
                                               .
                                               .
                                               .
                                  ) };
```

The keyword `CALL` in the SQLJ statement above is the SQLJ syntax to indicate that a stored procedure that does not return any values is being invoked. Any call to stored procedure using SQLJ is considered an executable statement. This means that all of the rules for a SQLJ executable statement apply to the `SimpleStoredProc` application.

To properly call the `insertStudent` stored procedure, we need to first declare a set of host expression variables that will hold the parameter values, which are going to be passed into the procedure. For this example we are declaring a set of variables and initializing them with the data elements for a single student. The value that we are initializing the variables with will be what gets passed into the `InsertStudent` stored procedure:

```
// initialize bind variables
Integer studentID = new Integer(100);
String studentFirstName = "John";
String studentLastName = "Huenick";
String studentStreet = "1342 WestLake Road";
String studentCity = "Pewaukee";
String studentState = "WI";
String studentZip = "53188";
```

After the host expression variables have been declared and populated with data, the `insertStudent` stored procedure will be invoked:

```
#sql { CALL insertstudent(:IN(studentID),
                          :IN(studentFirstName),
                          :IN(studentLastName),
                          :IN(studentStreet),
                          :IN(studentCity),
                          :IN(studentState),
                          :IN(studentZip))};
```

There are two things you must keep in mind when making a stored procedure call:

1. The Java data type of the host expression being passed in or out of the stored procedure should match the corresponding PL/SQL data type of the stored procedure. Oracle will perform implicit data type conversions, which can lead to unpredictable behavior in your application.

2. The host expression types of IN, OUT, and INOUT must match the type being expected by the PL/SQL stored procedure. Failure to properly describe these types in SQLJ will cause an error during translation.

SQLJ greatly simplifies the process of invoking a PL/SQL stored procedure. Let's now take a look at a basic PL/SQL stored function.

# Returning Values From PL/SQL Functions

Oracle allows you to write PL/SQL stored procedures both as subroutines that do not return a value, and functions that do. Let's write a PL/SQL function, called classCount, which will return the number of classes a student currently is taking. The classCount PL/SQL code is shown below. This function will calculate the number of credits the student is currently carrying, and is stored in a script names classCount.sql:

```
SQL> create or replace function classCount (studentId IN VARCHAR2)
  2    return number
  3    as
  4      total_credits number;
  5    begin
  6      select count(credits)
  7        into total_credits
  8        from student,
  9             class,
 10             student_class
 11      where student.student_id = student_class.student_id
 12        and student_class.class_id = class.class_id
 13        and student.student_id = studentId;
 14      return total_credits;
 15    end classCount;
 16  /

Function created.
```

Once the code has been compiled, let's write a SQLJ-based code to invoke the classCount function and display its value onto the screen.

## SQLJ and a PL/SQL Stored Function

Here is the code for the `SimpleStoredFunc` class:

```
package com.wrox.sqlj;

import oracle.sqlj.runtime.Oracle;
import java.sql.SQLException;

public class SimpleStoredFunc {

  public static void main(String args[]) {
    try {
      try {
        Oracle.connect("jdbc:oracle:oci8:@DATABASE", "username",
                       "password", true);

        // initialize bind variables
        Integer credits = new Integer(0);

        /*NOTE: This is where we are calling the stored function and
         *       retrieving the value retrieved from the stored procedure.
         */
        #sql credits = { VALUES classcount(:IN(args[0])) };

        // print out results
        System.out.println("The class count for student "
                            + args[0] + " is: " + credits);
      } catch(Exception e) {
        System.out.println(e.toString());
      } finally {
        Oracle.close();
      }
    } catch(SQLException sqle) {
      System.out.println("Error in closing the database connection: "
                          + sqle.toString());
    }
  }
}
```

Once compiled in the usual way, this class can be used by specifying on the command line which student ID we are interested in. The application will then compute how many classes that particular student is taking. Here are a couple of example invocations:

```
> java com.wrox.sqlj.SimpleStoredFunc 1
The class count for student 1 is: 4

> java com.wrox.sqlj.SimpleStoredFunc 4
The class count for student 4 is: 3
```

**299**

### How it Works

The SQLJ executable statement syntax for calling a PL/SQL function is different from the syntax for calling a PL/SQL stored procedure. The syntax for calling a PL/SQL function is:

```
#sql return value = { VALUES PL/SQL_function_name (
                                          parameter list) };
```

The SQLJ statement for the `classCount` function is:

```
// initialize bind variables
Integer credits = new Integer(0);

#sql credits = { VALUES classcount(:IN(args[0])) };
```

The first part of the SQLJ statement shown above is the value returned by the `classCount` function. This variable, called `credits`, is declared as a standard SQLJ host expression.

The next part of the SQLJ statement is the `VALUES` keyword. This keyword indicates to the SQLJ translator that the stored procedure being called is a function.

> Do not confuse when to use the **CALL** and **VALUES** keywords. The **CALL** keyword is for PL/SQL procedures and the **VALUES** keyword is for PL/SQL functions.

# SQLJ and Java Stored Procedures

Java stored procedures are invoked in the same manner as PL/SQL stored procedures. We're not going to discuss the pros and cons of using Java stored procedures here – that will come in Chapters 10 onwards. The goal here is to demonstrate how Java stored procedures can be written with SQLJ. Oracle has an embedded SQLJ translator and runtime environment embedded inside the database.

This means that you can easily port your SQLJ code into your database to create a Java stored procedure. Let's take our `IteratorExample` and rewrite it as a Java stored procedure. You will find that in reality this is a very easy process.

## The IteratorExample as a Java Stored Procedure

Writing and deploying a SQLJ stored procedure involves three steps:

❏ Write your SQLJ/Java stored procedure using the CREATE OR REPLACE JAVA SOURCE command.

❏ Compile the code into the Oracle database.

❏ Write and compile a PL/SQL wrapper for the loaded Java code.

### Step 1 – Writing the SQLJ/Java Stored Procedure

Let's create a new class file called `IteratorExampleSP`. The code in this class file is going to be based off the `IteratorExample.sqlj` file shown earlier in the chapter:

```
create or replace and compile java source named "IteratorExampleSP"
as
import oracle.sqlj.runtime.Oracle;

public class IteratorExampleSP {
  // use a static iterator
  #sql private static iterator StudentIterator(String student_id,
                                               String first_name,
                                               String last_name,
                                               String street,
                                               String city,
                                               String state,
                                               String zip);
  // gotten rid of the main() method and have made the
  // retrieveStudents method a static method
  public static void retrieveStudents() {
    try {
      StudentIterator students = null;

      // retrieve the data into the students iterator
      #sql students = { SELECT
                          student_id,
                          first_name,
                          last_name,
                          street,
                          city,
                          state,
                          zip
                        FROM
                          student};

      // printing out the results
      String holderString = "ID       FNAME   LNAME   STREET
                             CITY            STATE   ZIP";
      System.out.println(holderString);

      holderString = "---------------------------------------------
                      -------------------------------";
      System.out.println(holderString);

      // cycle through the returned results
      while (students.next()) {
        StringBuffer output = new StringBuffer(students.student_id());
        output.append("    ");
        output.append(students.first_name());
        output.append("    ");
        output.append(students.last_name());
        output.append("    ");
```

```
            output.append(students.street());
            output.append("      ");
            output.append(students.city());
            output.append("      ");
            output.append(students.state());
            output.append("      ");
            output.append(students.zip());

            System.out.println(output.toString());
        }

        // no longer need to close the database connection
        students.close();
    } catch(Exception e) {
        System.out.println(e.toString());
    }
  }
 }
}
/
```

### Step 2 – Compile the Java Stored Procedure and Load Into the Database

Oracle provides the command:

```
CREATE OR REPLACE AND COMPILE JAVA SOURCE
```

to enable the user to easily load a piece of Java code into the database. In order to load the Java stored procedure file into the database you must run the above command in SQL*PLUS. The above Java stored procedure was written into a text file called `IteratorExample.sql`, which is then run from SQL*Plus:

```
SQL> @IteratorExample

Java created.
```

If the Java stored procedure was successfully created, the message `Java Created` appears.

### Step 3 – Write and Compile a PL/SQL wrapper for your Java Code

In order to use a Java file as a stored procedure, you must write a PL/SQL wrapper that will tell Oracle the exact method name called when you are invoking the stored procedure. The PL/SQL wrapper for the `IteratorExampleSP` example is shown below:

```
SQL> create or replace procedure retrieveStudents
  2  as
  3  language java
  4  name 'com.wrox.sqlj.IteratorExampleSP.retrieveStudents()';
  5  /

Procedure created.
```

Every Oracle Java stored procedure must have at least one static method on a class. For more information on why this is, take a look at Chapter 10, *Java Stored Procedure Basics*. The above PL/SQL wrapper is essentially telling Oracle that every time a user executes the retrievestudents PL/SQL call, the retrieveStudents() method is invoked on the com.wrox.sqlj.IteratorExampleSP class loaded into Oracle.

Logging into SQL*Plus and issuing the above will create the retrieveStudents Java wrapper. Once this wrapper has been created, the retrieveStudents Java stored procedure can be called from SQL*Plus:

```
SQL> set serveroutput on
SQL> exec dbms_java.set_output( 100000 )

PL/SQL procedure successfully completed.
```

The first command tells Oracle that the user wants to see any output generated from the stored procedure. The second command tells Oracle to output all System.out.println() generated from a Java stored procedure into a buffer of 100,000 characters. The data in this buffer is then written out to the SQL*Plus console when the stored procedure is done executing. Finally, the third command executes the Java stored procedure. The resulting output is:

```
SQL> exec retrieveStudents
ID      FNAME    LNAME    STREET                  CITY          STATE   ZIP
------------------------------------------------------------------------------
1       Mary     Jones    1502 Westchisre Avenue  Clintonville  WI      53188
2       Dan      Smith    1802 Miller Street       Clintonville  WI      53188
3       Ryan     Smith    1802 Miller Street       Clintonville  WI      53188
4       Dave     Doe      1008 Morre Street        Waukesha      WI      53088
100     John     Huenick  1342 WestLake Road       Pewaukee      WI      53188

PL/SQL procedure successfully completed.
```

The IteratorExampleSP Java stored procedure behaves exactly like the IteratorExample application shown earlier, but it executes inside of the database.

At this point, let's switch gears and look at the SQLJ code in the IteratorExampleSP stored procedure.

## How It Works

The SQLJ code looks very similiar to the examples we have seen in previous sections. However, looks can be a little deceiving. If you look closely at the code, you will notice the following differences from the previous examples:

❑ There is no Oracle.connect() or Oracle.close() method call anywhere

❑ The StudentsIterator SQLJ declaration has been declared as a static method

## SQLJ Default Database Contexts and Java Stored Procedures

The IteratorExampleSP SQLJ code does not contain any calls to the Oracle.connect() or Oracle.close() methods. Since the IteratorExampleSP Java class is being used as a stored procedure in the Java database, you no longer have to worry about getting the default database context in your SQLJ code.

Oracle will manage the default database context for you. Even if your code includes calls to Oracle.connect() or Oracle.close(), the database server will ignore the call and hand out a database connection from its pool of database connections.

However, there are two things to keep in mind:

❑ You can still create a database context that is *not* the default database context. All of the normal SQLJ syntaxes still apply and you have to explicitly open and close the non-default database context. If the database context being created is not an Oracle database, you must load the JDBC drivers for that database into the Oracle database where the stored procedure is residing.To accomplish this, you must use the loadjava utility. The loadjava utility and how to load an external Java class into Oracle is covered in Chapter 9.

❑ Since Oracle controls the default database context, you can no longer tell SQLJ what type of auto-commit functionality you want. Oracle Java stored procedures using SQLJ always have auto-commit turned off.

## SQLJ Iterators and Java Stored Procedures

If you are going to use a SQLJ iterator in a Java class file that is going to be used as a Java stored procedure, you must declare your SQLJ iterators as static. Remember, Oracle requires a static method to be the entry point for a Java stored procedure because Oracle maps the PL/SQL wrapper for the stored procedure to a single, static method on a Java class.

Iterators that are going to be declared inside that class file must be declared as static if you want to use them from the method call acting as the entry point for Java stored procedure. This has nothing to do with SQLJ. Java requires that any method declared as static may only use other inner classes, instance-level variables, or methods inside that class if they are declared as static.

Since SQLJ is generating an inner class based on the SQLJ declaration for the StudentsIterator, it must be declared as a static or your SQLJ class will translate properly, but fail on compilation. To declare the StudentsIterator to be static you must use the following syntax:

```
#sql <access> static iterator iterator_name();
```

The syntax for a static iterator is the same as a normal SQLJ iterator, except for the keyword static right before the iterator keyword. The StudentsIterator iterator declaration for IteratorExampleSP is shown below:

```
// use a static iterator
#sql private static iterator StudentIterator(String student_id,
                                             String first_name,
                                             String last_name,
```

```
String street,
String city,
String state,
String zip);
```

### Final Thoughts on SQLJ and Java Stored Procedures

The important thing to take away from our discussion on Java stored procedures is that you can easily use SQLJ to write your Java stored procedures. Syntactically, there is no difference between writing a SQLJ application that runs outside of the database and an Oracle SQLJ Java stored procedure.

Keep in mind that stored procedures, Java or PL/SQL, are generally used when you want something to execute very close to the database. If you have a very database-intensive query that manipulates a great deal of data, running that query from a program residing outside of the database can be a very resource-intensive task for both the database server's CPU, and the network the database is residing on. Stored procedures help mitigate this by keeping all requests for data in the database.

In addition to this, using stored procedures allows you to write code that very easily reacts to events within the database. Suppose you want to audit whenever someone does some work on data within a particular table. You can use a combination of database triggers and stored procedures to very quickly capture who the user is, and what data changes they are making. This would not be possible with Java code that is written as an application residing outside of the database.

The key thing to keep in mind is that Oracle Java stored procedures run inside the database and are called differently to a standard Java application. These small differences can, if you are not aware of them, make writing your first SQLJ Java stored procedure a painful experience.

# New SQLJ Features in Oracle 9i

All of the code written for this chapter has been tested and run under Oracle 8.1.7 and Oracle 9.0.1. However, with the release of Oracle 9i, there are several new Oracle-specific SQLJ extensions that can provide a lot of power and flexibility for SQLJ-based applications. These extensions include:

❑ SQLJ optimization capabilities via the generation of optimized Oracle-specific code

❑ Full support for all Oracle-specific Java data types (in other words, RAW, ROWID, and so on)

❑ Full support for iterators being passed back and forth between stored procedure calls

❑ Support for dynamic SQL statements

❑ Scrollable iterators

These Oracle 9i-specific topics could easily take up a separate chapter or two each. We are only going to look at two of the five items shown above:

❑ Oracle 9i's support for dynamic SQL

❑ Oracle 9i's scrollable iterators

**305**

# Oracle 9i, SQLJ and Dynamic SQL

Earlier in the chapter the advantages and disadvantages of SQLJ vs. JDBC were discussed. One of the strengths of JDBC was its ability to handle dynamic SQL. A developer could build a SQL statement on the fly and then execute it.

However, with the release of Oracle 9i that advantage is now gone. Oracles 9i now offers a **meta-bind expression**. Meta-bind expressions allow the developer to statically define a SQLJ statement at development, and then append the meta-bind expression to the statement at run-time.

A meta-bind expression uses the syntax:

```
:{Java Bind Statement :: SQL Replacement code}
```

The Java **bind statement** is a variable that holds the piece of code that will be inserted into the SQLJ statement at run-time. The value inside of the Java bind statement can include:

❑  A dynamically created WHERE clause for SELECT, UDDATE, and DELETE statements.

❑  A table name in a SQL statement.

❑  A column name in a SELECT statement

The SQL replacement code is used during translation of the SQLJ code to Java as a placeholder. This placeholder ensures that the SQLJ translator does not throw any errors while translating the code. The second part of the meta-bind expression is the **SQL replacement code**.

Let's rewrite the SimpleSelectJDBC example, found in the *SQL vs. JDBC* section earlier in the chapter, using meta-bind expressions.

## Dynamic SQL with Oracle 9i SQLJ

The following code example will dynamically build a SQL statement using Oracle's 9i meta-expressions. If the user passes on the command line a student ID only, then the data for the student is retrieved. If no argument is passed in, then all of the data for the students in the application is returned.

```
package com.wrox.sqlj;

import oracle.sqlj.runtime.Oracle;

public class SimpleSelectMeta {

   #sql private iterator StudentIterator(String student_id,
                                         String first_name,
                                         String last_name,
                                         String street,
                                         String city,
                                         String state,
                                         String zip);
```

```
public void retrieveStudents(String[] args) {
  try {

    // make the database connection by using the default context
    Oracle.connect("jdbc:oracle:oci8:@DATABASE", "username",
                   "password", true);

    // declare meta-expression
    String metaExpression = "";

    // if a command line argument is passed in, build a WHERE clause
    if (args.length>0) {
      metaExpression = " WHERE student_id = " + args[0];
    }

    StudentIterator students = null;

    // retrieve the data into the students iterator
    #sql students = { SELECT student_id, first_name, last_name, street,
                             city, state, zip
                      FROM
                      student:{metaExpression :: WHERE student_id = '1'}
                    };

    // printing output
    System.out.println("ID FNAME   LNAME    STREET
                        CITY             STATE   ZIP");
    System.out.println("-------------------------------------------------
                        -------------------------------");

    // cycle through the returned results
    while (students.next()) {
      StringBuffer output = new StringBuffer(students.student_id());
      output.append("    ");
      output.append(students.first_name());
      output.append("   ");
      output.append(students.last_name());
      output.append("   ");
      output.append(students.street());
      output.append("   ");
      output.append(students.city());
      output.append("   ");
      output.append(students.state());
      output.append("   ");
      output.append(students.zip());

      System.out.println(output.toString());
    }

    students.close();
    Oracle.close();
  } catch(Exception e) {
```

```
      System.out.println(e.toString());
    }
  }

  public static void main(String[] args) {
    SimpleSelectMeta simpleSelectMeta = new SimpleSelectMeta();
    simpleSelectMeta.retrieveStudents(args);
  }
}
```

The above code can be compiled and translated using the standard `buildSQLJ` script:

> **buildSQLJ SimpleSelectMeta.sqlj**

Here are a some example invocations, with and without arguments passed on the command line:

```
> java com.wrox.sqlj.SimpleSelectMeta
ID      FNAME   LNAME   STREET                  CITY            STATE   ZIP
-----------------------------------------------------------------------------
1       Mary    Jones   1502 Westchisre Avenue  Clintonville    WI      53188
2       Dan     Smith   1802 Miller Street      Clintonville    WI      53188
3       Ryan    Smith   1802 Miller Street      Clintonville    WI      53188
4       Dave    Doe     1008 Morre Street       Waukesha        WI      53088

> java com.wrox.sqlj.SimpleSelectMeta 1
ID      FNAME   LNAME   STREET                  CITY            STATE   ZIP
-----------------------------------------------------------------------------
1       Mary    Jones   1502 Westchisre Avenue  Clintonville    WI      53188

> java com.wrox.sqlj.SimpleSelectMeta 3
ID      FNAME   LNAME   STREET                  CITY            STATE   ZIP
-----------------------------------------------------------------------------
3       Ryan    Smith   1802 Miller Street      Clintonville    WI      53188
```

## How it Works

The `SimpleSelectMeta` application starts by creating an instance of the `SimpleSelectMeta` class. It then calls the `retrieveStudents()` method, passing in the `args` variable passed into the main method.

```
public static void main(String[] args) {
  SimpleSelectMeta simpleSelectMeta = new SimpleSelectMeta();
  simpleSelectMeta.retrieveStudents(args);
}
```

Once inside the `retrieveStudents()` method, a default database connection is opened:

```
// make the database connection by using the default context
Oracle.connect("jdbc:oracle:oci8:@DATABASE", "username",
               "password", true);
```

At this point things are going to get interesting. A variable called `metaExpressions` is declared. This variable will hold the WHERE clause we are going to append to our SQLJ SELECT statement. The `metaExpressions` variable is initialized to be an empty string:

```
// declare meta-expression
String metaExpression = "";
```

If a command line is argument passed into the code, the `SimpleSelectMeta` application is going to build a WHERE clause to limit the query to only a specific student ID:

```
// if a command line argument is passed in, build a WHERE clause
if (args.length>0) {
  metaExpression = " WHERE student_id = " + args[0];
}
```

After the `metaExpression` has been built, a SQLJ executable statement is declared with the meta-expression at the end of it:

```
// retrieve the data into the students iterator
#sql students = { SELECT student_id, first_name, last_name, street,
                         city, state, zip
                  FROM
                  student:{metaExpression :: WHERE student_id = '1'}
                };
```

When the above expression is compiled, the SQLJ translator will, upon hitting the `metaExpression` shown above, validate the SQL statement by looking at the SQL statement with the right side of the meta-expression appended to it. So, as far as the Oracle SQL translator is concerned the SQL statement it is validating for the above executable statement is:

```
SELECT student_id, first_name, last_name, street, city, state, zip
  FROM student
 WHERE student_id = '1'}
```

However, at run-time, the SQLJ runtime engine will append whatever value is in the `metaExpression` variable we declared. So, if a command line argument of 2 is passed into the `SimpleSelectMeta` application, the SQL SELECT that is actually executed would look like:

```
SELECT student_id, first_name, last_name, street, city, state, zip
  FROM student
 WHERE student_id = 2
```

Using Oracle 9i's SQLJ and dynamic SQL gives you more flexibility in writing your applications. However, it does have a price. That price is that the dynamically generated piece of SQL code is not type or syntax-checked at compilation-time. This means that if it dynamically generates an invalid SQL statement, a run-time exception will be thrown.

# Scrollable Iterators in SQLJ

Before Oracle 9i, the only type of iterator available in Oracle's SQLJ implementation was a forward-only iterator. When using a forward-only iterator, the application must always start processing a record at the first record in the query. The code may move forward one record at a time, but it can never go back to a previous record in the query or jump further than one record at a time forward in the query.

Oracle 9i changes this with the introduction of the **scrollable iterator**. A scrollable iterator lets an application start at any point in the query result set, and even allows the application to jump any number of records forward or backward in a query result set.

To declare a scrollable iterator you use the following syntax:

```
#sql <modifier> iterator Iterator Name
                    implements sqlj.runtime.Scrollable
                with (sensitivity = sensitivity setting)
                    (parameter list);
```

The `classes` iterator shown in the previous example could be easily modified to be a scrollable iterator:

```
#sql private iterator StudentIterator
                    implements sqlj.runtime.Scrollable
                with (sensitivity = SENSITIVE)
                    (String student_id,
                     String first_name,
                     String last_name,
                     String street,
                     String city,
                     String state,
                     String zip);
```

The top line in the above syntax looks familiar. The second and third lines are new. The `implements` and `with` keyword are valid parts of a SQLJ `iterator` declaration. They have not been covered because they are considered advanced features in SQLJ. The `implements` keyword is telling the SQLJ translator that the iterator being declared in going to be a scrollable iterator.

The `with` keyword is being used to tell SQLJ what type of scrollable cursor is going to be created. A scrollable cursor is going to be one of two types:

❑   SENSITIVE

❑   INSENSITIVE

Setting the sensitivity to SENSITIVE means that the scrollable cursor can detect changes to data that the cursor is referencing. This means that parts of the cursor can be refreshed with changes made by another database user or process.

An INSENSITIVE setting means that the data is retrieved, but it is unable to tell whether or not the data it has retrieved has been modified by another concurrent user or process.

A scrollable iterator has the following methods available to it:

- ❑ next() – Moves to the next record in the iterator.

- ❑ previous() – Moves to the previous record in the iterator.

- ❑ first() – Moves to the first record in the iterator.

- ❑ last() – Moves to the last record in the iterator.

- ❑ absolute(int) – Moves to a specific record (as determined by the int value passed into the method) within the iterator. The absolute() method always starts counting from the first record in the iterator. If a negative value is passed into the method, the iterator will move that number of records back, starting from the end of iterator.

- ❑ relative(int) – Moves int number of records forward or back from the current record in the iterator.

- ❑ isFirst() – Returns true if the current record is the beginning of the iterator. It will return false if it is not.

- ❑ isLast() – Returns true if the current record is the last record in the iterator. It will return false if not.

> If you try moving beyond the first or last record in the iterator, it will behave as if you have called the **beforeFirst()** or **afterLast()** method. You will not point to a specific record and until you move to a valid record, any attempt to access the data in the iterator will result in a **SQLException** thrown.

This section on scrollable iterators only begins to cover the full depth and breadth of Oracle 9i's SQLJ scrollable iterator implementation. For a more thorough covering of the scrollable iterators, please refer to the Oracle 9i *SQLJ Developer's Guide and Reference*.

# Summary

SQLJ is a powerful tool for writing Java database applications. It allows the developer to write SQL code in a more natural form than the JDBC database API. However, SQLJ is not a replacement for JDBC. It is a sister technology that when used appropriately can take much of the headache and grunt work out of doing database application development.

In this chapter we have covered the basics writing Oracle SQLJ database applications. Topics covered include:

- ❑ The basic SQLJ syntax

- ❑ How to invoke the SQLJ translator to translate and compile your SQLJ source code

- ❑ How to use SQLJ executable statements to retrieve and manipulate data.

- ❑ How to use the default database context to connect to an Oracle database

- ❏ How to use SQLJ declarations to:
    - ❏ Create multiple database contexts
    - ❏ Look at how transactions work with SQLJ database contexts
    - ❏ Create Java helper classes called iterators to assist in manipulating data
- ❏ How to invoke PL/SQL stored procedures and functions with SQLJ
- ❏ Writing Java stored procedures with Oracle SQLJ
- ❏ Some of the new SQLJ features found in the SQLJ
    - ❏ Dynamic SQL using Oracle 9i
    - ❏ Scrollable iterators in SQLJ

While we covered quite a bit in this chapter, not everything was covered in regards to SQLJ. We did not:

- ❏ Fully explore all of the features in the SQLJ iterator statement
- ❏ Use SQLJ execution contexts to find out information about the execution environment in which a SQLJ statement is running
- ❏ The complexities of writing multi-threaded code in SQLJ
- ❏ The new features in the Oracle 9i release of SQLJ

For further information on these advanced topics, the reader is encouraged to look at the Oracle SQLJ Developer's Guide and Reference available on the Oracle web site, and *Professional Oracle 8i Application Programming* by *Wrox Press, ISBN 1-861004-84-2.*

Oracle 9i Java Programming

# Using the Oracle JVM

This chapter discusses a few of the more important issues regarding the Oracle JVM. It is not meant to fully detail how the JVM works since some of that information is not relevant to the programmer or is proprietary to Oracle Corporation. The JVM inside the database tries to be as 'normal' as possible, but there are some special considerations that need to be recognized. Running inside the database has its advantages and disadvantages – both of which need to be understood by developers. We will show you some aspects of how the JVM has evolved, its architecture, and how to load, resolve and execute code. We also discuss how to use the DBMS_JAVA package and some of the more useful features while also helping the developer debug their code and avoid common pitfalls.

## Historical Differences in the Oracle JVM

Oracle first introduced the JVM into the database in version 8.1.5. The code name for the project was **aurora** and this name is referenced in many of the Java classes provided by Oracle. Initial versions concentrated on getting the basics right while later versions added (or exposed in some cases) more features and optimizations. Along the way the Java sub-system has undergone a couple of name changes: JServer for databases up to version 8.1.7 and Oracle 9i JVM for 9i.

The 8.1.5 JVM is compliant with Sun's JDK 1.1.6. Successive versions of the database (up to and including Oracle 9i) are compatible with JDK versions through 1.2.1. Since Sun's JDK 1.3.x has been out for some time with 1.4 coming soon, care must be taken to only use the features and API's from JDK 1.2.1. You can use the newer Java compilers to generate 1.2.x-specific code but the same restriction on the API's is still required.

As an example; the method `java.lang.Double.doubleToRawLongBits()` is an unrecognized API in 1.2.x JDK's, so check with the API documentation for information about when a particular method or class was introduced. Every version is byte-code compatible with class files created by Sun's JDK compilers. That makes developing code largely the developers' choice – develop code outside the database then load the final class files afterwards or just directly use the Oracle JVM to compile, execute and debug.

Even though the initial JVM only supported JDK version 1.1.6, it was capable of supporting the more advanced JDBC 2.0 features because Oracle coded their implementation in the `oracle.jdbc2` package. Version 8.1.6 rendered this package redundant, since it supports the core JDBC and optional JDBC API's available in JDK 1.2.1.

An important optimization is the availability to developers of **JAccelerator**. It is also called **NCOMP** – for native compilation (covered in Chapter 15). This technology takes byte code and generates intermediate source code which is then compiled and deployed as shared libraries (for Unix systems) or DLL's (for Microsoft Windows systems). Therefore, it eliminates the need to repeatedly interpret essential classes. Every JVM uses this technology to speed up access to the core Java class libraries, Object Request Broker (ORB), and JDBC code. It has not been applied to the abstract windowing toolkit (AWT) or Swing classes since they are only included for compatibility and are not meant to be instantiated in the context of the server. Most developers are surprised to learn that NCOMP has been in the Oracle JVM since the beginning. However, it was only available to developers since version 8.1.7.

The ability to load Java code into the database is intrinsic to all JVM versions, but the flexibility of the tools has improved. For instance, versions 8.1.5 and 8.1.6 are subject to certain restrictions that versions 8.1.7 and later have removed. In 8.1.5 and 8.1.6:

❑ It is not possible to load code from compressed JAR or ZIP files so everything needs to be stored uncompressed (a small annoyance when trying to load third-party code)

❑ The ability to load the `java.*` packages is restricted to `SYS` and `SYSTEM` users (a restriction that can be bypassed by granting `JAVAUSERPRIV` and `JAVASYSPRIV` to the user

Version 8.1.7 added the capability of running the Oracle Servlet Engine so you could actually have a fully functioning web server inside the database. With the advent of Oracle's J2EE server (a component of 9iAS), the focus for the Oracle 9i JVM inside the database has moved towards more of a supporting role, in that respect. EJB support has always been present and has matured with the database. Versions 8.1.5 and 8.1.6 support EJB version 1.0 but only session beans. 8.1.7 and 9i support EJB version 1.1 with both session and entity beans.

Java has always been represented as supporting multiple languages using Unicode. Oracle can support multiple languages using NLS (National Language Support), but the JVM in 8.1.5 did not support NLS. This feature was added in 8.1.6.

The following table summarizes some of the differences between Oracle's database JVM implementations:

|  | 8.1.5 | 8.1.6 | 8.1.7 | 9i |
| --- | --- | --- | --- | --- |
| JDK version | 1.1.6 | 1.2.1 | 1.2.1 | 1.2.1 |
| `JAVA_POOL_SIZE` default | 20MB | 20MB | 20MB | 20MB |
| JAccelerator for core classes | Y | Y | Y | Y |
| JAccelerator for user code | N | N | Y | Y |
| Product name | JServer | JServer | JServer | Oracle 9i JVM |

|                                           | 8.1.5  | 8.1.6 | 8.1.7 | 9i  |
|-------------------------------------------|--------|-------|-------|-----|
| Support for Oracle Servlet Engine         | N      | N     | Y     | Y   |
| loadjava with compressed JAR/ZIP          | N      | N     | Y     | Y   |
| JDBC 2.0 support[1]                        | Y[2]   | Y     | Y     | Y   |
| Protected packages[3]                      | Y      | Y     | N     | N   |
| EJB version                               | 1.0    | 1.0   | 1.1   | 1.1 |
| EJB entity beans                          | N      | N     | Y     | Y   |
| EJB session beans                         | Y      | Y     | Y     | Y   |
| NLS support                               | N      | Y     | Y     | Y   |

[1] JDBC 2.1 core API and the JDBC 2.0 Optional Package API

[2] Subset of functionality provided in oracle.jdbc2 package

[3] Namely, java, javax, and oracle packages and sub-packages

# Memory Usage in the JVM

First, let's discuss how the Oracle database memory is structured and then describe how the dedicated and server modes of operation differ. When an Oracle instance is started, and you connect as a client, the Oracle process allocates memory structures and starts the various processes that manage the memory. Obviously, this allocation and management is transparent to you, the client. The Oracle instance allocates and manages the memory without any action on your part. Yet, you can have some influence on how that memory is allocated, and how you exercise that influence can impact how your database application performs. In this section of the chapter, we will examine some of the Oracle memory structures and how they impact your Java application. We'll begin by examining the System Global Area (SGA) and the various pools of memory allocated from the SGA. In particular, one pool that is of special interest to us is the Java pool.

## System Global Area

The System Global Area, or SGA, is the primary memory structure used by the Oracle instance. It contains a number of memory pools and buffers that are used by the database. Some of these pools and buffers (but not all) are shown in the illustration overleaf.

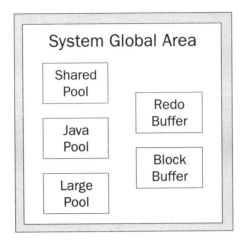

You can easily see the various parts of the SGA and how many bytes they use by querying the table
v$sgastat.

It is possible that your normal login may not have privileges to see this table. If that is
so, you will need to login as a user with DBA privileges, or get your DBA to grant
select privilege on the **v$sgastat** table.

```
SQL> select pool, name, bytes from v$sgastat
  2  order by pool, name;

POOL          NAME                               BYTES
-----------   --------------------------    ----------
java pool     free memory                     16105472
java pool     memory in use                    4866048
shared pool   Checkpoint queue                   73764
shared pool   KGFF heap                           5900
shared pool   KGK heap                           17520
shared pool   KQLS heap                         344072
shared pool   PL/SQL DIANA                      364000
shared pool   PL/SQL MPCODE                      64332
shared pool   PLS non-lib hp                      2096
shared pool   SYSTEM PARAMETERS                  62960
shared pool   State objects                     141932
...and so on
```

# The Java Pool

If you want to run Java in the database then you will have to create a session. Of course, sessions can be 'attached' to a user or can be run as a stand-alone process (for example, as a DBMS_JOB). Each session gets its own JVM. From a traditional JVM standpoint, that might sound bad but each Oracle JVM requires a very small memory footprint – typically quoted as little as 35KB (200KB for CORBA/EJB) per session.

How does the JVM get away with needing such a small amount of memory per session? It does it by placing all shared code and shared data required for execution in the **Java pool**. The amount of memory we can use for Java applications in the database is thus limited by the amount of memory allocated to the Java pool.

> *The Java session data for each user is also sometimes stored in the Java pool, depending on the mode in which Oracle is operating: dedicated mode or shared mode (a.k.a. Multi-Threaded Server or MTS). We delve into this in more detail in Chapter 15.*

Oracle estimates that each class in the database will need between 4 KB and 8 KB of Java pool memory. Thus the range of memory required for a Java application can be roughly determined by counting the number of classes and multiplying by 4 to get a low bound, and by 8 to get a high bound. Let's do another query against the v$sgastat table:

> **Even though the pool was introduced with 8.1.5, it was not part of the v$sgastat table until release 8.1.6. The query below will not work with an 8.1.5 database.**

```
SQL> compute sum of bytes on pool;
SQL> break on pool skip 1;
SQL> select * from v$sgastat where pool='java pool';

POOL          NAME                          BYTES
-----------   -------------------------     ----------
java pool     free memory                     16105472
              memory in use                    4866048
***********                                 ----------
sum                                          20971520
```

The total size of the Java pool can be determined by adding the free memory in the Java pool to the memory in use. Using the `compute sum...` and `break on pool...` statements above caused the sum to be computed and displayed for us. In the above query, we see that the total pool size is approximately 20 MB.

This memory is part of the SGA and the size of this is fixed using a database initialization parameter called JAVA_POOL_SIZE. The default size is 20 MB if the value is not defined. When running dedicated servers, the session-specific data is stored in the UGA, which is part of the PGA. For shared servers (MTS in pre-9i parlance), some of this UGA data *is* stored in the Java pool. You must use shared servers for CORBA/EJBs – see section 1.3 *Configuration* in %ORACLE_HOME%/relnotes/javavm/README_javavm.txt.

**319**

The shared pool is used when you load and resolve code or define call specifications. It is plausible that your development system will need a larger SHARED_POOL_SIZE than your production system since you most likely will not be loading and resolving code in production systems. In fact, the Oracle guidelines (*Oracle9i Java Developer's Guide*, Chapter 6, section *Java Memory Usage*, sub-section *Java Pool Memory*) suggest that you might be able to use as little as 10 MB for the Java pool, but they decline to accurately describe the circumstances defining that value. If you install the JVM for the first time (into a database that is not a default database from Oracle) then you might need a larger than normal Java pool since you will be loading and resolving thousands of core classes. This is also true if you deploy large numbers of EJBs, since they invoke the compiler (which requires lots of memory from the JAVA_POOL).

Even though the database shares some code and data between JVM's, you will not be able to share data with other JVM sessions. For example, you cannot store data in static class variables and expect to be able to access that data in another JVM session. Such "instance-wide" data structures are supposed to be available in later releases of the database.

## Limiting Available Memory to JVM Sessions

Since all JVM sessions share the same memory space, it is possible that some can be starved for memory while others consume too much. To prevent this you can use the JAVA_SOFT_SESSIONSPACE_LIMIT and JAVA_MAX_SESSIONSPACE_SIZE initialization parameters. The first parameter defaults to 1 MB and will trigger an alert if the JVM exceeds this limit. The second parameter defaults to 4 GB when undefined. If a JVM exceeds this limit it will be terminated with an out of memory error. Both alerts will be written to a trace file in the $ORACLE_BASE/admin/<SID>/udump directory. Execute the following command (as SYS or SYSTEM) to see your Java parameter settings.

```
SQL> show parameter java

NAME                             TYPE     VALUE
-------------------------------- -------- -----------------------------
java_max_sessionspace_size       integer  0
java_pool_size                   string   20971520
java_soft_sessionspace_limit     integer  0
```

Although the above example does not show it -- you can have one or both of the session space values listed with a value of zero. This indicates that the values have not been explicitly defined causing the default values to be in effect.

To demonstrate what happens when code exceeds these limits, the database initialization parameters in the $ORACLE_BASE/admin/<SID>/pfile/init<SID>.ora file were changed from the default (undefined) values to the following:

```
JAVA_SOFT_SESSIONSPACE_LIMIT=204800
JAVA_MAX_SESSIONSPACE_SIZE=409600
```

Next, the database was shutdown and restarted. The following SQL*Plus session transcript shows the Java code and PL/SQL wrapper being created and executed. This code simply allocates an array of bytes based on a user-supplied value.

```
SQL> create or replace and resolve java source named "mem_size" as
  2  public class mem_size{
  3    public static void alloc(int s) {
  4       byte[] b = new byte[s*1024];
  5       System.out.println(b.length);
  6    }
  7  }
  8  /

Java created.

SQL> create or replace procedure mem(p_size in number) as
  2      language java name 'mem_size.alloc(int)';
  3  /

Procedure created.

SQL> exec mem(400000)
BEGIN mem(400000); END;

*
ERROR at line 1:
ORA-29532: Java call terminated by uncaught Java exception:
java.lang.OutOfMemoryError
ORA-06512: at "USERNAME.MEM", line 0
ORA-06512: at line 1
```

The following information is from the trace file.

```
/home/oracle/admin/oaxaca/udump/oaxaca_ora_15269.trc
Oracle8i Enterprise Edition Release 8.1.7.0.0 - Production
With the Partitioning option
JServer Release 8.1.7.0.0 - Production
ORACLE_HOME = /home/oracle/product/817
System name:    SunOS
Node name:      oaxaca
Release:        5.8
Version:        Generic_108528-08
Machine:        sun4u
Instance name: oaxaca
Redo thread mounted by this instance: 1
Oracle process number: 15
Unix process pid: 15269, image: oracle@oaxaca (TNS V1-V3)

*** 2001-11-13 00:05:16.711
*** SESSION ID:(12.3) 2001-11-13 00:05:16.679
Session 11 exceeded soft sessionspace limit of 0x32000 bytes.
*** 2001-11-13 00:06:32.058
java.lang.OutOfMemoryError
  at mem_size.alloc(mem_size:3)
```

You can see (in the SQL*Plus transcript) the error that is generated when trying to allocate an array of memory beyond that allowed by the JAVA_MAX_SESSIONSPACE_SIZE parameter. What is not obvious is the warning that is generated when the code exceeded the JAVA_SOFT_SESSIONSPACE_SIZE value. This happened because the compiler used too much memory when creating the Java stored procedure. It still worked – silently. The alert message in the trace file shows the value 0x32000 (204800 bytes) was exceeded. You will have to empirically determine if you need to set a maximum session space value.

*In Chapter 15 we will take a look at the role of the Java Pool in maintaining session state across calls.*

## What to do with DBMS_SHARED_POOL

If you have a need to know the size and description of objects that are filling up your shared pool, you can use the DBMS_SHARED_POOL supplied PL/SQL package. By default it is not installed so you will have to run the %ORACLE_HOME%/rdbms/admin/dbmspool.sql script as SYS. These are some of the procedures in the package:

❑   DBMS_SHARED_POOL.SIZES (minsize NUMBER);

❑   DBMS_SHARED_POOL.KEEP (name VARCHAR2, flag CHAR DEFAULT 'P');

❑   DBMS_SHARED_POOL.UNKEEP (name VARCHAR2, flag CHAR DEFAULT 'P');

The first procedure will show all of the objects in the shared pool above the given size, which is measured in kilobytes. Following is an example showing all the objects over 100KB. Since the output is not very clear, spacing has been added between each object that was reported by the package. This package belongs to SYS so either run in that schema or grant the execute privilege to another user:

```
SQL> set serveroutput on size 100000
SQL> exec dbms_shared_pool.sizes(100);
SIZE(K) KEPT    NAME
------- ------  --------------------------------------------------------------
371             SYS.STANDARD                    (PACKAGE)
166             SYS./5ee89977_NamespaceRDBMS     (JAVA CLASS)
163             SYS.oracle/CDC/ChangeTable        (JAVA CLASS)
109 YES         SYS./5c3f9c09_SqljDecl            (JAVA CLASS)
104 YES         SYS.java/lang/Character           (JAVA CLASS)
101 YES         SYS.java/math/BigInteger          (JAVA CLASS)

PL/SQL procedure successfully completed.
```

If you have some Java code that you want to permanently keep in the shared pool then use the KEEP() procedure. This pins the object in the pool and keeps it from aging out. Consider pinning large frequently used Java classes or PL/SQL packages since loading and unloading them can cause the pool to become fragmented. Additionally, loading large objects in the pool can possibly displace many other objects (of greater cumulative size) in order to get contiguous space. Pin any code immediately after the database instance starts, to prevent fragmentation, by using an AFTER STARTUP ON DATABASE trigger. To keep or un-keep an object, the first parameter is the object name and for Java objects it is the "mangled" short name. The second parameter is the TYPE of object and can be any of the following (straight from the dbmspool.sql header):

| TYPE | Description |
|------|-------------|
| P | package/procedure/function |
| Q | sequence |
| R | trigger |
| T | type |
| JS | java source |
| JC | java class |
| JR | java resource |
| JD | java shared data |
| C | cursor |

You can undo this pinning using the UNKEEP() which takes the same parameters as KEEP().

*In order to obtain a detailed report on your memory usage patterns, you can use the* memstat *tool, which is discussed in Chapter 15.*

# Managing Code in the JVM

The JVM that Oracle has developed for the database could be considered a "complete" environment. This means that you can do all your development, testing, and deployment using this environment. In some cases, you should consider the database as your operating environment and forget (for the most part) about the host file system when compiling, loading, and executing code. A common mistake is to attempt to set the CLASSPATH for the Oracle JVM when it actually does not exist or make use of any environment variable by that name. That is, all code is resolved in the database – JARs and classes on the host file system might as well not exist. We will also see how the JVM handles resolution of classes.

## Invoker and Definer Rights

When defining a Java class or a PL/SQL call specification we have the option of saying how access control and privileges are to be determined. Both CREATE JAVA command and the loadjava utility allow you to specify this access control. When using invoker rights, the user who calls the code determines the access and privileges. That is, code defined with invoker rights is not bound to any particular schema and the user determines what data is accessible. This is useful when you want a common code base to act on different sets of data. It eliminates having to put complicated user-based logic in your code. When using definer rights, code is bound to a particular schema that dictates the access and privileges during execution.

**The default for Java code is invoker rights but the default for PL/SQL is definer rights.**

Put another way, a method defined with invoker rights is like a Visual Basic or Pro*C application with embedded INSERT, UPDATE, and DELETE statements. At run time, the program might see different tables depending on who logged in. A definer rights method is more like a PL/SQL stored procedure compiled with the default options. Regardless of who is logged in – when you run that procedure, it will access a consistent set of tables. Regardless of the type of access however (invokers' or definers') the actual subroutines and code executed will always be the same – that is fixed at compile time.

# Using CREATE JAVA and DROP JAVA SQL

There are a few ways to get code into the database. One way is to use the CREATE JAVA SQL syntax. With this SQL statement, a developer can:

❑ Load code from a BFILE, CLOB, BLOB which can be the result of a sub-query

❑ Load code directly 'in-line'

❑ Load .properties resource files

❑ Resolve loaded byte code with an optional user-supplied resolution specification (see the description of the -resolver option in the loadjava section)

❑ Compile source code (even SQLJ code) into byte code with one command

❑ Specify the rights assigned (invoker versus definer) when a caller executes the code

❑ Easily integrate Java object management into SQL scripts since it is more direct (and easier) to use than loadjava/dropjava

For example, the following simple Java source code is loaded in-line and has, by default, invoker rights. The AND COMPILE syntax for the CREATE JAVA SQL instructs the JVM to generate byte code from the Java source. The name of the source is in double quotes since it has lower case characters and we want to preserve the case. The PL/SQL code first records a starting timestamp, calls the Java procedure (which does nothing), and finally records an ending timestamp. The difference between timestamps is the approximate time required for the JVM sub-system to be 'cold started'. This startup time is longer the first time a JVM is started, but all subsequent JVM startups occur much faster. The semantics of defining a PL/SQL call specification are explained in Chapter 10.

```
SQL> create or replace and compile java source named "no_op_java" as
  2  public class no_op_java {
  3    public static void no_op() { }
  4  }
  5  /

Java created./

SQL> create or replace procedure no_op_java
  2  as language java name 'no_op_java.no_op()';
  3  /

Procedure created.

declare
```

```
    strt number;
    stop number;
 begin
   strt := dbms_utility.get_time();
   no_op_java();
   stop := dbms_utility.get_time();
   dbms_output.put_line('Elapsed (100th secs)= ' || (stop - strt));
 end;
 /
```

If you decide that you do not want the byte code or source in the database then you can use the DROP JAVA SQL statement. If you loaded and compiled a Java source file and then dropped it, the source code and corresponding compiled byte code will also be removed. The syntax for dropping Java is pretty simple – just indicate whether you want to drop a class, source code, or a resource and then the object name. Don't forget to double-quote the object name if it has lower case characters. You can also drop a class (byte code) or a resource. However, if you created the Java source and specified the AND COMPILE option in the SQL statement, you cannot drop just the class file. This example first shows an attempt to drop just the class file and then how to drop both the Java source and byte code for the no_op_java class:

```
SQL> drop java class "no_op_java";
drop java class "no_op_java"
                 *

ERROR at line 1:
ORA-29537: class or resource cannot be created or dropped directly


SQL> drop java source "no_op_java";

Java dropped.
```

# The DBMS_JAVA Package

The DBMS_JAVA package is actually a PL/SQL package but is documented in the *Oracle8i Java Developer's Guide*. It has numerous procedures and functions that developers can use to manage Java in the database (as well as others that are for internal use) – see http://download-eu.oracle.com/otndoc/oracle9i/901_doc/java.901/a90209/config.htm#1009372 for details.

Already in this book we have used the set_output utility of this package in order to redirect output to the SQL*Plus text buffer:

```
SQL> CALL dbms_java.set_output(5000);
```

We will discuss a few more as we progress through the chapter, but to start off, we'll take a quick look at the shortname and longname functions:

❑   FUNCTION longname (shortname VARCHAR2) RETURN VARCHAR2

❑   FUNCTION shortname (longname VARCHAR2) RETURN VARCHAR2

The name available from a query to the USER_OBJECTS view is referred to as the short name, the long name is held in a system table by Oracle and we can use the functions of DBMS_JAVA to evaluate and display each way. This occurs because Java names can get quite long (a Java name includes the complete package name) and all Oracle identifiers must be 30 characters or less. Therefore, the JVM generates hash values for longer names.

These functions permit us to convert between the short and long Java names. In fact, the longname and the shortname only differ where the shortname itself exceeds 30 characters (all). You will need to convert between these names in order to query Java objects reliably in the database.

Here is an example of the usage of each when logged in as the user SYS (who happens to own lots of Java code, if you have Java installed in the database):

```
SQL> column long_nm format a30 word_wrapped
SQL> column short_nm format a30

SQL> select dbms_java.longname(object_name) long_nm,
  2          dbms_java.shortname(dbms_java.longname(object_name)) short_nm
  3     from user_objects where object_type = 'JAVA CLASS'
  4       and rownum < 11
  5  /

LONG_NM                          SHORT_NM
-------------------------------- --------------------------------
com/visigenic/vbroker/ir/Const   /1001a851_ConstantDefImpl
antDefImpl

oracle/aurora/util/classfile/L   /1005bd30_LnkdConstant
nkd$Constant

oracle/sqlj/runtime/OraCustomD   /10076b23_OraCustomDatumClosur
atumClosure

oracle/aurora/mts/http/securit   /1019cfe7_RdbmsProtectionMappi
y/RdbmsProtectionMapping

10 rows selected.
```

As you can see, using LONGNAME on the OBJECT NAME turns it into the original class name for the Java class. If we take this long name and pass it through SHORTNAME, we get back the hashed-shortened name Oracle uses internally.

# Using loadjava and dropjava

It probably is not efficient to manually load or drop lots of code using CREATE JAVA and DROP JAVA SQL. If you have to load an entire JAR or ZIP file of source or byte code then use the loadjava program. Oracle recommends that you do not mix source and byte code for the same classes in the same JAR/ZIP file – see section 3.4.1, *Loadjava and Dropjava* in %ORACLE_HOME%/relnotes/javavm/README_javavm.txt. These two tools are actually implemented in Java. They connect to the database and transfer every file in the JAR/ZIP but they can also be used for single classes, resource files, property files, and source code. Here is a table of the most frequently used loadjava parameters:

| loadjava parameter | Description |
| --- | --- |
| -definer | Indicatesthat the code being loaded should use definers' rights. The default is to use invokers' rights. |
| -encoding <*encoding*> | Defines the encoding of a source code file. It has no effect on byte code. For 9i, the default is determined programmatically and is based on the JVM-wide file.encoding property. For 8.1.6 and 8.1.7, the default is latin1. |
| -force or -f | Forces all code to be reloaded without first checking for its existence. |
| -grant <*grants*> | Grants the EXECUTE permission to all listed users who have their names separated by a comma but with no whitespace. The user running loadjava needs to have the proper permission to do so. |
| -help or -h | Displays the list of available options. |
| -nousage | Makes loadjava skip printing a list of parameters when no arguments are given. This could be useful to verify that the program executes without error – possible for later use in a script. |
| -noverify | Tells loadjava to skip byte code verification. Can be potentially dangerous so use with caution and only with trusted code. To enforce this, the user must have the oracle.aurora.security.JServerPermission "Verifier" permission to bypass the verifier. |
| -oci8 or -oci or -o | Directs loadjava to use the OCI8/thick JDBC driver when connecting to database. Dictates how the -user parameter is formatted and is the default connection driver. |
| -order | Instructs loadjava to resolve classes starting with the lowest point in the class dependency tree. This helps to optimize the number of resolutions needed when loading. |
| -resolve or -r | Forces loadjava to resolve all classes at load time rather than at first use. |

*Table continued on following page*

| loadjava parameter | Description |
|---|---|
| `-resolver <resolver spec>` | Defines how `loadjava` will find references to other classes. This should be a single quoted string. The default is: current schema, `SYSTEM`, then `SYS` in this format:<br><br>`'(* <current schema>) (* PUBLIC))'`<br><br>This causes the `resolver` to first look for referenced classes in the current schema, then anything that is public which includes public synonyms for classes in other schemas. This includes all core classes in the `SYS` schema. You tell the `resolver` to look for particular classes by using class names (with optional wildcards) instead of just the default wildcard for all classes which is `*`. |
| `-schema <schema>` | Loads code into the given schema instead of the schema for the user executing `loadjava`. The user will need the following permissions:<br><br>`CREATE {ANY} PROCEDURE`, `CREATE {ANY} TABLE`, and `JServerPermission.loadLibraryInClass` for the class being loaded. |
| `-synonym or -s` | Creates public synonyms for all generated byte code loaded or compiled from loaded code. |
| `-thin or -t` | Directs `loadjava` to use the thin JDBC driver when connecting to database. Dictates how the `-user` parameter is formatted which has to be the standard JDBC URL notation. |
| `-tableschema <schema>` | Causes the `CREATE$JAVA$LOB$TABLE` and `JAVA$CLASS$MD5$TABLE` tables to be used (or created if this is the first time `loadjava` is run) from an alternate schema. |
| `-user <user/password@database>` | Who is connecting to the database and (by default) where classes and resources will be loaded. The format of this depends on the JDBC driver used. |
| `-verbose or -v` | Displays messages as `loadjava` is processing the files. Omitting this causes `loadjava` to be silent unless warning or errors are encountered. |

There are a handful of other parameters that are not described when using the -help option. They are listed below and are described fully in the *Oracle 9i Java Tools Reference* documentation:

| | |
|---|---|
| -andresolve | Compiles and resolves files in one pass (unlike -resolve) which will not invalidate dependent classes. If method specifications change then use -resolve. |
| -debug | Equivalent to javac -g and also logs all SQL loadjava is using. |
| -fileout <filename> | Sends all generated messages to the named file instead of the console. |
| -jarasresource | Treats the JAR as a single resource rather than breaking it into the constituent parts. |
| -noserverside | Disables enhancements that loadjava uses when run on the server. This forces loadjava to use JDBC driver calls for all object access. |
| -stdout | Sends all generated messages to STDOUT instead of the STDERR |
| -time | Generates a timestamp for all generated messages. |
| -unresolvedok | Causes loadjava to ignore resolution errors. Only meaningful when combined with -resolve option. |

And following is a table of common dropjava parameters:

| dropjava parameter | Description |
|---|---|
| -encoding <encoding> | Defines the encoding of a source code file. It has no effect on byte code. Default is determined programmatically and is based on the operating system platform. |
| -help or -h | Displays the list of available options. |
| -oci8 or -oci or -o | Directs dropjava to use the OCI8/thick JDBC driver when connecting to database. Dictates how the -user parameter is formatted and is the default connection driver. |
| -schema <schema> | Removes code from the given schema instead of the logged on users' schema. The user running dropjava needs to have the proper permission to do so. |
| -thin or -t | Directs dropjava to use the thin JDBC driver when connecting to database. Dictates how the -user parameter is formatted which has to be standard the JDBC URL notation. |
| -user <user/password@database> | Who is connecting to the database and (by default) where classes and resources will be removed. The format of this depends on the JDBC driver used. |
| -verbose or -v | Displays messages as dropjava is processing the files. Omitting this causes dropjava to be silent unless warning or errors are encountered. |

Here is a simple `loadjava` example that loads a single Java source file into the database (using, by default the OCI driver):

```
> loadjava -user username/password@database -verbose FileHandleDemo.java
initialization complete
loading  : FileHandleDemo
creating : FileHandleDemo
```

The subsequent SQL query shows that the JVM compiled the code but that the objects are marked `INVALID` since they have not been resolved. To rectify that, run the `ALTER JAVA SOURCE ...` `RESOLVE` SQL to force the JVM to resolve the Java classes:

```
SQL> column object_name format a20
SQL> select object_name, object_type, status
  2     from user_objects
  3     where object_name like '%FileHandle%';

OBJECT_NAME          OBJECT_TYPE          STATUS
-------------------- -------------------- -------
FileHandleDemo       JAVA CLASS           INVALID
FileHandleDemo       JAVA SOURCE          INVALID

SQL> alter java source "FileHandleDemo" resolve;

Java altered.

SQL> select object_name, object_type, status from user_objects where
  2     object_name like '%FileHandle%';

OBJECT_NAME          OBJECT_TYPE          STATUS
-------------------- -------------------- -------
FileHandleDemo       JAVA CLASS           VALID
FileHandleDemo       JAVA SOURCE          VALID
```

Having the Java code resolved after loading is just a matter of adding the `-resolve` (or -r) option to your `loadjava` command line syntax. The next example uses the following extra options but these are not necessary for resolving: `-time`, `-force`, and `-thin`.

```
> loadjava -user username/password@database -verbose -thin -resolve -force -time
/tmp/FileHandleDemo.java
[0.0 sec, 0.0 sec] initialization complete
[0.0090 sec, 0.0090 sec] loading  : FileHandleDemo
[0.149 sec, 0.158 sec] creating : FileHandleDemo
[1.044 sec, 1.202 sec] resolver :
[0.0070 sec, 1.209 sec] resolving: FileHandleDemo
```

From the subsequent SQL query we can now see the difference.

```
SQL> column object_name format a20

SQL> select object_name, object_type, status from user_objects where
  2    object_name like '%FileHandle%';

OBJECT_NAME          OBJECT_TYPE         STATUS
-------------------- ------------------- -------
FileHandleDemo       JAVA CLASS          VALID
FileHandleDemo       JAVA SOURCE         VALID
```

The following example loads Sun's activation framework into the database. This is one of the JAR files needed to use Sun's JavaMail API. Loading both of these into the database is desirable since they greatly help developers who need to send and receive mail from within the database. For Oracle 9i systems, this file is located in the %ORACLE_HOME%\lib directory.

> *Visit http://java.sun.com/products/javabeans/glasgow/jaf.html for more information about this API and to download it for use in non-9i systems. Visit http://java.sun.com/products/javamail/index.html if you are interested in the JavaMail API.*

```
> loadjava -user username/password@database -thin -force -noverify -resolve
/d01/oracle9/product/901/lib/activation.jar

    ORA-29552: verification warning: at offset 12 of
javax.activation.ActivationDataFlavor.<init> resolved FIELD<null> cannot Access
java.awt.datatransfer.DataFlavor.class$java$io$InputStream
verifier is replacing bytecode at javax.activation.ActivationDataFlavor.<init>:12
by a throw
at offset 12 of javax.activation.ActivationDataFlavor.<init> resolved FIELD<null>
cannot Access java.awt.datatransfer.DataFlavor.class$java$io$InputStream
at offset 18 of javax.activation.ActivationDataFlavor.<init> resolved FIELD<null>
cannot Access java.awt.datatransfer.DataFlavor.class$java$io$InputStream
verifier is replacing bytecode at javax.activation.ActivationDataFlavor.<init>:18
by a throw
at offset 18 of javax.activation.ActivationDataFlavor.<init> resolved FIELD<null>
cannot Access java.awt.datatransfer.DataFlavor.class$java$io$InputStream
at offset 30 of javax.activation.ActivationDataFlavor.<init> resolved FIELD<null>
cannot Access java.awt.datatransfer.DataFlavor.class$java$io$InputStream
verifier is replacing bytecode at javax.activation.ActivationDataFlavor.<init>:30
by a throw
at offset 30 of javax.activation.ActivationDataFlavor.<init> resolved FIELD<null>
cannot Access java.awt.datatransfer.DataFlavor.class$java$io$InputStream
```

What makes this activation.jar example interesting is the fact that loading it will cause the Oracle JVM byte code verifier to complain about some of the class files. The cryptic output above says there is a "verification warning". Fortunately, the byte code is correct since it has been tested outside the database in a conventional JVM environment and it comes from a trusted source. Why does the JVM complain? Most likely, the Oracle JVM software has a defect with this set of byte codes. The -noverify option can be used to bypass this condition but do not use this as a generic work-around for similar errors. It is quite possible that other code exhibiting similar verification errors is malicious – potentially causing the JVM to perform incorrectly or crash.

Here is the modified `loadjava` command. After the first error the remaining errors are the same as above and have been removed from the output for clarity:

```
> loadjava -user username/password@database -thin -force -resolve -noverify
activation.jar

Error while turning off verifier
    ORA-29532: Java call terminated by uncaught Java exception:
java.security.AccessControlException: the Permission
(oracle.aurora.security.JServerPermission Verifier ) has not been granted by
dbms_java.grant_permission to
SchemaProtectionDomain(USERNAME|PolicyTableProxy(USERNAME))
```

What happened is that USERNAME does not have the authority to turn off the verifier so we still see the errors. Connect as SYS or SYSTEM and grant the oracle.aurora.security.JServerPermission 'Verifier' permission to username.

```
SQL> exec
dbms_java.grant_permission('USERNAME','oracle.aurora.security.JServerPermission','
Verifier',null)

PL/SQL procedure successfully completed.
```

After granting the permissions, USERNAME will be able to load the activation.jar file without a problem and all the class files will be marked VALID.

To remove an entire JAR/ZIP file from the JVM, we can use dropjava. This example will silently complete if there are no errors. You can remove a JAR whether it is resolved or not. If you have loaded a JAR/ZIP of source code and had the code compiled/resolved, then removing the JAR/ZIP will also remove the compiled code.

```
> dropjava -u username/password activation.jar
```

If you look at the definition for the DBMS_JAVA package you will see that there are procedures named loadjava and dropjava. These are the entry points into Java code from Oracle that actually does the work for adding and removing Java code. Some of the Java code referenced by the PL/SQL wrapper functions and procedures in DBMS_JAVA is in a package named oracle.aurora.server.tools.loadjava, which implies that you can write your own Java that uses the same Java code. Furthermore, there are four other procedures and functions in DBMS_JAVA that assist in loading Java into the database. They are deploy_open, deploy_copy, deploy_close, and deploy_invoke and they also map to code in the same Java package. However, we will not cover any of this since it's not important to write alternate code loaders. What is important is to realize that many of the Java operations in the database can be used in your own code.

There are two tables that the JVM uses to hold the Java byte code and track the Java objects. The first table is named CREATE$JAVA$LOB$TABLE and it holds the fully qualified name of the object, the date and time it was loaded and the object itself. The other table is JAVA$CLASS$MD5$TABLE. Both tables do not exist by default, but will be created by loadjava the first time they are needed. Here are the definitions:

```
SQL> desc CREATE$JAVA$LOB$TABLE
 Name                              Null?    Type
 ---------------------------------  -------  --------------------

 NAME                                        VARCHAR2(700)
 LOB                                         BLOB
 LOADTIME                                    DATE

SQL> desc JAVA$CLASS$MD5$TABLE
 Name                              Null?    Type
 ---------------------------------  -------  --------------------

 NAME                                        VARCHAR2(200)
 MD5                                         RAW(16)
```

There is some documentation for these two tables, but they are really not of any concern during the normal development cycle and should not be directly altered. They are used by the loadjava and dropjava programs. Rows in JAVA$CLASS$MD5$TABLE map to rows in the USER_OBJECTS table.

The -debug option of loadjava is excellent for seeing how this utility works. What happens is that loadjava uses dbms_lob procedures to load the file to the database, then uses CREATE JAVA SQL to create the object (if the class does not currently exist). Your code can generate similar JDBC output by using the oracle.jdbc.driver.OracleLog class.

Every Java class that is created gets a distinct hash value which is stored in the MD5 column of the JAVA$CLASS$MD5$TABLE table. Hash values are similar to fingerprints – they uniquely describe objects. The loadjava utility uses them to determine if the Java currently being loaded is already present in the database. If present, loadjava will not overwrite the existing code. The -force option will override this default behavior and always (re)-load Java code, classes, resources, and so on.

It is important to note that even though you will not exercise direct control over these tables you do affect their contents. This means that if you use loadjava then do not use DROP JAVA SQL syntax since that will leave orphaned rows in these tables. If you find yourself in this situation then it's best to just determine what classes need to be removed and then execute loadjava and then dropjava to clean up the tables.

## Java Compile Options

You can specify compiler options using the loadjava command line as shown previously. You can also set a default option with the JAVA$OPTIONS table. Here is the table definition:

```
SQL> desc java$options;
 Name                              Null?    Type
 ---------------------------------  -------  --------------------

 WHAT                                        VARCHAR2(128)
 OPT                                         VARCHAR2(20)
 VALUE                                       VARCHAR2(128)
```

By default, the table does not exist but will be automatically created in the users' schema when you set the first option. An important concept to remember is that when you specify an option on the command line, it will override the table entry and will remove that value from the table. You should not directly modify this table. Instead, use the following procedures and functions from the DBMS_JAVA package to set, get, and reset the compiler options:

- ❏ procedure set_compiler_option(
      name VARCHAR2,
      option VARCHAR2,
      value VARCHAR2)

- ❏ function get_compiler_option(
      name VARCHAR2,
      option VARCHAR2) returns VARCHAR2

- ❏ procedure reset_compiler_option(
      name VARCHAR2,

      option VARCHAR2)

Options are also used for Java with SQLJ constructs. Currently, there are three options you can set:

- ❏ encoding
- ❏ online
- ❏ debug

The encoding option is similar to the -encoding option for loadjava. The debug option causes the JVM compiler to generate debugging information in the code (this is similar to the -g option with the Sun JDK compiler). The value of the online option indicates a fully qualified class name that will perform semantics checking for the affected classes being loaded.

The following example generates debugging information for any code in the wrox package and indicates to the compiler that you want to use two different encodings for your code in a hypothetical package named wrox.utility:

```
SQL> exec dbms_java.set_compiler_option('wrox.', 'debug', 'true')

PL/SQL procedure successfully completed.

SQL> exec dbms_java.set_compiler_option('wrox.utility', 'encoding', 'UTF8')

PL/SQL procedure successfully completed.

SQL> exec dbms_java.set_compiler_option('wrox.utility.nio', 'encoding',
  2 'SJIS')

PL/SQL procedure successfully completed.
```

The UTF8 encoding will affect any code (or sub-packages) in the wrox.utility package, except for the wrox.utility.nio code since that has its own encoding option. 'SJIS' is the 'shift JIS' character set for the Japanese language.

If you want to remove an option just call the reset_compiler_option procedure and the compiler will remove that row from JAVA$OPTIONS and revert back to the default value.

## Using the ALL_OBJECTS and USER_OBJECTS Tables

Now that you know how to add and remove code the next thing is to inspect the Java in the database. We can get a manifest of all Java by examining the rows in the USER_OBJECTS and ALL_OBJECTS tables. The following query shows a count of every different Java object types currently in the database. These counts will vary from machine to machine.

```
SQL> select object_type, count(*) from all_objects where object_type like
  2 'JAVA%' group by object_type order by object_type;

OBJECT_TYPE          COUNT(*)
------------------ ----------
JAVA CLASS              11891
JAVA DATA                 294
JAVA RESOURCE             195
JAVA SOURCE                19
```

We know that there are a large number of Java classes in the database, now let's see what is in our own schema. The following SQL query shows some of the Java objects in our schema. When the JVM cannot resolve the class dependencies (or the developer does not tell it to do so), the STATUS column will be INVALID.

```
SQL> select dbms_java.longname(object_name) long_name, object_type, status
  2    from user_objects where object_type like 'JAVA%' order by object_name,
  3    object_type;

LONG_NAME                                           OBJECT_TYPE     STATUS
------------------------------------------------- --------------- -------
com/sun/activation/registries/MimeTypeFile          JAVA CLASS      VALID
com/sun/activation/registries/MailcapParseException JAVA CLASS      VALID
.
.
BlobStuff                                           JAVA CLASS      VALID
BlobStuff                                           JAVA SOURCE     VALID
FileHandleDemo                                      JAVA CLASS      VALID
FileHandleDemo                                      JAVA SOURCE     VALID
.
.
META-INF/mailcap.default                            JAVA RESOURCE   VALID
META-INF/mimetypes.default                          JAVA RESOURCE   VALID
```

## Extracting Source Code

Another feature available since version 8.1.6 is the ability to extract the source code for any object of type JAVA SOURCE. It's just like getting the source code for non-wrapped PL/SQL. Source code can be retrieved from the USER_SOURCE or ALL_SOURCE tables. Here are their definitions:

```
SQL> desc user_source
 Name                       Null?    Type
 ------------------------- -------- ------------------
 NAME                                VARCHAR2(30)
```

```
    TYPE                              VARCHAR2(12)
    LINE                              NUMBER
    TEXT                              VARCHAR2(4000)

SQL> desc all_source
    Name                    Null?    Type
    --------------------- -------- ------------------
    OWNER                             VARCHAR2(30)
    NAME                              VARCHAR2(30)
    TYPE                              VARCHAR2(12)
    LINE                              NUMBER
    TEXT                .             VARCHAR2(4000)
```

This will not allow you to generate source code for Java class files, since the Oracle JVM does not have any reverse compilation features. If you want to get source code out of the database then you will have to put it in there first by loading the .java files. This SQL statement will get the source to the FileHandleDemo class and sort it by line number (We know this will work since a previous query showed that there is a JAVA SOURCE entry in the USER_OBJECTS table for the class):

```
select text from user_source where name = 'FileHandleDemo' order by line;
```

If you prefer, you can get the source code using more DBMS_JAVA functions and procedures. In Oracle 9.0.1 they can export Java source, class, or resource objects. For classes (byte code), it only makes sense to be able to export to a BLOB, but source code and resources can be exported to either a CLOB or a BLOB. These procedures use the oracle.aurora.rdbms.ExportSchemaObjects package to do the actual work so you could directly call them from within your Java code:

```
procedure export_source(name VARCHAR2, schema VARCHAR2, blob BLOB)

procedure export_source(name VARCHAR2, blob BLOB)

procedure export_source(name VARCHAR2, schema varchar2, clob CLOB)

procedure export_source(name VARCHAR2, clob CLOB)

procedure export_class(name VARCHAR2, schema VARCHAR2, blob BLOB)

procedure export_class(name VARCHAR2, blob BLOB)

procedure export_resource (name VARCHAR2, schema VARCHAR2, blob BLOB)

procedure export_resource(name VARCHAR2, blob BLOB)

procedure export_resource(name VARCHAR2, schema VARCHAR2, clob CLOB)

procedure export_resource(name VARCHAR2, clob CLOB)
```

The example below demonstrates the use of these procedures. First we extract 100 characters (using a CLOB) from the FileHandleDemo source code and then we extract the first 100 bytes from the same source code, but have it materialize through a BLOB:

```
SQL> set serveroutput on
SQL> declare
  2     c clob;
  3  begin
  4     dbms_lob.createtemporary(c, true);
  5     dbms_lob.open(c, dbms_lob.lob_readwrite);
  6     dbms_java.export_source('FileHandleDemo', c);
  7     dbms_output.put_line(dbms_lob.substr(c, 100));
  8     dbms_lob.close(c);
  9  end;
 10  /
import java.io.*;
  import java.sql.*;

  public class FileHandleDemo {


static FileOutputS

PL/SQL procedure successfully completed.

SQL> declare
  2     b blob;
  3  begin
  4     dbms_lob.createtemporary(b, true);
  5     dbms_lob.open(b, dbms_lob.lob_readwrite);
  6     dbms_java.export_source('FileHandleDemo', b);
  7     dbms_output.put_line(dbms_lob.substr(b, 100));
  8     dbms_lob.close(b);
  9  end;
 10  /
696D706F7274206A6176612E696F2E2A3B0D0A2020696D706F7274206A6176612E73716C2E2A3B0D
0A0D0A20207075626C696320636C6173732046696C6548616E646C6544656D6F207B0D0A0D0A2020
20207374617469632046696C6654F757470757453

PL/SQL procedure successfully completed.
```

## Resolving Java Classes

The resolver in the JVM is the functional equivalent of a CLASSPATH in a traditional JVM. If you want to know how the code is being resolved then we can use another DBMS_JAVA function called RESOLVER. It is defined like this:

```
function resolver(name VARCHAR2, owner VARCHAR2, type VARCHAR2) return VARCHAR2
```

The name must be the short name and it cannot be specified using a wildcard. The owner is the schema owner of the Java object and the type is either JAVA CLASS or JAVA SOURCE. First is an example showing the default resolver being used for the FileHandleDemo source code. The second example shows use of resolver for one of the classes that comes with the Oracle JVM.

```
SQL> select dbms_java.resolver('FileHandleDemo','USERNAME','JAVA SOURCE')
  2  RESOLVER from dual;

RESOLVER
```

```
------------------------------------------------------------------ ((*
USERNAME)(* PUBLIC))

SQL> select dbms_java.resolver('/10076b23_OraCustomDatumClosur','SYS',
  2  'JAVA CLASS') RESOLVER from dual;

RESOLVER
--------------------------------------------------------------------
((* SYS))
```

The format of each item in the `resolver` string is:

```
(<class files to resolve> <schema>)
```

So in the first example, we have:

```
((* SCOTT) (* PUBLIC))
```

This will cause the JVM to first look in the SCOTT schema for all classes and then look in the PUBLIC area. The JVM will throw an exception if it does not find the class files. If there is a need to just have particular classes resolved in a different schema, then you can specify a more granular `resolver`.

If you want to change the `resolver` after you have loaded the Java you can issue an ALTER JAVA DDL statement. You might want to do this if you have exported Java from one user and imported it with another user. In this example, the `resolver` might be invalid and you may have to update it for all your code.

To demonstrate, we setup three database user accounts: USER_A, USER_B, and USER_C. USER_A and USER_B each have a class named TestClass with a single method do_it() which displays a different message. USER_C has a class named TopClass which calls TestClass.do_it(). Here is the definition for USER_A:

```
SQL> connect user_a/user_a
Connected.
SQL> create or replace and resolve java source named "TestClass" as
  2  public class TestClass {
  3    public static void do_it() {
  4      System.out.println("This is from USER_A.TestClass.do_it()");
  5    }
  6  }
  7  /

Java created.

SQL> show errors
No errors.
```

Since users do not normally have `execute` authority on other users' code, we have to grant this explicitly to USER_C:

```
SQL> grant execute on "TestClass" to user_c;

Grant succeeded.
```

Here is the code for USER_B:

```
SQL> connect user_b/user_b
Connected.
SQL> create or replace and resolve java source named "TestClass" as
  2  public class TestClass {
  3    public static void do_it() {
  4       System.out.println("This is from USER_B.TestClass.do_it()");
  5    }
  6  }
  7  /

Java created.

SQL> show errors
No errors.

SQL> grant execute on "TestClass" to user_c;

Grant succeeded.
```

Here is the code for USER_C. Note that the resolver has been specified to first look in the schema for USER_C then USER_A and finally PUBLIC:

```
SQL> connect user_c/user_c
Connected.
SQL> create or replace and resolve java source named "TopLevel" resolver ((*
                              USER_C) (* USER_A) (* PUBLIC)) as
  2  public class TopLevel {
  3    public static void do_it() {
  4       TestClass.do_it();
  5    }
  6  }
  7  /

Java created.

SQL> show errors
No errors.
SQL> create or replace procedure resolve_test as
  2  language java name 'TopLevel.do_it()';
  3  /

Procedure created.
```

Below is the first execution and you can see that the resolver correctly uses TestClass.do_it from USER_A:

```
SQL> set serveroutput on size 10000
SQL> exec dbms_java.set_output(10000)

PL/SQL procedure successfully completed.

SQL> exec resolve_test
This is from USER_A.TestClass.do_it()

PL/SQL procedure successfully completed.
```

Next, we change the `resolver` to use USER_B instead of USER_A:

```
SQL> alter java source "TopLevel" resolver ((* USER_C) (* USER_B) (*
                        PUBLIC)) resolve;

Java altered.
```

Finally, we run the procedure (twice because of the Java session state) and you can see that the call to the PL/SQL wrapper now shows the `USER_C.TopLevel.do_it()` calling `TestClass` from USER_B.

```
SQL> exec resolve_test
BEGIN resolve_test; END;

*
ERROR at line 1:
ORA-29549: class USER_C.TopLevel has changed, Java session state cleared
ORA-06512: at "USER_C.RESOLVE_TEST", line 0
ORA-06512: at line 1


SQL> set serveroutput on  size 10000
SQL> exec dbms_java.set_output(10000)

PL/SQL procedure successfully completed.

SQL> exec resolve_test
This is from USER_B.TestClass.do_it()

PL/SQL procedure successfully completed.
```

By now you will realize that a lot of functionality exists in the DBMS_JAVA package and all of this is actually Java code. You can describe the package from a SQL*Plus prompt or you can just select the entire source to the DBMS_JAVA package header from the ALL_OBJECTS table. The second way has the added benefit of being able to see all the comments in the package header.

# Debugging and Common Pitfalls

This section is designed to help you be a more efficient Java developer when using the Oracle JVM. We want to highlight some of the ways you can debug your code and show you how to find out more about the memory usage of Java objects. We also will describe some of the common problems that almost every developer has when using the JVM. This includes those who are fairly accomplished Java programmers.

# Manipulating Debug Output

Not too many years ago all a developer had to help figure out what was wrong with their errant code was the basic character terminal (or file) and their brain. What usually ensued was a lot of debugging code (using `System.out.println()` calls in Java or `printf()` calls in C) to print variable values at strategic locations in the application logic. Then the integrated development environments came along, which brought us single stepping, memory and object browsing, and so on. Both of these techniques are available when developing with the Oracle JVM environment.

First, Java programmers know that calling `System.out.println()`, `System.err.println()`, or similar variants, will send output to the console. Code running in the JVM is non-interactive so the output must go somewhere. It doesn't go to `/dev/null` (or the equivalent on non-Unix systems). Rather, it goes to system-generated trace files in the `$ORACLE_BASE/<SID>/udump` directory. Trace files have useful information (that can be found elsewhere) but what is generally most important about these Java-related traces is the `System.out/System.err` output.

When working in SQL*Plus, the `SET SERVEROUTPUT ON` directive permits all output generated by `DBMS_OUTPUT` procedure calls to be displayed on the console. The PL/SQL wrapper procedure `DBMS_JAVA.SET_OUTPUT(buffersize NUMBER)` will redirect `System.out` and `System.err` output from the trace files to the console. The underlying code uses the `DBMS_OUTPUT` procedures. The `buffersize` parameter indicates how much output to buffer. If these two statements are used often then consider adding them to the `LOGIN.SQL` file.

Redirection is terminated when the JVM resets the state of your session. This happens when classes that have previously been executed are recompiled or reloaded. The following example demonstrates this behavior. The Java code has just one method to print the database version. It is loaded and the PL/SQL wrapper is created.

```
SQL> create or replace and compile java source named "prop" as
  2    public class prop {
  3      public static void db_ver() {
  4        System.out.println(System.getProperty("oracle.jserver.version"));
  5      }
  6    }
  7  /

Java created.
SQL> create or replace procedure db_ver
  2  as
  3  language java
  4  name 'prop.db_ver()';
  5  /

Procedure created.
```

Next, the output is redirected and the PL/SQL procedure executes as expected.

```
SQL> set serveroutput on size 10000
SQL> exec dbms_java.set_output(10000)
```

**341**

```
PL/SQL procedure successfully completed.

SQL> exec db_ver
9.0.1.0.0

PL/SQL procedure successfully completed.
```

Now, the Java source code is modified because a new method is added to print the JVM version. This Java code is re-loaded and a new PL/SQL wrapper is created.

```
SQL> create or replace and compile java source named "prop" as
  2    public class prop {
  3      public static void db_ver() {
  4        System.out.println(System.getProperty("oracle.jserver.version"));
  5      }
  6      public static void vm_ver() {
  7        System.out.println(System.getProperty("java.version"));
  8      }
  9    }
 10  /

Java created..

SQL> create or replace procedure vm_ver
  2  as
  3  language java
  4  name 'prop.vm_ver()';
  5  /

Procedure created.
```

The new PL/SQL procedure named VM_VER is executed. However, the Java class was already loaded into session memory because of the call to DB_VER. Re-loading the Java invalidated the Java session state. Therefore, an error about the session space being cleared is generated.

```
SQL> exec vm_ver
BEGIN vm_ver; END;

*
ERROR at line 1:
ORA-29549: class USERNAME.prop has changed, Java session state cleared
ORA-06512: at "USERNAME.VM_VER", line 0
ORA-06512: at line 1
```

Re-directing the output and re-executing VM_VER shows that the database has JDK version 1.2.1.

```
SQL> set serveroutput on size 10000
SQL> exec dbms_java.set_output(10000)
```

```
PL/SQL procedure successfully completed.

SQL> exec vm_ver
1.2.1

PL/SQL procedure successfully completed.
```

The following output is from the trace file. It was created after cleanly running both DB_VER and VM_VER.

```
/d01/oracle9/admin/ora901/udump/ora901_ora_2018.trc
Oracle9i Enterprise Edition Release 9.0.1.0.0 - Production
With the Partitioning option
JServer Release 9.0.1.0.0 - Production
ORACLE_HOME = /d01/oracle9/product/901
System name:    SunOS
Node name:      oaxaca
Release:        5.8
Version:        Generic_108528-08
Machine:        sun4u
Instance name: ora901
Redo thread mounted by this instance: 1
Oracle process number: 12
Unix process pid: 2018, image: oracle@oaxaca (TNS V1-V3)

*** 2001-10-18 02:06:43.342
*** SESSION ID:(7.1432) 2001-10-18 02:06:43.326
9.0.1.0.0
*** 2001-10-18 02:09:46.383
1.2.1
```

# JDBC Tracing using the OracleLog Class

Another useful debugging technique is to use the `oracle.jdbc.driver.OracleLog` class. This is a utility class that allows developers to control the types and amount of JDBC tracing output information that is generated. `OracleLog` sends this information to any `java.io.PrintStream` or `java.io.PrintWriter` based class. This includes `System.out`, `System.err`, `FilePrintStream`'s, etc. It can generate an enormous amount of data, which can slow your processing down significantly if lots of JDBC code is executed. What follows is some lines of JDBC debugging information generated by `loadjava`. Spacing has been added for clarity. The first line has a module mask and category mask which tells the logging code what and how muc to bedetailed.

```
DRVR OPER Enabled logging (moduleMask 0x0fffffff, categoryMask 0x0fffffff)

DRVR DBG1 SQL: "create table CREATE$JAVA$LOB$TABLE(name varchar2(700) unique, lob
blob, loadtime date)"

DRVR DBG1 Input SQL:  "create table CREATE$JAVA$LOB$TABLE(name varchar2(700)
unique, lob blob, loadtime date)"
```

```
DRVR DBG1 Output SQL: "create table CREATE$JAVA$LOB$TABLE(name varchar2(700)
unique, lob blob, loadtime date)"

DRVR DBG1 Before execute: m_currentRank=1, sql_kind=3, need_to_parse=true

DRVR DBG1 Input SQL:  "begin dbms_lob.write (?, ?, ?, ?); end;"

DRVR DBG1 Output SQL: "begin dbms_lob.write (:1, :2, :3, :4); end;"

DRVR DBG1 Before execute: m_currentRank=1, sql_kind=1, need_to_parse=true

DRVR DBG1 Send batch: batch=1, m_currentRank=0

DRVR DBG1 SQL: "create or replace  java class       using
'javax/activation/UnsupportedDataTypeException'"

DRVR DBG1 Input SQL:  "create or replace  java class       using
'javax/activation/UnsupportedDataTypeException'"
```

# Interactive Console-Based JVM Debugger

The debugging techniques discussed above are good but they still do not allow you to interactively debug server-side Java code. What Oracle provides is a debug–by–proxy architecture that allows you to remotely debug code in the JVM using the jdb program from Sun's JDK. There are a number of components to this. They are:

❑   jdb – command line debugger used to issue commands, view variables, and so on

❑   DebugProxy – server type of Java program that accepts connections from jdb and forwards them to the DebugAgent running in the database

❑   DebugAgent – Java in the database which accepts debugging commands from jdb (through a connection with the DebugProxy program)

To debug you would:

❑   Compile your code with the –g option (generates all debugging information for your Java) if you are using the client system JDK. You must load your code into the database and be prepared to tell jdb where the source is located so it can access it. It's usually simpler to just load and resolve the source code into the database using loadjava. Of course, specify the debug compiler option for your code before loading. These are settable using DBMS_JAVA procedures. If you loaded the source into the database then you do not have to specify a source location to jdb.

❑   Insure that the database user has been granted the JAVADEBUGPRIV role (when using 8.1.5) or has the proper JServerPermission (when using 8.1.6. and up). For example:

```
exec dbms_java.grant_permission('USERNAME',
'SYS:oracle.aurora.security.JServerPermission', 'Debug', ' ' )
```

❑ Start the client-side portion of the debugger called the "debug proxy" which is
`%ORACLE_HOME%/bin/debugproxy`. You can either let it pick a random port or specify your
own with the `-port` option. Step #8 in the following table shows that port 2222 is being used.

❑ Start the database `DebugAgent` using another `DBMS_JAVA` procedure called
`start_debugging`. This takes the following parameters:

   ❑ IP address or hostname of system running the DebugProxy

   ❑ Port `DebugProxy` is using to accept connections

   ❑ Time (in seconds) that the `DebugAgent` will wait for a request before stopping

❑ After you have started both the `DebugProxy` and `DebugAgent`, you will need to start `jdb`.
There are many options to `jdb` but for this example it just tells `jdb` to use the `-dbgtrace` flag
print to print all `System.out` calls. A password needs to be specified since `jdb` will connect to
an already running JVM. This is simply providing the password that `DebugProxy` generates
when it is connects with the `DebugAgent`. Step #10 in the table below shows this parameter.

❑ Within `jdb` a developer can suspend and resume threads, set breakpoints, inspect memory,
and so on. It's not a very fancy debugger but it gets the job done. Since we had to specify a
timeout value when starting the `DebugAgent`, the first command to issue in `jdb` is the
`suspend` command. This will allow you time to setup your environment and load the source
code before stepping into your methods.

Our example will use three Unix terminals. The purpose of the example is to display the 10th prime number
to `System.out`. It's a modified example that originally would generate any nth prime number. You should
note that `main()` is defined in this class. Trying to execute code without this did not work with `jdb`. It
makes sense since `jdb` is a Sun-provided tool and requires a common entry point into the program whereas
Java running in the Oracle JVM simply has to be statically defined. Here is the source code:

```java
public class prime {

  public static void nth_prime() throws Exception {
    int ctr = 0;
    int i = 2;
    int N = 10;

    for (; ctr < N; i++) {
      int divisor;
      int maxToTry = (int) Math.sqrt(i);

      for (divisor = 2; divisor <= maxToTry; divisor++) {
        if (i % divisor == 0) {
          break;
        }
      }

      if (divisor > maxToTry) {
        ctr++;
      }
    }

    System.out.println("The " + N + "th prime number is: " + (i - 1));
```

**345**

```
    System.exit(1);
  }

  public static void main(String[] args) throws Exception {
    nth_prime();
  }
}
```

There are three different UNIX terminals used for this example. It is possible to configure DebugProxy to run in the background and automatically start jdb but this example starts it manually. The three terminals are:

❑ Terminal 1 – where code is compiled and where the DebugAgent executes

❑ Terminal 2 – DebugProxy executes

❑ Terminal 3 – jdb executes

Here is the sequence of commands for the example. The commands are listed in detail since there are three different terminal sessions and it tends to get confusing. Steps #11 through #19 are jdb commands.

| Step # | Terminal # | Command |
|--------|-----------|---------|
| 1 | 1 | sqlplus username/password |
| 2 | 1 | set serveroutput on size 100000 |
| 3 | 1 | exec dbms_java.set_output(100000); |
| 4 | 1 | exec dbms_java.set_compiler_option('','debug','true'); |
| 5 | 1 | commit; |
| 6 | 1 | exec dbms_java.loadjava('-f -r -v /tmp/prime.java'); |
|   |   | Remember that the schema user needs to be granted the file read permission. |
| 7 | 1 | select * from user_objects where object_name='prime'; |
| 8 | 2 | debugproxy -port 2222 |
| 9 | 1 | call dbms_java.start_debugging( |
|   |   |         'oaxaca.us.oracle.com',2222,20); |
|   |   | This first parameter is the machine name. It does not represent a Java package specification. Numeric IP addresses are also allowable. |
| 10 | 3 | jdb -dbgtrace -password 4ugtm2 |
| 11 | 3 | suspend |
| 12 | 3 | load USERNAME:prime |

| Step # | Terminal # | Command |
|--------|-----------|---------|
| 13 | 3 | stop in prime:nth_prime |
| 14 | 3 | stop at prime:22 |
| 15 | 3 | run prime |
| 16 | 3 | where |
| 17 | 3 | list |
| 18 | 3 | cont |
| 19 | 3 | locals |
| 19 | 3 | cont |

This is the output from Terminal 1, connecting to the database as username/password.

```
SQL> set serveroutput on size 100000
SQL> exec dbms_java.set_output(100000);

PL/SQL procedure successfully completed.

SQL> exec dbms_java.set_compiler_option('','debug','true');

PL/SQL procedure successfully completed.

SQL> commit;

Commit complete.

SQL> exec dbms_java.loadjava('-f -r -v /tmp/prime.java');
arguments: '-kprb' '-localpathprefix' '/d01/oracle9/product/901/' '-f' '-r' '-v'
'/tmp/prime.java'
creating : source prime
resolving: source prime

PL/SQL procedure successfully completed.

SQL> select * from user_objects where object_name='prime';
OBJECT_NAME     SUBOBJECT_NAME     OBJECT_ID     OBJECT_TYPE     CREATED
-----------------------------------------------------------------------
prime                              33251         Java Class      18-NOV-01
prime                              33250         Java Source     18-NOV-01


LAST_DDL_TIME   TIMESTAMP                   STATUS    T  G  S
-----------------------------------------------------------------
18-NOV-01       2001-11-18:12:01:51         INVALID   N  N  N
18-NOV-01       2001-11-18:12:01:51         INVALID   N  N  N

SQL> call dbms_java.start_debugging('oaxaca.us.oracle.com',2222,30);

call completed
```

This is the output from terminal 2.

```
SQL> debugproxy -port 2222
Proxy Name:      oaxaca
Proxy Address:   138.1.112.74
Proxy Port:      2222

Agent Number:    1
Agent Name:      oaxaca
Agent Address:   138.1.112.74
Agent Port:      36341
Agent Password: 4ugtm2
```

This is the output from terminal 3. You can see that we have suspended the system then loaded the source code and set a few break points before continuing. After we run the program it stops at the first breakpoint which was set to the start of the nth_prime() method. We continue on to the next breakpoint and then inspect the local variables (some of which have gone out of scope). While we did not show it in this example, you can determine you current call stack by typing where on the jdb command prompt. The final line in the output is the 10th prime number.

```
# jdb -dbgtrace -password 4ugtm2
Initializing jdb...
[debugger: connected]
[debugger: loading classes ...]
> suspend
[debugger: listThreadGroups: 1 groups]
All (non-system) threads suspended.
> load USERNAME:prime
[debugger: reading 40 classes...]
0x7fffffc0:class(prime)
> stop in prime:nth_prime
[debugger: reading 56 classes...]
[debugger: getting (3) methods]
Breakpoint set in prime.nth_prime
> stop at prime:22
[debugger: reading 59 classes...]
Breakpoint set at prime:22
> run prime
[debugger: reading 60 classes...]
running ...
main[1]
Breakpoint hit: [debugger: lvar 0: slot=-1, name=ctr, sig=I, arg=false]
[debugger: lvar 1: slot=-1, name=i, sig=I, arg=false]
[debugger: lvar 2: slot=-1, name=N, sig=I, arg=false]
[debugger: lvar 3: slot=-1, name=divisor, sig=I, arg=false]
[debugger: lvar 4: slot=-1, name=maxToTry, sig=I, arg=false]
[debugger: lvar 0: slot=0, name=args, sig=[Ljava/lang/String;, arg=true]
prime.nth_prime (prime:5)
main[1] list
[debugger: getSourceFile: allocating 560 bytes.]
1
2     public class prime {
```

```
3
4              public static void nth_prime() throws Exception {
5      =>      int ctr = 0;
6              int i = 2;
7              int N = 10;
8
9              for (; ctr < N; i++) {
main[1] cont

Breakpoint hit: main[1] [debugger: lvar 0: slot=0, name=ctr, sig=I, arg=false]
[debugger: lvar 1: slot=1, name=i, sig=I, arg=false]
[debugger: lvar 2: slot=2, name=N, sig=I, arg=false]
[debugger: lvar 3: slot=-1, name=divisor, sig=I, arg=false]
[debugger: lvar 4: slot=-1, name=maxToTry, sig=I, arg=false]
[debugger: lvar 0: slot=0, name=args, sig=[Ljava/lang/String;, arg=true]
prime.nth_prime (prime:22)
main[1] locals
[debugger: getStackVariables: thread=main, currentFrame=0]
[debugger: getLocalVariables:]
[debugger:     stackframe=prime.nth_prime (prime:22)]
[debugger:     5 local vars]
Method arguments:
Local variables:
  ctr = 10
  i = 30
  N = 10
  divisor is not in scope
  maxToTry is not in scope
main[1] cont
The 10th prime number is: 29
```

As a side note, Oracle's JDeveloper 3.2 product integrates with this debugging architecture. This does not exclude other IDE's from doing the same.

As another option, you can develop and test your code outside the server using some third party IDE and then load the code into the server since the code (for the most part) behaves the same in either JVM. 'For the most part' implies that there are some differences between a normal JVM and the Oracle JVM.

A short (but not exhaustive) list includes:

❑   No 'true' multi-threading – but does not preclude the use of the threading API's

❑   No AWT/applet/Swing classes are allowed to be materialized (but can be used to generate off-screen images)

❑   `System.out()` and `System.err()` output – output goes to a file (by default) rather than a console.

# A Note on the Oracle Threading Model

Another differentiator of the Oracle JVM is that is does not have what one might consider a robust threading model. In fact, the Oracle JVM implements a threading model that is quite different from the traditional Java threading model. In Java, generally, you can start multiple threads that are executed either concurrently or in parallel, depending on the number of CPUs available to the system. To prevent multiple threads from accessing sensitive methods or code blocks, you have the option of synchronizing code, which effectively limits the number of concurrent threads to one.

What the Oracle JVM has is a non-preemptive scheduler where all Java threads are multiplexed onto a single operating system thread. It does not implement any method of concurrency when executing multiple threads inside the same application. Instead, different threads are scheduled in a queue, so that each thread executes until it is finished, and then the next thread takes over. Thread context switches only occur when a currently executing thread is blocked, such as when its `yield()` method is invoked or it performs an inherently blocking operation, such as receiving a packet from a socket (as we will study in more detail in Chapter 13, *Working with Operating System Resources*).

The idea behind the Oracle Java threading model is that it will in effect work the same whether you run your database with one or more processors. However, because of the nature of this model, it is generally not a good idea to write multi-threaded code within the database. Although not harmful, it will just not do any good, since Oracle runs the threads in a round-robin fashion, which effectively makes any multi-threaded Java program running within Oracle behave as if it was single-threaded. However, the database can very effectively schedule many JVM sessions so this isn't as large an issue as one might think. Developers just have to be aware of the differences.

# Summary

We've gone over details about how the Oracle JVM works, what it can and cannot do (and how it does the things it does). Some highlights regarding the evolution of the JVM from version 8.1.5. through Oracle 9i were also described. We've discussed many different ways to load and unload your Java code and third party JAR/ZIP files. The ability to set compile options helped us to debug source code (which we did using a few techniques). One of the more important discussions centered on how the JVM uses memory and how we can analyze this behavior with the DBMS_SHARED_POOL package. Finally, we have consistently shown that the DBMS_JAVA package is a very important set of routines for developers managing Java in the database.

Oracle 9i Java Programming

# Java Stored Procedure Basics

As an Oracle developer, you will of course be well versed in developing business logic in PL/SQL stored procedures. This chapter explores the relatively new alternative – the development of server-side business logic in Java. Indeed, one of the core services provided by the Oracle JVM is in making static methods of Java classes available to PL/SQL, as **Java stored procedures**.

The goal of this chapter is to demonstrate the basics of creating, publishing and executing Java methods as stored procedures and functions. Having done this we move on to demonstrate two basic, but useful and realistic examples of the use of Java stored procedures. One procedure will convert the time of a scheduled event to the time at your server (this will also demonstrate how to call a Java stored procedure from a trigger). This functionality is somewhat moot in Oracle 9i, which has introduced support for a TIMESTAMP WITH TIMEZONE type, but may nevertheless prove very useful to 8i users. The second demonstrates a very simple, but often required, e-mail address validation technique.

## Why use Java Stored Procedures?

In essence, the goal of the whole of section III of this book is to answer the question in the title. It is certainly true to say that the advent of Java in the Oracle database allows programmers to leverage their knowledge of Java in implementing the business logic on the server side. However, it is certainly not advocated here that Java be a replacement for the use of PL/SQL, and the debate about which to use when has been raging ever since Java was first introduced into the database. The argument generally goes like this. Use PL/SQL for:

❑ **Intensive database access**. SQL operations are faster than with Java, especially when a large amount of data is involved or bulk operations are being used. This is because SQL data types are in fact PL/SQL data types and SQL constructs are PL/SQL constructs. There is no "impedance mismatch". With Java *every* SQL data type must be mapped (converted) to some Java type.

Java is preferred for:

❑ **Intensive computation**. When working extensively with floating point numbers, or other types of numerical data types, Java performs better than PL/SQL. If you can do the computation in SQL, do so, but if you need to perform really complex maths, consider a Java stored procedure over a PL/SQL stored procedure.

❑ **Functionality not available in PL/SQL**, or for functionality that is available in PL/SQL but is limited in some way, or that is simply easier to implement in Java.

As discussed above, we will cover many examples of that last bullet point in this book. Chapters 12, 13 and 14 will discuss useful and correct uses for Java in the Oracle database and Chapter 17 investigates in detail when, in terms of performance, it is better to execute SQL from PL/SQ and when from Java.

It is important to note that the goal of the opening examples in this is to clearly elucidate the key principles of Java stored procedure development. These examples were chosen based on the sole criterion of achieving this goal. We do not claim that it is better to develop examples in Java as opposed to PL/SQL. Indeed, in terms of performance, the opposite may well be true. However, having provided this foundation, we do then move on to present two examples that represent realistic uses of Java (`TimeTranslator` and `mail_utility`). Hopefully this will whet your appetite for the chapters that follow in this section.

# An Overview of Java Stored Procedure Development

Stored procedures are essentially business methods, developed in PL/SQL or Java, which are stored in the Oracle database for general use by multiple clients to the database. Whether the procedure itself is written in Java or PL/SQL, it may be called from any client, be it Java or non-Java.

There are a number of ways in which we can load our Java code, containing the methods we wish to execute, into the database – each Java file or class being stored as a schema object:

❑ Source files (`.java` files) and `.sqlj` files are loaded as Java **source** schema objects

❑ Compiled `.class` Java files (bytecode) are loaded as Java **class** schema objects

❑ Data files, `.zip` files and `.jar` files are loaded as Java **resource** schema objects.

As we discussed in Chapter 1, we can load our code either using the `loadjava` utility or by directly creating and compiling the code in the database.

We cannot automatically call our static Java method as soon as the Java code is loaded into the database. First we establish the method as an entry-point to a call from SQL. In order to do this we must write a PL/SQL call specification. This is essentially a PL/SQL "wrapper" around the Java code, which publishes the Java method to the Oracle data dictionary and also contains the details of the name of the method, its parameter types and any return types. Java methods that return a value are published as functions and `void` methods are published as procedures.

At run time, the client code will call the Java method through the PL/SQL call spec (in other words, referencing the name of the call spec). The compiled Java code is injected into the JVM, Oracle looks up the call spec definition and then the appropriate Java method is executed. This process is illustrated in the following figure:

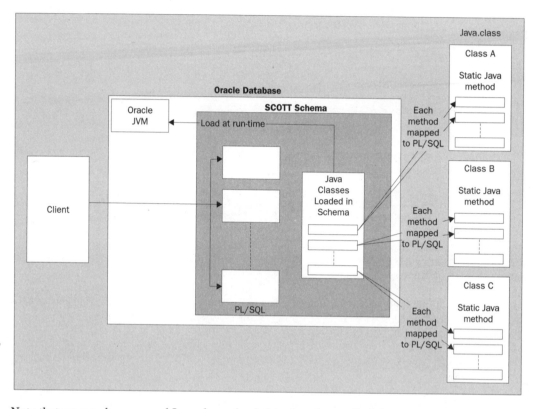

Note that we may have several Java classes loaded in the schema. Each Java class may contain several static methods and each static method is treated as a Java stored procedure.

# Executing Parameterless Java Methods

To illustrate all of this, we will walk through the process of writing our Java code, loading it into the database, writing the call spec and executing a Java method.

The example will use the EMP table from the SCOTT schema, which we recommend you emulate in your own user's schema (see Chapter 1). We'll publish and execute a Java method called raise() that will retrieve the value of the sal column for each row, into an updateable ResultSet, then will raise the salary of each employee, based on certain criteria.

# Loading the Java Class

We'll create a Java class called `RaiseSalary` that defines a `static` method called `raise()`. Note that the method is declared `static` so that it can be called without creating a class instance.

```
import java.sql.*;
import oracle.sql.*;
import java.math.*;

public class RaiseSalary {
  public static void raise() {
    Connection con = null;
    try {
```

We use the JDBC server-side internal driver (see Chapter 7 for details). Note that for the KPRB driver, `setAutocommit` is turned **off** by default.

```
// obtain oracle default connection
con = DriverManager.getConnection("jdbc:default:connection:");
```

Recall that the internal driver, and thus all of our SQL operations, will run within a default session and default transaction context. We are already "connected" to the database and the driver is pre-registered and pre-loaded on the server.

Next, we create a prepared statement that returns a bi-directional `ResultSet` that is insensitive to updates by others (`ResultSet.TYPE_SCROLL_INSENSITIVE`) and is updateable (`ResultSet.CONCUR_UPDATABLE`):

```
// Make PreparedStatement
// Fetch salary of all the employees
PreparedStatement ps =
  con.prepareStatement("select sal from emp",
                       ResultSet.TYPE_SCROLL_INSENSITIVE,
                       ResultSet.CONCUR_UPDATABLE);
```

Of course, the fact that the Java stored procedure creates a result set that can be updated, and that the query selects all rows from the table, means that it locks and needs a lock on the entire table. Any outstanding, non-committed transactions on the table would block it from executing. This is just a simple example, but in general we would obviously be much more selective with our query.

Next, execute our query and retrieve the results into our `ResultSet`:

```
ResultSet rs = ps.executeQuery();
```

We then iterate through each row in the `ResultSet`, raising the employee's salary depending on the range in which the current salary falls. If all of the updates succeed, we commit:

```
    while (rs.next()) {
      double Salary = rs.getDouble(1);

      // check for salary limits and increment salary
      if (Salary >= 0 && Salary <= 1000) {
        rs.updateDouble(1, Salary * 1.1);
      }
      if (Salary > 1000 && Salary <= 5000) {
        rs.updateDouble(1, Salary * 1.2);
      }
      if (Salary > 5001) {
        rs.updateDouble(1, Salary * 1.3);
      }
      rs.updateRow();
    }
    con.commit();
```

After all the rows are updated, the `ResultSet`, `Statement` and `Connection` objects are closed and any exceptions handled:

```
    // close ResultSet and Statement
    rs.close();
    ps.close();
  } catch (Exception e) {
    try {
      con.rollback();
    } catch (Exception ex) {
      ex.printStackTrace();
    }
    e.printStackTrace();

  }
 }
}
```

Compile the code and load the class into the database, as follows:

```
> javac RaiseSalary.java
> loadjava -user username/password RaiseSalary.class
```

The `loadjava` utility specifies the user name/password as a command line parameter under whose login the class is to be published. In this case the `RaiseSalary.class` will be published under the username schema, so a user who logs in as `username` will be able to call this stored procedure.

Alternatively we can load and compile our code in the database in one step, from SQL*Plus (download file: `RaiseSalary.sql`):

```
SQL> set define off
SQL> create or replace and compile
  2  java source named "RaiseSalary"
  3  as
  4
```

```
 5   import java.sql.*;
 6
 7   public class RaiseSalary {
 8     public static void raise() {

<...method definition here, as above...>

38     }
39   }
40   /
```

```
Java created.
```

Note that in order to get this to run we had to issue the set define off command to SQL*PLUS. The reason for this is that & is the substitution character in SQL*PLUS. If you do not issue this command it will attempt to do a character replacement and you will receive an error message along the lines that it can't convert boolean to int. The set define off command disables this behavior.

# Writing the Call Spec

Here we publish our raise() method as a stored procedure. The raise() method accepts no parameters and returns no value, so the PL/SQL call spec is very straight-forward in this case:

```
SQL> create or replace procedure call_raise as
  2    language java
  3    name 'RaiseSalary.raise()';
  4  /
```

```
Procedure created.
```

This code creates a procedure called call_raise defined in PL/SQL. The Java method that is called when you invoke the call_raise procedure is RaiseSalary.raise().

# Calling the Method from SQL*Plus

There are two ways of executing our Java method from SQL*Plus. One way is to call from PL/SQL, using the execute command:

```
SQL> exec call_raise
```

This, of course, is the equivalent of:

```
begin
   call_raise;
end;"
```

The RaiseSalary.raise method will be executed. This can be verified by executing the SQL SELECT statement on the SQL prompt:

```
SQL> select empno,sal from emp;
```

An alternate way is to use the SQL `call` command. The basic syntax for calling the Java stored procedure from SQL command prompt is given below:

```
SQL> call { procedure_name ([param[, param] ...])
   | function_name ([param[, param] …]) into :host_variable};
```

If the stored procedure returns a value to the caller, it must be published as a function, else it is published as a procedure. The parameter `param` can be a host variable or a literal (host variables must be preceded by a colon). The return value is captured into a `host_variable`.

Since our method accepts no parameters and returns no values, the call is simply:

```
SQL> call call_raise();
```

# Java Methods that take Parameters

In the previous section, we wrote a simple Java method that does not take any parameters and does not return any result to the user. In this section, we will modify the method to accept parameters and to return a result to the caller.

## Writing the Java Code

Following is the code for the new `CustomRaiseSal` class:

```java
import java.sql.*;
import oracle.sql.*;
import java.math.*;

public class CustomRaiseSal {
  public static int customRaise(double lowerLimit, double upperLimit,
                                double percentage) {
    int numRecordsUpdated = 0;
    Connection con = null;
    try {

      // obtain oracle default connection
      con = DriverManager.getConnection("jdbc:default:connection:");

      // Make Statement
      Statement stmt =
        con.createStatement(ResultSet.TYPE_SCROLL_INSENSITIVE,
                            ResultSet.CONCUR_UPDATABLE);

      // Fetch salary of all the employees
      ResultSet rs = stmt.executeQuery("select sal from emp");

      // Obtain all the ranges
      while (rs.next()) {
```

```
          double salary = rs.getDouble(1);

          // check for salary limits
          if (salary >= lowerLimit && salary <= upperLimit) {

            // increment the salary
            rs.updateDouble(1, salary + (percentage * salary / 100));
            numRecordsUpdated++;
          }
          rs.updateRow();
        }
        con.commit();

        // close ResultSet and Statement
        rs.close();
        stmt.close();
      } catch (Exception e) {
        try {
          con.rollback();
        } catch (Exception ex) {
          ex.printStackTrace();
        }
        e.printStackTrace();
        System.out.println(e);
      }

      // return No. Of Records Updated
      return (numRecordsUpdated);
  }
}
```

Much of the code is similar to that seen in our previous RaiseSalary class, so we will only discuss the relevant new points. Our new method is called customRaise(). It takes three arguments: the lower limit and upper limit of the salary range, and the percentage by which the salary is to be raised.

```
public class CustomRaiseSal {
  public static int customRaise(double lowerLimit, double upperLimit,
                                double percentage) {
```

If the employee salary lies between lowerLimit and upperLimit, it will be raised by a percentage factor. The number of records affected by executing this procedure will be returned to the client as an integer value.

The program iterates through all the records of the ResultSet, obtains the salary for each employee, increments the salary and updates the record:

```
        while (rs.next()) {
          double salary = rs.getDouble(1);

          // incrementing salary code...

          rs.updateRow();
        }
        con.commit();
```

Before we update the salary of the employee, we do the range checking. If the salary amount lies within the specified range, the salary is updated in the result set by calling the `updateDouble()` method of the `ResultSet`. The `numRecordsUpdated` variable keeps track of the rows affected.

```
// check for salary limits
if (salary >= lowerLimit && salary <= upperLimit) {

  // increment the salary
  rs.updateDouble(1, salary + (percentage * salary / 100));
  numRecordsUpdated++;
}
```

We compile and load the class source file as follows:

```
> javac CustomRaiseSal.java
> loadjava -user username/password CustomRaiseSal.class
```

# Publishing the Procedure

The following call spec will publish the `CustomRaise()` method to the Oracle data dictionary, as a function:

```
SQL> create or replace function call_customRaise(
  2    lowerlimit number, upperlimit number, percentage number)
  3    return number
  4    as language java
  5    name 'CustomRaiseSal.customRaise(double, double, double) return int';
  6  /

Function created.
```

In our call spec, corresponding SQL and Java parameters and return values must have compatible data types. The `int` and `double` Java types both map to the SQL NUMBER type.

Thus, while our `customRaise` Java method accepts three parameters of type `double` and returns an `int` to the caller, our PL/SQL wrapper maps each of these to a NUMBER, taking three parameters of type NUMBER and returning a NUMBER to the caller.

# Calling the Function from SQL*Plus

Again, we call our published Java method through PL/SQL. On the SQL prompt, first declare a variable of type `number` to receive the return value of the function and then execute the procedure:

```
SQL> var numrec number
SQL> execute :numrec:= call_customRaise(200,400,5)

PL/SQL procedure successfully completed.
```

The `customRaise` procedure receives three parameters and returns the result in the `numrec` variable:

```
SQL> print numrec

    NUMREC
----------
         3
```

Alternatively we can use the `call()` method:

```
SQL> call call_customRaise(200,400,5) into :numrec;

Call completed.
```

or:

```
SQL> set serveroutput on;
SQL> call dbms_output.put_line(call_customRaise(200,400,5))
  2  /
3
```

# Calling Java Stored Procedures from SQL DML

You may use Java stored procedures in SQL DML statements; for example, to format the output of a `SELECT` operation. Let's take a look at a quick example.

Create the `student_record` table and add a few records to it using the following SQL code:

```
CREATE TABLE student_record(
name varchar2(20),
m1 number(3),
m2 number(3),
m3 number(3),
m4 number(3)
);

INSERT INTO student_record VALUES('Smith',78,89,98,85);
INSERT INTO student_record VALUES('Mike',87,85,96,86);
```

The code for the Java class is shown below:

```
public class Student {
  public static double averageMarks(int m1, int m2, int m3, int m4) {

    // return average marks of the student
    return (m1 + m2 + m3 + m4) / 4;
  }
}
```

The `averageMarks` method accepts four integer parameters, specifying the marks scored by a student in various subjects, and computes the average mark scored. It returns this value to the caller as a `double`. Compile and load the Java class as normal.

The Java code is published as a function called `average_marks`:

```
SQL> create or replace function average_marks(
  2    m1 number, m2 number, m3 number, m4 number)
  3  return number
  4  as language java
  5  name 'Student.averageMarks (int, int, int, int)return double';
  6  /

Function created.
```

The `average_marks` function takes four parameters required by the `averageMarks()` method of our `Student` class. The return value of the method, which is in Java `double` format, is mapped to the SQL `NUMBER` data type.

We can execute our Java method from the following SQL `SELECT` statement:

```
SQL> select name, average_marks(m1,m2,m3,m4)
  2       as Average
  3    from student_record;

NAME                    AVERAGE
-------------------- ----------
Smith                        87
Mike                         88
```

You should bear in mind that if you execute DML in the same transaction that you use to execute SQL, then running DML will commit any outstanding work in the transaction. To illustrate this point, the following example creates a table called `foo` and then inserts ten rows. Next, a table named `bar` is created. Some would expect that you could rollback the ten rows since they were not committed but the example shows that creating `bar` automatically committed the insertions:

```
SQL> create table foo(x number);
Table created.
SQL> insert into foo (select rownum from all_objects where rownum <= 10);
10 rows created.
SQL> create table bar(x number);
Table created.
SQL> rollback;
Rollback complete.
SQL> select count(*) from foo;
  COUNT(*)
----------
        10
SQL>
```

# The Time Translator Java Stored Procedure

Imagine a content management system that uses Oracle for storing the content (images, text, etc.). When some part of a page is changed, a new HTML file is generated on the database server. Now, to modify the web page, users can log on to an administration site, through a browser. When they change content, a notification is sent to the database to create and publish a new HTML page. Simple. But, this system additionally has the feature to schedule content for a future time. For example, someone could log on and add a headline 'Merry Christmas' and have it pop in on Dec 25th - and they could do this in November, before you go on holiday!

However, the problem with this approach is that if we have people logging on from all over the world, and scheduling content for the future, then how do we translate their specified time to the time at the database server? In Oracle 9i we can use the TIMESTAMP WITH TIMEZONE data type, but if we are still using Oracle 8i then this is not available to us.

Fortunately Java provides us with a solution, which works for Oracle 8i as well as 9i. Using inherent features of the Java language, working with time zones is trivial. So, for example, say that someone in our New York department logs on and wishes to add a headline to our web site saying 'Happy Thanksgiving'. This user schedules the headline so that it is published exactly at noon on November 29th. So a notification is put in an EVENTS table instructing the server to re-cache at November 29th at 12:00, for a specified time zone, which in our case is East coast USA. Now, a trigger on the table runs a Java stored procedure, which compares the time zone with the server time zone, and re-calculates the time to re-cache according to that. Let's look at a Java stored procedure that would be useful in this scenario.

## Creating the Database Table

First we need to create a table for maintaining events. Whenever an event is recorded in the database table, we convert the event time into the server's local time. The server can use this time to callback the client at the specified time.

```
SQL> create table events (
  2      time_zone varchar2(100) not null,
  3      event_date date not null,
  4      event_job number
  5  );

Table created.
```

The events table contains three fields – the time_zone field specifies the time zone where the event is to take place, event_date specifies the server time for the event at which server should call back the client and the event_job specifies a unique event ID.

## The TimeTranslator Class

The translate method is a static method of TimeTranslator class. The complete source for the TrimeTranslator class is given opposite:

```
SQL> create or replace and compile java source named "TimeTranslator"
  2  as
  3
  4  import java.sql.Timestamp;
  5  import java.util.Calendar;
  6  import java.util.GregorianCalendar;
  7  import java.util.TimeZone;
  8
  9  public class TimeTranslator {
 10
 11    private static final int MS_SECOND = 1000;
 12    private static final int MS_MINUTE = 60 * MS_SECOND;
 13    private static final int MS_HOUR = 60 * MS_MINUTE;
 14
 15    public static Timestamp translate(Timestamp event, String id) {
 16      TimeZone serverZone = TimeZone.getDefault();
 17      TimeZone clientZone = TimeZone.getTimeZone(id);
 18
 19      GregorianCalendar clientEvent = new GregorianCalendar(clientZone);
 20      clientEvent.setTime(event);
 21      GregorianCalendar serverEvent = new GregorianCalendar(serverZone);
 22      serverEvent.setTime(event);
 23
 24      // Get the offset for the client time zone,
 25      // taking into account the daylight saving hours.
 26      int clientOffset =
 27        clientZone.getOffset(clientEvent.get(Calendar.ERA),
 28                             clientEvent.get(Calendar.YEAR),
 29                             clientEvent.get(Calendar.MONTH),
 30                             clientEvent.get(Calendar.DAY_OF_MONTH),
 31                             clientEvent.get(Calendar.DAY_OF_WEEK),
 32                     clientEvent.get(Calendar.HOUR_OF_DAY) * MS_HOUR
 33                     + clientEvent.get(Calendar.MINUTE) * MS_MINUTE
 34                     + clientEvent.get(Calendar.SECOND) * MS_SECOND
 35                     + clientEvent.get(Calendar.MILLISECOND));
 36
 37      // Get the offset for the server time zone,
 38      // taking into account the daylight saving hours.
 39      int serverOffset =
 40        serverZone.getOffset(serverEvent.get(Calendar.ERA),
 41                             serverEvent.get(Calendar.YEAR),
 42                             serverEvent.get(Calendar.MONTH),
 43                             serverEvent.get(Calendar.DAY_OF_MONTH),
 44                             serverEvent.get(Calendar.DAY_OF_WEEK),
 45                     serverEvent.get(Calendar.HOUR_OF_DAY) * MS_HOUR
 46                     + serverEvent.get(Calendar.MINUTE) * MS_MINUTE
 47                     + serverEvent.get(Calendar.SECOND) * MS_SECOND
 48                     + serverEvent.get(Calendar.MILLISECOND));
 49
 50      // Add the offset to the server time.
 51      serverEvent.add(Calendar.MILLISECOND, serverOffset - clientOffset);
 52      return new Timestamp(serverEvent.getTime().getTime());
 53    }
 54  }
 55  /

Java created.
```

The method computes the time of the event by adding to the current time the difference between the server and the client time zones:

```
serverEvent.add(Calendar.MILLISECOND, serverOffset - clientOffset);
```

The two offset values are calculated by calling the `getOffset()` method of the `TimeZone` class to take care of daylight saving, if any, for the zone. The server time zone is determined by calling the static `getDefault()` method:

```
TimeZone serverZone = TimeZone.getDefault();
```

The client time zone is determined by using the id passed by the client:

```
TimeZone clientZone = TimeZone.getTimeZone(id);
```

The `GregorianCalendar` class is used for constructing the `time` objects (see Appendix B for more details on this).

# Publishing the Java Method

The `translate()` method is published using the following PL/SQL code:

```
SQL> create or replace function translate_date (
  2      source date,
  3      time_zone varchar2
  4  ) return date
  5  as language java
  6  name 'TimeTranslator.translate(java.sql.Timestamp, java.lang.String)
  7  return java.sql.Timestamp';
  8  /

Function created.
```

# Writing the Trigger

The trigger `event_jobs` occurs whenever a row is inserted in the table. During the row insertion, we call the `translate_date` procedure to convert the local time to the server time:

```
SQL> -- Submit a job from a trigger.
SQL> create or replace trigger event_jobs
  2  before insert on events
  3  for each row
  4  declare
  5      jobno number;
  6  begin
  7      dbms_job.submit(
  8          jobno,
  9          're_cache();',    -- Replace this!
```

```
10        translate_date(:new.event_date, :new.time_zone) -- Only run once
11      );
12      :new.event_job := jobno;
13  end;
14  /

Trigger created.
```

In our example, the `re_cache()` procedure should be the produce we use to recache the HTML page in question. We will not provide an exact implementation for this procedure. However, in order that we may test the code, we need to create it:

```
SQL> -- Just a test.
SQL> create or replace procedure re_cache
  2  as
  3  begin
  4      null;
  5  end;
  6  /

Procedure created.
```

# Testing

We test the trigger by inserting a record in the database table by running the following PL/SQL code:

```
SQL> -- Test it!
SQL> declare
  2      jobno number;
  3  begin
  4      insert into events (event_date, time_zone)
  5      values (to_date('17.11.2001 12:00', 'dd.mm.yyyy hh24:mi'),
  6                      'Europe/Istanbul')
  7      returning event_job into jobno;
  8      dbms_output.put_line('Job: ' || jobno);
  9      commit;
 10  end;
 11  /
Job: 22

PL/SQL procedure successfully completed.
```

When you run the above code, a record will be added to the table with the appropriate time of event recorded in the table. On the client console, the `jobno` is printed.

# The e-mail Validation Stored Procedure

A simple and elegant example of how Java can be used to achieve something more elegantly than can be achieved in PL/SQL is to have Java validate e-mail addresses. While this is not impossible in PL/SQL, it is easier in Java simply because Sun has coded an address validation method in the JavaMail API which fully implements the RFC 822 mail addressing requirements.

What we can do is load that API into the database and create Java and PL/SQL functions to access the appropriate methods. You must load the `activation.jar` and `mail.jar` files into the database using `loadjava` (see Chapter 9 for an example of how to load these files). There seems to be a large number of files required to support this small operation, but the JavaMail API provides so much more than this example demonstrates. In fact, you can build an extremely functional e-mail client with the JavaMail API and have it run from within the database. For this example though, only the necessary classes will be loaded into memory.

Listed below is the Java source code. It will either return a 1 if the address is valid, 0, if the address is invalid, or –1 if some error occurred during the validation process. Note that it *always* returns a value so the PL/SQL will not have to handle any exceptions.

```
SQL> create or replace and resolve java source named "mail_utility" as
  2  import javax.mail.internet.*;
  3  import oracle.sql.NUMBER;
  4
  5  public class mail_utility {
  6
  7    public static NUMBER validate_address(String rfc822Address) {
  8      int rc = 0;
  9
 10      try {
 11        InternetAddress ia = new InternetAddress(rfc822Address);
 12        rc = 1;
 13      } catch (AddressException ae) {
 14        rc = 0;
 15      } catch (Exception e) {
 16        rc = -1;
 17      } finally {
 18        return new NUMBER(rc);
 19      }
 20    }
 21  }
 22  /

Java created.
```

and here is the PL/SQL wrapper function:

```
SQL> create or replace function validate_address(p_address in varchar2)
  2  return number
  3  as language java name
  4  'mail_utility.validate_address(java.lang.String)
  5  return oracle.sql.NUMBER';
  6  /

Function created.
```

The following is a few examples of the procedure in use:

```
SQL> declare
  2  begin
  3    dbms_output.put_line('Good = ' ||
                           validate_address('bob@anywhere.com'));
  4    dbms_output.put_line('Good = ' || validate_address('@a.com'));
  5    dbms_output.put_line('Good = ' || validate_address('bobby-k@s.org'));
  6    dbms_output.put_line('Good = ' || validate_address('bob(D)@s.org'));
  7    dbms_output.put_line('Good = ' ||
                           validate_address('bob:dole@kansas.org'));
  8    dbms_output.put_line('Good = ' ||
                           validate_address('bob dole@kansas.org'));
  9    dbms_output.put_line('Good = ' ||
                           validate_address('bob/dole@kansas.org'));
 10    dbms_output.put_line('Good = ' ||
                       validate_address('bob=@kansas.org'));
 11    dbms_output.put_line('Good = ' ||
                       validate_address('"Super Bob" <bob@kansas.org>'));
 12    dbms_output.put_line('Good = ' ||
                       validate_address('"Super Bob" a <bob@kansas.org>'));
 13    dbms_output.put_line('Good = ' ||
                       validate_address('"Super Bob Dole <bob@kansas.org>'));
 14  end;
 15  /
Good = 1
Good = 0
Good = 1
Good = 1
Good = 0
Good = 0
Good = 1
Good = 1
Good = 1
Good = 1
Good = 0

PL/SQL procedure successfully completed.
```

# Summary

The basic goal of this chapter was to lay a foundation in the creation and execution of Java stored procedures. The initial examples were kept simple in order to clearly illustrate the concepts of creating and loading Java classes and publishing methods as stored procedure or functions (depending on whether they returned a value). In addition to illustrating how to call Java procedures from PL/SQL, we showed how to call them from DML and from a database trigger. We ended with a couple of simple but useful examples of using Java in the database that have hopefully whet your appetite for the chapters to come.

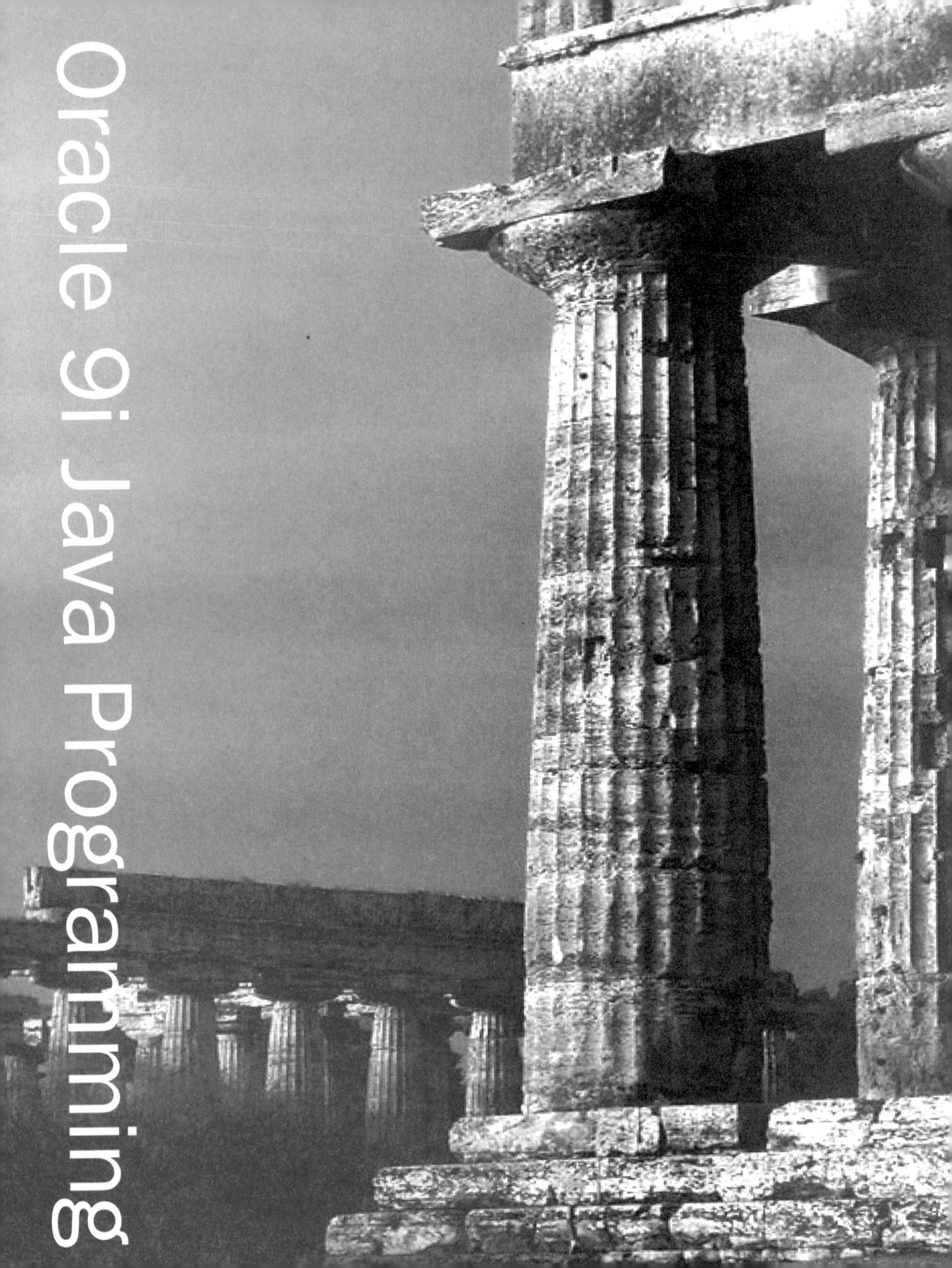
Oracle 9i Java Programming

# Oracle Java Security

In addition to the standard aspects of Oracle security, Java classes running inside the database are subject to strict security measures of the JVM that serve to protect vital system resources from code that is not trusted. These security measures are based on the Java 2 security architecture that provides fine-grained, policy-based access control to all code running inside the JVM, regardless of whether the class is loaded from the local file system or over the network.

Although the fundamental security concepts remain the same, certain differences exist between standard Java security and Oracle Java security, mostly due to the fact that the latter deals with code running within the boundaries of an already secure database. Most importantly, the Oracle JVM is *always* initialized with a security manager, while traditional JVMs by default are not. Therefore, knowledge of Java security is fundamental for any developer of Java applications that operate inside the Oracle database.

In this chapter, we will discuss the Oracle Java security model in detail. In short, we will:

❑ Discuss the basic attributes of any security system

❑ Provide an overview of the Java 2 security architecture

❑ Discuss Oracle Java security, compare it with traditional Java security, and illustrate how it affects Java classes inside the database

## Security Basics

Security is the practice of protecting vital resources and property from all forms of attack and plunder. There are many areas of security that apply to computer systems. For example, securing the network in which a system resides is an important area of security, which is usually addressed with proper setup of firewalls and layered networks. Intellectual security is another area, which deals with encryption and secure communications.

The area of computer security that we're concerned with in this chapter is how the Java compiler and runtime system restrict application programmers from creating subversive code. We are not concerned with encryption, secure sockets or user authentication – only with the security of the Java runtime environment.

# Common Security Attributes

Any good security practice, no matter what its nature, addresses a number of important attributes. Some of these key attributes are summarized below. Later in this chapter, at the end of the *Java Security Model* section, we will see how the Java security architecture addresses each of these issues.

❑ **Authentication** – The first task of any security system is to authenticate remote agents, such as users and code (for example, applets). A remote agent should not be permitted to pose as something other than what it is.

❑ **Authorization** – When a particular agent has been authenticated, it should be authorized. A good security architecture should provide administrators with the ability to decide what level of access to bestow upon an authenticated agent.

❑ **Containment** – When an agent has been authenticated and given proper authorization, the security system must ensure that the agent can only operate within the boundaries specified by the fine-grained authorization policy it has been bestowed.

❑ **Confidentiality** – A secure system should ensure that all attributes of a connection-time: frequency, data, queries, and so on, remain confidential.

*Note that the attributes mentioned above are by no means the only attributes of a successful security system – these are the ones that relate the most to Java security in the Oracle JVM.*

# Java Security Model

From its early days, security measures have been an integral part of the Java language. One reason for this is that Java was designed from the ground up for network computing. Networks greatly increase the risk of hostile attacks to any computer attached to them. This becomes especially true in an environment in which applications are transparently downloaded across a network and executed locally in the host environment, which is the case with Java applets.

But Java security is by no means limited to applets and other remote code of unknown origin. The current Java security model provides a framework of security policies and permissions that can be used to apply fine-grained security measures to any code running inside the JVM – be it an applet, an Enterprise JavaBean, a servlet or an ordinary class.

In this section, we will provide a concise overview of the basics of the Java security architecture. Specifically, this section will focus only on those aspects of standard Java security that directly relate to the Oracle Java security model, which will be discussed in detail later in this chapter. Therefore, all aspects of extended cryptography, code signing and certificate production will be left out in this context. In short, these are the main security issues that will not be discussed here:

❑ Code Signing

❑ Java Cryptography Architecture (JCA)

❑ Java Cryptography Extension (JCE)

❑ Java Secure Socket Extension (JSSE)

❑ Java Authentication and Authorization Service (JAAS)

For more information on these technologies, and a more detailed discussion of the Java security architecture, you can refer to another Wrox title, *Professional Java Security; ISBN 1-861004-25-7* that deals exclusively with these issues.

> **If you are already familiar with the basics of the Java security model, you can skip this section and directly advance to the section on Oracle Java security.**

In this section of the chapter we will look at how the Java security model has evolved over time, from the original sandbox model to today's fine-grained access control. We will also look at how Java security is implemented in the current generation of virtual machines. We will look first at the security that is inherent in the way the virtual machine loads and checks class files. The final part of this section will look at how to specify policies and permissions for classes in the virtual machine.

# Security Model Evolution

The current Java security model – Java 2 security – is based on fine-grained security policies implemented by assigning specific permissions to the runtime environment. This, however, has not always been so. The original Java security model granted limited privileges to Java applets downloaded from the network and a free reign to classes loaded from the local environment. As a result, developers were constrained when it came to developing web applications with applets and local code in a shared environment posed great risks of opening up security holes for malicious code.

The next version of Java security addressed the first issue to some extent, providing correctly digitally signed applets with the same level of access to system resources as local code. Unsigned or untrusted applets, however, were still given very limited access to the host environment. Although this model offered improvements over its predecessor, it was still largely flawed. Local code still had unlimited access to system resources and applets downloaded over the network were subject to a strict all-or-nothing security policy – either the applet had no access to the host environment or it had full access to all resources.

With the next evolution of the security model, Java 2 security, all code was potentially subject to fine-grained security policies, specified by the developer in a text-based policy file. The previously clear distinction between applets and local code was blurring, as both could be subject to the same security permissions and policies.

## *The Original Sandbox Model*

When Java was introduced, it was envisioned that many Java programs would be applets, which were small programs downloaded to a computer from a server. The language designers wanted to prevent malicious code from disrupting the local computer. Therefore, all code that was loaded and run from a server was untrusted and was subject to strict restrictions. The untrusted code was not allowed to read to or write from the local file system, and could not contact any server other than the server it came from. Code that was loaded and run from the local file system was trusted and did not have these restrictions. This model soon became known as the *sandbox model* – the term 'sandbox' referring to the strict boundaries in which remote code and applets were allowed to operate. The sandbox model is further illustrated in the following diagram.

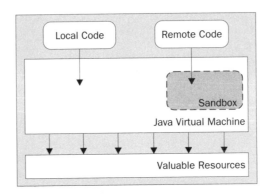

The situation improved somewhat with the release of JDK version 1.1, which introduced the concept of a *signed* applet. According to this concept, digitally signed applets were trusted to have full access to vital system resources, if the public key used to verify the signature was trusted. Unsigned and untrusted applets were still not trusted and could only access limited resources as before. Also, local code was still not subject to any security considerations, and was generally allowed to access any resource of the host environment, without explicit permission. The JDK 1.1 security model is shown in the following figure.

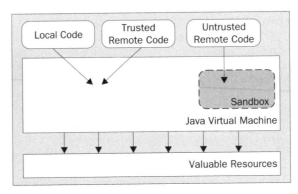

## Beyond the Sandbox

As time went by, it became apparent that the original sandbox security model had serious limitations. First of all, the *all-or-nothing,* security policy of the sandbox model did not provide the level of access control required by most applications. While untrusted remote code had restrained access to resources of the target environment, signed and "trusted" code had full access to *all* system resources, which was not always desirable. Secondly, the idea that local code should always be trusted, and provided with full access to vital resources, was not always applicable – especially not as the focus of Java shifted more and more towards the server-side, where more fine-grained security policies were needed.

These issues were addressed in version 1.2 of the Java Development Kit – also known as Java 2. The Java 2 security model extends and redefines many of the fundamental aspects of the previous model, and provides several new and important additions. Importantly, the new model provides an extension of security checks to include all levels of Java applications, including servlets, JavaBeans and applets.

In the new model, all code, regardless of whether it is local or remote, can be subject to policy-based, fine-grained access control that can be applied evenly to whole applications as well as different parts of the same program. Based on the policy-based access control, the security manager now has the ability to revoke or grant different components access to various system resources – such as writing a file in the file system, opening a socket to a specified URL and accessing environment variables.

> *It had actually been possible to accomplish this same level of access control in the previous Java security model. However, that had required the task of writing a customized extension of the core* `SecurityManager` *class, which was proven to be both time-consuming and error-prone.*

All code is arranged by the security model so that classes whose instances are granted the same permissions are grouped together into *protection domains*. In a secure application, each class loaded into the JVM is found a place in one or more protection domains. Domains can intersect, as general permissions, defined by global domains, can be overridden by a more definitive domain. This is further explained by the following diagram, which illustrates the structure of code, domains and security policies in the Java 2 security model.

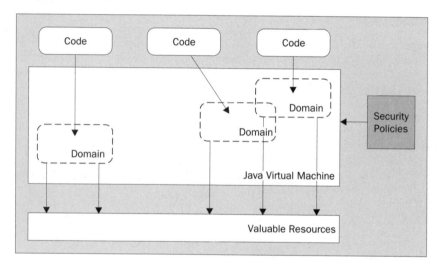

It should be noted that the use of fine-grained access control and security policies is purely optional in the new security model. By default, local applications are still unrestricted and applets run in a secured sandbox environment. It may be feasible in a development environment to maintain the default behavior, but once out in the open, each application should enable the security manager and maintain a policy-based, fine-grained access control.

To summarize, these are the main new features of the Java 2 security model:

❑ Security checks extended to include all Java programs

❑ Fine-grained access control

❑ Different parts of the same program can be given different levels of access

❑ Can specify which part of a resource a program can access

- ❑ Easily configurable security policy
- ❑ User can force application to use a security manager
- ❑ Easily extensible access control structure

> **Unless otherwise noted, the term *Java security* hereafter refers to *Java 2 security*.**

# Basic Java Security Architecture

The core of the Java security architecture is made up of three components: the bytecode verifier, the class loader architecture and the security manager. Each of these components plays a fundamental role in providing a secure computing environment.

The **bytecode verifier** is responsible for the inspection and verification of all code loaded into the JVM. The bytecode verifier performs many of the runtime checks that otherwise would have been left up to the class file interpreter.

The **class loader architecture** handles the task of loading classes from bytecode into the JVM. The class loader architecture consists of a number of different class loaders, which relate to each other with a tree-like structure. At the root of the class loader hierarchy, there is a single **primordial class loader**, which is responsible for loading the core classes of the Java platform.

Finally, the **security manager** is responsible for determining whether certain requests to access particular resources are to be allowed. By default, the JVM does not initialize a security manager (the exception is JVMs running in a browser), but this behavior can be overridden by an explicit request for security.

The basic Java security architecture is illustrated in the diagram on the right, which shows the interaction between the bytecode verifier, class loader and the security manager. Note that verified byte code bypasses the security manager if one has not been activated. The bytecode verifier and the class loader architecture, however, are fundamental to the core Java architecture, and exist whether a specific security policy is in effect or not.

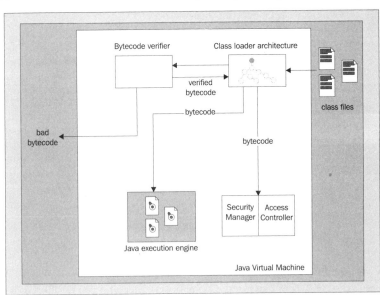

In the next few sections, we will discuss each of these three components in more detail.

## Bytecode Verifier

Before the class loader bothers to register a loaded class with the Java environment, the class must be passed by the bytecode verifier for inspection. The bytecode verifier analyzes the byte code stream of the specified class file and ensures that the class file has the correct format. Furthermore, the code structure and references are analyzed and verified against the rules of the Java language.

The process of bytecode verification takes place in two phases:

❑ In phase one, the bytecode verifier analyzes the internals of the class file and verifies that they adhere to the rules of the Java language. For example, the verifier makes sure that there is no overflow of operands on the stack, that the final classes are not subclassed, that the byte stream is not truncated, that no local variables are accessed before given a value, and so on.

❑ In the second phase of the verification process, the verifier will analyze all references to other classes from the class being analyzed. Not only will references themselves be verified for correctness, but also the relationship rules of the reference (for example, by determining whether a reference method has the appropriate visibility modifier).

By now, you might ask yourself why the verifier bothers to check variable state, operand overflow, and other such issues that should generally be left up to the compiler to verify. The reason for that is to prevent hostile class compilers from modifying byte code internals for malicious purposes. Also, byte code can easily be damaged or altered by anyone with the means to do so. Without explicit bytecode verification, such operations could have unexpected effects on the runtime environment.

Once a class has been verified and accepted, it is loaded through a class loader into the Java runtime environment. If a class fails the verification, then the program is terminated.

## ClassLoader Architecture

Class loaders are responsible for importing class bytecode into the Java virtual machine. The class loader architecture consists of a number of individual class loaders. Each class in the runtime environment is loaded by a specific class loader. Each class loader is in fact a class itself – implementation of the `java.lang.ClassLoader` abstract class – so in turn, each class loader must be loaded by another class loader. So if every class loader is loaded by another class loader, where does the first class loader come from?

### The Primordial Class Loader

At the top of the class loader hierarchy, resides the *primordial class loader* that bootstraps the class loading process. This class loader is integrated with the JVM and is responsible for loading the core classes of the Java platform. The primordial class loader is further illustrated in the following figure.

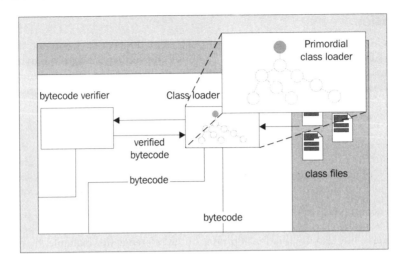

### Class Loader Implementations

The primordial class loader is generally written in a language such as C, and usually loads classes from the local file system in a platform-dependent manner. All other class loaders are implemented in Java and, as shown in the illustration above, are subclasses of the base class java.lang.ClassLoader. The Java API ships with a few implementations that are used in different class loading scenarios. Examples include java.security.SecureClassLoader and java.net.URLClassLoader.

## Security Manager

The Java 2 security architecture comes with a default security manager, which is easily configurable. This security manager is actually a Java class, named java.lang.SecurityManager. This class maps text-based permissions specified in a policy file to Permission objects in the runtime environment, and guards access to vital resources based on these Permission objects. The actual checking of permissions is performed by a class named java.security.AccessController. We will see more about permissions and the AccessController later.

> *Throughout this chapter, we will often refer to the "security manager." When used like this, we are not referring to the specific class* java.lang.SecurityManager, *but the collection of classes including* SecurityManager *and* AccessController *that manage security in the Java virtual machine.*

The security manager is responsible for applying fine-grained security policies throughout the Java runtime environment. The security manager determines whether a request to access a particular resource should be allowed or not, based on specified permissions. If such an access is permitted, the request proceeds as normal, but if the access is denied, a java.lang.SecurityException is thrown.

By default, most Java applications do not activate a security manager at startup time. Applets, however, are an exception to this. Browser JVMs initialize security managers by default, and usually deny the default security manager to be replaced (as that might open up security holes for malicious applets, that could replace the active security manager with a more relaxed version).

**378**

The JVM is designed so that only a single security manager can be running at a time. An application can access the default security manager through methods of the `java.lang.System` class, as shown here:

```
SecurityManager sman = System.getSecurityManager();
```

The previous method returns the active `SecurityManager` instance if it has been initialized, and `null` if not.

### Activating the Security Manager

Use of the default security manager can be specified during startup of a Java application. This is done by specifying the `java.security.manager` property when executing the application, as shown here:

```
> java -Djava.security.manager ApplicationName
```

If no security manager is installed, the program has normal access to all system resources (that is, full access for Java applications).

> Activating a security manager is a prerequisite for a secure application. Permissions and security policies specified do not take effect unless the security manager is initialized.

### Using the SecurityManager and AccessController Classes

Prior to Java 2, permission management and permission checking was performed through a subclass of the `SecurityManager` class. There were special methods for each type of permission, such as `checkRead()` to check for file read access, `checkConnect()` to check for connection access, and so on. This was not very flexible. If you needed a new type of permission in your program, you would have to write your own `SecurityManager` subclass and implement a `checkXXX()` method.

Java 2 introduced the new class `AccessController` to handle permission checking, leaving the `SecurityManager` to handle permission management. Permissions are now represented by `Permission` objects and both the `SecurityManager` and the `AccessController` have a new method, `checkPermisssion()`, to check permissions. Although you still need to create a subclass to represent a new permission for your program, sub-classing `Permission` is easier than subclassing `SecurityManager`.

> *For backwards-compatibility, the Java 2 `SecurityManager` still defines the JDK 1.x `checkXXX()` methods. However, if you are writing code that needs to check a permission you should call the `checkPermission()` method of `AccessController`.*

For example, to check whether some code has write privilege to a directory, you would use the `java.io.FilePermission` class, as shown here:

```
public boolean canWrite(String path) {
  try {
    FilePermission perm = new FilePermission(path,"write");
    AccessController.checkPermission(perm);
```

```
  } catch (SecurityException s) {
    return false;
  }
  return true;
}
```

*We will discuss permissions and the* `java.security.Permission` *class in more detail in the next section.*

# Details of the Security Architecture

By now, we have been discussing the foundations of the Java security architecture – the bytecode verifier, class loader architecture and the security manager. The last one of these, the security manager, is responsible for verifying the validity of requests for guarded resources of the system environment. In verifying such requests, the security manager compares the permissions of the requesting process with the action requested. These permissions are loaded into the runtime environment from a specified text-based policy file, which contains a description of the protection domains and permissions in effect for the JVM.

In this section we will discuss the foundation of the Java security infrastructure for fine-grained access control. This foundation consists of **policies**, **permissions**, and **protection domains**. The following diagram illustrates how these fit into the basic security model we discussed in the previous section.

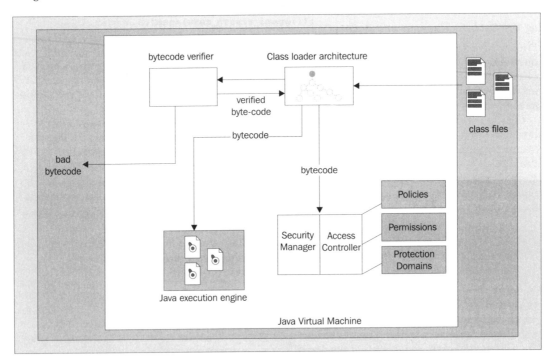

## Policies

In the Java security model, all classes are divided into protection domains. Protection domains can, for example, include all class files under a specific code base URL or all classes signed by a specific vendor. Each protection domain is then assigned permissions. Each permission specifies a permitted access to a particular resource, such as the right to write a given system property. The set of protection domains, along with the permissions assigned to each, constitute a **security policy**.

The Java security model provides a concrete security policy infrastructure that allows for a simplified configuration of runtime permissions and protection domains. A security policy is typically stored in a text-based policy file that follows a specific syntax specified by the Java security architecture.

### Policy Files

As we have already mentioned, a policy file is used to define which permissions are granted to specific domains of protection. A domain of protection is either defined by a URI (Uniform Resource Identifier), that indicates where the target code is to be found, or by a vendor name, that should match the target code's digital certificate.

A policy file is an ordinary ASCII file that contains a policy specification. Typically they have a name that ends with `.policy`, but that is not a requirement and they can have any name. The general policy file syntax is shown below.

```
[keystore "keystore URL", "keystore type";]

grant [signedBy "signer_names"] [, codeBase "URL" ]{
   permission permission_class_name "target_name", "action"
      [, signedBy "signer_names"];
   ....
   permission permission_class_name "target_name" , "action"
      [, signedBy "signer_names"];
};
```

Each policy file defines an optional key store entry and one or more permission entries, as shown above.

> *The keystore entry is the URL location of a set of keys and digital certificates. This allows permissions to be further restricted based on a digital signature. This topic is beyond the scope of this chapter. For more information on keystores please see http://java.sun.com/products/jdk/1.3/docs/guide/security/index.html.*

Each policy file can contain multiple `grant` blocks. Each grant can contain optional `signedBy` and `codeBase` elements. The `signedBy` element is used when code has been digitally signed. The `codeBase` element is used to grant permissions based on the URL that the code is loaded from. Within the `grant` block are one or more permission elements. Each permission element consists of the keyword `permission`, the class name of a permission, a target that the permission applies to, and an action if needed by the permission.

For example, here is one sample grant:

```
grant {

  permission java.io.FilePermission "/tmp/*", "read,write";
  permission java.util.PropertyPermission "java.home", "read";
  permission java.lang.RuntimePermission "accessClassInPackage.sun.*";

};
```

This grant specifies that all code executing in the runtime environment (no specific codeBase specified) should be able to read and write to all files in the /tmp folder, read the java.home system property and access any class in the external sun.* class hierarchy.

To use a custom policy file, the java.security.policy attribute is specified when the application is executed, as shown here:

```
> java -Djava.security.manager -Djava.security.policy=my.policy AppName
```

This example would execute the AppName class with a security manager that applied the security policy defined in the my.policy policy file. You can also specify multiple security policies files by listing each policy file in a properties file. The properties file is $JAVA_HOME/jre/lib/java.security (UNIX) or %JAVA_HOME%\jre\lib\java.security (Windows). Two policy files are used by default. Here are the two properties from the java.security file that specifies those policy files:

```
policy.url.1=file:${java.home}\lib\security\java.policy
policy.url.2=file:${user.home}\.java.policy
```

To add additional policy files, you would add additional properties with the name policy.url.n where n is replaced with a digit. The digits must be consecutively numbered. In the example above, the next policy file property would use the name policy.url.3.

## System-Wide Policy File

Each JRE comes with a system-wide policy file that stores initial permissions granted to all applications. This policy files is located under JAVA_HOME/jre/lib/security in a file called java.policy. Custom security policies do not override the permissions specified by the system-wide policy, they rather have a cumulative effect.

For example, for JDK 1.3, the system-wide policy file contains the following permissions:

```
// Standard extensions get all permissions by default
grant codeBase "file:${java.home}/lib/ext/*" {
  permission java.security.AllPermission;
};

// default permissions granted to all domains
grant {
```

```
    // Allows any thread to stop itself using the java.lang.Thread.stop()
    // method that takes no argument.
    permission java.lang.RuntimePermission "stopThread";

    // allows anyone to listen on un-privileged ports
    permission java.net.SocketPermission "localhost:1024-", "listen";

    // "standard" properties that can be read by anyone
    permission java.util.PropertyPermission "java.version", "read";
    permission java.util.PropertyPermission "java.vendor", "read";
    permission java.util.PropertyPermission "java.vendor.url", "read";
    permission java.util.PropertyPermission "java.class.version", "read";
    permission java.util.PropertyPermission "os.name", "read";
    permission java.util.PropertyPermission "os.version", "read";
    permission java.util.PropertyPermission "os.arch", "read";
    permission java.util.PropertyPermission "file.separator", "read";
    permission java.util.PropertyPermission "path.separator", "read";
    permission java.util.PropertyPermission "line.separator", "read";
    permission java.util.PropertyPermission
                                    "java.specification.version", "read";
    permission java.util.PropertyPermission
                                    "java.specification.vendor", "read";
    permission java.util.PropertyPermission "java.specification.name", "read";
    permission java.util.PropertyPermission
                                    "java.vm.specification.version", "read";
    permission java.util.PropertyPermission
                                    "java.vm.specification.vendor", "read";
    permission java.util.PropertyPermission
                                    "java.vm.specification.name", "read";
    permission java.util.PropertyPermission "java.vm.version", "read";
    permission java.util.PropertyPermission "java.vm.vendor", "read";
    permission java.util.PropertyPermission "java.vm.name", "read";
};
```

Note that we can use variable substitution in the file (line 2 above). If a property has been defined in the Java environment, the policy file can use the value of that property using the ${property_name} syntax.

## Permissions

In the Java security model, a **permission** represents access to a particular system resource. Each permission is represented by a permission object that is a subclass of java.security.Permission. Each instance of a permission has a name that refers to a target resource for which the permission is granted. Additionally, each instance can have a list of actions that define the set of operations that may be performed on the target resource.

Given the above, a runtime permission is identified by a

❑   Permission class type

❑   Permission name

❑   Permission actions

Different permissions exist for different resources. For example, a socket permission specifies access to connect to a particular network socket and a file permission specifies a list of actions for access to read, write or delete a particular file or file set. Below, we discuss those permissions that are relevant to the Oracle environment. Each of these extends the base class `java.security.Permission`, either explicitly or implicitly, by sub-classing the permission implementation `java.security.BasicPermission`.

- ❑ `java.security.Permission` – Abstract class for representing access to a system resource. All Java permission classes extend this class.

- ❑ `java.security.BasicPermission` – The `BasicPermission` class extends the `Permission` class, and can be used as the base class for permissions that want to follow the same naming convention as `BasicPermission`.

- ❑ `java.security.AllPermission` – The `AllPermission` is a permission that implies all other permissions. This permission should be granted with great care.

- ❑ `java.io.FilePermission` – This class represents access to a file or directory. A `FilePermission` consists of a pathname and a set of actions valid for that pathname.

  For the `FilePermission`, a path name consisting of a single "*" indicates all the files in the current directory (for example `/home/john/*`), while a path name consisting of a single "-" indicates all the files in the current directory and (recursively) all files and subdirectories contained in the current directory. (for example `/home/john/-`).

- ❑ `java.net.NetPermission` – This class is for various network permissions.

- ❑ `java.util.PropertyPermission` – This class represents access to a specified system property. With the default security manager, code has permission to read only a subset of system properties. You can grant read or write permission to the system properties with this permission.

  For this permission, the name value is the name of a given system property, such as `java.home` or `user.home`. The set of valid actions are `read` or `write`.

- ❑ `java.lang.reflect.ReflectPermission` – This permission defines access to reflective operations. Reflection is a way to dynamically learn class names and methods at runtime. It is usually not used directly by the application.

- ❑ `java.lang.RuntimePermission` – This class represents access to runtime permissions. These permissions affect the ability of code to modify the JVM or use system resources, such as stopping and starting threads, or loading shared native code libraries.

- ❑ `java.security.SecurityPermission` – This class represents access to a security operation. This includes such things as the ability to get or set the current security policy, or the ability to get or set digital keys.

- ❑ `java.io.SerializablePermission` – This class represents the ability to change the serializing and deserializing process. Serialization is the process of saving and loading object values.

- ❑ `java.net.SocketPermission` – This class represents access to a network via sockets. A `SocketPermission` consists of a host specification and a set of "actions" specifying ways to connect to that host. The name is the name or IP address of the host and can include a port or port range. The set of valid actions are `accept`, `connect`, `listen`, or `resolve`.

You can find the complete documentation on names and actions in the Java API documentation for each permission at http://java.sun.com/j2se/1.3/docs/api/index.html.

### Granting Permissions

Permissions are specified in a security policy file, as we discussed earlier. Policy files are modified to include new permission grants or revocations. New security policies, and thus permissions, take effect when the JVM is next initialized with the modified security policy.

## Protection Domains

Conceptually, a protection domain includes all classes whose instances are granted the same set of permissions. Protection domains are determined by the policy currently in effect. A protection domain is defined in a policy file by either specifying a specific code base URI where the target classes should be found, or a given vendor, whose certificate target classes shall be signed with. The Java application environment maintains a mapping from code (classes and instances) to their protection domains and then to their permissions.

> **Custom protection domains have no equivalent in Oracle Java security. In Oracle, all classes within the same database schema belong to the same protection domain.**

### Using CodeBase For Protection Domains

Using `codeBase`, we can give different classes different permissions and different levels of the same permission. For example, the policy file below creates two protection domains:

```
grant {
  permission java.util.PropertyPermission "user.dir", "read";
  permission file.io.FilePermission "<<ALL FILES>>", "read";
};

grant codeBase "file: /home/admin/-" {
  permission java.io.FilePermission "<<ALL FILES>>","read,write,delete";
};
```

Using this security policy, a class file that is located under the /home/admin/ root directory is granted full access to read, write and delete any file on the system. All other classes, however, are only permitted to read files.

# Oracle Java Security

Inside the database, there are two aspects of security concerning Java applications: database resource security and Java security.

Database resource security deals with securing database objects – such as tables, PL/SQL procedures and Java classes – from unauthorized access. A user can access resources and objects that belong to their own schema. A user must be granted special privileges – such as the GRANT EXECUTE privilege on Java classes – in order to access objects in other schemas.

Java security, on the other hand, deals with protecting resources of the runtime environment and operating system from Java applications running inside the Oracle JVM. However, inside an already secure database like Oracle, all Java code must obey strict security policies, that by default disallow unrestricted access to vital resources.

The Oracle Java security implementation builds on the Java 2 security model, and uses security policies and permission objects to protect operating system resources. The security model is automatically installed upon startup. Each database user must be assigned proper permissions to access operating system resources, such as files, system properties and network sockets.

# Overview

The Oracle Java security model implements the standard Java 2 security architecture. A few fundamental differences exist between the two, however. Traditional Java security was not designed for the enclosed environment of the database, as Oracle Java security. We have already mentioned that inside the Oracle JVM, a default security manager is always at hand and all code is subject to fine-grained access control and security policies. Other differences between the two models include the storage methods for security policies, definition of custom protection domains and class location. These differences, and others, are summarized in the following list.

- ❑ **Security Manager** – Traditional Java security does not initialize a security manager by default. The Oracle JVM, however, always comes with a security manager. The Oracle security manager should generally neither be customized nor overridden by the application. Standard Java security managers can easily be customized, without loss of security.

- ❑ **Security Policies** – In traditional Java security, security policies are defined in a text-based policy file that is specified by a command line option when starting the JVM. Policy files can be updated with any type of text editor.

  In Oracle, security policies are defined as individual permissions inside a central policy table. This policy table stores all security policies of the database. Each user is provided access to local permissions through a public database view. To update permissions in the policy table, a user must be granted a special permission. Given the proper permission, the user may update permissions through methods of the DBMS_JAVA PL/SQL package and the PolicyTableManager Java class.

- ❑ **Protection Domains** – All classes are divided into individual protection domains in traditional Java security. Each protection domain is assigned fine-grained permissions that in turn apply to each member of the domain. In Oracle, the equivalent of a protection domain is the database schema. All permissions are determined by the schema in which a class is loaded.

- ❑ **Permissions** – In traditional Java security, all permissions are positive, that is, they provide access to a resource that otherwise would not have been accessible. In Oracle, permissions can both be positive or limited. A limited permission restricts an otherwise positive permission, as we will see in more detail later.

- ❑ **Trusted Classes** – In Java security, all classes loaded from the class path are trusted. In Oracle, no classes are loaded from a class path – all classes are loaded within the database. Classes are trusted on a class-by-class basis according to granted permissions.

- ❑ **Signed Code** – Oracle Java security does not support signed code, which traditional Java security does.

## Sample Users

In what remains of this chapter, we will be giving short examples of how to apply Oracle Java security within the database. For that purpose, we create two database users, JOHN and PAUL, to whom we assign security roles and permissions later on.

To create the sample users, log on as SYS and execute the commands shown below:

```
connect sys/<your_password_here>;
create user JOHN identified by JOHN;
grant connect to JOHN;
create user PAUL identified by PAUL;
grant connect to PAUL;
```

# Permissions

In this section, we will discuss how permissions are stored, granted and revoked in the Oracle Java security model.

## Viewing and Storing Permissions

Unlike standard Java security, Oracle security permissions are not stored in text-based policy files. Instead, all Oracle JVM security permissions are stored as rows in a database table, which is called the *policy table*.

> The policy table did not exist in Oracle 8.1.5, since all security was provided through roles such as **JAVASYSPRIV, JAVAUSERPRIV, or JAVADEBUGPRIV.**

To specify security permissions in Oracle, the policy table is dynamically updated through either the DBMS_JAVA PL/SQL package or the PolicyTableManager Java class, methods of which are discussed in more detail below.

### The Policy Table

The USER_JAVA_POLICY view provides read access to those rows of the policy table that are relevant to the current user. Additionally, SYS (or any other user granted the DBA role) can view all user permissions, through the DBA_JAVA_POLICY view. Both views are identical in structure, as illustrated in the following figure.

| USER_JAVA_POLICY | DBA_JAVA_POLICY |
|---|---|
| KIND | KIND |
| GRANTEE_NAME | **GRANTEE** |
| TYPE_SCHEMA | TYPE_SCHEMA |
| TYPE_NAME | TYPE_NAME |
| NAME | NAME |
| ACTION | ACTION |
| ENABLED | ENABLED |
| SEQ | SEQ |

The following table describes the columns of the USER_JAVA_POLICY view. The DBA_JAVA_POLICY view is identical, except that the name of the grantee is stored in a column called GRANTEE and not GRANTEE_NAME, as it is for the USER_JAVA_POLICY view.

| Column name | Description |
| --- | --- |
| KIND | Specifies the nature of the permission. Can take either one of the values GRANT (positive permission) or RESTRICT (limited permission). |
| GRANTEE_NAME | The name of the user, schema, or role to which the permission is assigned. |
| TYPE_SCHEMA | The schema to which the permission applies. |
| TYPE_NAME | The full package name of the permission class, such as java.net.SocketPermission. |
| NAME | The target name of the permission. For example, for the java.io.FilePermission, the target name defines the subset of the file hierarchy to which the permission should apply. |
| ACTION | The action of the permission. For example, for java.util.PropertyPermission, the action attribute can take one or both of the values read and write. If no action is appropriate for a specific permission, the action attribute should be set to null. |
| ENABLED | This column shows whether the permission is enabled or disabled. Can take one of the values ACTIVE (enabled) or INACTIVE (disabled). |
| SEQ | Each permission granted is identified with a unique sequence number. |

### Viewing the Contents of the Policy Table

Each user can view relevant permissions from the policy table, by querying the USER_JAVA_POLICY view. Below, we will demonstrate a sample script that can be used with SQL*Plus to get a formatted output from the policy view.

```
SQL> column "grantee" format a10
SQL> column "permission type" format a25
SQL> column "permission name" format a40
SQL> column "action" format a10
SQL> column "g/r" format a3
SQL> set pagesize 50
SQL> set linesize 100

SQL> select
  2    substr(kind,1,1) "G/R",
  3    substr(type_name,instr(type_name,'.', -1)+1,
  4      length(type_name)) "Permission type",
  5    substr(grantee_name,1,10) "Grantee",
  6    substr(name,1,40) "Permission name",
  7    substr(nvl(action,'null'),1,10) "Action"
  8    from user_java_policy
  9  order by kind, type_name;
```

A sample output from this query is shown below. The first column shows whether the permission is granted (G) or restricted (R).

```
G/R  Permission type       Grantee  Permission name                    Action
---  --------------------  -------- --------------------------------   ------
 G   RuntimePermission     PUBLIC   createSecurityManager              null
 G   RuntimePermission     PUBLIC   exitVM                             null
 G   RuntimePermission     PUBLIC   modifyThreadGroup                  null
 G   RuntimePermission     PUBLIC   modifyThread                       null
 G   PropertyPermission    PUBLIC   *                                  read
 G   PropertyPermission    PUBLIC   user.language                      write
 G   JServerPermission     PUBLIC   LoadClassInPackage.*               null
 R   RuntimePermission     PUBLIC   loadLibrary.*                      null
 R   PolicyTablePermission PUBLIC   0:java.lang.RuntimePermission#lo   null
 R   JServerPermission     PUBLIC   LoadClassInPackage.java.*          null
 R   JServerPermission     PUBLIC   LoadClassInPackage.oracle.aurora   null
 R   JServerPermission     PUBLIC   LoadClassInPackage.oracle.jdbc.*   null
```

### Updating the Policy Table

The policy table that stores all Java permissions is just like any other table within Oracle. As such, explicit permission – Oracle-specific PolicyTablePermission – is needed to update the table. If you look at the example query result above in the **Permission type** column, you will see that one of the rows selected from the view is a PolicyTablePermission.

The Oracle JVM installs with a few default database roles, as we will discuss in more detail later. One of these roles, JAVA_ADMIN, is granted extensive PolicyTablePermission at the time of initialization. JAVA_ADMIN is automatically granted to the DBA role, and thus all members of that role. One such member, the SYS user, is additionally granted extended PolicyTablePermission beyond those of JAVA_ADMIN. We will discuss the JAVA_ADMIN role and the initial SYS user permissions in full detail later in this chapter.

Each user must be granted a specific PolicyTablePermission for every permission he is authorized to update the policy table with. For example, if a user should be able to grant others java.io.FilePermission, he must be granted explicit administrative rights to update the policy table for the java.io.FilePermission. Those rights would not allow him to grant java.net.SocketPermission, for example. For that, he would need explicit permission to update the policy table for java.net.SocketPermission.

Policy table permissions are granted through stored procedures. The stored procedures are implemented both in PL/SQL and Java. For each language, there are two variations of this method, one that provides the ID of the associated row in the policy table – either as a return value or an OUT parameter – and another one that does not. The row ID can be used later on to disable, enable or delete the permission in question.

The following two procedures of the DBMS_JAVA PL/SQL package are used to grant permissions to update the policy table. All of the parameters are required, and none may be NULL or empty strings.

```
PROCEDURE grant_policy_permission (
  grantee VARCHAR2,
  permission_schema VARCHAR2,
  permission_type VARCHAR2,
  permission_target VARCHAR2
);

PROCEDURE grant_policy_permission (
  grantee VARCHAR2,
  permission_schema VARCHAR2,
  permission_type VARCHAR2,
  permission_target VARCHAR2,
  key OUT NUMBER
);
```

In the same fashion, the following two methods of the `PolicyTableManager` Java class are used to grant permissions to update the policy table.

```
public long
oracle.aurora.rdbms.security.PolicyTableManager.grantPolicyPermission (
  java.lang.String grantee,
  java.lang.String permission_schema,
  java.lang.String permission_type,
  java.lang.String permission_target
);

public void
oracle.aurora.rdbms.security.PolicyTableManager.grantPolicyPermission (
  java.lang.String grantee,
  java.lang.String permission_schema,
  java.lang.String permission_type,
  java.lang.String permission_target,
  long[] key
);
```

The arguments to these methods are given in the following listing:

❑   `grantee` – The name of the user, schema, or role to which the grant applies. Can be a specific name, or `PUBLIC`, which applies to all users.

❑   `permission_schema` – The schema in which the permission is loaded. Usually, the `SYS` schema is used. An exception to this rule is when permission is granted on a custom permission class, not defined for `SYS`.

Before the policy table permission grantee can grant the specified permission to other users, the specified permission schema must have already been assigned the permission being granted (!). For example, if a specific `java.io.FilePermission` is granted in a schema that has *not* been granted that particular `java.io.FilePermission`, an exception will occur when the grantee tries to grant the permission to others. We will investigate this issue in more detail later, at the end of the *Granting Permissions* section.

permission_type – The permission class on which a permission is being granted. This argument requires a fully qualified name of the permission class. Oracle supported permission types are specified in the next section, *Supported Permission Types*.

❑ permission_target – The target name of the permission class on which the permission is being granted. The target name is different for each permission class.

For an example on how to grant administrative rights to update the policy table, log on as SYS and grant the following permissions to user JOHN:

```
SQL> -- Grant JOHN administrative rights to update the
SQL> -- policy table for the loadLibrary.xaNative permission
SQL> -- of java.lang.RuntimePermission
SQL> call dbms_java.grant_policy_permission (
  2    'JOHN',
  3    'JOHN',
  4    'java.lang.RuntimePermission',
  5    'loadlibrary.xaNative'
  6  );

SQL> -- Grant JOHN administrative rights to update the
SQL> -- policy table for the java.* permission
SQL> -- of java.util.PropertyPermission
SQL> call dbms_java.grant_policy_permission (
  2    'JOHN',
  3    'SYS',
  4    'java.util.PropertyPermission',
  5    'java.*'
  6  );
```

In the first call to GRANT_POLICY_PERMISSION, we grant permission to JOHN to modify the policy table for the RuntimePermission loadLibrary.xaNative (that is permission to load an external library named xaNative). The second parameter specifies the schema 'JOHN', so the RuntimePermission instance will be loaded to the JOHN schema. Previously, we ran a query on the USER_JAVA_POLICY table (see *Viewing the Contents of the Policy Table* above). If you run that query in the JOHN schema, you should see lines similar to this:

```
G/R Permission type      Grantee  Permission name                      Action
--- --------------------- -------- ------------------------------------ ------
R   RuntimePermission     PUBLIC   loadLibrary.*                        null
```

The R means the permission to load an external library has been revoked from the JOHN schema. What this means is that we've tried to give schema JOHN the policy permission to grant a permission, and that the permission itself has not been granted to JOHN. In other words, the JOHN schema does not contain an instance of RuntimePermission with the appropriate target name. We will see the impact of this later in the chapter.

We have also granted the policy table permission for PropertyPermission to JOHN. The PropertyPermission instance, as indicated by the procedure call, is loaded into the SYS schema. And in fact, SYS does have the PropertyPermission to read and write all properties. That is, there is an instance of PropertyPermission in the SYS schema with the target of all properties and an action of read and write.

**391**

Now, connect as JOHN and query the USER_JAVA_POLICY view for PolicyTablePermissions, which have been granted, as shown here:

```
SQL> connect JOHN/JOHN;

SQL> select name
  2      from user_java_policy
  3      where type_name like '%PolicyTablePermission'
  4        and kind = 'GRANT';
```

This query should return the two results, similar to the ones shown below:

```
NAME
--------------------------------------------------------
0:java.util.PropertyPermission#java.*
45:java. lang.RuntimePermission#loadLibrary.xaNative
```

The name field contains three different pieces of information. Each name field is structured like this (spaces added for clarity):

```
schema ID : permission class # permission target
```

The schema ID is the schema number of the schema where the specified permission class instance is loaded. The permission class is the fully qualified package name of the permission object. The permission target is the target to which the permission applies.

According to this, user JOHN has been granted the permission to grant PropertyPermission for properties with a name like java.*. The schema id for that permission is 0, which means the instance of PropertyPermission with the given target is loaded into the schema with id 0 (we will shortly see whose schema that is). JOHN also has permission to grant the RuntimePermission with a target of loadLibrary.xaNative. This permission, however, is loaded in the schema with id 45. To verify that these values correctly relate to the schemas we specified earlier when we called GRANT_POLICY_PERMISSION, you can query the DBA_USERS view (connected as SYS), as shown here:

```
SQL> connect SYS/<your_password_here>;

SQL> select username from dba_users where user_id = 45;

USERNAME
------------------------------
JOHN

SQL> select username from dba_users where user_id = 0;

USERNAME
------------------------------
SYS
```

## Supported Permission Types

The Oracle Java security model supports most of the standard Java permission types. The standard Java permissions were listed earlier in this chapter. Besides the standard Java permissions, the Oracle JVM additionally supports two Oracle-specific permissions, the `PolicyTablePermission` and the `JServerPermission`.

### oracle.aurora.rdbms.security.PolicyTablePermission

This permission is used to grant permission to modify the security policy table, as we have previously mentioned. A user that has been granted the right to modify the policy table can modify existing permissions and specify new ones. Initially, only those users that have been assigned the JAVA_ADMIN database role are granted the `PolicyTablePermission`.

For more information on how to grant the `PolicyTablePermission`, refer to the *Storing Permissions* section, above.

### oracle.aurora.security.JServerPermission

This permission is used to control access to various resources of the Oracle JVM. `JServerPermissions` are divided in three categories: *Class Loading Permissions, Runtime Permissions* and *Debugging Permissions.*

Class loading permissions grant abilities to load classes in the JVM and turn the Java bytecode verification on and off. The names that can be used with `JServerPermission` that apply to class loading are summarized in the following listing:

- ❏ `LoadClassInPackage` – This permission type grants the ability to load a class within a specified package. The package name is specified along with the permission type, for example, by specifying `LoadClassInPackage.SomePackage`.
- ❏ `Verifier` – This permission grants the ability to turn the bytecode verifier on or off.

The runtime permissions grant rights to specific runtime properties of the Oracle JVM. The names that can be used with `JserverPermission` that apply to the JVM are listed below. Most developers will only be concerned with the first, so we provide a short explanation for that and simply list the others.

- ❏ `JRIExtensions` – This permission grants the use of the MEMSTAT memory utility. MEMSTAT is discussed in more detail in Chapter 15.
- ❏ `Memory.Call`
- ❏ `Memory.Stack`
- ❏ `Memory.SGAIntern`
- ❏ `Memory.GC`

The final name that can be used with `JserverPermission` is for using a debugger.

- ❏ `Debug` – This permission grants the ability for debuggers to connect to a session.

# Initial Permissions

When the Oracle JVM is first initialized, several database roles are created. These roles, in addition to PUBLIC and the SYS user, are granted a few default permissions at initialization time. Each user is automatically granted the appropriate initial permissions, based on which roles he is member of.

For now, it will suffice to discuss the initial permissions granted to PUBLIC and the SYS user. Later in this chapter, in the *Security Roles* section, we will discuss the standard Java security roles, along with the initial permissions they are granted.

## PUBLIC Initial Permissions

The following permissions are initially assigned to PUBLIC, and hence all database users:

- ❑ java.util.PropertyPermission – Each user is *granted* permission to read any system property and additionally write the user.language permission of PropertyPermission.

- ❑ java.lang.RuntimePermission – All users are *granted* permission to halt the JVM, create new security managers and modify threads and thread groups. However, all users have *restricted* permission to load external libraries.

  Note that the process of loading external libraries, just as any other security-based operation, *would* have required explicit permission anyway. By specifying an explicit restriction, it is made sure that **no one** is granted permission to load custom external libraries in the database JVM, without explicitly overriding these restrictions. The only exception is the SYS user, who partially overrides this restriction, as we will see later.

- ❑ oracle.aurora.rdbms.security.PolicyTablePermission – All users are *restricted* from updating the policy table for the loadLibrary.* permission of java.lang.RuntimePermission. This restriction holds hands with the loadLibrary.* restriction on RuntimePermission, above.

  Since generally no one should be able to load external libraries, it is natural that no one has the ability to grant such permissions. The only exception is the SYS user, as we will see later.

- ❑ oracle.aurora.security.JServerPermission – Each user is *granted* permission to load custom classes and packages. However, this general permission is limited by *restricting* access to load classes in the core packages java.*, oracle.aurora.* and oracle.jdbc.*.

## SYS Initial Permissions

When the Oracle JVM is first initialized, the JAVA_ADMIN role is automatically granted to the DBA role. Furthermore, the SYS user, which is a member of DBA and thus JAVA_ADMIN, is granted a few additional permissions, which are illustrated below.

- ❑ java.lang.RuntimePermission – SYS is granted all RuntimePermissions. Specifically, SYS is granted explicit permission to create custom class loaders and to load a few isolated external libraries. The last permission overrides the restriction imposed on PUBLIC to load custom libraries. The library permissions granted to SYS are: loadLibrary.xaNative, loadLibrary.corejava and loadLibrary.corejava_dsdf.

Note that as SYS has full permission to update the policy table, it is possible to grant other users permission to load the aforementioned external libraries through SYS. This, however, is generally not recommended because external libraries are not subject to the same security restrictions as Java code.

- ❏ `java.lang.reflect.ReflectPermission` – SYS is granted all ReflectPermissions.

- ❏ `java.net.NetPermission` – SYS is granted all NetPermissions.

- ❏ `java.security.SecurityPermission` – SYS is granted all SecurityPermissions.

- ❏ `java.util.PropertyPermission` – SYS is granted all PropertyPermissions.

- ❏ `oracle.aurora.rdbms.security.PolicyTablePermission` – SYS is granted explicit access to modify the policy table for all permissions.

- ❏ `oracle.aurora.security.JServerPermission` – SYS is granted all JServerPermission types. Specifically, SYS is granted explicit permission to load classes in the core packages `java.*`, `oracle.aurora.*` and `oracle.jdbc.*`, which overrides the corresponding limitation imposed on PUBLIC.

## Granting Permissions

A user that has the administrative rights to update the policy table can grant permissions to other users, roles or schemas. If a granted permission already exists for the specified schema, no update occurs. Rather, the row identifier of the existing permission of the DBMS_JAVA is simply returned. If such an attempted overwrite takes place for a disabled permission, the permission is automatically enabled. More information on disabling, enabling and deleting permissions are provided below.

### Granting Permissions With PL/SQL

The following two procedures of the DBMS_JAVA PL/SQL package are used to grant permissions.

```
PROCEDURE grant_permission (
  grantee VARCHAR2,
  permission_type VARCHAR2,
  permission_name VARCHAR2,
  permission_action VARCHAR2
);

PROCEDURE grant_permission (
  grantee VARCHAR2,
  permission_type VARCHAR2,
  permission_name VARCHAR2,
  permission_action VARCHAR2,
  key OUT NUMBER
);
```

### Granting Permissions With Java

The following two methods of the `PolicyTableManager` Java class are used to grant permissions:

```
public long oracle.aurora.rdbms.security.PolicyTableManager.grant (
  java.lang.String grantee,
  java.lang.String permission_type,
  java.lang.String permission_name,
  java.lang.String permission_action
);

public void oracle.aurora.rdbms.security.PolicyTableManager.grant (
  java.lang.String grantee,
  java.lang.String permission_type,
  java.lang.String permission_name,
  java.lang.String permission_action,
  long[] key
);
```

In both PL/SQL and Java, the meaning of the parameters is as follows:

- ❏  `grantee` – the name, schema or role to which the grant applies, use `PUBLIC` for all users
- ❏  `permission_type` – the full package spec and name of the permission class
- ❏  `permission_name` – the target to which the permission applies
- ❏  `permission_action` – the valid action for the target
- ❏  `key` – sequence number of the permission returned from the table (in Java you pass in a variable of type `long[]` (array of long), and when the method returns the first element of the array will contain the sequence id)

### Granting Unauthorized Permissions

When a user is granted administrative permission to update the policy table for a specific permission type, care must be taken to properly specify the schema in which the permission instance is loaded (don't confuse this with the schema to which the grant should apply). When a policy table permission grantee tries to grant the specified permission to other users, a check is made on whether the specified schema has been assigned the permission being granted. That is, if specifying a policy table permission to schema A, and the permission instance is loaded in schema B, care must be taken that *schema B has been granted the intended permission*. If not, a security exception will be thrown when the grantee tries to grant the permission to others.

To illustrate this further, let's look at a simple example. Earlier in the chapter, we connected as SYS and granted two policy table permissions (*Updating the Policy Table* section). If you did not do that earlier, do it now.

Now, connect as JOHN and grant PAUL permission to read and write all property permissions that begin with "`java.`".

```
SQL> connect JOHN/JOHN;

SQL> call dbms_java.grant_permission (
  2    'PAUL',
  3    'java.util.PropertyPermission',
  4    'java.*',
  5    'read,write'
  6  );
```

When we granted the PropertyPermission, we said the instance of the PropertyPermission class with read and write action on target java.* was loaded in the SYS schema. Even though JOHN does not possess the permission to read and write java.* properties, this permission grant will succeed because SYS does have permission to read and write all properties.

Now, try to grant PAUL the loadLibrary.xaNative permission of java.lang.RuntimePermission. Since JOHN does not have this permission himself, this action will throw a security exception. That is, when we granted the policy table permission we indicated that the instance of RuntimePermission was loaded in the JOHN schema. Since JOHN does not have RuntimePermission to load external libraries, an instance of the class does not, in fact, exist in the JOHN schema and the grant to PAUL fails.

```
SQL> call dbms_java.grant_permission (
  2    'PAUL',
  3    'java.lang.RuntimePermission',
  4    'loadLibrary.xaNative',
  5    'null'
  6  );
call dbms_java.grant_permission (
     *
ERROR at line 1:
ORA-29532: Java call terminated by uncaught Java exception:
java.lang.SecurityException: policy table update
SYS:java.lang.RuntimePermission, loadLibrary.xaNative
```

## Restricting Permissions

In many cases, a general security permission is granted to a group of users. However, there are often exceptions to such general rules. To implement such exceptions, you can specify permission *restrictions*, that limit otherwise general permissions.

As with permission grants, restrictions can be specified both with Java and PL/SQL, as shown in the following two sections.

### Restricting Permissions With PL/SQL

The following two procedures of the DBMS_JAVA PL/SQL package can be used to restrict permissions.

```
PROCEDURE restrict_permission (
  grantee VARCHAR2,
  permission_type VARCHAR2,
  permission_name VARCHAR2,
  permission_action VARCHAR2
```

```
  );

  PROCEDURE restrict_permission (
    grantee VARCHAR2,
    permission_type VARCHAR2,
    permission_name VARCHAR2,
    permission_action VARCHAR2,
    key OUT NUMBER
  );
```

### Restricting Permissions With Java

The following two methods of the `PolicyTableManager` Java class can be used to restrict permissions.

```
public long oracle.aurora.rdbms.security.PolicyTableManager.restrict (
  java.lang.String grantee,
  java.lang.String permission_type,
  java.lang.String permission_name,
  java.lang.String permission_action
);

public void oracle.aurora.rdbms.security.PolicyTableManager.restrict (
  java.lang.String grantee,
  java.lang.String permission_type,
  java.lang.String permission_name,
  java.lang.String permission_action,
  long[] key
);
```

The parameters are the same as for granting permissions, described earlier under the *Granting Permissions With Java* section.

### Permission Restriction Example

For example, imagine a general rule that allows users to read all files in a shared directory, except for the password file and the access log. This type of permission could be defined by first specifying a general read permission to the whole shared directory, and then limiting the general rule by applying a read restriction on password and access.log files. This is further illustrated in the following example (which uses UNIX style paths, if you use Windows, change the paths as appropriate for your system):

```
SQL> connect SYS/<YOUR_PASSWORD_HERE>;

SQL> -- Give everyone (PUBLIC) read access to files
SQL> -- in the /usr/local/share directory
SQL> call dbms_java.grant_permission (
  2    'PUBLIC',
  3    'java.io.FilePermission',
  4    '/usr/local/share/-',
  5    'read'
  6  );
```

```
SQL> -- Limit everyone's access to read the password and access.log files
SQL> call dbms_java.restrict_permission (
  2      'PUBLIC',
  3      'java.io.FilePermission',
  4      '/usr/local/share/password',
  5      'read'
  6  );

SQL> call dbms_java.restrict_permission (
  2      'PUBLIC',
  3      'java.io.FilePermission',
  4      '/usr/local/share/access.log',
  5      'read'
  6  );
```

Now, imagine an exception to the limitation, namely that the file owner needs specific permission to both read and write the password file and the access log. To accomplish such a policy, we can explicitly grant a permission to override the limitation permission, without risking the overall security policy. The Oracle security manager combines all the security rules added to the policy table to understand each user's permissions.

This example is further illustrated in the following code snippet:

```
SQL> -- Grant user JOHN access to both read and write
SQL> -- the password file and the access log
SQL> call dbms_java.grant_permission (
  2      'JOHN',
  3      'java.io.FilePermission',
  4      '/usr/local/share/password',
  5      'read,write'
  6  );

SQL> call dbms_java.grant_permission (
  2      'JOHN',
  3      'java.io.FilePermission',
  4      '/usr/local/share/access.log',
  5      'read,write'
  6  );
```

Given the above security policy, our sample users would have the following permissions to the shared directory:

❑   JOHN – JOHN has permission to read all files in the shared directory. Additionally, JOHN may write to the password and access.log files.

❑   PAUL – PAUL has permission to read all files in the shared directory, except for the password and access.log files.

## Revoking Permissions

Permissions can be revoked either by temporarily disabling their functionality or by deleting them from the policy table.

### Disabling Permissions

The following procedure of the DBMS_JAVA PL/SQL package is used to disable a specific permission.

```
PROCEDURE disable_permission(key NUMBER);
```

A more general procedure to disable permissions is shown below. This method takes for arguments the attributes of the permission to disable. It searches the entire policy table for all rows that match the supplied parameters. As a result, more than one permission can be disabled by this method (for example, by only specifying permission_type, all permissions of the specified type are disabled).

```
PROCEDURE revoke_permission(
  permission_schema VARCHAR2,
  permission_type VARCHAR2,
  permission_name VARCHAR2,
  permission_action VARCHAR2
);
```

Corresponding methods are also provided through the PolicyTableManager Java class:

```
public void oracle.aurora.rdbms.security.PolicyTableManager.revoke (
  String schema,
  String type,
  String name,
  String action
);

public void oracle.aurora.rdbms.security.PolicyTableManager.disable(
  long number
);
```

### Deleting Permissions

> **Note that before a permission can be deleted, it must first be disabled, otherwise the deletion will have no effect.Unfortunately, no warning or error message is provided when this occurs.**

The following procedure of the DBMS_JAVA PL/SQL package is used to delete a specific permission.

```
PROCEDURE delete_permission(key NUMBER);
```

Permissions can also be deleted through the following method of the PolicyTableManager Java class:

```
public static void oracle.aurora.rdbms.security.PolicyTableManager.delete(long
number);
```

### Enabling Permissions

When a permission has been disabled, it can always be enabled again, through PL/SQL and Java methods. The following procedure of the DBMS_JAVA PL/SQL package is used to enable a specific permission, which has been previously disabled:

```
PROCEDURE enable_permission(key NUMBER);
```

A corresponding method of the PolicyTableManager Java class is shown below:

```
void oracle.aurora.rdbms.security.PolicyTableManager.enable(long number);
```

# Security Roles

A *role* is a set of database privileges granted to a database user with a single operation. Database privileges are granted to the role and users inherit the role's privileges by becoming members of that role. Roles are used to ease the management task of assigning a set of privileges to users. By managing roles, rather than updating multiple user accounts on an individual basis, we increase efficiency and ensure the integrity of the overall database security policy.

Traditional database roles can easily be extended to include all aspects of database privileges and security – including Oracle Java security. In fact, the Oracle JVM installs with four default database roles that can be used for Java security. In this section, we will discuss these default security roles and cover the process of creating custom roles for Java security.

## Built-in Security Roles

In Oracle 8.1.5, Java security was controlled by granting users the roles of JAVASYSPRIV, JAVAUSERPRIV and JAVADEBUGPRIV. Users that were granted the JAVASYSPRIV role had substantial control over database resources and the operating system. JAVAUSERPRIV, on the other hand, was more limited. The JAVADEBUGPRIV role was granted to those users that needed to invoke the internal Java debug agent.

It soon became obvious that these three database roles did not provide the level of security required by most enterprise applications. In the next version of Oracle, Java security was enforced by applying fine-grained permissions on a per-user basis. Thus, the new Oracle Java security model complied with the standard Java 2 security model, as we have already discussed.

For backwards-compatibility, the Oracle JVM still installs with the three original security roles. However, their implementations have changed, as they now exist as groups of ordinary Java permissions. In version 8.1.5, the Oracle security manager explicitly determined whether a particular database user existed as a part of a specific role, and provided resource access or threw security exceptions based on that determination. In more recent versions, the Oracle security manager complies with standard Java security checks, and determines resource access based on granted permissions.

In addition to the three aforementioned security roles, a fourth role is created when the Oracle JVM is installed. This role, JAVA_ADMIN, is granted permission to modify the policy table, and should therefore be used with great caution.

In the next three sections, we discuss the four built-in Java security roles in more detail.

## The JAVAUSERPRIV Role

This role allows a user to access files and sockets and both create and access Java classes. Specifically, the user is granted variations of three standard permissions, which are further illustrated below.

❑ `java.net.SocketPermission` – A user that has been granted this role may connect to and resolve any socket connection.

❑ `java.io.FilePermission` – A user that has been granted this role may read any file. No files may be written to.

❑ `java.lang.RuntimePermission` – A user that has been granted this role has the permission to modify thread groups, stop active threads (provided that it is already granted permission to access those threads), read file descriptors (and thereby read the particular file associated with the file descriptor), obtain policy information for a particular code source and both access and define any custom classes and packages (of course, neither Java Foundation Classes and packages nor Oracle libraries may be written to).

## The JAVASYSPRIV Role

This role gives a user access to privileged Java functionality and operating system resources. This role should be used with extreme caution. A user who is granted the `JAVASYSPRIV` role has the ability to open and accept direct socket connections, he may write to and delete any file accessible to the Oracle instance and he may instantiate new and manipulate existing class loaders for the JVM.

The exact permissions of the `JAVASYSPRIV` role are illustrated below:

❑ `java.io.SerializablePermission` – A user that has been granted this role may serialize any object and deserialize any file containing serialized data.

❑ `java.net.SocketPermission` – A user that has been granted this role may connect to and resolve any socket connection. Additionally, the user may listen to and accept connections from any socket that can access the database host.

❑ `java.io.FilePermission` – A user that has been granted this role may read, write, delete and execute any file.

❑ `java.lang.RuntimePermission` – A user that has been granted this role has the permission to instantiate custom class loaders, set class loaders for a specified thread context and retrieve the class loader for a particular class. The user may also set socket and stream factory implementations and replace standard input, output and error streams of the whole JVM. Additionally, the user may read and write any file descriptor on the system.

> It should be stressed that the **JAVASYSPRIV** database role should be used with caution. This role not only allows its grantees to damage JVM resources, it also risks the resources of the underlying database. If you want to grant extended privileges beyond those of **JAVAUSERPRIV**, you should consider applying fine-grained permissions by hand instead of granting **JAVASYSPRIV**.

### The JAVADEBUGPRIV Role

This role allows a grantee to invoke the Java debug agent, which is discussed in more detail in Chapter 9. This role is granted the following permissions:

- ❑    `java.net.SocketPermission` – A user that has been granted this role may connect to and resolve any socket connection.

- ❑    `oracle.aurora.security.JServerPermission` – A user that has been granted this role may debug Java code loaded in the database. Specifically, they are granted the `debug` action of the `JServerPermission`.

To receive permission to invoke the debug agent, a user must have been granted the `JAVADEBUGPRIV` role or the `debug JServerPermission`. Both methods are equivalent.

### The JAVA_ADMIN Role

This role is granted extensive permission to modify the policy table. When the Oracle JVM is first initialized, the `JAVA_ADMIN` role is granted to the `DBA` role. All members of the `DBA` role therefore have permission to update the policy table.

> **Show caution before you grant JAVA_ADMIN to others.**

Full administrative rights to update the policy table are granted to `JAVA_ADMIN` for the following permissions:

- ❑    `java.io.FilePermission`
- ❑    `java.io.SerializablePermission`
- ❑    `java.lang.reflect.ReflectPermission`
- ❑    `java.lang.RuntimePermission`
- ❑    `java.net.NetPermission`
- ❑    `java.net.SocketPermission`
- ❑    `java.security.SecurityPermission`
- ❑    `java.util.PropertyPermission`
- ❑    `oracle.aurora.rdbms.security.PolicyTablePermission`
- ❑    `oracle.aurora.security.JServerPermission`

### Granting Roles

To grant a specified user one of the three built-in security roles, you must log on to the database either as the `SYS` user or as a user that has been previously granted the intended role with administration options. For example:

```
SQL> grant javauserpriv to JOHN;
```

To grant administration options with a role, you must specify the `WITH ADMIN OPTION` option with the `GRANT` command. For example:

```
SQL> grant javasyspriv to PAUL with admin option;
```

**403**

## Custom Security Roles

In many cases, applying fine-grained security permissions to individual users can become time consuming and complicated, as the number of users accessing the database grows. Often, many users share common permissions, which it becomes useful to apply as a whole. For that purpose, you can create your own database role, and grant fine-grained permissions to the role. The following example illustrates this further.

```
SQL> connect SYS/<YOUR_PASSWORD_HERE>;

SQL> -- Create a generic database role
SQL> create role GENERIC_ROLE;

SQL> -- Grant permissions to the role
SQL> call dbms_java.grant_permission (
  2    'GENERIC_ROLE',
  3    'java.net.SocketPermission',
  4    'http://127.0.0.1',
  5    'accept,listen,connect,resolve'
  6  );

SQL> call dbms_java.grant_permission (
  2    'GENERIC_ROLE',
  3    'java.io.FilePermission',
  4    '/usr/local/share/-',
  5    'read'
  6  );

SQL> call dbms_java.grant_permission (
  2    'GENERIC_ROLE',
  3    'java.lang.RuntimePermission',
  4    'accessClassInPackage.*',
  5    'null'
  6  );

SQL> call dbms_java.grant_permission (
  2    'GENERIC_ROLE',
  3    'java.lang.RuntimePermission',
  4    'defineClassInPackage.*',
  5    'null'
  6  );

SQL> -- Grant the security role to users
SQL> grant GENERIC_ROLE to PAUL;
SQL> grant GENERIC_ROLE to JOHN;
```

## Extending Security Roles

In many cases, one or more users end up performing similar tasks while they work with the database. Thus, it is natural to group together users with similar intentions and grant security roles to whole groups.

However, things are not always so simple. Although a single security role might define the majority of permissions granted to a group of users, variations may exist. For example, imagine a generic security role that specifies users' access to JVM resources, class loaders, debugging options, network connections and more. Apart from these general permissions, a particular user might need permission to write files in a specific directory, or send requests to a particular network device, which other users should not be permitted to do. However, we neither want to create a custom security role for different users, nor apply fine-grained security permissions on a per-user basis.

A simple solution to this problem is to grant generic security roles to each user and add to the privileges defined by the security role by granting additional permissions to individual users. Permissions defined within the policy table have a cumulative effect, so granting additional permissions will only add to existing permissions acquired through the role.

The following example continues from the previous section, and assigns extended permissions to user JOHN, who was previously granted the GENERIC_ROLE role.

```
SQL> connect SYS/<YOUR_PASSWORD_HERE>;

SQL> -- Further extend the permissions granted to JOHN
SQL> call dbms_java.grant_permission (
  2     'JOHN',
  3     'java.io.FilePermission',
  4     '/home/john/-',
  5     'read,write,delete'
  6  );
```

# Building Custom Security Permissions

Up until now, the types of permissions we have been dealing with have been restricted to the standard Java and Oracle permission types, such as FilePermission and JServerPermission. However, there may be cases where it is necessary to implement custom security permissions to accomplish an intended security policy. In this section we will discuss the basic steps of implementing and employing custom permissions by illustrating a bug-tracking system that stores categorized bug reports as serialized objects in a file system.

## Overview

For many software projects, the process of reporting, tracking and organizing errors can often be more time-consuming than the actual process of fixing the faults. As projects grow larger, there is an increased need for a robust system of storing and managing bug reports.

In this section, we will develop a simple bug-tracking system that stores bug reports as serialized objects in the file system. The system is intended for internal use only, for the developers and testers of the underlying system (details of which are not relevant in this context). Each bug report is put in one of three categories – A, B or C – depending on which part of the system the bug relates to. Based on these three bug categories, different users are given different access to the system. For example, users working exclusively on part A should generally only be allowed to access A-class bugs. Moreover, access can be further restricted to the three fields of reading, writing and deleting. The testing team should have full access to read and write any bug report, while programmers should only be allowed to modify reports on bugs in the part of the system they are working on.

> *Of course, in a real-life scenario, this system could be much more complex. For example, when a specific report is marked 'in progress', it should be ensured that only the programmer claiming the bug should have permission to update the status, and so on.*

**405**

To manage the bug reports, we create a framework of Java classes that interact with the file system where the reports are stored. A specific database user, BUG_REPORTS, is created as the owner of these classes. Each class is made accessible for other parts of the database through a public synonym on which all users are granted execute privileges.

Each bug report is encapsulated in a BugReport object that is serialized and stored in a specific directory in the file system. (Writing to the file system allows us to demonstrate using FilePermission.) Only the dedicated BUG_REPORTS user is granted the permission to read, write and delete files in the bug reports directory. These files are accessed through appropriate methods of the BugReportManager class. Each I/O operation in the BugReportManager class is performed with the privileges of the class owner – namely BUG_REPORTS. Thereby, each database user can access the serialized files without being granted explicit file permissions. However, as we have already stated, we do control access to the serialized BugReport objects. This control is managed by having the security manager check the appropriate BugReportPermission of each invoker. BugReportPermissions are granted to individual bug categories – A, B or C – with a specified action of read, write or delete. If, when accessing the bug reports, the appropriate BugReportPermission is missing, a security exception is thrown. This is further illustrated in the following diagram, which shows user JOHN performing a read operation on a specified bug report.

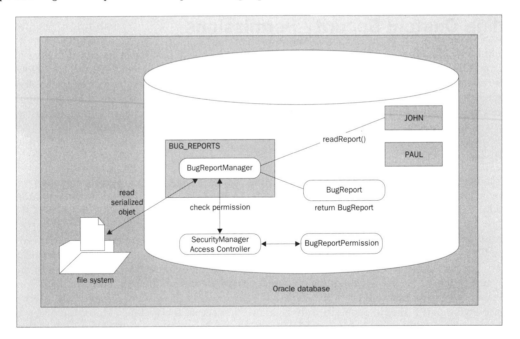

In the rest of this section we will guide you through the setup and deployment of the bug-tracking system.

## Accessing the Bug Reports

To store the class framework for the bug-tracking system, we create a special database user, BUG_REPORTS. A sample script for creating this user is shown below.

```
SQL> connect SYS/<YOUR_PASSWORD_HERE>;

SQL> create user BUG_REPORTS identified by BUG_REPORTS;
SQL> grant connect, resource to BUG_REPORTS;
SQL> grant create procedure to BUG_REPORTS;
SQL> grant create table to BUG_REPORTS;
SQL> grant create PUBLIC synonym to BUG_REPORTS;
SQL> grant drop PUBLIC synonym to BUG_REPORTS;

SQL> -- Need to grant create procedure to JOHN and PAUL also
SQL> grant create procedure to JOHN;
SQL> grant create procedure to PAUL;
```

### Grant File Permissions

The BUG_REPORTS user must be granted full permission to read, write and delete files in a chosen directory. In this setup, we use the `c:\temp` directory on the database server. You will need to supply an appropriate directory path for your system. This directory is specified again as a constant in the BugReportManager class.

```
SQL> call dbms_java.grant_permission (
  2     'BUG_REPORTS',
  3     'java.io.FilePermission',
  4     'C:\temp\*',
  5     'read,write,delete'
  6  );
SQL> commit;
```

> Make sure that the directory chosen to store the bug reports is writable by the database process.

In addition, the BUG_REPORTS user must be granted full permission to serialize objects.

```
SQL> call dbms_java.grant_permission (
  2     'BUG_REPORTS',
  3     'java.io.SerializablePermission',
  4     '*',
  5     'null'
  6  );
SQL> commit;
```

## Java Classes

In this section, we will investigate the Java class framework used for the bug-tracking system. This framework consists of seven classes. These classes, which are all members of the wrox.bugreports package, are summarized below:

❑ BugReport – The BugReport class encapsulates a single bug report.

❑ BugReportPermission – The BugReportPermission extends class java.security.BasicPermission. This class represents access to a bug report.

**407**

- ❑ `BugReportManager` – This class is the application's sole interface to the reports stored in the bug-tracking system. It interacts with the file system through privileged code blocks, that work on any one of the three helper classes shown below.

- ❑ `ReadAction` – This class implements the `java.security.PrivilegedAction` interface. It is used to read a bug report from a file.

- ❑ `WriteAction` – This class implements the `java.security.PrivilegedAction` interface. It is used to write a bug report to a file.

- ❑ `DeleteAction` – This class implements the `java.security.PrivilegedAction` interface. It is used to delete a bug report file.

- ❑ `BugReportTest` – This class is used to test the functionality of the bug-tracking system.

The relationships between each of the mentioned classes is further illustrated in the following UML diagram:

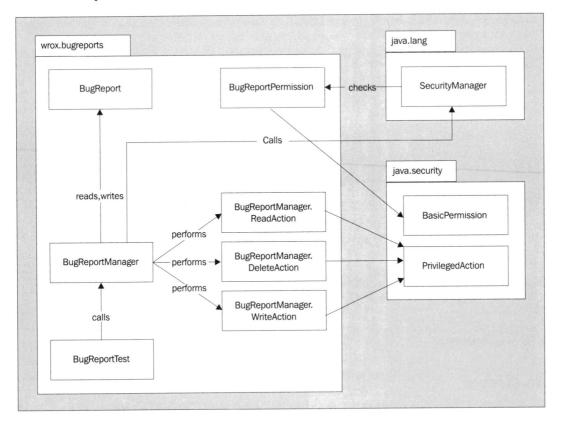

### BugReport

A `BugReport` instance represents a particular bug report. Each bug report contains the following set of attributes:

- ❑ **Bug class** – Each bug is assigned to a particular bug category, depending on which part of the underlying system it affects.

❑ **Date registered** – This is the date the report is created.

❑ **Status** – The status of the bug report. Can take any of the values `'unsolved'` (new report), `'in progress'` (someone has claimed the report and is trying to fix the bug), and `'solved'`. Corresponding constants declared in the `BugReport` class should be used.

❑ **Bug ID** – The bug report identifier is a value of type long that is constructed by calculating the current system time in milliseconds.

❑ **Title** – The title of the report.

❑ **Description** – A description of the bug.

❑ **Solution** – This is the solution to the bug, if it has been solved.

The `BugReport` class is shown in full detail below:

```
package wrox.bugreports;

import java.util.Date;
import java.io.Serializable;

public class BugReport implements Serializable {

  /** Bug class A constant */
  public static final char A_CLASS = 'A';

  /** Bug class B constant */
  public static final char B_CLASS = 'B';

  /** Bug class C constant */
  public static final char C_CLASS = 'C';

  /** Unresolved constant */
  public static final String UNSOLVED = "unsolved";

  /** In-progress constant */
  public static final String IN_PROGRESS = "in progress";

  /** Solved constant */
  public static final String SOLVED = "solved";


  // Instance variables.
  private char bugClass;
  private Date bugDate;
  private String bugStatus;
  private long bugID;
  private String bugTitle;
  private String bugDescription;
  private String bugSolution;

  public BugReport() {
    bugClass = ' ';
    bugStatus = "";
    bugID = -1L;
    bugTitle = "";
    bugDescription = "";
```

```
      bugSolution = "";

  }

  public long getBugID() {
    return bugID;
  }

  public String getBugTitle() {
    return bugTitle;
  }

  public String getBugDescription() {
    return bugDescription;
  }

  public String getBugSolution() {
    return bugSolution;
  }

  public char getBugClass() {
    return bugClass;
  }

  public String getBugStatus() {
    return bugStatus;
  }

  void setBugID(long bugID) {
    this.bugID = bugID;
  }

  void setBugDate(Date bugDate) {
    this.bugDate = bugDate;
  }

  public void setBugTitle(String bugTitle) {
    this.bugTitle = bugTitle;
  }

  public void setBugDescription(String bugDescription) {
    this.bugDescription = bugDescription;
  }

  public void setBugSolution(String bugSolution) {
    this.bugSolution = bugSolution;
  }

  public void setBugClass(char bugClass) {
    this.bugClass = bugClass;
  }

  public void setBugStatus(String bugStatus) {
    this.bugStatus = bugStatus;
  }
}
```

The BugReport class is essentially a data holder. There are variables for each of the attributes that were listed in the previous section, and setXXX() and getXXX() methods for each of the attributes.

### BugReportPermission Class

The `BugReportPermission` class represents access to a bug report. A `BugReportPermission` consists of a bug report class and a set of actions valid for that class of reports.

The reason why we create a custom permission, rather than just grant `java.io.FilePermission` to specified files in the root directory, is twofold. Firstly, this method allows us to better separate the business logic from the underlying persistence logic. If a user had direct access to the serialized files, he could easily bypass the business logic of the `BugReportManager` and convert the files directly to objects. However, by abstracting all the persistence logic in methods of the `BugReportManager` we can easily shift to other methods of persisting the bug reports without affecting the overall system. Also, by encapsulating the persistence logic, we ensure that minor changes in the inner structure of each file (for example, adding new fields to the `BugReport` class) do not affect the application.

Secondly, by securing the serialized bug report files, we ensure the integrity of the file format used to store the fields of each bug report. If users had direct access to write new and modify existing bug reports, we risk having a different format or file content which could upset the whole application.

The `BugReportPermission` extends the `java.security.BasicPermission` class, which in turn extends `java.security.Permission`. Exact class and method definitions are shown below:

```
package wrox.bugreports;

import java.security.Permission;
import java.security.BasicPermission;

public class BugReportPermission extends BasicPermission {

  public BugReportPermission(char bugClass, String actions) {
    super(String.valueOf(bugClass), actions);
  }

  public BugReportPermission(String bugClass, String actions) {
    this(bugClass.charAt(0),actions);
  }

  public boolean implies(Permission p) {
    return super.implies(p);
  }
}
```

This class is a simple one that implements the `BugReportPermission`. It has two constructors. One takes the bug report category as a character, the other takes a `String` parameter and uses the first char of the string as the category.

The method that is completely new is `implies(Permission)`. This method must be defined by subclasses of `Permission`. This method is used by the `AccessController` to determine whether a given permission is allowed based on a known valid permission. For example, if a known valid permission has a target name of `'a.b.*'` then this permission would allow a permission for `'a.b.xyz'` because of the wildcard.

## BugReportManager Class

The `BugReportManager` class is the sole interface the application has to access bug reports in persistent storage. The `BugReportManager` has three static methods – `readReport()`, `writeReport()` and `deleteReport()` – that allow the invoker to read, write and delete reports, respectively.

Each of the actual I/O operations of the `BugReportManager` is wrapped in an implementation of the `java.security.PrivilegedAction` interface, and executed as privileged code blocks. This means that all I/O operations are executed with the rights of the class definer, which in our case is user `BUG_REPORTS`. As we have already seen, `BUG_REPORTS` is granted full access to the directory that stores the bug reports, and therefore all I/O operations that are executed on behalf of `BUG_REPORTS` have full permission. For each of the three methods of the `BugReportManager`, there exists a corresponding class that implements the `java.security.PrivilegedAction` interface. These three inner classes are:

❑ `ReadAction` – For reading files; invoked as privileged code in `readReport()`

❑ `WriteAction` – For writing files; invoked as privileged code in `writeReport()`

❑ `DeleteAction` – For deleting files; invoked as privileged code in `deleteReport()`

The `PrivilegeAction` interface essentially tells the `AccessController` when to stop checking permissions. Usually, when permissions are checked, the `AccessController` checks every method call to ensure that all the methods that led to the current method have the privilege needed to perform the action. Code that is invoked as privileged indicates to the access controller that any calls prior to the privileged code do not need to be checked for permission.

These three inner classes are discussed later. Below is the opening declaration of the `BugReportManager` class:

```
package wrox.bugreports;

import java.io.File;
import java.io.FileInputStream;
import java.io.FileOutputStream;
import java.io.IOException;
import java.io.ObjectInputStream;
import java.io.ObjectOutputStream;
import java.security.AccessController;
import java.security.PrivilegedAction;
import java.sql.SQLException;
import java.text.DateFormat;
import java.util.Date;

public class BugReportManager {

    /** Static constants */
    static final String FILE_NAME = "bugReport";
    static File ROOT_DIR;

    static final String ROOT_DIR_PATH = "C:\\temp";
    static {
```

```
        // Assume this directory exists.
        ROOT_DIR = new File(ROOT_DIR_PATH);
    }

    public static BugReport readReport(long bugID) throws Exception {

        ReadAction ra = new ReadAction(bugID);
        AccessController.doPrivileged(ra);
        BugReport report = ra.getBugReport();

        if (report != null) {
            BugReportPermission perm =
                new BugReportPermission(report.getBugClass(),"read");
            SecurityManager sman = System.getSecurityManager();
            sman.checkPermission(perm);
        }
        return report;
    }

    public static boolean writeReport(BugReport report) throws Exception {
        BugReportPermission perm =
            new BugReportPermission(report.getBugClass(),"write");
        SecurityManager sman = System.getSecurityManager();
        sman.checkPermission(perm);

        WriteAction wa = new WriteAction(report);
        AccessController.doPrivileged(wa);
        return wa.wasWritten();
    }

    public static boolean deleteReport(BugReport report) throws Exception {
        BugReportPermission perm =
            new BugReportPermission(report.getBugClass(),"delete");
        SecurityManager sman = System.getSecurityManager();
        sman.checkPermission(perm);

        DeleteAction da = new DeleteAction(report);
        AccessController.doPrivileged(da);
        return da.wasDeleted();
    }
```

The class has static variables for the location of the bug report files. Remember to update the path of the root directory in your own deployment. In a real-life, enterprise bug-tracking system, this path value should be read from a properties file of some sort, for easier maintenance.

The `readReport()` method takes for an argument an ID of a specified bug report, and returns the corresponding `BugReport` instance, read from persistent storage. If the requested bug report is not found, this method returns `null`. To read the bug report, the `readReport()` method creates a new `ReadAction` instance and executes its `run()` method as privileged code. We discuss the `ReadAction` class in more detail later. If a bug report was successfully read, the invoker's permissions are checked against the class of the bug. If the required permission is not available, a security exception is thrown.

The `writeReport()` method takes for an argument a `BugReport` instance, which it writes to persistent storage. Before the object is serialized, the invoker's permissions are checked against the bug report class. If the invoker has permission to store the report, a new instance of the `WriteAction` class is constructed and its `run()` method executed as privileged code. Finally, the method returns whether the report was successfully serialized or not.

Finally, the `deleteReport()` method takes for an argument a `BugReport` instance, which it deletes from persistent storage. Before the corresponding file is deleted, the invoker's permissions are checked against the bug report class. Next, a new `DeleteAction` instance is constructed and its `run()` method executed as privileged code. The `deleteReport()` method returns true if the corresponding file was successfully deleted.

As part of the `BugReportManager` class, we now build three inner classes that allow read, write and delete actions on serialized files.

### BugReportManager.ReadAction Inner Class

The `ReadAction` inner class implements the `java.security.PrivilegedAction` interface for reading serialized files. A new `ReadAction` instance is constructed from a specified bug report ID. In its `run()` method, an attempt is made to read from the file system a serialized object that corresponds to the supplied bug ID. If that attempt is successful, a new `BugReport` instance is constructed from the object stream and made accessible to the invoker through the `getBugReport()` method.

```
static class ReadAction implements PrivilegedAction {

    private BugReport report;
    private Exception stored;
    private long bugID;

    public ReadAction(long bugID) {
        this.bugID = bugID;
    }
    public BugReport getBugReport() throws Exception {
        if (stored != null) {
            throw stored;
        }
        return report;
    }
    public Object run() {

        FileInputStream fis = null;
        ObjectInputStream ois = null;
        try {
            File f = new File(ROOT_DIR,FILE_NAME + bugID);
```

```
                    if (f.exists()) {
                        fis = new FileInputStream(f);
                        ois = new ObjectInputStream(fis);
                        report = (BugReport) ois.readObject();
                    }
            } catch (Exception e) {
                stored = e;
            } finally {
                try {
                    if (fis != null) fis.close();
                } catch (Exception ignored) {
                }
            }
            return null;
        }
    }
```

The getBugReport() method returns the BugReport instance read from persistent storage. As the run() method may not throw an exception, any exception caught during the read process is stored and thrown through the getBugReport() method.

This method implements the run() service of the PrivilegedAction interface. This method is executed when the ReadAction instance is supplied as an argument to the doPrivileged() method of java.security.AccessController.

The run() method tries to read the specified object from the file system. Any exception that may occur during the read process is stored and later thrown by the getBugReport() method.

### BugReportManager.WriteAction Inner Class

The WriteAction inner class implements the java.security.PrivilegedAction interface for writing serialized files. A new WriteAction instance is constructed from a specified BugReport instance. In its run() method, an attempt is made to serialize the object and store it as a file in the specified root directory. If the supplied BugReport instance has not been assigned with a bug ID, a new ID is obtained and assigned to the object. After the attempted write, the invoker can call the wasWritten() method, that returns true if the write was successful, but false otherwise.

```
static class WriteAction implements PrivilegedAction {

    private boolean wasWritten;
    private BugReport report;
    private Exception stored;

    public WriteAction(BugReport report) {
        this.report = report;
        wasWritten = false;
    }

    public boolean wasWritten() throws Exception {
        if (stored != null) {
            throw stored;
```

```
            }
        return wasWritten;
    }

    public Object run() {

        FileOutputStream fout = null;
        ObjectOutputStream out = null;
        try {

            // Get a new report ID if this is a new report.
            if (report.getBugID() == -1) {
                report.setBugID((new Date()).toString().hashCode());
                report.setBugDate(new Date());
            }

            // Write the object to file.
            File f = new File(ROOT_DIR,FILE_NAME + report.getBugID());
            if (!f.exists()) {
                f.createNewFile();
            }
            fout = new FileOutputStream(f);
            out = new ObjectOutputStream(fout);
            out.writeObject(report);
            wasWritten = true;

        } catch (Exception e) {
            stored = e;
        } finally {
            try {
                if (out != null) out.flush();
            } catch (Exception ignored) {
            }
            try {
                if (fout != null) fout.close();
            } catch (Exception ignored) {
            }
        }
        return null;
    }
}
```

The wasWritten() method returns true if the specified BugReport instance was successfully serialized and written to a file. The file is named with the bugID forming part of the name. The bug id is generated with the current system time in milliseconds. For our simple example, using the system time creates unique increasing numeric ids. As with the getBugReport() method of the ReadAction class, this method throws any exceptions that may have been stored from the write process of the run() method.

The run() method tries to write the specified object to a file. Any exception that may occur during the write process is stored and later thrown by the wasWritten() method.

### BugReportManager.DeleteAction Inner Class

The DeleteAction class implements the java.security.PrivilegedAction interface for deleting serialized files. A new DeleteAction instance is constructed from a specified BugReport instance. In the run() method, an attempt is made to delete from the file system a serialized object that corresponds to the supplied BugReport instance. After the delete attempt, the invoker can call the wasDeleted() method that returns true if the deletion was successful, but false otherwise.

```java
static class DeleteAction implements PrivilegedAction {

    private boolean wasDeleted;
    private BugReport report;
    private Exception stored;

    public DeleteAction(BugReport report) {
        this.report = report;
        wasDeleted = false;
    }

    public boolean wasDeleted() throws Exception {
        if (stored != null) {
            throw stored;
        }
        return wasDeleted;
    }

    public Object run() {

        try {

            File f = new File(ROOT_DIR,FILE_NAME + report.getBugID());
            if (f.exists()) {
                wasDeleted = f.delete();
            }

        } catch (Exception e) {
            stored = e;
        }
        return null;
    }
    }
}
```

The wasDeleted() method returns true if the persistent state of the specified BugReport instance was successfully deleted. As with the wasWritten() method of the WriteAction class, this method throws any exceptions that may have been stored from the delete process of the run() method.

The run() method tries to delete the serialized file that stores the specified object. Any exception that may occur during the delete process is stored and later thrown by the wasDeleted() method.

### BugReportTest Class

To test the functionality of the bug-tracking system, we create a simple class that provides static methods for reading and writing a specified bug report. The BugReportTest class contains two methods, testRead() and testWrite(), that read and write, respectively, a dummy bug report. Both methods return String values. For the testRead() method, the return value either corresponds to the title of the bug report read, if the read was successful, or the string representation of an exception thrown, if the read failed. Similar goes for testWrite() – either it returns an indication of whether the object was written or a string representation of an exception thrown.

```
package wrox.bugreports;

public class BugReportTest {
  public static String testRead() {
    try {
      BugReport report = BugReportManager.readReport(1);
      return report.getBugTitle();
    } catch (Exception e) {
      return "Error: " + e.toString();
    }
  }

  public static String testWrite() {
    try {
      BugReport report = new BugReport();
      report.setBugTitle("Generic A class bug");
      report.setBugClass('A');
      report.setBugID(1);
      if (BugReportManager.writeReport(report)) {
      return "success";
      } else {
      return "failure";
      }
    } catch (Exception e) {
      return "Error: " + e.toString();
    }
  }
}
```

## Deployment

In this section, we go through the deployment of the sample bug-tracking application.

### Deploy the Java Classes

You can choose any method you wish to deploy the Java classes to the database – for example, compile them externally and use loadjava to load the .class files or build a JAR file from the compiled .class files and load the JAR file to the database. Alternately, you could use the PL/SQL syntax CREATE OR REPLACE AND COMPILE. In any case, you must ensure that:

❑   There exists a public synonym for the BugReportTest class, and

❑   All users have execute privileges on the BugReportTest class.

If you have not done so already, connect as the SYS user, create the bug_reports user and grant the following permissions:

```
drop user bug_reports cascade;
create user bug_reports identified by bug_reports;
grant connect, resource to bug_reports;
grant create public synonym to bug_reports;
grant drop public synonym to bug_reports;

call dbms_java.grant_permission (
 'BUG_REPORTS',
'java.io.FilePermission',
'C:\temp\*',
 'read,write,delete'
 );

call dbms_java.grant_permission (
 'BUG_REPORTS',
 'java.io.SerializablePermission',
 '*',
 'null'
 );
```

As an example, we'll show you how to use loadjava to load and compile the source files directly to the database. You can use these commands for your own deployment – just remember to supply the correct Oracle SID and use the JDBC Thin driver, if the OCI driver is not available.

```
> loadjava -user bug_reports/bug_reports@database -resolve -grant PUBLIC -synonym
BugReport.java

> loadjava -user bug_reports/bug_reports@database -resolve -grant PUBLIC -synonym
BugReportPermission.java

> loadjava -user bug_reports/bug_reports@database -resolve -grant PUBLIC -synonym
BugReportManager.java

> loadjava -user bug_reports/bug_reports@database -resolve -grant PUBLIC -synonym
BugReportTest.java
```

The loadjava commands shown above will create the synonym and grant execute privilege as it loads the Java classes. If you do not use the syntax above, or you create the classes directly in the database with create or replace and compile, you can create the synonym and grant execute privilege like this:

```
SQL> create PUBLIC synonym "wrox/bugreports/BugReportTest"
  2  for "wrox/bugreports/BugReportTest";
SQL> grant execute on "wrox/bugreports/BugReportTest" to PUBLIC;
```

### Grant Bug Permissions

When all Java classes have been loaded into the database, it is time to grant our existing users appropriate BugReportPermissions.

Connect as the BUG_REPORTS user and start by granting BUG_REPORTS administrative rights to update the policy table for BugReportPermission, as shown below:

```
SQL> connect BUG_REPORTS/BUG_REPORTS;

SQL> call dbms_java.grant_policy_permission (
  2      'BUG_REPORTS',
  3      'BUG_REPORTS',
  4      'wrox.bugreports.BugReportPermission',
  5      '*'
  6  );
```

Next, grant BUG_REPORTS full BugReportPermission.

```
SQL> call dbms_java.grant_permission (
  2      'BUG_REPORTS',
  3      'BUG_REPORTS:wrox.bugreports.BugReportPermission',
  4      '*',
  5      'read,write,delete'
  6  );
```

To illustrate the use of our custom permission, we grant our two users JOHN and PAUL different permissions. JOHN is assigned read and write access to A-class bugs, while PAUL only has read access to B-class bugs.

```
SQL> call dbms_java.grant_permission (
  2      'JOHN',
  3      'BUG_REPORTS:wrox.bugreports.BugReportPermission',
  4      'A',
  5      'read,write,delete'
  6  );

SQL> call dbms_java.grant_permission (
  2      'PAUL',
  3      'BUG_REPORTS:wrox.bugreports.BugReportPermission',
  4      'B',
  5      'read'
  6  );
```

### Write a Sample Report

Next, while you are still connected as BUG_REPORTS, create a PL/SQL call spec for the testWrite() method of BugReportTest, as shown below.

```
SQL> create or replace function write_report return varchar2
  2  as language java
  3  name 'wrox.bugreports.BugReportTest.testWrite() return java.lang.String';
  4  /
```

Enable server output and execute the function.

```
SQL> set serveroutput on;
SQL> call dbms_output.put_line substr((write_report,1,255);
```

We use the `substr` function simply to limit the output to 255 characters and avoid line length overflow errors. If everything goes as expected, you should get a message of success on the screen:

```
success
```

### Verify Permissions

Next, connect as user JOHN, create a sample call spec for the `testRead()` method and execute the function.

```
SQL> connect JOHN/JOHN;
SQL> create or replace function read_report return varchar2
  2  as language java
  3  name 'wrox.bugreports.BugReportTest.testRead() return
                                             java.lang.String';
  4  /

SQL> set serveroutput on;
SQL> call dbms_output.put_line(read_report);
```

Since JOHN has permission to read A-class bug reports, you should get the following output:

```
Generic A class bug
```

Then, connect as PAUL, create an identical call spec and execute the function.

Note that we must create local call specs for each database user. It is not possible to create a single spec for one user and have each user access this spec through a public synonym, as we did with the Java classes owned by BUG_REPORTS. The difference between the two is that when the public Java classes are accessed through a local call spec, they are invoked from the Java address space of the invoking user. On the other hand, accessing a joint call spec through a synonym would mean that each Java class accessed was invoked through the Java address space of the user that owned the PL/SQL spec. As a result, all Java permissions would be resolved for the PL/SQL spec owner, and the not the true invoker. Therefore, we must use separate call specs for each user, as we do for JOHN and PAUL.

```
SQL> connect PAUL/PAUL;
SQL> create or replace function read_report return varchar2
  2  as language java
  3  name 'wrox.bugreports.BugReportTest.testRead() return
                                             java.lang.String';
  4  /

SQL> set serveroutput on;
SQL> call dbms_output.put_line(read_report);
```

PAUL has only permission to read B-class bug reports, so this call should throw a security exception:

```
Error: java.security.AccessControlException: the Permission
(wrox.bugreports.BugReportPermission A ) has not been granted by
dbms_java.grant_permission to
SchemaProtectionDomain(PAUL|PolicyTableProxy(PAUL))
```

## Troubleshooting

If things are not working as expected, you should search for the source of your problems among the following known issues:

### Public Synonym Permission

Do not forget to grant the CREATE PUBLIC SYNONYM and DROP PUBLIC SYNONYM privileges to the BUG_REPORTS user. The latter is necessary if you for some reason need to redeploy the Java classes to the database, such as when you change the directory in which to store the bug reports. When you load classes in the database that already exist, and specify the -synonym option for loadjava, existing public synonyms are dropped and recreated. If inadequate privileges are granted to the BUG_REPORTS user, the database will issue an error when loading the classes:

```
ORA-01031: insufficient privileges
```

### Execute Permission

If users JOHN and PAUL are not granted EXECUTE privilege on the Java classes owned by user BUG_REPORTS (for example, by specifying the -grant option of the loadjava command), a security exception will occur when they try to execute the Java call spec:

```
Error: java.security.AccessControlException: the Permission
(wrox.bugreports.BugReportPermission A ) has not been granted by
dbms_java.grant_permission to
SchemaProtectionDomain (BUG_REPORTS|PolicyTableProxy(BUG_REPORTS))
```

This can be solved by granting EXECUTE privilege on the Java classes:

```
SQL> connect BUG_REPORTS/BUG_REPORTS;

SQL> grant execute on "wrox/bugreports/BugReport" to public;
SQL> grant execute on "/50676a0b_BugReportManager_SJP" to public;
SQL> grant execute on "/7e98109d_BugReportPermission" to public;
SQL> grant execute on "/5d26c202_BugReportManager" to public;
SQL> grant execute on "wrox/bugreports/BugReportTest" to public;
```

The names used in these grant statements can be determined by performing a query on the USER_OBJECTS table:

```
SQL> select object_name
  2    from user_objects
  3   where object_name
  4    like '%BugReport%';
```

### Write Permission

If the directory that you specified to store the bug reports is not writable by the database process (such as by the operating system user that started the Oracle instance), you will get an `IOException` when you try to write a new bug report. This can be solved by widening the permissions on the directory, for example by executing `chmod` on a UNIX operating system. Windows users will likely not have this problem.

### Session state cleared

This occurs when a Java class is recompiled. When the class is recompiled, any state associated with the class is cleared. The error message will look something like this:

```
ERROR at line 1:
ORA-29549: class BUG_REPORTS.wrox/bugreports/BugReportTest has changed, Java
session state cleared
```

Simply rerun the call that caused the error and a new state will be created.

# Summary

In this chapter we have covered the Oracle Java security model used by the JVM to restrict unwanted operations by Java classes running inside the database.

We began this chapter by discussing some of the basic concepts of computer security. Next, we covered the basics of the Java security model, from its early days as a sandbox model to the fine-grained, policy-based system of modern Java security.

However, the major focus of this chapter was on the Oracle Java security model. This model implements the traditional Java security model and adapts it to the database-specific needs of the Oracle JVM. We discussed how permissions are stored within the database and what methods and requirements are necessary when granting and revoking Java permissions. Furthermore, we covered the default security roles that the Oracle JVM is installed with, and illustrated how custom security roles can be created to suit the needs of different applications.

Finally, we ended our discussion of Oracle Java security by illustrating a sample bug-tracking system that employed user-defined Java permissions loaded within the database to maintain a highly specific, custom security policy.

While this chapter has covered quite a lot of material, there is much more that we have not covered. Readers who are interested in more details on security in Java should read another Wrox title, *Professional Java Security; ISBN 1861004257;* and visit
http://java.sun.com/products/jdk/1.3/docs/guide/security/index.html.

Oracle 9i Java Programming

# Using Java Utilities

With the choice of three mature programming languages when working from within the Oracle database, PL/SQL, C-based external procedures and Java, it is no wonder some developers are confused regarding when it is appropriate to use which. With Java being the latest addition to the database programming language spectrum, it is natural to attempt and determine specifically the role of that language in working with Oracle. In that context, people often tend to compare Java with PL/SQL, the alternative to programming from within the database. This, however, is like comparing apples with oranges. PL/SQL and Java were created for different purposes, and should generally be used accordingly. Probably most of the confusion regarding the issue of PL/SQL or Java relates to the issue of using Java for database access or not. Generally, it is our opinion that when working with the database, you should use PL/SQL whenever you can. The tight integration with the SQL execution engine –PL/SQL datatypes are just SQL datatypes, which means that PL/SQL will always outperform Java when it comes to working with SQL, since it requires numerous expensive conversions of both language and data in order to accomplish the same goals using Java.

Rather than comparing Java with PL/SQL in terms of database access, you should compare them in terms of functionality. In this area, the biggest advantage of PL/SQL – its tight integration with the Oracle database – becomes its biggest weakness. Unlike Java, PL/SQL was not designed to be a general-use programming language. Working with Oracle is just one of the many tasks of Java, which means that it can offer more extensive functionality than that of PL/SQL, which is generally limited to database-related chores. For example, by using Java, we can dynamically generate images, transport files over FTP or use the database for mail storage, which is not possible to do with PL/SQL.

Therefore, it is more natural to compare Java not with PL/SQL, but rather the traditional method of extending the functionality of PL/SQL programs: C-based external procedures. The role of both Java and C in relation to Oracle is similar – to solve tasks that are impossible to accomplish using PL/SQL alone. However, as we will see in more detail in Chapter 13, there are a number of reasons why you should choose Java in favor of C-based procedures. For example, Java runs, just like PL/SQL, within the address space of the database, while C procedures have to be controlled as external processes in the operating system, which makes them inherently harder to maintain. Additionally, C-based external procedures have to be compiled specifically for each platform – a DLL on Windows won't work on UNIX, for example – which is not true of Java.

It is the intent of this chapter to provide a clear definition of the true advantage of using Java when working within the Oracle database. Additionally, we will seek to touch upon some of the areas at which Java excels, in relation to various utilities and extensions, such as mail transport and image generation.

In many parts of this chapter, we will introduce some of the Java APIs related to these areas, without providing extensive coverage. The idea is to provide enough information on each API for you to see how it fits in the overall Java API structures and how you can use it in your own Oracle Java applications. To fully explore the usage for each API, we encourage you to study the Java API documentation, which is accessible on-line at http://java.sun.com/products/jdk/1.2/docs/api/index.html.

# Defining the Role of Java

Ever since Java was first integrated with Oracle, the PL/SQL vs. Java argument has been the source of constant debate. Both these languages are highly sophisticated, with a wide range of available utilities. Most of the things you can do in PL/SQL you can also do in Java, and vice versa. However, there are things which you either just can't accomplish with one of the languages, or it is much more easy to do with the other. In this section, we will go through these issues and iterate some of the arguments for each language, in order to determine where Java fits best.

## Advantages of PL/SQL

PL/SQL is an extension to the industry standard SQL query language. PL/SQL utilizes the same data types and language constructs used by SQL, which makes it ideal for seamless implementation of extensive database operations. Owing to the similarities with SQL, database operations in PL/SQL are much faster than they would be using Java, since there is no impedance mismatch between PL/SQL and SQL – they both use the same data types, as we have mentioned.

Additionally, PL/SQL comes with a wide variety of built-in packages, which address both common as well as highly specific aspects of Oracle programming. Many of these packages have no equivalent in Java (although they can be easily called from Java).

## Advantages of Java

Java has been one of the fastest growing computer languages in recent years. Java is object-oriented with inherent support for automatic garbage collection, polymorphism, inheritance, and multithreading.

Many of the services provided by Java are developed as general specifications, rather than concrete implementations, which makes the language less reliant on individual service vendors. An example of this is the EJB (Enterprise JavaBeans) specification, where Java provides interfaces, some classes and a specification, which vendors like IBM and BEA adhere to. Through an open-source community process, there is virtually no limit to the extensions and utilities developed for the Java language, many of which can be useful within the database (PL/SQL also has open-source extensions, but these are more related to database chores than those of Java). In our opinion, this is the biggest advantage of Java in the database – functionality that either does not exist or is very limited in PL/SQL.

Java applications inside the database can utilize either one of two standards for access to a relational database, SQLJ or JDBC. Although database access performed with these methods will be considerably slower than PL/SQL, partly because of the overhead of data conversion, it is less of an issue when running Java inside Oracle, where queries do not have to travel a across network on their way to the database.

And finally, Java has much more powerful capabilities of accessing system resources outside the database – such as files, operating system commands and network sockets – than PL/SQL. We will illustrate that further in the next chapter, *Working with OS Resources.*

## Wrap Up

Both PL/SQL and Java can be used on their own to successfully build applications inside the database. Despite their inherent dissimilarities, the two languages still have much in common and can easily work together.

To conclude, we have gathered a few guidelines on where you should use each language when working within the boundaries of Oracle:

❑ **Use PL/SQL for Intensive Database Access** – PL/SQL is built around the database, it uses the same datatypes and constructs as SQL. PL/SQL operations are faster than with Java, especially when a large amount of data is involved or bulk operations are being used.

❑ **Use PL/SQL for Oracle Specific Functionality** – Many capabilities of PL/SQL have no parallel in Java. This is especially true for some of the built-in PL/SQL packages, such as DBMS_LOCK and DBMS_ALERT.

❑ **Use Java to Access System Resources** – Java has much better capabilities for accessing external resources than PL/SQL, such as files and sockets. Additionally, Java allows for more fine-grained security policies, which are often necessary when working with vital resources.

❑ **Use Java for Functionality Not Available in PL/SQL** – This goes also for functionality that is available, but more limited in PL/SQL, such as mail transport or image generation, as we will discuss in this chapter. Many of the Java standard extensions and libraries can be useful in the database, as we will see later.

> PL/SQL was designed for the database, while Java was not. As a result, PL/SQL is better for tasks that involve resources of the database, while Java suits better for operations not directly related to Oracle.

# Java Utilities

One of the biggest advantages of using Java in the database is the vast collection of utilities and extensions available to the language. Java language extensions are backed up by a whole community of Java users, which leads to rapid advancements and a widespread industry support for new technologies.

It is the intent of this chapter to provide you with a short overview of some of the alternative Java APIs that you might come to use in the database. The following list illustrates some of the database-related highlights of the current API collection:

❑ **Graphics and Imaging** – There is a widespread support for imaging technologies for Java. For example, apart from the standard AWT classes, which allow for simple imaging capabilities, there are APIs for Advanced Imaging, Java 2D and Java 3D. For a database running on a host with an active display device, it can be useful to generate images in the database. For example, imagine a scenario where every morning the database gathers statistics of some sort from the previous day and generates graphs from that information. Such graphs could then be encoded – for example, as GIF or JPEG – and stored as BLOBs in the database. We will illustrate an application for doing that later in this chapter.

❑ **Messaging** – Java provides two basic APIs for messaging: JavaMail, for e-mail transfer and the Java Messaging Service (JMS) for a more general type messaging system (similar to DBMS_AQ in Oracle). JavaMail is discussed in more detail later when we implement a stored procedure for sending messages with BLOB attachments in a simpler manner than is possible with PL/SQL.

❑ **Security** – In the previous chapter, we mentioned some of the security extensions available to the Java language. To recap, these include Java Authentication and Authorization Service (JAAS), Java Cryptography Extension (JCE), Java Cryptography Architecture (JCA) and Java Secure Socket Extension (JSSE). The cryptography extensions can be especially useful within the database, for handling sensitive information.

❑ **XML** – Java provides an extensive set of APIs for XML handling. For example, JAXP (Java API for XML Processing) and JAXB (Java Architecture for XML Binding), while they can be used in conjunction with the standard Oracle XDK for Java.

We will be looking exclusively at two of those technologies here – namely image generation and mail transport with JavaMail. However, we do encourage you to explore further the possibilities of the other utilities mentioned. In doing that, you can start by visiting the Java products page, at http://java.sun.com/products/, which should lead you to the appropriate resources.

# Generating Images

The ability to dynamically generate custom images can be useful in database applications. For example, from persistent information stored in database tables, it may be useful to construct all sorts of charts that can be distributed to interested clients. Traditionally, such images are generated from a client application outside the database, but with the advent of Java stored procedures, we can now do so from within the context of Oracle.

However, why should one ever want to generate images within the database? Isn't it much more simple to do so at the client, or at least outside the database?

While it may be so in many cases, there are times where it may be more feasible to use a stored procedure in the database to dynamically generate images. By doing that, for example in an application where a number of clients need to access an image generated from information stored in the database, we encapsulate the business logic behind the generated image that would otherwise have to be stored on each client. Additionally, in certain cases related to the distribution of dynamic images, it is simply more efficient to run the logic from within the database. We will look at one such particular example at the end of this chapter, when we discuss the possibility of having a database job automatically send generated charts to a list of recipients, by using image generation, JavaMail and PL/SQL job scheduling together.

# Working with Images in Java

The Java platform has support for various graphics and image APIs. In addition to the Java AWT (Abstract Windowing Toolkit) and Java 2D imaging libraries, which are bundled with version 1.2 and higher of the JDK, there are various other extensions for advanced graphics and image processing available for install at your own discretion, such as Java 3D and Advanced Imaging:

- ❑ **Java AWT** – The Abstract Window Toolkit, or AWT, is a collection of GUI classes for the Java platform. The AWT has been around since the early days of Java, and is therefore widely available. Though the AWT is mostly composed of components related to GUI controllers and applets, it also contains classes related to the manipulation of images.

- ❑ **Java 2D** – The Java 2D image API extends the AWT with increased functionality for image manipulation, including support for alpha channels (transparency), color conversions and various other conversion operations. Java 2D originally had to be obtained separately, but has been a part of the JDK since version 1.2. In Oracle terms, this means version 8.1.6 and up.

- ❑ **Java 3D** – The Java 3D API is an extension for building and working with three-dimensional environments and objects. Java 3D has to be installed separately. The API and relevant documentation can be downloaded at http://java.sun.com/products/java-media/3D/index.html.

- ❑ **Java Advanced Imaging** – For any developer considering advanced image manipulation, beyond that of simple two-dimensional charts and icons, Java Advanced Imaging is the answer. This API provides a high-level model for various aspects of image processing, such as geometric warping, scaling, filtering, and contrast enhancement. Java Advanced Imaging does not come with any current JDK. It can be downloaded freely at http://java.sun.com/products/java-media/jai/index.html.

It is not our intention in this section to teach you every aspect of image processing with Java, as that would need at least a chapter of its own. Rather, in this section we will illustrate the basic steps necessary for generating a custom, off-screen image with the Java AWT. Even though the Java 2D API also comes as a part of Java 2, it is significantly more complex to use than the AWT, being more advanced. However, when you have mastered the image aspects of the AWT, there is nothing to stop you from directly advancing to Java 2D, or even better, installing Java 3D or the Advanced Imaging API.

## Oracle Support for the AWT

Before we go any further, however, you should note that there is a limitation to the support Oracle has for the AWT. Obviously, it makes no sense to support that part of the AWT that deals with GUI, such as applets, since there is no notion of a display device in the database. However, the functionality of the AWT we are concerned with – generating off-screen images, stored in byte buffers in memory – should very well be available. Such is usually the case with Java in server applications, for example Java Servlets on the middle tier that are used to generate custom charts and buttons. Indeed, according to the Oracle Java documentation, the Oracle JVM does have support for the off-screen parts of the AWT. For example, at http://download-west.oracle.com/otndoc/oracle9i/901_doc/java.901/a90210/01_intro.htm, it states:

*A server cannot provide GUIs, but it can supply the logic that drives them. For example, the Oracle JVM does not supply the basic GUI components found in the JDK's Abstract Windowing Toolkit (AWT). However, all AWT Java classes are available within the server environment.* **So, your programs can use AWT functionality, as long as they do not attempt to materialize a GUI on the server.**

According to this, there should be no problem in using the AWT for our desired functionality. However, in our experience, the reality is different. For example, on some versions of Oracle 8i, you will get `java.lang.UnsatisfiedLinkError` when you try to access some of the imaging functionality – an error that indicates that necessary native libraries are not at hand and though this is not a problem with 9i, using the AWT on that version will often give strange results, such as invalid graphics context for images, and so on. In addition, all of the standard imaging Java APIs we discussed earlier rely on some part of the AWT in one way or another. This means that you cannot, for example, install Java Advanced Imaging and expect that to work if the AWT is not working.

Fortunately, there is a solution to this problem. As we have already stated, one of the biggest advantages of Java in the database is the wide range of third-party and open-source components that can readily be loaded and used in your applications. Before the advent of Java, if Oracle did not come with a specific functionality, that was usually the end-of-the-road – you just had to hope that functionality would come with the next Oracle upgrade. Using Java, you can virtually take any piece of code that has already been developed, load it up and use it in the database just like any other integrated functionality. This capability can help us to overcome the limitations of the Oracle Java AWT implementation (or lack thereof). Currently, there is readily available a number of third-party AWT extensions that allow you to bypass the use of native graphics resources of the server system to some extent. In this section we will illustrate the use of one such particular extension, **PJA** or **Pure Java AWT**, which implements the off-screen functionality of the AWT using pure Java. This package is free for distribution under the GNU General Public License. We will discuss the setup and usage of PJA in more detail below.

> Note however, that even with the use of PJA, you might encounter problems on some versions of Oracle 8i. This is because even though the PJA does not make use of native resource when working with images, it does require the existence of some fundamental libraries to be compatible with the AWT framework. So, if you repeatedly get something like `java.lang.UnsatisfiedLinkError` when running your imaging procedures, that might indicate that your version of the Oracle JVM is not fit to work with graphics. Since this problem is not bound to all versions of Oracle 8i, you might try to upgrade your system to a more recent version. Since Oracle 9i does guarantee all the necessary native libraries, that is most obvious candidate for an upgrade (not to mention a lot of other performance and functionality upgrades, of course).

## Problems with UNIX Display

In order to generate off-screen images in Java, the server in question must be running a graphical display. Traditionally, when working with Java on a server with no display device (which is true for many UNIX systems), this problem can be solved by running virtual display software on the server, and setting the `DISPLAY` environment property accordingly. However, this approach will not work for Java stored procedures in Oracle, since they cannot rely on native graphical resources. As we have already stated, we need some third-party software in order by bypass those native resources in Oracle, as we will be doing below with PJA. But by using such software and thereby eliminating the need for native graphical resources, we in turn eliminate the need for a display device, so no virtual display is required for UNIX systems. Graphical display independence is a common feature of the AWT alternatives we will discuss below.

# Using the Pure Java AWT

To overcome the limitations of using AWT in the Oracle JVM, we need to install an extension that can eliminate the dependency on native graphical resources when generating images from our Java stored procedures. The extension we choose to use in this chapter is called Pure Java AWT, or PJA. PJA is a class library for drawing off-screen graphics, implemented entirely in Java (although it does require some fundamental native graphics libraries to exist, as we previously noted). PJA is developed by a company called eTeks (http://www.eteks.com/index_us.html), although it is free for distribution under the GNU Public License.

## Installation

PJA can be downloaded at http://www.eteks.com/pja/en/. The PJA archive is not available in a UNIX format (tar), so you will have to download a Zip or Sea file on your Mac or Windows workstation and transfer the files from there to your database server, if it is running UNIX.

In any case, the PJA archive that you download contains the two necessary PJA jar files, documentation and Javadoc and the PJA source code. We encourage you to browse through the documentation and Javadoc, since the information we provide in this chapter will be rather limited.

To install PJA for use in your stored procedures, you need to load the two supplied JAR files into a specific schema, and create a public synonym for each class they contain. Using loadjava, this can be accomplished as illustrated below:

```
> loadjava -user username/password@database -resolve -synonym pja.jar
> loadjava -user username/password@database -resolve -synonym pjatools.jar
```

The reason why you have to create a public synonym for these archives, is that some of the core Java classes will need to dynamically load an instance of the PJA graphics environment implementation, as we will see later. Since all core classes belong to SYS, you need the public synonym if your classes are to be found from another schema (such as the SYS schema).

Do not forget to grant the CREATE PUBLIC SYNONYM and DROP PUBLIC SYNONYM privileges to the user whose schema the PJA jar files are loaded into. The latter is necessary if you for some reason need to redeploy the Java classes to the database. When you load classes in the database that already exist, and specify the -synonym option for loadjava, existing public synonyms are dropped and recreated. If inadequate privileges are granted to the user in question, the database will issue an error when loading the classes:

```
ORA-01031: insufficient privileges
```

To grant these privileges, log on as any member of the DBA role (such as SYS) and issue the following grants:

```
SQL> grant create public synonym to username;
SQL> grant drop public synonym to username;
```

## How Does it Work?

Most graphics functions in the standard AWT, such as the methods of the `Graphics` class that we will discuss below, are implemented with native graphical functions that vary according to the operating system in question. This is true even when drawing off-screen images. While this may be perfectly acceptable in most cases, it is not when working with Java in Oracle, for reasons we stated above. Therefore, when working with graphics in our Java stored procedures, we need some means of bypassing the native functions of the AWT. This is exactly what PJA does for us. PJA implements some of the fundamental services of the AWT using pure Java, which eliminates our dependency on native graphical resources. Note, however, that PJA does not (and will never) pass Sun's `JavaPureCheck` tool test, and is therefore according to the definition not 100 percent Java The reason for this is that PJA needs to extend some of the internal Sun graphics classes, which in turn rely on native resources, as you can read about in the supplied PJA FAQ. This means that even though you use PJA to bypass the direct use of native resources in the AWT, you might encounter problems on some versions of Oracle 8i, where these libraries do not seem to be supplied, as we have already noted.

So, now we know that PJA implements some of the AWT functionality using 'pure Java'. But there are other advantages. Since the Java imaging model relies on native graphics resources, a certain problem arises when it is used on servers with no graphical display, which is traditional of UNIX machines. Traditionally, this has meant that you had to install a specific "virtual display" on the UNIX host, as we discuss in more detail below. However, using PJA, that is not necessary. Since it is written in Java, PJA can generate off-screen images without the existence of a display device – either virtual or real.

Finally, perhaps the biggest advantage of using PJA, and the reason why we have chosen to use that rather than some of its many alternatives, is that it extends the fundamental AWT class model. This means that if you have prior knowledge of working with the AWT, there is no need for you to learn anything new, since all of the standard classes, such as `java.awt.Graphics` and `java.awt.Color`, work as before.

Now that we have discussed how it works and what its advantages are, let's see how you actually use the PJA. To enable the use of PJA, instead of the supplied AWT implementation, you need only set a few system properties, which specify the behavior of the AWT. These properties are:

- ❑ `awt.toolkit` – Specifies the AWT toolkit in use; for PJA, this should equal `com.eteks.awt.PJAToolkit`.

- ❑ `java.awt.graphicsenv` – Allows the change of the `java.awt.GraphicsEnvironment` default implementation, which is necessary for servers with no graphical display, and Java stored procedures in the database in general. For PJA, this property should be set to `com.eteks.java2d.PJAGraphicsEnvironment`.

- ❑ `java.awt.fonts` – Specifies the path where True Type Fonts files will be loaded from. This property varies according to the operating system, as we will see below.

To use the PJA in your procedures, you need to set these system properties somewhere (only once per session). For example, for a database running on Windows NT/2000:

```
System.setProperty(
    "java.awt.graphicsenv",
    "com.eteks.java2d.PJAGraphicsEnvironment"
```

```
);
System.setProperty("awt.toolkit", "com.eteks.awt.PJAToolkit");
System.setProperty("java.awt.fonts", "C:\\WINNT\\Fonts");
```

The only varying property is of course the path to the True Type fonts directory. The PJA documentation contains more information how to work with fonts in the AWT. Let's provide another example of a font path, this time for the Solaris platform:

```
String solarisPath = "/usr/openwin/lib/X11/fonts/Type1:"
    + "/usr/openwin/lib/X11/fonts/TrueType";
System.setProperty("java.awt.fonts", solarisPath);
```

Note that the Oracle Java security model requires specific permissions in order to set system properties. To grant your user the necessary permissions for working with PJA, you need to issue the following grants:

```
connect sys/<sys-password>;

call dbms_java.grant_permission (
    'USERNAME',
    'java.util.PropertyPermission',
    'java.awt.graphicsenv',
    'read,write'
);

call dbms_java.grant_permission (
    'USERNAME',
    'java.util.PropertyPermission',
    'awt.toolkit',
    'read,write'
);

call dbms_java.grant_permission (
    'USERNAME',
    'java.util.PropertyPermission',
    'java.awt.fonts',
    'read,write'
);
```

## Other Alternatives

Although we will only be using the PJA to implement our examples in this section, that is not to say there are no alternatives. On the contrary, you can use any third-party imaging package with Oracle, given that it works with your respective version of the JDK (1.2 in all current releases, except Oracle 8.1.5, which uses JDK 1.1). For example, a company called Visualize Inc. (http://www.visualizeinc.com/) provides a range of imaging products for Java. One such, called JV-Pub, consists of a class library that enables you to generate various types of custom charts in your server-side Java applications, in a number of image formats. Just as PJA, JV-Pub eliminates the need for an X server when deployed on UNIX.

# Generating Images

The Java AWT packages contain a large number of graphical classes and methods. However, only a small subset of those is of any importance when creating simple off-screen images. The most fundamental of those is the abstract `Image` class. To construct an `Image` instance when using the PJA, we use a non-abstract class called `PJAImage`. In the next few paragraphs we will discuss these in more detail.

## Image Class

The abstract `Image` class represents a particular graphical image in Java. Through methods of the `Image` class, you can obtain information on the image in question, such as width and height. To draw to the image, you obtain an instance of the `Graphics` class, which we discuss in more detail below, through the `getGraphics()` method of the image. The `Image` class is abstract and must be obtained in a implementation-specific manner.

When using PJA to extend the AWT, you can construct a new image with the `com.eteks.awt.PJAImage` class, as shown here:

```
Image img = new PJAImage(width, height);
```

For more information on using the `PJAImage` class, consult the PJA documentation.

Note that you have no means of relating a new `Image` instance to a physical image file on disk or other persistent storage – not through methods of the `Image BufferedImage` class, that is. Later in this section, when we will look at methods of image encoding, we will see how you can take an off-screen image in memory and write it to a file or `BLOB` in the database.

Once you have constructed a new `Image` instance, you can draw to it through its associated `Graphics` class instance, obtained with the `getGraphics()` method inherited from the `Image`. In the next section, we will look at the `Graphics` class in more detail.

# Drawing with the Graphics Class

The `Graphics` class is the cornerstone of drawing in Java, as it provides the framework for all graphics operations. An instance of the `Graphics` class represents a particular graphics context, such as an off-screen image, a printable document or a screen. Through its methods, you can alter the properties of the graphics context in question, such as the background color, the size and location of the drawing area, the active foreground color, and the font type in use. In order to draw to a particular graphics context, you must obtain the associated `Graphics` instance. However, as `Graphics` is an abstract class, you will not able to construct an instance of it by hand. Rather, since each class that represents a graphical output device contains a reference to the graphical context in question, you must obtain a `Graphics` instance through the output class instance you are working with. For example, when working with off-screen images, you obtain a `Graphics` instance through the `getGraphics()` method of the `Image` class, as we demonstrated above.

In the next few paragraphs we will study the coordinate system and drawing methods of the `Graphics` class in more detail.

## The Graphics Coordinate System

When drawing to a particular context with the Graphics class, you specify the position of the shapes that you draw according to a two-dimensional coordinate system. Each point in the graphics context is thus identified by two factors, the x and y coordinates. However, unlike the ordinary Cartesian coordinate system you may be familiar with from algebra, the coordinate system used by the Graphics class has a reverse y-axis, so that the y-coordinates increase when you move down the axis. This is illustrated in the following figure.

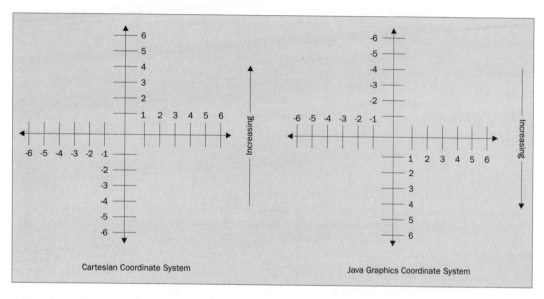

Cartesian Coordinate System

Java Graphics Coordinate System

In the Graphics coordinate system, however, coordinates never take negative values. Thus, the upper left corner of each graphics context is defined to be the coordinate (0,0). The coordinates range from 0 to *width*-1 in the x-direction, and from 0 to *height*-1 in the y-direction, as we show in the figure below.

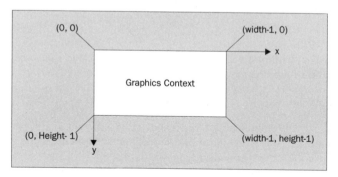

## Fonts and Colors

When drawing shapes or text to a particular graphics context with the Graphics class, you work with the font face and color currently active. To alter either the active font or color, you call the setFont() or setColor() methods of the Graphics class, respectively, supplying for arguments an instance of java.awt.Font or java.awt.Color.

**435**

### Font

The JDK 1.2 allows for very delicate methods for constructing a new Font instance. The most simple of these is to invoke one of two Font class constructors, supplying the name, style and size of the font in question. For example:

```
Font f = new Font("Serif", Font.PLAIN, 10);
```

When supplying a font name, you can either use a logical font name or a font face name. Here, we will only be using logical names, since font faces vary between operating systems. The available logical names for the Font class are:

- ❑ Dialog
- ❑ DialogInput
- ❑ Monospaced
- ❑ Serif
- ❑ SansSerif
- ❑ Symbol

The style attribute is one of the many style constants declared by the Font class, such as Font.BOLD or Font.ITALIC. The size argument declares the size of the font in question, measured in pixels.

### Color

The simplest method for constructing a custom Color instance is to supply the colors red, green and blue components, according to the RGB color model, in a Color class constructor. Each component can be in the range 0-255. For example, to construct a pure red color, you can call:

```
int r = 255;
int g = 0;
int b = 0;
Color red = new Color(r,g,b);
```

Additionally, for working with basic colors, you can instead choose to use some of the predefined Color object constants of the Color class, such as Color.blue and Color.green.

## Drawing Methods

Once you have obtained an instance of the Graphics class, representing the graphical context of an off-screen image, you can utilize its methods to draw text and shapes on to the image associated. In short, using methods of the Graphics class, you can draw:

- ❑ text
- ❑ lines
- ❑ rectangles
- ❑ polygons

- ❏ circles

- ❏ arcs

- ❏ other images

and much more. In the next few paragraphs, we will illustrate the most trivial methods of the `Graphics` class, for drawing simple shapes and text. Note that the `Graphics` class is not limited to the topics in our discussion – we will only illustrate the most fundamental drawing operations in this context, and leave it up to you to continue from there. For full information on the methods of the `Graphics` class, consult the JDK 1.2. online Javadoc documentation, at http://java.sun.com/products/jdk/1.2/docs/api/java/awt/Graphics.html.

*Note that in the examples below, we assume that **g** is an instance of Graphics, previously obtained from a BufferedImage.*

### Text

Through the `drawString()` method of the `Graphics` class, you can draw strings on a specified location in the graphics context, using the currently active font face. For example:

```
g.drawString("This is a text, at location x = 100, y = 200", 100, 200);
```

### Lines

You draw a line with the `drawLine()` method, which takes for arguments the beginning point and end point coordinates of the line in question. For example, to draw a line that stretches diagonally from the upper left corner of an image to the point (100, 200), you can call:

```
g.drawLine(0, 0, 100, 200);
```

### Rectangles

You can draw a rectangle with the `Graphics` class with two different methods, depending on whether you want your rectangle to be filled or not. To draw the outlines of a rectangle, you can issue:

```
int startx = 100;
int starty = 100;
int width = 50;
int height = 80;

g.drawRect(startx, starty, width, height);
```

Similarly, to draw a filled rectangle, you call:

```
int startx = 100;
int starty = 100;
int width = 50;
int height = 80;

g.fillRect(startx, starty, width, height);
```

**437**

## Ovals

You draw an oval, either a circle or ellipse, with `Graphics` through either one of the `drawOval()` or `fillOval()` methods, depending on whether you want a filled oval or not. Both methods take four arguments:

❑　**x** – the x-coordinate of the upper left corner of an imaginary rectangle encompassing the oval

❑　**y** – the y-coordinate of the upper left corner of an imaginary rectangle encompassing the oval

❑　**width** – the width of the oval

❑　**height** – the height of the oval

The meaning of these arguments is further illustrated in the following diagram:

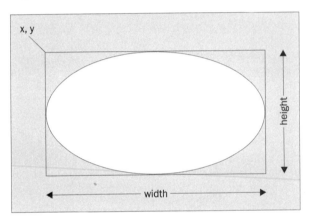

For example, to draw a yellow circle, 100 pixels in diameter, with a red outline, you could run:

```
int x = 0;
int y = 0;
int width = 100;
int height = 100;
g.setColor(Color.yellow);
g.fillOval(x, y, width, height);
g.setColor(Color.red);
g.drawOval(x, y, width, height);
```

## Arcs

It can often be useful to work with isolated arcs or filled circle slices when drawing images, as we will see later in this chapter, as we develop a stored procedure for generating custom pie charts. Some thought must be given before you start drawing arcs, however. Both the `drawArc()` and `fillArc()` take five arguments, which are:

❑　**x** – the x-coordinate of the upper left corner of an imaginary rectangle encompassing the circle on which the arc lies

- ❑ **y** – the y-coordinate of the upper left corner of an imaginary rectangle encompassing the circle on which the arc lies

- ❑ **width** – the width of the circle on which the arc lies

- ❑ **height** – the height of the circle on which the arc lies

- ❑ **start angle** – the angle at which the angle starts

- ❑ **arc angle** – the number of degrees the arc spans

The start angle specified is interpreted so that zero degrees is at the 3 o'clock position, and a positive value indicates a counter-clockwise rotation and vice versa. Both the arc angle and the start angle are specified in degrees (in other words, not radians). The following figure illustrates an arc which starts at angle 90° and stretches on for another 90 degrees.

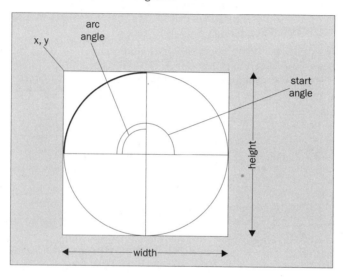

To draw a corresponding angle (using some arbitrary values for width, height and position), you can issue:

```
int x = 0;
int y = 0;
int width = 100;
int height = 100;
g.drawArc(x, y, width, height, 90, 90);
```

The `fillArc()` method works as `drawArc()`, except that it fills a sector delimited by the arc and lines lying from the center of the circle to each end of the arc, with the currently active color. We will use this method extensively later, when we draw pie charts.

### Further Drawing Methods

In previous paragraphs, we have illustrated a few of the fundamental drawing methods of the `Graphics` class. We have, however, just scratched the surface of the `Graphics` class drawing capabilities. For example, this class additionally has support for drawing polygons, clipping and merging images, which we encourage you to study further.

# Image Encoding

Once we have constructed a new instance of Image, and drawn to its graphics context through the associated Graphics instance, we must take measures to somehow export the image to a particular image format, in order to use it. Of the various image formats available, the two most related to the types of images we are concerned with are the GIF and JPEG image formats. Each of those is suited for different purposes. JPEG suits best for complex, multi-colored images, such as photographs, while GIF is better suited for images with few colors and little variation, such as charts and buttons.

However, there is no built-in image encoder with the Oracle JVM. Traditional Sun JVMs ship with a Sun-specific JPEG encoder and decoder implementations, which are unfortunately not available for Oracle. There is, however, a big selection of free or open-source encoder implementations available, so this is usually not a problem. Below, we will illustrate one such particular, which we will be using in our examples.

## Using the ACME Encoders

ACME Laboratories, http://www.acme.com/, provides a number a free, open-source image encoder and decoder implementations, for such image formats as GIF, JPEG and PPM. These implementation are simple to install and even more simple to use. In addition, both the ACME GIF and JPEG encoders automatically ship with the PJA JAR files we have previously discussed – so if you choose to use PJA, no additional setup is required!

> **This is yet another advantage of using PJA – only one package has to be installed, along with image encoders and everything.**

### Installing ACME

If you are not using PJA in your procedures, but you still want to install the ACME encoders, you can download the whole ACME Java software library from http://www.acme.com/resources/classes/Acme.tar.gz. This URL points to an archive that has been compiled using UNIX tar and gzip. Even though there is no WinZip version available, you can fortunately open a tar.gz archive using all recent versions of WinZip. If you are using UNIX, you can extract the archive by issuing:

```
gunzip Acme.tar.gz
tar -xvf Acme.tar
```

This will create a directory called Acme, with the source and class files of the ACME library. Using Windows, you can simply double-click the downloaded archive. Doing that, you should get a prompt like the one shown here:

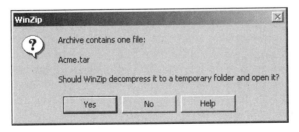

By pressing **Yes**, you should be able to extract the archive contents to a location of your choice. This too will create a folder called `Acme`, with all the source and class files.

In most cases when creating custom images with Java, at least the source of images we will be doing in this chapter, it is most appropriate to use the GIF image compression. Additionally, we will not need to decode images; so just uploading the GIF encoder will suffice (for your own application, feel free to experiment with the `Acme` classes).

To load the classes necessary for a GIF encoder, follow the steps below (assuming you are in the subfolder of the extracted `Acme` folder). On a Windows platform, issue:

```
> cd Acme\JPM\Encoders
> loadjava -user username/password@database -resolve ImageEncoder.java

> cd ..\..\
> loadjava -user username/password@database -resolve IntHashtable.java

> cd JPM\Encoders
> loadjava -user username/password@database -resolve GifEncoder.java
```

### Using the ACME GIF Encoder

Once you have uploaded the ACME GIF encoder classes into your database schema, either directly or indirectly with the PJA JAR files, you can encode your custom images. In order to do so, you must have a valid output stream to a persistent resource, such as a file. In the example below, we assume that such a stream has already been initialized. Later in this section, we will provide a more robust example, as we illustrate how to write images to `BLOB` fields in the database.

```java
import java.io.*;
import java.awt.*;
import java.awt.image.*;
import com.eteks.awt.*;
import Acme.JPM.Encoders.GifEncoder;

...

OutputStream out;
// Obtain output stream.

// Construct and encode the image.
Image img = new PJAImage(300, 300);
img.getGraphics().drawString("Sample image", 10, 10);
GifEncoder encoder = new GifEncoder(img, out);
encoder.encode();
out.flush();
out.close();
```

By flushing and closing the stream, we will effectively write the image to the target destination.

**441**

# Constructing Images in Oracle

Now that we have illustrated generally how we can generate images with Java, how can we use that knowledge when working with the database? Ideally, we would like to implement a generic Java class that would allow us to generate custom images from a given input. Such input will almost always come from tables in the database. Therefore, we have a few options when it comes to implementing such a client:

- ❑ Write a specific Java class for each image type, and have it read from the database how the image should be drawn.

- ❑ Write a general Java class that takes for argument the necessary attributes of the image.

Although the latter method may be more general, it is much easier to encapsulate the graphics logic in a specific type of class. However, to allow for some customization, we can easily implement simple setter methods for the manipulation of colors, fonts, and similar, instead of using a single static method, with a large collection of input arguments. Such a method will always limit our manipulation of the image, and cause problems when more arguments have to be added.

> *This would more easily be done with general method that adds arguments to a collection. For example assume a method called* addColor() *in a class that draws line charts. Such a method would allow us to specify colors for an arbitrary number of data sets, rather than assuming only, for example, one or two possible sets.*

However, a common problem with working with Java classes in the database is that PL/SQL can only work with static Java methods, not objects. It is generally not feasible to have setter methods work on static variables – imagine for example what happens if you work with two images simultaneously. Setting an attribute for one image would immediately overwrite the similar value for the other one.

A particular solution to this problem, which we will employ in our examples below, is to define a class with static methods that transparently work, with a collection of objects behind the scenes. Through static methods of such a class, we can silently look up an object corresponding to some specified identifier, and pass the method call on the object. That way, we can maintain state between method calls from the PL/SQL context, and thereby use standard Java mutator and accessor methods to set image and graphics properties.

For example, assume we have a class like the following:

```
public class MyImage {

  private static Color activeColor;
  private static BufferedImage img;
  private static Graphics g;

  public static void setActiveColor(int r, int g, int b) {
    activeColor = new Color(r, g, b);
  }

  // More methods...
}
```

Now, if you are simultaneously working with two images, and call setActiveColor() for each, the latter call will overwrite the value set with the prior call. A solution to this is to use static wrapper methods, like those shown here:

```java
import java.util.Hashtable;

public class MyImage {

    private Color activeColor;
    private BufferedImage img;
    private Graphics g;
    private static long sequence = 0;
    private static Hashtable images = new Hashtable();

    public static long createImage() {
        Long imageID = new Long(sequence++);
        images.put(imageID, new MyImage());
        return imageID.longValue();
    }

    // Static method.
    public static void setActiveColor(long imageID, int r, int g, int b) {
        ((MyImage) images.get(new Long(imageID))).setActiveColor(r, g, b);
    }

    // Instance method.
    private void setActiveColor(int r, int g, int b) {
        activeColor = new Color(r, g, b);
    }

    // More methods...

}
```

Using this class, a client obtains an image ID with a call to the createImage() method, which initializes a MyImage object and stores it in a hash table. The client must store the associated image ID, and use it in every call to the static methods of the MyImage class. Each such method looks up a matching MyImage instance, and delegates its call to the corresponding instance method.

Of course, there is nothing in this that prevents clients from using a wrong image ID in a call to static methods. However, we can reduce that possibility, and make the image handling more transparent at the same time, by declaring a corresponding PL/SQL object type, which stores the ID locally. For example:

```sql
SQL> create or replace function wrap_create_image
  2  return number
  3  as language java
  4  name 'MyImage.createImage() return long';
  5  /

SQL> create or replace procedure wrap_set_active_color (
  2     image_id in number,
```

```
   3     r in number,
   4     g in number,
   5     b in number
   6   )
   7   as language java
   8   name 'MyImage.setActiveColor(long,int,int,int)';
   9   /

SQL> create or replace type MyImage
   2   as object (
   3   image_id number,
   4     static function create_image return MyImage,
   5     member procedure set_active_color (
   6     r in number,
   7     g in number,
   8     b in number
   9   )
  10  );
  11  /

SQL> create or replace type body MyImage
   2   as
   3     static function create_image
   4   return MyImage
   5     is
   6     begin
   7       return MyImage(wrap_create_image());
   8     end;
   9     member procedure set_active_color (
  10      r in number,
  11      g in number,
  12      b in number
  13    )
  14    is
  15    begin
  16      wrap_set_active_color(image_id,r,g,b);
  17    end;
  18  end;
  19  /
```

We will illustrate this design pattern more closely in the next section, where we develop an application for generating pie charts from a custom SQL query.

# Generating a Pie Chart from a Query

In this section, we will illustrate a particular use of the methods we have discussed in this section, by implementing a simple Java class for generating a pie chart GIF image from a custom SQL query, and corresponding PL/SQL procedures and objects. In short, our application consists of the PieChart Java class, which makes use of PJA and the ACME GIF encoder we set up earlier to encode a custom pie chart image, and write it to a supplied BLOB locator. The PieChart class follows the same design pattern we illustrated in the previous section, that is, by maintaining objects in a static hash table, and using static methods as wrappers for corresponding instance methods.

For mapping the `PieChart` class methods to PL/SQL procedures, we use a specific package, `UTL_PIECHART`. However, we never use this package directly, as we will define a specific PL/SQL type that encapsulates a particular `PieChart` Java instance. These components are further illustrated in the following figure:

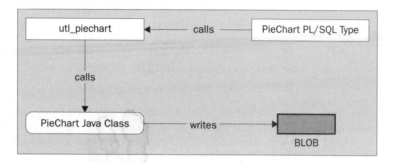

## PieChart Java Class

Each `PieChart` instance encapsulates the properties of a particular pie chart. All of the `PieChart` instance methods are private – you access a particular instance through static wrapper methods, as we illustrated above. When a new `PieChart` instance has been created, you can alter its properties through a few setter methods, although all charts follow the same fundamental layout (in your own application, you might allow for more customization). This basic layout is illustrated in the diagram below:

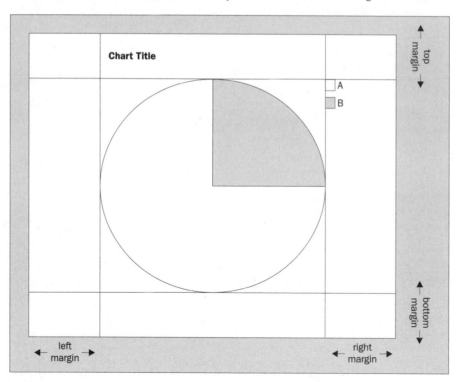

The application can alter the following attributes of a pie chart:

❑   chart title

❑   pie slice colors

❑   background color

❑   foreground color

However, all these attributes have default values, so no explicit settings are needed (except for the chart title, which should describe the chart).

To actually draw the chart, you invoke the generate() method of the PieChart class. This method takes for arguments a custom SQL query string and a BLOB locator instance. By executing the query, the generate() method draws a pie chart from the results and writes them out to the supplied BLOB locator. We will illustrate this in more detail below.

### Declarations

You should alter the default margin and font size values for your own implementation.

```
package com.wrox.image;

import java.sql.*;
import java.util.*;
import java.io.*;
import java.awt.*;
import java.awt.image.*;
import Acme.JPM.Encoders.GifEncoder;
import oracle.sql.BLOB;
import oracle.jdbc.driver.*;
import com.eteks.awt.*;

public class PieChart {

    // Class variables.
    private static Connection conn;
    private static long c = 0;
    private static Hashtable charts;
    private static final int type = BufferedImage.TYPE_INT_RGB;
    private static final int BORDER = 10;
    private static final int LEFT_MARGIN = 50;
    private static final int RIGHT_MARGIN = 100;
    private static final int BOTTOM_MARGIN = 50;
    private static final int TOP_MARGIN = 100;

    // Instance variables.
    private Color bgColor;
    private Color fgColor;
    private Graphics g;
    private Image img;
    private int height;
```

```
private int width;
private int graphHeight;
private int graphWidth;
private int sum;
private int radius;
private int[] data;
private String title = "No title specified";
private String[] labels;
private Vector colors = new Vector();
```

### Constructor

A new `PieChart` instance is constructed from the width and height attributes of the resulting image. The `PieChart` constructor constructs a new `BufferedImage` and stores its `Graphics` instance locally.

```
private PieChart(int width, int height) {
   this.width = width;
   this.height = height;
   graphHeight = height - TOP_MARGIN - BOTTOM_MARGIN;
   graphWidth = width - LEFT_MARGIN - RIGHT_MARGIN;
   radius = Math.min(graphHeight, graphWidth) / 2;
   img = new PJAImage(width, height);
   g = img.getGraphics();
   bgColor = Color.white;
   fgColor = Color.black;
}
```

### Creating a Chart

A new `PieChart` instance is created with the static `createChart()` method. This method returns a chart identified which is used when altering the chart properties. In this method, we set the system properties required for the PJA, as we have previously discussed.

> Note that you need to alter the path to the fonts directory for your own system, as we have mentioned before.

```
public static long createChart(int width, int height) throws Exception {

   // Initialize properties.
   if (charts == null) {
      charts = new Hashtable();
      System.setProperty("awt.toolkit", "com.eteks.awt.PJAToolkit");
      System.setProperty(
        "java.awt.graphicsenv",
        + "com.eteks.java2d.PJAGraphicsEnvironment"
      );

      // Change this for your own system!
      System.setProperty("java.awt.fonts", "C:\\WINNT\\Fonts");
```

```
        }

        try {
            Long chartID = new Long(c++);
            charts.put(chartID, new PieChart(width,height));
            return chartID.longValue();
        } catch (Error e) {
            e.printStackTrace();
            throw e;
        }
    }
```

## Adding Custom Colors

The addColor() method adds a custom color to the chart's collection of colors. When generating the chart, the generate() method checks this collection for colors, and if none exist, it uses the default colors.

```
public static void addColor(long chartID, int r, int g, int b) {
    ((PieChart) charts.get(new Long(chartID))).addColor(r, g, b);
}

    private void addColor(int r, int g, int b) {
        colors.add(new Color(r, g, b));
    }
```

## Altering Chart Properties

The following setter methods alter some of the pie chart properties, as we have discussed before.

```
public static void setBackgroundColor(long chartID, int r, int g, int b) {
    ((PieChart) charts.get(new Long(chartID))).setBackgroundColor(r, g, b);
}

private void setBackgroundColor(int r, int g, int b) {
    bgColor = new Color(r, g, b);
}

public static void setForegroundColor(long chartID, int r, int g, int b) {
    ((PieChart) charts.get(new Long(chartID))).setForegroundColor(r, g, b);
}

    private void setForegroundColor(int r, int g, int b) {
        fgColor = new Color(r,g,b);
    }

public static void setTitle(long chartID, String title) {
    ((PieChart) charts.get(new Long(chartID))).setTitle(title);
}

    private void setTitle(String title) {
    this.title = title;
}
```

### Initializing the Chart

The init() and drawTitle() methods initialize the chart's graphics properties. These are called from the generate() method, below.

```
private void init() {
  g.setColor(bgColor);
  g.fillRect(0, 0, width, height);
  g.setColor(fgColor);
  drawTitle();
}


private void drawTitle() {
  g.drawString(title, LEFT_MARGIN, TOP_MARGIN / 2);
}
```

### Generating the Chart

When all properties have been set, you call the generate() method, supplying a custom SQL query and the destination BLOB locator to which the image should be written. Some assumptions are made of the SQL query supplied, namely:

❏   The result set must contain only two columns

❏   The first column should be the label of a particular pie sector

❏   The second column should be the associated sector value

Invalid queries will cause an exception to be thrown.

```
private void generate(String query, BLOB blob) throws Exception {
  init();

  // Initialize database resources.
  if (conn == null) {
    conn = DriverManager.getConnection("jdbc:oracle:kprb:@");
  }
```

When executing the query, the generate() method first evaluates how many rows it returns, in order to initialize data arrays. It does so by using a scrollable resultset.

```
PreparedStatement pstmt = conn.prepareStatement(
  query,
  ResultSet.TYPE_SCROLL_INSENSITIVE,
  ResultSet.CONCUR_READ_ONLY
);
try {
  ResultSet rs = pstmt.executeQuery();
  if (rs.last()) {
    data = new int[rs.getRow()];
    labels = new String[rs.getRow()];
    sum = 0;
```

```
        rs.beforeFirst();
        for (int i = 0; rs.next(); i++) {
          labels[i] = rs.getString(1);
          data[i] = rs.getInt(2);
          sum += data[i];
        }
      }
      rs.close();
    }
    finally {
      pstmt.close();
    }
```

When all data has been fetched, we generate the pie and consequently draw its legend. We will discuss that process in more detail below.

```
      drawPie();
      drawLegend();
```

When the pie has been constructed, we obtain an output stream to the supplied BLOB locator and write the image contents, GIF-encoded, to the stream.

```
      BufferedOutputStream out =
        new BufferedOutputStream(blob.getBinaryOutputStream());
      GifEncoder encoder = new GifEncoder(img, out);
      encoder.encode();
      out.flush();
      out.close();
    }
```

## Drawing the Chart

The drawPie() method draws the pie chart from the supplied input values. It does so by using the fillArc() method we have discussed before.

```
    private void drawPie() {

      Color defaultColor = Color.yellow;
      int startAngle = 0;
      int arcAngle;
      for (int i = 0; i < data.length; i++) {

        // Set the active color.
        if (colors.size() > i) {
          g.setColor((Color) colors.elementAt(i));
        } else {
          defaultColor = defaultColor.lighter();
          g.setColor(defaultColor);
        }
        arcAngle = (360 * data[i]) / sum;
        g.fillArc(LEFT_MARGIN, TOP_MARGIN,
```

```
        2 * radius, 2 * radius,
        startAngle, arcAngle
      );
      startAngle += arcAngle;
    }
  g.setColor(fgColor);
}
```

### Drawing the Chart Legend

When we have drawn the pie chart, we draw a legend to the right of the chart, using the supplied labels.

```
private void drawLegend() {

  Color defaultColor = Color.yellow;
  int x = width - RIGHT_MARGIN;
  int y = TOP_MARGIN;
  int offset = 10;
  for (int i=0; i < labels.length; i++) {

    // Set the active color.
    if (colors.size() > i) {
      g.setColor((Color) colors.elementAt(i));
    } else {
      defaultColor = defaultColor.lighter();
      g.setColor(defaultColor);
    }

    // Draw a small rectangle.
    g.fillRect(x,y,offset,offset);
    g.setColor(fgColor);
    g.drawRect(x,y,offset,offset);

    // Draw the label.
    g.drawString(labels[i], x + 2*offset,y + offset);

    y += 2*offset;
  }
 }
}
```

## Loading the PieChart Class

Once we have written the `PieChart` class, we must load it into the database. This can be accomplished with `loadjava`, as illustrated here:

```
>loadjava -user username/password@database -resolve PieChart.java
```

## UTL_PIECHART PL/SQL Package

For publishing the static methods of the `PieChart` class, we define a specific PL/SQL package, `UTL_PIECHART`.

### Package Header

The UTL_PIECHART package header is illustrated below:

```
SQL> create or replace package utl_piechart
  2  is
  3    function create_chart (
  4      width in number,
  5      height in number
  6    ) return number;
  7    procedure add_color (
  8      chart_id in number,
  9      r in number,
 10      g in number,
 11      b in number
 12    );
 13    procedure set_background_color (
 14      chart_id in number,
 15      r in number,
 16      g in number,
 17      b in number
 18    );
 19    procedure set_foreground_color (
 20      chart_id in number,
 21      r in number,
 22      g in number,
 23      b in number
 24    );
 25    procedure set_title (
 26      chart_id in number,
 27      title in varchar2
 28    );
 29    procedure generate (
 30      chart_id in number,
 31      query in varchar2,
 32      dest_blob in blob
 33    );
 34  end;
 35  /
```

The UTL_PIECHART package body is straightforward. Each procedure and function in the body publishes a corresponding method in the PieChart Java class. We have omitted the package body in these pages, but on the Wrox website (http://www.wrox.com/) you can download the full package declaration, along with the body.

## PieChart PL/SQL Type

Ideally, when using the PieChart class from PL/SQL, we would like to access its "setter" methods without having to worry about the chart ID in question. Previously in this section, we discussed an alternative method for doing that, by creating a specific PL/SQL type which would encapsulate a single PieChart Java class instance. Below, we define a corresponding PieChart PL/SQL type.

### Type Header

The `PieChart` type header is shown below. It stores the chart ID as a member variable. To construct a new `PieChart` instance, you use the static `CREATE_CHART()` function, as we will show below:

```
SQL> create or replace type PieChart
  2  as object (
  3     chart_id number,
  4     static function create_chart (
  5        width in number,
  6        height in number
  7     ) return PieChart,
  8     member procedure generate (
  9        query in varchar2,
 10        dest_blob in blob
 11     ),
 12     member procedure add_color (
 13        r in number,
 14        g in number,
 15        b in number
 16     ),
 17     member procedure set_background_color (
 18        r in number,
 19        g in number,
 20        b in number
 21     ),
 22     member procedure set_foreground_color (
 23        r in number,
 24        g in number,
 25        b in number
 26     ),
 27     member procedure set_title (
 28        title in varchar2
 29     )
 30  );
 31  /
```

### Type Body

The `PieChart` type body is shown below. Each member method calls the corresponding `UTL_PIECHART` procedure, using the stored chart ID.

```
SQL> create or replace type body PieChart
  2  as
  3      static function create_chart (
  4          width in number,
  5          height in number
  6      ) return PieChart
  7      is
  8      begin
  9          return PieChart(utl_piechart.create_chart(width,height));
 10      end;
```

```
11        member procedure generate (
12              query in varchar2,
13              dest_blob in blob
14        )
15        is
16        begin
17              utl_piechart.generate(chart_id,query,dest_blob);
18        end;
19        member procedure add_color (
20              r in number,
21              g in number,
22              b in number
23        )
24        is
25        begin
26              utl_piechart.add_color(chart_id,r,g,b);
27        end;
28        member procedure set_background_color (
29              r in number,
30              g in number,
31              b in number
32        )
33        is
34        begin
35              utl_piechart.set_background_color(chart_id,r,g,b);
36        end;
37        member procedure set_foreground_color (
38              r in number,
39              g in number,
40              b in number
41        )
42        is
43        begin
44              utl_piechart.set_foreground_color(chart_id,r,g,b);
45        end;
46        member procedure set_title (
47              title in varchar2
48        )
49        is
50        begin
51              utl_piechart.set_title(chart_id,title);
52        end;
53   end;
54   /
```

## Using the Application

Now that we have created all the components for your pie chart image generator, it is time to test its functionality. For example, assume we have a database table for storing images, as declared below:

```
SQL> create table images (
  2      image_id number,
  3      image_value blob,
  4      constraint pk_images primary key (image_id)
  5  );
```

Now, we need a query to generate our chart. Using already available tables, we could, for example, select:

```
SQL> select owner, count(*) from all_objects group by owner;
```

and get a list of database users, along with the number of database objects that belongs to them. To use this query to generate a chart, we could run the following:

```
SQL> declare
  2     pc PieChart := PieChart.create_chart(300,500);
  3      id number := 1;
  4      image_loc blob;
  5  begin
  6     -- Prepare the BLOB record.
  7     insert into images values (id, empty_blob());
  8     select image_value
  9       into image_loc
 10       from images
 11      where image_id = id;
 12     -- Construct the chart.
 13     -- Use a light gray background color.
 14     pc.set_background_color(230, 230, 230);
 15     pc.set_title('Objects created by Owner');
 16     pc.generate(
 17       'select owner, count(*) from all_objects group by owner',
 18       image_loc
 19     );
 20     commit;
 21  end;
 22  /
```

That's all it takes to generate a pie chart! In your own, real-life applications, you might want to use code similar to the following to generate charts for various statistics. By using triggers and database jobs (through the DBMS_JOB package) you can easily make sure that information gets dynamically updated, either instantly as your data gets changed or at regular intervals. We will explore further uses of dynamic images at the end of this chapter, when we illustrate the pie chart application in conjunction with our custom SMTP mail client.

## Viewing Generated Images

When you have generated an image, and verified that some content has been added to the BLOB locator supplied, you probably want to view the results. In the next chapter, we will illustrate the use of Java to work with operating system resources, such as files. Specifically, we will in that chapter implement a simple stored procedure that allows you to write a given BLOB to a file in the database server file system. Another alternative to viewing the images, especially if you do not have direct access to the Oracle server file system, is to have a stored procedure send them to you as a mail attachment. We will illustrate that at the end of this section, after we have implemented our JavaMail mail client.

# Sending e-Mail Messages from the Database

Sending e-mail messages is a very common procedure in Oracle database applications. Such applications commonly deal with customer- or client-related business information, and may from time to time have to contact or notify the clients or customers in question. In doing that, it is much more feasible to integrate with a mail transport component that operates within the boundaries of the database, rather than having to reach out and interact with OS-specific programs and utilities.

When working with the Oracle database, you have two choices when it comes to sending e-mail messages from your stored procedures. You can either use the built-in PL/SQL package UTL_SMTP, if you are using Oracle version 8.1.6 or later, or you can implement your own package by using the JavaMail API, which is the standard e-mail extension for Java. In many cases, it is sufficient to use UTL_SMTP. However, there may be times where a custom mail transport application built using Java is either more simple to use or more efficient than one implemented on top of UTL_SMTP. At the end of this section, we will illustrate this further when we implement a PL/SQL package, which uses JavaMail to send messages that can take a BLOB locator for an attachment.

## The UTL_SMTP Package

The standard UTL_SMTP PL/SQL package, which was first introduced with Oracle 8.1.6, provides functionality for sending e-mail messages over SMTP (Simple Mail Transport Protocol) from the database. In Oracle 8i, UTL_SMTP was implemented on top of the UTL_TCP package, which was in turn implemented with Java sockets. As a result, in order to use UTL_SMTP in Oracle 8i, you must make sure that you have installed and enabled the Oracle JVM. In Oracle 9i, UTL_TCP is implemented using native sockets, so both that package and UTL_SMTP are independent of Java.

Although it can often be sufficient to use UTL_SMTP when sending e-mail messages from the database, there are a number of reasons why you should choose JavaMail instead. Firstly, JavaMail hides from you the details of the underlying MIME message structure, which is not true for UTL_SMTP. With UTL_SMTP, each e-mail message has to be constructed according to the RFC822 Internet specification, which most people are not familiar with. For example, consider the following code snippet, which constructs a simple message using UTL_SMTP:

```
declare
    mail_host varchar2(30) := 'mail.myhost.com';
    mail_conn utl_smtp.connection;
    message varchar2(1000);
    frm varchar2(100) := 'myself@myhost.com';
    t varchar2(100) := 'you@yourhost.com';
    subject varchar2(100) := 'This is a subject line';
    body varchar2(100) := 'This is message body';
    crlf char(2) := chr(13) || chr(10);

begin
    mail_conn := utl_smtp.open_connection(mailhost, 25);

    -- Construct the message.
    message := '' ||
        'Date: ' || to_char(sysdate, 'dd Mon yy hh24:mi:ss') || crlf ||
```

```
         'From:  ' || frm || crlf ||
         'Subject: ' || subject || crlf ||
         'To: ' || t || crlf ||
         body;

    -- Send the message.
    utl_smtp.helo(mail_conn, mail_host);
    utl_smtp.mail(mail_conn, frm);
    utl_smtp.rcpt(mail_conn, t);
    utl_smtp.data(mail_conn, message);
    utl_smtp.quit(mail_conn);
end;
/
```

Now, even though this example did not take up many lines of code, you may have noticed all the trouble we had to go through just in order to correctly format the message. The whole message had to be supplied as a single string, where each line was terminated by a <CR><LF> sequence, as required by the RFC821 specification. A corresponding example, using JavaMail, is illustrated below:

```
String mailhost = "mail.myhost.com";
String from = "myself@myhost.com";
String to = "you@yourhost.com";
String subject = "This is a subject line";
String body = "This is message body";

System.getProperties().put("mail.smtp.host",host);
Session session = Session.getInstance(System.getProperties(),null);

// Construct the message.
MimeMessage message = new MimeMessage(session);
message.setFrom(new InternetAddress(from));
message.setRecipients(Message.RecipientType.TO,InternetAddress.parse(to));
message.setSubject(subject);
message.setText(body);
message.setSentDate(new Date());

// Send the message.
Transport.send(message);
```

Instead of constructing the message by hand, by joining individual message parts in a single string, we used specific methods to specify each part of the message. This makes the code more readable and less prone to errors.

When using attachments with UTL_SMTP, things get even more complex. In that case, each file must be identified with a specific MIME header, followed by the file contents. For example:

```
file_name varchar2(100);

...
```

**457**

```
message := '' ||
    'Date: ' || to_char(sysdate, 'dd Mon yy hh24:mi:ss') || crlf ||
    'From: ' || from || crlf ||
    'Subject: ' || subject || crlf ||
    'To: ' || to || crlf ||
    'Mime-Version: 1.0' || crlf ||
    'Content-Type: multipart/mixed; '' ||
    'boundary="DMW.Boundary.605592476"' || crlf ||
    '--DMW.Boundary.605592476' || crlf ||
    'Content-Type: text/plain; name="message.txt"; ' ||
    'charset=US-ASCII' || crlf ||
    'Content-Disposition: inline; filename="message.txt"' || crlf ||
    'Content-Transfer-Encoding: 7bit' || crlf ||
    '' || crlf ||
    body || crlf ||
    '--DMW.Boundary.605592476' || crlf ||
    'Content-Type: application/octet-stream; name="' ||
    file_name || '"' || crlf ||
    'Content-Disposition: attachment; filename="' ||
    file_name || '"' || crlf ||
    'Content-Transfer-Encoding: 7bit' || crlf || crlf;

-- Append the file contents.

...
```

You get the point. Not only does this make the code obscure to read, it also makes it more vulnerable to changes and thus more likely to cause errors. This is not the case with JavaMail, where sending file attachments is trivial:

```
File f;

...

Multipart mp = new MimeMultipart();
MimeBodyPart mtxt = new MimeBodyPart();
mtxt.setText(text);
mp.addBodyPart(mtxt);

// Attach the file.
MimeBodyPart attachment = new MimeBodyPart();
FileDataSource fds = new FileDataSource(f);
attachment.setDataHandler(new DataHandler(new FileDataSource(f)));
attachment.setFileName(fds.getName());
mp.addBodyPart(attachment);
message.setContent(mp);

...
```

So, to conclude, we say that one of the advantages of using JavaMail rather than UTL_SMTP is simplicity – especially when working with file attachments (this is probably not a big issue when not dealing with attachments). Another advantage of JavaMail is that is much more general than UTL_SMTP, which, as the name implies, is only useful for sending e-mail over the SMTP protocol. JavaMail, on the other hand, is a general-use messaging specification, which can be implemented for any type of protocol. In fact, the JavaMail distribution we will be working with in our examples below does include support for other protocols than SMTP, such as POP3. This could allow us to implement a **mail store** within the database. The advantages of storing messages in database tables, rather than flat files which is more traditional, are obvious, since that would allow us to more easily search through and filter the message contents. Furthermore, by using interMedia to index the message tables, we could also categorize and search through file attachment, in addition to the actual message subject and body.

We could easily devote a whole chapter to the JavaMail subject alone. However, in this section, we are mainly interested in using JavaMail for mail transport over SMTP, since that reflects the vast majority of database messaging applications.

# JavaMail

The JavaMail specification provides a collection of abstract classes that model a mail system. The API provides a platform and protocol independent framework to build Java technology-based mail and messaging applications.

While the JavaMail abstract classes and interfaces are not directly usable (due to their abstract nature), it is up to the mail providers implementing the API to provide the functionality needed to communicate with specific protocols. Actually, implementations for the most commonly used mail protocols, including SMTP (Simple Mail Transport Protocol), POP3 (Post Office Protocol 3), IMAP (Internet Message Access Protocol) and MIME (Multipurpose Internet Mail Extensions), are available for download from Sun, in addition to various other third-party implementations.

Mail services are divided into two categories: **transport** and **storage**. Transport services have the capability of delivering messages to a specified destination, such as mailboxes, where it is the role of the storage services to keep track of all incoming and outgoing deliveries. The most commonly used transport protocol is the SMTP protocol, while the POP3 and IMAP protocols are probably the most widely used mail protocols for storing. Using supplemented or custom implementations of the JavaMail interfaces, allows applications to access these various message protocols in virtually the same manner.

## Installation

Currently, JavaMail is not included in any standard distribution of the Java Runtime or Development Kit, including the Oracle Java runtime environment. The implementation distribution has to be downloaded separately from Sun's JavaMail page, at http://java.sun.com/products/javamail/. The distribution archive contains lots of documentation and examples, in addition to the mail.jar archive, which contains the actual class files. The JavaMail distribution archive includes implementations of the core JavaMail API packages as well as implementations of the IMAP, POP3, and SMTP transport service providers, as we have already mentioned.

In addition to the core `mail.jar` archive, you will also need the JavaBeans Activation Framework (JAF) extension, in order to use JavaMail. This extension consists of the `activation.jar` file, which includes the `javax.activation` package. This archive is available for download at http://java.sun.com/beans/glasgow/jaf.html. Just as the JavaMail archive, the `activation.jar` file ships in an archive containing lots of supplementary content, which is not directly required for the setup of JavaMail.

> *We did mention previously that the* `UTL_SMTP` *package was implemented with Java in Oracle 8i. However, it was not implemented on top of JavaMail, but Java sockets, which explains the absence of JavaMail in the Oracle Java runtime environment.*

### Loading JavaMail into the Database

Before you can start to use JavaMail in your Oracle applications, you must load the `mail.jar` and `activation.jar` libraries into the database. When using Oracle 8.1.5, special care must be taken, since the aforementioned libraries use compression, which will cause problems on that database version. On that platform, you must unpack and repack the files **without compression**. This is how you can do it on the UNIX platform:

> *Note that we must remove the* `MANIFEST.MF` *file since the* `jar` *command will attempt to write its own manifest file.*

```
$ jar xvf activation.jar
$ rm activation.jar
$ rm META-INF/MANIFEST.MF
$ jar cf0 activation.jar META-INF javax com
$ rm -rf META-INF javax com
$ jar xvf mail.jar
$ rm mail.jar
$ rm META-INF/MANIFEST.MF
$ jar cf0 mail.jar META-INF javax com
$ rm -rf META-INF javax com
```

And this is how you do it on Windows:

```
> jar xvf activation.jar
 extracted: META-INF/MANIFEST.MF
   created: META-INF/
 extracted: META-INF/mailcap.default
 extracted: META-INF/mimetypes.default
   created: javax/
   created: javax/activation/
 extracted: javax/activation/ActivationDataFlavor.class
       .              .
       .              .
       .              .
 extracted: com/sun/activation/viewers/ImageViewerCanvas.class
 extracted: com/sun/activation/viewers/TextEditor.class
 extracted: com/sun/activation/viewers/TextViewer.class
```

```
> del activation.jar
> del META-INF\MANIFEST.MF
> jar cf0 activation.jar META-INF javax com
> del META-INF javax com
>\META-INF\*, Are you sure (Y/N)? y
>\javax\*, Are you sure (Y/N)? y
>\*, Are you sure (Y/N)? y

> jar xvf mail.jar
extracted: META-INF/MANIFEST.MF
  created: META-INF/
extracted: META-INF/javamail.default.providers
   .             .
   .             .
   .             .
created: com/sun/mail/handlers/
extracted: com/sun/mail/handlers/text_html.class
extracted: com/sun/mail/handlers/text_plain.class
extracted: com/sun/mail/handlers/text_xml.class
extracted: com/sun/mail/handlers/multipart_mixed.class
extracted: com/sun/mail/handlers/message_rfc822.class

> del mail.jar
> del META-INF\MANIFEST.MF
> jar cf0 mail.jar META-INF javax com
> del META-INF javax com


\meta-inf\*, Are you sure (Y/N)? y
\javax\*, Are you sure (Y/N)? y
\com\*, Are you sure (Y/N)? y
```

Once you have repacked the JAR files, you can load them into the database, for example by using `loadjava`. Again, special concern must be taken with Oracle 8.1.5, since the classes contained by these archived are protected from non-dba users in version 8.1.5 (that is classes in the `javax.*` packages). Therefore, using 8.1.5, you must load the archives into the SYS schema, and use a public synonym, as shown below:

```
> loadjava -user sys/syspasswd@database -synonym -resolve -noverify
 -verbose activation.jar
> loadjava -user sys/syspasswd@database -synonym -resolve -noverify
 -verbose mail.jar
```

For more recent Oracle versions, you should load these archives into your user's schema. Loading these archives will take a few minutes on most platforms, as they are quite large and the JVM has to resolve all the class files that the archives contain.

# Using Java to Send Mail with BLOB Attachments

Once the `mail.jar` and `activation.jar` classes have been loaded into the database, we can use them for our Java stored procedures. In this section, we will implement a Java SMTP mail client, which allows us to send mail with BLOB attachments. Using this class to send mail from the database, especially when working with attachments, is significantly easier than using UTL_SMTP, as we will see below.

Our Java mail clients consist of a class called SMTPExtensions. In addition to that class, we must implement a specific type of mail data source, for handling BLOB locators. However, before we start working on those classes, we must look at the security permissions necessary for running JavaMail in the database.

## Security Considerations

When working with JavaMail, there are generally two types of permissions that need to be granted. Firstly, you need a socket permission to connect to the SMTP mail host you specify, and secondly, you need a permission to modify system properties, since you need to add to the properties collection the name of the mail host in question. In order to grant these permissions, you need to log on as SYS or any other DBA role member, and make the following procedure calls:

```
SQL> call dbms_java.grant_permission (
  2      'USERNAME',
  3      'java.util.PropertyPermission',
  4      '*',
  5      'read,write'
  6  );

SQL> call dbms_java.grant_permission (
  2      'USERNAME',
  3      'java.net.SocketPermission',
  4      'your.mailhost',
  5      'connnect,resolve'
  6  );
```

Note that you have to modify the value of your.mailhost to match the mail host you'll use in your call to the SEND_MAIL() procedure below.

> *For more information on Java security and permissions, you should consult* Chapter 11, Oracle Java Security.

## BlobDataSource Java Class

To work with BLOB attachments in our SMTP mail client, we implement a specific extension to the javax.activation.DataSource interface, which defines a generic type of data source, such as a mail attachment.

### Declarations

```
import javax.activation.DataSource;
import oracle.sql.BLOB;

public class BlobDataSource implements DataSource {

  private BLOB blob;
  private String name;
```

### Constructor

Each `BlobDataSource` instance is identified by a BLOB locator and a corresponding file name.

```
public BlobDataSource(BLOB blob, String name) {
    this.blob = blob;
    this.name = name;
}
```

### Content Type

The `getContentType()` method returns the content-type information required by a `DataSource`. For all files, we can use `"application/octet-stream"`.

```
public String getContentType() {
    return "application/octet-stream";
}
```

### Returning a BLOB Input Stream

The `getInputStream()` method returns an `InputStream` from the `DataSource`. In our implementation, we use the `getBinaryStream()` method of the BLOB locator.

```
public InputStream getInputStream() throws IOException {
    try {
        return blob.getBinaryStream();
    } catch (SQLException e) {
        throw new IOException(e.getMessage());
    }
}
```

### File Name

The `getName()` method returns the name of the `DataSource`, that is the name of the BLOB attachment (as displayed in the mail message).

```
public String getName() {
    return name;
}
```

### Returning an Output Stream

Finally, we must implement the `getOutputStream()` method of the `DataSource` interface. However, this implemention is in fact never used, but supplied only in order to fully implement the `DataSource` interface.

```
public OutputStream getOutputStream() throws IOException {
    return new ByteArrayOutputStream(0);
}
}
```

## SMTPExtensions Java Class

Our actual SMTP mail client is illustrated below. It consists of a single static method, `sendMail()`, which takes for arguments the properties of the mail message that should be sent. It currently supports only a single `BLOB` attachment, but adding more attachment would be trivial.

```
package com.wrox.mail;

import java.util.*;
import javax.activation.*;
import javax.mail.*;
import javax.mail.internet.*;
import oracle.sql.BLOB;

public class SMTPExtensions {

    public static void sendMail(String host, String to,
        String from, String cc, String bcc, String subject,
        String text, BLOB blob, String blobName)
        throws AddressException, SendFailedException, MessagingException {

        // Create the JavaMail session
        Properties properties = System.getProperties();
        properties.put("mail.smtp.host",host);
        Session session = Session.getInstance(properties,null);

        // Construct the message
        MimeMessage message = new MimeMessage(session);
        message.setFrom(new InternetAddress(from));
        message.setRecipients(
            Message.RecipientType.TO,
            InternetAddress.parse(to)
        );
        message.setSubject(subject);

        // Add CC, if specified.
        if (cc != null) {
            message.setRecipients(
                Message.RecipientType.CC,
                InternetAddress.parse(cc)
            );
        }

        // Add BCC, if specified.
        if (bcc != null) {
            message.setRecipients(
                Message.RecipientType.BCC,
                InternetAddress.parse(bcc)
            );
        }
```

If any attachments are specified, we must construct a multi-part message, adding a part for the `BLOB` attachment as well as for the actual text of the message.

```
        if (blob != null && blobName != null) {

            Multipart mp = new MimeMultipart();

            // Add the text to the multi-part.
            MimeBodyPart mtxt = new MimeBodyPart();
            mtxt.setText(text);
            mp.addBodyPart(mtxt);

            // Attach the file attachment.
            MimeBodyPart attachment = new MimeBodyPart();
            BlobDataSource bds = new BlobDataSource(blob,blobName);
            attachment.setDataHandler(new DataHandler(bds));
            attachment.setFileName(bds.getName());
            mp.addBodyPart(attachment);
            // Add the MultiPart to the message.
            message.setContent(mp);
```

If there are no attachments, we just set the text stand-alone.

```
        } else {
            message.setText(text);
        }
```

Finally, we set the current date and send the message.

```
        message.setSentDate(new Date());
        Transport.send(message);
    }
}
```

*Note that we could have declared different overloaded* sendMessage() *methods, for different combinations of input arguments (such as when no arguments are specified), but chose not to for the sake of simplicity. In your own implementation, you may choose to use different methods for this purpose, and different PL/SQL call specs, correspondingly.*

## Loading the Java Classes

Once the Java classes are ready, we must load them into the database. This can be accomplished with loadjava, as illustrated below:

```
> loadjava -user username/password@database -resolve BlobDataSource.java
> loadjava -user username/password@database -resolve SMTPExtensions.java
```

## SMTP Extensions PL/SQL Package

To publish our Java mail client to a PL/SQL procedure, we define a specific package, UTL_SMTP, as illustrated below. This package contains only a single procedure, SEND_MAIL().

```
SQL> create or replace package utl_smtp_ext
  2  is
  3    procedure send_mail (
  4      p_host varchar2,
  5      p_to varchar2,
  6      p_from varchar2,
  7      p_cc varchar2,
  8      p_bcc varchar2,
  9      p_subject varchar2,
 10      p_text varchar2,
 11      p_attachment blob,
 12      p_attachment_name varchar2
 13  );
 14  end;
 15  /

SQL> create or replace package body utl_smtp_ext
  2  is
  3    procedure send_mail (
  4      p_host varchar2,
  5      p_to varchar2,
  6      p_from varchar2,
  7      p_cc varchar2,
  8      p_bcc varchar2,
  9      p_subject varchar2,
 10      p_text varchar2,
 11      p_attachment blob,
 12      p_attachment_name varchar2
 13  )
 14    as language java
 15      name 'com.wrox.mail.SMTPExtensions.sendMail(java.lang.String,
 16        java.lang.String, java.lang.String, java.lang.String,
 17        java.lang.String, java.lang.String, java.lang.String,
 18        oracle.sql.BLOB, java.lang.String)';
 19  end;
 20  /
```

## Using the Mail Client

To illustrate how we can use our database mail client for sending messages with BLOB attachments, we declare a simple table for storing files.

```
SQL> create table files (
  2    file_id number,
  3    file_name varchar2(500),
  4    file_value blob
  5  );
```

In the following example, we insert a new text file to the FILES table and use the BLOB locator as an attachment to the SEND_MAIL() procedure.

```
SQL> declare
  2         buffer raw(255) := utl_raw.cast_to_raw('Some nonsense...');
  3         amt binary_integer := 32767;
  4         pos integer := 1;
  5         id number := 10;
  6         lob_loc blob;
  7         name varchar2(500) := 'Nonsense.txt';
  8  begin
  9
 10         -- Create a new BLOB file.
 11         insert into files values (id, name, empty_blob());
 12         select file_value into lob_loc
 13         from files
 14         where file_id = id
 15         for update;
 16
 17         dbms_lob.write (lob_loc, utl_raw.length(buffer), pos, buffer);
 18         commit;
```

To send the message, you call the SEND_MAIL() procedure, supplying appropriate arguments. If you are developing Oracle applications at your workplace, you can get the name of a valid SMTP mail host from your company's network administrator. If working at home, you should contact your local ISP for information on the mail host. In many cases, the mail host is simply called *mail.your-isp*, where *your-isp* is the web site of the ISP in question. You can also get information on your mail host by viewing the information you have entered in your mail program. For example, using Microsoft Outlook, you can go to **Tools | Accounts**, select the properties of your mail account, and search for 'Outgoing Mail Server (SMTP)'. Other programs should store this information in a similar fashion.

```
 19         -- Send a message, using the BLOB for attachment.
 20         utl_smtp_ext.send_mail(
 21             p_host => 'mail.foo.com',
 22             p_to => 'recipent@foo.com,
 23             p_from => 'sender@foo.com',
 24             p_cc => null,
 25             p_bcc => null,
 26             p_subject => 'Re: Nonsense',
 27             p_text => 'Here you get your attachment...',
 28             p_attachment => lob_loc,
 29             p_attachment_name => name
 30         );
 31
 32         --dbms_output.put_line('Result: ' || result);
 33  end;
 34  /
```

# Tying it All Together

In this chapter we have been looking at common Java utilities and extensions that can be used when working with stored procedures in the Oracle database. Specifically, we illustrated the use of Java for dynamic image generation and mail transport from within the database. At the end of each section, we illustrated a particular usage of the technology in question by implementing an example application. Although our examples have been presented mostly in isolation, they will most likely be a part of a greater whole when put to use in the enterprise. As we end this chapter, we would like to further demonstrate that point by illustrating a particular usage of mail transport and image generation – **together** – from within the database.

## Mail Sending with Custom Image Attachments

At the beginning of this chapter, we illustrated an application that allows us to generate pie chart images from a custom SQL query string. Since the image in question is written to a supplied BLOB locator, it is natural to use the pie chart application in conjunction with our BLOB attachment mail transport client. In fact, this may well be a more practical use of dynamic images, rather than storing them in fields in the database, where they have to be extracted specifically for use.

For example, assume you need to design an application for a large retail chain that allows you to dynamically generate a pie chart of the proportion of total sales for each outlet in the chain, and send it through e-mail to a specific list of recipients (such as the board of directors). Using the two applications we have developed in this chapter, this is trivial. For example, assume that all sales are logged down into a table called SHOPS_SALES, which ties to the SHOPS table as illustrated here (of course, this is extremely simplified):

```
SQL> create table shops (
  2     shop_id number,
  3     location varchar2(500),
  4     constraint pk_shops
  5     primary key (shop_id)
  6  );

SQL> create table shops_sales (
  2     shop_id number,
  3     sale_date date default sysdate,
  4     sale_amount number,
  5     constraint fk_shops_sales_shop_id
  6     foreign key (shop_id) references shops
  7  );
```

Before going further, add some data to those tables:

```
SQL> insert into shops values (1, 'New York');
SQL> insert into shops values (2, 'London');
SQL> insert into shops values (3, 'Milan');

SQL> insert into shops_sales (shop_id, sale_amount) values (1, 500);
```

```
SQL> insert into shops_sales (shop_id, sale_amount) values (1, 500);
SQL> insert into shops_sales (shop_id, sale_amount) values (2, 100);
SQL> insert into shops_sales (shop_id, sale_amount) values (2, 8000);
SQL> insert into shops_sales (shop_id, sale_amount) values (2, 600);
SQL> insert into shops_sales (shop_id, sale_amount) values (3, 5000);

SQL> commit;
```

Now, by issuing the following query:

```
SQL> select s.location, sum(ss.sale_amount)
  2  from shops s, shops_sales ss
  3  where s.shop_id = ss.shop_id
  4  group by s.location;
```

you get a list of shops and respective total sales. To generate a pie chart with this information, and have it sent through e-mail to a specified recipient, you might declare the following (replacing foo lines with your own values):

```
SQL> declare
  2      pc PieChart := PieChart.create_chart(300,500);
  3      image_loc blob;
  4      query varchar2(200);
  5      name varchar2(500) := 'SalesByLocation.gif';
  6  begin
  7
  8      -- Construct the query.
  9      query := 'select s.location, sum(ss.sale_amount) ' ||
 10          'from shops s, shops_sales ss ' ||
 11          'where s.shop_id = ss.shop_id ' ||
 12          'group by s.location';
 13
 14      -- Get a temporary BLOB.
 15      dbms_lob.createtemporary(image_loc, true, dbms_lob.session);
 16
 17      -- Construct the chart.
 18      pc.set_title('Sales Share by Location');
 19      pc.generate(query, image_loc);
 20
 21      -- Send the e-mail.
 22      utl_smtp_ext.send_mail(
 23          p_host => 'mail.foo.com',
 24          p_to => 'directorys@foo.com',
 25          p_from => 'database@foo.com',
 26          p_cc => null,
 27          p_bcc => null,
 28          p_subject => 'Sales Overview',
 29          p_text => 'See attached image.',
 30          p_attachment => image_loc,
 31          p_attachment_name => name
 32      );
 33
 34  end;
 35  /
```

**469**

Now, to automate this process, you might for example declare a database job that runs at the beginning of every month and sends an image attachment to the directors that illustrates a summary of last month's sales. To declare the job, you make use of the built-in DBMS_JOB PL/SQL package, which we discuss in more detail in Chapter 17, *Using PL/SQL and Java Together*. But as you can see from this, there is virtually no limit to the possibilities of Java stored procedures in the database.

# Summary

In this chapter, we have made an attempt at defining the role of Java within the spectrum of programming languages available for Oracle. Our main conclusion is to use Java for tasks that are either not possible to accomplish with PL/SQL or are more limited with that language – given that you can solve it in Java.

After defining the advantages of using Java, we set off to illustrate some of their uses. Specifically, we implemented a stored procedure for generating dynamic images from within the database, and another one for simplified mail transport over SMTP, using BLOB data for attachments. At the end of this chapter, we tied those two examples together by illustrating a sample use of both sending automated messages with JavaMail, using charts generated from the database.

In the next chapter, we will continue our discussion of the uses of Java stored procedures, when we discuss methods of working with operating system resources, which is another big advantage of Java, as we will see.

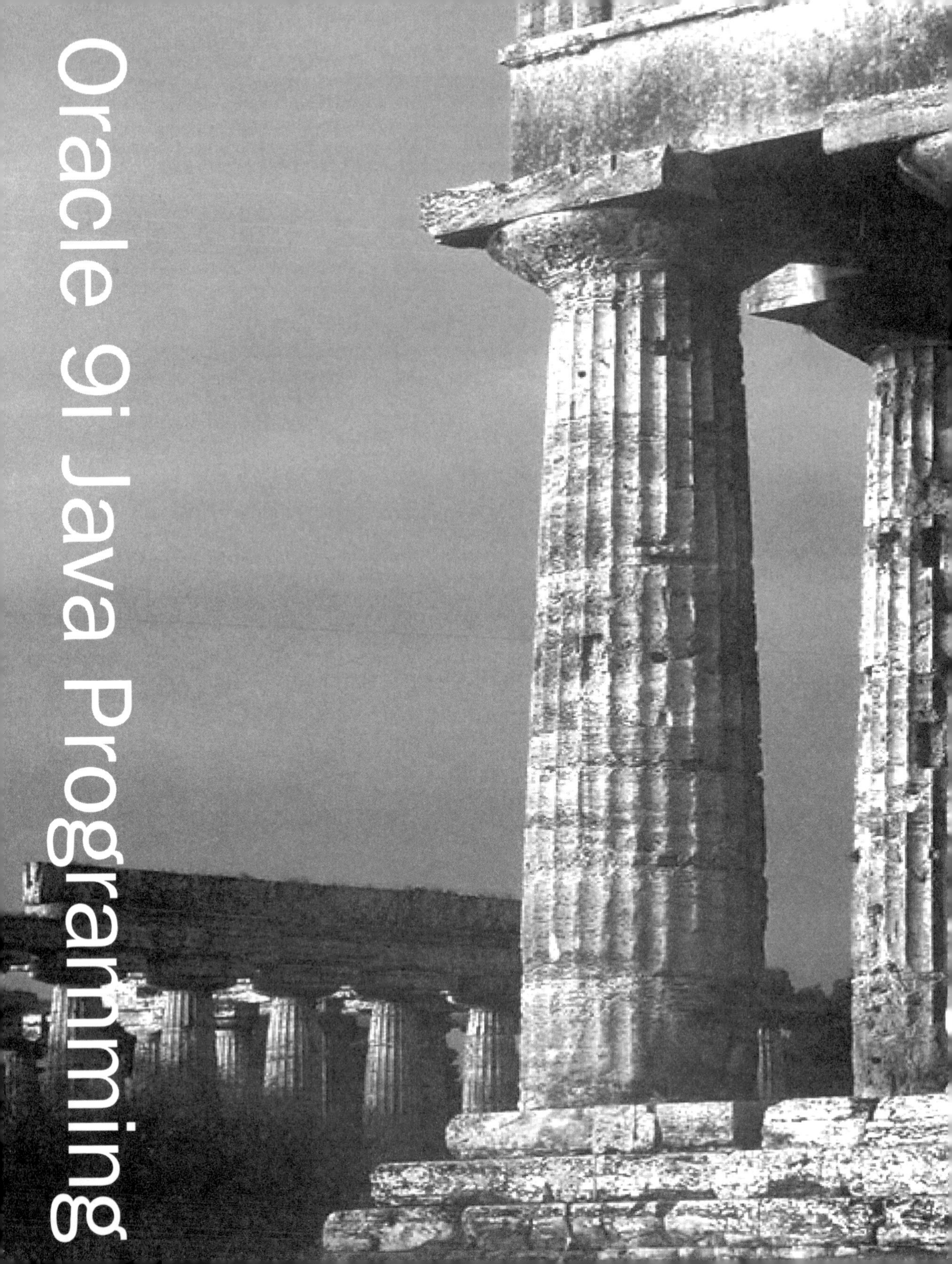
Oracle 9i Java Programming

# Working with Operating System Resources

The ability to interact with the database server operating system is one of the areas in which PL/SQL is rather lacking. For example, PL/SQL is unable to work with binary files and directories, is unable to reach out of the database to run executables, and until recently, PL/SQL has had rather limited support for working with sockets. As a result, developers have traditionally had to turn to a second language to perform non-trivial tasks outside the boundaries of the database.

The Oracle database came with the functionality of running external C-based procedures from PL/SQL in version 8.0. Of course, in version 8i and upwards, we have an integrated JVM, which allows Java programs to execute securely within the database. Both C-based external procedures and Java stored procedures complement most of the limitations of operating resource handling with PL/SQL. However, in most cases, Java is preferred to C for a number of reasons, including:

- ❑ C-based procedures run as a separate operating system process while Java procedures run within the address space of the database

- ❑ C-based procedures require specific listener configuration while Java procedures by default need to no setting up

- ❑ C-based procedures require an external compiler while Java procedures can be compiled and resolved by tools provided with Oracle

- ❑ C-based procedures are platform-dependent – a particular DLL compiled for Windows will not run on a UNIX system – while the same Java procedure runs on whatever platform is supported by Oracle

Whenever you are working within the Oracle database and need functionality not readily available in PL/SQL, you should consider using Java. In most cases, that will adequately address your problem, with minimal set up and overhead. However, if you find yourself in a situation where Java is unable to provide the specific functionality you require, you should either rethink what it is you want to accomplish or turn to C-based external procedures.

In this chapter, we will discuss some important issues of which you need to be aware when dealing with system resources. We will discuss the capabilities of Java for working with resources of the database server operating system, in other words, **files**, **sockets**, **host commands**, and **executables**. Whenever applicable, we will compare Java's approach to working with a specific type of resource with a corresponding aspect of PL/SQL. Specifically, we will:

- ❏ Discuss file handling in Java

- ❏ Compare Java I/O with the PL/SQL `UTL_FILE` package

- ❏ Implement a Java stored procedure for getting a directory listing in PL/SQL

- ❏ Write a Java stored procedure for writing `LOB` fields to files

- ❏ Study methods of executing external programs from the database

- ❏ Develop a stored procedure for dynamically running SQL*Loader

- ❏ Look at ways of issuing operating system commands from the database

- ❏ Implement a procedure for extracting operating system environment variables

- ❏ Discuss socket programming with Java

- ❏ Implement a procedure that can be used to notify external clients of changes to database structures

# Guidelines for Resource Handling

When working with operating system resources from within the database, there are a few important points to bear in mind. The guidelines that we discuss in the next few paragraphs apply to most of the topics we cover in this chapter.

## Security

Java programs operating inside the boundaries of the database JVM are subject to **fine-grained security policies** that serve to protect vital resources from unauthorized access. These security policies are implemented as Java permission objects, which are granted to individual users and roles. Each permission applies to a specific set of actions on a specific set of resources, such as the permission to read and write a specific file in the file system. Permissions are either **positive**, granting access to a resource, or **restrictive**, limiting resource access. Permissions are granted by users that have the administrative rights to update the database permission storage for specific permission types. More information on permissions and security policies are provided in Chapter 11, *Oracle Java Security*.

The Oracle Java security model serves to protect vital resources from unpermitted access of Java programs within the database. Some of the most vital resources that the security policies apply are the resources of the operating system. Therefore, before you start writing code that makes use of the external resources of the operating system, you must be aware of the permissions required. In each of the examples we provide in this section, we illustrate what permissions are needed and how these are granted. Preliminary knowledge of the Oracle Java security model can therefore be very helpful, although not strictly required, before you start testing the code we will be using hereafter.

# Resource Lifetime

One of the main features of the Java language is its use of an **automatic garbage collector**. Unlike languages such as C++, when working with Java you don't have to destroy objects explicitly after use. The JVM determines when a specific object is not being referenced by any other object, at which point the object is garbage collected. Of course, you can always speed up the garbage collection process by nulling your objects after use, but that is not strictly necessary.

This rule, however, does not apply to external resources represented by Java objects. Resources such as file streams, database cursors, and sockets must *always* be closed explicitly after usage, because the resource manager in question (for example a database or an operating system) does *not* automatically shut down the resource when the associated object is closed.

Generally, always close all operating system resources immediately after you use them. To ensure that your resources are closed, no matter what exceptions may be thrown in the surrounding code, practice using the `finally` block around all code working with resources, because statements put in a `finally` block are always executed, no matter what exceptions might occur in other parts of the program. For example:

```
InputStream is = null;
try {
  // perform I/O operations
} finally {
  if (is != null) {
    try {
      is.close();
    } catch (IOException ignored) {
    }
  }
}
```

Whenever exception handling is omitted in our examples in this chapter, it is done for the sake of clarity. In your own applications, make sure all exceptions are handled appropriately. For more details on exceptions and what to do with them, take a look at Chapter 6, *Handling Exceptions*.

# Java and Files

Often, it may be useful to access files in the operating system from *within* the database. For example, you might want to maintain text-based property files outside the database, export binary files stored in BLOB fields to a tape device, or provide dynamic means of data import. This all requires extensive means to access and manipulate operating system files and directories.

The built-in UTL_FILE PL/SQL package provides some functionality for file access, but is limited in many ways. These limitations, however, are not in place for Java, which provides an extensive framework of classes for file access and manipulation. In this section, we will:

❑ Discover the classes of the Java File API, their purpose and their usage

❑ Look at working with I/O operations such as working with path names and directories and manipulating files

❑ Use this knowledge to implement a few simple examples, where Java can complement the missing aspects of file handling in PL/SQL, namely listing the contents of a directory and writing a LOB to a file

# Limitations of the UTL_FILE Package

The UTL_FILE built-in package provides limited operating system I/O functionality for PL/SQL programs. With this package, you can read and write text files at predefined directories in the operating system of the Oracle database server. These predefined directories are specified as arguments in the database init.ora file. In many cases, the I/O services provided by UTL_FILE can be more than adequate. However, this package has a number of serious limitations, which make it more feasible to look for alternatives. A few of those limitations are summarized below:

❑ **File Permissions**
The UTL_FILE package can only read and write files in directories that have been explicitly specified in the init.ora file for the database. If a directory has been specified by the utl_file_dir variable in the init.ora file, *all users* of that database instance can *both read and write* any files in the specified directory. This may not always be desirable; usually a more fine-grained permission policy is required. Additionally, it is not possible to specify recursive directories in the init.ora file – each directory in a tree must be explicitly named. Of course, this means that minimal changes to the file system – such as renaming a directory or moving files from one location to another – require changes to init.ora, which in turn requires a database restart, which is not acceptable in an enterprise environment.

❑ **File Types**
The UTL_FILE package can only manipulate text files – *no binary files* can be handled.

❑ **Line Buffer**
The UTL_FILE package limits the length of lines that can be written. Although this is usually not an issue, it is a limitation nonetheless.

❑ **Directory Limitations**
It is not possible to create a new directory or even list the contents of a directory with UTL_FILE.

Fortunately there are alternatives to UTL_FILE. Java comes with an inherent file I/O support, which overcomes all of the limitations of UTL_FILE. We have already seen in the security chapter, how the Oracle Java fine-grained security model allows you to specify dynamic file permissions that can apply recursively to whole directories, as well as individual files. Additionally, Java provides an extensive set of classes for file handling that allow for the manipulation of both text-based *and* binary files, as well as directory listing and traversing. In the next few sections we will study these capabilities of Java, as we explore the Java file manipulation API in detail.

# Security

Before you start working with files in the operating system, you must be granted the appropriate file permissions. The `java.io.FilePermission` was discussed in detail in Chapter 11, *Oracle Java Security*. For example, to grant user USERNAME access to read and write all files in the /home directory and all its subdirectories, you need to grant the following permission (whilst logged in as a user who has been granted the DBA role):

```
SQL> call dbms_java.grant_permission (
  2    'USERNAME',
  3    'java.io.FilePermission',
  4    '/home/-',
  5    'read,write'
  6  );

Call completed.
```

> Since all Java code runs as the Oracle software owner, you could potentially use Java to overwrite or damage files of the Oracle kernel or data files. This is one of the greatest dangers with file access from Java stored procedures. As a result, you should generally never grant a user unrestricted file permissions – at least not for writing.

# The Java File API

All of the Java file manipulation classes belong to the `java.io.` package. Not all of the `java.io` classes relate to files, however, many of them deal with fundamental handling of **streams** and general I/O operations. If you are not familiar with the basics of stream handling with Java – including the basic operations of `java.io.InputStream` and `java.io.OutputStream`, on which the file I/O is built then please refer to the *Input and Output* section in Appendix B for details.

In the next few paragraphs, we will study each of the fundamental file classes to some extent. For a more detailed description of each class, you should refer to the Java 2 Javadoc API.

> *The new Java 2 Standard Edition, version 1.4, which was in its beta stage of development at the time of this writing, adds an extensive set of new classes to a whole new I/O package, `java.nio` – Java Non-Blocking I/O. This package addresses some of the aspects of Java I/O that have been lacking, such as support for pipes and a more sophisticated handling of stream buffers. Oracle, however, currently supports only JDK 1.2, so it might be some time before these classes can be used in the database.*

## The File Class

The `File` class is used as an abstract representation of a file in the operating system, be it a text file, binary file, or even a whole directory. The `File` class can be used to create new files and directories in the file system, given that the appropriate `FilePermission` is granted. The `File` class contains methods to study some of the properties of the file in question, such as the date it was last modified, the name of the file, and the files it contains, if it is a directory. Additionally, it contains methods to manipulate the file, such as setting it to be read-only or simply deleting it. Note, however, that in order to write to a file, you must use the `FileOutputStream`, which we study below.

The `File` class is further illustrated in the UML diagram shown below:

| File | File (continued) |
|---|---|
| +pathSeparator: String<br>+pathSeparatorChar: char<br>+separator: String<br>+separatorChar: char | + getPath(): String<br>+ hashCode(): int<br>+ isAbsolute(): boolean<br>+ isDirectory(): boolean<br>+ isFile(): boolean<br>+ isHidden(): boolean |
| + File(parent: File, child: String)<br>+ File(pathname: String)<br>+ File(parent: String, child: String) | + lastModified(): long<br>+ length(): long<br>+ list(): String[]<br>+ list(filter: FilenameFilter):String[]<br>+ listFiles(): File[] |
| + canRead(): boolean<br>+ canWrite(): boolean<br>+ compareTo(pathname: File): int<br>+ compareTo(Object o): int<br>+ createNewFile(): boolean<br>+ delete(): boolean<br>+ deleteOnExit()<br>+ equals(Object obj): boolean<br>+ exists(): boolean<br>+ getAbsoluteFile(): File<br>+ getAbsolutePath(): String<br>+ getCanonicalFile(): File<br>+ getCanonicalPath(): String<br>+ getName(): String<br>+ getParent(): String<br>+ getParentFile(): File | + listFiles(filter: FileFilter): File[]<br>+ listFiles(filter: FilenameFilter): File[]<br>+ mkdir(): boolean<br>+ mkdirs(): boolean<br>+ renameTo(dest: File): boolean<br>+ setLastModified(time: long): boolean<br>+ setReadOnly(): boolean<br>+ toString(): String<br>+ toURL(): URL<br><br>+ createTempFile(prefix: String, suffix: String): File<br>+ createTempFile(prefix: String, suffix: String, directory: File): File<br>+ listRoots(): File[] |

## The FileDescriptor Class

Each machine-specific sink of bytes that you can manipulate through Java, such as files and sockets, has an associated low-level file structure in the operating system. The `FileDescriptor` class provides a handle to such a structure. This class should generally *not* be managed directly by the application.

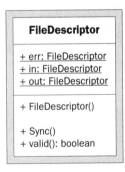

| FileDescriptor |
|---|
| + err: FileDescriptor<br>+ in: FileDescriptor<br>+ out: FileDescriptor |
| + FileDescriptor() |
| + Sync()<br>+ valid(): boolean |

## The FileInputStream and FileOutputStream Classes

To read the contents of a file in a file system, you construct an instance of the `FileInputStream`, which is an extension of the standard `java.io.InputStream` class. You can construct a `FileInputStream` instance from either a `File` object or by supplying the path to an existing file.

Just as the `FileInputStream` is used to read contents of a file, you use the `FileOutputStream` class to write to a file. This class extends the standard `java.io.OutputStream` and should be used identically. When you create a new `FileOutputStream`, by specifying a path to a file or a `File` object, you can optionally specify that the bytes you write to the output stream should be appended to the end of the file, rather than written to the front. This can be useful, for example, when you need to write information to a log file. We will discuss that issue further in our examples at the end of the file section.

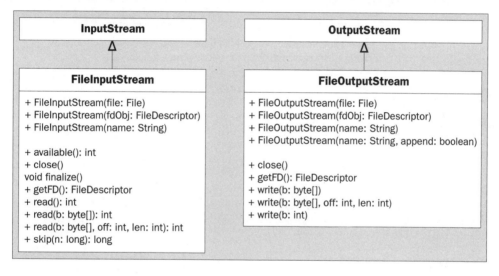

## The FileReader and FileWriter Classes

The `FileReader` and `FileWriter` classes extend `java.io.Reader` and `java.io.Writer` respectively, and are used to read from and write to text-based files. To read from and write to binary files, use `FileInputStream` and `FileOutputStream` instead. Both classes assume that the default character encoding is being used.

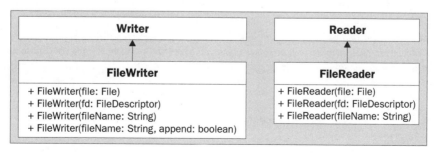

### The FileFilter and FilenameFilter Interfaces

Lastly, we have the interfaces `FileFilter` and `FileNameFilter`, used in conjunction with the `list()` and `listFiles()` methods of the `File` class to filter a specific set of files. Specifically, if you need only to filter by the name of the files in question, you should use an instance of a `FileNameFilter` implementation. On the other hand, if you need more detailed filtering, such as by modification date or file size, you should use an instance of a `FileFilter` implementation.

There is no standard implementation available for either one of these interfaces – to implement your own filter, you have to define the appropriate action for its `accept()` method. We provide an example of such an implementation later in this section.

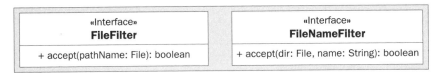

# I/O Operations

When working with files, there are a handful of basic operations that you encounter over and over again. In this section, we will study more closely how Java addresses these.

## Working with Path Names

Unfortunately, not all operating system use the same syntax for file paths. This means that you cannot hard-code file paths in your code and expect it to work on a different platform. For example, on a Windows system, file names in a path are separated by a back-slash, while on UNIX, they are separated by a forward-slash. For example:

```
// on Windows
C:\Program Files\Oracle

// on UNIX
/usr/local/oracle
```

This means that code like the one shown here, which is intended for use on a Windows platform, will not work on other platforms.

> *Note that the double back slash is needed, as otherwise the compiler might think you are using an escape character. This, however, applies only when you **construct** a string in Java that contains a back-slash. When supplying a path name to a Java method from a PL/SQL procedure, you use just a single back-slash.*

```
String path = System.getProperty("user.dir") + "\\logs\\error.log";
File log = new File(dir);
```

To address this problem, the `File` class provides a few static variables, which can be used to construct file paths that adjust to the operating system in question, as shown here:

```
String path = System.getProperty("user.dir")
  + File.seperatorChar
  + "logs"
  + File.seperatorChar
  + "error.log";
File log = new File(dir);
```

> Of course, this is usually only appropriate in the first place if you are working with a
> file that is relative to some predefined location or environment variable, such as
> **$JAVA_HOME**. If you need to specify the absolute path of a file, you will always need to
> include some platform-specific information (in other words, **C:\**), which means that
> the name separator will not matter. Therefore, always try to use relative file names
> with Java – at least if you want your application to be portable.

In the examples at the end of the file section, we develop a PL/SQL package of file handling extensions, which includes a procedure to return the current path separator from the File Java class. Additionally, later in this chapter, when we study methods to execute operating system commands from a Java context, we will develop a sample class that you can use to retrieve the value of environment variables from the underlying software account (in other words, the Oracle user account).

### Relative Paths

When you construct a new File object in Java, you can use a relative path to identify the file. In a traditional JVM, a relative path is resolved from the location in which the JVM was initiated (where the Java executable was run). For Oracle, you do not explicitly initiate the JVM, so this obviously does not apply there. In fact, Oracle does not even use the corresponding base directory between individual platforms. The Oracle documentation states that relative path names are resolved relative to ORACLE_HOME, but experience shows that on a Windows platform, for example, relative paths are resolved relative to ORACLE_HOME/DATABASE/. The lesson from this is that you should not count on relative path names, at least not if you want your application to be stable between individual database versions. Instead, use absolute path names, preferably by extracting operating system environment variables, as we will illustrate later in this chapter.

## Working with Directories

As we have previously mentioned, one of the limitations of using PL/SQL for file handling is the lack of methods for working with directories. Consequently, this is one of the areas where a conjunction with Java is most useful. In the next few paragraphs we will illustrate how you can use Java to work with operating system directories and their contents. Later, we will use that knowledge to implement a method that allows you to return a filtered list of files from a specified directory, as a PL/SQL array.

### Creating a Directory

To create a directory, you instantiate a new File object, which represents your directory, and invoke either its mkdir() or mkdirs() method, depending on what exactly it is you want to accomplish. The first method only creates a new directory, if the specific parent directory exists, while the latter method creates the specific directory, along with all missing parent directories. For example:

```
File dir = new File("newdir");
dir.mkdir();
```

## Identifying a Directory

To determine whether a specific file is a directory or a file, you call the `isDirectory()` method of the `File` class, which returns True if the file is indeed a directory.

```
File dir = new File("tmp");
if (dir.isDirectory()) {
  File dump = new File(dir,"core");
  dump.createNewFile();
} else {
  System.err.println("The 'tmp' directory is a file!");
}
```

## Listing Directory Contents

To list the contents of a directory, you can invoke one of two methods of the `File` class. The first method, `list()`, returns an array of strings naming the files and directories in the specified directory. The second method, `listFiles()`, works just like the first method, except that it returns an array of `File` objects representing the files and directories in the specified directory. Both methods return null if the `File` object on which they are invoked is not a directory. The following example shows a method that takes for an argument the path of a directory and prints to the standard output stream the contents of the directory:

*Note that for Oracle you will have to redirect the standard output streams to a specific location, or else all output that is written to those streams will end up in a common trace file. To redirect the output to the SQL\*Plus screen, you first call SET SERVEROUTPUT ON in your SQL\*Plus session, followed by a call to DBMS_JAVA.SET_OUTPUT(), with an appropriate output buffer, as we discussed in Chapter 1 and 9.*

```
public void dir(String path) throws SQLException {

  File dir = new File(path);
  if (dir.isDirectory()) {
    File[] files = dir.listFiles();
      for (int i=0; i < files.length; i++) {
        System.out.print(files[i].getName() + "   ");
        if (files[i].isDirectory()) {
          System.out.print("<DIR>" + tab);
        }
      System.out.println();
    }
  }
}
```

Both methods of listing contents of a directory are overloaded with a variant that takes for an argument a specific file filter. Both `list()` and `listFiles()` have variants that take a `FilenameFilter` argument, but `listFiles()` additionally has a variant that takes a `FileFilter` argument. To use these overloaded methods, you have to implement your own filter class. For example, suppose you have the following filter class, which implements `FilenameFilter`:

```
import java.io.File;
import java.io.FilenameFilter;

public class CvsFilter implements FilenameFilter {

  public boolean accept(File dir, String name) {
    return (!dir.getName.equals("CVS") &&!name.equals("CVS")
            &&!name.startsWith(".#"));
  }
}
```

To use this filter in your code, you supply it as an argument to either the `list()` or `listFiles()` method of the `File` class, as shown here:

```
File cvsRoot = new File("/usr/local/cvs/source");
FilenameFilter filter = new CvsFilter();
String[] files = cvsRoot.list(filter);
```

# Writing to a File

To write to a file in Java, we start by creating a new `FileOutputStream`, supplying either a specified file object or a path to a file as an argument. The file output stream can then be used directly, through its `write()` methods, or indirectly, by using it to construct a more specific `InputStream` implementation, such as `java.io.PrintStream`. In the next few paragraphs, we will illustrate a few such methods of file writing.

*The `java.io` package contains many more output stream and output writer variations. For more information, consult the Java 2 documentation.*

### Direct Output with the FileOutputStream

The first step in file writing is to construct a `FileOutputStream` instance. The `FileOutputStream` can be used to directly write byte contents to the specified file, using its standard `write()` methods. For example:

```
String message = "This is my first letter";
File letter = new File("personal","letter1.txt");
letter.createNewFile();

FileOutputStream out = new FileOutputStream(letter);
out.write(message.getBytes());
out.flush();
out.close();
```

As always when working with Java output streams, you should flush and close the stream after you have completed your writing, as we illustrated in this example.

By default, a new file output stream writes to a new file, in other words, any previous contents of the file being written to are discarded. However, this behavior can be altered by setting the appending Boolean argument to one of the `FileOutputStream` constructors. This can be useful when writing information to a log file (although we recommend using the database for logging). For example, in the code below we redirect the standard Java output stream to a file in the file system of the database server. The output will be appended to the end of the file.

```
System.setOut(new PrintWriter(new FileOutputStream("out.log"), true));
```

*Note that in order to redirect the standard Java output streams to a file, the user must be granted the `setIO` action of `java.lang.RuntimePermission`.*

## Using a Buffered Output Stream

When working with streams in Java, considerable performance can be gained by using a **buffered stream**. Each time you write to such a stream, the piece of data written is added to an internal byte buffer, rather than written to the intended destination. Only when the buffer has reached its capacity, is an actual write operation made, and the buffer is flushed. When buffering a file output stream, this can greatly reduce the number of disk access operations required, thus reducing the time it takes to write to the file. In Java, a buffered output stream is represented by a `BufferedOutputStream` object. Such an object can be constructed from a `FileOutputStream`, as shown here:

```
String message = "This is my second letter";
File letter = new File("personal","letter2.txt");
letter.createNewFile();

BufferedOutputStream out = new BufferedOutputStream(
    new FileOutputStream(letter)
);

// write this line a number of times to the file, thus illustrating the
// advantage of using a buffered output stream.
for (int i=0; i < 1000; i++) {
  out.write(message.getBytes());
}
out.flush();
out.close();
```

Note that although you can specify the internal buffer capacity when you construct a new `BufferedOutputStream` instance, the default size (512 bytes) works well in most cases.

## Using a Print Stream

As you may have noticed with the two types of output streams we have been working with so far, `FileOutputStream` and `BufferedOutputStream`, we need to convert the desired output to a byte array each time a write is made. At best, this may be inconvenient, or inefficient at worst, since you often have to convert the output to a string before you construct the byte array, which can incur overhead. For example, assume you have to write to a file some output you need to construct from a diverse set of data types – characters, strings, numbers, and so on, as illustrated below:

```
public void writeToFile(String s1, int i, String s2,
    boolean b, String s3, long l)
    throws IOException{

    File f = new File("tmp","results.out");
    f.createNewFile();
```

```
        String s = s1 + ": " + i + "\n" + s2 + ": " + b + "\n" + s3 + ": " + l;
        FileOutputStream out = new FileOutputStream(f);
        out.write(s.getBytes());
        out.flush();
        out.close();
    }
```

To avoid having to work directly with byte arrays, you can use the `PrintStream` class, which allows you to directly print various data types to the stream, without converting them first to bytes. For example, we could rewrite our previous `writeToFile()` method by using a `PrintStream`, as follows:

```
    public void writeToFile(String s1, int i, String s2,
        boolean b, String s3, long l)
        throws IOException{

        File f = new File("tmp","results.out");
        f.createNewFile();

        PrintStream out = new PrintStream(new FileOutputStream(f));
        out.print(s1);
        out.print(": ");
        out.println(i);
        out.print(s2);
        out.print(": ");
        out.println(b);
        out.print(s3);
        out.print(": ");
        out.println(l);
        out.flush();
        out.close();
    }
```

## Cascading Streams

Note that there is nothing to stop you from cascading any number of different output streams. For example, you can cascade the `PrintStream`, the `BufferedStream`, and the `FileOutputStream`, to enjoy the functionality of the `PrintStream` and the efficiency of the `BufferedOutputStream`, when writing to a file in the operating system! For example:

```
    File f = new File("tmp","results.out");
    f.createNewFile();

    PrintStream out = new PrintStream(
      new BufferedOutputStream(
        new FileOutputStream(f)
      )
    );
```

### Writing Text-Based Files

Another alternative to FileOutputStream when working with text-based files is to use the FileWriter class. As we have mentioned before, using the FileWriter is nearly identical to using the FileOutputStream, except that you work with character arrays, rather than byte arrays. Thus, if your file contents are already stored in a character array, it is logical to use the FileWriter. For example:

```
String message = "This is my fourth letter";
File letter = new File("personal","letter4.txt");
letter.createNewFile();

FileWriter writer = new FileWriter(letter);
writer.write(message.toCharArray());
writer.flush();
writer.close();
```

Note that you can use FileWriter to construct a PrintWriter instance, which is analogous to the PrintStream we used above, except that it should only be used to write character streams, and not byte streams. For example:

```
String message = "This is my fifth letter";
File letter = new File("personal","letter5.txt");
letter.createNewFile();

PrintWriter writer = new PrintWriter(new FileWriter(letter));
writer.println(message);
writer.flush();
writer.close();
```

## Reading from a File

To read from a file, you follow a similar procedure to when you write to a file. You can either use a FileInputStream or a FileReader instance to directly work with the byte or character contents of a file, or wrap an instance of these classes in a more specific subclass of either the java.io.InputStream or java.io.Reader, respectively. In the following paragraphs, we will illustrate a few such methods. This discussion resembles our discussion of file writing in most cases, except, of course, that we are reading from rather than writing to a file.

### Direct Input with the FileInputStream

You can directly read the byte contents of a file by using a FileInputStream instance, initialized for a specific file in the database server's file system. The process of file reading follows the same principles as general stream reading in Java. For example, you can obtain the number of available bytes by calling the available() method inherited from java.io.InputStream, and mark a position in the stream, which you can later revert to with the reset() method.

If you are working with small files (the exact definition depending on your requirements, but generally less than a few MBs), you can read the whole file content at once by constructing a byte array whose size matches the number of available bytes. For example:

```
File letter = new File("personal","letter1.txt");
FileInputStream in = new FileInputStream(letter);

-- the available() method does not block the file
-- from other simultaneous processes.
byte[] b = new byte[in.available()];
in.read(b);
in.close();
String message = new String(b);
```

However, when working with larger files, you should generally process the file contents in a few steps. Of course, that assumes you are not going to store the file contents in a memory structure anyway, as we did in the previous example using a String, since it would not make any difference how many reads you would make. Generally speaking, when working with large files in the database, you usually read and process the file contents in small amounts at a time, possibly by appending to a LOB field in the database. The following example illustrates how we read from a file using a 512-byte buffer:

```
File letter = new File("personal","letter2.txt");
FileInputStream in = new FileInputStream(letter);

byte[] b = new byte[512];
int amountRead = in.read(b);
while (amountRead != -1) {
  -- do something with the bytes read
  amountRead = in.read(b);
}
in.close();
```

Note that when using a small buffer to read from a file, you must keep track of the amount of bytes read. If, for the last read operation, you do not completely fill the byte buffer (which happens only if the number of bytes in the source file is an integer multiple of the size of the byte buffer array), you must make sure you use only those bytes in the buffer that were actually read. For example, if you have a byte array of 10 elements, and you read a file containing 14 bytes, you will fill the byte array for the first read attempt, but a successive read will fill only the first four elements of the array. Thus, you must make sure you take only those four bytes from the array. We will see an example of this below, when we illustrate file copying with Java.

### Using a Buffered Stream

Similar to our discussion of the BufferedOutputStream for file writing, you can use a BufferedInputStream for reading buffered input. For example:

```
File letter = new File("personal","letter3.txt");
BufferedInputStream  in = new BufferedInputStream(
  new FileInputStream(letter)
);

-- deliberately use a smaller buffer than that of the input stream.
byte[] b = new byte[256];
int amountRead = in.read(b);
while (amountRead != -1) {
```

**487**

```
      -- do something with the bytes read
      amountRead = in.read(b);
   }
   in.close();
```

### Reading Text-Based Files

Finally, when reading text-based files, it may be more convenient to handle character arrays, rather than arrays of bytes. For this purpose, you can use the `FileReader` class, as we illustrate below:

```
File letter = new File("personal","letter4.txt");
FileReader reader = new FileReader(letter);
char[] c = new byte[256];
int amountRead = in.read(c);
while (amountRead != -1) {
   -- do something with the characters read
   amountRead = in.read(c);
}
reader.close();
```

## Moving a File

From time to time, you may need to move a file to another location. In Java, this can be done by invoking the `renameTo()` method of the `File` object in question, supplying as an argument the destination target. For example:

```
File log = new File("logs","error.log");
File old = new File("old","old-error.log");
old.createNewFile();
if (!log.renameTo(old)) {
   System.err.println("Unable to move the log file!");
}
```

## Copying a File

Unfortunately, there is no explicit method for copying files in the Java I/O API. However, this is trivial to accomplish by working with two simultaneous file streams – a stream of input from the source file and another stream of output to the destination file. Using two streams simultaneously in this fashion is the recommended method for copying files in Java. A common beginner's mistake is to work only with a single stream at a time, in other words, reading all the contents of the source file in a byte array, closing the input stream and then writing the byte array to the destination file. This is often done in order to reduce the overhead of keeping two file streams open at the same time. The truth is, however, that the little overhead associated with the file streams is minimal compared to the memory that is required for storing the input file in byte array variables. Since files can potentially become very large, such an improper copying method can easily eat up all of the Java memory pool, thus affecting other parts of the database.

The key to efficiently copying files in Java is to choose the proper buffer size to use when fetching and writing the byte contents. Using too small a buffer results in too frequent disk writes, while a too large buffer can consume too much shared memory. Usually, you can avoid explicitly setting the buffer size by using Java's inherent implementations of buffered input and output streams, `BufferedInputStream` and `BufferedOutputStream`, respectively, and using a byte array of a smaller or equal size to copy the data between the two files. The following example further illustrates this:

```
-- Copy the access log to a tape. The destination file
-- on the tape should be identified with the current
-- system time in milliseconds, in standard Java format.
File source = new File("/var/logs/access.log");
File destination = new File(
  "/dev/rmt/0/access"
  + System.currentTimeMillis()
  + " .log"
);
destination.createNewFile();

-- prepare input and output streams
BufferedInputStream in = new BufferedInputStream(
  new FileInputStream(source)
);
BufferedOutputStream = new BufferedOutputStream(
  new FileOutputStream(destination)
);

-- read half MB at a time
byte[] buffer = new byte[512];
int amountRead = in.read(buffer);
while (amountRead != -1) {

  -- note that we write only the number of bytes actually read
  out.write(buffer, 0, amountRead);
  amountRead = in.read(buffer);
}

buffer = null;
out.flush();
out.close();
in.close();
```

# Working with Files in the Database

At the beginning of the *Files* section, we mentioned some of the limitations of file handling with PL/SQL, most notably the lack of methods for handling directories and binary files. In this sub-section we will illustrate a few uses of Java to complement the aspects of file handling lacking in PL/SQL. Whereas before the addition of Java to the Oracle database, you had to implement and compile external C procedures, you can now accomplish the same with a few lines of Java code embedded within the runtime environment of Oracle. Again, this is one of the true advantages of Java in the database: small but useful procedures that extend the functionality of Oracle's more robust database language, PL/SQL.

## *Listing Directory Contents*

It can often be useful to list the contents of specified directory in the file system of the database server from a stored procedure. Using Java, we can implement such a procedure and publish it in PL/SQL. In the next few paragraphs, we will illustrate that process in more detail. Specifically, we will write a procedure that accepts as an argument, the name of a specified directory and returns an array of file names for that directory. Additionally, we will develop an overloaded version of the basic procedure, which takes for a second argument, a string expression that can be used to filter the set of files that should be returned.

### Defining the Varray

When working with a file name list in our methods below, we will use a specific table type (SQL table type, not PL/SQL table type), as defined below. Using a table type, rather than for example a VARRAY, allows us to list an unlimited number of files, although that number is most likely limited to some arbitrary value for most operating systems.

```
SQL> create type files
  2  as
  3  table of varchar2(512);
  4  /

Type created.
```

### The File Extensions Class

In our example, we will use a simple class, FileExtensions, which contains the desired methods:

```
package com.wrox.util.file;

import java.io.File;
import java.io.FilenameFilter;
import java.io.IOException;
import java.sql.Connection;
import java.sql.DriverManager;
import java.sql.SQLException;
import oracle.sql.ARRAY;
import oracle.sql.ArrayDescriptor;

public class FileExtensions {

    private static ArrayDescriptor arrdesc;
    private static ARRAY arr;
    private static Connection conn;
```

The list() method returns an instance of oracle.sql.ARRAY, which we later map to our specific FILES table type in the PL/SQL package below. The list() method has two variations; one that takes for an argument only the name of the directory to list and another one which takes for an additional argument the expression used to filter the file names of the resulting list. The first method effectively relays its call to the second method, as we can see.

```
public static ARRAY list(String dir) throws IOException, SQLException {
  return list(dir, null);
}
```

The latter `list()` method starts by initializing the `ArrayDescriptor` for the `FILES` table type, if that has not already been done. Note that we store the `ArrayDescriptor` object in a static variable, shared among different calls. Initializing an `ArrayDescriptor` object is inherently expensive, in our experience, and it would be very ineffective to do so per call.

*Note that we prove more tangible evidence of the cost of initializing an `ArrayDescriptor` in Chapter 17 PL/SQL vs. Java.*

Next, the `list()` method determines whether it should directly list all the files in the specified directory or filter the list according to a supplied criteria. In the latter case, it constructs an instance of the `ExpressionFilter` class, which we discuss below.

```
public static ARRAY list(String dir, String expr)
  throws IOException, SQLException {

  // initialize the array descriptor
  if (arrdesc == null) {
    conn = DriverManager.getConnection("jdbc:oracle:kprb:@");
    arrdesc = ArrayDescriptor.createDescriptor("FILES", conn);
  }

  if (expr == null) {
    return new ARRAY(arrdesc, conn, (new File(dir)).list());
  } else {
    FilenameFilter f = new ExpressionFilter(expr);
    return new ARRAY(arrdesc, conn, (new File(dir)).list(f));
  }
}
}
```

In addition to the two `list()` methods, we add a method to the `FileExtensions` class which returns the path separator for the current operating system. This method can be used in conjunction with another method we develop later in this chapter for extracting operating system environment variables, in order to write platform-independent applications.

```
public static String getPathSeparator() {
  return File.pathSeparator;
}
}
```

## The Expression Filter

Just by allowing us to get a directory listing from a PL/SQL procedure, our Java program would be of great use. However, there may be times where you need to filter the directory contents according to a specified criteria, for example, list only those files that end with `.sql`. With Java, such a task is trivial to accomplish by creating an appropriate implementation of the `FilenameFilter` interface, which we discussed earlier. In our case, we want to define a `FilenameFilter` implementation that filters the specified file set, according to an expression similar to a SQL `LIKE` predicate. For example, using our above example, we would like to filter the file names according to the expression:

**491**

```
%.sql
```

The `ExpressionFilter` class below implements `FilenameFilter` for that purpose. An instance of `ExpressionFilter` is constructed by supplying the specified expression. Note that the expression applies to the file name only – to filter according to other attributes of the file in question, such as size or creation date, we would need to implement the `FileFilter` interface.

```java
package com.wrox.util.file;

import java.io.File;
import java.io.FilenameFilter;
import java.io.IOException;
import java.util.StringTokenizer;

public class ExpressionFilter implements FilenameFilter {

  private static final char WILDCARD = '%';
  private String expr;
  private String[] tokens;

  public ExpressionFilter(String expr) {
```

The `ExpressionFilter` constructor splits the expression up in token, according to the number of wild card characters (%). Note that the expression is considered case-insensitive, which is why we store it in uppercase (we will be matching against the file name in uppercase later).

```java
    this.expr = expr.toUpperCase();
    StringTokenizer tok = new StringTokenizer(this.expr,
      String.valueOf(WILDCARD));
    tokens = new String[tok.countTokens()];

    for (int i = 0; i < tokens.length; i++) {
      tokens[i] = tok.nextToken();
    }
  }
```

The `accept()` method takes for arguments the directory `File` object and the name of the file in question. If the file name matches the specified expression, the method returns `true`.

```java
  public boolean accept(File dir, String name) {
    int pos = 0;
    int temp;
    String uname = name.toUpperCase();

    for (int i = 0; i < tokens.length; i++) {
      temp = uname.indexOf(tokens[i], pos);
      if (temp == -1) {
        return false;
      }
      pos = temp + tokens[i].length();
```

```
        }

        // Determine whether there is a wild card
        // at the end of the expression.
        return pos != uname.length()
              && expr.charAt(expr.length() - 1) != WILDCARD;
    }
}
```

### Loading the Java Classes into the Database

Once the two Java classes have been created, they must be loaded into the database, for example by using loadjava. The following example illustrates this:

```
> loadjava -user user/pass@sid -oci8 -resolve ExpressionFilter.java
> loadjava -user user/pass@sid -oci8 -resolve FileExtensions.java
```

Note that the order in which you load the two classes is important, since FileExtensions depends on ExpressionFilter.

### The UTL_FILE_EXT Package

To publish the Java methods in the database, we define a specific PL/SQL package, UTL_FILE_EXT. This package contains functions that return an array of file names for a specified directory, with or without a file name expression. Additionally, a third method returns the OS-dependent path separator, as we have previously discussed. The UTL_FILE_EXT package is defined below:

```
SQL> create or replace package utl_file_ext
  2  is
  3
  4     function dir_list (
  5       p_directory in varchar2
  6     ) return files;
  7
  8     function dir_list (
  9       p_directory in varchar2,
 10       p_expr in varchar2
 11     ) return files;
 12
 13     function get_path_separator
 14     return varchar2;
 15
 16  end;
 17  /

Package created.

SQL> create or replace package body utl_file_ext
  2  is
  3
  4     function dir_list (
```

```
  5        p_directory in varchar2
  6     ) return files
  7     as
  8     language java
  9     name 'com.wrox.util.file.FileExtensions.list(java.lang.String)
 10        return oracle.sql.VARRAY';
 11
 12     function dir_list (
 13        p_directory in varchar2,
 14        p_expr in varchar2
 15     ) return files
 16     as
 17     language java
 18     name 'com.wrox.util.file.FileExtensions.list(java.lang.String,
 19        java.lang.String) return oracle.sql.VARRAY';
 20
 21     function get_path_separator
 22     return varchar2
 23     as
 24     language java
 25     name 'com.wrox.util.file.FileExtensions.getPathSeparator()
 26        return java.lang.String';
 27
 28  end;
 29  /
```

```
Package body created.
```

### Using the Package

With the UTL_FILE_EXT package, you can get a listing of files in a specified directory in any of your PL/SQL programs, given that you have been granted read permission on the directory in question. For example, suppose you want to display the contents of the ORACLE_HOME/sqlplus/admin/ directory, on a Windows server with ORACLE_HOME set to C:\oracle\ora81:, you should see something similar to the following:

```
SQL> declare
  2     l_list files;
  3  begin
  4     l_list := utl_file_ext.dir_list('C:\oracle\ora81\sqlplus\admin');
  5     for i in 1..l_list.count loop
  6        dbms_output.put_line(l_list(i));
  7     end loop;
  8  end;
  9  /
glogin.sql
help
plustrce.sql
pupbld.sql
sqlplus.ini

PL/SQL procedure successfully completed.
```

Using the overloaded `DIR_LIST()` method, you could for example, list only those files whose names start with p and end with `.sql`, as illustrated here:

```
SQL> declare
  2    l_list files;
  3  begin
  4    l_list := utl_file_ext.dir_list(
                        'C:\oracle\ora81\sqlplus\admin','p%.sql');
  5    for i in 1..l_list.count loop
  6      dbms_output.put_line(l_list(i));
  7    end loop;
  8  end;
  9  /
plustrce.sql
pupbld.sql

PL/SQL procedure successfully completed.
```

## Writing a LOB to a File

The `DBMS_LOB` PL/SQL package, which we use for working with LOBs stored in the database, is useful for many purposes. However, this package has one large limitation, namely the lack of methods for writing LOBs to files in the database server operating system. In this section, we will develop a Java stored procedure and a corresponding PL/SQL package to address these issues.

### The LobExtensions Class

The `LobExtensions` class illustrated below contains a few variations of a method called `writeToFile()`. This method takes for arguments a specific LOB instance (in other words, CLOB or BLOB) and the path to a destination file in the database server file system:

```java
package com.wrox.util.file;

import java.io.BufferedInputStream;
import java.io.BufferedOutputStream;
import java.io.File;
import java.io.FileOutputStream;
import java.io.IOException;
import java.io.InputStream;
import java.sql.SQLException;
import oracle.sql.BLOB;
import oracle.sql.CLOB;

public class LobExtensions {

  public static long writeToFile(BLOB blob, String parent, String fileName)
    throws IOException, SecurityException, SQLException {

    return writeToFile(blob, parent + File.separatorChar + fileName);
  }

  public static long writeToFile(BLOB blob, String path)
```

```
      throws IOException, SecurityException, SQLException {

  BufferedInputStream in =
    new BufferedInputStream(blob.getBinaryStream());
  return writeToFile(in, new File(path));
}

public static long writeToFile(CLOB clob, String parent, String fileName)
  throws IOException, SecurityException, SQLException {

  return writeToFile(clob, parent + File.separatorChar + fileName);
}

public static long writeToFile(CLOB clob, String path)
  throws IOException, SecurityException, SQLException {

  BufferedInputStream in =
    new BufferedInputStream(clob.getAsciiStream());
  return writeToFile(in, new File(path));
}
```

All of the real work of different `writeToFile()` methods is accomplished with the private, internal `writeToFile()` method below, which takes for arguments the input stream that should be written and the `File` object representing the file to write to.

```
private static long writeToFile(InputStream in, File f)
  throws IOException, SecurityException, SQLException {

  long bytesWritten = 0;

  // read 256 bytes at a time
  byte[] buffer = new byte[256];
  BufferedOutputStream out =
    new BufferedOutputStream(new FileOutputStream(f));

  try {

    // read from the input stream and write to the output stream
    int i = in.read(buffer);
    while (i != -1) {
      out.write(buffer, 0, i);
      bytesWritten += i;
      i = in.read(buffer);
    }

    // flush the output stream
    out.flush();

    // close file resources
  } finally {
    if (in != null) {
```

```
        try {
          in.close();
        } catch (IOException ignored) {}
      }

    if (out != null) {
        try {
          out.close();
        } catch (IOException ignored) {}
      }
    }

  return bytesWritten;
  }
}
```

## Loading the Java Class into the Database

Once the Java class has been created, it must be loaded into the database, for example by using loadjava, as we have done before:

```
> loadjava -user user/pass@sid -oci8 -resolve LobExtensions.java
```

## The UTL_LOB_EXT Package

The UTL_LOB_EXT PL/SQL package maps the public methods of the LobExtensions class to PL/SQL procedures:

```
SQL> create or replace package utl_lob_ext
  2  is
  3
  4    function write_to_file (
  5      p_lob_loc in blob,
  6      p_directory in varchar2,
  7      p_file_name in varchar2
  8    ) return number;
  9
 10    function write_to_file (
 11      p_lob_loc in blob,
 12      p_path in varchar2
 13    ) return number;
 14
 15    function write_to_file (
 16      p_lob_loc in clob,
 17      p_directory in varchar2,
 18      p_file_name in varchar2
 19    ) return number;
 20
 21    function write_to_file (
 22      p_lob_loc in clob,
 23      p_path in varchar2
 24    ) return number;
 25
```

```
26  end;
27  /

Package created.
```

The package body is illustrated below:

```
SQL> create or replace package body utl_lob_ext
  2  is
  3
  4    function write_to_file (
  5      p_lob_loc in blob,
  6      p_directory in varchar2,
  7      p_file_name in varchar2
  8    ) return number
  9    as
 10    language java
 11    name 'com.wrox.util.file.LobExtensions.writeToFile(
 12      oracle.sql.BLOB, java.lang.String,
 13      java.lang.String) return long';
 14
 15    function write_to_file (
 16      p_lob_loc in blob,
 17      p_path in varchar2
 18    ) return number
 19    as
 20    language java
 21    name 'com.wrox.util.file.LobExtensions.writeToFile(
 22      oracle.sql.BLOB, java.lang.String) return long';
 23
 24    function write_to_file (
 25      p_lob_loc in clob,
 26      p_directory in varchar2,
 27      p_file_name in varchar2
 28    ) return number
 29    as
 30    language java
 31    name 'com.wrox.util.file.LobExtensions.writeToFile(
 32      oracle.sql.CLOB, java.lang.String,
 33      java.lang.String) return long';
 34
 35    function write_to_file (
 36      p_lob_loc in clob,
 37      p_path in varchar2
 38    ) return number
 39    as
 40    language java
 41    name 'com.wrox.util.file.LobExtensions.writeToFile(
 42      oracle.sql.CLOB, java.lang.String) return long';
 43
 44  end;
```

```
   45  /

Package body created.
```

## Using the Package

Once all necessary components have been created, it is time to test the functionality of our package. In the example below we create a sample BLOB table, insert a new BLOB into the table and then write that BLOB to a file. Note that you need to alter the path to the destination file to suit your own platform. Note also that you need write permission for the specified file (as we have discussed before), or else the procedure throws a security exception.

```
SQL> create table blobs (
  2      id number,
  3      b blob
  4  );

Table created.

SQL> declare
  2      buffer raw(255) := utl_raw.cast_to_raw('Some nonsense...');
  3      amt binary_integer := 32767;
  4      pos integer := 1;
  5      new_id number := 10;
  6      lob_loc blob;
  7      length number;
  8  begin
  9
 10      -- ceate a new BLOB
 11        insert into blobs values (new_id, empty_blob());
 12        select b
 13          into lob_loc
 14          from blobs
 15         where id = new_id
 16           for update;
 17
 18      dbms_lob.write (lob_loc, utl_raw.length(buffer), pos, buffer);
 19      commit;
 20
 21      -- write the BLOB to a file, change this for your own setup
 22      length := utl_lob_ext.write_to_file(lob_loc, 'C:\nonsense.dump');
 23
 24  end;
 25  /

PL/SQL procedure successfully completed.
```

When this is run, and all necessary permissions have been granted, it should produce a new binary file in the specified location.

# Running OS Commands and Executables

In this section, we will discuss methods of executing **external programs** from Java applications running within the database. This should not be confused with methods of remote method invocation or interoperability between languages, such as calling a C++ function from a Java method. Rather, in this context, we are referring to the process of running operating system executables, such as notepad.exe or ps.sh, from a procedure within the database. Such can be especially useful in relation to Oracle-specific executables, as we will see in an example later, when we develop a procedure for running SQL*Loader on a specified input file.

Although the methods we develop in this chapter apply to all external programs executable by the Oracle software account, there is one class of programs we have particular interest in, namely **command-line interpreters**. A command-line interpreter is a common term for a program employed by users of the operating system in question to work with files, programs, and other operating system resources. For example, the DOS prompt is the inherent command-line interpreter for the Windows platform, while on a UNIX system, you can choose between various interpreters (or shells), such as the Korne and Bourne shells. Since a command-line interpreter provides you with an environment in which you can perform various platform-dependent operations and potentially run other programs, you should *think twice before using one* from your stored procedures. The reason for this is that these programs in some sense bypass the security system of the Java runtime environment, because if you have been granted access to a particular command-line interpreter, you can use that to perform actions which you have otherwise not been permitted, such as remove important files or run insecure programs. Still, we find it useful at times to use a particular command line interpreter not to run other programs, but rather to issue a command from its inherent command set. With some tricks and clever thinking, we can even do this securely, as we will illustrate later in this section.

In short, we will be looking at:

❑ Issues regarding running an external command or program, including the runtime environment and processes involved

❑ Writing a procedure stored in the database from which we call the SQL*Loader utility

❑ Things issuing operating system commands

❑ Implementing a Java stored procedure for extracting environment variables from the operating system

## Running an External Program

The process of running an operating system executable from Java involves the use of two core classes, java.lang.Runtime and java.lang.Process. In short, the intended executable is provided as an argument to the exec() method of the Runtime class, which effectively runs the program as a separate process. The exec() method returns a Process instance which encapsulates this native process and contains methods for its management. For example, through public methods of the Process class the application can provide the process with input, read its stream of output and extract error messages if the command does not succeed. The Runtime and Process classes are further illustrated in the UML diagram below (note that deprecated methods have been omitted):

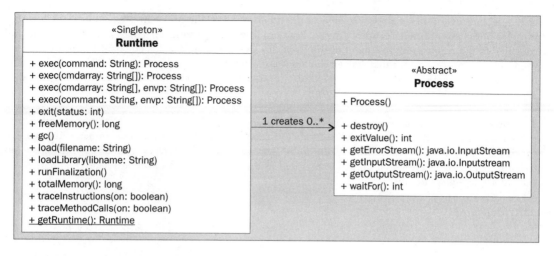

## The Runtime Environment

The `Runtime` class allows the application to interface with the environment in which it is running. For example, through methods of the `Runtime` class, the application can load dynamic libraries, get information on memory usage, and execute custom scripts in the runtime environment. The last of these is the subject of this section.

The `Runtime` class follows the **Singleton design pattern**, in that there exists only a single instance of `Runtime` for each JVM and the application is not allowed to create a new instance. An instance of the `Runtime` class is accessible through the static `getRuntime()` method, as shown here:

```
Runtime rt = Runtime.getRuntime();
```

> *A **Singleton** is a design pattern that constrains a class to a single unique instance which clients can reference by calling a static method. Further discussion on the Singleton pattern can be found in various design books, such as* Design Patterns *by Erich Gamma, Richard Helm, Ralph Johnson, and John Vlissides, ISBN 0201633612 published by Addison Wesley.*

### Executing Commands

The `Runtime` class contains four variations of a method called `exec()`, which can be used to execute external programs from a Java application. The four `exec()` method variations are illustrated below:

```
public Process exec(String command);
public Process exec(String[] cmdArray);
public Process exec(String command, String[] envp);
public Process exec(String[] cmdArray, String[] envp);
```

The last method variation takes for arguments an array of commands that should be executed and an array of environment properties, where each element in the array has the format:

```
name=value
```

**501**

Often, it is necessary to set a specific environment before a specific program is executed, which is the purpose of the environment property array. If an environment variable specified in this array is already specified in the runtime environment of the JVM (for the Oracle JVM, this equals the environment of the Oracle software account that started the database), the specified value overrides the existing value for the process created by the `exec()` method (in other words, it does not override the existing value *permanently*, only for the sub-process created).

The three first `exec()` methods all relay their functionality to the last method. When an environment properties array is not specified, a null reference is used instead. When a single command line string is specified, it is split up by the default token of the `StringTokenizer` class (which is a whitespace) and transformed to an array, which in turn is supplied as the first argument to the last `exec()` method, the second argument set to null.

### Security Concerns

The `Runtime.exec()` method can execute any executable file in the file system, given two security prerequisites:

❏ The specified file is executable by the user who initialized the JVM, which is the Oracle software account

❏ The code running the `exec()` method has been granted the execute permission of `java.io.FilePermission` for the intended file

The first prerequisite is dependent on the operating system in question (for example, on a UNIX system, `chmod` with the appropriate permissions should be executed on the intended file). The latter prerequisite is a matter of setting the appropriate Java security permissions for the database user who owns the piece of code running the `exec()` method. In Chapter 11, we discuss the details of the Oracle Java security model, including the `java.io.FilePermission`. To be able to execute a file, an explicit `execute` permission has to be granted through the `java.io.FilePermission`. For example, consider the following code fragment that grants user `USERNAME` execute privileges on the Notepad application file, under a Windows OS:

```
SQL> call dbms_java.grant_permission (
  2     'USERNAME',
  3     'java.io.FilePermission',
  4     'C:\Windows\Notepad.exe',
  5     'execute'
  6  );

Call completed.
```

Note that by granting an **execute** permission on a specific command language interpreter, as we will discuss later, you effectively bypass the security constraints of the JVM, since the specified interpreter can be used to execute programs not directly executable by the database user in question. We will discuss this in more detail later in this section.

In addition to an `execute FilePermission`, there is an additional security permission grant required for Java applications that wish to execute external programs through the `Runtime.exec()` method. Since the program executed might produce output, the code performing the execution must be granted explicit `writeFileDescriptor RuntimePermission` to write *all* file descriptors. This is because it is generally not known what kind of output the child process creates, and where that output is written. For example, continuing from our previous example, here is how USERNAME is granted the necessary `RuntimePermission`:

```
SQL> call dbms_java.grant_permission (
  2     'USERNAME',
  3     'java.lang.RuntimePermission',
  4     '*',
  5     'writeFileDescriptor'
  6  );

Call completed.
```

Generally, because of these extensive permissions needed in order to execute external programs, you should carefully consider to whom you permit this ability. Even though the program intended to execute may be harmless, it opens up security holes to allow code from within the JVM to execute it externally. For example, great harm can easily be done if a harmless executable is replaced with a more malicious version, which is often the intent of many modern viruses.

Also, as we mentioned before, you should note that the process spawned by a call to `Runtime.exec()` executes under the security domain of the account used to start up the database, in other words, the Oracle software account. This account is granted extensive operating system permissions, most notably full permission to both read and write all files in the Oracle file hierarchy. Thus, there is nothing stopping a process executed from the Oracle JVM potentially altering or removing vital files of the database – such as data, tablespaces, and redo files.

> To emphasize, you should show great care when executing external programs from the JVM.

So, because of these security considerations, why are we illustrating this process of running external programs in the first place? Well, in short, although potentially unsafe, this feature of Java has its uses. For example, it can be useful to execute a particular Oracle program, such as SQL*Loader, from a stored procedure triggered by the database. Although someone could potentially replace the SQL*Loader executable with a harmful program that overwrites important data files, that same person could obviously have done the same damage in the first place, since they had write permission to the ORACLE_HOME/bin directory!

There is more potential that a malicious user or virus would write a new program with the same name as an existing program, and place it somewhere in the library path of the software account in question – in our case, Oracle – so that it appears before the *actual* program. For example, assume that a particular Oracle software account has the following two environment variables set (on a UNIX system):

```
ORACLE_HOME=/usr/local/oracle
PATH=/usr/bin:/usr/local/sbin:$ORACLE_HOME/bin.
```

Assuming that some virus has write access to the `/usr/local/sbin` directory, it could write a file called `sqlldr.sh` to that directory, which means that if a user logged on to the Oracle account would execute the SQL*Loader executable as shown here:

```
> sqlldr userid=username/password control=sample.ctl
```

it would in fact execute the wrong program, the one placed by the virus, which in turn would be run with privileges of the Oracle account!

*This type of software intrusion has been rightly compared to the famous Trojan horse.*

However, there is a simple solution to this. By identifying all executables with their absolute path, we can avoid this type of attack. We will employ this method in all of our examples in this section, and encourage you to do the same.

## Processes

The `exec()` method of the `Runtime` class is used to execute a specified command from the Java context. The command is executed as a separate operating system process, specifically, a *child process* of the JVM process. The `exec()` method returns an instance of the `java.lang.Process` class, which encapsulates the child process that is created by the command execution. Through methods of the `Process` class, the application can read input from the process, send output to the process, wait for the process to complete, check the process exit status, and potentially destroy the process.

*That the process created by the `exec()` method is a child process of the JVM process means that it should terminate if the parent process is terminated.*

### Process Management

When a child process has been created through the `Runtime.exec()` method, it can be managed through methods of the `Process` class. Specifically, these methods allow the application to:

- **Destroy the Process**
  The child process can be forcibly terminated with a call to the `destroy()` method.

- **Obtain the Process Exit Value**
  The `exitValue()` method returns the exit value for the sub-process. Although the exit value returned is generally OS-specific (for example, on the Windows OS, a value of 2 specifies a `file not found` error), a value of 0 always specifies a normal process termination, while any non-zero value indicates a failure. The specific nature of a process failure can be determined by processing the process error stream, as we will discuss later.

  If the external process represented by the `Process` instance has not terminated, a call to the `exitValue()` method will throw an `IllegalStateException`. To wait until a process terminates, the `waitFor()` method should rather be used.

- **Wait for the Process to Finish**
  Usually, a process takes some time to finish. For example, a process that runs SQL*Loader with a large input file might take a few seconds to terminate. A common mistake when working with processes in Java, is to directly call `exitValue()` after the process has been started. If the process has not been terminated, this will throw an `IllegalStateException`.

To securely wait for a process to terminate normally, the waitFor() method should rather be used. This method waits for the process to terminate and then returns the return value, which would have been obtained from exitValue() after the process had finished. Generally, the only time you should use exitValue() instead of waitFor() is when you don't want your program to get blocked by waiting on an external process that may never complete. If you want to wait for a process to complete, but still avoid blocking the whole application, you should consider running a thread that monitors the process and throws an exception if a specific maximum waiting time has been reached. This is further illustrated below.

> Note that although a specified process terminates successfully – in other words, with an exit value of zero – this does not necessarily mean that the command that was run by the process executed with the intended results, even though this is often the case. The process exit value only indicates that the process itself, and thereby the executed command, did not terminate abnormally. A utility executed by a process might exit normally even though its results were not what the application expected. In such a case, the application should investigate the output from the process, as well as its exit value, to successfully determine the correct course of action.

The following example illustrates a Windows process that executes the Oracle export program for the USERNAME database schema. As this process might take some time to finish, depending on the size of the USERNAME schema, we call the waitFor() method to securely allow it to terminate:

```
public boolean export(String expFile) throws Exception {

    String[] cmds = {
      "C:\\Oracle\\Ora81\\bin\exp",
      "username/password",
      "file=" + expFile
    };
    Process proc = Runtime.getRuntime().exec(cmds);
    return (proc.waitFor() == 0);
}
```

In other cases, it may not be acceptable to wait too long for a process to terminate. Consider the following example, which illustrates a class that is used to ping a specific host name to determine whether the host can be reached through the network. This class effectively calls the UNIX ping utility, using the specified host name as an argument. If a specified host cannot be reached through the network, the ping request might time-out. Generally, if the host is not reached within a few seconds, it is considered unreachable. To use the waitFor() method to wait for the process to finish may block the invoking method for much more time than the time it takes to determine whether the host is unreachable (according to our definition, that is). Therefore, we have the ping() method repeatedly check whether exitValue() returns an exit value or throws an exception. When the ping() method has waited on the process for a few seconds without any results, it should force it to terminate, and indicate that the host specified could not be reached. This is further illustrated in the code below:

```
public class Ping {

  public static boolean ping(String host) {
```

```
        // 5 seconds time interval,
        return ping(host, 5000);
    }

    public static boolean ping(String host, long timeFrame) {

        // Start the process.
        int val;
        Process proc = null;
        try {

            // Change this path for your own system.
            proc = Runtime.getRuntime().exec("C:\\Windows\\ping " + host);

        } catch (Exception e) {
            return false;
        }

        // Wait either for the process to end
        // or the specified time limit to pass.
        if (proc != null) {
            long startTime = System.currentTimeMillis();
            while ((System.currentTimeMillis() - startTime) < timeFrame) {
                try {

                    // Check the process exit value.
                    // If the process has not terminated,
                    // this will throw an IllegalStateException.
                    val = proc.exitValue();
                    return (val == 0);

                } catch (IllegalStateException ignored) {}
            }

            // The request has timed out,
            // terminate the process.
            proc.destroy();
            return false;
        }
        return false;
    }
}
```

In short, an application calls the static ping() method of the Ping class which runs the ping command on the host name specified. This method returns true if the host was successfully contacted, but false if either the host was not contacted or if the process timed out.

Although this may seem simple, there is one big defect to our current version of the Ping class – namely what happens when the ping process returns within the specified time limit, and returns an indication of success (in other words, a return value of zero), but the host was still *not* reached. In the next section, we will investigate that issue further.

### Process I/O

All standard I/O operations of the child process are redirected to the parent process through standard Java streams, which are made accessible through public methods of the `Process` class. These methods, along with the respective I/O operations, are illustrated below.

> Note that `Process` class I/O terminology is relative to the parent process, and not the child process. That way, you use `getOutputStream()` to write information *to* the child process, while `getInputStream()` returns a stream of output *from* the child process.

❑ `getOutputStream()`
This method returns an output stream to the child process as a `java.io.OutputStream` instance. You use the `getOutputStream()` method to write instructions to the child process. This stream is compatible with `stdout`.

❑ `getInputStream()`
This method returns a stream of output from the child process. For example, if you issue a `dir` command through `Runtime.exec()`, the sub-process output stream should include the directory listing relative to the directory where the JVM was initialized. This stream is compatible with `stdin`.

❑ `getErrorStream()`
This method returns a stream of error messages from the child process. This stream is compatible with `stderr`.

For example, the following example executes the `ping` utility and writes the appropriate output to the standard output device:

*If you try to run this code snippet from SQL\*Plus, you should first call SET SERVEROUTPUT ON and then DBMS_JAVA.SET_OUTPUT(), with an appropriate buffer size. More on this in Chapter 9 Using the Oracle JVM.*

```
InputStream is;
BufferedReader br;
String line=null;

// change this for your own system
Process proc = Runtime.getRuntime().exec("C:\\Windows\\ping -nonsense");
int exitValue = proc.waitFor();

// process output stream
is = proc.getInputStream();
br = new BufferedReader(new InputStreamReader(is));
while ((line = br.readLine()) != null) {
  System.out.println(line);
}
is.close();
```

This piece of code should produce output similar to the following (exact details of course vary between individual platforms):

```
Pinging localhost [127.0.0.1] with 32 bytes of data:

Reply from 127.0.0.1: bytes=32 time<10ms TTL=128
Reply from 127.0.0.1: bytes=32 time<10ms TTL=128
Reply from 127.0.0.1: bytes=32 time<10ms TTL=128
Reply from 127.0.0.1: bytes=32 time<10ms TTL=128

Ping statistics for 127.0.0.1:
    Packets: Sent = 4, Received = 4, Lost = 0 (0% loss),
Approximate round trip times in milli-seconds:
    Minimum = 0ms, Maximum =  0ms, Average =  0ms
```

The next example executes an erroneous command – the Oracle export utility with an invalid option – and writes the resulting error message to the standard error stream:

> *The reason why we could not use* ping *for this example is that it never sends output to the standard error stream, as we will see later.*

```
InputStream is;
BufferedReader br;
String line=null;

Process proc = Runtime.getRuntime().exec("exp usename/password
                                   nosuchargument");
int exitValue = proc.waitFor();

// Process output stream.
is = proc.getErrorStream();
br = new BufferedReader(new InputStreamReader(is));
while ((line = br.readLine()) != null) {
    System.err.println(line);
}
is.close();
```

This code should produce an output to the standard error stream, similar to the one shown here:

```
LRM-00108: invalid positional parameter value 'nosuchargument'
EXP-00019: failed to process parameters, type 'EXP HELP=Y' for help
EXP-00000: Export terminated unsuccessfully
```

Remember that in our Ping example from the previous sub-section, we mentioned the ping process could possibly terminate with a return value of zero, even though the host name specified was unavailable. The reason for this is that the ping utility does not exit abnormally when a specified host cannot be reached. Rather, this utility will write the results of the contact attempt to the standard output stream. When a specified host is unreachable, the ping utility will provide an output that states Request timed out. In our Ping sample class, we must appropriately handle such output, as shown in the modified code for the ping() method below:

```
if (proc.exitValue() == 0) {
  StringBuffer output = new StringBuffer();
  BufferedReader reader;
  try {
    reader = new BufferedReader(
      new InputStreamReader(
        proc.getInputStream()
      )
    );
    while (reader.ready()) {
      output.append(reader.readLine());
    }
    is.close();
  } catch (IOException ignored) {
  }

  // Determine ping results.
  return (output != null &&
    output.toString().indexOf("Request timed out") == -1);
} else {
  return false;
}
```

## Running SQL*Loader from a Procedure

To illustrate the use of running external programs from a stored procedure within the database, we will implement a simple Java class which runs the Oracle SQL*Loader data import utility to load into the database data from text-based files in the file system. This section is *not* intended as an introduction to the SQL*Loader program. For more information on the subject, you should consult the Oracle documentation.

### Why use SQL*Loader?

Instead of running SQL*Loader as an external process, we could just as well implement a PL/SQL or Java procedure which reads specified input and control files, and inserts each line in the input file to the table specified by the control file. This way, the data import process would be within our transaction control, unlike what happens when we run SQL*Loader.

While these are all valid arguments, the main reason we choose to import data from file with SQL*Loader is *performance*. SQL*Loader is very efficient and can be used to load vast amounts of data into the database in very short time. With a specific command line option, it can even load data using a direct path to the database blocks, bypassing the SQL engine altogether. This is the fastest way possible for loading data into the database.

> *Of course, you could potentially write a C-based procedure for direct path load through OCI, but that is far more complex than what we will illustrate here.*

### Database Objects

In our SQL*Loader application, each call to the program will be identified by a unique transaction ID, stored in the LOADER_TRANSACTIONS database table, below. This table additionally stores the name of the control file in question and the date the transaction took place:

```
SQL> create table loader_transactions (
  2     transaction_id number,
  3     control_file varchar2(1000),
  4     transaction_date date default sysdate,
  5     constraint pk_loader_transactions
  6        primary key (transaction_id)
  7  );

Table created.
```

To generate new transaction IDs, we create a specific sequence and add a trigger to the LOADER_TRANSACTIONS table:

```
SQL> create sequence transaction_seq;

Sequence created.

SQL> create or replace trigger loader_transactions_seq
  2  before insert on loader_transactions
  3    for each row
  4  begin
  5    select transaction_seq.nextval into :new.transaction_id
  6       from dual;
  7  end;
  8  /

Trigger created.
```

The SQL*Loader program logs down all its activity in a log file in the file system. Additionally, it writes down a log of bad or discarded input rows in specific files. We are interested in this information, but not willing to go to the file system to view it. Therefore, we create specific tables for each file type, which will contain a row for each line in the respective output file:

```
SQL> create table loader_log (
  2     transaction_id number,
  3     line_number number,
  4     line varchar2(500),
  5     constraint pk_loader_log
  6        primary key (transaction_id, line_number),
  7     constraint fk_loader_log_tx_id
  8        foreign key (transaction_id) references loader_transactions
  9  );

Table created.

SQL> create table loader_bad (
  2     transaction_id number,
  3     line_number number,
  4     line varchar2(500),
  5     constraint pk_loader_bad
  6        primary key (transaction_id, line_number),
```

```
  7    constraint fk_loader_bad_tx_id
  8      foreign key (transaction_id) references loader_transactions
  9  );

Table created.

SQL> create table loader_discard (
  2    transaction_id number,
  3    line_number number,
  4    line varchar2(500),
  5    constraint pk_loader_discard
  6      primary key (transaction_id, line_number),
  7    constraint fk_loader_discard_tx_id
  8      foreign key (transaction_id) references loader_transactions
  9  );

Table created.
```

### The SqlLoader Java Class

The SqlLoader Java class contains a single public method, load(), which takes for arguments the user name and password of the schema to load into, and the name of the control file in question:

```
package com.wrox.util.loader;

import java.io.*;
import java.sql.*;

public class SqlLoader {

  private static Connection conn;

  public static long load(String userName, String password,
                          String controlFile) throws Exception {

    BufferedReader err;
    CallableStatement cstmt;
    File ctrlFile = null;
    File logFile = null;
    File badFile = null;
    File discardFile = null;
    long txid = -1;
    String line;
    String parent = "";
    StringBuffer buffer;
    Process proc;

    // initialize the connection
    if (conn == null) {
      conn = DriverManager.getConnection("jdbc:oracle:kprb:@");
    }
```

The `load()` method starts by checking whether the specified control file really exists. If not, an exception is thrown:

```
ctrlFile = new File(controlFile);
if (!ctrlFile.exists()) {
  throw new Exception("The specified control file does not exist!");
}
parent = ctrlFile.getParent();
```

Next, a new transaction ID is obtained from the CREATE_TRANSACTION() function in the UTL_LOADER PL/SQL package which we will discuss later:

```
try {

  // insert a new transaction
    conn.prepareCall(
      "begin ? := utl_loader.create_transaction(?); end;");
  cstmt.registerOutParameter(1, Types.NUMERIC);
  cstmt.setString(2, controlFile);
  cstmt.execute();
  txid = cstmt.getLong(1);
```

We make sure that all output files are created in the same directory as the control file. These files are uniquely identified by the current transaction ID.

```
  // initiate the output file objects
  logFile = new File(parent, "loader" + txid + ".log");
  badFile = new File(parent, "loader" + txid + ".bad");
  discardFile = new File(parent, "loader" + txid + ".discard");
```

Next, we prepare the SQLLDR execution. Note that we hard-code the path to the SQLLDR executable in our code (we don't want to locate the program by the Oracle software account's library path, due to the reasons we discussed earlier in this section), but a better alternative would be to load the interpreter name from the database, as we will do later in this chapter, for the Environment class.

Note also that in our current implementation, we are by no means utilizing all the options of the SQL*Loader program. For the sake of simplicity, we will use only the most standard options (in other words, specify schema, control file and output files). Of course, in your own implementation, you might add more features and options to this class.

```
String[] cmds = {

  // Note that we hard-code this at the moment.
  "C:\\Oracle\\Ora81\\bin\\sqlldr", userName + "/" + password,
    "control=" + controlFile,
    "log=" + logFile.getAbsolutePath(),
    "bad=" + badFile.getAbsolutePath(),
    "discard=" + discardFile.getAbsolutePath()
};
```

Next, we execute the command and wait for the process to finish. If it returns a non-zero exit value, we throw an exception, supplying the error stream we obtain from the process.

```
// execute the program
proc = Runtime.getRuntime().exec(cmds);

// determine the return value
if (proc.waitFor() != 0) {

  // process the error stream and throw an exception accordingly
  err =
    new BufferedReader(new InputStreamReader(proc.getErrorStream()));
  buffer = new StringBuffer();
  while (err.ready()) {
    buffer.append(err.readLine());
  }
  err.close();
  throw new Exception(buffer.toString());
}
```

If the execution was successful, we process each of the output files with a call to the private `processFile()` method, defined below. This method reads the respective file and for each row, inserts a new row in a corresponding database table. Note that if the call was successful, we will only need to process the actual log file. This is reflected in the `processFile()` method, where we check whether the specified file really exists:

```
processFile(logFile, "loader_log", txid);
processFile(badFile, "loader_bad", txid);
processFile(discardFile, "loader_discard", txid);

conn.commit();

// rollback
} catch (Exception e) {
conn.rollback();
throw e;

// delete all files on exit
} finally {

if (logFile.exists()) {
  logFile.delete();
}

if (badFile.exists()) {
  badFile.delete();
}

if (discardFile.exists()) {
  discardFile.delete();
}
}

return txid;
}
```

To process each output file, we use the same private method, processFile(), as we have already mentioned. This method takes for arguments the File object to process, the name of the table to insert into, and the current transaction ID. It reads each line of the file in question and inserts it into the specified table. For that purpose, we use JDBC, with update batching.

*The reason why we choose to use Java rather than PL/SQL to read the output files, is because of the file access limitations of PL/SQL. As you may remember from our file section at the beginning of this chapter, PL/SQL can only access files in directories directly specified in the database's init.ora configuration file. Since our SQL\*Loader class takes for an input a custom control file, it is much easier for us to grant file access permission to a Java procedure, through its dynamic security model, rather than update the init.ora file for each new control file.*

```
    private static void processFile(File f, String table,
                                    long txid) throws Exception {

    if (f.exists()) {

        PreparedStatement pstmt = conn.prepareStatement(
          "insert into "
          + table + " (" + "transaction_id, line_number, line) "
          + "values (?, ?, ?)");

        BufferedReader reader =
          new BufferedReader(new InputStreamReader(new FileInputStream(f)));
        int i = 1;
        while (reader.ready()) {
          pstmt.setLong(1, txid);
          pstmt.setInt(2, i++);
          pstmt.setString(3, reader.readLine());
          pstmt.addBatch();
        }
        pstmt.executeBatch();
        pstmt.close();
      }
    }
  }
```

### Loading the Java Class into the Database

Once the Java class has been created, it must be loaded into the database, for example by using loadjava, as we have done before:

```
> loadjava -user username/pass@database -oci8 -resolve SqlLoader.java
```

### The UTL_LOADER Package

Once we have loaded the SqlLoader class into the database, we create a PL/SQL package, UTL_LOADER, for various methods. We have already mentioned the CREATE_TRANSACTION() function, which inserts a new row into the LOADER_TRANSACTIONS table. Additionally, we define a LOAD() procedure, which maps the load() method of the SqlLoader class. The UTL_LOADER package is illustrated below:

```
SQL> create or replace package utl_loader
  2  is
  3    function create_transaction (
  4      p_control_file varchar2
  5    ) return number;
  6
  7    function load (
  8      p_user_name varchar2,
  9      p_password varchar2,
 10      p_control_file varchar2,
 11      p_direct_path number
 12    ) return number;
 13
 14  end;
 15  /

Package created.

SQL> create or replace package body utl_loader
  2  is
  3
  4    function create_transaction (
  5      p_control_file varchar2
  6    ) return number
  7    is
  8      txid number;
  9    begin
 10
 11      insert into loader_transactions (control_file)
 12      values (p_control_file)
 13      returning transaction_id into txid;
 14
 15      return txid;
 16
 17    end;
 18
 19    function load (
 20      p_user_name varchar2,
 21      p_password varchar2,
 22      p_control_file varchar2,
 23      p_direct_path number
 24    ) return number
 25    as
 26    language java
 27    name 'com.wrox.util.loader.SqlLoader.load(
 28      java.lang.String, java.lang.String,
 29      java.lang.String, int) return long';
 30
 31  end;
 32  /

Package body created.
```

## Using the Package

You can use the UTL_LOADER PL/SQL package or the SqlLoader Java class directly in your applications to dynamically invoke the SQL*Loader utility. As an example, we will illustrate a sample scenario that uses the UTL_LOADER package to load data from a file to the database.

First, we begin by creating a sample table which holds one numeric column and another character column:

```
SQL> create table demo (
  2     x number,
  3     y varchar2(500)
  4  );

Table created.
```

For this table, we use the following control file, called demo.ctl (in our case, using Windows 98, located on the desktop, at C:\WINDOWS\Desktop). This control file also contains all of the data we are going to load in:

```
load data
infile *
into table demo (
  x,
  y
)
begindata
1          Number one
2          Number two
3          Number three
4          Number four
```

Before we can use our UTL_LOADER package, we must grant the corresponding schema appropriate permissions. Aside from an execute permission for the SQLLDR executable, and a permission to read and write file descriptors (as we have discussed before), the schema must have full permission to read, write, and delete files in the directory of the control file. This is illustrated below, where we are logged on as the SYSTEM user, assuming user USERNAME is being used:

```
SQL> call dbms_java.grant_permission (
  2     'USERNAME',
  3     'java.io.FilePermission',
  4     'C:\Oracle\Ora81\bin\sqlldr',
  5     'execute'
  6  );

Call completed.

SQL> call dbms_java.grant_permission (
  2     'USERNAME',
  3     'java.lang.RuntimePermission',
  4     'writeFileDescriptor',
  5     '*'
  6  );

Call completed.
```

```
SQL> call dbms_java.grant_permission (
  2    'USERNAME',
  3    'java.lang.RuntimePermission',
  4    'readFileDescriptor',
  5    '*'
  6  );

Call completed.

SQL> call dbms_java.grant_permission (
  2    'USERNAME',
  3    'java.io.FilePermission',
  4    'C:\WINDOWS\Desktop\*',
  5    'read,write,delete'
  6  );

Call completed.
```

Next, we can run the LOAD() function, as illustrated below:

```
SQL> declare
  2    txid number;
  3  begin
  4    txid := utl_loader.load('username', 'password',
  5                            'C:\WINDOWS\Desktop\demo.ctl', 0);
  6    dbms_output.put_line('Transaction ID: ' || txid);
  7  end;
  8  /

PL/SQL procedure successfully completed.
```

Now, we can query the LOADER_LOG table for the last transaction to see how this process went:

```
SQL> select line
  2    from loader_log
  3    where transaction_id = (
  4      select max(transaction_id)
  5        from loader_transactions
  6    )
  7    order by line_number;

LINE
-------------------------------------------------------------------------------


SQL*Loader: Release 8.1.6.0.0 - Production on Tue Nov 6 12:25:06 2001

(c) Copyright 1999 Oracle Corporation.  All rights reserved.

Control File:    C:\WINDOWS\Desktop\demo.ctl
Data File:       C:\WINDOWS\Desktop\demo.dat
  Bad File:      C:\WINDOWS\Desktop\loader1.bad
  Discard File: C:\WINDOWS\Desktop\loader1.discard
 (Allow all discards)
```

```
Number to load: ALL
Number to skip: 0
Errors allowed: 50
Bind array:     64 rows, maximum of 65536 bytes
Continuation:   none specified
Path used:      Conventional

Table DEMO, loaded from every logical record.
Insert option in effect for this table: INSERT

   Column Name                          Position  Len  Term Encl Datatype
   ------------------------------------ --------- ---- ---- ---- -----------------
X                                          1:10   10                  CHARACTER
Y                                         11:20   10                  CHARACTER


Table DEMO:
  4 Rows successfully loaded.
  0 Rows not loaded due to data errors.
  0 Rows not loaded because all WHEN clauses were failed.
  0 Rows not loaded because all fields were null.


Space allocated for bind array:                    1536 bytes(64 rows)
Space allocated for memory besides bind array:        0 bytes

Total logical records skipped:          0
Total logical records read:             4
Total logical records rejected:         0
Total logical records discarded:        0

Run began on Sat Nov 03 12:25:06 2001
Run ended on Sat Nóv 03 12:25:07 2001

Elapsed time was:     00:00:00.18
CPU time was:         00:00:00.00

47 rows selected.
```

Further queries on the LOADER_BAD and LOADER_DISCARD tables should return no results, if everything went well.

### Common Problems

When you invoke the load() method you must make sure that you supply the full path to the control file, and not just the actual file name. If not, you might get an error like the following:

```
ORA-29532: Java call terminated by uncaught Java exception: java.lang.Exception:
SQL*Loader-500:
Unable to open file (demo.dat)SQL*Loader-553: file not foundSQL*Loader-509: System
error: The system cannot find the file specified.
ORA-06512: at "USERNAME.UTL_LOADER", line 18
ORA-06512: at line 4
```

Additionally, you must make sure that all Java permissions are appropriately granted. For example, if you don't explicitly grant a permission to write file descriptors, you might get the following error:

```
ORA-29532: Java call terminated by uncaught Java exception:
java.security.AccessControlException:
the Permission (java.lang.RuntimePermission writeFileDescriptor ) has not been
granted by dbms_java.grant_permission to
SchemaProtectionDomain(USERNAME|PolicyTableProxy(WROX_6020))
ORA-06512: at "USERNAME.UTL_LOADER", line 18
ORA-06512: at line 4
```

### Further Thoughts

An interesting example of how our application can be used is to use the UTL_LOADER package in conjunction with the UTL_FILE_EXT package we defined earlier in this chapter, by creating a procedure which regularly scans a specified directory (using the UTL_FILE_EXT.LIST() function), possibly run as a job with the DBMS_JOB package, and checks whether any input files have been modified. If so, it invokes the SQL*Loader for the corresponding control files. This can be useful in a scenario where an external process regularly dumps data in a specified directory, which in turn has to be fed to the database. We leave this idea as an exercise for you to implement!

# Issuing Operating System Commands

The intent of this section is to illustrate how the Runtime class can be used to execute OS-dependent shell commands, such as dir, echo, and copy under DOS, and ps, ls, and grep under the Bourne shell.

A common misconception with the Runtime class and operating system commands is to pass only the specified command as an argument to the exec() method, and omit the specific command language interpreter. For example:

```
// this will not work!
Process proc = Runtime.getRuntime().exec("mkdir holm");
```

The reason why this code does not work is that the mkdir command is a part of the command language interpreter and *not* a standalone executable. In other words, there is no executable called mkdir.exe or mkdir.sh located in the current environment path. To specify commands that are part of a command language interpreter, the command line interpreter executable *must* be specified as the *first* executable in the command array argument to Runtime.exec(). Following the interpreter executable, there must a flag specifying that a child process *should* be created. For the DOS command interpreter, this flag should be /C, while for the UNIX Bourne shell, this flag should be -c. Next, there should be specified the commands to execute, along with any arguments. For example:

```
// this will work
String[] cmds = {
  "C:\\Windows\\command.com",
  "/C",
  "mkdir",
  "holm"
};
Process proc = Runtime.getRuntime().exec(cmds);
```

On a Windows 95/98 operating system this code will work, given that the appropriate file permissions are granted.

> **To emphasize, in order to issue operating system commands, you must specify the command language interpreter in question as the first argument to `Runtime.exec()`, followed by the command in question.**

## Further Security Concerns

The security concerns we had for the process of running external programs from Java in general are especially strong in regard to operating system or shell commands. This is because in order to issue operating system commands, you must be granted the permission to execute the respective command language interpreter. By doing that, you can violate other security constraints, since you can use the command line shell to issue arbitrary commands and executables, given that the Oracle software account has permission to do so. Thereby, a harmless grant to allow some user access to environment variables through a command line would in fact, allow that user to remove or alter vital resources of the file system, including all of the Oracle file hierarchy. Therefore, use great caution before granting permission to command language interpreters.

In spite of these precautions, it can be useful to reach out of the database and execute operating system functions. This is especially true in relation to environment variables, which are otherwise not accessible through either Java or PL/SQL. We have seen in this chapter how important is it to obtain the value for certain environment variables, such as ORACLE_HOME, in order to avoid hard-coding path names in our applications. In fact, at the end of this section, we will implement a stored procedure for doing just that. Such a process can be secured, for example, by creating a specific user for the procedure in question, and allowing other users to run just that procedure with definer rights (rather than invoker rights, as is the default behavior for Java). The security of the database is not compromised in any way by doing this, since the schema in question is protected by the security constraints of the Oracle database (for example by the user name and password). By securing access to the specified schema, which is something we need to do with all of our schemas, we can make sure this specific permission to run the command language interpreter does not get violated. Again, we will illustrate this in more detail at the end of this section.

## Common Command Language Interpreters

The most common DOS command language interpreters are listed below.

*In all of our Windows examples in this section, we will be using the Windows 95/98 command language interpreter.*

❑ **Windows NT/2000 – C:\WINNT\system32\cmd.exe**
This is the DOS command line interpreter for Windows NT and all later Windows variations that build on that operating system, such as Windows 2000.

❑ **Windows 95/98/ME – C:\Windows\command.com**
This is the DOS command interpreter for Windows 95 and all later Windows variations that build on that operating system, such as Windows 98.

Some common UNIX shells, along with the location of their respective command language interpreter executable, are listed below. In all of our UNIX/Linux examples in this section, we will be using the Bourne shell.

❑ **Bourne shell – /bin/sh**
This is the most simple and compact of the UNIX shells.

❑ **Korne shell – /bin/ksh**
The Korne shell is a superset of the Bourne shell that allows for editing of the command line.

❑ **C shell – /bin/csh**
The C shell uses C-language syntax and conveniences.

## *Accessing Environment Variables*

An environment variable defines some aspect of a user's working environment, such as the location of important applications, default text editor to use, shell command aliases or the address of a display device.

It may often be useful to obtain information on the operating system working environment from a Java application. For example, for a Java stored procedure in the database, it can be necessary to obtain the value of ORACLE_HOME, to locate specific files and libraries to work with. Generally, there are three ways to access environment variables through Java programs:

❑ **Standard System Properties**
The getProperty() method of the System class returns the value of a specified system property. Available system property names can be determined by calling System.getProperties().propertyNames(), which returns an Enumeration of property names. The array of environment properties made available through the System class consists of a subset of variables from the working environment combined with a set of properties specific to the Java runtime environment. Roughly, the system properties can be divided in three categories:

  ❑ **Java Runtime Properties** – These are the properties of the Java runtime environment. For example, java.version specifies the JRE version, java.class.path specifies the class path of the runtime environment, and java.library.path specifies the JVM library path (equals the PATH environment variable).

  ❑ **User Environment Properties** – These are some of the properties of the user that initialized the JVM. For example, user.name specifies the user account's login name, user.language specifies the user's language code, and user.dir specifies the directory in which the user was located when the JVM was initialized.

  ❑ **Operating System Properties** – These are the properties of the underlying operating system. For example, os.name specifies the operating system name and os.version specifies the internal operating system version.

> You should note that not all of the standard system properties are available for Oracle Java programs. Later in this section, we will create a PL/SQL call spec for the System.getProperty() method, which you can use to verify the existence of specific properties.

❏ **JVM Initialization Parameters**

When a JVM is initialized through the `java` executable, specific system properties can be specified by the user with the `-D` command line flag. Properties specified in this manner are later accessible through the `System.getProperty()` method. For example, executing:

```
java -DsomeProperty=someValue MyClass
```

would run the `MyClass` Java class, which could access the `someProperty` property through the `getProperty()` method of the `System` class.

> This method of supplying properties to the JRE is not available for Java stored procedures in the database, as the user has no control over the initialization of the Oracle JVM.

❏ **Accessing Environment Variables from the Command Line**

Finally, one can access the value of specific environment variables by executing an *echo* command from a command line through the `exec()` method of the `Runtime` class.

The last method of accessing environment variables is the subject of this section. Specifically, in the paragraphs that follow, we will develop a Singleton Java class called `Environment` that the application can use to echo the value of a specific environment variable.

## System Properties

In many cases, it may be sufficient to obtain system properties from the Java context, without reaching out of the database, as we will illustrate later in this section. For that purpose, you can use the `System.getProperty()` method we discussed earlier. Note, however, that in order to use this method, you must be granted a specific permission. For example, to grant user USERNAME permission to read all system properties, you should log on as the SYSTEM user and issue the following:

```
SQL> call dbms_java.grant_permission (
  2     'USERNAME',
  3     'java.util.PropertyPermission',
  4     '*',
  5     'read'
  6  );

Call completed.
```

To obtain system properties from the SQL console, you can create the following PL/SQL function:

```
SQL> create or replace function get_system_property (
  2     property_name varchar2
  3  ) return varchar2
  4  as
  5  language java
  6  name 'java.lang.System.getProperty(java.lang.String)'
```

```
    7     return java.lang.string';
    8  /
```

```
Function created.
```

For example, if you are running your Oracle on a Solaris operating system, calling the
GET_SYSTEM_PROPERTY() function for the os.name system property should return SunOS, as shown
below:

```
SQL> set serveroutput on
SQL> call dbms_output.put_line(get_system_property('os.name'));
SunOS

Call completed.
```

> *Note that the value returned from a call to System.getProperty('os.name') from
> within the database might not be consistent with the value of a similar call from a Java program
> running outside the database. For example, it is known that when running Oracle 8.1.6 on the
> Windows 98 operating system, a call to System.getProperty('os.name') from inside
> the database returns the value of Windows 95, even though a regular Java application on the
> same machine gets the value Windows 98 when making a similar call. A similar problem exists
> for Oracle on Windows XP.*

## Extracting Environment Variables

In this section, we will implement a Java stored procedure for extracting environment variables from the
operating system. For this purpose, we create a specific database schema in which we create all objects and
grant permissions to run operating system commands. In the paragraphs below, we assume that we are
using a schema named USERNAME, as suggested in the opening *Setting Up* chapter of the book.

Our environment variables procedure consists of a single Java class, Environment, and a corresponding
PL/SQL call spec. The Environment class stores references to all environment variables that it has
already extracted, in order to avoid unnecessary processing. Since different operating systems use different
command language interpreters, we define a specific table that stores different interpreter types and
corresponding operating systems. When determining which operating system is currently in use, we use
the method of extracting system properties, which we illustrated above.

### Storing Command Line Interpreters

We use the COMMAND_INTERPRETERS table below to store command line interpreters for different
operating systems. The operating system names we use match those we would obtain with a call to
System.getProperty(), using the os.name property name.

```
SQL> create table command_interpreters (
    2     os_name varchar2(500),
    3     interpreter varchar2(500)
    4  );

Table created.
```

As an example, we add some interpreters for a few common operating systems:

```
SQL> -- Windows 95
SQL> insert into command_interpreters (os_name, interpreter)
  2  values ('Windows 95','c:\windows\command.com');

1 row created.

SQL> -- Windows NT
SQL> insert into command_interpreters (os_name, interpreter)
  2  values ('Windows NT','C:\WINNT\System32\cmd.exe');

1 row created.

SQL> -- Linux
SQL> insert into command_interpreters (os_name, interpreter)
  2  values ('Linux','/bin/sh');

1 row created.

SQL> -- Solaris
SQL> insert into command_interpreters (os_name, interpreter)
  2  values ('SunOS','/bin/sh');

1 row created.
```

## The Environment Class

The Environment class provides the application with methods to access operating system environment variables. The Environment class can be used to access every variable in the environment of the Oracle software account (in other words, the operating system user that started the database).

The Environment class follows the Singleton design pattern, in that there exists only a single Environment instance per JVM (we discussed the Singleton pattern earlier in this chapter). Clients, however, never access the Environment instance directly. Rather, they do this through the static echo() method, as shown here:

```
String display = Environment.echo("display");
```

The Environment class declaration is shown below:

```
package wrox.util;

import java.io.IOException;
import java.io.InputStream;
import java.util.Arrays;
import java.util.Hashtable;
import java.sql.Connection;
import java.sql.DriverManager;
import java.sql.PreparedStatement;
import java.sql.ResultSet;
```

```
    import java.sql.SQLException;

public class Environment {

    // Singleton instance.
    private static Environment instance;

    // Instance variables.
    private boolean argumentSeperate;
    private Hashtable env;
    private String[] cmdBase;
    private String prefix;
    private String suffix;
```

As we want only a single Environment instance to exist for each JVM, we declare the Environment constructor with a private visibility modifier. That way, only the Environment class can initialize itself. The Environment constructor initializes the environment variable hash table storage and calls the private setCommandSyntax() method, which we discuss below:

```
    private Environment() throws SQLException {
      env = new Hashtable();
      setCommandSyntax();
    }
```

The static echo() method is the only public method of the class. This method obtains a new Environment instance by calling the static getInstance() method, and relays its call to the execute() method:

```
    public static String echo(String variable)
       throws  IllegalArgumentException, SecurityException,
               IOException, SQLException {

       return getInstance().execute(variable);
    }

    public static Environment getInstance() throws SQLException {
      if (instance == null) {
        instance = new Environment();
      }
      return instance;
    }
```

The setCommandSyntax() method sets the command line syntax used to extract the environment variables. The reason we can't hard-code our syntax is that different operating systems use different arguments for the Runtime.execute() method. Not only do they use different command language interpreters, but they also use different flags for indicating a child process and different methods for indicating command arguments. UNIX systems specify a child process with the -c flag, while Windows systems use the /C flag for that purpose. Windows systems enclose environment variables with the % sign, while UNIX systems add only a $ prefix. Finally, on a Windows system you must specify the argument to the echo command as a separate element in the command array, while on a UNIX system, you append the argument to the echo command. This is further illustrated below:

> Note that you have to grant your user a **RuntimePermission** to read system properties, as we discussed earlier, for this class to work.

```
private void setCommandSyntax() throws SQLException {

    String interpreter = null;
    String osName = System.getProperty("os.name");
    #sql {
      select interpreter
      into :interpreter
      from command_interpreters
      where os_name = :osName
    };

    // This is a Windows system.
    if (osName.startsWith("Win")) {
      prefix = "%";
      suffix = "%";
      cmdBase = new String[4];
      cmdBase[0] = interpreter;
      cmdBase[1] = "/C";
      cmdBase[2] = "echo";
      cmdBase[4] = "echo";

    // This is a UNIX system.
    } else {
      prefix = "%";
      suffix = "%";
      cmdBase = new String[3];
      cmdBase[0] = interpreter;
      cmdBase[1] = "-c";
      cmdBase[2] = "echo ";
    }
  }
```

The `execute()` method shown below is used to obtain the value of a specified environment variable. The specified variable name is case-insensitive and should *not* be specified in an OS-specific manner. That is, instead of:

```
String oracleHome = Environment.echo("$ORACLE_HOME");
```

you should use:

```
String oracleHome = Environment.echo("ORACLE_HOME");
```

If the specified environment variable is not declared for the Oracle software account (whose environment we are working with, since we are operating within the Oracle JVM), the `execute()` method throws an `IllegalArgumentException`. A `SecurityException` is thrown if the invoker is not permitted to execute command line functions from Java. Finally, the method throws an `IOException` if an error occurs while running the `echo` command (in other words, incorrect command line syntax is being used):

```
private String execute(String variable)
    throws IllegalArgumentException, SecurityException, IOException {
```

First, the `execute()` method determines whether the specified environment variable has previously been retrieved. In that case, the stored value is returned. The operating system environment that the JVM is accessing equals the environment set when the database was started. This environment cannot change unless the database is restarted, which means that we can allow ourselves to store up caches of variable values to save unnecessary processing.

```
if (env.containsKey(variable)) {
    return (String) env.get(variable);
} else {
```

If the specified variable is not available, we prepare the command execution, based on the command line syntax declared for the current OS:

```
String osVariable = prefix + variable + suffix;
String value = null;

String[] cmd = new String[cmdBase.length];
System.arraycopy(cmdBase,0,cmd,0,cmdBase.length);
cmd[cmd.length-1] += osVariable;

// Execute the command array.
Process proc = Runtime.getRuntime().exec(cmd);

// Determine success.
boolean success;
try {
    success = (proc.waitFor() == 0);
} catch (InterruptedException e) {
    success = false;
}
```

If the execution was successful, we read the output from the process. This output should match the value of the specified environment variable:

```
if (success) {
    InputStream is = null;
    try {
        is = proc.getInputStream();
        byte[] b = new byte[is.available()];
        is.read(b);
        value = new String(b).trim();
```

If either there is no output available or if the output read equals the name of the environment variable (for example, on a Windows system, calling echo %NO_SUCH_VARIABLE% will simply return %NO_SUCH_VARIABLE%), we throw an `IllegalArgumentException`, which should indicate that the specified variable is not set for the current environment:

```
            if (value.length() == 0 || value.equals(osVariable)) {
              throw new IllegalArgumentException(
                "Environment variable '" + variable + "' not set!");
```

Otherwise, we store the variable value in the hash table:

```
            } else {
              env.put(variable.toUpperCase(),value);
            }
```

Finally, we make sure all resources are closed down:

```
          } finally {
            if (is != null) {
              is.close();
            }
          }
```

If the command execution was unsuccessful, we read the specified error message and throw a new `IOException`, using the error stack read:

```
        } else {

          String error = "";
          InputStream is = null;
          try {
            is = proc.getErrorStream();
            byte[] b = new byte[is.available()];
            is.read(b);
            error = new String(b).trim();
          } finally {
            if (is != null) {
              is.close();
            }
          }
          throw new IOException(error);
        }
```

However, if everything goes as expected, we return the environment variable value:

```
        return value;
      }
    }
  }
```

## Load the Class into the Database

For the Java class to work inside Oracle, you must load it into the database. For example, you can use `loadjava` as shown below.

> Note that you should specify the **-definer** option to **loadjava**, if you intend to grant other users execute permission on this class without having to grant these users permission to execute the command language interpreter. This is recommended, as we have discussed before.

```
> loadjava -user username/password -oci8 -resolve -definer Environment.java
```

### Grant Necessary Permissions

When you have successfully loaded the class into the database, you must log on as the SYSTEM user and grant the schema in which you loaded the class (in our case, the user USERNAME) the permissions needed to execute command line functions, as we have discussed before. Remember to use the appropriate command language interpreter, as outlined below:

```
SQL> call dbms_java.grant_permission (
  2    'USERNAME',
  3    'java.io.FilePermission',
  4    -- 'C:\WINNT\system32\cmd.exe',   -- Windows NT/2000
  5    -- '/bin/sh',    -- Linux/UNIX
  6    'C:\Windows\COMMAND.COM',   -- Windows 95/98
  7    'execute'
  8  );

Call completed.

SQL> call dbms_java.grant_permission (
  2    'USERNAME',
  3    'java.lang.RuntimePermission',
  4    '*',
  5    'writeFileDescriptor'
  6  );

Call completed.

SQL> call dbms_java.grant_permission (
  2    'USERNAME',
  3    'java.lang.RuntimePermission',
  4    '*',
  5    'readFileDescriptor'
  6  );

Call completed.
```

### Create a Call Spec

Next, you should log on as the specified class owner (in other words, USERNAME), and create a PL/SQL call spec for the Environment class:

```
SQL> create or replace function echo(
  2    p_variable varchar2
  3  ) return varchar2
  4    as
```

```
5    language java
6    name 'com.wrox.util.Environment.echo(java.lang.string)
7      return java.lang.string';
8  /
```

```
Function created.
```

To test this procedure, try to execute with a known environment variable. For example:

```
> set serveroutput on;
> call dbms_output.put_line(echo('ORACLE_HOME'));
```

```
C:\Oracle\Ora81
```

This call should print the value of the ORACLE_HOME environment variable on the screen (in this case, C:\Oracle\Ora81) if everything goes as expected. If, instead of the environment variable value, you get a Java error message, you should take appropriate action, depending on the exception type:

❑   java.security.SecurityException
    The database user does not have permission to execute command line functions from the Oracle JVM. Check their execute permissions.

❑   java.io.IOException
    An error occurred while executing the echo command. Make sure the specified command syntax is correct.

❑   java.lang.IllegalArgumentException
    The environment variable you specified is not set for the Oracle software account.

### Using the ECHO Procedure

Now that we have developed a secure procedure (in the sense that we can grant other users execute privileges without violating security constraints through the command prompt) for extracting environment variables, there are all sorts of things we can use it for. Most notably, we will benefit from being able to extract the value of ORACLE_HOME in our programs, *without* hard-coding. Additionally, you might find this useful to locate Oracle-specific log and trace files, such as alert.log and the user trace file, and process their contents into the database, where they can be more easily manipulated.

# Sockets

In the early days of Java, special focus was put on a new realm of technology, known as the Internet. As a result, Java has always maintained a strong support for network computing. HTTP, FTP, Telnet, and SMTP services are made easy through simple APIs, which are either part of the core Java packages or widespread standard extensions.

However, no matter what network protocol you use with Java, the actual work is always accomplished through low-level communication handles known as **sockets**. A socket is an endpoint in a duplex communication between processes on a network. The socket is used by these processes to perform network operations through the underlying operating system. There are generally two types of sockets we are concerned with; **stream sockets** and **datagram sockets**. Stream sockets provide reliable means of data transport between two interconnected processes on a network, while datagram sockets provide a more lightweight and elementary service from transmitting and receiving individual packets of data. Stream sockets operate over the TCP protocol while datagram sockets use the UDP network protocol. Java has inherent support for both these types of sockets, through standard classes of the `java.net` core package.

It is not the intent of this section to study every aspect of network computing with Java. Rather, this section will focus exclusively on those areas of Java that deal with low-level network communication performed through sockets. However, detailed knowledge of sockets and network protocols is not required for the examples in this section. Aside from illustrating how Java can be generally used for socket programming, thus addressing the needs of users of older versions of Oracle 8i for which the `UTL_TCP` PL/SQL package lacked performance, we will illustrate those areas where Java can add to the functionality provided by PL/SQL. Specifically, we will illustrate the uses of **multicast datagram sockets**, used to broadcast a message to a large recipient group, when we implement a simple stored procedure at the end of this section.

❑ **Stream Sockets**
A stream socket is a socket over which data can be continuously transmitted. Stream sockets are used for TCP communications. A stream socket connects with another socket by specifying a foreign network address and port and hoping that there is a socket listening for incoming connections at the other end. Such a socket is known as a **client socket**. A socket, that awaits an incoming connection from a client connection is known as a **server socket**.

❑ **Datagram Sockets**
For communications over the UDP protocol, datagram sockets are needed. A datagram socket is attached to a particular port address and can be used either for transmission or reception of UDP packets. A UDP packet, or datagram, is a term describing a general packet of data, which contains information on its destination and origin.

# Socket Handling with PL/SQL

The `UTL_TCP` package, which was introduced with Oracle 8.1.6, allows PL/SQL code to open a socket connection over the TCP protocol to any server accepting connections. In Oracle 8i, `UTL_TCP` was implemented with Java, and had some performance issues in versions 8.1.5 and 8.1.6, which made it more feasible to use Java directly for working with sockets. In Oracle 8.1.7, most of these issues had been addressed, and in Oracle 9i, `UTL_TCP` was implemented with native socket support, which greatly increases its efficiency.

Although useful, the `UTL_TCP` package is limited in many ways. First of all, as the name implies, it only supports socket communications over the TCP transport protocol, which may not always be appropriate. Secondly, `UTL_TCP` is not permitted to accept connections initiated from outside the application. This means that `UTL_TCP` is only capable of using client sockets – server sockets are not permitted. These issues are further summarized below:

❏ **Performance**

In Oracle 8.1.5 and 8.1.6, UTL_TCP had performance issues, which makes it more feasible to use Java for those versions. More recent Oracle versions, however, have addressed these issues.

❏ **Socket Duplexity**

PL/SQL does not support server sockets, in other words, a PL/SQL program is not allowed to accept connections initiated from *outside* the program. Java supports both client sockets and server sockets, allowing programs both to accept as well as initiate connections. There are, however, limitations to the use of server sockets in Oracle, as we will illustrate later.

❏ **Transport Protocol**

PL/SQL only supports the TCP transport protocol, while Java supports both TCP and UDP. Although TCP is far more widely used than UDP, it may be necessary to develop sockets that make use of the fast delivery of UDP. In fact, we will illustrate an example thereof later in this section.

Due to these limitations of PL/SQL, it can sometimes be better to use Java for socket programming inside the database. The Java language, as we will see later, has a wide support for working with sockets. Aside from inherent support for both the TCP and UDP transport protocols, and the option of writing both the client and server end of streams sockets, the Java socket framework allows you to create your own custom socket implementations through simple class extensions. This may be useful say, if you need to operate over a specific transport protocol, through a custom firewall, and so on, although we will not pursue that issue further in this context.

This, however, is not to say that you should always choose Java rather than PL/SQL when working with sockets. On the contrary, following the general guidelines of using PL/SQL and Java we introduce in Chapter XX, we say that *if you can accomplish your goal in PL/SQL you should do so*, as long as it is not at the cost of either performance or functionality. This, of course, assumes that you are operating from PL/SQL in the first place – if you are operating from Java, you should stick to that. So if you need to work with TCP client sockets from your PL/SQL procedures, and you are using Oracle 8.1.7 or 9i, you should go for UTL_TCP. However, if you are working with an earlier Oracle version or if you need functionality not available in PL/SQL, Java should be your choice.

# Socket Security

As with all other operating system resource specific permissions are required in order to work with sockets. Specifically, you need to grant each user connecting to or accepting connections from some external network host an explicit permission to either connect to and resolve or listen to and accept connections from the specified host. All these permissions are specified as actions to the java.net.SocketPermission. For example:

```
SQL> call dbms_java.grant_permission (
  2     'USERNAME',
  3     'java.net.SocketPermission',
  4     '199.99.123.11',
  5     'connect,resolve,accept,listen'
  6  );

Call completed.
```

This would grant user USERNAME full permission to connect to and accept connections from the specified IP address. All the examples in this section assume that the appropriate socket permissions have been granted.

# Stream Sockets (TCP Sockets)

A stream socket in Java is represented either by a java.net.Socket or a java.net.ServerSocket instance, depending on whether the socket in question acts as a client or a server, respectively. These two classes are further illustrated in the following figure:

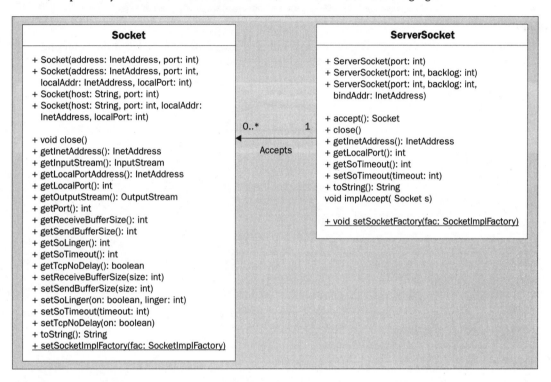

In short, an application initiates a client socket by constructing a Socket instance that listens to a specified address, through a specified port. If on the other end of the communication line, there exists a corresponding ServerSocket, listening for incoming connections, the two sockets set up a dedicated connection. Through this connection, the sockets can write data to each other, and read each other's previously written datagrams, through the standard socket input and output streams obtained through the getInputStream() and getOutputStream() method of the Socket class.

## Client Sockets

A Socket instance can be created with one of the four non-deprecated public constructors. For example:

```
Socket s = new Socket("localhost", 4545);
```

Optionally, you can specify to which local port and address the client socket should be bound. All `Socket` constructors can throw any one of three exceptions:

❑ `SecurityException`
If the schema has not been granted the appropriate `SocketPermission`

❑ `IOException`
If any I/O exception occurs when connect the socket

❑ `UnknownHostException`
If the host specified either does not exist or is unreachable

### Socket I/O

If a client socket has been successfully created, and there exists a server socket at the other end of communication, you can write data to and read data from the socket connection. For example:

```java
import java.io.*;
import java.net.*;

...

Socket s = null;
InputStream in = null;
OutputStream out = null;
try {

  s = new Socket("localhost", 4545);
  out = s.getOutputStream();
  in = s.getInputStream();

  out.write((new String("Is anyone out there?")).getBytes());
  byte[] b = new byte[in.available()];
  in.read(b);
  System.out.println("Answer from server: " + new String(b));

} finally {
  if (in != null) {
    try {
      in.close();
    } catch (IOException ignored) {
    }
  }
  if (out != null) {
    try {
      out.close();
    } catch (IOException ignored) {
    }
  }
  if (s != null) {
    try {
      s.close();
    } catch (IOException ignored) {
    }
  }
}
```

Note that in order to get the output to your SQL console in this example, you will need a prior call to `DBMS_JAVA.SET_OUTPUT()` and `DBMS_OUTPUT.ENABLE()`, as we have discussed before.

> **Always make sure that resources are properly closed, including input and output streams from the socket connection. Operating system and network resources are not automatically shut down when the database session is ended, as we have mentioned before.**

## Server Sockets

A `ServerSocket` can be instantiated with one of three constructors, illustrated in the previous UML diagram. Each of these constructors specifies the port to which the socket listens. If a port number of 0 is specified, the server socket will bind to any free port on the server (which is generally not useful, since the client needs to know the address of the server). The `backlog` argument specifies the number of client sockets that may be put in a queue for a connection at any time. If an `InetAddress` is specified, the server socket will be bound to the specified port on that address. This may be appropriate, for example, when you have more than one network interface on a server.

### Accepting Connections

A `ServerSocket` accepts a connection through the `accept()` method. This method listens for connections that have been made to the server socket. If an incoming connection is detected, this method accepts it and returns the `Socket` instance associated.

You should note that the `accept()` method **blocks** – in other words, the processing stops at that operation – until a connection is made. Server sockets usually run as dedicated server processes, so this is not usually a problem. For example, consider the following code, which illustrates a dedicated server socket:

```
PrintWriter out = null;
Socket client;
ServerSocket server = null;
try {

  // create a new server socket
  server = new ServerSocket(4545);

  // continuously listen for incoming connections
  while (true) {
    client = server.accept();
    out = new PrintWriter(client.getOutputStream(),true);
    out.println("Hello");
    out.close();
    client.close();
  }
} catch (Exception e) {
} finally {
  if (server != null) {
    server.close();
  }
}
```

The time to block – the time that may elapse between incoming connections – is by default not limited. However, a maximum waiting time for an incoming connection can be specified by calling the `setSoTimeout()` method with an appropriate millisecond argument (a value of zero specified an infinite timeout). If such a timeout interval is specified before an `accept()` attempt is made, and no client attempts connection before that time has elapsed, an `java.io.InterruptedIOException` is thrown. This does not, however, invalidate the server socket in any way. This is further illustrated in the following example:

```
try {

  // create a new server socket
  server = new ServerSocket(4545);

  // set a time-out interval, one minute
  server.setSoTimeout(60 * 1000);

  // continuously listen for incoming connections, unless we time-out
  while (true) {
    client = server.accept();
    out = new PrintWriter(client.getOutputStream(),true);
    out.println("Hello");
    out.close();
    client.close();
  }
} catch (InterruptedIOException interruption) {
  System.out.println("Connection timed out, closing socket...");
  return;
} finally {
  if (server != null) {
    server.close();
  }
}
```

If a client attempts a connection to a server socket that is currently engaged in communication with another client, it is put on hold. By default, a server socket can accept up to 50 connections in a queue at any given time. However, the default value can be overridden, by specifying a new backlog value when constructing the `ServerSocket`, as shown here:

```
// only accept three connections in a queue
ServerSocket s = new ServerSocket(4545, 3);
```

If a client attempts a connection to a server socket whose queue is full, the client is refused connection, in other words, a `java.net.ConnectException` is raised.

### Server Sockets in the Database

When using server sockets within the database, care must be taken with how the database is configured or else the socket might perish once a session is terminated. Specifically, a server socket can only exist across calls if it is initiated with a **dedicated** server connection. You will not be able to run a server sockets for more than a single call at a time with a **shared** connection, at the end of which the socket connection is terminated. If an attempt is made to use a `ServerSocket` instance between calls in a shared connection, the system will throw an `IOException`, indicating that the underlying connection was terminated.

> You should note that Oracle does not place any such restrictions upon client sockets. Client sockets are by nature outbound, unlike server sockets, and can persist across database calls.

Even if you are running a dedicated database instance, you may find that server sockets are not as useful within the Oracle JVM as they are outside the database. This stems from the fact that the Oracle JVM does not allow for multi-threading within individual database sessions, as we discuss further in Chapter 9 *Using the Oracle JVM*. Traditionally, a single server socket is used to handle multiple client connections. In Java run outside Oracle, this is usually implemented as stated in the pseudo-code below:

```
open server socket
loop forever
  listen for an incoming connection
  if a connection is made
    start a new thread which handles the client connection
```

Using this method, we ensure that a client can make connection with the server socket, even if it is currently working with another client. In Oracle Java, this is *not* possible because of the threading limitations we have mentioned (even if it is possible through some means, it will not be trivial to set up).

This, of course, does not mean that server sockets have no purpose within the database. On the contrary, they can be used effectively in communication between two individual sockets, such as between two database sessions. Our point is just that they can't be used effectively to handle multiple clients, as we have illustrated.

## Example Uses of Stream Sockets with Oracle

We have previously mentioned that all application-level Java networking functionality is implemented with sockets – in fact, stream sockets, most of the time. This goes also for more specific networking services, such as database drivers. For example, the Oracle JDBC thin driver is implemented entirely through Java sockets. Specifically, this driver uses TCP stream sockets to imitate the behavior of the Oracle Net8 TTC protocol, which is used to connect to the database from an outside resource.

In your own database applications, you will find that sockets can be useful for many purposes. For one, you can use such sockets to easily communicate between Java components in different database sessions (and thus different JVMs), without the use of any PL/SQL-specific functionality. Additionally, you can use sockets to notify clients outside the database of updates or changes to database structures, thereby limiting the number of times each client needs to initiate a database connection and issue a query. For that purpose, however, we usually find it more efficient to use datagram sockets, which require less overhead than stream sockets. In the next section, we will study the use of datagram sockets with Java in more detail.

# Datagram Sockets (UDP Sockets)

Datagram sockets are created in Java as DatagramSocket objects. A DatagramSocket interacts with other sockets by transmitting independent packets of data – in other words, datagrams – each of which stores the address and port number of the intended recipient. A DatagramSocket can be used to both to send and receive datagram packets, unlike stream sockets, where a separate socket class is required for both the client and the server. For datagram sockets, there is no built-in client-server relationship, although these sockets are often implemented in such a manner. Communication between two datagram sockets on a network does not require a dedicated connection – a datagram socket can transmit packets to any number of recipient sockets, in any specific order without any need for connection set up.

Often, it may be useful to transmit a datagram to more than one recipient, similar to specifying carbon copy recipients to your e-mail messages. For that purpose, Java provides an extension to the DatagramSocket, MulticastSocket, which allows datagrams to be **multicast** to a group of sockets. There is very little difference in using a standard DatagramSocket and a MulticastSocket; for the latter, you just have to make sure that the specified recipient address is indeed the address of a multicast socket group. This can be one of biggest advantages of using Java sockets in Oracle, since it requires less overhead than sending a message over TCP to multiple recipients. We will illustrate an example of this later in this chapter when we implement a stored procedure, which can notify a number of listeners of changes that have been made to database tables.

The DatagramSocket class encapsulates datagrams as DatagramPacket objects. The DatagramPacket class, along with DatagramSocket, is further illustrated in the following diagram:

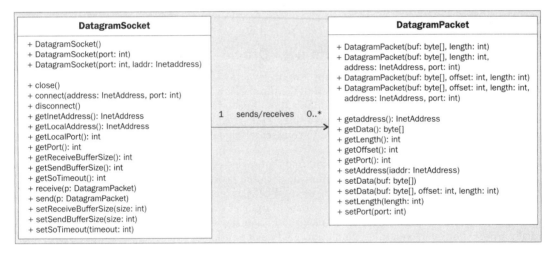

## Datagram Packets

A datagram packet in Java is encapsulated as a DatagramPacket instance. A DatagramPacket instance contains information on the address and port number to which it should be routed and the data which it contains. A DatagramPacket is routed from one machine to another based solely on information contained within that packet. For example, the following code constructs a DatagramPacket destined to reach port number 6770 on the local host, containing the string Hello as internal data:

```
byte[] data = {'H', 'e', 'l', 'l', 'o'};
InetAddress target = InetAddress.getLocalHost();
DatagramPacket packet = new DatagramPacket(data,data.length,target,6770);
```

When you initiate a `DatagramPacket` that should be used to receive an incoming datagram, you specify the length of the internal package buffer. If you use this instance to receive a packet containing more data than the specified buffer can hold, the incoming data is truncated:

```
// 256 byte buffer
byte[] buffer = new byte[256];
DatagramPacket incoming = new DatagramPacket(buffer,buffer.length);
```

## Datagram Sockets

A datagram socket is represented as a `DatagramSocket` instance in Java. Similar to the `Socket` and `ServerSocket`, the `DatagramSocket` constructors either specify an address and port to which the socket should bind, or omit these arguments, in which case a default value is supplied (localhost and port 80).

### Reading from and Writing to a Datagram Socket

Once a valid `DatagramSocket` has been constructed, you can construct a `DatagramPacket` and send it off to the specified target address. Additionally, you can use the same `DatagramPacket` object to receive incoming packets from other sockets. This is further illustrated in the following example:

```
byte[] data = {'H', 'e', 'l', 'l', 'o'};
byte[] buffer = new byte[256];
InetAddress target = InetAddress.getLocalHost();
DatagramPacket packet = new DatagramPacket(data,data.length,target,6770);
DatagramSocket socket = new DatagramSocket(5454);
String result = null;
try {

  // send the packet
  socket.send(packet);

  // waiting for response
  packet = new DatagramPacket(buffer, buffer.length);
  socket.receive(packet);
  result = new String(packet.getData());

} finally {
  socket.close();
}
```

As you can see from this, it is fairly simple to send and receive packets with `DatagramSocket`. No input and output streams, as for stream sockets – just some simple `send()` and `receive()` methods and that's all!

As for the `ServerSocket accept()` method, the `receive()` method of `DatagramSocket` blocks until a packet is received. Therefore, to set up a `DatagramSocket` that listens continuously for incoming packets, we can use a similar method as before with the `ServerSocket`. For example, the following example illustrates a datagram socket that receives and stores datagram packets storing information on pixels in an image frame. The socket receives packets until more time than the specified time-out interval elapses between transmissions (we discuss socket time-out in more detail in the next section). The information extracted from each packet is used to specify a particular pixel in a 300 x 300 image frame. Each pixel is identified by an x-y coordinate and an RGB color value.

```
int x = 0;
int y = 1;
int r = 2;
int g = 3;
int b = 4;
int width = 300;
int height = 300;
Object[][] image = new Object[width][height];

DatagramPacket incoming;
DatagramSocket server = new DatagramSocket(5454);
int bufferLength = 5;
byte[] data;
byte[] pixel;

try {

    // 30 second time-out
    server.setSoTimeout(30*1000);

    // continuously wait for an incoming packet
    while (true) {
        incoming = new DatagramPacket(new byte[bufferLength],bufferLength);
        server.receive(incoming);
        data = incoming.getData();

        // construct the pixel, store the RGB
        // value, and place in the correct coordinate
        if (((int) data[x]) <= width && ((int) data[y]) <= height) {
            pixel = new byte[3];
            pixel = System.arraycopy(data,r,pixel,pixel.length);
            image[(int) data[x]][(int) data[y]] = pixel;
        }
    }

// time-out, end of transmission
} catch (InterruptedIOException timeout) {
} finally {
    socket.close();
}
```

### *Multicast Sockets*

A multicast socket is a datagram socket that has the capability of joining groups of other multicast sockets. A multicast socket can send messages to a specific socket group, which effectively sends the message to all sockets in the group. A multicast socket need not be a member of a group to send messages to it.

In Java, a multicast socket is represented by the `MulticastSocket` class, which extends `DatagramSocket`. A `MulticastSocket` is used just like a `DatagramSocket` – by constructing a `DatagramPacket`, sending the packet, and so on. Two methods of the `MulticastSocket` are of special interest, however. Those are the methods `joinGroup()` and `leaveGroup()`, which allow the socket to join and leave a specified multicast group, respectively. A multicast group is represented by a specific IP address. Sockets that wish to join the group invoke the `joinGroup()` using the specified address. For example:

```
InetAddress group = InetAddress.getByName("212.30.198.1");
MulticastSocket mcs = new MulticastSocket(5555);
mcs.joinGroup(group);

byte[] alert = {'a', 'l', 'e', 'r', 't'};
DatagramPacket pkg= new DatagramPacket(alert, alert.length, group);
mcs.send(pkg);
mcs.leaveGroup(group);
```

It can be useful to use multicast sockets when communicating with a broad number of clients, as we will do in an example at the end of this section.

# Socket Timeout

A common risk when programming with sockets is that a socket blocks and hangs infinitely on a dead connection. This may happen, for example, when a `Socket` tries to read input from a disconnected or unavailable server socket, or when a `DatagramSocket` waits indefinitely for an incoming datagram packet. The effects of hanging a socket are perhaps more dramatic when programming within the boundaries of the database, since the active database session risks being hung as well.

Fortunately, there is a simple solution to this problem. Each of the socket classes `Socket`, `ServerSocket` and `DatagramSocket`, contain a method called `setSoTimeout()`, which allows you to specify a timeout interval for the socket. This method accepts as an argument an integer value, which represents the maximum number of milliseconds an operation may block for. If a time-out value has been set, and an operation has blocked the socket for more time than the specified time-out value, an `InterruptedIOException` will be thrown. This exception will not have any effect on the underlying socket. This is further shown in the following snippet:

```
DatagramPacket packet = new DatagramPacket(new byte[512],512);
DatagramSocket socket = new DatagramSocket(5454);

// 5 second time-out
socket.setSoTimeout(5*1000);
```

```
try {
  socket.receive(packet);
} catch (InterruptedIOException timeout) {
  // timed-out
}
```

To recap, the blocking methods that are subject to possible time-out checks, are:

```
ServerSocket.accept();
SocketInputStream.read();
DatagramSocket.receive();
```

## What Happens if a Socket Hangs?

If a socket, which has been specified with an infinite time-out value, hangs on a connection, the active database session will also hang. Furthermore, any attempts at killing an active session hung by a non-interruptable Java operation, will most likely fail, as shown here:

```
ALTER SYSTEM KILL SESSION '9,9'
*
ERROR at line 1:
ORA-00031: session marked for kill
```

The ORA-00031 error specifies that the session specified in the ALTER SYSTEM KILL SESSION command cannot be killed immediately because it is involved in an operation that may not be interrupted, such as socket communications. The session is marked to be killed as soon as the operation in question is finished. However, in the case of a failed socket, a time-out may never happen, which means that the session must be implicitly killed by shutting down the database.

# Using Multicast Sockets to Notify Listeners

In many cases, it may be feasible to implement a generic procedure to notify a set of external clients when changes have been made to particular database tables. The term *client* refers in this context to some process outside the database, such as a Java applet connecting to Oracle through the thin JDBC driver. Such a client might store cached data from the database in a local memory structure, so that it would not have to constantly query the database, with an associated overhead.

For internal clients (for example, other database users), we can use PL/SQL packages such as DBMS_ALERT to notify database changes. Using that for an external process, would mean that we needed to keep an open database connection, even while not polling the database. Since Net8 connections are expensive in terms of memory (and other resources), this is usually not acceptable.

A better alternative is to use Java to trigger a message sent to a group of multicast sockets when a table is updated. In this section, we will illustrate a stored procedure for doing just that.

## The Notification Class

The following Java class contains a single method, notify(). This method takes for an argument the IP address of the multicast group that should be notified and the message that should be sent:

```
SQL> create or replace and resolve java source named "NetworkExtensions"
  2  as
  3
  4  import java.net.*;
  5  import java.io.*;
  6
  7  public class NetworkExtensions {
  8
  9    public static void notify(String ip, int port, String msg) throws
                                                            Exception {
 10        InetAddress group = InetAddress.getByName(ip);
 11        MulticastSocket mcs = new MulticastSocket();
 12        byte[] b = msg.getBytes();
 13        DatagramPacket pkg = new DatagramPacket(b, b.length, group, port);
 14        mcs.send(pkg);
 15        mcs.close();
 16    }
 17  }
 18  /

Java created.
```

Note that the socket *does not have to join the group* in order to send it a packet.

## The NOTIFY Procedure

A corresponding PL/SQL call spec is illustrated below:

```
SQL> create or replace procedure notify (
  2     p_group varchar2,
  3     p_port number,
  4     p_message varchar2
  5  )
  6  as
  7  language java
  8  name 'com.wrox.util.net.NetworkExtensions.notify(
  9     java.lang.String, int, java.lang.String)';
 10  /

Procedure created.
```

## Using the Procedure

With the NOTIFY() procedure, you can add a trigger to a table that clients use to access information. For example, assume you had a live stock ticker, which displayed stock information from the database. Since we don't want to keep an open connection to the database, we would let the ticker select from the database once it is initialized, and then initiate a multicast socket and have it join a specific multicast group, defined for the database. Once the stock information changes, a trigger on the corresponding table would run the NOTIFY() procedure, which in turn would notify all stock tickers of the changes. Each ticker would then open a database connection, or use an already open one, and fetch the modified rows. For example, consider the following trigger:

```
SQL> create table stock_data (
  2    ...
  3  );

Table created.

SQL> wrox_6020> create or replace trigger stock_data_notify
  2    after insert or update on stock_data
  3    for each row
  4    begin
  5
  6    -- let the clients know what row ID was changed,
  7    -- so that they can directly access the modified rows.
  8    notify('some-ip-address', 80, :new.rowid);
  9
 10    end;
 11    /

Trigger created.
```

> Note that you will need to grant the schema running the NOTIFY() procedure a
> NetPermission to connect to and resolve the given multicast address, as we
> discussed previously in the sockets section.

# Summary

In this chapter, we have discussed how Java can be used to work with resources of the database server operating system, in other words, files, sockets and operating system executables. Wherever possible, we have illustrated how to use Java to advantage by complementing some of the lacking aspects of resource handling with PL/SQL, such as in relation to the built-in UTL_FILE and UTL_TCP packages.

Generally, this chapter has focused on those areas where the advantages of using Java have made it a more feasible option than PL/SQL. In the next chapter, we will take a new course, and investigate some problems that can only be solved with the close cooperation of both languages.

Oracle 9i Java Programming

# Using PL/SQL and Java Together

In previous chapters we have focused on those aspects of the Java language that make it more suitable than PL/SQL for specific tasks within the database. Generally, Java offers more capabilities for interacting with operating system and network resources and is generally preferred to PL/SQL when performing intensive calculations or string handling. On the other hand, PL/SQL is preferred over Java when it comes to transaction-intensive operations and SQL integration with the database.

There are cases, however, where an intended result can only, or can more gracefully, be accomplished through the use of both PL/SQL and Java. In this chapter, we will study two such scenarios in detail. Specifically, we will:

❑   Develop an FTP Java client that runs inside the Oracle database, which makes use of PL/SQL for scheduling automatic transfer and processing of file content from a remote server. We will then demonstrate a sample use of the FTP client by developing an application that gathers and stores page request statistics from a set of distributed HTTP servers.

❑   Implement an application that makes use of both PL/SQL and Java to compress large documents stored in the database. We will then illustrate how we can integrate our compression utilities with interMedia Text in order to preserve the searching capabilities of compressed content.

## File Transfer Application

Imagine that you are required to set up an application that would wake up at regular intervals and transfer a file from a remote FTP server down to the file system of the database server, where its contents would be processed and stored in tables within the database. To accomplish this, which language would you use: PL/SQL or Java?

With PL/SQL you could make use of the built-in DBMS_JOB package to schedule specific tasks at regular intervals. PL/SQL, however, offers no options for file transfer over FTP. You might attempt to implement your own FTP client using the UTL_TCP socket package, but you would probably not get anywhere with that, since PL/SQL does not permit server sockets, which are necessary for FTP transfer.

Java has many options for network programming, including support for FTP. However, there are no means of task scheduling with Java. You might try to use a suspended thread for that purpose, but that would not be stable enough (for example, if for some reason the database goes down and then back up, your thread will have been terminated and must be manually started all over again). Additionally, the Oracle Java threading model does not support thread concurrency, as we saw in Chapter 9, *Using the Oracle JVM*, which means that we would not be able to run more than one task in the background at a time.

Of course, we could in either case resort to native functions of the underlying operating system in order to accomplish our task. With PL/SQL, we could call external C-based procedures that interact with FTP software of the operating system, and with Java, we could make use of OS-dependent utilities to schedule automatic file transfer (such as CRON for UNIX). However, such solutions would not only be unreliable and platform-dependent, they would also impose limitations on the functionality of our application, since we could not integrate easily with the language of our choice and the external software in question.

Therefore, we may conclude that the ideal solution to this problem is the joint cooperation of both PL/SQL and Java. With that combination, we would use Java to perform the actual file transfer and processing, while PL/SQL would be responsible for the automatic scheduling of individual transfers. That way, all our application logic would reside within the database, which gives us a stable and platform independent approach. So, to summarize, the main reasons we choose to use a combination of PL/SQL and Java to implement our FTP client application, are:

❑ **Simplicity** – By using the 'best of both worlds', we avoid complex implementation of specific services for either language

❑ **Platform Independence** – Running all the application logic within the database makes the application independent of platform, since we do not have to resort to OS-specific utilities for either scheduling or FTP transfer

❑ **Performance** – By storing all code within the database, we avoid unnecessary database calls over a network and minimize costly integration with external operating system resources

# Overview

In this section we will develop a generic-use Java FTP client, running inside the Oracle database, by using the readily available internal Sun network packages. Instead of working with files stored physically in the database server file system, we will implement the client so that it makes use of files stored in BLOB fields in the database, either by downloading from or uploading to a remote FTP server.

When we have developed the Java class framework we will make use of the built-in DBMS_JOB PL/SQL package for the scheduling of automatic file transfer at specified points in time. Finally, we will illustrate a specific use of our FTP client, by demonstrating an application that regularly gathers log files from a set of remote HTTP servers. This application extends the default download handler used by our FTP client, in order to process each log file and store its content in specific log tables. The following diagram provides an overview of the structure of our FTP client application.

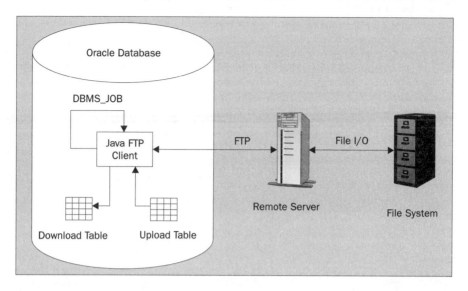

In this section we will implement the database tables, Java classes, and PL/SQL procedures that make up our FTP application. However, before we begin writing any code, it is necessary to obtain some rudimentary knowledge of the technology we will be working with. Therefore, we will begin our study of database file transfer with a brief introduction to the FTP protocol.

# What Is FTP?

FTP, the **F**ile **T**ransfer **P**rotocol, is a general-use protocol for the transfer and handling of files from one computer to another over a network. FTP is implemented using the lower level TCP transfer protocol. Therefore, you can only use FTP for file transfer over a TCP/IP network, such as the Internet.

FTP is a client-server protocol. A client makes a connection to a server, which must be configured to accept incoming FTP requests. If a connection is made, the client may both transfer files to and retrieve files from the server, given that appropriate file system permissions are granted at both ends of the connection. The server is unable to communicate with the client on its own initiative; direct contact by the server always comes as a response to a prior client request.

For a single FTP connection, two distinct TCP sessions are used. One session is responsible for the transfer of file data while the other is dedicated to the transfer and reception of specific FTP commands. The command transfer connection remains open for the duration of the whole FTP session, while the data transfer connection is open only when needed – that is, when files are being transferred.

For each of the two TCP sessions of a single FTP connection, there is a corresponding handler within the FTP software at each end of the connection (client and server).

*You should note that the fact that there are two TCP sessions at work within the FTP software does not indicate that the software is capable of multiprocessing – transmitting files at the same time as the client browses for another directory at the remote server. Most FTP utilities can only process one task at a time, either upload or download a file, or issue a specific FTP command.*

These handlers are referred to as the **protocol interpreter** and the **data transfer process**, and are responsible for communication and data transfer, respectively. The protocol interpreter communicates with the corresponding interpreter at the other end of the connection according the communication transmission procedure specified by the FTP protocol. The set of commands specified by the FTP protocol is used for the client to traverse the file system of the server, download or upload specific files, specify the file transfer mode, change which local directory files should be transferred to, and more. The server corresponds to each valid FTP command according to the communication specification.

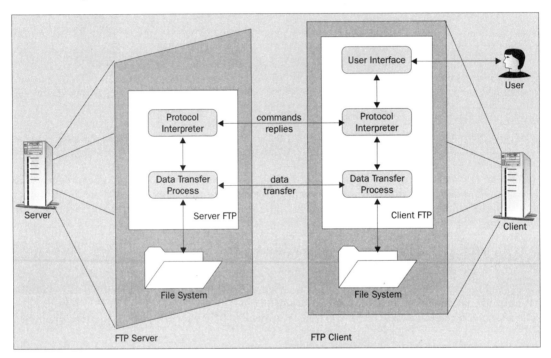

The data transfer process handles the transmission of data from the client to the server or vice versa. The data transfer can be specified for either binary or character type files. The binary transfer mode will usually not damage character files, while character transfer mode will almost definitely corrupt binary files. The data connection used by the data transfer process can transmit data in both directions – that is, the client can both upload files to and download files from the server. Just remember that data transfer can only be initiated from the client side, as we have already mentioned.

*For more information on basic networking concepts and TCP sockets, refer to Chapter 13, Working with Operating System Resources.*

## The Procedure of File Transfer

Each time a client wants to transfer a file to or receive a file from an FTP server, a standard communication procedure takes place. This is further illustrated in the listing below.

**1.** The client requests a connection with the server.

**2.** If the server address is accessible, and the server is configured so that it may accept FTP requests, the client is prompted for a username and password.

**3.** If the username is valid and a matching password is supplied, the client is permitted access to the FTP server.

**4.** Now the client may browse through any directory in the server's file hierarchy, which the remote user account is granted permission to access.

**5.** When the client has located the intended directory, it may either download files to a local directory or upload files to the specified remote directory. If the user account has inadequate permissions to write files to the specified destination, an exception is thrown.

**6.** The client repeats steps 4 and 5 as needed.

**7.** Finally, the client sends a hang-up signal, and terminates the connection.

As an example, we illustrate a sample dialogue from an FTP session between a Windows client and a UNIX server:

*Note that the specified server* `ftp.someserver` *does not exist in reality.*

```
> ftp ftp.someserver
Connected to ftp.someserver.
220 someserver FTP server (SunOS 5.7) ready.
User (ftp.someserver:(none)): wrox
331 Password required for wrox.
Password:
230 User wrox logged in.
ftp> dir
200 PORT command successful.
150 ASCII data connection for /bin/ls (213.220.69.187,1031) (0 bytes).
total 292
drwxrwxrwx   6 wrox     other        512 Nov 12 22:00 .
drwxr-xr-x   7 root     other        512 Oct 15 11:01 ..
-rw-------   1 wrox     other       6857 Nov 12 17:54 .bash_history
-rwxrwxrwx   1 wrox     other       1418 Aug  8 13:38 .profile
-rw-------   1 wrox     other         14 Sep  9 13:21 .sh_history
drwx------   2 wrox     other        512 Oct 18 13:49 .ssh
drwxr-xr-x   2 wrox     other       1024 Nov 12 18:37 logs
-rw-r--r--   1 wrox     other      48404 Nov  6 20:48 sqlnet.log
226 ASCII Transfer complete.
ftp: 1165 bytes received in 0.11Seconds 10.59Kbytes/sec.
ftp> get sqlnet.log
200 PORT command successful.
150 Opening ASCII mode data connection for sqlnet.log(48404 bytes).
226 Transfer complete.
ftp: 48404 bytes received in 1.54Seconds 31.43Kbytes/sec.
ftp> quit
```

When we implement an FTP client in the database with Java, later in this section, we will get a better idea of how this procedure is implemented.

# Java FTP Transfer

Given the Java language's inherent support for network computing, you may be surprised to find that there are no documented FTP classes in the core Java API. The `java.net` package contains low-level handlers for various socket types and higher-level abstractions for connections to HTTP and JAR resources, but no visible FTP handlers.

If you look at the core `java.net.URL` class, which represents an abstract network URL, and see that a few of its constructors accept a custom network protocol and file name as arguments, you might be tempted to use the URL class for file transfer over FTP, by supplying 'ftp' as the protocol name. This, however, is generally not recommended, mainly because the FTP protocol requires more specific permissions than protocols commonly used by `java.net.URL`, such as HTTP. Using the URL class for file transfer over FTP, you have no way of altering the transfer mode (binary or ASCII), uploading files or making more than one transaction per connection. This is further illustrated in the code snippet below:

```
import java.net.URL;
import java.io.InputStream;

/* The most general URL constructor takes for arguments
   the name of the protocol used, the name of the remote
   host, the port of the remote host, and the file which
   should be read. */

URL detailedUrl = new URL('http', 'www.wrox.com', 80, 'index.asp');

/* However, a URL object can also be constructed by
   supplying the whole URL as a single String. By default,
   an HTTP connection is made to port number 80, so the
   port number can simply be omitted. */

URL simpleURL = new URL('http://www.wrox.com/index.asp');

/* This, will work, but only with the default settings of
   the FTP server in question. Since this is a text file,
   we should be able to download it properly. */

URL asciiUrl = new URL(ftp://user:pass@ftp.someserver/home/pub/file.txt');
InputStream is = asciiUrl.openConnection();
byte[] content = new byte[512];
int amoundRead = in.read(content);
while (amountRead != -1) {
  // Handle the content...
  amountRead = in.read(content);
}
in.close();

/* Here we will run into problems. If we try to read from this
   URL, we will find that the binary file in question (an image)
   has been corrupted. */

URL binUrl = new URL(ftp://user:pass@ftp.someserver/home/pub/image.jpg');
```

So why does the Java language, which has been widely credited for networking capabilities, not come with built-in support for such a widely used application protocol as FTP? The answer is that it does in fact come with built-in implementation of FTP. The problem is just that this implementation is not a part of the public Java API, but rather the internal Sun JDK implementation. To discover more about this issue, we must take a closer look at the structure of the Java networking API, and see what takes place behind the scenes.

## Java Networking Behind the Scenes

Now, suppose we attempt to use the URL class to retrieve a file from some FTP server, as we have previously demonstrated. In the example below we use a URL instance to connect to an imaginary FTP server, which requires a login name and password:

> *If you want to test this for yourself, you should replace bolded literals with real values. Make sure that your setup does not automatically log you on, such as through a netrc setup.*

```
import java.net.URL;
import java.io.InputStream;

public class FtpTest {

  public static void main(String[] args) throws Exception {
    URL url = new URL('ftp', 'ftp.someserver', 'some-file');
    InputStream in = url.openStream();
    byte[] b = new byte[1024];
    in.read(b);
    in.close();
    System.out.println(new String(b));
  }
}
```

As you may have noticed, we deliberately omitted the username and password of the remote FTP software account in the URL constructor. As a result, if we attempted to execute this method (again, using real values), an exception similar to the following would be thrown:

```
> java FtpTest
Exception in thread 'main' sun.net.ftp.FtpLoginException: user
        at sun.net.ftp.FtpClient.login(FtpClient.java:286)
        at sun.net.www.protocol.ftp.FtpURLConnection.connect
                                (FtpURLConnection.java:91)
        at sun.net.www.protocol.ftp.FtpURLConnection.getInputStream
                                (FtpURLConnection.java:96)
        at java.net.URL.openStream(URL.java:798)
        at FtpTest.main(FtpTest.java:8)
```

If we analyze the stack trace shown above, from the bottom up, we see that the error occurs in the URL.openStream() method, which is called from FtpTest.main(), as we may have assumed. However, if we trace the source of the error, we see that it originally occurs in a method called login() in a class named FtpClient in the sun.net.ftp package. Where does that class come from?

Each URL instance interacts with an instance of a specific stream handler class, which extends the abstract java.net.URLStreamHandler base class. The URLStreamHandler class is a superclass of all stream protocol handlers. When a new URL instance is created, the constructor allocates it a specific URLStreamHandler subclass instance, based on the protocol specified. The first time a protocol name is encountered when constructing a URL the appropriate stream protocol handler is explicitly loaded. All subsequent constructions of URL objects using that particular protocol will use the same stream handler class.

When locating and loading a new stream handler class for a specific protocol, the system follows a very specific sequence of operations. It starts by determining whether an instance of the java.net.URLStreamHandlerFactory interface has been set up for the application, and proceeds to set up a new stream handler factory if it has not. If the stream handler factory does not return a valid stream handler for the protocol in question, the system tries to locate a valid stream handler among a list of specified system packages.

If all of the previous steps fail to find a valid stream handler for the protocol in question, as a last resort, the constructor attempts to load and instantiate a class named:

```
sun.net.www.protocol.myprotocol.Handler
```

where *myprotocol* is the protocol specified. If this last step fails, which means that an unsupported protocol has been specified, the URL constructor throws a MalformedURLException.

When you specify 'ftp' as an argument to the URL constructor, the system will try to locate a valid FTP stream handler, which it will find in the sun.net.www.protocol.ftp internal package. This stream handler will instantiate a sun.net.www.protocol.ftp.FtpURLConnection instance that in turn interacts with an instance of sun.net.ftp.FtpClient, to handle the FTP request. These internal classes are the key to custom FTP handling with the traditional JDK. We will discuss those issues in more detail in the next subsection.

## Sun Internal Packages

The FTP classes we mentioned above are just a few classes in a whole hierarchy of internal Java packages located under the sun.* root package. These packages are not part of the official JDK documentation, because they are a Sun-specific implementation, which is specifically not a part of the Java technology API standard. Therefore, Sun does not guarantee that these classes will remain available in future releases of the JDK, and even if they are, they may be subject to change without notice.

Despite these obvious limitations, there may be cases where it is useful to use the internal Sun packages, as we will be doing in our FTP implementation in this chapter. The sun.net.ftp package has been a part of the Java language from its early days. Already, many developers use this and other internal Sun packages, especially since the core API falls short of providing a solution to such trivial network services as FTP. Most or all of the internal Sun packages are available in all current versions of Oracle 8i and 9i, so when we start using those for our FTP client application later on, there is no setup required.

If you, for some reason, want to use another API for handling file transfer over FTP, there are a wide variety of packages available for that purpose. Among them is a product called NetComponents, from ORO Software, which is free for download at http://www.savarese.org/oro/. NetComponents is a set of Java packages that allow for easy access to the most commonly used Internet protocols, including FTP.

You should note that even though we have stated that Sun does not guarantee that the internal networking classes will remain available in future releases of Java, there is little chance of that not happening – too many people are already dependent on these resources. In any case, if you choose to use a third-party FTP implementation instead of the Sun classes, you are probably not any better off with regard to possible depreciation or lack-of-support – software companies come and go, and may also change their code without notice.

### Using the Sun FTP API

Since the Sun classes are undocumented, there is no standard on-line Javadoc you can browse to familiarize yourself with their use. However, the source code for these classes can be freely downloaded, and does in fact ship with some JDK versions. From the source, you can easily build your own custom Javadoc documentation. If you do not want to download the whole JDK source code, which is quite large, there are a number of on-line resources that allow you to view the internal source code of the JDK, including http://www.sourcebot.com/sourcebot/sun/.

The class of the Sun FTP package in which we are most interested, is the FtpClient class, which we have already mentioned. A new FtpClient instance is usually constructed by specifying the host name, and possibly the port number, of the FTP server to which the client should connect. For example:

```
FtpClient fc = new FtpClient('ftp.someserver');
```

When a new FtpClient has been initialized, it must log on to the remote site through its login() method:

```
try {
   fc.login('user', 'password');
} catch (FtpLoginException f) {
}
```

The login() method throws an FtpLoginException if the login attempt fails.

Once the client has logged on to the server, it may browse through the file system, either upload or download files, and specify the file transfer mode, with the cd(), put() or get(), and ascii() or binary() methods, respectively. The put() and get() methods return input and output streams, such as java.io.InputStream and java.io.OutputStream, which have to be processed in order to read or write the file in question. This is further demonstrated below:

```
// Specify a remote directory.
fc.cd('/home/pub');

// Read a text file.
fc.ascii();
InputStream in = fc.get('textfile.txt');

// Write a binary file.
fc.binary();
OutputStream out = fc.put('binary.exe');
...

// Close the server.
fc.closeServer();
```

There are many additional methods of the FtpClient class – including methods for remote directory listing and custom command issuing – that we will not be using in this context.

**555**

# Writing the Database FTP Client

We have discussed the options available when it comes to writing a database FTP client in Java. The internal Sun FTP package is readily available in all current Oracle versions, and requires no specific installation or setup. Therefore, it is a good candidate for building our FTP client application.

In short, our FTP application consists of Java classes, database tables and a PL/SQL package. For storing the FTP servers available for transfer, we use a table called FTP_SERVERS. For each server stored in the FTP_SERVERS table, we have a set of files that should be either uploaded to or downloaded from the server. These files are specified in the FTP_SERVER_UPLOADS and FTP_SERVER_DOWNLOADS tables, respectively. All files that we upload to remote servers are stored in a BLOB field in the UPLOADS database table. By default, we store each file that we download in a similar fashion in a BLOB field in the DOWNLOADS database table. However, when it comes to download, we may sometimes want to override the default behavior, and process the file contents directly as we download them. For that purpose, we can specify a custom download class (we discuss that below) for each file in the FTP_SERVER_DOWNLOADS table, which is then used each time the file is downloaded. At the end of this section we will see an example of this, when we implement a custom download class for processing log files from remote HTTP servers, directly as they are downloaded.

For each of the FTP_SERVERS, FTP_SERVER_UPLOADS and FTP_SERVER_DOWNLOADS tables, we define corresponding Java classes, Server, Upload and Download, respectively. Both the Download and Upload classes extend the abstract Transfer class, which represents a general FTP transfer. An instance of the Server class represents a server declared in the FTP_SERVERS table, along with all corresponding attributes. Each Server instance contains reference to the corresponding Download and Upload objects. The Server class additionally serves as a static entry point for a FTP transfer, that is, clients call the static Server.executeTransfer() method with a specified server ID in order to execute all transfers declared for the server in question.

Finally, we declare a PL/SQL package called UTL_FTP for accessing the Java methods from a PL/SQL context. The UTL_FTP package, along with all previous components of our application, is further illustrated in the following figure:

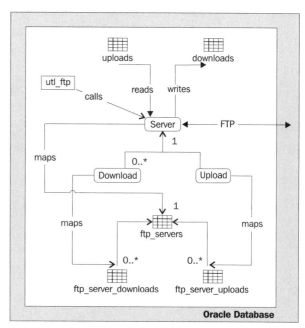

All objects used in this application can be loaded in whatever schema suits you. As you will see later on, when we develop the Java classes used in our application, we will make use of the Logging API (defined in *Appendix C*) for logging down errors that may occur during the FTP transfer. However, before we actually start developing those classes, we must set up the database tables that they make use of. We will do so in the next subsection.

## Database Structure

The following database diagram illustrates the relationship between the tables in our FTP application:

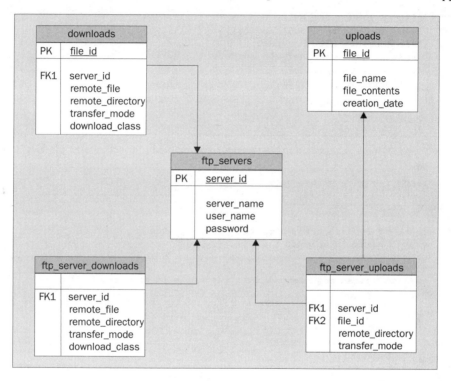

### FTP Servers

As we previously mentioned, we use the FTP_SERVERS database table to store the FTP servers that we want to access. For each FTP server we store various attributes, such as the server name and the name of the remote software account to use. This is further illustrated in the following listing:

```
SQL> create table ftp_servers (
  2     server_id number not null,
  3     server_name varchar2(100) not null,
  4     user_name varchar2(100) not null,
  5     password varchar2(100) not null,
  6     constraint pk_ftp_servers
  7       primary key (server_id)
  8  );

Table created.
```

To associate each file with a unique server ID, we can optionally define a specific sequence and have a trigger automatically set the sequence value for each row. However, as we will see later, it may be more useful to relate each server with the ID of the background job being used to regularly upload files to and download files from that server.

## Upload Files

The UPLOAD table defines the files that we wish to upload to remote servers:

```
SQL> create table uploads (
  2     file_id number not null,
  3     file_name varchar2(500) not null,
  4     file_contents blob not null,
  5     creation_date date default sysdate,
  6     constraint pk_uploads
  7       primary key (file_id)
  8  );

Table created.
```

Additionally, we define a sequence and a trigger for automatically inserting new file IDs:

```
SQL> create sequence upload_seq;

Sequence created.

SQL> create or replace trigger uploads_new_sequence
  2  before insert on uploads
  3  for each row
  4  begin
  5    select upload_seq.nextval into :new.file_id from dual;
  6  end;
  7  /

Trigger created.
```

## Download Files

By default, we store each file that we download in the DOWNLOADS database table. Note that there is no need for a temporary directory for downloads, unlike uploads. For each download file we store a reference to the server it was downloaded from. Note that instead of additionally storing a reference to the FTP_SERVER_DOWNLOADS table, we physically store the remote file name and directory this file was obtained from.

> *This is because we can alter the files specified in the FTP_SERVER_DOWNLOADS and FTP_SERVER_UPLOADS tables if we need to change the transfer set for a specific server. In that case, we would not want to lose the information on the download files.*

```
SQL> create table downloads (
  2     file_id number not null,
  3     server_id number not null,
  4     remote_file varchar2(500) not null,
```

```
    5   remote_directory varchar2(500) not null,
    6   file_contents blob not null,
    7   creation_date date default sysdate,
    8   constraint pk_files
    9     primary key (file_id),
   10   constraint fk_downloads_server_id
   11     foreign key (server_id) references ftp_servers
   12 );

Table created.
```

Since we will often need to look up a specific file by its server ID, remote file name and remote directory, we create a (unique) index on those same fields:

```
SQL> create unique index download_idx on downloads (
  2   server_id, remote_file, remote_directory);

Index created.
```

As before, we define a sequence and a trigger for automatically inserting new file IDs:

```
SQL> create sequence download_seq;

Sequence created.

SQL> create or replace trigger downloads_new_sequence
  2   before insert on downloads
  3   for each row
  4   begin
  5     select download_seq.nextval into :new.file_id from dual;
  6   end;
  7   /

Trigger created.
```

### Specifying Files for Upload

The FTP_SERVER_UPLOADS table specifies the files that should be uploaded to a remote server. Each record in this table stores a reference to a file in the UPLOADS table.

```
SQL> create table ftp_server_uploads (
  2   server_id number not null,
  3   file_id number not null,
  4   remote_directory varchar2(500) not null,
  5   transfer_mode char(1) default 'B' not null,
  6   constraint fk_ftp_server_u_server_id
  7     foreign key (server_id) references ftp_servers,
  8   constraint fk_ftp_server_u_file_id
  9     foreign key (file_id) references uploads,
 10   constraint chk_upload_transfer_mode
 11     check (transfer_mode in ('B','A'))
 12 );

Table created.
```

Note that we need to store in this table the mode of file transfer to be used for this file. This can take one of two values: 'B', which stands for binary, and 'A', which stands for ASCII (text-based). We use a CHECK constraint to ensure that these values are properly set.

### Specifying Files for Download

The FTP_SERVER_DOWNLOAD table specifies the files that should be downloaded from a remote server. For each download file we store the name of the class that should process the file when downloaded. By default, we wish to store each file downloaded directly in the DOWNLOADS table, above. Therefore, we use the com.wrox.ftp.Download class to process the download file.

*Later in this chapter, we will implement an extension of this class, which can be used to directly process log files, as we have previously mentioned.*

```
SQL> create table ftp_server_downloads (
  2      server_id number not null,
  3      remote_directory varchar2(500) not null,
  4      remote_file varchar2(500) not null,
  5      transfer_mode char(1) default 'B' not null,
  6      download_class varchar2(500) default 'com.wrox.ftp.Download'
                                              not null,
  7      constraint fk_ftp_server_d_server_id
  8        foreign key (server_id) references ftp_servers,
  9      constraint chk_download_transfer_mode
 10        check (transfer_mode in ('B','A'))
 11  );

Table created.
```

Now that we have created the necessary database objects, it is time to develop the Java classes of our application.

## Java Classes

Our FTP application consists of four Java classes, as we have already stated:

❑   **Server** – Encapsulates a remote server stored in the FTP_SERVERS database table

❑   **Transfer** – An abstract class that defines methods for a generic FTP transfer

❑   **Upload** – Encapsulates a single file to upload, stored in the FTP_SERVER_UPLOADS table

❑   **Download** – Encapsulates a single file to download, stored in the FTP_SERVER_DOWNLOADS table

These classes and the relationship between them are further illustrated in the following UML diagram:

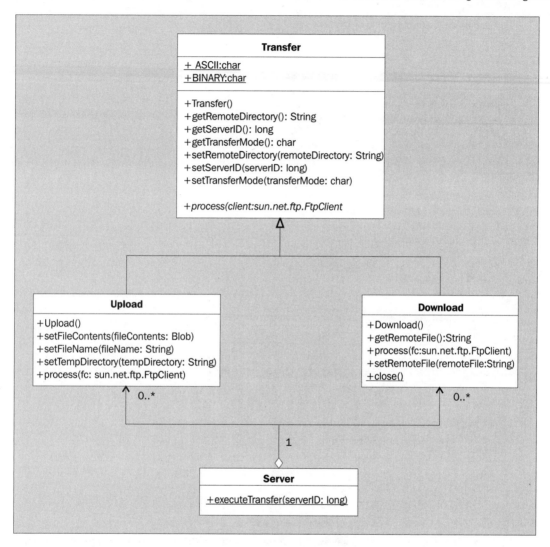

### Transfer

The abstract Transfer class defines generic methods used by the Download and Upload classes below. Through polymorphism, the Server class can execute a file upload and download in a uniform manner, by invoking the process() method of the Transfer class.

```
package com.wrox.ftp;

import java.sql.Connection;
import sun.net.ftp.FtpClient;
```

```java
public abstract class Transfer {

  // Binary transfer mode
  public static final char BINARY = 'B';

  // ASCII transfer mode
  public static final char ASCII = 'A';

  protected char transferMode;
  protected String remoteDirectory;
  protected long serverID;

  public String getRemoteDirectory() {
    return remoteDirectory;
  }

  public char getTransferMode() {
    return transferMode;
  }

  public long getServerID() {
    return serverID;
  }

  public void setRemoteDirectory(String remoteDirectory) {
    this.remoteDirectory = remoteDirectory;
  }

  public void setTransferMode(char transferMode) {
    this.transferMode = transferMode;
  }

  public void setServerID(long serverID) {
    this.serverID = serverID;
  }

  public abstract void process(FtpClient client) throws Exception;
}
```

### Upload

The Upload class extends Transfer for uploading files. Each Upload instance represents a particular row in the FTP_SERVER_UPLOADS database table, with the corresponding attributes.

```java
package com.wrox.ftp;

import java.io.*;
import java.sql.*;
import sun.net.ftp.FtpClient;

public class Upload extends Transfer {
```

```
// Instance variables.
private Blob fileContents;
private char transferMode;
private String fileName;
private long serverID;

public void setFileName(String fileName) {
  this.fileName = fileName;
}

public void setFileContents(Blob fileContents) {
  this.fileContents = fileContents;
}
```

The Upload class implements the process() method of the Transfer class by uploading the specified file in the FTP_SERVER_UPLOADS table to the remote server through the supplied FtpClient instance. A new file is uploaded by invoking the put() method of the FtpClient with a given file name. The put() method returns an output stream to which we write the contents of the upload file, which was read from the supplied BLOB locator. Note that we use for that purpose buffered input and output streams:

```
public void process(FtpClient fc) throws Exception {

  BufferedInputStream in = null;
  BufferedOutputStream out = null;

  try {

    // Upload the file.
    out = fc.put(fileName);
    in = new BufferedInputStream(fileContents.getBinaryStream());
    byte[] buffer = new byte[512];
    int amountRead = in.read(buffer);
    while (amountRead != -1) {
      out.write(buffer, 0, amountRead);
      amountRead = in.read(buffer);
    }
    out.flush();

  } finally {
    if (in != null) {
      try {
        in.close();
      } catch (IOException ignored) {}
    }
    if (out != null) {
      out.close();
    }
  }
}
```

## Download

The `Download` class extends `Transfer` for downloading files:

```
package com.wrox.ftp;

import java.io.*;
import java.sql.*;
import oracle.jdbc.driver.OracleCallableStatement;
import oracle.jdbc.driver.OracleTypes;
import oracle.sql.BLOB;
import sun.net.ftp.FtpClient;

public class Download extends Transfer {

  // Shared statement and connection.
  protected static Connection conn;
  protected static PreparedStatement pstmt;

  // Instance variables.
  protected String remoteFile;

    public String getRemoteFile() {
    return remoteFile;
  }

  public void setRemoteFile(String remoteFile) {
    this.remoteFile = remoteFile;
  }
```

The `Download` class implements the `process()` method of the `Transfer` class by retrieving a file from the supplied `FtpClient` and storing the file contents in the `DOWNLOADS` database table. To avoid unnecessary parsing of statements, we define a static `PreparedStatement` instance used to insert into the `DOWNLOADS` table. This statements is closed through the static `close()` method, below, at the end of an FTP transaction (as we will see with the `Server` class later).

```
public void process(FtpClient fc) throws Exception {
```

The `process()` method uses a `CallableStatement` (a subclass of `PreparedStatement`, which is thus more general) to call the `GET_DOWNLOAD_FILE()` function of the `UTL_FILE` PL/SQL package, which we will study later. This function takes for arguments a server ID, name of a remote file and remote directory, and returns an updatable `BLOB` locator for a corresponding download file.

*The reason why we use a PL/SQL function for this functionality, rather than issuing the respective statements through JDBC, is that we potentially have to work with a lot of intermediary results and statements in the function that are not directly related to the BLOB locator with which we are concerned (that is, we have to insert a new file record if one does not exist, keep track of the file ID, and so on). We will discuss the arguments for when to use PL/SQL and when to use JDBC (or SQLJ) from a Java program in more detail in Chapter 17, PL/SQL vs. Java.*

```
if (pstmt == null) {
  conn = DriverManager.getConnection("jdbc:oracle:kprb:@");
  pstmt = (OracleCallableStatement)
  conn.prepareCall("begin ? := utl_ftp.get_download_file(?,?,?); end;");
}

BufferedInputStream in = null;
BufferedOutputStream out = null;

try {

  // Execute the function.
  ((OracleCallableStatement) pstmt).registerOutParameter(1,
          OracleTypes.BLOB);
  pstmt.setLong(2, serverID);
  pstmt.setString(3, remoteFile);
  pstmt.setString(4, remoteDirectory);
  pstmt.execute();
  out =
    new BufferedOutputStream(((OracleCallableStatement) pstmt)
      .getBLOB(1).getBinaryOutputStream());
```

Once it has obtained a BLOB locator for a download file, the process() method reads the output from the remote file and writes it to the BLOB:

```
  in = new BufferedInputStream(fc.get(remoteFile));
  byte[] buffer = new byte[512];
  int amountRead = in.read(buffer);
  while (amountRead != -1) {
    out.write(buffer, 0, amountRead);
    amountRead = in.read(buffer);
  }
  out.flush();
  out.close();
  conn.commit();

} catch (SQLException e) {
  conn.rollback();
  throw e;

} finally {
  if (in != null) {
    try {
      in.close();
    } catch (IOException ignored) {}
  }
  if (out != null) {
    out.close();
  }
}
}
```

The static `close()` method is invoked at the end of each transfer in the `Server` class, below. It closes the statement, if it has been opened.

```
public static void close() throws SQLException {
  if (pstmt != null) {
    pstmt.close();
    pstmt = null;
  }
 }
}
```

### Server

The `Server` Java class represents a remote FTP server, whose information is stored in the `FTP_SERVERS` database table previously discussed. A new `Server` instance can only be constructed through the static `executeTransfer()` method, below (the `Server` class constructor has private visibility):

```
package com.wrox.ftp;

import java.sql.*;
import java.util.*;
import sun.net.ftp.FtpClient;
import com.wrox.util.logging.*;

public class Server {

  // Instance variables.
  private long serverID;
  private String serverName;
  private String userName;
  private String password;
  private HashSet transfers;
```

Note that we make use of the Logging API (`com.wrox.util.logging.*`) described in Appendix C, for logging down errors that may occur during FTP transfer. This becomes necessary since our transfers will be run in the background, initiated by a server job.

The `Server` constructor takes for an argument the ID of a specific server stored in the `FTP_SERVERS` database table. It calls the private `load()` method, discussed below, to read to the server and transfer information from the database.

```
private Server(long serverID) throws SQLException {
  this.serverID = serverID;
  transfers = new HashSet();
  load();
 }
```

The private `load()` method queries the database for server information, using the server ID supplied as an argument to the class constructor, using JDBC for database access. This method issues three SQL statements. The first selects information on the server itself, the second selects a list of the files that should be downloaded and the third selects the list of files that we will upload to the server For each upload and download specified, the `load()` method constructs a corresponding `Upload` or `Download` object and stores it in the `transfers` hash set.

```
private void load() throws SQLException {

    Connection conn = DriverManager.getConnection("jdbc:oracle:kprb:@");
    PreparedStatement pstmt = null;
    ResultSet rs;
    String className;
    Download dl;
    Upload ul;

    try {

      // Select server information.
      pstmt =
        conn.prepareStatement("select server_name, user_name, password "
                              + "from ftp_servers "
                              + "where server_id = ? ");
      pstmt.setLong(1, serverID);
      rs = pstmt.executeQuery();
      if (rs.next()) {

        // Set server information.
        serverName = rs.getString("server_name");
        userName = rs.getString("user_name");
        password = rs.getString("password");
      }

      // Select download information.
      pstmt = conn.prepareStatement("select remote_directory, remote_file, "
                              + "transfer_mode, download_class "
                              + "from ftp_server_downloads "
                              + "where server_id = ? "
                              + "order by remote_directory");
      pstmt.setLong(1, serverID);
      rs = pstmt.executeQuery();
      while (rs.next()) {
```

*Note that we order our results by the remote directory column. Thus, if more than one file should be downloaded from the same directory, we can avoid moving unnecessarily through the remote file system (there is probably not much overhead associated with that task, but it never hurts to reduce network processing). We adopt a similar approach with the upload files.*

As we have discussed before, we want to be able to instantiate a new Download instance, based on a class name stored in the database. While dynamic class loading is a commonplace task in a traditional Java environment (using the Class.forName() method), other rules apply when working within Oracle. The reason for this is that classes in Oracle are located on a per-schema basis, and not from a single class path, as is the case with traditional JVMs. An attempt to load a class in schema B from schema A with a simple Class.forName() call will therefore not work, as the two classes use two distinct class loaders. Therefore, when dynamically loading a specific class, we need somehow to specify not only the name of the class in question, but also the class loader or schema to which it belongs. Alternatively, we could achieve the same results by storing our classes in other schemas and using a public synonym.

While Oracle supplies methods for inter-schema class loading, we will, for the sake of simplicity, put the restriction on the Download extensions used that they must be loaded into the same schema as the other classes of the application. In other words, if you load the Server, Download and Upload into schema A, you should not use the Download extensions that are loaded into schema B. To ensure that we use the appropriate class handler, we retrieve the class handler of the Server class and supply it as an argument to the forName() method:

```
        className = rs.getString("download_class");
        try {
          dl =
            (Download) Class.forName(className, true,
              getClass().getClassLoader()).newInstance();
        } catch (Exception e) {
          throw new SQLException("Class " + className + " does not exist!");
        }

        dl.setRemoteFile(rs.getString("remote_file"));
        dl.setRemoteDirectory(rs.getString("remote_directory"));
        dl.setTransferMode(rs.getString("transfer_mode").charAt(0));
        dl.setServerID(serverID);
        transfers.add(dl);
      }


      // Select upload information.
      pstmt =
conn.prepareStatement("select fsu.remote_directory as remote_directory, "
                  + "u.file_name as file_name, "
                  + "u.file_contents as file_contents, "
                  + "fsu.transfer_mode as transfer_mode "
                  + "from ftp_server_uploads fsu, uploads u "
                  + "where fsu.file_id = u.file_id "
                  + "and fsu.server_id = ? "
                  + "order by fsu.remote_directory");
      pstmt.setLong(1, serverID);
      rs = pstmt.executeQuery();
      while (rs.next()) {

        // Create a new Upload object.
        ul = new Upload();
        ul.setFileName(rs.getString("file_name"));
        ul.setRemoteDirectory(rs.getString("remote_directory"));
        ul.setTransferMode(rs.getString("transfer_mode").charAt(0));
        ul.setFileContents(rs.getBlob("file_contents"));
        ul.setServerID(serverID);
        transfers.add(ul);
      }
```

```
    } finally {
      if (pstmt != null) {
        pstmt.close();
      }
    }
  }
```

The static `executeTransfer()` method is the only public method of the `Server` class. This method acts as a static entry point for FTP transfers. The `executeTransfer()` method takes for an instance a specific server ID, constructs a corresponding `Server` instance and invokes its private `executeTransfer()` method, below. Note that we use the Logging API to log down errors at this stage, since this will be run in the background. All other methods in our application throw errors, so all errors that occur should reach the `executeTransfer()` method.

```
public static void executeTransfer(long serverID) {
  try {
    (new Server(serverID)).executeTransfer();
  } catch (Exception e) {
    try {
      Logger l =
        LogManager.getInstance().getLogger("com.wrox.ftp.Server");
      l.log(e, LogLevel.ERROR);
    } catch (SQLException ignored) {}
  }
}
```

The private `executeTransfer()` method is illustrated below. This method creates a new `FtpClient` instance, according to the server information, and attempts to log on.

```
private void executeTransfer() throws Exception {

  FtpClient fc = null;
  String currentDir = null;
  String remoteDir;
  Transfer t;

  try {

    // Create a new FTP client and log on.
    fc = new FtpClient(serverName);
    fc.login(userName, password);
```

If the logon is successful, the method next iterates through all the `Transfer` objects (`Download` or `Upload`) and executes the `process()` method of the corresponding implementation through polymorphism. Note that we keep track of the current directory in which we are positioned, so that we don't have to unnecessarily move through the remote file system if we are currently positioned in the target directory.

```
    for (Iterator i = transfers.iterator(); i.hasNext(); ) {

      t = (Transfer) i.next();

      // Determine transfer mode.
      if (t.getTransferMode() == Transfer.ASCII) {
```

```
      fc.ascii();
    } else {
      fc.binary();
    }

    // Move to the specified directory,
    // but only if it is different from
    // the current directory we are in.
    remoteDir = t.getRemoteDirectory();
    if (currentDir == null ||!remoteDir.equals(currentDir)) {
      fc.cd(remoteDir);
      currentDir = remoteDir;
    }

    // Process the file.
    t.process(fc);
  }
```

Finally, all resources are closed down, including the shared statement used by all `Download` instances:

```
    finally {

      try {
        Download.close();
      } catch (Exception e) {}

      try {
        fc.closeServer();
      } catch (Exception e) {}
    }
  }
}
```

## Load the Classes Into the Database

Before we go any further, we should load the classes comprising our FTP application to the database. This can be accomplished with `loadjava`, as illustrated here:

```
> loadjava -user username/password@database -resolve Transfer.java
> loadjava -user username/password@database -resolve Download.java
> loadjava -user username/password@database -resolve Upload.java
> loadjava -user username/password@database -resolve Server.java
```

## Security Considerations

When working with operating system resources, such as TCP sockets used in FTP transfer, we must be granted explicit Java permissions, as we have discussed in previous chapters in this book. Specifically, for using FTP, we must be granted a socket permission to connect to the specified FTP server and additionally, to accept connections on all ports between 1024 and 65535 (the highest available port) on the database server. This is further illustrated with an example:

```
SQL> connect sys/<your-password>;

SQL> call dbms_java.grant_permission (
  2     'username',
  3     'java.net.SocketPermission',
  4     'ftp.someserver',  -- change this!
  5     'accept,connect'
  6  );

Call completed.

SQL> call dbms_java.grant_permission (
  2     'username',
  3     'java.net.SocketPermission',
  4     'localhost:1024-',
  5     'listen,resolve'
  6  );

Call completed.
```

For more information on the SocketPermission or Java permissions in general, consult Chapter 11, *Oracle Java Security*.

## UTL_FTP PL/SQL Package

When the Java classes have been loaded into the database we can create the UTL_FTP PL/SQL package, which we use to invoke FTP transfers from the PL/SQL context. The UTL_FTP package specification is declared below:

```
SQL> create or replace package utl_ftp
  2  is
  3
  4     function get_download_file (
  5       p_server_id in number,
  6       p_remote_file in varchar2,
  7       p_remote_directory in varchar2
  8     ) return blob;
  9
 10     procedure execute_transfer (
 11       p_server_id in number
 12     );
 13
 14  end;
 15  /

Package created.
```

We discussed the GET_DOWNLOAD_FILE() function before, in relation to the Download class. The EXECUTE_TRANSFER() procedure provides a call spec for the Server.executeTransfer() method.

**571**

```
SQL> create or replace package body utl_ftp
  2  is
  3
  4    function get_download_file (
  5      p_server_id in number,
  6      p_remote_file in varchar2,
  7      p_remote_directory in varchar2
  8    ) return blob
  9    is
 10      l_blob blob;
 11      l_file_found boolean := true;
 12      l_rowid rowid;
 13    begin
 14
 15      begin
 16
 17        select file_contents
 18          into l_blob
 19          from downloads
 20         where server_id = p_server_id
 21           and remote_file = p_remote_file
 22           and remote_directory = p_remote_directory
 23           for update;
 24
 25        -- Erase the original file.
 26        dbms_lob.trim(l_blob,0);
 27
 28      exception when others then
 29        l_file_found := false;
 30      end;
 31
 32      -- Create a new file record.
 33      if not l_file_found then
 34        insert into downloads (
 35          remote_file, remote_directory,
 36          server_id, file_contents)
 37        values (
 38          p_remote_file, p_remote_directory,
 39          p_server_id, empty_blob())
 40        returning rowid into l_rowid;
 41
 42        -- Select for update.
 43        select file_contents
 44          into l_blob
 45          from downloads
 46         where rowid = l_rowid
 47           for update;
 48      end if;
 49
 50      -- Return the BLOB locator.
 51      return l_blob;
 52    end;
 53
```

```
54    procedure execute_transfer (
55      p_server_id in number
56    )
57    as language java
58    name 'com.wrox.ftp.Server.executeTransfer(long)';
59
60  end;
61  /
```

```
Package body created
```

# The Role of PL/SQL

It is the intention of this section to illustrate a general-use FTP client application operating from within the database, which can be used to schedule automatic file transfer and processing at regular intervals. So far, we have developed the Java classes and created the database tables necessary for the FTP client, but we have not yet demonstrated how it can be scheduled for automatic file transfer. One of the advantages of running our client within the database is that we can make use of the inherent job system of Oracle. Within the database, jobs can be scheduled for execution through the built-in DBMS_JOB PL/SQL package, which you are probably familiar with. If not, you can consult the Oracle *Supplied PL/SQL Packages and Types Reference* for more information (either as part of the documentation supplied with your database or from http://download-west.oracle.com/otndoc/oracle9i/901_doc/appdev.901/a89852/dbms_job.htm#ARPLS019).

Make sure that your database is properly configured for running background jobs, otherwise DBMS_JOB will not work. Specifically, you will need to set two parameters in the database's init.ora configuration file:

❑ job_queue_processes – The number of background processes that are available to run jobs. This can take any value between 0 (no jobs) and 36.

❑ job_queue_interval – This is the number of seconds the job queue processes wait before they check for a new job to execute. After each check, the processes are put to sleep for this many seconds.

After you have modified these parameters, you must restart your database.

## Scheduling an FTP Transfer

Using the UTL_FTP package we just declared, we can submit a recursive FTP transfer job with a call to the SUBMIT() procedure of DBMS_JOB. In doing that, it may be useful to use the job ID obtained from the SUBMIT() procedure as an ID for the server in the FTP_SERVERS table. Thus, we can easily relate database jobs with the FTP servers they are connecting to (such as USER_JOBS with FTP_SERVERS). Additionally, we reduce the risk of submitting a job with an invalid server ID. For example, consider the following code that submits a file transfer every 24 hours, for the server and files specified. First, it calls the DBMS_JOB.SUBMIT() procedure, and uses the associated job ID to insert a new row in the FTP_SERVERS table. Then, it adds a new file specification in the FTP_SERVER_DOWNLOADS table, and inserts a new file in the UPLOADS table. Finally, it adds a row to the FTP_SERVER_UPLOADS table, using the new file.

*Note that the values presented in this example are not real – you need to supply your own if you want to replicate this example.*

```
SQL> declare
  2      job number;
  3      buffer raw(255) := utl_raw.cast_to_raw('Some nonsense...');
  4      amt binary_integer := 32767;
  5      pos integer := 1;
  6      lob_loc blob;
  7      new_file number;
  8  begin
  9
 10      -- Submit a job.
 11      dbms_job.submit(
 12        job,
 13        'utl_ftp.execute_transfer(job);',
 14        trunc(sysdate),
 15        'trunc(sysdate) + 1'
 16      );
 17
 18      -- Create a new server
 19      insert into ftp_servers (
 20        server_id, server_name, user_name, password)
 21      values (
 22        job, 'ftp.someserver', 'user', 'pass');
 23
 24      -- Specify a download file.
 25      insert into ftp_server_downloads(
 26        server_id, remote_directory, remote_file)
 27      values (
 28        job, '/export/home/files', 'server.log');
 29
 30      -- Create a new file.
 31      insert into uploads (
 32        file_name, file_contents)
 33      values (
 34        'report.txt', empty_blob())
 35      returning file_id into new_file;
 36
 37      -- Write to the BLOB.
 38      select file_contents into lob_loc
 39        from uploads
 40       where file_id = new_file
 41         for update;
 42      dbms_lob.write (lob_loc, utl_raw.length(buffer), pos, buffer);
 43
 44      -- Specify an upload.
 45      insert into ftp_server_uploads (
 46        server_id, file_id, remote_directory)
 47      values (
 48        job, new_file, '/export/home/files');
 49
```

```
50   commit;
51
52 end;
53 /
```

PL/SQL procedure successfully completed.

Now, if want to test the application, without scheduling a job for doing that, you might want to specify a simple download by hard-coding a server ID like this:

```
SQL> -- Create a new server
SQL> insert into ftp_servers (
  2        server_id, server_name, user_name, password)
  3 values (
  4        1, 'ftp.someserver', 'user', 'pass');

1 row inserted.

SQL> -- Specify a download file.
SQL> insert into ftp_server_downloads (server_id, remote_directory, remote_file)
  2 values (1, '/export/home/files', 'server.log');

1 row inserted.

SQL> commit;

Commit complete.
```

Then, try to execute the transfer:

```
SQL> call utl_ftp.execute_transfer(1);

call completed.
```

To determine whether the download proceeded or not, you can look at the last entry in the error messages view:

```
SQL> select message_id, message
  2    from my_log_messages
  3   where message_id = (
  4    select max(message_id) from my_log_messages
  5 );

no rows selected
```

If everything works as expected, this query should return no rows for the Server class.

In the next section, we will illustrate a further example of using our application, as we implement a specific Download class extension that can be used to process access logs from remote HTTP servers.

# Archiving Access Logs

There are many practical uses of running an FTP client from within the database. Due to the scheduling abilities of the PL/SQL language, we can set up regular processing of data from remote servers, which allows us to gather statistics in database tables which would otherwise only be accessible as files distributed on different machines on a network.

An example of data that it may be useful to gather in such a fashion is information on web page requests from a set of HTTP servers. Such information is typically written to log files, which are then rotated on a regular interval, such as once per day. It is hard to make any use of such information when it is stored in files in the file system. It would be much more useful if we could store the data in a database where it could be analyzed and grouped according to specific criteria. A possible approach to this problem is to have each server process the log files at regular intervals, and store the page request information in a central database, as illustrated in the following figure:

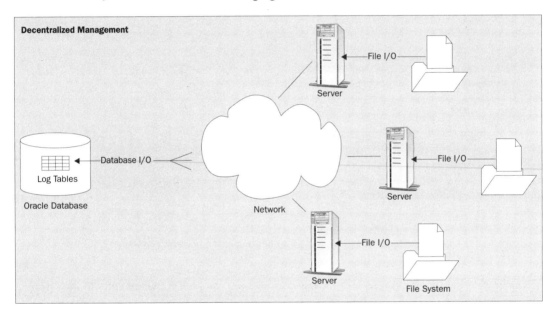

Such an approach, however, has its drawbacks:

❏ **Database I/O** – The database update has to take place over the network. This incurs a lot of overhead. Additionally, the data has to be transported over the network as database calls, which adds much more data to the actual transfer than if the file contents were transferred in one stream, with FTP.

❏ **Decentralized Management** – Each server has to manage its own database access. Minimal changes to the database environment need to be reflected in a number of places.

Another possible solution is to have the database retrieve the raw access logs at regular intervals, and process them locally, within the database. That way, we minimize network traffic and database I/O and put the log file management in a central location. Although this may possibly not be a suitable approach for all applications (depending, for example on the spatial distribution of servers and network setup – FTP is not always an option), this illustrates a useful way for using our FTP application in a real-life situation. This is further demonstrated in the figure below:

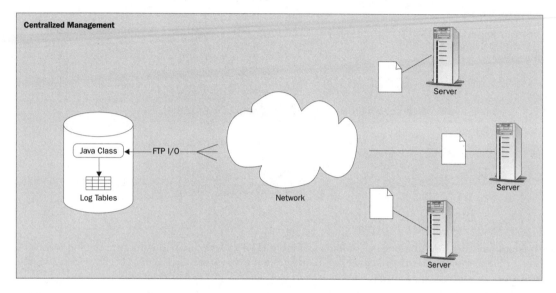

In this section we will implement such an approach by building on our database FTP application. Specifically, we will develop an extension of the `Download` class, which we use to process and store page request information from remote access logs transferred over FTP into the database.

Before we start writing the `Download` extension class, we shall study briefly what information we need from the access logs and develop a specific log format accordingly.

## Log Format

Various pieces of information can be obtained about each page request to a web server. For example, we can obtain the time the request took place, the page that was requested and the host name of the client making the request. Not all of the information available for use is necessary in all cases, and in this example we will only make use of a specific subset of the request headers that would be otherwise available. In our application we will require that each server logs four distinct elements of each request, as specified below:

❑ **Time** – The time the request takes place

❑ **Remote Host** – The name of the remote host making the request

❑ **HTTP Header** – The HTTP header used for the request. The header consists of three elements:

    ❑ *HTTP Method* – For example, GET or POST

- ❑ *HTTP URI* – The Uniform Resource Identifier (URI) of the resource requested, relative to the document root of the web site
- ❑ *HTTP Version* – For example, `HTTP/1.0`
- ❑ **User Agent** – The full name of the user agent used to make the request. This information may be further processed at will, in order to retrieve further details on the operating system and web browser of the client.

For our application, each server should log this information according to the following comma-delimited format:

```
Time,Remote host,HTTP header,User agent
```

For example, these would be two entries that adhered to our log format:

```
25.09.2001 15:46:22,212.30.192.1,GET /htdocs/index.html HTTP/1.1,Mozilla/4.0
(compatible; MSIE 5.5; Windows NT 5.0)

25.09.2001 15:49:12,212.67.160.157,GET /htdocs/welcome.html HTTP/1.0,Mozilla/4.0
(compatible; MSIE 5.5; Windows 98)
```

## Configuring the Apache HTTP Server

It is not our intention to illustrate for each available HTTP server how to configure the log format according to our standards. However, we illustrate that process for the Apache HTTP server, which is open-source and one of the most widely used HTTP servers in the world today.

To specify the log file format for an Apache server, changes must be made to its `httpd.conf` configuration file (located under `APACHE_HOME/conf/`). In this file, add or replace existing access log specifications with the one shown below.

```
LogFormat '%{%d.%m.%Y %H:%M:%S}t,%h,%r,%{User-Agent}i' common

SetEnvIf Request_URI \.jsp$ page=jsp
SetEnvIf Request_URI \.html$ page=html
SetEnvIf Request_URI \.htm$ page=htm
CustomLog logs/clients_access_log common env=page
```

The `LogFormat` line above specifies:

- ❑ **%t** – The time a request is made, using the format *dd.mm.yyyy hh:mi:ss*,
- ❑ **%h** – The remote host,
- ❑ **%r** – The HTTP header,
- ❑ **%{User-Agent}i** – The user agent.

After these changes, you must restart the Apache server for the changes to take effect.

To let the server automatically rotate the log files on a regular interval, you can make use of a small program that ships with most Apache versions, which is called `rotatelogs`. This is a simple program that is used to rotate Apache logs without having to kill the server. This program is typically located in either the APACHE_HOME/bin or APACHE_HOME/support directory, depending on your version. To use `rotatelogs` with your Apache server, you should add the following specification somewhere in its `httpd.conf` file (assuming `rotatelogs` is in APACHE_HOME/bin):

```
TransferLog '|/apache-home/bin/rotatelogs /path-to-logs/logname time',
```

where the time is specified in seconds. For example (replace bold words to better suit your own setup):

```
TransferLog '|/usr/apache/bin/rotatelogs /usr/apache/logs/old-access 86400'
```

At the end of each rotation time (here after 24 hours) a new log is started and the old log is moved to the file specified in the line above, with the current system time as a suffix (for example, /usr/local/apache/logs/old-access.xxx). For more information on the Apache HTTP server, refer to the Apache web site, at http://www.apache.org/.

If the `rotatelogs` utility is not available in your current version of Apache, you can download the Apache source from http://httpd.apache.org/ and copy the `rotatelogs` program from there to your own setup.

## Extending the Download Class

Now that we have defined the format used by our access logs, it is time to implement the actual log handler class. This class, `AccessLog`, extends the `Download` class we have previously used. In its `process()` method, it reads the byte stream from the remote log file and inserts each entry in a database table called ACCESS_LOG, which is defined below.

### Access Log Table

The ACCESS_LOG table, along with an associated sequence and sequence trigger, is illustrated below:

```
SQL> create table access_log (
  2    server_id number not null,
  3    request_id number not null,
  4    remote_host varchar2(255) not null,
  5    time date not null,
  6    http_method varchar2(10) default 'GET' not null,
  7    file_name varchar2(255) default 'none' not null,
  8    http_version varchar2(10) default 'HTTP/1.0' not null,
  9    user_agent varchar2(255) not null,
 10    constraint pk_access_log primary key (request_id),
 11    constraint fk_ftp_server foreign key (server_id) references
                                                      ftp_servers
 12  );

Table created.

SQL> create sequence access_log_seq;
```

```
Sequence created.

SQL> create or replace trigger access_log_new_sequence
  2  before insert on access_log
  3     for each row
  4  begin
  5    select access_log_seq.nextval into :new.request_id from dual;
  6  end;
  7  /

Trigger created.
```

### AccessLog Class

The `AccessLog` class is declared below:

```java
package com.wrox.ftp;

import java.io.*;
import java.sql.*;
import java.util.Date;
import java.util.StringTokenizer;
import oracle.jdbc.driver.OracleConnection;
import oracle.jdbc.driver.OraclePreparedStatement;
import sun.net.ftp.FtpClient;

public class AccessLog extends Download {

    /** The date format used */
    public static final String DATE_FORMAT = "dd.mm.yyyy HH24:MI:SS";
```

The `AccessLog` class overrides the `process()` method of the `Download` class, for processing an access log. It reads each line of the access log, splits it up and stores it in the database. For that purpose we use JDBC because of its inherent support for bulk inserts.

```java
    public void process(FtpClient fc) throws Exception {

        BufferedReader reader = null;
        int noLineTokens = 4;
        int noHeaderTokens = 3;
        String line;
        String remoteHost;
        String httpMethod;
        String fileName;
        String httpVersion;
        String userAgent;
        String time;
        StringTokenizer lineTokens;
        StringTokenizer headerTokens;

        try {
```

**580**

Once we have obtained a connection to the database, we prepare the database INSERT statement. This statement is shared among all AccessLog instances in the current transaction.

```
if (pstmt == null) {
    conn = DriverManager.getConnection("jdbc:oracle:kprb:@");
    pstmt = conn.prepareStatement("insert into access_log ("
                        + "server_id, remote_host, "
                        + "time, http_method, file_name, "
                        + "http_version, user_agent) "
                        + "values (?,?,to_date(?, '"
                        + DATE_FORMAT + "'),?,?,?,?)");
```

Following that, we set the number of batches to execute. In our example, we use 20 statements in a batch. Note that we use the Oracle-specific batch update model, which performs batch execution when either the batch limit has been reached or a commit is made (for more information on Oracle batch updates, refer to Chapter 5, *Using JDBC*).

```
    ((OraclePreparedStatement) pstmt).setExecuteBatch(20);
}
```

Next, we process each line of the log file, and add a new entry to the batch.

```
reader =
  new BufferedReader(new InputStreamReader(fc.get(remoteFile)));
line = reader.readLine();
while (line != null) {
  lineTokens = new StringTokenizer(line, ",");

  // Do not proceed if some information is missing.
  if (lineTokens.countTokens() == noLineTokens) {

    // Read the time value.
    time = lineTokens.nextToken();

    // Read the name of the remote host.
    remoteHost = lineTokens.nextToken();

    // Read and process the HTTP header.
    headerTokens = new StringTokenizer(lineTokens.nextToken(), " ");
    if (headerTokens.countTokens() == noHeaderTokens) {
      httpMethod = headerTokens.nextToken();
      fileName = headerTokens.nextToken();
      httpVersion = headerTokens.nextToken();
    } else {
      httpMethod = "";
      fileName = "";
      httpVersion = "";
    }

    // Read the name of the user agent.
    userAgent = lineTokens.nextToken();
```

```
        // Prepare the SQL statement.
        pstmt.setLong(1, serverID);
        pstmt.setString(2, remoteHost);
        pstmt.setString(3, time);
        pstmt.setString(4, httpMethod);
        pstmt.setString(5, fileName);
        pstmt.setString(6, httpVersion);
        pstmt.setString(7, userAgent);
```

Note that since we set the Oracle-specific execute batch value for the `PreparedStatement` instance, calling `executeUpdate()` will effectively send a batch of 20 statements to the database, each time such a count has been reached.

```
        pstmt.executeUpdate();
      }

      // Read the next line.
      line = reader.readLine();
    }
    conn.commit();

  } catch (SQLException e) {
    conn.rollback();
    throw e;
  }
```

Finally, all resources are closed down:

```
  finally {

    // Close the file I/O stream.
    if (reader != null) {
      try {
        reader.close();
      } catch (IOException ignored) {}
    }
  }
}
```

### Using the AccessLog

In order to set up and use the log handler, you must load the `AccessLog` class in the database and configure a specific file in the `FTP_SERVER_DOWNLOAD` database table, so that it uses the `AccessLog` class. For example:

```
> loadjava -user username/password@database -resolve AccessLog.java
```

```
SQL> -- Create a new server
SQL> insert into ftp_servers (
  2    server_id, server_name, user_name, password)
  3  values (2, 'ftp.someserver', 'user', 'pass');

1 row inserted.
```

```
SQL> -- Specify a download file.
SQL> insert into ftp_server_downloads (
  2     server_id, remote_directory, remote_file, download_class)
  3     values (2, '/usr/local/apache/logs', 'access.log',
  4     'com.wrox.ftp.AccessLog');

1 row inserted.

SQL> commit;

Commit complete.
```

As before, try to execute the transfer:

```
SQL> call utl_ftp.execute_transfer(2);
```

*At the Wrox web site, you can download the source code for the whole FTP application.*

# Data Compression

When storing a large number of files in the database, it may be feasible to apply some sort of binary compression to their contents, in order to take up less disk space.

The PL/SQL language has no support for any compression algorithm, while Java in fact supports more than one. However, for some LOB operations, such as getting a temporary LOB, you need to call functions in the DBMS_LOB built-in PL/SQL package. As a result, in order to implement a database utility that can be used to both compress and decompress large database objects, we need the collaboration of both PL/SQL and Java.

In this section we will develop such an application, and illustrate its use in a sample scenario. Furthermore, at the end of this section, we will give an example of measures that must be taken when we have applied compression to the contents of a particular database table, so that other parts of the database can still work with its content as before. Specifically, we will give an example of how to customize a search index with interMedia Text so that compressed documents can still be indexed and searched as before.

## Java Compression API

The core java.util.zip package provides classes for reading and writing the standard ZIP and GZIP file formats. These formats can be used for the compression of any type of data, be it a file in a file system or a BLOB field in a database.

Both the ZIP and GZIP formats build on the DEFLATE compression algorithm, which is also made available through Java. There is, however, a fundamental difference between ZIP and GZIP. GZIP can only be used to compress a single entry – be it one file or an archive of multiple files – while ZIP is used to compress (and archive) any number of entries. Therefore, we find it more appropriate to use the GZIP format in our database compression application, because we will be dealing with single LOB entries at a time.

**583**

## GZIP Compression

The GZIP specification defines a compressed data format that can be used to compress any single source of bytes. Java provides two classes for the GZIP handling, `GZIPInputStream` and `GZIPOutputStream`, for reading and writing data in GZIP format. The `GZIPInputStream` and `GZIPOutputStream` extend the base `InputStream` and `OutputStream` I/O Java classes, and are used accordingly.

# Java Classes

Our compression/decompression application consists of two freestanding classes, `Compressor` and `Decompressor`. These classes are used to compress and decompress, respectively, a source of binary data, stored as a `BLOB` in the database. For the compression method, we will actually overwrite the source `BLOB` with its compressed counterpart, while for the decompression procedure, we simply switch the two `BLOB` locators, so that the caller may think he is handling the uncompressed source, while in fact he is only handling an uncompressed copy of the source, stored as a temporary `BLOB` that will persist only for the current session (the user should not be able to decompress the actual data). The two Java classes, along with the `UTL_GZIP` PL/SQL package that we use to publish them, are illustrated in the following diagram:

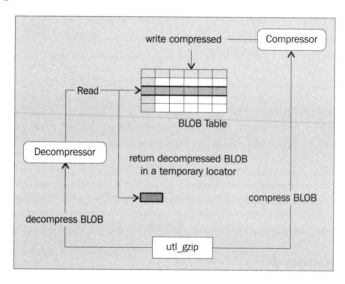

In the next few paragraphs, we will study our two Java classes in more detail.

## Compressor

The `Compressor` class is used to compress binary data stored in a `BLOB` column in a database table. It does so through the static `doCompress()` method. The reason why this class accepts only binary (`BLOB`) data for compression, is that we commonly compress data at its current location – that is, by overwriting the uncompressed source with the compressed output – which means that the data type will be `BLOB` anyway, even though the source of the data is text-based (since the compressed output is binary in nature).

### Declarations

The `Compressor` class is designed to be a `Singleton` – with a private constructor and a single static Compressor instance. We discussed the Singleton design pattern in more detail in Chapter 13, *Working with Operating System Resources*.

```
package com.wrox.gzip;

import java.io.*;
import java.sql.*;
import java.util.zip.*;
import oracle.jdbc.driver.*;
import oracle.sql.*;

public class Compressor {

    // Singleton instance.
    private static Compressor instance;

    // Instance variables.
    private OracleConnection conn = null;
    private OracleCallableStatement cstmt = null;
```

The `Compressor` constructor obtains a connection and prepares the callable statement we use to get a temporary BLOB. This statement is closed when the `Compressor` instance is garbage collected (when the session ends), since we implement a `finalize()` method below that closes the statement (a `finalize()` method is always called when an object is garbage collected).

The reason for our Singleton design is that we wish to share the callable statement among all calls to the compressor method below. By doing that, we greatly reduce the SQL parsing overhead, as we will discuss in Chapter 16, *SQL Tuning and Analyzing Queries*.

```
    private Compressor() throws SQLException {

        conn =
          (OracleConnection) DriverManager.getConnection("jdbc:oracle:kprb:@");

        // Create a temporary BLOB, with a call to the
        // dbms_lob.createtemporary() procedure.
        cstmt = (OracleCallableStatement) conn.prepareCall("begin
                  dbms_lob.createtemporary(?, true, dbms_lob.session); end;");
    }
```

### Compressing the Data

The `compress()` method is used to compress the underlying data of a specified BLOB locator. It returns a locator to a temporary BLOB that contains the compressed data. This temporary BLOB persists only through the duration of the current transaction (after which it becomes invalid for use).

This method relies on the built-in PL/SQL package DBMS_LOB in order to store the compressed binary data. BLOB locators are used only as pointers to actual binary data, which means that use of BLOB locators, rather than storing binary objects in local variables, is preferred in terms of (less) memory usage. If we were to rely solely on Java, we would either have to read the original binary data in a local memory structure (such as byte[]), or store it in a persistent storage, such as the file system, for the duration of the transaction. The first method is very memory-extensive as binary data stored as BLOB can become as large as 4 GBs. Obviously, loading even a fraction of such data in a shared memory would not only risk the session executing this method, but all Java sessions running inside the database, as they all share a common pool of memory. The latter method, storing the uncompressed binary data in an external data source, would not be very preferable in terms of performance. An I/O operation on a BLOB locator within the database will always perform faster than any comparable operation on an external entity, such as a file in a file system. Additionally, for doing that, we would need to grant our users permissions to write files in the operating system, which may not always be preferable. Generally, if we can do something in the database, without limiting either functionality or performance, we should do it.

Therefore, in terms of both performance and memory usage, it is necessary to use two BLOB locators in this method: the supplied locator which points to the original (uncompressed) data, and a temporary locator (exists through the current session) which points to the compressed data. We create this temporary locator through the DBMS_LOB PL/SQL package, as you will see below.

In JDBC 2.0, there are a number of limitations to LOB handling. For example, using JDBC it is not possible to write to a LOB, only read from it. These limitations, however, are not in place in the Oracle-specific JDBC extensions. Since we need to write to a BLOB locator later in this method, we therefore choose to use the Oracle JDBC extensions in our database access. For more information on the Oracle JDBC extensions, consult Chapter 7, *Handling Complex Types*.

```
public BLOB compress(BLOB blob) throws SQLException, IOException {

    BLOB compressedBlob = null;
    byte[] buffer;
    GZIPOutputStream out = null;
    BufferedInputStream in = null;
    int amountRead;
    OracleResultSet rs;
```

Before anything else, this method makes sure the supplied BLOB locator is not null. If that is the case, an appropriate null value is returned.

```
    if (blob == null) {
      return null;
    }
```

Next, we create the temporary BLOB, which we use to store the compressed data. We do that with a call to the DBMS_LOB.CREATETEMPORARY procedure, which accepts a given BLOB locator as an IN/OUT argument. This temporary BLOB will exist for the duration of the current session (the current call), unless we explicitly delete it at the end of the transaction, as we will be doing later in the UTL_GZIP package.

*The temporary BLOB will generally be used only to replace the original BLOB value. Therefore, there is no need to have it persist for any longer than required.*

```
try {

    cstmt.registerOutParameter(1, oracle.jdbc.driver.OracleTypes.BLOB);
    cstmt.setBLOB(1, compressedBlob);
    cstmt.execute();
    compressedBlob = cstmt.getBLOB(1);
```

If we successfully obtained an empty BLOB locator, we proceed to compressing the data. We do so by constructing a new GZIPOutputStream from the output stream of the source BLOB, and writing the compressed byte stream (in chunks of data) to the temporary BLOB, as shown below:

```
if (compressedBlob != null) {
  System.out.println("a");
  out = new GZIPOutputStream(compressedBlob.getBinaryOutputStream());
  buffer = new byte[blob.getBufferSize()];
  in = new BufferedInputStream(blob.getBinaryStream(), buffer.length);
  amountRead = in.read(buffer);
  while (amountRead != -1) {
    out.write(buffer, 0, amountRead);
    amountRead = in.read(buffer);
  }
  out.flush();
}
```

Finally, we make sure all resources are shut down:

```
} finally {

  // Close the output stream.
  if (out != null) {
    try {
      out.close();
    } catch (IOException ignored) {}
  }

  // Close the input stream.
  if (in != null) {
    in.close();
  }
}

  return compressedBlob;
}
```

For running the decompress() method, we declare a static method which uses the static Singleton instance:

```
    public static BLOB doCompress(BLOB blob)
            throws SQLException, IOException {
      if (instance == null) {
        instance = new Compressor();
      }
      return instance.compress(blob);

    }
```

### Closing Resources

As we have previously mentioned, we define a `finalize()` method for closing down resources.

```
    public void finalize() {
      try {
        cstmt.close();
      } catch (SQLException ignored) {}
    }
  }
```

## Decompressor

The `Decompressor` class resembles the previous `Compressor` class in many ways, except that it is used to decompress an already compressed source of data to a temporary `BLOB` locator, which is designed to persist throughout the lifetime of the current database session. The application uses the temporary `BLOB` locator to access the decompressed value of a compressed `BLOB`, stored in some database table – that is, after a particular `BLOB` record in some table has been compressed, it is never actually decompressed, but rather a copy of the `BLOB` is decompressed and stored in a temporary locator. The `Decompressor` class performs data decompression through the static `doDecompress()` method, which we will see below.

### Declarations

Like the `Compressor` class, `Decompressor` is designed as a Singleton. Its private constructor obtains database resources, as before:

```
package com.wrox.gzip;

import java.io.*;
import java.sql.*;
import java.util.zip.*;
import oracle.jdbc.driver.*;
import oracle.sql.*;

public class Decompressor {

  // Class variable.
  private static Decompressor instance;

  // Instance variables.
  private OracleConnection conn = null;
  private OracleCallableStatement cstmt = null;
```

```
private Decompressor() throws SQLException {

  conn =
    (OracleConnection) DriverManager.getConnection("jdbc:oracle:kprb:@");

  // Create a temporary BLOB, with a call to the
  // dbms_lob.createtemporary() procedure.
  cstmt = (OracleCallableStatement) conn.prepareCall("begin
          dbms_lob.createtemporary(?, true, dbms_lob.session); end;");
}
```

### Decompressing Data

The decompress() method of the Decompressor works basically like the compress() method of Compressor, except that it performs decompression, rather than compression.

```
public BLOB decompress(BLOB blob) throws SQLException, IOException {

    BLOB decompressedBlob = null;
    byte[] buffer;
    GZIPInputStream in = null;
    BufferedOutputStream out = null;
    int amountRead = -1;
    OracleResultSet rs;
```

Again, if the supplied BLOB locator is null, we return null.

```
    if (blob == null) {
      return null;
    }
    try {
      cstmt.registerOutParameter(1, oracle.jdbc.driver.OracleTypes.BLOB);
      cstmt.setBLOB(1, decompressedBlob);
      cstmt.execute();
      decompressedBlob = cstmt.getBLOB(1);
```

If the new BLOB was successfully obtained, we decompress the supplied source BLOB and write the decompressed data to the temporary BLOB.

```
      if (decompressedBlob != null) {
        in = new GZIPInputStream(blob.getBinaryStream());
        out = new BufferedOutputStream(
            decompressedBlob.getBinaryOutputStream(), blob.getBufferSize());
        buffer = new byte[blob.getBufferSize()];
        try {
          amountRead = in.read(buffer);
        } catch (EOFException eof) {
          amountRead = -1;
        }
```

```
        while (amountRead != -1) {
          out.write(buffer, 0, amountRead);
          try {
            amountRead = in.read(buffer);
          } catch (EOFException eof) {
            amountRead = -1;
          }
        }
        out.flush();
      }
```

As before, we make sure all resources are shut down each time:

```
      } finally {

          // Close the output stream.
          if (out != null) {
            try {
                out.close();
            } catch (IOException ignored) {
            }
      } finally {

        // Close the output stream.
        if (out != null) {
          try {
            out.close();
          } catch (IOException ignored) {}
        }

        // Close the input stream.
        if (in != null) {
          in.close();
        }
      }

    return decompressedBlob;
  }
```

As we did for the Compressor class, we define a static method for decompressing:

```
public static BLOB doDecompress(BLOB blob)
      throws SQLException, IOException {
  if (instance == null) {
    instance = new Decompressor();
  }
  return instance.decompress(blob);
}
```

### Closing Resources

Again, we define a `finalize()` method for closing down resources:

```
public void finalize() {
  try {
    cstmt.close();
  } catch (SQLException ignored) {}
}
}
```

## Load the Classes Into the Database

When all the Java classes have been created, they must be loaded into the database:

```
>loadjava -user username/password@database -resolve Compressor.java
>loadjava -user username/password@database -resolve Decompressor.java
```

# Publishing the Classes

Before we can start compressing BLOBs in the database, there are a few PL/SQL procedures and functions we must create. Firstly, we must create call specifications for both of the doCompress() and doDecompress() methods. Additionally, we need a couple of procedures that take a BLOB locator as an IN/OUT argument, and either compress or decompress its underlying data.

To organize these procedures and functions together, we create a specific PL/SQL package, UTL_GZIP. In the next two subsections we will further illustrate the structure of this package.

## Package Header

The UTL_GZIP package header (specification) is shown below:

```
SQL> create or replace package utl_gzip
  2  is
  3
  4    function get_compressed (
  5      p_blob_loc in blob
  6    ) return blob;
  7
  8    function get_decompressed (
  9      p_blob_loc in blob
 10    ) return blob;
 11
 12    procedure do_compress (
 13      p_uncompressed in out nocopy blob
 14    );
 15
 16    procedure do_decompress (
 17      p_compressed in out nocopy blob
 18    );
 19
```

```
20   end;
21   /

Package created.
```

## Package Body

In the next few paragraphs, we will study the procedures and functions that make up the UTL_GZIP package.

```
SQL> create or replace package body utl_gzip
  2  is
```

### GET_COMPRESSED

The GET_COMPRESSED function is a wrapper for the Compressor.doCompress() Java method.

```
 3      function get_compressed (
 4        p_blob_loc in blob
 5      ) return blob
 6      as language java
 7      name 'com.wrox.gzip.Compressor.doCompress
 8        (oracle.sql.BLOB) return oracle.sql.BLOB';
```

### GET_DECOMPRESSED

The GET_DECOMPRESSED function is a wrapper for the Decompressor.doDecompress() Java method.

```
 9      function get_decompressed (
10        p_blob_loc in blob
11      ) return blob
12      as language java
13      name 'com.wrox.gzip.Decompressor.doDecompress
14        (oracle.sql.BLOB) return oracle.sql.BLOB';
```

### DO_COMPRESS

This procedure takes for an argument a BLOB instance whose source should be compressed.

```
15      procedure do_compress (
16        p_uncompressed in out blob
17      )
18      is
19        l_compressed blob;
20        l_length integer;
21
22      begin
23
24        -- Get a compressed, temporary BLOB locator.
25        l_compressed := get_compressed(p_uncompressed);
```

```
26
27       -- Erase the original lob. Otherwise, we will
28       -- append the new data to the existing one.
29       dbms_lob.trim(p_uncompressed,0);
30
31       -- Get the length of the compressed data.
32       l_length := dbms_lob.getlength(l_compressed);
33
34       -- Copy the compressed data to the destination BLOB.
35       dbms_lob.copy(p_uncompressed, l_compressed, l_length, 1, 1);
36
37       -- Free the BLOB locator.
38       dbms_lob.freetemporary(l_compressed);
39
40     exception when others then
41        rollback;
42   end;
```

### DO_DECOMPRESS

This procedure takes for an argument a BLOB instance whose source should be decompressed. This method, however, does in fact not decompress the actual source of the BLOB. Rather, it returns a reference to a temporary BLOB locator which points to a decompressed version of the source BLOB specified, in other words, the application cannot decompress the actual content once it has been compressed.

```
43     procedure do_decompress (
44       p_compressed in out com.wrox.gzipblob
45     )
46     is
47     begin
48       p_compressed := get_decompressed(p_compressed);
49     end;
50
51   end;
52   /

Packages body created.
```

## Using the UTL.GZIP Package

There are many ways of using the UTL_GZIP package, once the application has been set up properly. Ideally, we would like to keep the compression transparent to the application. This can be done when compressing new content, by setting a trigger on the table in question, which would activate the UTL_GZIP.DO_COMPRESS procedure when new data is inserted. However, we have no way of activating a trigger before a SELECT statement, which means that other parts of the database have to be aware of possible compression before selecting such content. For example, instead of:

```
SQL> declare
  2    id number;
  3    blob_loc blob;
  4  begin
```

```
 5    select img_id, img_value
 6      into id, blob_loc
 7      from images;
 8  end;
 9  /
```

we would need to add:

```
SQL> declare
  2     id number;
  3     blob_loc blob;
  4  begin
  5     select img_id, img_value
  6       into id, blob_loc
  7       from images;
  8  utl_gzip.do_decompress(blob_loc);
  9  end;
 10  /
```

# Testing the Application

To verify that our compression utility really works, we create a small test that measures the size of documents before and after compression. We create a specific table for that purpose, as shown here:

```
SQL> create table documents (
  2      document_id number not null primary key,
  3      document blob
  4  );

Table created.
```

To evaluate the compression we create a sample document and measure its size (in bytes) before and after compression. Additionally, we verify that the original size of the document stays intact after we decompress it.

```
SQL> set serveroutput on;
SQL> declare
  2
  3  blob_loc blob;
  4  buffer raw(255) := utl_raw.cast_to_raw(
                                'This is a new line of text!\n\r');
  5
  6  begin
  7
  8    -- create a new document.
  9    insert into documents (document_id, document)
 10    values (1, empty_blob());
 11
 12    -- write to the new blob.
```

```
13    select document
14      into blob_loc
15      from documents
16     where document_id = 1
17       for update;
18
19    for i in 1..500 loop
20       dbms_lob.writeappend(blob_loc, utl_raw.length(buffer), buffer);
21    end loop;
22
23    -- Print out the size of the uncompressed blob.
24    dbms_output.put_line('Size of document before compression: ' ||
25       dbms_lob.getlength(blob_loc) || ' bytes'
26    );
27
28    -- Compress the document.
29    utl_gzip.do_compress(blob_loc);
30
31    -- Print out the size of the compressed blob.
32    dbms_output.put_line('Size of document after compression: ' ||
33       dbms_lob.getlength(blob_loc) || ' bytes'
34    );
35
36    -- Decompress the blob.
37    utl_gzip.do_decompress(blob_loc);
38
39    -- Verify that the size of the decompressed blob
40    -- equals the original document size.
41    dbms_output.put_line('Size of document after decompression: ' ||
42       dbms_lob.getlength(blob_loc) || ' bytes'
43    );
44
45    commit;
46  end;
47  /
```

If you run this code, you should get an output that is something like this:

```
Size of document before compression: 15500 bytes
Size of document after compression: 104 bytes
Size of document after decompression: 15500 bytes
```

This shows that our application works as expected. In fact, by compressing the document, we reduce its size to around 7 percent of the original document size! Of course, the actual amount of compression varies with document format and size.

# Indexing and Searching Compressed Content

Our data compression strategy unfortunately has some side effects. Most notably, by compressing the data, we have limited our ability to index and search the source content. Since we are working with BLOB content in the first place, an obvious candidate for indexing would be interMedia Text. After we compress the source content, thereby messing up its internal byte structure, we will not be able to directly use interMedia text for indexing.

Does this then mean that by applying compression, we have no possibility of searching the data? Not at all. In this section we will demonstrate how you can extend the functionality of interMedia Text so that it can also work for content that has been highly compressed.

## Using interMedia Text

This section is not intended to be a guide to interMedia Text. For that purpose, we would need a separate chapter or a book of its own. If you are not familiar with interMedia Text, take a look at http://technet.oracle.com/products/intermedia/index.htm. In either case, you should read through the examples presented here, as they might give you an idea of how you can make use of PL/SQL to integrate the compression strategy with other parts of the Oracle database.

> *Note that if you are using Oracle Personal Edition on Windows 95/98, you will not be able to use interMedia text, as it does not ship for those platforms. On other platforms, you may have to install the interMedia text option, if that has not been done at database creation time.*

When you create an interMedia Text index, you can optionally specify a particular data store for the index – that is, how the text that is to be indexed should be stored. By default, it is assumed that you are using a DIRECT_DATASTORE, which stores data internally in a table column. However, alternatives exists, as illustrated below:

❑ DETAIL_DATASTORE – This data store is used when indexing content with a master-detail relationship. A master table stores header information and one or more rows in a detail table are used to store the actual documents.

❑ FILE_DATASTORE – This type of data store is used when indexing files stored externally in the operating system. The names of the files to index are stored in the text column, one per row.

❑ NESTED_DATASTORE – You use this type of data store when indexing data stored in a nested table.

❑ URL_DATASTORE – This type of data store is used to index data stored externally in files located on an intranet or on the Internet. URLs pointing at the files in question are stored in the text column.

❑ USER_DATASTORE – This type of data store works in conjunction with a user-defined stored procedure, which synthesizes the source content at index creation time

Of all these data store variants, we are only interested in the last one, USER_DATASTORE, as we can use that to index content in compressed form, as we shall see below.

### Using the USER_DATASTORE Object

The USER_DATASTORE object is used in conjunction with a user-defined stored procedure to synthesize data during indexing. For example, we might use a procedure to join related information to a document that is to be indexed, so that the whole set will be searched together. Additionally, we can define a procedure that interacts with the decompress procedures of our UTL_GZIP package, so that interMedia text can index a set of documents, even though they have been compressed.

When using the USER_DATASTORE, you must supply the following attributes to the index:

❑ **Procedure Name** – This is the name of the procedure that synthesizes the content to be indexed. This procedure must be owned by the CTXSYS internal interMedia text user. Moreover, it must be executable by the index owner.

❑ **Output Type** – This is the data type of the content that should be indexed. Can be either CLOB, BLOB, or VARCHAR2.

The procedure specified must follow certain standards. It should take two arguments; a ROWID IN variable and an IN/OUT variable of the type you specified as output type. For example:

```
procedure foo_proc(rid IN ROWID, loc in out blob);
```

To create an index based on the procedure above, on a table called FOO_DOCS, you would specify attributes and options as shown here:

```
ctx_ddl.create_preference('foo_ud', 'user_datastore');
ctx_ddl.set_attribute('foo_ud ', 'procedure', 'foo_proc');

create index foo_idx ON foo_docs(doc) indextype is
ctxsys.context parameters('datastore foo_ud');
```

Of course, you first would have needed to create the procedure in the CTXSYS schema and grant the index owner executive rights to that procedure.

## Indexing Compressed Documents

Now that we have seen how the USER_DATASTORE object can be used with interMedia Text to customize the synthesis of indexed content, we can implement our own stored procedure to use with an index on a compressed documents table.

For example, suppose we want to index the DOCUMENTS table we have been working with earlier. Specifically, we want to index all the documents contained in this table. The problem remains, that those documents are stored compressed in the database, so special measures must be taken.

First, we must log on as the user that owns the UTL_GZIP package and grant the CTXSYS owner executive rights on that package. This must be done, because CTXSYS must be the owner of the stored procedure used in the interMedia text index, and that procedure must interact with the UTL_GZIP package. Additionally, we must grant CTXSYS SELECT permission on the DOCUMENTS table, as illustrated below:

```
SQL> connect username/password;
Connected.
SQL> grant execute on utl_gzip to ctxsys;

Grant succeeded.

SQL> grant select on documents to ctxsys;

Grant succeeded.
```

**597**

Next, we log on as CTXSYS and create the following procedure:

```
SQL> connect ctxsys/password;
Connected.

SQL> create or replace procedure indexcompressed (
  2     riw in rowid,
  3     blob_loc in out blob
  4  )
  5  is
  6     temp_blob blob;
  7  begin
  8
  9     select document
 10       into temp_blob
 11       from username.documents
 12      where rowid = riw;
 13
 14     blob_loc := username.utl_gzip.get_decompressed(temp_blob);
 15
 16  end;
 17  /

Procedure created.
```

This procedure basically takes the specified row ID and writes the uncompressed BLOB value to the blob_loc OUT variable.

Finally, we log on again as the owner of the DOCUMENTS table, and create the interMedia Text index. Under normal circumstances this index creation might take some time, but with the additional compression overhead added, you may assume a very long time for this operation if there are many documents currently loaded.

```
SQL> call ctx_ddl.create_preference('documents_ud', 'user_datastore');

Call completed.

SQL> call ctx_ddl.set_attribute('documents_ud', 'procedure',
                                 'indexCompressed');

Call completed.

SQL> call create index foo_idx ON documents(document) indextype is

Call completed.

SQL> call ctxsys.context parameters('datastore documents_ud');

Call completed.
```

That's basically all it takes. Now you can use our compression filter to limit the size of your documents and still enjoy the power of interMedia Text for indexing and searching the very same content.

# Summary

In this chapter we have explored issues that were solved with the joint collaboration of PL/SQL and Java. In the first half of the chapter we demonstrated a database FTP application, which made use of the PL/SQL DBMS_JOB package to schedule automatic transfer of remote files over FTP. The actual file transfer and processing was handled by Java.

In the latter half of this chapter, we implemented a simple utility, which made use of the GZIP compression abilities of Java and the inherent LOB handling features of PL/SQL, to compress and decompress large objects stored in the database. At the end of that section we demonstrated how we could integrate this compression utility with the interMedia Text software, to allow for full indexing and searching of highly compressed documents in the database.

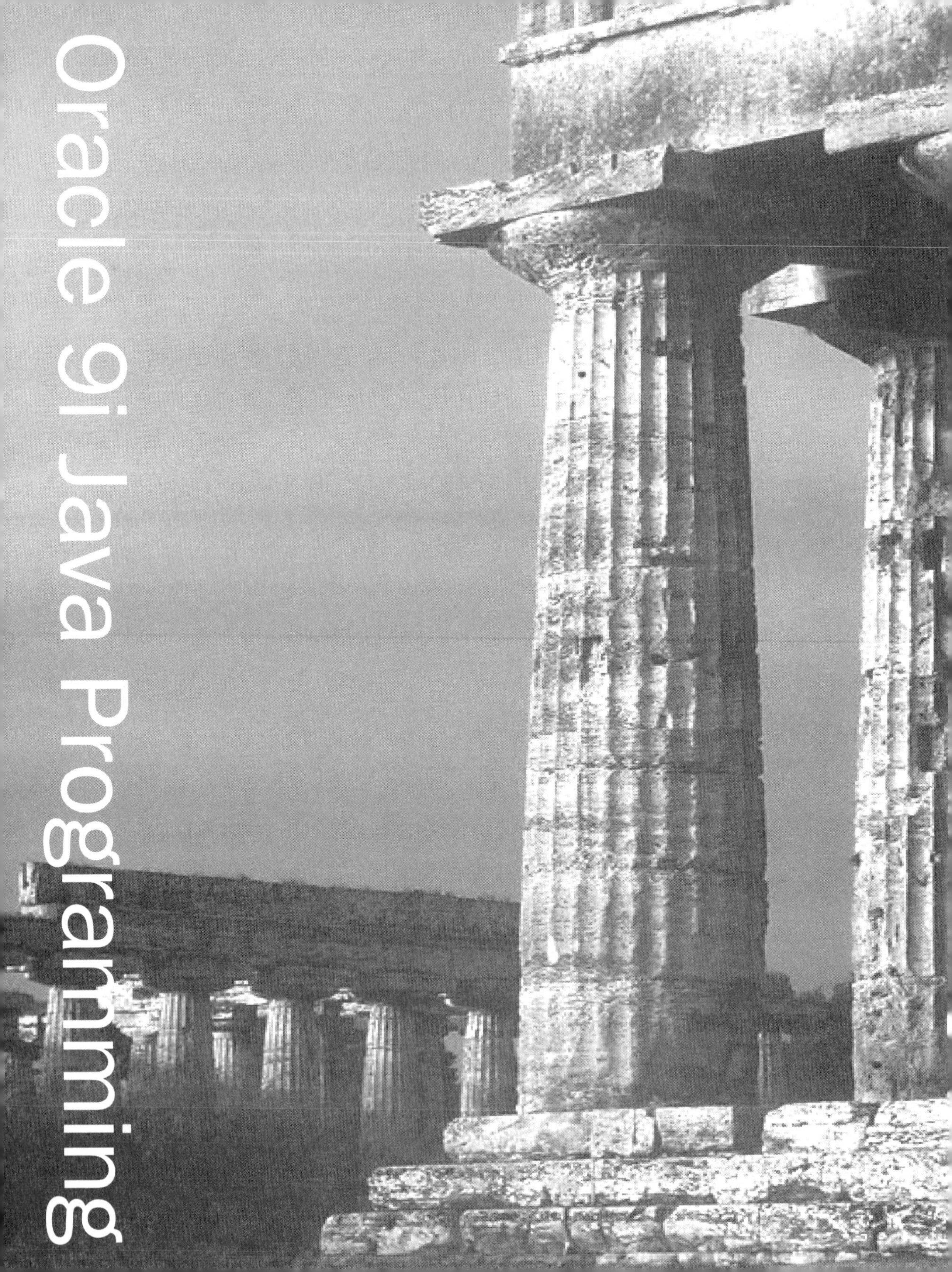
Oracle 9i Java Programming

# Java Application Performance

*"We should forget about small efficiencies, say about 97% of the time: premature optimization is the root of all evil." Knuth, Donald, Dec 1974, Structured Programming with go to Statements, Computing Surveys, Vol. 6 No. 4, pg. 268*

In the past, one of the arguments against Java has been that as an interpreted language, it is slow. The decision to make Java an interpreted language was an intentional design decision on the part of Java's creators. They wanted a language that could easily be run on multiple platforms. The trade-off was an interpreted language that was originally slower than languages such as C and C++.

Naturally it didn't take long for developers to find a way to create native compiled code out of Java code. One of the leaders in that field has been the Symantec Corporation with their Just-In-Time compiler. This compiler became a part of the Java Virtual Machine reference implementation a few years ago. With the release of Java 2 version 3 (Java 1.3) the reference implementation now uses Sun's HotSpot virtual machine. Execution speed of Java code has been improved to such a degree that it is now a viable language for many, if not all, applications.

However, compiling into native code is just one facet of the performance equation. An inefficiently implemented algorithm can be so bad that no amount of native code can improve its performance. In those cases it is up to the programmer to test and understand the code, and find another, more efficient, way to implement the algorithm. In fact, most of the time you should write correct code first, optimize the code second, and then attempt to improve performance through compilation last.

Performance optimization is a big topic; big enough to fill an entire book of information on how to make Oracle and Java perform better. In this chapter we will look at just a few ways to improve your Java programs:

❑ **Object Creation** – We look at a common Java idiom and how it causes tremendous drains on memory and resources. We then look at a better way to implement the code.

❑ **Static variables and serialization** – We examine how session state is preserved across calls to the database and performance considerations of this mechanism.

❑ **Measuring memory usage** – We try out a database procedure that analyzes how our Java classes and applications use memory.

❑ **JDBC Driver performance** – we compare performance of the OCI and thin JDBC drivers for reading and writing LOBS.

❑ **ncomp** – We show how to use Oracle's tool for creating shared libraries of compiled Java code that can be loaded into the database.

# Object Creation and Performance

The quote at the beginning of this chapter expresses a common sentiment among experienced programmers. Most of the time, there is a small amount of code that causes the biggest drain on time and resources. It makes no sense to optimize code before you know where you can get the biggest benefit. However, in my experience, there are a few Java idioms that can be so misused that it does make sense to optimize as you implement. One of those idioms is the concatenation of string references. As we will see, when string references are concatenated, the JVM is forced to create numerous temporary objects that can potentially waste large amounts of memory and processor time.

One of the most expensive operations to perform in the Java environment is to create an object. Creating an object involves allocating heap memory and initializing data structures. If this is the very first instance, the class may need to be loaded and verified. Optimizing the usage of objects and memory is thus a key place to look when trying to optimize the performance of your class.

## String vs. StringBuffer

One of the first web applications I worked on was an internal system (it was not a public internet system) that provided a web-based management front-end for a data management system. The data consisted of photographic images stored on tapes. The main purpose of the database was to store metadata about the images. The web interface allowed the users to create queries against the metadata, using any number of columns to form the WHERE clause (we always returned the same columns in the result). The result was returned as an HTML page to the users. From the result, they could find images that they wanted to view or work with. They would then access the image in memory (if it was still there) or order the tape that contained the image to be loaded so they could access the image.

When we first developed the query interface, the system analysts specified to show all the results of any given query, no matter how many rows are returned. Early in development, this was no problem, as there was not that much data in the tables. Soon, however, the number of rows started running into the thousands. That, and the way we first coded the user interface, combined to create a big problem for us. Queries were taking minutes to return results to the clients. Sometimes the query would appear to never return. When I investigated the problem, I found that the code we had written was causing OutOfMemoryErrors in the JVM. We were creating thousands of temporary objects, and making thousands of memory allocations that caused our application to run slowly, and to run out of memory. A faulty exception handler was catching the error, but never returning any response, so to the user it appeared that the query never returned.

We can simulate the problem I described above with this next class. Create the Java class StringDemo1 as shown in the source code opposite:

```
SQL> create or replace and compile
  2  java source named "StringDemo1"
  3  as
  4  import java.sql.*;
  5  public class StringDemo1 {
  6    public static void getAllObs() {
  7      long start = System.currentTimeMillis();
  8      System.out.println("Entered  StringDemo1.getAllObs() at " + start
  9                          + " milliseconds");
 10      Connection conn = null;
 11      String html = "<html><body><table>";
 12      try {
 13        String url = "jdbc:default:connection:";
 14        conn = DriverManager.getConnection(url);
 15        String sql = "select * from all_objects";
 16        Statement stmt = conn.createStatement();
 17        ResultSet rset = stmt.executeQuery(sql);
 18          while (rset.next()) {
 19            html += "<tr>";
 20            html += "<td>" + rset.getString(1) + "</td>";
 21            html += "<td>" + rset.getString(2) + "</td>";
 22            html += "<td>" + rset.getString(3) + "</td>";
 23            html += "<td>" + rset.getString(4) + "</td>";
 24            html += "<td>" + rset.getString(5) + "</td>";
 25            html += "<td>" + rset.getString(6) + "</td>";
 26            html += "<td>" + rset.getString(7) + "</td>";
 27            html += "<td>" + rset.getString(8) + "</td>";
 28            html += "<td>" + rset.getString(9) + "</td>";
 29            html += "</tr>";
 30            if (html.length() > 300000) {
 31              break;
 32            }
 33          }
 34        html += "</table></body></html>";
 35      } catch (Exception e) {
 36        e.printStackTrace();
 37      }
 38      finally {
 39        try {
 40          conn.close();
 41        } catch (Exception ignored) {}
 42      }
 43      long end = System.currentTimeMillis();
 44      System.out.println("Complete StringDemo1.getAllObs() at " + end
 45                          + " milliseconds");
 46      System.out.println("Total milliseconds=" + (end - start));
 47      System.out.println("final length = " + html.length());
 48      System.out.println();
 49    }
 50  }
 51  /

Java created.
```

**603**

When the Java class is successfully compiled, create a call specification:

```
SQL> create or replace procedure string_demo1
  2     as language java name 'StringDemo1.getAllObs()';
  3  /

Procedure created.
```

Use the following PL/SQL statements to set the environment so that output is directed to the console:

```
SQL> set serveroutput on
SQL> call dbms_java.set_output(2000);

Call completed.
```

*All the examples in this chapter which are called from SQL\*Plus will use the two statements above so that output is directed to the console. You can put these statements into a `login.sql` file so that they are automatically executed when you login. Information about `login.sql` can be found in Chapter 3 of the SQL\*Plus User's Guide and in Chapter 1 Getting Started of this book.*

Now, call the procedure. Take this time to get up and stretch, look out the window (if you have one), or stroll down to the break room for a snack. As you can see from the display below, the procedure took over two minutes to execute on my machine.

```
SQL> exec string_demo1;
Entered  StringDemo1.getAllObs() at 1003416672435 milliseconds
Complete StringDemo1.getAllObs() at 1003416804295 milliseconds
Total milliseconds=131860
final length = 300178

PL/SQL procedure successfully completed.
```

The code in this example is similar to code that you've seen in previous examples throughout the book. It uses the SQL\*Plus CREATE OR REPLACE AND COMPILE statement to load and compile the Java class directly in the database. Since it runs inside the database, it has a static method, getAllObs() that can be called from SQL\*Plus. The method queries the ALL_OBJECTS table and creates a string from the results. The code could have queried any table, but the ALL_OBJECTS table is a large table, which ensures the string will be large. The code also computes and displays the total time it takes to query the database and create the string, and it prints the length of the string that is created.

Since this code is designed to run inside the database, we get the default connection from the database, and use it to get a Statement object. With the Statement object, we execute the query as shown below:

```
String sql = "select * from all_objects";
Statement stmt = conn.createStatement();
ResultSet rset = stmt.executeQuery(sql);
```

The query results are returned in a `ResultSet` object. In my database, the `ALL_OBJECTS` table contains more than 20,000 rows, so I know that the string created from the results will be quite large, although the code stops building the string once it goes over 300,000 characters. The value of 300,000 was chosen so that the code would spend a noticeable amount of time, but not all day, creating the string.

For each row in the `ResultSet`, and each column in each row, the code concatenates HTML tags and the column value to the string, simulating the building of an HTML page that will be used to display the query results on a client browser. Here are the first couple of lines of code that creates the string:

```
html += "<tr>";
html += "<td>" + rset.getString(1) + "</td>";
```

String objects in Java behave differently from other objects. For example, the `String` class is the only class in the Java environment for which you can use a literal to access the object. A string literal in Java code is an instance of the `String` class, and it is treated as if it were a reference to the `String` object for that literal; in other words, you can access all the methods of the `String` class using just a string literal:

```
int x = "This is a String literal".length();     // x is 24
char c = "This is a String literal".charAt(3);    // c is 's'
int y = "This is a String literal".indexOf("a S"); // y is 8
```

No other class in Java has this feature. You can't access an `Integer` object using a literal `int`:

```
int x = 14.intValue(); //won't compile
```

The other way that strings are unique in Java is that they are the only class for which the '+' and '+=' operators are defined. When the compiler sees this code:

```
String s = "a" + "b";
```

The compiler knows that you want to create a single string by concatenating two literal strings. In fact, the compiler does the concatenation at compile time, creating byte code as if you had programmed:

```
String s = "ab";
```

When you are using `String` references, though, the compiler has to do something different, and this relates to the fact that string objects are immutable. Let's look at the code above again:

```
html += "<td>" + rset.getString(1) + "</td>";
```

It appears that we are changing the string html by adding three strings to it, but that is not what is occurring. Even though many Java programmers would refer to "the string html," html is not a `String`; it is a variable of type `String` that references a string object. What really occurs in the above code is that the compiler creates a new `String` object and assigns the reference to the variable html. It must create a new `String` object because the original `String` object cannot be changed.

So the first problem in the example code arises from the fact that as soon as each line completes, there are at least two string objects on the memory heap: the original string object (which will soon be reclaimed by the system) and the new string. We could reduce the number of string objects that are created by using a single line of code for all the columns in a row rather than separate lines for each column in a row:

```
html += "<tr>" + "<td>" + rset.getString(1) + "</td>" +

...the next 7 lines in a similar manner

        "<td>" + rset.getString(9) + "</td>" + "</tr>";
```

However, there is another problem that is not addressed by the change above. When a new `String` is created from an existing `String`, a buffer is created to hold the new string as it is being built up; the buffer is sized to be exactly the length of the original `String`. As soon as you append a single character, a new buffer is allocated, the old buffer is copied to the new buffer, and then the new material is appended. So when we use string concatenation to create new strings, we cause at least one additional method call to resize the `buffer`. We create at least two additional objects (the first buffer and the resized buffer) over and above the original string and the new `String`. The number of method calls, and additional objects created will depend on how many times the `append()` method is called. It is all this object creation and extra memory use that caused the `StringDemo1` class to take several minutes to create the final string.

So, in the web application where I found this problem, the first thing we needed to do was clean up our code. Eliminating all the excess object creation and memory allocation would have to be the first step. Yet we still needed to create dynamic web pages. How does one create dynamic strings in Java? The answer is the `StringBuffer` class.

## Creating Dynamic Strings

Since the `String` objects are immutable, the creators of Java included the `StringBuffer` class in the core Java API. The `StringBuffer` class is a class that acts as a buffer for the creation and manipulation of dynamic strings. In fact, even if you don't explicitly use the `StringBuffer`, the compiler uses it for you whenever you concatenate string references. In the section above, I said that if you have source code like this:

```
html += "<td>" + rset.getString(1) + "</td>";
```

A new `String` is created and the reference is assigned to the variable `html`. The Java compiler creates the new `String` by treating the source code as if you had coded this:

```
StringBuffer sb = new StringBuffer(html);
sb.append("<td>").append(rset.getString(1)).append("</td>");
html = sb.toString();
```

The `StringBuffer(String)` constructor creates a `StringBuffer` that is sized to the same number of characters as are contained in the string argument. As soon as `append()` is called, the `StringBuffer` object must resize its internal buffer to hold additional characters. Due to the additional method calls, additional buffer objects, and additional memory allocation, string concatenation tends to be very inefficient. In the next example, we'll see how to use the `StringBuffer` to dramatically improve the performance of Java code that dynamically creates strings.

By taking control of the `StringBuffer` creation, we can eliminate all the waste caused by string concatenation and caused by allowing the compiler to create `StringBuffer` method calls. The `StringBuffer` has a constructor that takes an integer parameter:

```
StringBuffer html = new StringBuffer(300200);
```

This parameter instructs the `StringBuffer` object to initialize its internal buffer to be the specified number of characters. As long as we do not append more than that many characters to the `StringBuffer`, there will be no additional method calls to resize the buffer, and no reallocation of memory. The performance improvement is impressive, as we will see in the `StringDemo2` class.

Modify the `StringDemo1` class as shown below to create the `StringDemo2` class:

```
SQL> create or replace and compile
  2  java source named "StringDemo2"
  3  as
  4  import java.sql.*;
  5  public class StringDemo2 {
  6    public static void getAllObs() {
  7      long start = System.currentTimeMillis();
  8      System.out.println("Entered  StringDemo2.getAllObs() at " + start
  9                          + " milliseconds");
 10      Connection conn = null;
 11      StringBuffer html = new StringBuffer(300200);
 12      html.append("<html><body><table>");
 13      try {
 14        Class.forName("oracle.jdbc.driver.OracleDriver");
 15        String url = "jdbc:default:connection:";
 16        conn = DriverManager.getConnection(url, "username","password");
 17        String sql = "select * from all_objects";
 18        Statement stmt = conn.createStatement();
 19        ResultSet rset = stmt.executeQuery(sql);
 20        while (rset.next()) {
 21          html.append("<tr>");
 22          html.append("<td>").append(rset.getString(1));
 23          html.append("</td>");
 24          html.append("<td>").append(rset.getString(2));
 25          html.append("</td>");
 26          html.append("<td>").append(rset.getString(3));
 27          html.append("</td>");
 28          html.append("<td>").append(rset.getString(4));
 29          html.append("</td>");
 30          html.append("<td>").append(rset.getString(5));
 31          html.append("</td>");
 32          html.append("<td>").append(rset.getString(6));
 33          html.append("</td>");
 34          html.append("<td>").append(rset.getString(7));
 35          html.append("</td>");
 36          html.append("<td>").append(rset.getString(8));
 37          html.append("</td>");
 38          html.append("<td>").append(rset.getString(9));
 39          html.append("</td>");
```

```
40          html.append("<td>").append(rset.getString(10));
41          html.append("</td>");
42          html.append("<td>").append(rset.getString(11));
43          html.append("</td>");
44          html.append("<td>").append(rset.getString(12));
45          html.append("</td>");
46          html.append("<td>").append(rset.getString(13));
47          html.append("</td>");
48          html.append("</tr>");
49          if (html.length() > 300000) {
50             break;
51          }
52        }
53        html.append("</table></body></html>");
54      } catch (Exception e) {
55        e.printStackTrace();
56      }
57      finally {
58        try {
59          conn.close();
60        } catch (Exception ignored) {}
61      }
62      long end = System.currentTimeMillis();
63      System.out.println("Complete StringDemo2.getAllObs() at " + end
64                          + " milliseconds");
65      System.out.println("Total milliseconds=" + (end - start));
66      System.out.println("final length = " + html.length());
67      System.out.println();
68    }
69 }
70
71 /
```

When the Java class is successfully compiled, create a call specification:

```
SQL> create or replace procedure string_demo2
  2    as language java name 'StringDemo2.getAllObs()';
  3  /
```

Use the following PL/SQL statements to set the environment so that output is directed to the console:

```
SQL> set serveroutput on
SQL> call dbms_java.set_output(2000);
```

Now, call the procedure:

```
SQL> exec string_demo2;
Entered  StringDemo2.getAllObs() at 1003419696403 milliseconds
Complete StringDemo2.getAllObs() at 1003419699107 milliseconds
Total milliseconds=2704
final length = 300158
```

As I said, the improvement is dramatic, from 132 seconds (131860 milliseconds) to 3 seconds (2704 milliseconds). That's more than a 40X improvement.

No matter how easy it is to do string concatenation:

```
String a = "a";
String b = "b";
String s = a + b;
```

Avoid the temptation! As we saw in the example above, sometimes a little work on the part of the programmer can yield huge performance improvements.

In this case, we created a `StringBuffer` object that was large enough to hold the string we wanted to create. As we append to the `StringBuffer`, the object never needs to resize its buffer, so all the expensive memory reallocations and object creation that occurs with string concatenation is eliminated.

Owing to this dramatic difference in execution times, it makes sense to keep this in mind whenever you are concatenating `String` references in Java. If the method is going to be called rarely, you can choose to use the '+' operator to concatenate strings. If however, the method will be called a lot, you will definitely want to consider using a `StringBuffer` in the code.

To do this in your own code, you'll need to estimate how large the string is that you want to create could possibly be. In the example above it was easy because I somewhat arbitrarily sized the `StringBuffer` to 300,200 characters without worrying about how many rows would be returned. I chose this value because I knew, from runs of the previous example, that this size would be large enough to hold the string that was created by the code. In your own code, you'll need to look at how many rows you want to display to the user, and how large each row could be. You can test that estimate by printing out the size of each completed `StringBuffer`.

If you're getting strings from some source other than a table, it will be harder to make the estimate, but even a rough estimate will be better than starting with the default buffer size. When you use the constructor:

```
StringBuffer sb = new StringBuffer();
```

The default size is 16 characters. Every time the buffer resizes, it adds 1 to the current size and then doubles it. So the progression of buffer sizes is 16, 34, 70, 142, 286, 574, 1150, and so on. Suppose the actual string size is going to be 1000 characters, but your rough estimate comes out to 500. Even with your estimate being 50% too low, you've still eliminated 5 calls to the resize method.

Keep in mind that using `StringBuffers` is not a cure all. You can still consume all the memory in the system and cause the program to crash by appending enough characters to the `StringBuffer`. In the application I worked on, our second step in the solution was to page all queries. When a query returned rows, we only showed a certain number (it was a user configurable parameter) to the user. If the number of rows returned was more than the number displayed, we gave the user a Next button to get the next set of rows from the query. Using these techniques, we eliminated all memory problems from the application.

In both `StringDemo1` and `StringDemo2`, all the objects, were created within the scope of the `getAllObs()` method. The memory used for these objects was released when the method completed. Recall from the *Java Classes and Objects* chapter, that there are other variables that can be used in a class. These are instance and class variables. Instance variables are any class member variables that are not static. Instance variables exist as long as the instance exists. For Java in the database, that lifetime is normally as long as the call is active. When the call completes, the instance is released and instance variables are out of scope. However, class variables (static class member variables) must maintain state between calls. That topic is examined next.

# Java Memory Usage In The Database

When a call to the database completes, the Java session state must be saved. Before we look at how the state is saved, it will be helpful to review how Oracle allocates memory for Java. When you connect as a client to an Oracle instance, the Oracle process allocates memory structures and starts the various processes that manage the memory. The Oracle instance allocates and manages the memory without any action on your part.

> *For more information on the Oracle database memory structure please refer to* Chapter 9 *Using the Oracle JVM. In this section we will discuss in particular one pool that is of special interest to us, the* `Java pool`.

Whether or not Java session data is located in the `Java pool` depends on the mode in which Oracle is operating: dedicated mode or MTS mode.

## Java pool and Dedicated Server

When running in dedicated server mode, the `Java pool` is used for the common parts of each Java class. For example, all instances of a class will execute the same code for a given method. That code does not need to be replicated for each session. It is thus kept in the `Java pool` and shared between all sessions. Static (or class) data is also kept in the `Java pool`. Oracle estimates that each class in the database will need 4K to 8K of `Java pool` memory (Oracle Java Developer's Guide, Java Application Performance chapter. You can find this document with the database documentation or online at http://technet.oracle.com/docs/content.html). Thus, when using Oracle in dedicated mode, the range of memory required by the `Java pool` for a Java application can be determined by counting the number of classes and multiplying by 4 to get a low bound, and by 8 to get a high bound. The session-specific data, such as the value of instance variables, is kept in the process memory of the server.

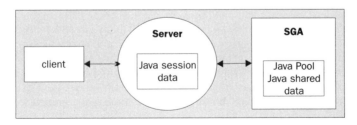

## Java pool and MTS

The situation is much different in the MTS case. As in dedicated server mode, the `Java pool` is used for the shared part of each Java class. However, since any server can process a client's request, all the servers need access to the client's session data. When running Java in a shared server database, the session specific Java data is thus stored in the `Java pool`.

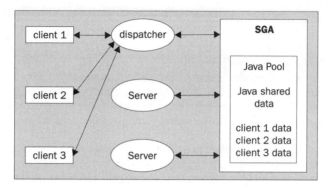

Determining your memory requirement here is now a bit more involved. You will need to determine how much memory your application will use per session, and then multiply that by the number of sessions you expect to support. That number must be smaller than your `Java pool` size. The memory needed for each session is determined by how much Java session state must be saved for each session; this is dependent on the amount of static variables used by your application. The next section looks at static variables in a little more detail. Later in this chapter, we will examine how to determine memory usage of your Java classes or application.

# Static Variables

Recall from Chapter 2, *Java Classes and Objects*, that a class can have static variables, which are also known as class variables. Static variables are specific to a class and not to any specific instance of a class. All instances of a class share the static variables. Thus, if one instance changes the value of a static variable, that change is seen in all other instances. You can release all instances of an object, and then later create a new instance, and this new instance will see the same value of the static variable. This creates an issue for Java classes running in the database. Suppose that you make a call to some Java code in the database, and that Java code initializes, changes, or simply just uses some static data. When the call is complete, that call memory is released back to the pool. If the database didn't do something to preserve the state of the class, the next call would find that the state had been lost. In this section of the chapter, we'll examine how the database maintains session state.

*JVMs outside the database do not have this issue. All static data is kept in the JVM memory space for the life of the JVM.*

## *End Of Call Migration*

Oracle maintains the session state across calls by migrating all static variable objects and data to session memory (the Java pool) at the end of the call to your Java stored procedure. Oracle calls this an end of call migration. When a call is completed, it goes through all the static variables of the classes in use, and writes the objects or data to session memory. If the objects reference other objects or data, those are also written to session memory. This continues until all objects that are reachable through static variables have been migrated.

This can be time and memory consuming if you have lots of objects so there exists a mechanism for selectively pruning this data. Oracle calls this the EndOfCallRegistry notification process. A developer will register interest on each object they want to be managed using the oracle.aurora.memoryManager.EndOfCallRegistry class using a method named registerCallback(). When the call ends, the JVM iterates over all registered objects and invokes the act() method. This method is part of the oracle.aurora.memoryManager.Callback interface and is where a developer is free to do what they want with the object. Typically, you will either just set the variable to null or, possibly, save the data in a table. You cannot create or execute JDBC statements at the end of a call. What you gain in space savings in the Java pool is offset by the time required to rebuild the data structures the next time you make another call. There are no firm trade-off guidelines.

In the following example, we'll look at a simple class that demonstrates that Oracle preserves state across calls. Create the StaticFieldDemo class as shown below:

```
SQL> create or replace and compile
  2  java source named "StaticFieldDemo"
  3  as
  4  public class StaticFieldDemo {
  5    static int sfield;
  6    public static void initField() {
  7      if (sfield == 0) {
  8        System.out.println("Initializing sfield in initfield ");
  9        sfield = 42;
 10      }
 11      System.out.println("Value of sfield Initialized  =" + sfield);
 12    }
 13    public static void testStaticField() {
 14      StaticFieldDemo.initField();
 15      StaticFieldDemo sfd = new StaticFieldDemo();
 16      sfd.initField();
 17 System.out.println("Value of sfield in testStaticField =" + sfd.sfield);
 18    }
 19    public static void main(String[] args) {
 20      StaticFieldDemo.testStaticField();
 21    }
 22  }
 23  /

Java created.
```

When the Java class is successfully compiled, create a call specification:

```
SQL> create or replace procedure static_demo
  2    as language java name 'StaticFieldDemo.testStaticField()';
  3  /

Procedure created.
```

Use the following PL/SQL statements to set the environment so that output is directed to the console:

```
SQL> set serveroutput on
SQL> call dbms_java.set_output(2000);

Call completed.
```

Now, call the procedure.

```
SQL> exec static_demo;
Initializing sfield
Value of sfield=42
Value of sfield=42
Value of sfield=42

PL/SQL procedure successfully completed.

SQL> exec static_demo;
Value of sfield=42
Value of sfield=42
Value of sfield=42

PL/SQL procedure successfully completed.
```

When the class is first loaded, the static variable sfield has a value of 0. This is because the Java Language Specification requires that all class and instance variables have an initial value. So even though the code did not explicitly initialize the variable sfield, the compiler inserted code to initialize it for us. The default initialization for numeric variables is 0, the default for references is null, and the default for Boolean is false.

Our entry point into the class is the testStaticField() method. This calls the initField() method to initialize the sfield variable. That method then prints the new value. Notice that because the initField() method is static, we can do this without creating an instance of the class.

Next, we do create an instance of the class, and show that calling the initField() from the instance does not reinitialize the variable, because sfield is common to all instances and is no longer equal to zero. Finally, we print out the value of the variable one more time, accessing it through the instance we created. I did this to show that sfield is shared by the class instance sfd. Note that accessing a static field in this manner is not encouraged. One reason for this is that using sfd.sfield could mislead other developers into thinking sfield is an instance variable. The accepted way to access a static field is to use the class name StaticFieldDemo.sfield.

When we call the procedure a second time, we see that even when the `testStaticField()` method calls the `initField()` method again, the value of the variable `sfield` still has its value of 42. We can see this because the message `Initializing sfield` is not printed during the second call. Thus, the value of the variable has been retained across calls.

The code on the previous page also contains a `main()` method. You can use this method to run the class outside the database. If you do this, you will see a different behavior. Each time you run the class, a new JVM process is created. Regardless of how many times you execute the class, the message `Initializing sfield` will be printed every time. The value of `sfield` is not retained when one JVM process terminates and a new process is created.

### FileDescriptor Objects

The preceding discussion might suggest that you can save any variable between calls. Unfortunately this is not true for some objects related to system resources. For example, `FileDescriptor` objects automatically become invalid between calls since the Oracle JVM closes any file that is still open at the end of a call. The following example shows how a `FileDescriptor` becomes invalidated between calls. The code opens a file and keeps it in a static variable. Since we are in the same JVM session, it is expected that it would still be valid between calls but the two sequential calls to `write_a_line` show that this is not the case.

First, the Java and two PL/SQL procedures are created:

```
SQL> create or replace and compile java source named "FileHandleDemo"
  2  as
  3  import java.io.*;
  4  import java.sql.*;
  5  public class FileHandleDemo {
  6    static FileOutputStream w = null;
  7    private static void showFD() {
  8      FileDescriptor fd = w.getFD();
  9      if (fd == null) {
 10        System.out.println("file descriptor is null");
 11      } else {
 12        System.out.println("file descriptor: handle=" +
 13          fd.toString() + ", valid=" + fd.valid());
 14      }
 15    }
 16    public static void write_a_line(String s) {
 17      if (w == null) {
 18        System.out.println("opening file...");
 19        w = new FileOutputStream("/tmp/t.txt");
 20        String msg = "opened file...";
 21        w.write(msg.getBytes());
 22      } else {
 23        System.out.println("file was opened already...");
 24      }
 25      showFD();
 26      w.write(s.getBytes());
 27      showFD();
 28    }
 29    public static void close_it() {
```

```
30       if (w == null) {
31          System.out.println("file is closed already");
32       } else {
33          System.out.println("closing file");
34          showFD();
35          w.close();
36       }
37       w = null;
38    }
39  }
40  /
```

```
SQL> create or replace procedure
  2     write_a_line(p_text in varchar2)
  3     as language java
  4     name 'FileHandleDemo.write_a_line(java.lang.String)';
  5  /

SQL> create or replace procedure
  2  close_it as language java name 'FileHandleDemo.close_it()';
  3  /
```

The result of two sequential calls to the PL/SQL procedure can be seen below:

```
SQL> set serveroutput on size 1000000
SQL> exec dbms_java.set_output(1000000);

PL/SQL procedure successfully completed.
SQL> exec write_a_line('hello');
opening file...
file descriptor: handle=java.io.FileDescriptor@cf9566cf, valid=true
file descriptor: handle=java.io.FileDescriptor@cf9566cf, valid=true

SQL> exec write_a_line('doggie');
file was opened already...
file descriptor: handle=java.io.FileDescriptor@cf9566cf, valid=false
java.io.IOException
at java.io.FileOutputStream.writeBytes(FileOutputStream.java)
at java.io.FileOutputStream.write(FileOutputStream.java)
at FileHandleDemo.write_a_line(FileHandleDemo:29)
BEGIN write_a_line('doggie'); END;


*
ERROR at line 1:
ORA-29532: Java call terminated by uncaught Java exception: java.io.IOException
ORA-06512: at "USERNAME.WRITE_A_LINE", line 0
ORA-06512: at line 1
```

Note that the file was opened the first time but the file descriptor is not valid. That is why the java.io.IOException is thrown.

```
SQL> exec close_it
closing file
file descriptor: handle=java.io.FileDescriptor@cf9566cf, valid=false
```

`java.net.ServerSocket` objects are subject to the "end of call" cleanup routines if the database is running in shared server mode but the dedicated server mode will not invalidate the `java.net.ServerSocket` objects. Client `java.net.Socket` objects can persist between calls in either dedicated or shared modes. Developers usually focus on these since it's more likely to have Java stored procedures running in the database connecting to other servers rather than being a server itself (which is what can be done with `ServerSocket`).

### How Static Variables Affect Performance

When you are accessing a database in dedicated server mode, this end-of-call migration will seldom be an issue. Java session data is stored in the process memory of the server. There is obviously a limit on the session memory in the server process. It is unlikely, however, that the data from a single user's Java session will exhaust this memory.

On the other hand, when the database is operating in shared mode, this is more of an issue. Recall that Java session state for all users is stored in the `Java pool`. If your application supports thousands of concurrent users and uses a large amount of memory for session state, it will be very easy to exhaust the memory allocated to the `Java pool`. The total memory is thus a sum of the memory required for common Java data plus the product of the number of sessions and the amount of memory needed for each session.

Not only does this consume memory resources, it imposes additional workload on the memory manager, which must read and write the session data. Another way to look at the impact of static variables is that the more session memory needed for each session, the fewer concurrent users can be supported by your application.

In either case, shared mode or dedicated mode, it can be important to be able to measure how much memory is needed by your Java application running in the database.

# Measuring Memory Usage

A common question on Java newsgroups and mailing lists is how to determine the size of an object in memory. Some languages make this easy. The C and C++ languages, for example, have a `sizeof` operator that can tell the program exactly how many bytes are being used by an object. Java, on the other hand makes it extremely difficult to determine this information. There is no operator or function that can do this. Mainly, this is because Java has no pointers, and manages memory for the programmer, so there's almost never a need for that data.

When we run Java in the database, however, that information becomes more important. As I've mentioned, Oracle stores Java data in the `Java pool`, which is limited in size. Also, as we just saw, additional memory is used to preserve state across calls. If we're running in MTS mode, with lots of concurrent users, this memory usage could become critical.

Oracle has addressed this problem with a utility that can analyze and report on memory usage in our Java classes and applications. This tool is the Memory Profiling Utility, or MemStat, tool. MemStat accesses the static variables of a class or classes, and records memory usage for each primitive and object. If an object refers to other objects, MemStat follows the object chain until it has enumerated all the objects and primitives that will be migrated to session memory at the end of a call.

The MemStat utility is accessed through a Java class provided by Oracle. This class is the oracle.aurora.memstat.MemStat class. It defines three methods for analyzing and reporting memory usage for your Java application.

| Method Signature | Method Purpose |
|---|---|
| MemStat.writeDump(Class MyClass,<br>                  String outputPath,<br>                  String filePrefix) | Analyzes and reports memory usage for the given class. |
| MemStat.writeDump(String outputPath,<br>                  String filePrefix) | Analyzes and reports memory usage for all classes in the session at the point that the method is called. |
| MemStat.writeDumpAtEOC(String outputPath,<br>                       String filePrefix) | Analyzes and reports memory usage for all classes in the session at the end of the call. |

The String parameters in each of the method calls above tell the MemStat utility where to write the report information.

In this next example, we'll look at how to use MemStat to examine the memory usage for a single class. We will also briefly examine how to read the report produced by MemStat.

To effectively use MemStat, you will need permission to access all private as well as public static variables, permission to access the JVM to determine which classes are loaded, and permission to write to the directory where the final report will be printed. Have a DBA grant the permissions below to your login. In the FilePermission grant, you will need to change the directory to the directory you want to use for this example. More information on permissions can be found in Chapter 11 *Oracle Java Security*.

The first call allows memstat to read the private variables in every class. ReflectPermission affects reflection, which is the technique where class names and methods can be dynamically accessed at runtime. By suppressing access checks, the schema USERNAME has permission to read private variables.

```
SQL> call dbms_java.grant_permission ('USERNAME',
  2    'SYS:java.lang.reflect.ReflectPermission',
  3    'suppressAccessChecks', null);
```

Granting the JserverPermission with name JRIExtensions gives USERNAME permission to run the memstat class.

```
SQL> call dbms_java.grant_permission ('USERNAME',
  2    'SYS:oracle.aurora.security.JServerPermission',
  3    'JRIExtensions', null);
```

The final call gives us permission to write to a system directory.

```
SQL> call dbms_java.grant_permission ('USERNAME',
  2    'SYS:java.io.FilePermission',
  3    'c:\Project\memstat','read,write');
```

Notice above that the grantee parameter ('USERNAME') is case sensitive. You must use all caps as shown. Specifying the user as 'username' or 'Username' will not work.

Create the MemStatDemo class as shown below:

> If you create the class outside the database and use loadjava to load it into the
> database, you will need to add another library to the classpath in addition to
> classes12.zip to get the class to compile. This library is
> %ORACLE_HOME%/javavm/lib/aurora.zip.

```
SQL> create or replace and compile
  2    java source named "MemStatDemo"
  3    as
  4    import java.util.LinkedList;
  5  import oracle.aurora.memstat.MemStat;
  6  public class MemStatDemo {
  7    static Integer si = new Integer(42);
  8    static Double sd = new Double(Math.PI);
  9    static String[] ss = null;
 10    static LinkedList sll = null;
 11    MemStatDemo() {
 12      ss = new String[30];
 13      sll = new LinkedList();
 14      for (int i = 0; i < 30; i++) {
 15        ss[i] = "String" + i;
 16        sll.add(ss[i] + i);
 17      }
 18    }
 19    public static void report() {
 20      MemStatDemo msd = new MemStatDemo();
 21      try {
 22    MemStat.writeDump(MemStatDemo.class, "c:/Project/memstat", "msdemo");
 23      } catch (Exception e) {
 24        e.printStackTrace();
 25      }
 26    }
 27  }
 28  /
```

When the Java class is successfully compiled, create a call specification:

```
SQL> create or replace procedure memstat_demo
  2     as language java name 'MemStatDemo.report()';
  3  /
```

Use the following PL/SQL statements to set the environment so that output is directed to the console:

```
SQL> set serveroutput on
SQL> call dbms_java.set_output(2000);
```

Now, call the procedure:

```
SQL> exec memstat_demo;
Analyzing class: MemStatDemo
Analysis finished in 2023 ms.
Writing class analysis report...
Writing file: msdemo
Writing file: msdemo1
Writing file: msdemo2
Writing file: msdemo3
Writing file: msdemo4
```

We'll look very briefly at the class. At this point in the book, there should be very little that is unfamiliar here. The main thing to notice is the `import` statement for the `MemStat` package. This is the package that contains the `MemStat` class. This package is contained in the `aurora.zip` library file.

```
import oracle.aurora.memstat.MemStat;
```

Next the class declares some static variables, including an array of strings and a `LinkedList` of strings. A `LinkedList` object is a Java collection object that keeps object references in a list. Each entry in the list contains a link, or reference, to the next object. When `MemStat` analyzes the memory usage it will need to report on all the `Strings` in the array and all the strings in the `LinkedList`, not just on the array or `LinkedList` itself. The constructor handles the job of initializing the array and the `LinkedList`. The `report()` method calls the constructor, and then calls the `writeDump()` method to run the report.

In this example, we used the `writeDump(Class, String, String)` method. The first parameter is the `Class` instance of the class we wish to evaluate. Every class in Java has a special object associated with it; this object is an instance of `Class` that represents the class. Every class in Java has a variable `class` (inherited from the `Object` class) that points to the instance of `Class`. Thus, since we wanted memstat to report on all the variables used by `MemStatDemo`, we passed the `Class` object for `MemStatDemo` using this syntax:

```
MemStat.writeDump(MemStatDemo.class, "c:/Project/memstat", "msdemo");
```

However, we could have instructed memstat to report on any class. We would simply pass the appropriate `Class` instance of any class in the JVM. That is, we could have called:

```
MemStat.writeDump(String.class,    // to report on String, or
MemStat.writeDump(NcompDemo.class, // to report on NcompDemo, or
MemStat.writeDump(AnyClass.class,  // to report on a class named AnyClass
```

The two string parameters are used to tell `MemStat` where to write the report. The first parameter is the directory where the report will be written. This should, of course, be a directory to which you have read and write permission. The `MemStat` report can be quite large, so the `MemStat` utility breaks the report into sections. The second parameter tells `MemStat` what file prefix to use for all the files that are created.

If you look at the output from the call, you can see that five files were created. The first file used the file prefix with nothing appended; each of the next files had an incremental numerical suffix appended. Each of the report files is formatted as an HTML file, so you can view the report by opening the first page in any web browser.

```
Writing file: msdemo
Writing file: msdemo1
Writing file: msdemo2
Writing file: msdemo3
Writing file: msdemo4
```

In the screen shot below, you can see part of the first page of the report. We don't have space here to examine every facet of the report. We will look briefly at two tables in the first page of the report. For more details on how to interpret the report, consult the *Oracle Java Developer's Guide*.

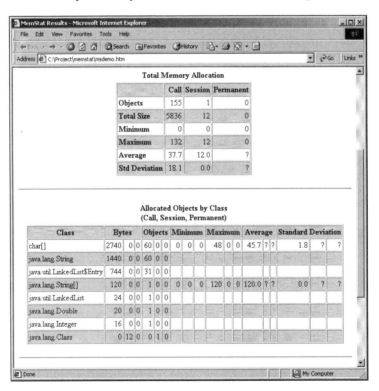

**Total Memory Allocation**

|  | Call | Session | Permanent |
|---|---|---|---|
| Objects | 155 | 1 | 0 |
| Total Size | 5836 | 12 | 0 |
| Minimum | 0 | 0 | 0 |
| Maximum | 132 | 12 | 0 |
| Average | 37.7 | 12.0 | ? |
| Std Deviation | 18.1 | 0.0 | ? |

**Allocated Objects by Class**
**(Call, Session, Permanent)**

| Class | Bytes | | | Objects | | | Minimum | | | Maximum | | | Average | | | Standard Deviation | | |
|---|---|---|---|---|---|---|---|---|---|---|---|---|---|---|---|---|---|---|
| char[] | 2740 | 0 | 0 | 60 | 0 | 0 | 0 | 0 | 0 | 48 | 0 | 0 | 45.7 | ? | ? | 1.8 | ? | ? |
| java.lang.String | 1440 | 0 | 0 | 60 | 0 | 0 | | | | | | | | | | | | |
| java.util.LinkedList$Entry | 744 | 0 | 0 | 31 | 0 | 0 | | | | | | | | | | | | |
| java.lang.String[] | 120 | 0 | 0 | 1 | 0 | 0 | 0 | 0 | 0 | 120 | 0 | 0 | 120.0 | ? | ? | 0.0 | ? | ? |
| java.util.LinkedList | 24 | 0 | 0 | 1 | 0 | 0 | | | | | | | | | | | | |
| java.lang.Double | 20 | 0 | 0 | 1 | 0 | 0 | | | | | | | | | | | | |
| java.lang.Integer | 16 | 0 | 0 | 1 | 0 | 0 | | | | | | | | | | | | |
| java.lang.Class | 0 | 12 | 0 | 0 | 1 | 0 | | | | | | | | | | | | |

The table (Total Memory Allocation) above shows the total statistics for the report. Most of the tables in the report show information for call memory, session memory and permanent memory. This table shows that there are 155 objects in call memory and one object in session memory. The total memory used by these objects is 5836 bytes for call memory, and 12 bytes for session memory. Remember, that these statistics apply only to the objects that are reachable through static class variables.

The next table gives statistics for each object class. Each statistic, `bytes` for example, has three columns under it. The first column is for call memory, the next is session memory, and the third is permanent memory. Thus, for the class `String`, 1440 bytes of call memory are used, and 0 bytes of session and permanent memory are used. Again for string, there are 60 objects in call memory and 0 objects in session and permanent memory. Also, don't forget that even though this table shows data for call memory, all of that call memory is migrated to session memory at the end of the call.

## Other memstat Methods

In the example above, we used `MemStat` to report memory usage statistics for a single class. The `MemStat` class also defines two other methods that can be used to analyze memory usage.

```
MemStat.writeDump(String, String)
```

The `writedump(String, String)` method is used when you want a memory analysis of all objects in the current session. This method immediately analyzes all the current classes and provides the same output we saw above. This won't include classes created after `writeDump()` is called, and may include classes which will no longer be in use when end-of-call migration is performed. For that reason, it may not be an accurate measure of the memory that will be migrated to session memory.

```
MemStat.writeDumpAtEOC(String, String)
```

The `writeDumpAtEOC(String, String)` will cause `MemStat` to perform the memory analysis right before end-of-call migration occurs. It analyzes all classes which will be migrated, and thus is an accurate measure of the memory needed to store session state.

## Memory Considerations

Obviously, this one Java class with its one static `int` variable or a few static strings is not going to consume a great deal of session memory. However, end of call migration can be memory intensive. If you have a lot of objects that are referenced by static variables, and some of these objects reference other objects, the number of objects that need to be migrated could be large. This not only uses session memory, but also takes processing resources as the memory manager migrates objects to and from session memory.

Ideally, the objects that can be migrated should be objects that are relatively small but expensive to build. The key here is small. As the object grows larger or easier to construct, you will want to consider recreating the objects for each call rather than relying on end-of-call migration to save and restore the object state.

# JDBC Driver Comparisons

In the *Connecting to Oracle through JDBC* chapter, we looked at the difference between JDBC drivers. Recall that the JDBC specification defines four types of drivers:

❑   **Type 1** – Connects to a database through the ODBC API

❑   **Type 2** – Connects to a database through a native code library

❑   **Type 3** – Connects to a database through a middleware proxy

❑   **Type 4** – Connects to a database through 100% Java code

In some cases, you will not have a choice over which driver to use. If your application needs to run on a multitude of client platforms, and you cannot control the client's platform, you will need to use a Type 4 driver. Using the Oracle Thin (Type 4) driver means the driver can be used on any platform because it is 100 percent Java and it can be deployed with the application. If you are writing Java stored procedures or Java code such as EJBs that will deployed in the database, you will use the KPRB (internal) Oracle driver.

At other times, you may have a choice. If you are developing an application that will be deployed to client platforms, and you have the opportunity to install Oracle client software on every platform, then you can choose to use either the OCI (Type 2) or thin driver. However, JDBC books and examples you find on the Internet tend to use the thin driver exclusively. I have recommended to other developers that they use the OCI driver whenever they have the choice, and the thin driver only when they need to. In this section of the chapter, we will provide some concrete data that supports this choice of OCI over thin.

For the series of benchmarks in this section, the tests were run on two different client-server architectures. Each set of tests is run with a Java client running on a Sun server, and connecting to an Oracle 8.1.7 database running on the same machine. The programs were run on the same machine where the database resides in an attempt to mitigate network latencies.

The tests were also executed with a client and server on different machines so we can see how the tests perform over a 10-base-T network. The client was a Windows 2000 machine and the same Sun machine as above was the server. The specifications for the both machines are shown in the table below.

| Server | Client |
| --- | --- |
| Sun Ultra 60 | Dell Workstation |
| 2 450 MHz CPU's | 1 500 MHz Pentium 3 |
| 512 MB RAM | 384 MB RAM |
| Solaris 8 | Windows 2000 Workstation |
| JDK 1.3.1_01 | JDK 1.3.1_01 |

A number of different tests were performed on each architecture. The first set of tests looked at writing LOB data to the database. The write test times how fast a BLOB (from memory) can be written to a new database row ten times. The BLOB is a memory-based byte array materialized as an InputStream. By using a BLOB from memory, we remove any uncertainty resulting from trying to read a BLOB from some source such as a file. Garbage collection is disabled and the JVM is started with the same amount of heap memory in an attempt to remove any potential variables.

The next set of tests looks at reading BLOB data. The read test times how fast a BLOB can be read from a database row. Each test was executed using the thin and OCI8 drivers ten times for four different BLOB sizes. The BLOB is just read – nothing is done with the contents. Again, garbage collection is disabled and the JVM has 32MB of memory. Here is how the table was initially populated.

# LOB write test

Start by creating a table to hold the BLOB data for the write test.

```
SQL> create table lobtest (
  2     id number,
  3     data BLOB
  4  );
```

Here is the Java class we will use to write test the performance of each driver when writing data to the database:

```
import java.io.*;
import java.lang.*;
import java.sql.*;
import java.util.*;
import java.text.NumberFormat;
import oracle.jdbc.driver.*;
import oracle.sql.BLOB;

public class lob_write_test {
  static String sql =
    "begin insert into lobtest(id, data) values(?, empty_blob()) return data into ?; end;";

  public static void main(String[] argv) {
    try {

      // Setup program parameters and input blob
      int lobsize = Integer.parseInt(argv[0]);
      int iter = Integer.parseInt(argv[1]);
      byte[] data = new byte[lobsize * 1024];
      Arrays.fill(data, (byte) 64);

      // Setup connection and record time
      long start = System.currentTimeMillis();
      DriverManager.registerDriver(new OracleDriver());
      Connection conn = DriverManager.getConnection(argv[2], "username",
```

```
                       "password");
      conn.setAutoCommit(false);
      System.out.println(System.currentTimeMillis() - start);

      long prepTime = System.currentTimeMillis();
      OracleCallableStatement ocs =
        (OracleCallableStatement) conn.prepareCall(sql);
      ocs.setInt(1, lobsize);
      ocs.registerOutParameter(2, OracleTypes.BLOB);
      System.out.println(System.currentTimeMillis() - prepTime);

      long totalIterTime = 0;

      for (int i = 0; i < iter; i++) {
        long iterStartTime = System.currentTimeMillis();
        InputStream is = new ByteArrayInputStream(data);
        ocs.executeUpdate();
        BLOB blob = ocs.getBLOB(2);
        OutputStream os = blob.getBinaryOutputStream();

        int bufSize = blob.getBufferSize();
        byte buffer[] = new byte[bufSize];
        int length;

        while ((length = is.read(buffer, 0, bufSize)) != -1) {
          os.write(buffer, 0, length);
        }

        is.close();
        os.close();
        conn.commit();
        long iterTime = System.currentTimeMillis() - iterStartTime;
        totalIterTime += iterTime;
        System.out.println(iterTime);
      }

      ocs.close();
      conn.close();
      System.out.println(totalIterTime / iter);
      System.out.println(System.currentTimeMillis() - start);
      System.exit(0);
    } catch (Exception e) {
      e.printStackTrace();
    }
  }
}
```

This class should be compiled and run outside the database. Here is the usage syntax for the class:

```
java -ms32m -mx32m -noclassgc lob_write_test lob_size iterations driver
```

The Java virtual machine is started with the `java` program. The `-ms32m` specifies the starting memory size as 32 MB, and `-mx32m` sets the maximum memory size at 32 MB. The argument `-noclassgc` disables class garbage collection. Next is the name of the class that will be executed. We pass three arguments to the class: the size of the LOB to write to the database in KB, the number of times the program is to write the LOB, and the driver to use for the database connection. So, for example, to test writing a 1000 KB (1 MB) BLOB to the database 10 times using the OCI driver to connect to the database with SID database, you would use:

```
> java -ms32m -mx32m -noclassgc lob_write_test 1000 10 jdbc:oracle:oci8:@database
```

The class starts by creating a byte array of the desired size as shown here:

```
byte[] data = new byte[lobsize * 1024];
Arrays.fill(data, (byte) 64);
```

Note that the size that is passed on the command line is multiplied by 1024 (1 KB). After the array is created, the call to `Array.fill()` initializes the array with data.

Next we get a connection to the database, and use the connection to create a `CallableStatement`. The timing for both of these actions is output. Inside the loop, we use the `CallableStatement` to insert a BLOB placeholder into the table and then return the BLOB locator.

```
static String sql = "begin insert into lobtest(data) " +
                    "values(empty_blob()) return data into ?; end;";

public static void main(String[] argv) {
   try {

      ...

      OracleCallableStatement ocs =
         (OracleCallableStatement) conn.prepareCall(sql);
      ocs.registerOutParameter(1, OracleTypes.BLOB);
```

Through the BLOB locator, we can stream BLOB data to the table. This is done by getting an `OutputStream` from the BLOB to which we can write data. When you write to a stream it must be an output stream. So, to write to the BLOB, the program gets an `OutputStream` from the BLOB locator.

```
InputStream is = new ByteArrayInputStream(data);
ocs.executeUpdate();
BLOB blob = ocs.getBLOB(1);
OutputStream os = blob.getBinaryOutputStream();

...

while ((length = is.read(buffer, 0, bufSize)) != -1) {
    os.write(buffer, 0, length);
}
```

**625**

This program was run a number of times with various LOB sizes, but always 10 iterations of writing to the database. Each lob size was tested with the thin driver and the OCI driver. The lob sizes passed to the program on the command line were 10000, 1000, 100, 10. (Remember that the program actually multiplies those figures by 1024.)

Here are the results for the client running on the Sun server (all times in milliseconds):

|  | THIN 10000K | OCI8 10000K | THIN 1000K | OCI8 1000K | THIN 100K | OCI8 100K | THIN 10K | OCI8 10K |
|---|---|---|---|---|---|---|---|---|
| Time to connect: | 1348 | 869 | 1257 | 694 | 1032 | 612 | 969 | 610 |
| Statement prepare: | 56 | 57 | 55 | 54 | 54 | 55 | 54 | 56 |
| Avg. time: | 36082 | 33894 | 3616 | 3383 | 559 | 390 | 206 | 92 |
| Total time: | 362241 | 339889 | 37485 | 34593 | 6683 | 4582 | 3096 | 1602 |

Looking at the table, you can see that there is some performance gain when using the OCI driver. The OCI driver is faster at getting a connection; both drivers perform the same when preparing the statement; and then again the OCI driver is usually faster at writing the data.

Running the same tests with the Windows platform as the client gives these results (all times in milliseconds):

|  | THIN 10000K | OCI8 10000K | THIN 1000K | OCI8 1000K | THIN 100K | OCI8 100K | THIN 10K | OCI8 10K |
|---|---|---|---|---|---|---|---|---|
| Time to connect: | 2483 | 1663 | 3815 | 1472 | 2653 | 1462 | 2424 | 1442 |
| Statement prepare: | 131 | 130 | 141 | 120 | 131 | 120 | 130 | 120 |
| Avg. time: | 41945 | 40448 | 4126 | 4022 | 533 | 460 | 132 | 100 |
| Total time: | 422107 | 406284 | 45295 | 41910 | 8121 | 6199 | 3886 | 2573 |

Although the differences between BLOB writes are not as significant here, there is still a noticeable difference between the two drivers in the amount of time it takes to get a connection to the database.

# LOB read test

The read test class is similar to the write test class. The big difference, of course, is that we are reading the lobtest table here. For this class to be able to read lob data, you must have run the previous class to fill the table with data. Here is the lob_read_test class:

```
import java.io.*;
import java.lang.*;
import java.sql.*;
import java.util.*;
import oracle.jdbc.driver.*;
```

```java
import oracle.sql.*;

public class lob_read_test {
  static String sql =
    "select data from lobtest where ID = ? and rownum < 2";

  public static void main(String[] argv) {
    try {

      // Setup program parameters
      int lobsize = Integer.parseInt(argv[0]);
      int iter = Integer.parseInt(argv[1]);

      // Setup connection and record time
      long start = System.currentTimeMillis();
      DriverManager.registerDriver(new OracleDriver());
      Connection conn = DriverManager.getConnection(argv[2], "username",
                  "password");
      conn.setAutoCommit(false);
      System.out.println("Time to connect: "
                        + (System.currentTimeMillis() - start));

      long prepTime = System.currentTimeMillis();
      OraclePreparedStatement ops =
        (OraclePreparedStatement) conn.prepareStatement(sql);
      ops.setNUMBER(1, new NUMBER(lobsize));
      System.out.println("Statement prepare: "
                        + (System.currentTimeMillis() - prepTime));

      long totalIterTime = 0;

      for (int i = 0; i < iter; i++) {
        OracleResultSet rs = (OracleResultSet) ops.executeQuery();

        while (rs.next()) {
          long iterStartTime = System.currentTimeMillis();
          BLOB blob = rs.getBLOB(1);
          InputStream is = blob.getBinaryStream();

          int bufSize = blob.getBufferSize();
          byte buffer[] = new byte[bufSize];
          int length;

          while ((length = is.read(buffer, 0, bufSize)) != -1);

          is.close();
          long iterTime = System.currentTimeMillis() - iterStartTime;
          totalIterTime += iterTime;
          System.out.println("Iteration " + j + ": " + iterTime);
        }

        rs.close();
      }
```

```
            ops.close();
            conn.close();
            System.out.println("Avg. time: " + (totalIterTime / iter));
            System.out.println("Total time: "
                             + (System.currentTimeMillis() - start));
            System.exit(0);
        } catch (Exception e) {
            e.printStackTrace();
        }
    }
}
```

The command line syntax for executing this class is the same as it was for the lob_write_class:

```
> java -ms32m -mx32m -noclassgc lob_read_test lob_size iterations driver
```

The program performs a select on the lobtest table. From the resultset, it gets the BLOB locator and uses the locator to get an InputStream from which it can read the binary data. Then, it simply reads the data using the read() method of the InputStream. It does not process the data in any way.

This program was run a number of times with various LOB sizes, but always with 10 iterations of reading the LOB from the database. Each LOB size was tested with the thin driver and the OCI driver. The LOB sizes passed to the program on the command line were 10000, 1000, 100, 10. (Remember that the program actually multiplies those figures by 1024.)

Here are the results for the client running on the Sun server (all times in milliseconds):

| | THIN 10000K | OCI8 10000K | THIN 1000K | OCI8 1000K | THIN 100K | OCI8 100K | THIN 10K | OCI8 10K |
|---|---|---|---|---|---|---|---|---|
| Time to connect: | 1152 | 804 | 1153 | 804 | 1172 | 825 | 1161 | 824 |
| Statement prepare: | 80 | 89 | 80 | 87 | 81 | 89 | 83 | 86 |
| Iteration 0: | 2699 | 1362 | 487 | 149 | 190 | 49 | 127 | 39 |
| Avg. time: | 2415 | 1158 | 257 | 94 | 54 | 13 | 27 | 6 |
| Total time: | 25397 | 12491 | 3815 | 1847 | 1806 | 1061 | 1533 | 986 |

And the same set of read tests with the Windows client:

| | THIN 10000K | OCI8 10000K | THIN 1000K | OCI8 1000K | THIN 100K | OCI8 100K | THIN 10K | OCI8 10K |
|---|---|---|---|---|---|---|---|---|
| Time to connect: | 2664 | 1753 | 2664 | 1732 | 2644 | 1732 | 2624 | 1703 |
| Statement prepare: | 170 | 170 | 171 | 170 | 170 | 170 | 170 | 160 |

| | THIN 10000K | OCI8 10000K | THIN 1000K | OCI8 1000K | THIN 100K | OCI8 100K | THIN 10K | OCI8 10K |
|---|---|---|---|---|---|---|---|---|
| Avg. time: | 14462 | 13332 | 1493 | 1353 | 190 | 139 | 46 | 20 |
| Total time: | 147492 | 135255 | 17766 | 15452 | 4717 | 3304 | 3255 | 2083 |

I also did some "normal" SQL queries and updates to see how they are affected by the thin and OCI8 drivers. To test, I select all rows from SCOTT.EMP and then for each row, I update the row 20 times with the same values. I do this entire process 20 times and get the average time for each iteration. Once again, I ran the test without the garbage collector, with 32MB of memory, and ran each test on NT and Solaris. Additionally, this test was run with various default batch sizes of 1, 5, 10, 20, and 40.

As you can see, the results for the read test are similar to those for the write test. The OCI driver is always faster at getting a connection. Both drivers are the same when it comes to creating a Statement object. The OCI driver is generally faster than the thin driver at reading LOB data from the database.

# EMP Test

The finally test involves reading and writing data to the EMP table. For this set of tests we also used batch updates to see how that affected performance. Here is the class:

```java
import java.io.*;
import java.lang.*;
import java.sql.*;
import java.util.*;
import oracle.jdbc.driver.*;
import oracle.sql.*;

public class emp_rw_test {
  static String sqlQuery = "select * from emp";
  static String sqlUpdate =
    "update emp set hiredate=?, sal=?, job=? where empno=?";

  public static void main(String[] argv) {
    try {

      // Setup connection and record time
      int iter = Integer.parseInt(argv[0]);
      int batchSize = Integer.parseInt(argv[1]);
      long start = System.currentTimeMillis();
      DriverManager.registerDriver(new OracleDriver());
      OracleConnection conn =
        (OracleConnection) DriverManager.getConnection(argv[2], "username",
            "password");
      conn.setAutoCommit(false);
      conn.setDefaultExecuteBatch(batchSize);
      System.out.println("Time to connect: "
                  + (System.currentTimeMillis() - start));

      long prepTime = System.currentTimeMillis();
```

```
      OraclePreparedStatement opsQuery =
        (OraclePreparedStatement) conn.prepareStatement(sqlQuery);
      OraclePreparedStatement opsUpdate =
        (OraclePreparedStatement) conn.prepareStatement(sqlUpdate);
      System.out.println("Statement prepare: "
                        + (System.currentTimeMillis() - prepTime));

      long totalIterTime = 0;

      for (int i = 0; i < iter; i++) {
        OracleResultSet rs = (OracleResultSet) opsQuery.executeQuery();

        while (rs.next()) {
          long iterStartTime = System.currentTimeMillis();
          rs.getNUMBER(1);
          rs.getString(2);
          rs.getString(3);
          rs.getNUMBER(4);
          rs.getDATE(5);
          rs.getNUMBER(6);
          rs.getNUMBER(7);
          rs.getNUMBER(8);

          for (int x = 0; x < 20; x++) {
            opsUpdate.setDATE(1, rs.getDATE(5));
            opsUpdate.setNUMBER(2, rs.getNUMBER(6));
            opsUpdate.setString(3, rs.getString(3));
            opsUpdate.setNUMBER(4, rs.getNUMBER(1));
            opsUpdate.executeUpdate();
          }

          long iterTime = System.currentTimeMillis() - iterStartTime;
          totalIterTime += iterTime;
        }

        rs.close();
      }

      opsQuery.close();
      opsUpdate.close();
      conn.commit();
      conn.close();
      System.out.println("Avg. time: " + (totalIterTime / iter));
      System.out.println("Total time: "
                        + (System.currentTimeMillis() - start));
      System.exit(0);
    } catch (Exception e) {
      e.printStackTrace();
    }
  }
}
```

The class above is executed with the following command syntax:

```
> java -ms32m -mx32m -noclassgc emp_rw_test iterations batch_size driver
```

The first argument to the program is the number of times to read and write the EMP table. The second parameter is the batch size. The batch size tells the driver how many statements to send to the database in each batch. The final argument is the driver.

After this program gets the connection, it uses the connection to set the batch size:

```
conn.setDefaultExecuteBatch(batchSize);
```

Normally when you call the executeUpdate() method of the Statement, the driver immediately sends the SQL to the database for execution. When you set the batch size, the Oracle driver does something different. When batching is in effect, executeUpdate() does not send the SQL immediately to the database. Rather, the SQL is added to a list of SQL statements, and the batch is not sent until the number of statements reaches the batch size. At that time, all the statements are sent to the database together for execution.

So, the program queries the EMP database, and then reads the various column values from the table. After it does this, it sets the parameters for an update statement and calls the executeUpdate() method; it does this 20 times for each row. Remember that this simply adds the update SQL to the batch until the batch size is equal to the size set with the setDefaultExecuteBatch() method. Once the default size is reached, the driver sends the batch of statements to the database where they are executed. Thus, we would expect to see that a batch size of 1 (executing each statement immediately) is less efficient than larger batch sizes (executing n statements in the same batch).

The timing results obtained for the Solaris client are:

|  | THIN | OCI8 | THIN | OCI8 | THIN | OCI8 | THIN | OCI8 | THIN | OCI8 |
|---|---|---|---|---|---|---|---|---|---|---|
| Batch Size | 1 | 1 | 5 | 5 | 10 | 10 | 20 | 20 | 40 | 40 |
| Time to connect: | 1165 | 798 | 1176 | 800 | 1167 | 799 | 1171 | 797 | 1194 | 806 |
| Statement prepare: | 44 | 43 | 43 | 44 | 45 | 43 | 44 | 44 | 45 | 44 |
| Avg. time: | 3886 | 3304 | 2693 | 3262 | 2765 | 2412 | 4165 | 2645 | 2862 | 2486 |
| Total time: | 12088 | 9699 | 9154 | 8707 | 8969 | 8272 | 10997 | 8564 | 9030 | 8510 |

In general, the OCI driver is faster than the Thin driver. (There does appear to be an anomaly with a batch size of 5.) Also, as expected, we see that as batch size increases, execution time decreases. In other words, a batch size of 40 is more efficient than a batch size of 1.

The same program run on the Windows client gave these results:

|  | THIN | OCI8 | THIN | OCI8 | THIN | OCI8 | THIN | OCI8 | THIN | OCI8 |
|---|---|---|---|---|---|---|---|---|---|---|
| Batch Size | 1 | 1 | 5 | 5 | 10 | 10 | 20 | 20 | 40 | 40 |
| Time to connect: | 2574 | 1703 | 2654 | 1672 | 2564 | 1672 | 2544 | 1673 | 2554 | 1673 |

*Table continued on following page*

**631**

|  | THIN | OCI8 | THIN | OCI8 | THIN | OCI8 | THIN | OCI8 | THIN | OCI8 |
|---|---|---|---|---|---|---|---|---|---|---|
| Statement prepare: | 110 | 110 | 110 | 111 | 110 | 110 | 110 | 110 | 100 | 110 |
| Avg. time: | 4649 | 4721 | 4616 | 2713 | 2977 | 2659 | 2890 | 2526 | 2716 | 2826 |
| Total time: | 15322 | 13480 | 12768 | 9944 | 10035 | 9824 | 10175 | 9414 | 10175 | 9103 |

## Driver Comparison Summary

We've shown here that there really is a difference between the two drivers. In almost every test case explored, there is a statistically significant performance difference between the OCI and the thin drivers.

When you have a choice, and you need the fastest performance, you should choose the OCI driver. Because the OCI driver uses native code libraries, it executes faster than the thin driver.

# Oracle Native Compiler (ncomp)

There may well come a time when you have done everything you can do and there is still a performance problem. At that point, you may need to investigate compiling your Java bytecode to native machine code. It is commonly accepted that native machine code will run faster than interpreted byte code. If you've been running Java code in a JVM outside the database, you've actually already been compiling bytecode to machine code with a Just-In-Time compiler. This compiler converts byte code to machine code at run-time.

In contrast to the Just-In-Time compiler provided with many Java Virtual Machines, Oracle has been using an Ahead-Of-Time compiler since they began supporting Java in the database (since Oracle 8.1.5). The entire set of core Java libraries have been precompiled to machine code and are used instead of interpreted class files. However, prior to Oracle 8.1.7, this tool was not made available to developers outside of Oracle. Starting with Oracle 8.1.7, the tool, known as ncomp, was made available for any developer to use. Later in this section we will look at an example using native compilation with an Oracle 8.1.7 database running on Windows NT. However, this material in general applies to Oracle 8.1.7 on Solaris and Oracle 9i on Solaris and Windows.

> *In this section, we will frequently refer to compiling the code. This term can have two different meanings. When we compile Java source with javac, or with "create or replace and compile" we are compiling Java source to Java bytecode that is platform independent. When we compile Java code with the Oracle native compiler, we are compiling Java byte-code to machine code that is specific to a platform. I will attempt to make the distinction clear when the context does not indicate which compilation I mean.*

# Just In Time and Ahead Of Time

The Just-In-Time (JIT) compiler has been a standard part of the Java environment since the days of Java 1.1. A JIT compiler takes bytecode and compiles it to machine code as it is interpreted by the JVM. For example, assume that your Java application calls a method of a class. Right before the method is executed the first time, the JIT compiler would compile the method to native machine code, and then execute it for you, without compiling any other methods of the class. The compiled code is then cached in the JVM process memory. If that method is called again, the compiled code is again executed. However, when the program ends and the JVM terminates, the machine code is thrown away. The next time you run the program, the compiler would need to compile the code again.

One of the signs that a Just-In-Time compiler is in use is a stack trace from an exception that has the phrase "Compiled code" in place of the line numbers as shown below:

```
java.lang.ArrayIndexOutOfBoundsException: 5
    at ArrayDemo.getElement(ArrayDemo.java:15)
    at ArrayDemo.main(ArrayDemo.java, Compiled Code)
Exception in thread "main"
Process ArrayDemo exited abnormally with code 1
```

Normally, a stack trace shows the methods and source code line numbers of all the method calls that led to the exception. When a method is compiled to machine code, the line number information is lost in the compilation process. So instead, the phrase "Compiled code" is used in place of the line number.

> *The JIT compiler can be disabled. For all releases of Java 2, you can disable the JIT compiler at the command line by using* java -Djava.compiler=NONE myapp. *An alternate technique is to set the system property* JAVA_COMPILER *to NONE.*

Oracle has coined the term Ahead-Of-Time for their compiler. With Oracle's Ahead-Of-Time compiler, the bytecode is compiled to machine code long before a client ever calls it. Oracle converts the Java bytecode to platform independent C code. The C code is then compiled and linked with platform specific code into a shared library for a particular platform. For Windows, this will be a .dll file, for Solaris, a .so file. The shared library is loaded into the database, where it is executed in place of calls to interpreted Java bytecode. In contrast to a JIT, the shared library is always available to the virtual machine and does not need to be recompiled every time the database is restarted.

The tool that compiles Java bytecode to a native code shared library is ncomp. Oracle's documentation for the ncomp tool states that the speed increase from natively compiling Java code will depend upon how CPU intensive the Java code is. The more CPU intensive your code is, the more of a speed increase you can expect. They also list a number of factors that affect the speed increase. Two of those factors are:

- ❑ Use of numerics
- ❑ Amount of array accessing

> *You can see the complete list and read more information about ncomp in* the Oracle Java Tools Reference *or the* Java Developer's Guide. *Both documents can be found in the database documentation that came with your database, or on Oracle's web site,* http://technet.oracle.com/docs/content.html.

If we create a class that uses a large number of array accesses and floating point arithmetic, we should have a class that is CPU intensive and can benefit from native compilation. The class below will create a 1000x1000 array of doubles, and a 1000x1 array of doubles, and multiply the two arrays. This will result in more than a million array accesses and 1000 floating point multiplications.

We'll start by developing a class named `NcompDemo` that we will run in the database without compiling to machine code.

> *For the first part of this example, I will show how to create the class directly in the database. If you prefer, you can compile it outside the database and use the loadjava tool as we've done in other places in this book.*

It's a relatively straightforward class with just a couple of methods. A `runIt()` method creates and fills two arrays with random doubles. A `doMultiply()` method multiplies the two arrays and returns the result. The first significant point about this class is the package declaration:

```
SQL> create or replace and compile
  2      java source named "NcompDemo"
  3        as
  4        package com.wrox;
```

Some of the classes you see in this chapter and other chapters will not have a package declaration. While this is normally not a big deal in Java, it can cause problems later when we try to natively compile this class. When you natively compile this class later, you will see that Oracle creates the shared library file based on the package. Only a single shared library is loaded for each package. If this class had no package, and you later compiled another class with no package, the newer shared library would be used and the older shared library would not be used.

The first method shown in the class is the `runIt()` method:

```
  5  public class NcompDemo {
  6    public static int num = 1000;
  7    public static void runIt() {
  8      double[][] matrix1 = new double[num][num];
  9      double[] matrix2 = new double[num];
 10      double[] result = null;
 11      long start = System.currentTimeMillis();
 12      for (int i = 0; i < num; i++) {
 13        matrix2[i] = Math.random();
 14        for (int j = 0; j < num; j++) {
 15          matrix1[i][j] = Math.random();
 16        }
 17      }
```

This method declares the three arrays that will be used, a 1000 X 1000 array, a 1000 X 1 array, and an array to hold the result of calling `doMultiply()`. Then two `for` loops are used to fill the arrays with random doubles. When the arrays are ready, they are passed to the `doMultiply()` method, which looks like this:

```
18        result = doMultiply(matrix1, matrix2);
19        long end = System.currentTimeMillis();
20        System.out.println("Time to fill and multiply matrices = "
21                          + (end - start) + " millis");
22    }
23 public static double[] doMultiply(double[][] matrix1, double matrix2[]) {
24        double[] result = new double[num];
25        for (int i = 0; i < num; i++) {
26          for (int j = 0; j < num; j++) {
27            result[i] += matrix1[i][j] * matrix2[j];
28          }
29        }
30        return result;
31    }
```

The doMultiply() method again has some for loops, this time to multiply the two matrices. When the multiplication is complete, the result is returned to the runIt() method. The program then computes the total time it took to fill and multiply the arrays, and prints that result to the screen.

The last method in the class is the main(String[] args) method:

```
32    public static void main(String[] args) {
33        NcompDemo.runIt();
34    }
35 }
36 /
```

This method can be used to run this program outside the database. If the code does not successfully compile, use the SHOW ERRORS PL/SQL statement to determine and correct the problem. When the Java class is successfully compiled, create a call specification:

```
SQL> create or replace procedure compile_demo
  2  as language java name 'com.wrox.NcompDemo.runIt()';
  3  /
```

Use the following PL/SQL statements to set the environment so that output is directed to the console:

```
SQL> set serveroutput on
SQL> call dbms_java.set_output(2000);
```

Now, call the procedure as shown below. As you can see from the display, the procedure took over 21 seconds to execute on my system. This example was run on a Pentium III 450 MHz with 192 MB of RAM, running NT 4. The database was Oracle8i Enterprise Edition Release 8.1.7.0.0 – Production. The results could be different depending on the hardware configuration and OS versions.

```
SQL> exec compile_demo;
Time to fill and multiply matrices = 21261 millis
```

**635**

I actually ran the code several times on my system, and the average time was 21.3 seconds. Remember this number for later, when we see how the compiled code performs.

You might find it interesting to compile and run the program outside the database and compare the run times. On my system, it ran almost 5 times faster outside the database with a JIT compiler than without a JIT.

# Compiling the Class to Native Code

Now let's look at how to compile the class to a shared library and run the compiled code in the database. Unfortunately, even though the compiler has been in use since Oracle 8.1.5, the Windows release of Oracle 8.1.7 was a little incomplete. In this section, I'll try to provide complete instructions on how to use ncomp in a Windows environment. If you have Oracle 9i for Windows, you will find that Oracle has fixed at least one of the problems I had to overcome with 8.1.7. If you are running Oracle on Solaris, you should be able to use Oracle's documentation to compile the Java code with little difficulty. Information on running ncomp can be found in *the Oracle Java Tools Reference* or the *Java Developer's Guide*.

> **The native compiler is only available with Oracle 8.1.7 Enterprise Edition or later, and is only available for Solaris or Windows. The instructions in this section were developed for Oracle 8.1.7 on Windows NT.**

Before you perform any of the following steps, check for the existence of the file orajox8.lib in the Oracle directories. This file was not included in the original Oracle 8.1.7.0.0 release. If you are using Oracle 9i for Windows, you need orajox9.lib, and this file is part of the 9i release. Without the file, you will not be able to create the compiled library. If you have this file, ensure it is located in the %ORACLE_HOME%\lib directory. If you do not have this file, you will have to get it as part of the 8.1.7.1.1 patch. If you have a license from Oracle, you can get the patch directly from them. Next, you will need a C/C++ compiler. At this time, it appears that only the Windows Visual C/C++ compiler is supported for native compiling on the Windows platform. I used Windows Visual C++ 6.0. Obtain a copy and install it to a directory on your system. To make the compilation process easier, do NOT install Visual C++ to a directory with spaces in the name. If you already have it installed in a directory like Program Files uninstall it and reinstall it to a directory like C:\msdev.

> *It is probably possible to perform the native compilation from a directory with spaces in the name. However, when I ran into the problem, I chose to reinstall Visual C++ from C:\Program Files to C:\msdev. Thus these directions assume you are running Visual C++ from a directory without spaces in the name.*

Ensure your environment has the correct settings as shown opposite:

| Environment Variables | Addition Required |
|---|---|
| `JAVA_HOME` | Set to the location where your JDK is installed |
| `CLASSPATH` | Include the appropriate JDK JAR files in your `CLASSPATH` as follows:<br>For JDK 1.1, include `%JAVA_HOME%\lib\classes.zip`.<br>For JDK 1.2, include the `%JAVA_HOME%\lib\tools.jar` and `%JAVA_HOME%\lib\dt.jar` files. |
| `MSDEV_HOME` | Set to the location of MS Visual C++ |
| `PATH` | Add the JDK binary path: `%JAVA_HOME%\bin`<br>Add the JDK library path: `%JAVA_HOME%\lib`.<br>Add the Visual C++ path `%MSDEV_HOME%\VC98\Bin`<br>Add the Visual C++ path `%MSDEV_HOME%\Common\MSDev98\Bin` |

To be able to compile and load the shared library, the user will need the DBA role. Have your DBA grant the DBA role to the user who will be compiling and loading the Java code.

```
SQL> grant dba to username;
```

Open the file `%ORACLE_HOME%\javavm\jahome\Settings_windows_nt.properties` for editing. You will need to make the following general edits:

- ❏ Change forward slashes (/) to double back slashes (\ \) in directory paths
- ❏ Add aliases for Windows utility commands and programs such as copy or del

For example, part of one of the lines from the file looked like this before the change:

```
LINK_COMMAND = $(visual.c.home)/bin/LINK   /DLL /OUT:$@ \
```

We need to change the path separator character from '/' to '\\'. The back-slash is doubled because otherwise, the single slash acts as an escape. We don't change the slashes that signal command options in the line (/DLL for example) or the single slash at the end of the line which signals that the command continues on the next line. Here's how the line looks after the change:

```
LINK_COMMAND = $(visual.c.home)\\bin\\LINK   /DLL /OUT:$@ \
```

Here is how the file looks on my system after I performed the edits. Pay close attention to which slashes are unchanged forward slashes, which have been changed to double back-slashes, and which are single back-slashes. You will also need to change the `visual.c.home` property so that it uses the correct directory for your system:

```
file.extension.exe = exe
file.extension.obj = obj
library.prefix = "ora"
file.extension.dll = dll

EXPORTS_COMMAND =

visual.c.home = C:\\msdev\\VC98
oracle.home = $(ORACLE_HOME)

LINK_COMMAND = $(visual.c.home)\\bin\\LINK  /DLL /OUT:$@ \
/LIBPATH:$(visual.c.home)\\lib /DEF:$(*:b).def $< \
$(oracle.home)\\lib\\orajox8.lib

CFLAGS =   $<  -Fo$@ $(c.compile.include) \
$(c.compile.flags.platform) $(c.compile.flags.aurora)

CC = $(visual.c.home)\\bin\\cl

COMPILE.c = $(CC) $(CFLAGS) $(CPPFLAGS) -c

c.compile.flags.platform =
c.compile.flags.aurora =

makefile.maker = $(one.c.unit.per.dll.makefile.maker)

loadjava = $(oracle.home)\\bin\\loadjava.bat $(loadjava.options)

load-incr-dumper-class.command = \
 $(oracle.home)\\bin\\loadjava.bat $(loadjava.basic.options) \
 -u $(SCHEMA)/$(PASSWORD) $(incremental.dumper.classlist)

cp.command = cp.bat
ls.command = cmd /c dir
rm.command = cmd /c del
rmdir.command = cmd /c rmdir /S /Q
du.command = du -k
ls.libs.command = cmd /c dir lib
```

Note that the last six lines need to be added to the file for Oracle 8i. The properties file in Oracle 9i includes those lines already and does not need further editing. If you are using Oracle 8i for Windows, you will need a batch file that calls the Windows `copy` command. If you have Oracle 9i for Windows, Oracle has included their own `copy` program, `ocopy`, which will work with `ncomp`.

So, for Oracle 8i, create the `cp.bat` file. This file allows the compilation process to use the Windows copy program. The file should look like this:

```
@echo off
cmd /c copy %1 %2
```

Copy the `cp.bat` file to the directory `C:\project\wrox`.

Create the `NcompDemo.java` source file in `C:\Project\wrox`. Use the Java compiler to compile the Java `NcompDemo` class. Assuming you've put the source code into the directory `C:\project\wrox`, you would compile the source like this:

```
C:\Project\wrox> javac -d . NcompDemo.java
```

The `-d .` option above specifies the root directory for the class file. If you omit it, then the class file will be located in the same directory as the source. But since the class is in a package, we need the directory structure to match the package structure. The `-d` option specifies the root of the package directories; the `.` means the current directory. So, specifying the `-d .` will cause the compiler to create the directory `\com\wrox\` at the current location (`C:\project\wrox`) and place the class file into that directory. When `javac` completes, the path to the class will be `C:\project\wrox\com\wrox\NcompDemo.class`.

You can specify the classes to be compiled in one of three ways. You can put the files to be compiled into a .zip file, you can put them into a file similar to a .zip but with a .jar extension, or you can put the names of the classes into a file that `ncomp` reads. For this example I created a .jar file. The `NcompDemo.jar` file is created with the Java jar program like this:

```
C:\Project\wrox> jar cvf NcompDemo.jar com\wrox\NcompDemo.class
added manifest
adding: com/wrox/NcompDemo.class(in = 1219) (out= 767)(deflated 37%)
```

In the command line above, the `c` option creates a new archive, `v` specifies verbose output, and `f` specifies the name of the `.jar` file for the archive. The last parameter gives the name of the class we are adding to the `.jar` file.

> **Even though we are putting the class file into the .jar, it is only used by ncomp to get the name of the file to be compiled. The byte code itself comes from the database.**

And now, the moment you've been waiting for, it's time to try to use `ncomp` to natively compile your code. In the command line below, `ncomp` is the name of the batch file that controls the compilation; the option `-user username/password` is the username and the password of the user whose schema contains the Java class; the name `NcompDemo.jar` is the `.jar` file that contains the classes to be compiled:

```
C:\Project\wrox> ncomp -user usename/password NcompDemo.jar
```

> **If you did not previously create or load the NcompDemo class file in the database as shown in the previous section, use the -load option with the command above.**

The compilation process will print a lot of information to the console, as well as a lot of information to the log file. The log file is named `ncomp.log` and is located in the current directory, which is `C:\Project\wrox` for this example. What you are looking for is a line printed to the console similar to the following when the process completes:

```
# Deployment History, produced by query:
# select timestamp, status, dll_name  from jaccelerator$dlls order by dll_name
Fri Oct 19 14:33:59 MDT 2001 installed /orajox8_e9a6aaeeb8_wrox_com_wrox.dll
```

The lines that start with # are comment lines. The process is querying the database as shown in the second comment. If the dll was created and loaded properly, the query will return at least one row from the jaccelerator$dlls table. The status you want to see is "installed" with the library named similarly to what is shown above: the first part of the name is orajox8, the next part is the timestamp in hex, and the name finishes with the package specification of the package that was compiled and loaded.

Before we run the code, here are some suggestions if the process fails:

❑   Ignore any error messages such as The syntax of the command is incorrect. This particular message will display when you run the ncomp process the first time.

❑   Pay attention to any error messages in the ncomp.log file. In particular look for any Java exceptions, especially java.io.IOExceptions, in the file. Look at the command that preceded the exception to see if you missed any slashes that caused the command to be parsed incorrectly.

❑   Ignore any exceptions in the log that occur because of the touch command such as:

```
touch com_wrox.log -- got java.io.IOException: CreateProcess: touch
com_wrox.log  error=2when executing action:  touch com_wrox.log
```

touch is a UNIX command. It simply updates the timestamp of a file, and the dll can be created even if touch does not exist.

❑   If any dialog boxes appear on the screen warning that a shared library could not be located, check you path environment to ensure it includes the path to the file that could not be found.

We are almost at the point where we can try running the compiled library. Before we can do that, we need to ensure that the Oracle JVM is configured to load the .dlls. The information on how to enable and disable the shared libraries can be found in the Readme document in the %ORACLE_HOME%\javavm directory. It states that to enable the shared library, you would have the DBA execute the following commands.

```
SQL> alter java class "java/io/Serializable" if needed check;
SQL> alter system flush shared_pool;
SQL> alter system flush shared_pool;
SQL> alter system flush shared_pool;
```

There are times when you may need to have the database stop using compiled libraries. For example, if you need to debug your Java code, you will probably want to use the interpreted code rather than the compiled library. The SQL to do this is similar to above. After executing the SQL shown below, your DBA will also need to flush the shared pool as shown above.

```
SQL> alter java class "java/io/Serializable" check;
```

With the shared libraries enabled, log in as the user who created the compiled library, and execute the code again.

```
SQL> set serveroutput on
SQL> call dbms_java.set_output(2000);

SQL> exec compile_demo;
Time to fill and multiply matrices = 14461 millis
```

There's a noticeable improvement here. I ran this code a number of times and got an average execution time of 14.6 seconds. We've improved the execution time of this code by about 30%.

# Important Facts to Consider with Native Compilation

The release notes document, %ORACLE_HOME%/relnotes/javavm/README_javavm.txt for Oracle 9i, discusses some issues and tips/tricks when converting Java byte code into the shared libraries. The Oracle Technology Network (OTN) also has some good information. Some of the more important topics from these documents are:

❑ What happens when NCOMPing Java classes in the default package (UnnamedPackage). Basically, you need to be careful because NCOMPing one class might un-NCOMP others.

❑ How to pick safe levels of C-code optimizations. Oracle suggests that exceedingly aggressive optimization of generated C-code can produce incorrect binaries. However, this is not specific to NCOMPing or Oracle. Rather, it is a caveat of many optimizing compilers.

❑ Which JDK releases to avoid – Solaris releases of JDK 1.1.7p, 1.2, 1.2.1p, 1.2.2_05a and 1.1.3 with native threads. There are no listed JDK's to avoid for Windows NT.

❑ How to manage file space in %ORACLE_HOME%/javavm/admin directory using a Java stored procedure. This displays the fully qualified name of the shared libraries in use (for a given user), which allows you to remove libraries not in use.

# When Compiling Doesn't Help

There are times, of course, when native compiling will not be able to improve your application performance. As I mentioned above, the Oracle documentation lists a number of situations that will be more likely to benefit from native compilation. One situation where native compilation does not help is when the bottleneck is within the database itself.

For example, consider this Java class Bottleneck:

```
public class Bottleneck {
  public static void import() {
    String[][] data = new String[1000][5]
    File file = new File("datafile.dat");
    //assume we have code that opens and reads
    //the data file, and stores the contents in
    //the 2D array named data
    for (int i = 0; i < data.length; i++) {
```

```
        String sql = "insert into data_table " +
          "(col1, col2, col3, col4, col5) " +
          "values ('" +  data[i][0] +
          "', '" + data[i][1] +
          "', '" + data[i][2] +
          "', '" + data[i][3] +
          "', '" + data[i][4] +
          "')";
        Statement stmt = conn.createStatement();
        stmt.executeUpdate(sql);
      }
    }
  }
```

The Java class above creates a thousand SQL INSERT statements that use literal data, and then uses a Statement object to insert the data into some table. Since this code creates 1000 unique SQL statements, each statement will have to be parsed, the table and column names will have to be resolved for each statement, security is checked for each statement, and so on. This creates a lot of work for the database, and compiling this Java code to machine code will not lessen that work to any degree. The way to resolve the problem here is not to compile the code, but to make proper use of bind variables and PreparedStatements. As discussed in Chapter 5 *Using JDBC*, when you use a PreparedStatement, the database will reuse the already parsed SQL if it later sees the same SQL statement. When the database reuses SQL, all of the work of parsing, resolving, optimizing, and so on, does not need to be redone, and so is more efficient.

# Summary

I have tried to show in this chapter how a program often has more effect on the performance of the application than any other factor.

We looked at what is probably the most common misuse of the language, and one of the most dramatic examples of a performance improvement. This example of Strings versus StringBuffers is a specific case of a more general problem. It is relatively expensive to allocate memory and create objects. Any time we can reuse objects, we can improve our Java programs.

There are actually many additional techniques that can be used to make Java programs run faster. However, many of them will not be able to show the same dramatic performance improvement we saw in this chapter. You can learn more about these techniques at these web sites:

❑ http://www-2.cs.cmu.edu/~jch/java/optimization.html

❑ http://www.protomatter.com/nate/java-optimization/

❑ http://www.javaworld.com/jw-04-1997/jw-04-optimize.html

❑ http://www.javaworld.com/javaworld/jw-09-1998/jw-09-speed.html

An opposite viewpoint is here:

❏    http://billharlan.com/pub/papers/A_Tirade_Against_the_Cult_of_Performance.html

The original paper by Don Knuth that contains the quote from the start of this chapter can be found at this web site:

❏    http://pplab.snu.ac.kr/courses/PL2001/papers/p261-knuth.pdf

That quote is the reason why this chapter did not cover the many optimizations recommended by the web sites above. Recall the problem I talked about in the first section: the `OutOfMemoryError` caused by String concatenation. If we had just assumed that the problem was caused by Java being slow, we might have spent a lot of time using all kinds of little tricks to make the Java code faster. None of that would have had a noticeable impact, since the problem was not that the bytecode was slow, but that the code we wrote was unnecessarily creating hundreds of objects and wasting megabytes of memory.

The key is to write code that is first correct and error-free. Then you must understand what part of the code is consuming most of the processing time. There are several tools that can help you determine this information. However, you can often get what you need with the simple `System.out.println` statement. That is what we did with the examples in this chapter. We knew how much time was needed to create the strings in the string demo classes because we printed that information from inside the classes.

In the *Static Variables* section, we saw how the Oracle JVM preserves session state across calls. It does this by storing the static class variables in session memory. We also examined one way to determine how much memory our Java classes and programs are using. The `MemStat` procedure is a useful tool in your Oracle Java toolkit. It can help you locate places where you can reduce the memory used by your classes. The less session memory consumed by your classes, the more concurrent users can be supported by your application.

We also looked at the performance difference between the OCI (Type 2) and Thin (Type 4) drivers. In some cases, you will not have a choice of which driver your application uses. When you do have a choice, you should choose the OCI driver. As we saw in numerous tests, the OCI driver generally performs faster than the thin driver. The primary reason for this is that the OCI driver uses native code libraries to connect to the database.

After improving your code, checking your memory usage, and optimizing your end of call migration, if you still need a performance improvement, you can look at compiling your Java bytecode to native machine code. Using Oracle's native compilation tool `ncomp`, you can create a native shared library (a DLL for Windows or a Shared Library for UNIX) by compiling your code. This works best for code that is CPU intensive and is not bound by any database process.

Oracle 9i Java Programming

# SQL Tuning and Analyzing Queries

Most people agree that tuning is an integral aspect of database programming. However, the order in which tuning should appear in the database development process is sometimes regarded as a matter of opinion, which it most certainly is not. Too many people look at tuning as a post-production process when the fact is that it is most effective at the earliest stages of design, development and testing. Once a system is up and running, it is much more complex to tune it than if it were still in design and development. Considerations such as the fact that people are relying on the system to do their jobs, that the system must remain available and come into play – limiting what you may and may not do. In fact, when a system has been deployed, it is considerably more difficult just to locate the source of the contention, than it is to get it fixed. One reason for this, is that there are several different levels at which an Oracle application can be tuned, including:

- ❑   Data Model
- ❑   Business Logic
- ❑   SQL Statements
- ❑   Database Instance
- ❑   Memory, CPU and I/O

The area of database tuning with which we are concerned in this chapter is the tuning of SQL statements processed by the application. Even if the SQL is not the actual performance bottleneck, it may often be useful to start a database performance analysis at the SQL level, instead of working from one end to the other. From the results of that analysis, it can be easier to determine whether you should move upwards (towards tuning the business rules and data model), downwards (tuning the database instance or operating system resources), or whether the source of your problem does in fact lie within the SQL itself.

So far in this book, we have been mainly looking at issues at the business logic layer, working with PL/SQL and Java within the database. When aiming at the optimization of SQL access for your application, design decisions at the business layer can indeed have a dramatic effect. This mainly relates to the choice of programming language or technology used to issue and handle the SQL processing – such as PL/SQL or Java, JDBC or SQLJ, and so on. As a result, you may find it natural to begin your optimization at the business layer, by selecting your method of SQL access, and then move on to tuning the actual SQL statements being worked with. In this chapter, we in fact propose quite the opposite. Start by tuning your SQL, to the point that no further optimization can be accomplished. Only then, evaluate the results and determine what method you should use for execution. We will see in the next chapter, *PL/SQL and Java: Benchmarking SQL Execution*, a common rule of thumb for when you should use PL/SQL rather than Java for database access is when you have to execute a series of statements, which would be more efficient by wrapping the whole set in a PL/SQL procedure. In that chapter, we will see how the impedance mismatch between SQL types and Java types that exists in Java (but not PL/SQL) can impede performance – additionally, the network round trips necessary for a Java implementation (when the Java executes outside of the database) can additionally impede performance. However, as we will illustrate at the end of this chapter, you can often reduce the initial number of SQL statements with careful examination and rewriting. Therefore, it is natural to begin analyzing and tuning the actual SQL – *before* you choose which language you want to use to execute it.

This chapter is divided into three parts. In the first part, we will discuss the first steps of SQL tuning – namely, the use of bind variables and indexes. These two issues are fundamental to any tuning strategy. While taking these steps does not guarantee optimal performance, not taking them will definitely guarantee lack thereof. Therefore, you should always develop your applications by using bind variables in all SQL statements and properly indexing the tables you use when necessary.

Next, we will introduce some of the most useful tools and utilities available for analyzing and measuring the performance of your SQL. Proper knowledge and use of these tools form the basis for advanced measures of SQL tuning, which we will study in the third section of the chapter. There, we will build on the foundations we laid in the first section, and illustrate more advanced steps in the tuning strategy. Specifically, we will study the details of the Oracle optimizer, and how you should tune your SQL according to your chosen optimizer approach. Additionally, we will illustrate some common caveats of using SQL that can be easily bypassed by properly rewriting your statements.

Lastly, we'll close up with a section on advanced SQL constructs and how to efficiently use SQL to its fullest. One important concept we'll look at here is the fact that doing as much as you can in a single SQL statement will generally outperform many times the same operation done in a "procedural" fashion. That is, you sometimes have to think in SQL (in sets) when developing a database application and SQL is inherently non-procedural. If you can achieve that type of thinking, you'll have gone a long way.

# First Steps In SQL Tuning

One of the reasons many people refrain from tuning their applications, is that with the whole range of tuning techniques available for the Oracle database, it is hard to know where the tuning process should start. Knowing that there is a problem – either potential or existing – is one thing, properly identifying its roots is something totally different. A novice Oracle developer could easily end up spending a lot of time and resources on tuning strategies that simply won't do any good, because they fail to properly address the source of the contention.

Earlier, we made a point that it is often most appropriate to begin tuning attempts at the SQL level, by properly analyzing the processing behavior of the SQL statements being run against the database. Of course, if you already know or suspect that the source of a particular performance problem has roots in other parts of the database system, you should target your efforts accordingly. In any case, considering the inherent bottleneck potential of SQL, it should be the goal of any developer to make sure that all his SQL statements are as optimized as possible.

Of all the approaches to SQL tuning, some of the most important ones are:

❑   Writing reusable SQL statements by always making use of bind variables and when applicable – stored procedures

❑   Appropriate use of indexes

❑   Doing all you can in a single SQL statement, avoiding procedural code whenever possible

Aside from being the most important steps, these are also usually the most simple to implement. Starting from scratch, with no tuning, to a highly tuned application, these basic steps will get you very far. It's that simple! Then, by adding a few of the more advanced tuning methods we study later in this chapter, you can end up, with little effort, with a fully optimized application.

However, before we can start tuning our SQL, it is necessary to understand how SQL statements are processed by Oracle. In the next few paragraphs, we will study the basics of that process.

# Oracle SQL Processing

When a SQL statement is issued against the Oracle database, it is the role of the **SQL compiler** to check the statement's syntax and determine how it is most efficiently executed. Once the compiler has properly verified and compiled the statement, it is sent off to the **SQL execution engine**, which is responsible for the execution of the compiled statement and the retrieval of results, if any.

The following diagram illustrates the process of SQL processing in the Oracle database:

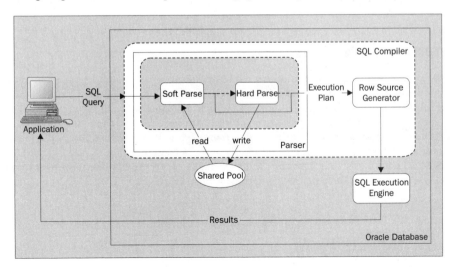

Each time a statement is received by the compiler, a **soft parse** occurs. During this phase, the compiler verifies the syntax and semantics of the statement's text and determines whether the user that issues the statement has permission to access the objects it references. At the end of the soft parse phase, the compiler calculates the hash value of the statement, which is used to identify it within the database. Next, the compiler searches the library cache of the **shared pool** to determine whether a statement with the same hash value exists. That is the case if an identical statement has already been issued against the database and stored in the library cache. If the compiler finds the statement in the library cache, it retrieves the information on the statement stored within the cache. This information includes the statement's **execution plan**, which is a set of algorithms used to identify the way in which the statement should be executed (we will discuss execution plans in more detail a little later). After the information has been obtained from the library cache, the next step is the **row source generator**, which generates a tree of row sources – where each row source maps to a specific row in a table – from the execution plan. The row source generator in turn passes the row source tree on to the execution engine, which executes the statement according to the tree. This is the most preferred sequence of events in the execution of a SQL statement, since it requires the least resources and takes the least time to perform.

If the SQL compiler does not find the specified statement in the library cache during the soft parse, a **hard parse** must be performed. A hard parse is the process of optimizing the statement, determining its ideal execution plan, and then storing the results in the library cache. This process can be the most time-consuming step in the whole execution of a SQL statement in many cases. For example, for a simple INSERT statement, 90% of the total execution time might be spent parsing the statement if you do not use bind variables. During a hard parse, the compiler must perform numerous calculations while optimizing the statement, which take up a considerable amount of system resources. Even worse is the impact this has on other parts of the database, as shared memory resources must be locked during the parsing process, when the compiler writes the statement along with its execution plan in the library cache. This is because each time a particular process updates a part of the shared pool, it gets a specific **latch** (a lightweight serialization device) for the pool, which indicates that the memory block referenced is being used. As a result, other processes that wish to access the block must be put on a queue for the duration of the latch. Excessive number of latches set during hard parses can therefore end up causing contention to the whole shared pool – with dramatic effects on the overall performance of the database.

Later, we will expand our knowledge of the Oracle SQL parsing process, and investigate the components that are put to work during the hard parsing phase in more detail.

# Fundamental Tuning Strategies

From what we have seen, the first step of any database tuning effort should be the elimination of unnecessary parsing, both hard and soft. Reduction of hard parses can be easily implemented by using **bind variables**, rather than hard-coded literals, in all SQL statements. Once the cost of hard parsing has been eliminated, with the appropriate use of bind variables, the next step of tuning should focus on the reuse of statements in your application. Soft parsing, while less important than hard parsing, still implies considerable work. You will lessen the soft parse burden by using Prepared and CallableStatements in your Java code and reusing those prepared statements over and over. Your goal is to parse a statement once per session – never more than once.

The next step in the tuning process will be the optimization of the SQL execution plan generated by the compiler. The execution plan tells the engine how it should execute the statement and fetch its results. Inefficient execution plans can therefore dramatically slow down the database. There are many ways of optimizing the execution plan, some of which involve the proper configuration of the Oracle **optimizer** – which is the process responsible for calculating the statement's execution plan – as we will study in detail later in this chapter. However, the first step in tuning the execution plan should be the careful planning of **indexes**, which can be used by the optimizer to speed up access to the data. Proper use of indexes can greatly increase the performance of the application, while their improper use can do just the opposite. Therefore, you should choose your indexes wisely, as we will illustrate later on.

These two fundamental aspects of SQL tuning – using bind variables and indexes – are the topics of this section.

# Using Bind Variables To Reuse Statements

The most important aspect of building successful and scalable database applications is the proper use of bind variables. Bind variables greatly eliminate the need for hard parsing in the database. So, you greatly reduce both the system resources required to execute your SQL statements and the time you lock shared memory resources from other parts of the database.

> **The importance of bind variables cannot be overstressed. Without their use, your applications will not scale – it's as simple as that.**

## Why Are Bind Variables So Important?

We have already illustrated the basic process of executing a SQL statement in Oracle. If the statement is being executed for the first time, the SQL compiler must perform a hard parse, which is a very resource- and time-consuming process. When the compiler evaluates a given SQL statement to determine its unique hash value, it looks at the text of the statement. Two statements that vary only in hard-coded literal values, are seen as two different statements by the compiler. This means that if you execute:

```
SQL> select * from dept where deptno = 10;
```

and moments later:

```
SQL> select * from dept where deptno = 20;
```

the compiler will perform two hard parses. Obviously, in a production environment, you can end up issuing the same statement with different literal values thousands of times – with according overhead.

In most databases, both the number of database objects and the characteristics of each object are usually limited. Although these things change with time – new tables are added; existing columns are dropped; and so on – such changes are usually not very rapid. As a result, there is generally a limit to the number of different actions that can be taken with SQL. That is, there are a finite number of questions (queries) you will ask of the data. On the other hand, however, there is virtually no limit to the data that can be contained by the database, and thus no limit to the possible statement-literal combinations. So, if you code "select * from emp where empno = 1234;"(using literals) and there are lots of employees – you have lots of queries to parse. If you code "select * from emp where emp = :x;", you have but one query.

This is where bind variables fit into the picture. With the use of bind variables, each statement is stored only once within the shared pool, which means that less memory is required for the library cache, less contention results from the locking of shared pool latches, and less resources are taken for hard parsing statements. With bind variables, we could rewrite the above statement using a bind variable as:

```
SQL> select * from dept where deptno = :b1;
```

and have it executed as often as required, by substituting the requested department number, with little overhead.

## Measuring the Advantages of Using Bind Variables

To give you a tangible demonstration of the advantages of using bind variables, we set up a simple example in which we measure the time it takes to execute a set of statements without bind variables and compare it with the time it takes to execute the same set of statements with bind variables.

For this example, we will use a small Java class that we will insert into a sample table using three different approaches:

❑ No bind variables, we will just use a simple `Statement` and execute a string

❑ Using bind variables, but soft parsing each time (not following the parse *once* per session rule)

❑ Using bind variables and parsing only *once* per session, not once per statement

We will load this Java class into the database and execute it as a Java stored procedure. Additionally we will be using the database utility `TKPROF`, explained in more detail later, to get detailed statistics regarding the performance of each approach.

For our example, we must create a sample table `NUM_STR` that is designed to hold a numerical column and a string column.

```
SQL> create table num_str (
  2      num number not null,
  3      str varchar2(100) not null
  4 );
```

In our examples, we will measure the time it takes to insert 10,000 records into our `NUM_STR` table, with and without bind variables and with and without reusing our parsed statement. To ensure that no previous operations affect our measurements, we should flush the shared pool memory, thereby removing all parsed statements from the library cache.

> Note that you must be logged on as a member of the DBA group, or a user that has been explicitly granted the `ALTER SYSTEM` privilege, in order to flush the shared pool.

```
SQL> alter system flush shared_pool;
```

The Java code we need to perform our test is as follows. It is a small class with three methods implementing the three tests we discussed above. We'll look at each in turn:

```
SQL> create or replace and compile java source named "binds"
  2  as
  3  import java.sql.*;
  4  import oracle.jdbc.driver.*;
  5  import oracle.sql.*;
  6
  7  class binds {
  8    static Connection conn = null;
  9
 10    public static void no_binds(int n) throws Exception {
 11      if (conn == null) {
 12        conn = DriverManager.getConnection("jdbc:oracle:kprb:", "", "");
 13
 14      }
 15      Statement stmt = conn.createStatement();
 16      for (int i = 0; i < n; i++) {
 17        stmt.execute("insert into num_str values " + "(" + i
 18                     + ", 'This is record#' || " + i + ")");
 19      }
 20    }
```

This is our first test; it simply creates a unique SQL statement for each insertion and inserts as many rows as we tell it to. Next, onto the routine that will use bind variables by utilizing a `PreparedStatement` – but it will still parse the statement each and every time:

```
 21    public static void binds_but_overparses(int n) throws Exception {
 22      if (conn == null) {
 23        conn = DriverManager.getConnection("jdbc:oracle:kprb:", "", "");
 24
 25      }
 26      PreparedStatement ps;
 27      for (int i = 0; i < n; i++) {
 28        ps = conn.prepareStatement("insert into num_str values
                                    ( ?, 'This is record#' || ? )");
 29
 30        ps.setInt(1, i);
 31        ps.setInt(2, i);
 32        ps.execute();
 33        ps.close();
 34      }
 35    }
```

That is much better than not using bind variables as we will see – but it still isn't the correct way. Until now, we have been focusing on the reduction of hard parses in the execution of SQL statements. We have already said that the hard parse is the most time- and resource-intensive phase in the execution of a new SQL statement, but we haven't mentioned how much weight the soft parse has in that process. In fact, as we will soon demonstrate, the soft parse *does* count for a considerable amount of time when we execute SQL. For each statement, the compiler must verify both the syntax and the semantics of the statement, and determine whether the process that issued the statement has permission to access the objects it refers to. Additionally, during the soft parse phase, the compiler must calculate the SQL hash value for the statement and attempt to look it up in the database library cache. So even though the statement is found in the cache, we are still performing a series of operations that must add up to some processing time. So how can we reduce the number of soft parses?

To reuse the SQL cursor for bulk SQL operations in Java – thereby performing only a single soft parse for each execution of the statement – we will use JDBC and declare the `PreparedStatement` instance globally, outside the loop executing the statement. This means that for N calls to either `executeUpdate()` or `executeQuery()` of the `PreparedStatement`, you have only a single call to `Connection.prepareStatement()`. The overhead of keeping an open cursor is minimal compared to the benefits of reducing the soft parse process.

In order to maximize efficiency, we must maximize reuse of the statement itself. We'll accomplish this in the last method named aptly enough `the_right_way`:

```
36    static PreparedStatement ps;
37
38    public static void the_right_way(int n) throws Exception {
39      if (conn == null) {
40        conn = DriverManager.getConnection("jdbc:oracle:kprb:", "", "");
41
42      }
43      if (ps == null) {
44        ps = conn.prepareStatement("insert into num_str values
                                        ( ?, 'This is record#' || ? )");
45
46      }
47      for (int i = 0; i < n; i++) {
48        ps.setInt(1, i);
49        ps.setInt(2, i);
50        ps.execute();
51      }
52    }
53  }
54  /
```

The last bit of setup we must do before testing with each of these methods is to create the PL/SQL wrapper procedures that enable us to call each method easily:

```
SQL> create or replace procedure no_binds( n in number )
  2  as language java
  3  name 'binds.no_binds( int )';
  4  /

SQL> create or replace procedure binds_but_overparses( n in number )
  2  as language java
  3  name 'binds.binds_but_overparses( int )';
  4  /

SQL> create or replace procedure the_right_way( n in number )
  2  as language java
  3  name 'binds.the_right_way( int )';
  4  /
```

To actually test, what we will do is run a script such as:

```
SQL> truncate table num_str;
SQL> alter system flush shared_pool;
SQL> exec &1(1)
SQL> alter session set max_dump_file_size = unlimited;
SQL> alter session set timed_statistics=true;
SQL> alter session set sql_trace=true;
SQL> exec &1(10000)
SQL> exit
```

and pass it no_binds, binds_but_overparses and the_right_way in turn. After each execution, we will use TKPROF to format the resulting trace file to see the performance characteristics of each. Note; TKPROF was not included with earlier Windows versions of Oracle9i. If you do not have it installed then please contact Oracle support, quoting bug report number #2007918.

We will explain TKPROF in detail later on in this chapter, but to run it you just need to be in the following trace file directory:

```
> cd c:\Oracle\admin\database\udump
```

You then run it using the following command:

```
> tkprof ORA24425.trc tkprof_report.txt
```

Where 24425 is the server process ID of the session for which the trace was enabled. Now we can read the tkprof_report.txt file, and view the report. For our system the outcome of the three runs was:

OVERALL TOTALS FOR ALL RECURSIVE STATEMENTS (no_binds)

| call | count | cpu | elapsed | disk | query | current | rows |
|---|---|---|---|---|---|---|---|
| Parse | 10000 | 9.21 | 9.06 | 0 | 0 | 0 | 0 |
| Execute | 10000 | 1.13 | 1.52 | 0 | 10032 | 10364 | 10000 |
| Fetch | 0 | 0.00 | 0.00 | 0 | 0 | 0 | 0 |
| total | 20000 | 10.34 | 10.58 | 0 | 10032 | 10364 | 10000 |

Misses in library cache during parse: 10000

OVERALL TOTALS FOR ALL RECURSIVE STATEMENTS (binds_but_overparses)

| call | count | cpu | elapsed | disk | query | current | rows |
|---|---|---|---|---|---|---|---|
| Parse | 10000 | 0.80 | 0.93 | 0 | 0 | 0 | 0 |
| Execute | 10000 | 2.06 | 1.94 | 0 | 10032 | 10364 | 10000 |
| Fetch | 0 | 0.00 | 0.00 | 0 | 0 | 0 | 0 |
| total | 20000 | 2.86 | 2.87 | 0 | 10032 | 10364 | 10000 |

Misses in library cache during parse: 1

```
OVERALL TOTALS FOR ALL RECURSIVE STATEMENTS (the_right_way)

call      count      cpu    elapsed  disk      query     current        rows
-------  ------  --------  ---------- -----  ---------- ----------  ----------
Parse         0    0.00      0.00       0          0          0           0
Execute   10000    1.42      1.42       0         32      10364       10000
Fetch         0    0.00      0.00       0          0          0           0
-------  ------  --------  ---------- -----  ---------- ----------  ----------
total     10000    1.42      1.42       0         32      10364       10000

Misses in library cache during parse: 0
```

As you can see – the results are rather dramatic. The test without bind variables is clearly the loser, we spent over 10 CPU seconds executing what the right approach did in less than 1.5 CPU seconds! The difference is measurably large. In the code sample above, we are performing a series of database operations – ten thousand in fact, which require only a single lookup in the shared library cache. We have already mentioned that each access to the shared pool sets a latch that effectively prevents other processes from accessing the memory block being accessed. Normally, all database locks can potentially cause contention, but when we are repeatedly locking up parts of a central memory structure used by *all* parts of the database, we can dramatically affect the processing of the database as a whole. This means that if we run our tests against a multi-user database, we would expect them to affect other concurrent users, in different levels though, since each user had to be put on a queue when asking for that part of the library cache we were working with. By reducing hard parses, we take the biggest step in cutting down the time we hold up the library cache, and by reducing soft parses, that time has been as good as eliminated.

## Methods of Using Bind Variables

With different methods of database access, there are different methods of variable binding in SQL. We've already explored it with JDBC above, now we'll look at other environments.

With static SQL, written either in PL/SQL or SQLJ, it is natural to use bind variables, as any variable of the language in question can be mixed freely with SQL types in the statement. More explicit measures must be taken with dynamic SQL, in either JDBC or PL/SQL, as we will illustrate below.

### Static SQL with PL/SQL

Use of bind variables is straightforward in static SQL executed in PL/SQL, by using PL/SQL variables instead of literals. For example:

```
SQL> set define off

SQL> declare
  2      l_dname varchar2(50) := 'RESEARCH & DEVELOPMENT';
  3      l_deptno number := 20;
  4  begin
  5      update emp set dname = l_dname where deptno = l_deptno;
  6      commit;
  7  end;
```

## Dynamic SQL with PL/SQL

For dynamic SQL in PL/SQL, bind variables are specified by using a colon (:) as a prefix to a specific variable name. The method of specifying the value for a declared bind variable varies with the method used to construct the SQL. For native dynamic SQL (constructed with the EXECUTE IMMEDIATE command), you specify variable values with the USING clause of EXECUTE IMMEDIATE, as illustrated below:

```
SQL> set define off

SQL> declare
  2        l_dname varchar2(50) := 'RESEARCH & DEVELOPMENT';
  3        l_deptno number := 20;
  4  begin
  5        execute immediate('update dept set dname = :bv1 where deptno = :bv2')
  6        using l_dname, l_deptno;
  7  end;
```

For dynamic SQL constructed with the DBMS_SQL package, you specify bind variable values using the DBMS_SQL.BIND_VARIABLE procedure:

```
SQL> set define off

SQL> declare
  2        l_dname varchar2(50) := 'RESEARCH & DEVELOPMENT';
  3        l_deptno number := 20;
  4        l_status integer;
  5        l_cur := integer;
  6  begin
  7        l_cur := dbms_sql.open_cursor;
  8        dbms_sql.parse(
  9            l_cur,
 10            'update dept set dname = :bv1 where deptno = :bv2',
 11            dbms_sql.native
 12        );
 13        dbms_sql.bind_variable(l_cur, ':bv1', l_dname);
 14        dbms_sql.bind_variable(l_cur, ':bv2', l_deptno);
 15        l_status := dbms_sql.execute(l_cur);
 16        dbms_sql.close_cursor(l_cur);
 17  exception when others then
 18        dbms_sql.close_cursor(l_cur);
 19  end;
```

## SQLJ

Just as with static SQL in PL/SQL, it is straightforward to use bind variables in SQLJ programs. Any Java variable of the appropriate type may serve as a SQL bind variable. In SQLJ, bind variables are prefixed by a colon within SQL statements. No further measures need to be taken – the Java variable is just used as it is, by simply adding a colon prefix. For example:

```
String deptName = "RESEARCH & DEVELOPMENT";
int deptNo = 20;
#sql {
  update dept set dname = :deptName where deptno = :deptNo;
  commit;
};
```

# Using Indexes

Indexing is crucial to any database application. Indexes are required to enforce data uniqueness, to avoid locking conflicts caused by foreign key constraints, and to speed up query execution. The last of these issues will be the focus of this section.

## How Does an Index Work?

A relational database table index works just like any other real-life index you are accustomed to. For example, at the end of this book, you will find an index of all the topics that are discussed in these pages. If you need to find information on the DBMS_JAVA PL/SQL package, for example, you look up the package name in the index, which tells you on which pages this package is mentioned. Without the index, you would have to scan through every page of this book and search every sentence for an indication of the package you seek for. Obviously, it takes less time to find a topic by using the index, and the same applies to an index a database table.

When you create an index in Oracle, you specify the **key** to which it should apply. An index key can be a single column or multiple columns, for which the relative order in which the columns are declared in the index is important – a topic we'll investigate below. When you have more than one column as the index key, the index is said to be a **composite index**. Additionally, you can use an index key (a function that takes for arguments one or more of the columns in the table). Such an index is only allowed for the **function-based** index type, which we will look at later.

## Pros and Cons of Indexes

As we have already seen, the main benefit of having an index on a table is that it generally allows those rows within the table that are looked up by the index to be located more efficiently than if the whole table had to be scanned (there are exceptions to this, as we will see later). For this purpose, there are many different types of indexes, each of which serves best for a particular data set.

However, an index does not come for free. Each time you modify the data contained with an indexed table (such as update, delete, or insert rows), Oracle must maintain the integrity of the index, which requires more work than without an index – the index is a complex data structure which must be maintained. Normally, this is not a problem, unless you end up with an excessive set of indexes on a single table, in which case you will begin to affect operations on its contents.

So, to conclude, using an index on a table will, in most cases:

❑ Speed up queries that look up rows by the index

❑ Slow down data manipulation – inserts, updates and deletes – to some extent

In each case, the benefits of using an index must be weighed against its cost. Generally, if the table in question has more queries than inserts and updates, you should index it by the columns most frequently used in the query predicates. However, if the table is rarely queried, and you are more worried about the performance of data manipulation operations, you should avoid using indexes – at least in excessive numbers.

## Oracle Index Types

With the variety of index types available for Oracle, care must be taken to choose the proper index for each scenario. The index types supported by Oracle are:

❑ **B*Tree Indexes** – A B*Tree (B "star" tree) index is the standard index used by Oracle, and by far the most commonly used. A B*Tree index works similar to a traditional binary tree, and provides fast access to one or many rows in a table. It is created with the CREATE INDEX statement and may be created when you add a primary key or foreign key constraint to a table. Additionally, you can supply the UNIQUE keyword when you create a B*Tree index, which effectively guarantees uniqueness within the index. For example:

```
SQL> create index hiredate_idx on emp(hiredate);
SQL> create unique index dname_idx on dept(dname);
SQL> create index ename_idx on emp(ename) desc;
```

A **regular** B*Tree index can only be ordered in ascending order. If you specified DESC in the CREATE INDEX clause for an index, Oracle will in fact create a function-based index, using an underlying B*Tree structure. As a result, to create an index in descending order, you must follow the same guidelines as for a function-based index (set privileges, use the Cost Based Optimizer, and so on), as we discuss below.

❑ **Bitmap Indexes** – A bitmap index associates a key value with a set of row IDs, which are stored as a bitmap. A bitmap index should be used for columns that have low cardinality. For example, a column with only two distinct values – such as 'Y' and 'N' – is a perfect candidate for a bitmap index. When you have a table with such low-cardinality columns, and you frequently specify the target column in a predicate, you should create a bitmap index. Additionally, bitmap indexes should be used for READ MOSTLY database tables as they are highly non-concurrent when updated due to their inherit structure and design. A bitmap index is created with the BITMAP keyword to the CREATE INDEX statement. For example:

```
SQL> create bitmap index gender_idx on persons (gender);
```

❑ **Function-Based Indexes** – A function-based index is an index based on a custom expression. The expression may include any combination of functions, either built-in or user-defined. A function-based index is created in much the same way as a "regular" index – for example:

```
SQL> Create index upper_ename_idx on emp(UPPER(ename));
```

That will create a function-based index that indexes the uppercase value of ENAME in the EMP table.

❑ **Domain Indexes** – A domain index is a custom index that is created using a specific API. You can create a custom domain index yourself, although we will not discuss that process in these pages. When you create a domain index, you implement methods that tell the SQL compiler details of the index structure (such as how selective it is), which the optimizer uses when deciding whether or not to use the index. An example of a domain index is the interMedia Text index, which is used to index text objects within the database.

Of the four index types we just mentioned, special care must be taken with function-based indexes.

## Function-Based Indexes

When you create an index on one or more columns in a table, you are only indexing the actual contents of those columns. In other words, you can only use the index if you use the columns in an expression in the specific manner in which they were defined in the index. If you create an index on the ENAME column in the EMP table, you could access a row by the index if you wrote a query like:

```
SQL> select * from emp where ename = 'MARTIN';
```

However, assume you wanted to select all employees whose name was MARTIN, Martin, martin, MarTin and so on (in mixed case). You could write that sort of query like:

```
SQL> select * from emp where upper(ename) = 'MARTIN';
```

This statement would work, but it would not use your index. By using the UPPER() function in the WHERE clause, you ruled out the possibility of using the index, since the index applies only to the ENAME column *as it is*. This applies to all built-in Oracle functions (such as. SUBSTR(), LOWER(), INSTR(), arbitrary expressions involving the columns (such as. COL1 + 2*COL2, UPPER(COL1) || '_' || COL2), and custom user-defined functions. This is easy to understand if you think of it in real terms. Just as you would not be able to look up a name in a phone book if you spelled it out backwards, you would not be able to use the ENAME index in a predicate which used it as an argument to a custom REVERSE() function (which would reverse the order of characters in a given string), as shown here:

```
SQL> select * from emp where reverse(ename) = 'NITRAM';
```

Although you can often rewrite a SQL statement to avoid using an expression in a predicate, there are times where it is mission-critical to use a particular expression in the WHERE or ORDER BY clause of a statement. To use such an expression and still enjoy the performance benefits of an index, you can create a function-based index on the table in question, using the specified expression. For example, if you have to be able to query the DEPT table for a specific department by its name, and you want your query to be case-insensitive, you could issue a statement like:

```
SQL> select * from dept where upper(dname) = upper(:bv1);
```

Without a function-based index, this statement would perform a full table scan on the DEPT table and execute the UPPER() function twice per row. In the case of a table containing thousands of rows, and possible a more complex expression predicate, this can dramatically affect performance.

Now, to solve that problem, you can create a function-based index on the DEPT table, using the UPPER(DNAME) expression as the indexed value:

```
SQL> create index dpet_upper_dname on dept (upper(dname));
```

A function-based index pre-computes the value of the index expression for each row, which means that it not only allows you to avoid a full table scan, it significantly reduces the number of times you have to evaluate the functional expression in question. Generally, consider using a function-based index on a table if you frequently use one of the columns in the table as an argument to a specific expression in a query predicate.

Unlike B*Tree and bitmap indexes, there is some setup involved with function-based indexes. If you attempted to create the above function index without going through the setup, the database probably will throw an error, as shown here:

```
create index emp_upper_ename on emp (upper (ename))
                                          *
ERROR at line 1:
ORA-01031: insufficient privileges
```

To be able to create function-based indexes, and have them actually used by the Oracle optimizer, you must:

❑ Grant your user the QUERY_REWRITE privilege

❑ Use the Cost-Based Optimizer (CBO)

❑ Set the following parameters on either a session-level (by using ALTER SESSION, for which you need to have the ALTER SESSION privilege) or instance-level (by modifying the database init.ora configuration file and restarting the database):

```
QUERY_REWRITE_ENABLED=TRUE
QUERY_REWRITE_INTEGRITY=TRUSTED
```

The first parameter tells the optimizer that it may rewrite the query to use the function-based index. The latter parameter tells the optimizer that it should trust the expression you provide with an index. If these are not set as illustrated, your index will be created, but never used.

As mentioned above, the cost-based optimizer approach must be used for a function-based index to be used. This means that you should gather statistics on the table in question before you use the index – in order to give the cost-based optimizer the information it needs to do its job.

Finally, some points to consider when using a function-based index:

❑ If the index expression includes references to a public synonym for a function in another schema, you must take care not to define later a function with the same name in your own schema. This will disable the index. If you enable or rebuild the index, it will attempt to use the original function referenced by the synonym, ignoring the local function.

❑ Take care when using a function that converts character data for an index. The index will use the NLS settings currently in effect when indexing the table in question. If these settings later change, the index may return incorrect results for older entries.

We will revisit function-based indexes later in this chapter, when we look at problems with implicit type conversion and unnecessary use of functions in statement predicates.

## Using Composite Indexes

A composite index is an index that contains more than one column as a key. Oracle allows up to 32 columns to make up a composite index. A primary key is often specified as a composite index, especially in the case of join tables, which connect together two or more tables (like a CUSTOMER_ADDRESSES table that joins together the CUSTOMERS and ADDRESSES tables).

A composite index created on a series of columns is typically only used by a SQL statement if the statement involves a construct that uses a **leading portion** of the index. The leading portion of an index is one or more of the columns used by the index, in the same order as they were specified at index creation time. As a result, the order in which columns are specified for an index is important. For example, look at the following table, which is indexed by columns A, B and C, in that order:

```
SQL> create table t (
  2   a number,
  3   b number,
  4   c number
  5  );

SQL> create index tidx on t (a,b,c);
```

> *In terms of performance, you should specify the order of the columns in a composite index from the most likely to be queried to the least.*

A leading portion of the TIDX index can be any one of the following three column combinations:

❑   A

❑   A, B

❑   A, B, C

However, these combinations do not make up a leading portion of the index:

❑   B

❑   C

❑   B, C

This means that if you write a statement that specifies only a criterion for column B, the statement will *generally* not be able to make use of the index in the execution plan.

> *Oracle9i added a new feature, the index skip scan. This feature does allow a query that specifies a criterion for column B to use the index that begins with A under certain special conditions. It is beyond the scope of this chapter to describe this fully, you can refer to http://download-west.oracle.com/otndoc/oracle9i/901_doc/server.901/a87503/optimops.htm#51553 for a full description.*

For example:

```
SQL> -- These statements will use the index.
SQL> select * from t where a = :bv1;
SQL> select * from t where a = :bv1 and b = :bv2;
SQL> select * from t where a = :bv1 and b = :bv2 and c = :bv3;

SQL> -- These statements will in GENERAL not use the index.
SQL> select * from t where b = :bv1;
SQL> select * from t where c = :bv1;
SQL> select * from t where b = :bv1 and c = :bv2;
```

*Note that the order in which the predicates appear in the statement does not matter – only the existence of each predicate. That is, you can say "where a = :bv1 and b = :bv2" or "where b = :bv2 and a = :bv1", the order of the conditions in the predicate is not relevant.*

A phone book is an example of a real-world composite index you should be familiar with. Suppose you have a company phone book that specifies an index on the name, address and occupation of each employee, ordered accordingly. If you search for a phone number only by the name of the employee, you would end up with a set of possible candidates, which you would have to scan through to get the desired result (that is, you would probably have to call each number you get and determine whether it belongs to the person you are looking for). However, it would be more efficient to include the address and occupation in your search, in which case you would more likely end up with a single phone number. The same argument applies to a composite table index – the more columns of the index you supply in your predicates, the more you narrow your search. And just as you can't generally use a table index unless you use the leading portion of the index, you cannot search the phone book by using only an address or occupation – unless you resort to a full page scan.

*Note that a phone book index does not have to be unique; there is nothing that prevents two people with the same name and the same occupation from living together, though that is probably not very common.*

So what are the advantages of using a composite index? A composite index can be useful if you have two or more columns in a table with poor selectivity, that combined make up better selectivity. Additionally, a composite index can greatly reduce the I/O required for a query if all of the columns selected are contained within the index (in which case, the cost-based optimizer will select the column values directly from the index). Generally, you should consider using a composite index on a set of columns that are frequently selected together in your queries, separated by the AND operator.

However, composite indexes come with their cost. Whereas there is always a performance trade-off when updating a table with an index, this trade-off magnifies when you add more columns, since more work must take place for each update.

## Problems With Indexes

Unfortunately, the mere task of indexing does not always increase the performance of your application. To actually do any good, an index must of course be used. It is far too common to see people apply indexes to solve a particular performance problem, only to find out later that those same indexes are never being used by the optimizer. So how can you make sure that your precious indexes are being used as expected? We will investigate that further later in this chapter, when we study the details of the Oracle SQL processing architecture – specifically, the different approaches of SQL optimization performed by the SQL compiler during the parsing phase.

Indexes should not be applied without an estimation of what it is that they should accomplish. In some cases, using an index might even slow down the process of accessing your data. Such can be true if you access an excessive number of rows as a percentage of the table via an index or have a table containing small amounts of data, where a full table scan will outperform retrieval by index at any time.

### Indexing Small Tables

If you were to locate a particular topic in this book by a page number, it would be far more efficient to look it up in the index at the end of the book, rather than scanning through all its pages, as we have previously mentioned. On the other hand, if you had to find a particular headline in a three-page advertising brochure, it would probably be more efficient to just flip through the pages, rather than use an index at the back. The same argument applies to database tables. If you have a table that contains a limited number of rows, a full table scan would probably outperform an index lookup at any given time. To perform an index lookup, you must begin by scanning the index for the specified key, reading the row ID of the respective row, and then reading the row from the table by using the row ID. A full table scan, on the other hand, would probably only require a single read operation, since the table contained only a few rows.

Such an example, where a full table scan would probably be more efficient than an index lookup, is a table that defines a set of limited templates or object types, which are referenced by the respective ID in other tables. For example, you could have a table called COUNTRIES, which contained only a COUNTRY_NAME and a COUNTRY_CODE. This table could contain at most a few hundred rows, but more likely just a few dozens, depending on the business requirements, which means that a full table scan would always outperform an index lookup.

To avoid using an index for a given table, you can either avoid creating the index in the first place, or tell the optimizer to perform a full table scan, by supplying a specific optimizer hint, as we will observe later.

# First Steps in SQL Tuning Wrap-Up

So, to conclude, you should first focus your tuning efforts at optimizing the parsing stage of the SQL execution process. Aside from being the most obvious process to optimize, it is also the most time-consuming, which means that even minor efforts spent on tuning the parsing process will usually result in considerable performance gain. The most important, single operation related to the tuning of the parsing process, is the use of bind variables in SQL statements. While the mere presence of bind variables won't ensure that your application will scale, their absence will definitely ensure that it will not. Even though bind variables reduce the number of hard parses performed for your SQL statements, they do not directly reduce the number of soft parses. The time taken for soft parses to check the syntax of a statement and look up its execution plan in the library cache can add up considerably when performing a series of operations. Therefore, whenever possible, you should avoid soft parses by caching up your SQL cursor and reusing it as often as necessary within the same execution context.

When you have optimized the parsing process, you should turn your attention to tuning the actual execution of your SQL. The first step in doing that is to set up appropriate indexes to your tables. Carefully chosen indexes can significantly speed up access to your data by reducing the table scans and reads necessary for retrieval. However, whereas efforts at tuning the parsing process are rather straightforward to implement, more care must be taken with indexes. Every index will add overhead to data manipulation performed on the table, which may become intolerable at a particular point. In some cases an index may even slow down the process of retrieval, as we saw previously when we compared an index with a full table scan on small tables.

# Analyzing Queries

Before we can move on to more advanced areas of SQL tuning, it is necessary to get familiar with some of the Oracle tools and utilities for analyzing the execution plan and processing of SQL. Specifically, in this section, we will study:

- ❑ **EXPLAIN PLAN** – This command can be used to view the execution plan as selected by the optimizer for a given SQL statement

- ❑ **AUTOTRACE** – This is similar to EXPLAIN PLAN, but more simple to use and adds additional information (AUTOTRACE is a part of the SQL*PLUS program)

- ❑ **SQL Trace** – This utility writes all SQL activity for either a given session or the whole database instance down to a raw trace file in the file system

- ❑ **TKPROF** – Used in conjunction with SQL Trace, TKPROF is a command line tool that can be used to generate reports from raw trace files.

# Explain Plain and Autotrace

Often, it can be useful to generate statistics on the execution plan for a given SQL statement, without much trouble. For this purpose, Oracle provides a command, EXPLAIN PLAN, which can be invoked through SQL. The EXPLAIN PLAN command takes the execution plan of the specified statement and stores it in a specific database table – called the PLAN_TABLE –, which can later be queried for the plan of a specific statement.

When working with SQL*PLUS, there is another alternative for viewing the execution plan of a given statement, a command called AUTOTRACE. The AUTOTRACE command can be used to activate automatic execution plan tracing for the current session, which will effectively display the plan for each statement issued. The advantages of AUTOTRACE over EXPLAIN PLAN is that you don't have to query the plan table specifically to get the actual output – it is just displayed automatically on your screen. Additionally, you can view many statistics regarding the execution of your query such as physical and logical I/O performed.

Both EXPLAIN PLAN and AUTOTRACE are designed to interpret exactly what a SQL statement will do. EXPLAIN PLAN provides little information to help decide whether the given plan is a good idea, or not. AUTOTRACE on the other hand can give us a great deal of information about the execution characteristics of a query. As a result, EXPLAIN PLAN is very limited as a tuning tool. However, it can be useful when comparing two semantically equal, but syntactically different statements, since they allow you to see what execution plan is chosen for each.

## Explain Plan

The EXPLAIN PLAN command executes the Oracle optimizer against a SQL statement and inserts the execution plan for the statement into another table, usually referred to as the **plan table**. The plan table is, by default, named PLAN_TABLE. Below, we will guide you through the setup of the default plan table that ships with Oracle.

## Setting Up the Plan Table

The EXPLAIN PLAN statement requires the presence of the plan table in order to store the descriptions of the row sources. The script to create this table can be found in a file named utlxplan.sql in the ORACLE_HOME/rdbms/admin/ directory. Assuming you are located in ORACLE_HOME/bin/, open up SQL*PLUS as the user you wish to explain for, and issue the following command:

```
SQL> @%ORACLE_HOME%/rdbms/admin/utlxplan.sql

Table created.
```

This is all the setup required for EXPLAIN PLAN.

## Using Explain Plan

When you have created the plan table, you can issue the EXPLAIN PLAN command for an arbitrary SQL statement you wish to analyze, as shown here:

```
SQL> explain plan
  2    set statement_id=identifier
  3    for
  4    statement;
```

This will explain the plan for the specified statement into the PLAN_TABLE table (this is by default, but you can optionally specify another destination table). Later, you can select the execution plan from the plan table, by supplying the specified identifier. For example, suppose you explained a plan as illustrated here:

```
SQL> explain plan
  2    set statement_id='depts_emps'
  3    for
  4    select e.ename, d.dname
  5      from emp e, dept d
  6    where e.deptno = d.deptno
  7    order by e.ename;

Explained.
```

To display the explain plan for the given statement, you could write a custom query which selects from the PLAN_TABLE, for a specified statement identifier. For example, using SQL*PLUS, the following script will prompt for an identifier and display the execution plan for the statement associated:

```
SQL> select
  2       lpad(' ',level-1) ||
  3       operation || ' ' ||
  4       options || ' ' ||
  5       object_name "Plan"
  6  from plan_table
  7  connect by prior id = parent_id
  8       and prior statement_id = statement_id
  9  start with id = 0
 10       and statement_id = '&identifier'
 11  order by id;
```

Assuming you saved the above query in a script file named `ep.sql`, you should get a plan similar to the one shown here:

```
SQL> @ep
Enter value for identifier: depts_emps
old  10:        and statement_id = '&identifier'
new  10:        and statement_id = 'depts_emps'

Plan
----------------------------------------------------------


SELECT STATEMENT
 SORT ORDER BY
  MERGE JOIN
   SORT JOIN
    TABLE ACCESS FULL DEPT
   SORT JOIN
    TABLE ACCESS FULL EMP

7 rows selected.
```

So what does this execution plan tell us? To read from the plan, it is best to advance bottom-up. From that, we can see that in order to execute this statement, the database must perform a full table scan on the EMP table (which we could have guessed, since we are selecting all its rows), and for each row in EMP, we must perform another full table scan on DEPT. The two tables are sort joined and the results merged and finally sorted.

By default, the demo tables that come with SQL*Plus (EMP and DEPT) are not built with indexes. To fix that, we create primary keys for both EMP and DEPT and a foreign key to EMP, as shown here:

```
SQL> alter table dept
  2        add constraint pk_dept primary key (deptno);
SQL> alter table emp
  2        add constraint pk_emp primary key (empno);
SQL> alter table emp
  2        add constraint fk_emp_dept foreign key (deptno) references dept;
```

Now, if we re-execute the DELETE FROM PLAN_TABLE, run the EXPLAIN PLAN for this statement again, and select the plan generated from the plan table as before, we should get:

```
Plan
---------------------------------------------------
SELECT STATEMENT
 SORT ORDER BY
  NESTED LOOPS
   TABLE ACCESS FULL EMP
   TABLE ACCESS BY INDEX ROWID DEPT
    INDEX UNIQUE SCAN PK_DEPT

6 rows selected.
```

This looks much better (but we all know that looks can be deceiving and we'll see that in the next section). Now we are scanning the EMP table as before (which is what we want anyway), but for each row we access the DEPT table through the foreign key, by the row ID.

## Autotrace

When using SQL*Plus for database access, you can make use of the built-in AUTOTRACE command to get a report on the execution plan used by the optimizer for a given statement, rather than using EXPLAIN PLAN. Of the two, AUTOTRACE is simpler to use, since it does not require you to select the plan from the plan table. Rather, the plan is displayed directly on the screen after a successful statement, along with optional statistics.

### Setting Up Autotrace

To use the AUTOTRACE command with SQL*Plus, you must create the PLUSTRACE role for the SYS account and grant that role to those schemas that should be able to use the utility. The script to set up the PLUSTRACE role is located under the ORACLE_HOME/sqlplus/admin/ directory. Assuming you are located in ORACLE_HOME/bin/, you would set up this role as illustrated:

```
SQL> connect sys;

SQL> @..%ORACLE_HOME%/sqlplus/admin/plustrce
```

Next, you should grant the PLUSTRACE role to those schemas that should be able to use the utility. In the following example, we grant PLUSTRACE to PUBLIC, which allows everyone to use it (no security considerations to keep in mind, so this is generally recommended):

```
SQL> grant plustrace to public;
```

### Autotrace Options

Once you have created and granted the PLUSTRACE role, you can enable AUTOTRACE by issuing the SQL*Plus command SET AUTOTRACE. This command has a few options:

❑   SET AUTOTRACE OFF – This disables AUTOTRACE. This is the default option.

❑   SET AUTOTRACE ON – This enables AUTOTRACE. For each DML command, AUTOTRACE generates a report, which includes both the optimizer execution path and the SQL statement execution statistics.

❑   SET AUTOTRACE ON EXPLAIN – This enables AUTOTRACE for reports which show only the optimizer execution path.

❑   SET AUTOTRACE ON STATISTICS – This enables AUTOTRACE for reports that show only the SQL statement execution statistics.

❑   SET AUTOTRACE TRACEONLY – This enables AUTOTRACE for reports that include both the optimizer execution path and the SQL statement execution statistics. However, unlike SET AUTOTRACE ON, this option suppresses the printing of the user's query output, if any.

## Using Autotrace

To illustrate the use of AUTOTRACE, let's look at the same query we worked with in the section on the EXPLAIN PLAN:

```
SQL> set autotrace traceonly;

SQL> select e.ename, d.dname
  2    from emp e, dept d
  3    where e.deptno = d.deptno
  4    order by e.ename;
```

This should produce an output similar to the following:

```
Execution Plan
----------------------------------------------------------
   0      SELECT STATEMENT Optimizer=CHOOSE
   1    0   SORT (ORDER BY)
   2    1     NESTED LOOPS
   3    2       TABLE ACCESS (FULL) OF 'EMP'
   4    2       TABLE ACCESS (BY INDEX ROWID) OF 'DEPT'
   5    4         INDEX (UNIQUE SCAN) OF 'PK_DEPT' (UNIQUE)


Statistics
Statistics
----------------------------------------------------------
      0  recursive calls
      2  db block gets
     29  consistent gets
      0  physical reads
      0  redo size
   1119  bytes sent via SQL*Net to client
    503  bytes received via SQL*Net from client
      2  SQL*Net roundtrips to/from client
      1  sorts (memory)
      0  sorts (disk)
     14  rows processed
```

We can immediately see that the execution plan on the upper half of the report matches the plan generated by EXPLAIN_PLAN earlier. The statistics on the lower half of the report are recorded by AUTOTRACE when the statement is executed and indicate the system resources required to execute the statement. The most important of these statistics are summarized below:

❑ **DB Block Gets** – This is a count of logical reads that include access for block updates and requests for segment header information. Combined with consistent gets, below, these two make up the number of logical reads.

❑ **Consistent Gets** – This is a count of logical reads or block accesses that can be retrieved without read consistency problems. If the data being read is altered during the duration of the query (for example, by another process), this count is increased.

❑ **Physical Reads** – This is a count of the physical reads from disk necessary to satisfy the logical reads discussed above. Together, the three counts can be used to determine the *cache hit ratio* (the number of times data was found in the cache divided by the number of read attempts), as:

```
((consistent gets + db block gets) - physical reads) /
(consistent gets + db block gets)
```

For example, in our report above, the cache-hit ratio was exactly 1.0 – all the data was found in the cache (as a result of our previous execution of this statement, presumably). Generally, this number should be as near to one as possible. A low cache ratio indicates that not enough memory has been allocated for the buffer cache.

❑ **Bytes Sent/Received via SQL*Net to/from the Client** – These two counts (measured in bytes) indicate the network traffic generated by the statement.

❑ **SQL*Net Roundtrips to/from Client** – This is the number of message round trips transmitted over the network during the execution of the query. These transmissions can cause network latency, especially when working in a three-tier scenario (shouldn't be too expensive in our case, working with Java inside the database).

Looking at the results, we can see that we performed 29 `consistent gets` on this particular query. If you recall, earlier we made a comment about "looks can be deceiving", it would appear that this plan is the good plan – it uses an index (and indexes are "good"). In this case however, these tables are so small that the index actually impedes performance. If we analyze the tables and rerun the query:

```
SQL> analyze table emp compute statistics;
SQL> analyze table dept compute statistics;
SQL> select e.ename, d.dname
  2  from emp e, dept d
  3  where e.deptno = d.deptno
  4  order by e.ename;

Execution Plan
----------------------------------------------------------
   0      SELECT STATEMENT Optimizer=CHOOSE (Cost=7 Card=14 Bytes=252)
   1    0   SORT (ORDER BY) (Cost=7 Card=14 Bytes=252)
   2    1     HASH JOIN (Cost=3 Card=14 Bytes=252)
   3    2       TABLE ACCESS (FULL) OF 'DEPT' (Cost=1 Card=4 Bytes=44)
   4    2       TABLE ACCESS (FULL) OF 'EMP' (Cost=1 Card=14 Bytes=98)


Statistics
----------------------------------------------------------
      0  recursive calls
      4  db block gets
      2  consistent gets
      0  physical reads
      0  redo size
   1119  bytes sent via SQL*Net to client
    503  bytes received via SQL*Net from client
```

```
 2  SQL*Net roundtrips to/from client
 1  sorts (memory)
 0  sorts (disk)
14  rows processed
```

We can see we can do much better by not using an index. Notice also the new information displayed by AUTOTRACE here. Each step of the plan has three pieces of extra information:

❑ COST: relative cost of executing that part of the query plan. Used by the COST based optimizer when choosing among many alternate plans for the same query.

❑ CARD: Short for cardinality, it is an estimate of the number of rows this part of the plan will produce. Note how it estimates four rows for the full scan of DEPT and 14 rows for the full scan of EMP. After the HASH JOIN it estimates all 14 rows will be output. This information is derived from the statistics we collected on the table.

❑ BYTES: An estimation of the size of the data produced by each step in bytes. This is cardinality times average row size.

# SQL Trace and TKPROF

Together, the SQL Trace facility and the TKPROF command line utility enable detailed tracing of the activity that takes place within the database. In short, SQL Trace is used to write performance information on individual SQL statements down to trace files in the file system of the database server. Under normal circumstances, these trace files are hard to comprehend directly. For that purpose, you use the TKPROF utility to generate text-based report files from the input of a given trace file.

## SQL Trace

The SQL Trace facility is used to trace all SQL activity of a specified database session or instance down to a trace file in the database server operating system. Each entry in the trace file records a specific operation performed while the Oracle server process is processing a SQL statement. SQL Trace was originally intended for debugging, and is still well suited for that purpose, but can just as equally be used to analyze the SQL activity of the database, for tuning purposes.

### Setting Up SQL Trace

SQL Trace can be enabled for either a single session or a whole database instance. It is, however, rarely enabled at a database level, since that would cause serious performance problems – remember that SQL Trace writes every SQL statement processed to a log file, with according I/O activity.

Enable tracing for a session at a selected interval – avoid having tracing in effect for long periods of time. This is because of the increased I/O overhead that results from its use. To enable tracing for the current session, you should issue ALTER SESSION, as shown here:

```
SQL> alter session set sql_trace=true;
```

Likewise, to disable the current trace operation, you execute:

```
SQL> alter session set sql_trace=false;
```

## Adding Timing Functionality

There is another important parameter that should be set before using SQL Trace, namely TIMED_STATISTICS. This parameter specifies whether Oracle should measure the execution time for various internal operations. Without this parameter set, there is much less value to the trace file output. As with other parameters, you can set TIMED_STATISTICS either on an instance-level (in init.ora) or session-level. The former should not affect performance, so it is generally recommended. On a session-level, you would issue:

```
SQL> alter session set timed_statistics=true;
```

## Controlling the Trace Files

The trace files generated by SQL Trace can eventually grow quite large. A few global initialization parameters, set in init.ora for the database instance or session settings, affect the trace files. If enabled, SQL Trace will write to a file in the operating-system directory indicated by the USER_DUMP_DEST initialization parameter. You should note that trace files for USER processes (dedicated servers) go to the USER_DUMP_DEST directory. Trace files generated by Oracle background processes such as the shared servers used with MTS and Job queue processes used with the job queues will go to the BACKGROUND_DUMP_DEST. It should further be noted that trace files from these background processes are generally useless – do not use SQL_TRACE with a shared server configuration! That is because your session will hop from shared server to shared server – generating trace information not in one but in *many* trace files rendering it useless.

Trace files are usually named:

```
ora<spid>.trc,
```

where *<spid>* is the server process ID of the session for which the trace was enabled.

On Windows, the following query may be used to retrieve your sessions trace file name:

```
SQL> select c.value || '\ORA' || to_char(a.spid,'fm00000') || '.trc'
  2    from v$process a, v$session b, v$parameter c
  3   where a.addr = b.paddr
  4     and b.audsid = userenv('sessionid')
  5     and c.name = 'user_dump_dest';
```

Whereas on Unix, this query can be used to retrieve it:

```
SQL> select c.value || '/' || d.instance_name || '_ora_' ||
  2              to_char(a.spid,'fm99999') || '.trc'
  3    from v$process a, v$session b, v$parameter c, v$instance d
  4   where a.addr = b.paddr
  5     and b.audsid = userenv('sessionid')
  6     and c.name = 'user_dump_dest';
```

You should note that naming conventions for trace files might differ between individual versions of Oracle and SQL Trace. Therefore, if the trace file function above does not seem to indicate the correct trace file, you can always search for the server process ID in the names of existing files, or locate the most recent file, if you are working on a local development database.

The size of the trace files is restricted by the value of the MAX_DUMP_FILE_SIZE initialization parameter set in init.ora for the database instance. You may also alter this at the session level using the ALTER SESSION command, for example:

```
SQL> alter session set max_dump_file_size = unlimited;
Session altered.
```

# TKPROF

The TKPROF utility takes a SQL Trace trace file as input and produces a text-based report file as output. It is a very simple utility, summarizing a large set of detailed information in a given trace file so that it can be understood for performance tuning.

## Using TKPROF

TKPROF is a simple command line utility that is used to translate a raw trace file to a more comprehensible report. In its simplest form, TKPROF can be used as shown here:

```
>tkprof <trace-file-name> <report-file-name>
```

Other options are available – specifically, various useful sorting options – which we will not discuss in this context. For more information on the options associated with TKPROF, you can simply issue:

```
>tkprof
```

and a list of options will be displayed:

*Additionally, you can lookup the TKPROF on-line documentation, at http://download-west.oracle.com/otndoc/oracle9i/901_doc/server.901/a87503/sqltrace.htm.*

## Generating a Report

To illustrate the joint use of TKPROF and SQL Trace, we will set up a simple example. Specifically, we will trace the query we used previously in our EXPLAIN PLAN examples, and generate a report from the resulting trace file. First, we must log on to SQL*PLUS as the intended user, and then execute the code below:

```
SQL> set serveroutput on;
SQL> select c.value || '\ORA' || to_char(a.spid,'fm00000') || '.trc'
  2    from v$process a, v$session b, v$parameter c
  3    where a.addr = b.paddr
  4      and b.audsid = userenv('sessionid')
  5      and c.name = 'user_dump_dest';
SQL> -- remember the output of the above query so we can tkprof it later

SQL> alter session set timed_statistics=true;
SQL> alter session set sql_trace=true;

SQL> select e.ename, d.dname
```

```
  2   from emp e, dept d
  3   where e.deptno = d.deptno
  4   order by e.ename;

SQL> exit;
```

Next, we log on to the command prompt, go to the specified trace file directory, and use TKPROF to generate a report:

```
>cd c:\Oracle\admin\database\udump
>tkprof ORA24425.trc tkprof_report.txt

TKPROF: Release 8.1.6.0.0 - Production on Sun- Okt 14 03:25:44 2001

(c) Copyright 1999 Oracle Corporation.  All rights reserved.
```

Now we can read the tkprof_report.txt file, and view the report.

### Analyzing the Output from TKPROF

Continuing from our previous example, we proceed to analyze the contents of the tkprof_report.txt report file.

At the top of the report, we see the actual SQL statement we issued.

```
select e.ename, d.dname
from emp e, dept d
where e.deptno = d.deptno
order by e.ename
```

Next, we get the execution report for the statement. This report (included below) is illustrated for the three different phases of Oracle SQL processing: parse, fetch and execute. This corresponds to the SQL processing architecture we discussed earlier.

For each processing phase, we see: the number of times that phase occurred; the CPU time elapsed for the phase; the real-world time that elapsed; the number of physical I/O operations took place on the disk; the number of blocks processed in 'consistent-read' mode; the number of blocks read in 'current mode' (reads that occur when the data is changed by an external process during the duration of the statement processing); and the number that were affected by the statement.

What all of these figures mean, depends on the type of statement being executed.

❑  **SELECT Statement** – Here, most of the work should take place during the FETCH phase. ROWS represents the rows that were returned by the query.

❑  **INSERT, DELETE or UPDATE Statement** – For these statements, most of the work should take place during the EXECUTE phase. ROWS represents the rows that were affected by the modification that took place.

When looking at the execution report, there are a few 'red flags' you should watch out for:

❑ **Many Statements Executed But Once** – This might indicate that you are not using bind variables in your SQL. If you were, the same statement would appear executed more than once.

❑ **Large Difference between CPU Time and Elapsed Time** – This indicates that the process spent a lot of time just *waiting* for something to finish. There are numerous explanations for that; such as, because of contention in the shared pool, which can be a result of not using bind variables, another is a wait for physical I/O to occur.

❑ **High Disk Count** – This might indicate that the buffer cache is not big enough. Try to trace the statement again. If the DISK count is still high, consider resizing your buffer cache.

The execution report is shown below:

| call | count | cpu | elapsed | disk | query | current | rows |
| --- | --- | --- | --- | --- | --- | --- | --- |
| Parse | 1 | 0.00 | 0.00 | 0 | 0 | 0 | 0 |
| Execute | 1 | 0.00 | 0.00 | 0 | 0 | 0 | 0 |
| Fetch | 2 | 0.00 | 0.00 | 0 | 15 | 4 | 7 |
| total | 4 | 0.00 | 0.00 | 0 | 15 | 4 | 7 |

Following the execution report, we can see optimizer approach used (CHOOSE, we will discuss that later) and the user ID of the session that enabled the trace (you can match this ID against the ALL_USERS table to get the actual user name).

```
Misses in library cache during parse: 0
Optimizer goal: CHOOSE
Parsing user id: 78
```

Additionally, we see the number of times the statement was not found in the library cache. The first time a statement is executed this count should be one, but zero in subsequent calls if bind variables are used. Again, watch out for the absence of bind variables – a large number of library cache misses would indicate that.

Finally, the report displays the execution plan used for this statement. This information is nearly identical to that of AUTOTRACE and EXPLAIN PLAN, with the important difference that the number of actual rows flowing out of each step in the plan is revealed to us. Note, though, that instead of referencing the name of the DEPT table primary key, as we saw for example with AUTOTRACE, the trace report displays only the object ID of the index. If you look up this object ID, it should in fact reveal that this is in fact the PK_DEPT index.

*There is an option for TKPROF to have all objects' names spelled out – the EXPLAIN option – but it is not generally recommended for use.*

```
Rows      Row Source Operation
-------   -----------------------------------------------------
    7     SORT ORDER BY
    7      NESTED LOOPS
    8       TABLE ACCESS FULL EMP
    7       TABLE ACCESS BY INDEX ROWID DEPT
   14         INDEX UNIQUE SCAN (object id 21669)
```

# Advanced SQL Tuning

Once you have taken the first steps of SQL tuning, and armed yourself with the analyzing utilities, it is time to explore some of the more advanced issues of SQL tuning. In this section we will study some of those issues, including:

❑ The functionality of the rule-based optimizer, and how it fails to provide for a reflective SQL optimization

❑ The advantages of the cost-based optimizer, and how you generate statistics to use with it

❑ Methods of rewriting and tuning your SQL statements, to reflect your choice of optimizer approach

We start this section, however, by expanding our view of the Oracle SQL processing architecture.

# Details of Oracle SQL Processing

When performing a hard parse on a statement, Oracle makes a choice of one of two SQL **optimizer approaches**, used to optimize the statement and generate its optimal execution plan. These two optimizer approaches are:

❑ **The Rule-Based Optimizer (RBO)** – This optimizer uses a set of predefined rules to determine the best execution plan for a statement. It does not take into account the actual status of the objects in question, just their definition. Additionally the syntax of the query counts heavily using the RBO – a simple reorder of the tables in the FROM clause can and will result in a radically different plan. As a result, the RBO often generates far from optimal execution plans, and should generally not be used.

❑ **The Cost-Based Optimizer (CBO)** – This optimizer generates an execution plan based on available statistics on the objects in question. If no statistics are available, the optimizer synthesizes best guess statistics for objects based on heuristics and sizes of extents. The CBO should generally be used for all applications.

The optimizer is further illustrated in the following diagram.

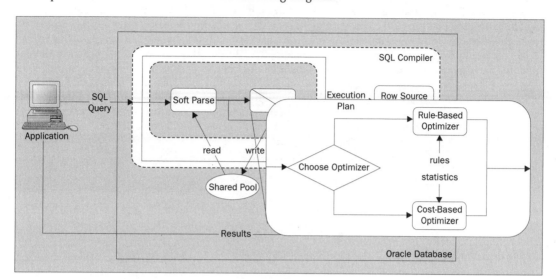

In the next few sections, we will study both optimizer approaches in more detail. We will start by the rule-based approach, and later advance to the cost-based approach.

# The Rule-Based Optimizer

The rule-based optimizer (RBO) chooses an execution plan for SQL statements based on the access paths available and the ranks of these access paths (if there is more than one way, then the RBO uses the operation with the lowest rank). An access path is a method of getting to the data in the table – for example, you might access the table via an INDEX, a FULL SCAN, or by ROWID. If no statistics are available, and you are not accessing any objects that force the use of the CBO such as a partitioned table, an index organized table, a table with a non-default degree of parallelism to name a few – the RBO is used, otherwise the CBO is used.

When building an execution plan for a specific SQL statement, there is a limited amount of information available to the rule-based optimizer. Specifically, there are three main sources of information that the optimizer can access:

❑ The text of the actual SQL statement

❑ Rudimentary information about the objects referenced in the statement, such as the structure of tables and views and the data types of columns being referenced

❑ Basic information about the indexes associated with the tables referenced by the SQL statement

**675**

This is further illustrated in the following diagram. The SQL statement in the diagram depicted selects three columns from the standard EMP and DEPT tables. If the RBO were to optimize this statement, it would know only that two of the columns are of type VARCHAR2 and one of type NUMBER, and that the two tables referenced have no indexes of any kind (that is true for the default demo tables as set up in the SCOTT schema). From this rudimentary information, the RBO would have to assess a proper execution plan for the statement in question. This plan would be the same as long as the statement does not change and no changes are made to the tables referenced. In other words, using the RBO, we would execute this statement the same way for a table containing a handful of rows as we would for a table containing vast amounts of data. The RBO makes no evaluation of the magnitude of data contained by individual objects or the state of referenced indexes, since it has no means of accessing such information.

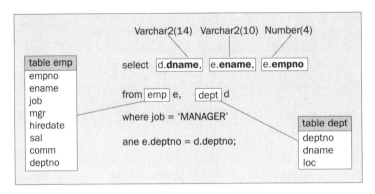

The rule-based optimizer works on each parsed SQL statement by using a set of predefined rules of access, hence its name. These rules, however, are based on established theory, rather than empirical analysis of the actual data structure being referenced. As a result, it is more than likely that the rule-based optimizer will not give you the ideal access path for each statement – as demonstrated above with AUTOTRACE where the cost-based optimizer arrived at the better plan easily. For a more precise evaluation of a statement, more information is needed. That is where the cost-based optimizer, which we will study in the next section, enters the picture.

For further details on the behavior of the RBO, we suggest you read the *Oracle8i Designing and Tuning for Performance Guide* or the *Oracle9i Performance Guide and Reference*. As it is not the recommended approach when using Oracle, we will not be covering it in any more detail here.

# The Cost-Based Optimizer

The cost-based optimizer approach generates the optimal execution plan for a SQL statement based on statistics for the objects referenced by the statement. When determining an execution plan, the CBO will first set up a whole set of possible plans, calculate the cost for each, and then choose the lowest-scoring one.

The cost-based approach is recommended for all Oracle applications. It generally allows for more optimal execution plans than the rule-based approach, since it can more closely reflect the actual status of referenced objects. In addition, most new features added to Oracle since version 7.3 of the database are available only via the cost-based optimizer, including features such as:

❑   Bitmapped indexes

❑   Function-based indexes

❑   Index Organized Tables

❑   Partitioned Tables

❑   Parallel Query

❑   Fine Grained Auditing

An interesting feature of the cost-based optimizer is the ability for us to **hint** a query – to suggest a better way to get the results, to help the optimizer out. Hints are embedded in a query in the form of a comment, for example:

```
SQL> set autotrace traceonly explain

SQL> select e.ename, d.dname
  2    from emp e, dept d
  3   where e.deptno = d.deptno
  4   order by e.ename
  5  /

Execution Plan
----------------------------------------------------------
   0      SELECT STATEMENT Optimizer=CHOOSE (Cost=4 Card=383 Bytes=11107)
   1    0   SORT (ORDER BY) (Cost=4 Card=383 Bytes=11107)
   2    1    MERGE JOIN (Cost=3 Card=383 Bytes=11107)
   3    2     SORT (JOIN) (Cost=3 Card=14 Bytes=98)
   4    3      TABLE ACCESS (FULL) OF 'EMP' (Cost=2 Card=14 Bytes=98)
   5    2     SORT (JOIN) (Cost=3 Card=82 Bytes=1804)
   6    5      TABLE ACCESS (FULL) OF 'DEPT' (Cost=2 Card=82 Bytes=1804)

SQL> select /*+ index( d PK_DEPT ) */ e.ename, d.dname
  2    from emp e, dept d
  3   where e.deptno = d.deptno
  4   order by e.ename
  5  /

Execution Plan
----------------------------------------------------------
   0      SELECT STATEMENT Optimizer=CHOOSE (Cost=17 Card=383 Bytes=11107)
   1    0   SORT (ORDER BY) (Cost=17 Card=383 Bytes=11107)
   2    1    NESTED LOOPS (Cost=16 Card=383 Bytes=11107)
   3    2     TABLE ACCESS (FULL) OF 'EMP' (Cost=2 Card=14 Bytes=98)
   4    2     TABLE ACCESS (BY INDEX ROWID) OF 'DEPT' (Cost=3 Card=82
Bytes=1804)
   5    4      INDEX (UNIQUE SCAN) OF 'PK_DEPT' (UNIQUE) (Cost=1 Card=82)

SQL> set autotrace off
```

As you can see, left to its own devices, the cost-base optimizer would prefer to full-scan both small tables and sort merge them together. However, we can influence the optimizers opinion by telling it we would really like it to use a specific index on a certain table – in this case, to do that, we used:

```
SQL> select /*+ index( d PK_DEPT ) */ e.ename, d.dname
```

There are a plethora of hints available to us to use if we so choose. Rather then present an exhaustive list, we'll refer you to the Oracle performance documentation at http://download-west.oracle.com/otndoc/oracle9i/901_doc/server.901/a87503/optimops.htm.

## Gathering Optimizer Statistics

We have already mentioned that the CBO depends on the existence of statistics to work properly. But how can we gather such statistics? We will investigate that in the next couple of sections.

### The DBMS_STATS Package

The built-in PL/SQL package DBMS_STATS can be used to generate and manage statistics for a single object, all objects in a specified schema, or even all objects within the database. The statistics gathered by DBMS_STATS can reside in the dictionary or in a table created in a custom schema for this purpose.

For the purpose of gathering statistics, the package has five public procedures, as illustrated:

- ❑ **GATHER_INDEX_STATS** – Gathers statistics for indexes
- ❑ **GATHER_TABLE_STATS** – Gathers table, column, and index statistics
- ❑ **GATHER_SCHEMA_STATS** – Gathers statistics for all objects in a schema
- ❑ **GATHER_DATABASE_STATS** – Gathers statistics for all objects in a whole database.
- ❑ **GATHER_SYSTEM_STATS** – Gathers CPU and I/O statistics for the system (this procedure is new with Oracle9i)

Aside from these, DBMS_STATS has numerous other methods, which are, for example, used to import and export statistics. Each of the mentioned procedures, along with any others, are fully documented in the *Oracle 9i Supplied PL/SQL Packages and Types References Guide,* at http://download-west.oracle.com/otndoc/oracle9i/901_doc/appdev.901/a89852/toc.htm so we will not repeat that material here. Rather, we give you an example of how to generate statistics, by looking at the GATHER_SYSTEM_STATS() procedure.

### Example: Gathering System Statistics

System statistics are expecially important, as they affect every SQL statement in the database. System statistics are gathered for the I/O and CPU performance of the database system. The GATHER_SYSTEM_STATS() procedure is used to gather system statistics, as shown:

```
SQL> exec dbms_stats.gather_system_stats( interval => 10 );
```

Here we have specified we would like Oracle to monitor the system over a ten minute interval and collect the system CPU and I/O performance during that interval. It will use this information in the future when developing query plans.

### The ANALYZE Statement

In addition to the DBMS_STATS package, you can use the ANALYZE command to gather statistics on a single object. However, we recommend using DBMS_STATS, which has more functionality then the ANALYZE command, such as the ability to gather statistics in parallel – a feat that ANALYZE by itself cannot accomplish.

You can use ANALYZE to gather statistics on a single object, as demonstrated here:

```
SQL> analyze table emp compute statistics;
SQL> analyze index pk_dept compute statistics;
```

# Which Optimizer To Use?

In short, the answer to this is simply "use the cost-based optimizer".

## Selecting an Optimizer

You select an optimizer, either globally or per session, with the OPTIMIZER_MODE parameter. This parameter can take values, as defined in the following list:

- ❑ CHOOSE – With this mode, the optimizer chooses between a cost-based approach and a rule-based approach based on whether statistics are available or not. To use the CBO, it is enough to have statistics for a single table referenced in a statement. In that case, the optimizer will guess the statistics for the remaining objects. However, if no statistics are available, the RBO will be used. This is the default optimizer mode.

- ❑ ALL_ROWS – This mode lets the optimizer use a cost-based approach for all SQL statements, regardless of the presence of statistics. Furthermore, the optimizer will optimize statements with a goal of best throughput, by trying to use as few resources as possible.

- ❑ FIRST_ROWS_n – Available with Oracle 9i and up, this will cause the optimizer to use a cost-based approach, regardless of the presence of statistics. Furthermore, it will optimize with a goal of best response time to return the first N number of rows, where N can take one of the values 1, 10, 100, or 1000.

- ❑ FIRST_ROWS – This mode is available only for backward compatibility and should generally not be used. It optimizes the query to get the first set of rows as quickly as possible.

- ❑ RULE – This mode lets the optimizer use a rule-based approach for all SQL statements, with or without statistics. It can and will be ignored if you are accessing an object that forces the use of the cost-based optimizer such as a partitioned table. This mode is not recommended.

As we previously said, you can set the optimizer mode on a database level (defined in the init.ora file) or per session (defined by the ALTER SESSION command).

# Writing Effective SQL

One of the beauties of the SQL language is that the same SQL statement can be written in numerous different ways and still produce the same results. Depending on the actual syntax being used, the only difference between two semantically equal SQL statements would be the manner in which the statements are processed and the results retrieved. In other words, given a semantically correct but performance-faulty statement, there is a great possibility that you can alter its text and achieve much better performance.

Of course, there are other factors than the actual syntax of a statement that count to performance. Indexes, bind variables, table statistics and optimizer hints are very important in this sense, as we have already seen. However, there are some factors that must be taken into consideration when writing SQL, which relate only to the structure of the actual text of the statement. These factors include:

- ❏   Limiting the number of database calls

- ❏   Avoiding unnecessary use of functions in predicates

- ❏   Avoiding implicit type conversion

In the next few paragraphs, we will study these issues in more detail.

## Limiting the Number of Database Calls

To minimize database calls, it is preferable to join multiple SQL statements in to one, whenever possible. That is especially true when issuing SQL from a Java context – through either JDBC or SQLJ – where network overhead and implicit type conversion between SQL and Java types must take place for each call. In this section, we will illustrate two methods that can be used for that purpose.

### Never Do In Procedural Code What Can Be Accomplished In a Single SQL Statement

Frequently, developers with a procedural background resort to procedural methods in the database. This is not the best approach in most cases. SQL is a set oriented language – it is not procedural in nature. You should strive to allow a single SQL statement to perform as much work as possible, without introducing procedural code.

For example, suppose you were tasked with creating the routines to archive information from one table to another. You simply must select all old data from one table and put it into another table and then delete the old data from the source table. One approach (in pseudo code) would be:

```
Open a select statement to get all of the rows
Loop
    Fetch data into some variables
    Insert into history_table those values
    Delete from source-table
          where primary key = (primary key from those values)
End loop;
Close query
Commit;
```

This would be highly inefficient for a couple of reasons:

❏ Excessive roundtrips between the database and your application. If there were 100,000 rows or more, this would take more then 300,000 round trips!

❏ Excessive code – that pseudo code, with bind variables and error checking would be quite a few lines of code to write, debug, and maintain

A much more desirable approach would be simply:

```
Insert into history select * from source
        where timestamp_column > some_threshold;
Delete from source where timestamp_column > some_threshold;
Commit;
```

Now, your code is much simpler – three statements, one bind variable. We'll have three round trips, a lot less code. We could in fact go one step further. This routine deals 100% with SQL data – it is all data manipulation. We could wrap that code in a stored procedure using PL/SQL and place it in the database. We'll now get our code in Java down to simply:

```
Call stored-procedure passing the threshold
```

Now, we have one bind, one round trip, and very little code at all to write, debug and maintain. Not only that, but it runs many times faster then the procedural approach.

When you find yourself writing lots of code with a great deal of SQL in it, step back and look at what you are doing. See if there isn't a single SQL statement that can do the work of 100 lines of procedural code hiding in there – you might be surprised.

## Hierarchical Queries

A good example of how you can exploit the powers of SQL to avoid the procedural approach to your database queries is to use the Oracle-specific CONNECT BY PRIOR clause when working with hierarchical data – i.e. where each row below the top level relates to a single parent row from the same table. The CONNECT BY PRIOR clause is a very underused feature of Oracle. With it, you can select a structured subtree of data, either in whole or part, with a single SQL statement – where a corresponding procedural approach would require an increasing amount of queries with an increasing number of levels. To illustrate the use of this feature we will set up a simple example of a Java class that reads hierarchical data from a table and maps each row to a Java object. The table we use in this example contains a collection of web pages, connected to the parent page through a foreign key:

```
SQL> create table pages (
  2       page_id number not null,
  3       name varchar2(500) not null,
  4       parent number,
  5       constraint pk_pages primary key (page_id),
  6       constraint fk_page_parent foreign key (parent) references pages
  7  );
```

*Note that we can identify top-level pages (those pages with no parent) with the fact that their PARENT is NULL.*

**681**

Each page stored in the PAGES table is mapped to an instance of the Page Java class, illustrated below. Each Page instance stores a page ID and name, and additionally a list of all subpages, if any.

```java
import java.util.Vector;

public class Page {
  private long pageID = -1;
  private String name = "";
  private Vector subpages = new Vector();

  public Page(long pageID, String name) {
    this.pageID = pageID;
    this.name = name;
  }

  public void addSubPage(Page p) {
    subpages.addElement(p);
  }

  public long getPageID() {
    return pageID;
  }
}
```

Next, we define a class, PageManager, for retrieving a specified part of the web tree, starting from a given root page. Since each Page object contains a list of its subpages, and each subpage in turn contains a list of its subpages, we implement our method so that it returns a Page instance, reflecting the page ID we specified as the root.

By using an all-too-common procedural approach, we could implement our PageManager as illustrated below. The getSubtree() method takes for an argument the ID of a specified root page, and returns a corresponding Page object. To add subpages to each Page instance, we use the private addSubPages() method. By recursively calling the addSubPages() method for each Page instance initialized, we can traverse the tree down to its leaves.

```java
import java.sql.*;

public class PageManager {

  private static Connection conn;
  private static PreparedStatement pstmt1;
  private static PreparedStatement pstmt2;

  public static Page getSubtree(long rootID) throws SQLException {

    // Initialize database objects.
    if (conn == null) {
      conn = DriverManager.getConnection("jdbc:oracle:kprb:@");
      pstmt1 =
        conn
          .prepareStatement("select page_id, name from pages where parent = ?");
```

```
      pstmt2 =
        conn.prepareStatement("select name from pages where page_id = ?");
    }

    // Select the page objects, starting with the specified page.
    Page root = null;
    pstmt1.setLong(1, rootID);
    ResultSet rs = pstmt1.executeQuery();
    if (rs.next()) {
      root = new Page(rootID, rs.getString("name"));
      addSubPages(root);
    }
    rs.close();
    return root;
  }

  private static void addSubPages(Page parent) throws SQLException {
    Page p;
    pstmt2.setLong(1, parent.getPageID());
    ResultSet rs = pstmt2.executeQuery();
    while (rs.next()) {
      p = new Page(rs.getLong("page_id"), rs.getString("name"));
      addSubPages(p);
      parent.addSubPage(p);
    }
    rs.close();
  }

  public static void close() throws SQLException {
    if (pstmt1 != null) {
      pstmt1.close();
    }

    if (pstmt2 != null) {
      pstmt2.close();
    }
  }
}
```

This sort of *bad* database programming is far too common, especially with developers that have a background in procedural programming. Obviously, if we are working with a large web tree, we could end up with hundreds or even thousands of database queries for each call to getSubtree(), using the procedural approach.

Fortunately, by rewriting our PageManager class so that it makes use of the CONNECT BY PRIOR clause when fetching the pages, we can **limit that count to a single query**. CONNECT BY PRIOR returns all nodes in a hierarchy that appear below a node specified with its START WITH predicate. The START WITH predicate is inclusive, so that the specified root is also returned. The results of such a query are returned so that each parent node is followed by a list of the respective child nodes, if any. This is best explained with an example. First, we add some sample rows to the PAGES table, as shown here:

```
SQL> insert into pages values (1, '1', null);
SQL> insert into pages values (2, '1.1', 1);
SQL> insert into pages values (3, '1.1.1', 2);
SQL> insert into pages values (4, '1.1.2', 2);
SQL> insert into pages values (5, '1.2', 1);
SQL> insert into pages values (6, '1.3', 1);
SQL> insert into pages values (7, '1.2.1', 5);
SQL> insert into pages values (8, '1.2.2', 5);
SQL> insert into pages values (9, '1.1.3', 2);
SQL> commit;
```

To select the whole tree using CONNECT BY PRIOR, we could issue:

```
SQL> select lpad(name, level*4) name, page_id, parent
  2  from pages
  3  start with page_id = 1
  4  connect by prior page_id = parent
  5  ;
```

```
NAME                            PAGE_ID    PARENT
------------------------------  ---------- ----------
   1                                1
      1.1                           2          1
         1.1.1                      3          2
         1.1.2                      4          2
         1.1.3                      9          2
      1.2                           5          1
         1.2.1                      7          5
         1.2.2                      8          5
      1.3                           6          1

9 rows selected.
```

Using this method in our PageManager class, instead of the previous procedural approach, we need to rewrite its getSubtree() method, as illustrated below:

```java
import java.sql.*;
import java.util.Hashtable;

public class PageManager {

  private static Connection conn;
  private static PreparedStatement pstmt;

  public static Page getSubTree(long rootID) throws SQLException {

    // Initialize database objects.
    if (conn == null) {
      conn = DriverManager.getConnection("jdbc:oracle:kprb:@");
      pstmt = conn.prepareStatement("select page_id, parent, name "
                        + "from pages "
                        + "start with page_id = ? "
                        + "connect by prior page_id = parent");
    }
```

Note that since we traverse the resultset down to the leaf nodes, as illustrated in our previous query example, we need to keep track of the parent `Page` objects by their page ID. To do that, we use a `Hashtable` object, which stores a reference to all `Page` objects that have been initialized. To avoid unnecessary lookup in the hash table, we store a reference to the current parent `Page` object. That way, when iterating through a level of pages that have no subpages (for example, the subpages of the page called "1.1", in our example above), we can always make use of the same `Page` object.

```
Hashtable pages = new Hashtable();
long pageID;
long parentID;
Page currentParent;
Page root = null;
Page p;
pstmt.setLong(1, rootID);
ResultSet rs = pstmt.executeQuery();
if (rs.next()) {
  root = new Page(rootID, rs.getString("name"));
  currentParent = root;
  do {

    parentID = rs.getLong("parent");
    pageID = rs.getLong("page_id");
    if (parentID != currentParent.getPageID()) {
      currentParent = (Page) pages.get(new Long(parentID));
    }
    p = new Page(pageID, rs.getString("name"));
    currentParent.addSubPage(p);
    pages.put(new Long(pageID), p);

  } while (rs.next());
  }
  rs.close();
  return root;
}

public static void close() throws SQLException {
  if (pstmt != null) {
    pstmt.close();
  }
}
}
```

For more information on the syntax and usage of the CONNECT BY PRIOR clause, consult the Oracle documentation at http://download-west.oracle.com/otndoc/oracle9i/901_doc/server.901/a90125/queries2.htm.

### The RETURNING Clause

Oracle 8.0 introduced a valuable addition to the INSERT, DELETE and UPDATE operations – namely, the RETURNING clause. The RETURNING clause is used to return a specified list of values into bind or PL/SQL variables. This can be used to an advantage by limiting the number of statements required when performing a SELECT before or after a DML operation.

For example, without the RETURNING clause, it is necessary to issue two SQL statements when inserting a new sequence value to a table. For example, if we assume that we have a sequence DEPT_SEQ that should be used to generate primary keys for the DEPT table, we would need to execute two SQL statements to use the sequence to add a new department record, as shown in these examples:

```
SQL> -- First select the sequence value, then insert...
SQL> select dept_seq.nextval into did from dual;
  2  insert into dept (dept_id, dept_name)
  3  values (did, 'Maintenance');
SQL> commit;

SQL> -- or insert first, then select the sequence value.
SQL> insert into dept (dept_id, dept_name)
  2  values (dept_seq.nextval, 'Maintenance');
SQL> select dept_seq.currval into did from dual;
SQL> commit;
```

By using the RETURNING clause with the INSERT statement, it should suffice to use only a single SQL statement:

```
SQL> insert into dept (dept_id, dept_name)
  2  values (dept_seq.nextval, 'accounting');
SQL> returning dept_id into did;
SQL> commit;
```

This limits the number of database calls to one, instead of two, as previously. Obviously, there are more uses for the RETURNING clause, but the sequence-insert example we just illustrated is probably the most common scenario that can benefit from its use.

## Avoid Unnecessary Use of Functions in Predicates

Generally, avoid using an expression containing functions on database columns as a predicate to SQL statements. Such statements will cause the optimizer to ignore possible indexes on the columns specified, which will dramatically affect the execution plan and thus performance. Earlier, we discussed function-based indexes, which can be used when there is a large need for a function in a query predicate. However, function-based indexes should always be thought of as a last resort – they are expensive to build and take up resources when the table is modified. If possible, you should rewrite the statement in question, so that it can be used without the use of a function in its predicates, and still achieve the same results.

### TRUNC

The TRUNC() function can be used to truncate a given numeric or date value according to a specific format – that is, remove all decimals or date fractions that are of less magnitude than a specified decimal place or date format. A common mistake with SQL is to use the TRUNC() function with a column value in a WHERE clause predicate, for example when selecting a list of rows on a specified numerical or date range. This, of course, has the effect that the optimizer must perform a full scan on the table, and execute the TRUNC() function twice for each row in the table (as we will see below). Of course, a possible solution is to create a function-based index on the specified column, but that is not desirable. A function-based index should be used only when an expression cannot be avoided, which is not the case here, as we will illustrate.

For example, suppose we create an index on the HIREDATE column of the EMP table, as shown here:

```
SQL> create index hiredate_idx on emp (hiredate);
```

Now, say you wanted to select a list of all employees that have been hired over the past year. An obvious, but non-performable, approach is to use the TRUNC() function on the HIREDATE column:

```
SQL> select * from emp where trunc(hiredate,'yyyy') = trunc(sysdate,'yyyy');
```

This is not an acceptable way to write this statement. Rather, it can be rewritten by using the BETWEEN operator, for the same results:

```
SQL> select * from emp
  2   where hiredate between
  3   trunc(sysdate,'yyyy')
  4   and add_months(trunc(sysdate,'yyyy'),12) - 1/(24*60*60);
```

> *Note that we subtract one second from the latter date, since otherwise we would be taking January 1st on the year after into account.*

In the former expression, we not only made a full table scan, but we also executed the TRUNC() function many times. In the latter case, we make it not only possible for the optimizer to use the HIREDATE index, we also limit the number of times we execute the TRUNC() function to two. For a large data set, that can result in a tremendous performance gain.

## *Avoid Implicit Type Conversion*

More subtle than the explicit use of functions in query predicates, is the often unintentional use of implicit type conversion. Implicit type conversion is a "feature" of Oracle that usually does more harm than good. An implicit type conversion occurs when you match a character column with a numeric literal or vice versa. For example:

```
SQL> select * from t where character_column = number;
```

Oracle takes this query and rewrites it, so that the CHARACTER_COLUMN column in the predicate is passed as an argument to the TO_NUMBER() function, which makes it possible to match it against a numeric literal, as we did in this example. Although the query works as expected, the type conversion has the result that the optimizer is unable to use any conventional index that possibly exists for the CHARACTER_COLUMN column. To explore this issue further, we set up a simple example. We create a table that stores famous quotations from equally famous individuals. Each quotation is identified by a number, stored in the ID column.

```
SQL> create table quotations (
  2   id varchar2(500) not null,
  3   quotation varchar2(1000) not null,
  4   quoted_after varchar2(500) not null,
  5   constraint pk_quotations primary key (id)
  6   );
```

We deliberately define the ID primary key column as a VARCHAR2. By specifying a primary key constraint, we automatically apply an index to the ID column.

Now, let's add a few quotations to the table:

```
SQL> insert into quotations
  2  values (
  3  '1',
  4  'Only two things are infinite, the universe and human stupidity, '
  5  || 'and I''m not sure about the former.',
  6  'Albert Einstein'
  7  );

SQL> insert into quotations
  2  values (
  3  '2',
  4  'C makes it easy to shoot yourself in the foot; C++ makes ' ||
  5  'it harder, but when you do, it blows away your whole leg',
  6  'Bjarne Stroustrup'
  7  );

SQL> commit;
```

To query the table for a specific quotation, you could issue a statement like the one shown here:

```
SQL> select quotation, quoted_after from quotations where id = '1';
```

If you view the execution plan for this statement, you will see that:

```
Execution Plan
----------------------------------------------------------
   0      SELECT STATEMENT Optimizer=CHOOSE
   1    0   TABLE ACCESS (BY INDEX ROWID) OF 'QUOTATIONS'
   2    1     INDEX (UNIQUE SCAN) OF 'PK_QUOTATIONS' (UNIQUE)
```

However, you may find out that you can also specify your statement without the quotes, as shown here:

```
SQL> select quotation, quoted_after from quotations where id = 1;
```

This will work just as fine as the first query. However, there is a big difference here. In the latter query, Oracle applied an *implicit type conversion* to the specified literal, which means that in fact it is transformed by the compiler as:

```
SQL> select quotation, quoted_after from quotations where to_number(id) = 1;
```

This becomes obvious if we look at the execution plan for the statement:

```
Execution Plan
----------------------------------------------------------
   0      SELECT STATEMENT Optimizer=CHOOSE
   1    0   TABLE ACCESS (FULL) OF 'QUOTATIONS'
```

As you should know from our discussion of indexes, a conventional B*Tree index is only created for the actual values contained by the column or the list of columns that make up the index key. Thus, by using the TO_NUMBER() function, we make access by the index unavailable. Potentially, we could of course create a function-based index on the ID column, from the value of TO_NUMBER(ID), but that should be avoided. Rather, you should use the first statement, so that it does not cause an implicit type conversion.

*Of course, you should also rewrite the statement so that it makes use of bind variables, rather than literals!*

# Summary

In this chapter we have discovered some of the fundamental aspects of SQL tuning. It should however not be seen as an exhaustive source of tuning strategies – for that, you would more likely need a book of its own! Rather, it was the intent of this chapter to guide you through some of the first steps of SQL optimization and tuning. Based on the nature of your own database, such tuning efforts may eventually result in:

❑   Addition of bind variables to your SQL

❑   Definition of indexes to better support the SQL statements

❑   Rewriting of SQL statements to provide a more efficient execution plan

❑   Eventually, the realization that the SQL itself cannot be tuned any better

Once you have fully optimized your SQL, you should evaluate the performance of the database, and base on that evaluation the next steps in your tuning efforts. If you decide that the execution plan is the most efficient possible, but performance is still not acceptable, then that must mean that either the data model does not efficiently support the SQL or the underlying database instance or operating system need to be tuned.

To conclude, you should generally start your database tuning efforts by looking at the SQL of your application. Beside the fact that it has the most potential for bottlenecks, further tuning efforts can be most efficiently deduced from that examination.

Oracle 9i Java Programming

# PL/SQL and Java: Benchmarking SQL Execution

Generally, for intensive data access operations, such as complex analysis or updates of database tables, you can expect PL/SQL to perform significantly better than Java. To write a stored procedure that generates and stores statistics from a set of base tables, you should definitely choose PL/SQL. However, when you need to perform a task that is either impossible or harder to accomplish with PL/SQL, you should go for Java. For example, you may have to write a procedure that generates an off-screen image from a given set of inputs or returns a list of files in a specified directory in the file system. For these tasks, Java will be the right choice.

This clear division between the two languages tends to blur when you are working with Java stored procedures that need to interact with resources of the database. For that purpose, Java provides you with two open standards for relational database access, JDBC and SQLJ, both of which we discussed in Section II *SQL and Java*. However, unlike PL/SQL, Java was not designed specifically for working with the Oracle database. For each SQL statement you issue from Java, there are numerous conversions of both data and language required to achieve the intended results. With PL/SQL, all SQL operations work seamlessly as PL/SQL shares the same syntax and constructs as Oracle SQL. Normally, when working in a client-server environment with Oracle and Java, this means that you will *gain* performance by running your SQL statements together in PL/SQL procedures, rather than issuing them directly from the Java application.

For Java stored procedures, this is partially true. However, as we will see later, there is much *less* overhead with each SQL statement when running Java code *within* the database, than if the same statement were run from a Java application *outside* the database. In fact, much of the overhead of working with SQL in server-side Java stems from the *cost* of data conversion associated, and not network latency, as is the case with traditional JDBC drivers. The reason for this is that the server-side JDBC driver you use in Java stored procedures has been highly optimized with native compilation, and can directly access the Oracle SQL execution engine through internal library calls.

As a result, each scenario that deals with database access from a Java class must be evaluated before you can deduce whether you will gain more performance by using PL/SQL for database access instead of issuing multiple statements from Java. If you are working with a lot of intermediary results – data that you need only for the duration of a transaction – that otherwise would have to be fetched from the database to the JVM, you should definitely go for PL/SQL, since you thereby avoid expensive conversion of SQL data to Java types. However, if you are using a large number of input variables for each statement or if you need to work with all of the obtained results in your Java program, you will probably not gain any performance by wrapping those statements in a PL/SQL procedure. In such cases, choice of design rather than performance, will be the decisive factor in determining whether to use PL/SQL or not.

In this chapter, we will look at these issues in more detail and provide evidence for each of our claims by performing benchmarks of different aspects of database access from the Oracle JVM. Note that the intent of this chapter is only to compare the performance of Java with PL/SQL in terms of database access from Java programs within the Oracle database. We have already compared the general pros and cons of each language in some of the chapters in Section III *Using Java in the Database* of this book. To recap, we say there that:

❑   When working with database objects, you should use PL/SQL if you can

❑   If you need to perform a task that is impossible or hard to accomplish with PL/SQL, you should go for Java if that provides you with the desired functionality

As previously stated, this chapter consists mostly of benchmarks of different aspects of SQL access from Java stored procedures, and a discussion of their results. For our benchmarks, we will be performing the following set of measurements:

❑   Compare the time it takes to issue multiple SQL statements with the time it takes to execute a single PL/SQL procedure that issues all of the statements at once, from Java stored procedures within the database. In doing that, we will:

    ❑   Perform the same comparison with Java classes outside the database, in order to demonstrate the advantages of the server-side JDBC drivers

    ❑   Measure the cost of passing data from Java stored procedures to a PL/SQL procedure and compare it with the cost of passing variables from one PL/SQL procedure to another

It is our aim to use the results of our benchmarks to illustrate that:

❑   The performance of executing multiple statements from Java closely matches that of running a single PL/SQL procedure for all the statements, when passing the same amounts of data as input and output and working with the server-side JDBC driver

❑   The biggest overhead of issuing SQL statements from Java stored procedures is the cost associated with the conversion of Java types to SQL types and vice versa

From these two general conclusions, we will then deduce that for optimal performance when running SQL from Java stored procedures, you should *choose the method of database access that requires the least amount of data conversion.*

Finally, we should mention that the performance measures discussed in this chapter should generally *not* be your first step on the way to tuning your database application. Rather, you should always start by optimizing the actual SQL statements *before* you choose which method you use to issue them, as we study in more detail in Chapter 16 *SQL Tuning and Analyzing Queries*. If your statements are not optimized, choosing between PL/SQL and Java makes very little difference.

# Comparing PL/SQL and JDBC

When accessing the Oracle database from a Java application in a traditional 3-tier environment, the performance gain of using PL/SQL procedures rather than issuing multiple SQL statements directly from the Java classes is obvious. For each database call, the JDBC driver must make at least a single round trip to the database – to issue the specified statement and return the results – and possibly many more, when dealing with large result sets. As with all communication over a network, latency can be a huge bottleneck. For each statement issued, the network traffic can be potentially decreased by properly taking advantage of the JDBC driver in question, such as by bulk processing and pre-fetching rows. However, the fact remains that for n distinct statements issued through a Java application at the middle tier, you must make at least n database round trips. Additionally, for each statement, the JDBC driver in question must translate the statement and all the supplied arguments from Java types to Oracle SQL types, which will accumulate when passing large amounts of data from one language to the other. As a result, using PL/SQL to group together as many statements as possible in a single procedure can greatly increase performance. Instead of adding a network round trip for each statement you issue, you might suffice with a single database call for a single procedure.

However, when working with Java stored procedures inside the Oracle database, the advantages of using PL/SQL rather than issuing SQL directly from the Java context are not so obvious. Although it is true that SQL-intensive procedures that have little interaction with the Java layer and produce a lot of intermediary results perform much better with PL/SQL than with Java, the same may not always be true when the Java business logic must integrate tightly with the database. In fact, when working with a set of SQL statements that each require either input from and/or return output to the invoking Java method, the throughput of JDBC or SQLJ will *generally* match closely that of invoking a PL/SQL procedure from the same method. This is because for Java stored procedures, the network latency bottleneck is non-existent. In fact, generally the most limiting factor of SQL processing from Java within the database is the cost associated with data type conversion from Java to SQL and vice versa. Therefore, the advantages of grouping a set of SQL statements as a PL/SQL procedure should always be evaluated against the unavoidable cost of converting the input and output necessary.

When we say *unavoidable*, we mean just that. If you have N statements that each require a distinct input parameter (such as a bind variable), you can either execute each statement from Java with a single argument at a time – performing n one-variable data type conversions – or call a single PL/SQL procedure, supplying all the n arguments at once – which requires a single n-variable conversion. If both methods are properly coded, by using bind variables and avoiding unnecessary soft parses by caching statements, the end result should be the same. Thereby, if each of your SQL statements needs to integrate with the Java context – by taking input parameters or returning output – you gain little or no performance by grouping them together as a PL/SQL procedure, since the unavoidable cost of data type conversion will always be the limiting factor. However, as we stated before, if your SQL statements need not integrate directly with the Java program or if they produce a lot of intermediary results, which would otherwise have to be fed back to the Java method in question, PL/SQL will increase the performance.

Of course, there is more to database design than mere performance. Maintainability is also an important factor. By separating business logic from the persistence logic – in other words, putting all of your SQL in PL/SQL procedures – you will attain better control over changes at the persistence level in the database. We will discuss this issue in more detail at the end of this chapter.

These claims would not be worth much if we could not provide tangible evidence to support them. Therefore, in this section, we will perform measurements of the time it takes to execute a given set of statements, n times in a row. For each set of measurements, we will compare the time taken to execute the statements directly from JDBC with the time it takes to execute a corresponding PL/SQL stored procedure. Additionally, for the JDBC tests, we will put our focus on the impact of soft parsing, which can be avoided by sharing instances of statement objects (we discussed soft parsing in detail in Chapter 16 *SQL Tuning and Analyzing Queries*). Furthermore, to illustrate the advantages of the server-side KPRB driver, and support our claim that this driver reduces much of the overhead associated with the traditional client-side drivers (the term *client-side* referring only to the fact that these drivers are used outside the database, not necessarily at the client tier), we will conduct our measurements both inside and outside the database, in which case we use the OCI JDBC driver.

To better illustrate the performance differences between the server-side and client-side drivers, we will begin our analysis by providing a short overview of the different JDBC driver types supported by Oracle.

> Note that we use JDBC for database access in all of our benchmarks. There is no specific reason for that; we could just as well have used SQLJ. Both methods eventually access the database through a specific JDBC driver, so both should achieve similar results.

# Oracle JDBC Drivers

As we saw in Chapter 4 *Connecting to Oracle with JDBC*, Oracle provides three general types of JDBC 2.0-compliant database drivers. Two of those, OCI and Thin, are intended for client-side development (that is, outside the database, as we have already mentioned), while the third one, KPRB, is suited only for Java applications inside the Oracle database. These three driver types are further illustrated in the following listing:

> *Each JDBC driver belongs to a certain driver type, ranging from one to four, according to the underlying implementation. More information on the different JDBC driver types is provided at* http://java.sun.com/products/jdbc/driverdesc.html.

❑ **OCI Driver**
The Oracle OCI driver provides a part-Java, part-native JDBC implementation, which makes it a Type 2 JDBC driver. It interacts with the Oracle database through the Oracle Call Interface (OCI) by invoking C-language routines in the Oracle OCI libraries. As a result, Oracle client software has to be installed for each client connecting with Oracle through the OCI driver. This makes the OCI driver platform-specific, and supported only on those platforms for which the Oracle client software is supported.

❑   **Thin Driver**
The Oracle Thin driver is a pure Java implementation, which makes it a Type 4 JDBC driver. The JDBC thin driver uses Java TCP sockets to connect directly to the database, by emulating the Oracle SQL*Net protocol. Thus, the thin driver requires a TCP/IP listener up and running at the database server, which is usually the case anyway. No software is required on the client-side (the tier in which the driver is operated), other than a suitable JRE. As a result, the thin driver is platform-independent and can thus be used both in a traditional 3-tier setup, or even in a 2-tier setup without an Oracle client, such as a Java applet accessed through a browser.

In addition to the traditional client-side thin driver, an identical server-side variation is used internally by the Oracle JVM, such as to access remote database instances. This should not be confused with the server-side KPRB driver that we use in our Java stored procedures. We will not study the server-side thin JDBC driver in further detail.

❑   **KPRB Driver**
The server-side Oracle KPRB driver is built into the Oracle JVM and is intended only for Java code inside the database. The KPRB driver uses native Java methods to call C-language routines in the internal KPRB C-library. This library is a part of the Oracle server process, which means that it can communicate directly with the Oracle SQL engine, avoiding unnecessary network traffic. As a result, this driver offers tremendous performance gain over the traditional client-side drivers, as we will illustrate in our measurements below.

The internal KPRB driver can only be used to access the same database as it is loaded in. Since it makes use of native methods of the database, the KPRB driver is defined as a Type 2 JDBC driver.

*You should note that we don't mention the Oracle JDBC-ODBC bridge in this discussion, as that type of driver should generally never be used, not even at the development stage. Using the KPRB driver inside the database or the thin driver outside the database is usually much more simple than using the JDBC-ODBC bridge anyway, not to mention the performance differences!*

The aforementioned three JDBC driver types are further illustrated in the following diagram:

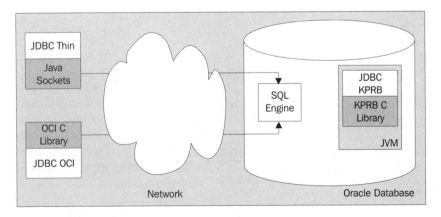

While these three JDBC drivers are implemented differently, they are all JDBC 2-compliant and are thus inherently similar. In other words:

- ❑ They support the same syntax and API

- ❑ They support generally the same Oracle extensions (there are some exceptions to this, for example with PL/SQL table types, as noted in the Oracle *JDBC Developer's Guide and Reference*)

However, certain fundamental differences exist between the driver types, mainly between the two client-side drivers on one hand and the server-side driver on the other. Most notable are:

- ❑ The client-side drivers by default commit after each statement that has been issued, while the server-side driver does not.

- ❑ The server-side drivers use the same session and transaction context as the underlying database session. Therefore, there is no connection management within the Java context. Additionally, there is no need to explicitly close the database connection when working with the server-side drivers. This is different from the client-side drivers, which work with a distinct Net8 connection and transaction context per `Connection` object.

  Note, however, that for the server-side driver, statements and result sets persist across calls and have to be explicitly closed in order to release database cursors. This is true for both the server-side and client-side drivers. However, for the server-side driver, statements should generally *not* be closed immediately after use, a common practice when using the client-side drivers, but rather, they should be closed at the end of a session. By sharing statements at the session-level (as we illustrated in Chapter 16 *SQL Tuning and Analyzing Queries* and some of our other examples in this book), we limit the amount of soft parsing for SQL statements, which can become a bottleneck.

We will explore these differences in more detail below, when we set up our timing measurements.

# Benchmark Setup and Preparation

Before we guide you through the benchmark process and results, we will briefly study the setup and preparation for each of the measurements.

## SQL Statements

In all of our timing measurements, we will be using a set of three SQL statements, which we execute either as a PL/SQL block or as individual statements with JDBC. These statements access the demo database tables which come with SQL*Plus, and are by default set up for the SCOTT database schema. To create these tables for your own schema, you can run the demobld.sql script, which is located under ORACLE_HOME/sqlplus/demo. However, some adjustments to these tables are necessary, as the DEPTNO columns in the EMP and the DEPT tables accept only two-digit numbers. As you will see below, we will be inserting larger values in our measurements, so we need to modify these columns to better suit that purpose. For example, if you are running SQL*Plus on a Windows platform, you can issue:

```
SQL> @[ORACLE_HOME]/sqlplus/demo/demobld
Building demonstration tables.  Please wait.
Demonstration table build is complete.

SQL> alter table emp modify (deptno number(3));
```

```
Table altered.

SQL> alter table dept modify (deptno number(3));

Table altered.
```

The three SQL statements we will be working with are illustrated below:

```
-- create a new department
insert into dept (deptno, dname, loc)
values (:bv1, :bv2, :bv3);

-- move Smith and Scott to the new department
update emp set deptno = :bv1
where ename in ('SMITH','SCOTT');

-- select the number of departments
select count(*) from dept;
```

The PL/SQL function we will use to group these statements together is illustrated below.

```
SQL> create or replace function plsql_wrapper (
  2      p_dname varchar2,
  3      p_loc varchar2,
  4      p_deptno number
  5  ) return number
  6  as
  7      cnt number;
  8  begin
  9
 10      -- create a new department
 11      insert into dept (deptno, dname, loc)
 12      values (p_deptno, p_dname, p_loc);
 13
 14      -- move Smith and Scott to the new department
 15      update emp set deptno = p_deptno
 16      where ename in ('SMITH','SCOTT');
 17
 18      -- select the number of departments
 19      select count(*) into cnt from dept;
 20      return cnt;
 21
 22  end;
 23  /

Function created.
```

## Logging the Results

To eliminate isolated variations, we execute each of our measurements a number of times (five times, on average), and take the average value of the time for each measurement. To easily work with the accumulated results, we store the results of each measurement in a database table, which is created as illustrated below:

```
SQL> create table measurements (
  2    name varchar2(500) not null,
  3    x number not null,
  4    y number not null
  5  );

Table created.
```

Once all the measurements are over, we will gather the statistics with the following query:

```
select name, x, avg(y)
  from measurements
 group by name, x;
```

However, a better approach is to use an inner query, so that we get the measurement names as columns. For example:

```
select x, cnt, java, plsql
  from (
    select x,
      trunc( avg ( decode(name, 'JDBC with KPRB', y, null) ),1) java,
      trunc( avg ( decode(name, 'PL/SQL with KPRB', y, null) ),1) plsql,
      count(x) cnt
      from measurements
     group by x
);
```

We will illustrate this further below, when we actually gather the results.

## The Benchmark Process

Each series of measurements in our benchmarks below will be executed for 1, 10, 20, 30, 40, and 50 consecutive executions. This is done in order to compare the time difference between using JDBC only and using PL/SQL with JDBC with an increasing number of statements. The reason for this is to illustrate whether the performance of the two methods will differ when an increasing number of statements is being executed. From those results, we can see whether it makes more difference to use PL/SQL with few statements or a number of statements.

In fact, as you will see below, we will illustrate that such a level does not exist. The only noticeable difference between 'few' and 'many' statements is when soft parsing is made per execution (in other words, when a PreparedStatement is constructed on a method-level, rather than at a class-level). In that case, the 'single statement case' (actually, three statements, since we are working with groups of three) performs dramatically worse than its PL/SQL counterpart. Since this is actually the issue most relevant to the largest number of Java developers, we will emphasize further on this below.

Once we have executed all of our measurements a fair number of times, we will plot a scatter graph of execution time vs. statements.

## Hardware Setup

Finally, a note on the hardware setup used in our benchmarks below. In all cases, we use an Oracle Personal database, version 8.1.7, on a Windows 98 platform. The database server has an 850 MHz Intel Pentium III CPU, and 256 MB of memory.

# Benchmarking the Client-Side Drivers

To benchmark the client-side JDBC drivers, we will create two Java classes that execute our SQL statements N times in a row, for each N in the set 1, 10, 20, 30, 40, and 50, as we discussed previously in the *Benchmark Setup and Preparation* section. Each measurement will be logged to the MEASUREMENTS table.

> Note that in these measurements, we use *only* the OCI JDBC driver. Using the thin driver would have led to similar results, since the two drivers perform similarly when working with 'traditional' SQL statements like those we will be using, in other words, no LOBs, arrays and so on.

## Using JDBC

To measure the time it takes to execute our set of statements through JDBC, we will use a simple Java class, JdbcTest, as illustrated below. To limit the number of soft parses, we declare all connection and statement objects at the class-level, and share them for all executions.

```
import java.sql.*;

public class JdbcTest {

    private static Connection conn;
    private static PreparedStatement pstmt1;
    private static PreparedStatement pstmt2;
    private static PreparedStatement pstmt3;
    private static PreparedStatement pstmt4;
```

The static main() method is invoked from the command line. This method loads the OCI JDBC driver, obtains a database connection, and calls the execute() method for different number of executions, as many times as we specify with an argument from the command line:

```
public static void main(String[] args) throws Exception {

    // load the driver
    Class.forName("oracle.jdbc.driver.OracleDriver");

    // get a connection
    conn = DriverManager.getConnection(
            "jdbc:oracle:oci8:@DATABASE", "username", "password");

    // disable auto-commit
    conn.setAutoCommit(false);
```

**699**

```
      pstmt1 = conn.prepareStatement("insert into dept (deptno, dname, loc) "
                                    + "values (?, ?, ?)");
      pstmt2 = conn.prepareStatement("update emp set deptno = ? "
                                    + "where ename in ('SMITH','SCOTT')");

      pstmt3 = conn.prepareStatement("select count(*) from dept");
      pstmt4 = conn.prepareStatement("insert into measurements (name, x, y) "
                                    + "values (?, ?, ?)");

      // execute the tests
      try {

        for (int i = 0; i < Integer.parseInt(args[0]); i++) {
          execute(1);
          execute(10);
          execute(20);
          execute(30);
          execute(40);
          execute(50);
        }

      } finally {
        pstmt1.close();
        pstmt2.close();
        pstmt3.close();
        pstmt4.close();
        conn.close();
      }
    }
```

The execute() method takes for an argument the number of executions to make. It goes into a for loop and executes the specified number of statements. To measure the time it takes to execute, it uses the current system time, obtained with a call to System.getCurrentTimeMillis():

```
    public static void execute(int count) throws SQLException {

      ResultSet rs;
      int cnt;

      // start the measurements
      long timestamp = System.currentTimeMillis();
      long time;

      // execute a series of statements
      for (int i = 0; i < count; i++) {

        // create a new department
        pstmt1.setInt(1, 50 + i);
        pstmt1.setString(2, "DEPT #" + i);
        pstmt1.setString(3, "CITY #" + i);
```

```
        pstmt1.executeUpdate();

        // move Smith and Scott to the new department
        pstmt2.setInt(1, 50 + i);
        pstmt2.executeUpdate();

        // select the number of departments
        rs = pstmt3.executeQuery();
        cnt = rs.next() ? rs.getInt(1) : 0;
        rs.close();
    }
```

Finally, the results of the measurements are logged in the database:

```
    time = System.currentTimeMillis() - timestamp;
    pstmt4.setString(1, "JDBC with OCI");
    pstmt4.setInt(2, count);
    pstmt4.setLong(3, time);
    pstmt4.executeUpdate();
    conn.commit();
    }
}
```

## Using PL/SQL

As with the JDBC measurements above, we will write a specific class to measure the execution time when using a PL/SQL stored procedure to issue our SQL statements. The PlSqlTest class is illustrated below. It resembles JdbcTest in most cases, except that it uses a CallableStatement to invoke the PL/SQL procedure, rather than a PreparedStatement to issue each statement:

```
import java.sql.*;

public class PlSqlTest {

    private static CallableStatement cstmt;
    private static Connection conn;
    private static PreparedStatement pstmt;

    public static void main(String[] args) throws Exception {

        // load the driver
        Class.forName("oracle.jdbc.driver.OracleDriver");

        // get a connection
        conn = DriverManager.getConnection(
                "jdbc:oracle:oci8:@DATABASE", "username", "password");

        // disable auto-commit
        conn.setAutoCommit(false);

        cstmt = conn.prepareCall("begin ? := plsql_wrapper(?,?,?); end;");
```

```
      cstmt.registerOutParameter(1, Types.NUMERIC);
      pstmt = conn.prepareStatement("insert into measurements (name, x, y) "
                                + "values (?, ?, ?)");

      // conduct the measurements
      try {

        for (int i = 0; i < Integer.parseInt(args[0]); i++) {
          execute(1);
          execute(10);
          execute(20);
          execute(30);
          execute(40);
          execute(50);
        }

      } finally {
        pstmt.close();
        cstmt.close();
        conn.close();
      }
    }

    public static void execute(int count) throws SQLException {

      // start the measurements
      long timestamp = System.currentTimeMillis();
      long time;
      int cnt;

      // execute a series of statements
      for (int i = 0; i < count; i++) {
        cstmt.setString(2, "DEPT #" + i);
        cstmt.setString(3, "CITY #" + i);
        cstmt.setInt(4, 50 + i);
        cstmt.execute();
        cnt = cstmt.getInt(1);
      }

      // log down the time this took
      time = System.currentTimeMillis() - timestamp;
      pstmt.setString(1, "PL/SQL with OCI");
      pstmt.setInt(2, count);
      pstmt.setLong(3, time);
      pstmt.executeUpdate();
      conn.commit();
    }
  }
```

## Results

Once we have executed both these measurements a specific number of times, we gather the average value for each measurement, as illustrated below:

```
SQL> select x, java, plsql, plsql-java, trunc( (plsql-java)/java*100, 1) pct
  2    from (
  3      select x,
  4        trunc( avg ( decode(name, 'JDBC with OCI', y, null) ),1) java,
  5        trunc( avg ( decode(name, 'PL/SQL with OCI', y, null) ),1) plsql
  6        from measurements
  7      group by x
  8  );
```

|          X |       JAVA |      PLSQL | PLSQL-JAVA |        PCT |
| ---------- | ---------- | ---------- | ---------- | ---------- |
|          1 |       61,9 |       62,4 |        0,5 |        0,8 |
|         10 |        458 |      220,7 |     -237,3 |      -51,8 |
|         20 |      863,3 |        438 |     -425,3 |      -49,3 |
|         30 |       1358 |      695,2 |     -662,8 |      -48,8 |
|         40 |     1763,5 |      917,1 |     -846,4 |      -48,0 |
|         50 |       2310 |     1170,4 |    -1139,6 |      -49,3 |

```
6 rows selected.
```

The last column in our query illustrates the difference in time between the JDBC and PL/SQL measurements, as a proportion of the time for the JDBC benchmark. This means that if you use JDBC to issue each of your SQL statements, this would be the proportional increase or decrease in time you would expect if you instead executed the statements as a PL/SQL function. Since a negative value indicates a time decrease, we can see that by using PL/SQL with the client-side drivers, we always gain performance. In fact, using PL/SQL on average decreased the execution time by around 40 percent for our specific set of measurements. Note however, that for the single execution case, the two methods gave similar results. This clearly indicates that the performance gain of using PL/SQL *increases* with the number of executed statements, as we might have suspected.

A graph of execution time vs. statements, for both the JDBC and PL/SQL measurements, is illustrated below:

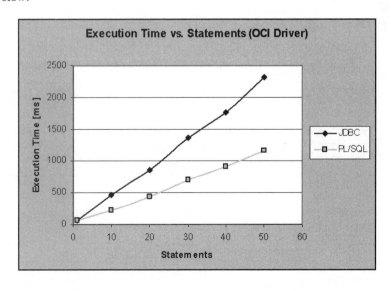

# Benchmarking the KPRB Driver

Now that we have benchmarked the client-side OCI JDBC driver, it is time to perform identical measurements for the server-side driver. For these benchmarks, we take the two classes we used in the previous section, and make a few minor adjustments to reflect the server-side environment, such as changing the JDBC URL used to obtain the connection, removing the `main()` method, and a few other alterations. Both classes are loaded into the database by using the `CREATE JAVA` command from the SQL*Plus command prompt, as we illustrate below.

## Using JDBC

The Java class used in our JDBC benchmarks is illustrated below. This class resembles the `JdbcTest` class we used in the previous benchmarks on the OCI driver. In the code below, we highlight only those lines that were actually changed from the original version (in addition, we remove the `main()` method, as previously stated):

```
SQL> create or replace and compile java source named "JdbcTest"
  2  as
  3
  4  import java.sql.*;
  5
  6  public class JdbcTest {
  7
  8    private static Connection conn;
  9    private static PreparedStatement pstmt1;
 10    private static PreparedStatement pstmt2;
 11    private static PreparedStatement pstmt3;
 12    private static PreparedStatement pstmt4;
 13
 14    public static void execute(int count) throws SQLException {
 15
 16      // initialize resources
 17      if (conn == null) {
 18        conn = DriverManager.getConnection("jdbc:oracle:kprb:@");
 19
 20        pstmt1 =
 21          conn.prepareStatement("insert into dept (deptno, dname, loc) "
 22                                + "values (?, ?, ?)");
 23        pstmt2 = conn.prepareStatement("update emp set deptno = ? "
 24                                + "where ename in ('SMITH','SCOTT')"
 25
 26        pstmt3 = conn.prepareStatement("select count(*) from dept");
 27        pstmt4 =
 28          conn.prepareStatement("insert into measurements (name, x, y) "
 29                                + "values (?, ?, ?)");
 30      }
 31
 32      ResultSet rs;
 33      int cnt;
 34
 35      // start the measurements
```

```
36        long timestamp = System.currentTimeMillis();
37        long time;
38
39        // execute a series of statements
40        for (int i = 0; i < count; i++) {
41
42          // create a new department
43          pstmt1.setInt(1, 50 + i);
44          pstmt1.setString(2, "DEPT #" + i);
45          pstmt1.setString(3, "CITY #" + i);
46          pstmt1.executeUpdate();
47
48          // move Smith and Scott to the new department
49          pstmt2.setInt(1, 50 + i);
50          pstmt2.executeUpdate();
51
52          // select the number of departments
53          rs = pstmt3.executeQuery();
54          cnt = rs.next() ? rs.getInt(1) : 0;
55          rs.close();
56        }
57
58        // log the time this took
59        time = System.currentTimeMillis() - timestamp;
60        pstmt4.setString(1, "JDBC with KPRB");
61        pstmt4.setInt(2, count);
62        pstmt4.setLong(3, time);
63        pstmt4.executeUpdate();
64
65        conn.commit();
66      }
67
68      public static void close() throws SQLException {
69        pstmt1.close();
70        pstmt2.close();
71        pstmt3.close();
72        pstmt4.close();
73      }
74    }
75  /
```

```
Java created.
```

To close down resources, we declare a static close() method, as illustrated above. When the Java class has been created, we must create a PL/SQL call specification, as illustrated below:

```
SQL> create or replace procedure jdbc_execute(p_count number)
  2  as language java
  3  name 'JdbcTest.execute(int)';
  4  /

Procedure created.
```

```
SQL> create or replace procedure jdbc_close
  2  as language java
  3  name 'JdbcTest.close()';
  4  /

Procedure created.
```

To execute the measurements, we invoke the JDBC_EXECUTE() procedure for different numbers of executions, as previously with the client-side measurements. To do that, we declare a procedure, as shown below:

```
SQL> create or replace procedure run_jdbc (
  2      cnt number
  3  )
  4  as
  5  begin
  6    for i in 1..cnt loop
  7       jdbc_execute(1);
  8       jdbc_execute(10);
  9       jdbc_execute(20);
 10       jdbc_execute(30);
 11       jdbc_execute(40);
 12       jdbc_execute(50);
 13    end loop;
 14    jdbc_close();
 15  end;
 16  /

Procedure created.
```

## Using PL/SQL

As before with the JDBC benchmarks, we use a slightly modified version of the PlSqlTest class from the client-side benchmarks to measure the execution time for PL/SQL issued through JDBC in the database. The highlights of the new PlSqlTest class are illustrated below.

```
SQL> create or replace and compile java source named "PlSqlTest"
  2  as
  3
  4  import java.sql.*;
  5
  6  public class PlSqlTest {
  7
  8    private static CallableStatement cstmt;
  9    private static Connection conn;
 10    private static PreparedStatement pstmt;
 11
 12    public static void execute(int count) throws SQLException {
 13
 14       // initialize resources
```

```
15      if (conn == null) {
16        conn = DriverManager.getConnection("jdbc:oracle:kprb:@");
17        cstmt = conn.prepareCall("begin ? := plsql_wrapper(?,?,?); end;");
18        cstmt.registerOutParameter(1, Types.NUMERIC);
19      pstmt = conn.prepareStatement("insert into measurements (name, x, y)"
20                                    + "values (?, ?, ?)");
21      }
22
23      int cnt;
24
25      // start the measurements
26      long timestamp = System.currentTimeMillis();
27      long time;
28
29      // execute a series of statements
30      for (int i = 0; i < count; i++) {
31        cstmt.setString(2, "DEPT #" + i);
32        cstmt.setString(3, "CITY #" + i);
33        cstmt.setInt(4, 50 + i);
34        cstmt.execute();
35        cnt = cstmt.getInt(1);
36      }
37
38      // log the time this took
39      time = System.currentTimeMillis() - timestamp;
40      pstmt.setString(1, "PL/SQL with KPRB");
41      pstmt.setInt(2, count);
42      pstmt.setLong(3, time);
43      pstmt.executeUpdate();
44      conn.commit();
45    }
46
47    public static void close() throws SQLException {
48      cstmt.close();
49      pstmt.close();
50    }
51  }
52  /
```

```
Java created.
```

Once the class has been created, we create the PL/SQL call spec:

```
SQL> create or replace procedure plsql_execute(p_count number)
  2  as language java
  3  name 'PlSqlTest.execute(int)';
  4  /
```

```
Procedure created.
```

```
SQL> create or replace procedure plsql_close
  2  as language java
```

```
    3   name 'PlSqlTest.close()';
    4   /

Procedure created.
```

Similar to the JDBC measurements earlier, we create a procedure for running the tests a specified number of times:

```
SQL> create or replace procedure run_plsql (
    2       cnt number
    3   )
    4   as
    5   begin
    6       for i in 1..cnt loop
    7           plsql_execute(1);
    8           plsql_execute(10);
    9           plsql_execute(20);
   10           plsql_execute(30);
   11           plsql_execute(40);
   12           plsql_execute(50);
   13       end loop;
   14       plsql_close();
   15   end;
   16   /

Procedure created.
```

## Results

As before, we gather the average value for each measurement once we have repeated the whole process a few times, as illustrated with the following query:

```
SQL> select x, java, plsql, plsql-java, trunc( (plsql-java)/java*100, 1) pct
    2       from (
    3           select x,
    4               trunc( avg ( decode(name, 'JDBC with KPRB', y, null) ),1) java,
    5               trunc( avg ( decode(name, 'PL/SQL with KPRB', y, null) ),1) plsql
    6           from measurements
    7           group by x
    8   );
```

| X | JAVA | PLSQL | PLSQL-JAVA | PCT |
|----------|----------|----------|----------|----------|
| 1 | 27,6 | 28,9 | 1,3 | 4,5 |
| 10 | 179 | 187,3 | 8,3 | 4,4 |
| 20 | 374,1 | 347,3 | -26,8 | -7,7 |
| 30 | 504,3 | 501,5 | -2,8 | -0,6 |
| 40 | 633,8 | 651,8 | 18 | 2,8 |
| 50 | 880,4 | 907,8 | 27,4 | 3,0 |

```
6 rows selected.
```

As for the client-side measurements, the last column in the table shows the difference in time between the JDBC and PL/SQL benchmarks, as a proportion of the time for the JDBC measurements. As we can see from the table, these results differ greatly from we obtained with the client-side drivers, as the time it took to execute the statements with JDBC closely matched the time it took to execute the statements with PL/SQL through JDBC! In fact, the proportional time difference was on average positive by only 1.1 percent, which is well within the margin of error.

A graph of execution time vs. statements for both the JDBC and PL/SQL measurements is shown below. This graph illustrates how the results for both benchmarks are closely related with time:

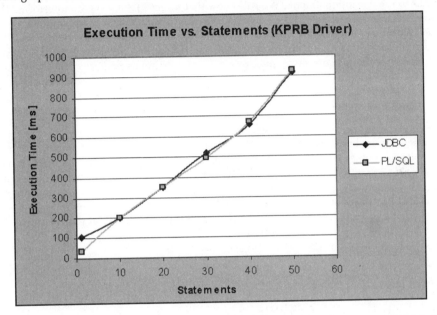

These results may come as a surprise. What we illustrated here is that for our specific set of SQL statements, it does not matter in terms of *performance* whether you use PL/SQL or JDBC to execute them. These results differ from what we obtained with the client-side OCI driver before, as it was clear by then that PL/SQL greatly increased the performance. This clearly illustrates the advantages of the server-side KPRB JDBC driver. We have already mentioned that by using the KPRB driver, we eliminate the inherent network latency commonly associated with database calls across the client-side JDBC drivers, but other factors also count when comparing the drivers. The KPRB JDBC driver can directly access the KPRB C libraries of the Oracle server process by making native internal calls. This reduces the time it takes the driver to access the Oracle SQL execution engine. In addition, all of the core Java API in the Oracle JVM – including all of the JDBC and SQLJ classes – are natively compiled and optimized by using the NCOMP Oracle native compiler, as we discussed in Chapter 15 *Java Application Performance*. Together, these factors greatly increase the performance of the KPRB driver, towards that of PL/SQL, as we can see from our measurements.

One should, however, avoid making too general an assumption about the results of these measurements. They only illustrate that for our specific set of SQL statements, we gained equal throughput with JDBC as we did with PL/SQL through JDBC. That is not the same as to say that server-side JDBC is as fast as PL/SQL. On the contrary, we could clearly see by directly measuring the execution time for the PLSQL_WRAPPER() procedure that PL/SQL still outperforms JDBC, when executed within the PL/SQL context, in other words, not from Java. This is an important point. In our benchmarks we were executing a PL/SQL procedure from a Java class. For the OCI driver, network latency and external calls to the execution engine dramatically slowed down the JDBC SQL execution. For the server-side JDBC driver, the networking bottleneck is non-existent and each SQL statement is executed with internal calls to the execution engine. We still know that direct PL/SQL will outperform JDBC though. This indicates that for server-side JDBC, we still have a bottleneck, which can be related to the amount of work being done, rather than the amount of calls being made, as is true for the client-side drivers. In fact, this bottleneck relates to the amount of data being converted from Java to the SQL execution engine, as we will study in more detail in our next set of benchmarks.

# Effects of Soft Parsing

Before we go on to our next set of benchmarks, I would like to make a note on the effect of soft parsing, which we discussed in detail in Chapter 16 *SQL Tuning and Analyzing Queries*. In our benchmarks above, we shared statement objects between calls, by putting them at the class level, rather than parsing them per method call. Closing statements immediately after use is a common mistake when working with Java procedures in the database, since the overhead of repeatedly soft parsing those statements for each call will eventually be a large bottleneck. To illustrate that point, we repeat our server-side tests, but declaring statement objects inside each execute() method, rather than at the class level. The modified JdbcTest2 and PlSqlTest2 classes are illustrated below.

## JdbcTest2

Changes in this class from the previous JdbcTest class have been highlighted:

```
SQL> create or replace and resolve java source named "JdbcTest2"
  2  as
  3
  4  import java.sql.*;
  5
  6  public class JdbcTest2 {
  7
  8    public static void execute(int count) throws SQLException {
  9
 10      Connection conn = DriverManager.getConnection("jdbc:oracle:kprb:@");
 11      PreparedStatement pstmt1 = null;
 12      PreparedStatement pstmt2 = null;
 13      PreparedStatement pstmt3 = null;
 14      PreparedStatement pstmt4 = null;
 15      ResultSet rs;
 16      int cnt;
 17
 18      // start the measurements
 19      long timestamp = System.currentTimeMillis();
 20      long time;
```

```
21
22        try {
23
24          // prepare the statements
25          pstmt1 =
26            conn.prepareStatement("insert into dept (deptno, dname, loc) "
27                                 + "values (?, ?, ?)");
28          pstmt2 = conn.prepareStatement("update emp set deptno = ? "
29                                 + "where ename in ('SMITH','SCOTT')");
30
31          pstmt3 = conn.prepareStatement("select count(*) from dept");
32
33          // execute a series of statements
34          for (int i = 0; i < count; i++) {
35
36            // create a new department
37            pstmt1.setInt(1, 50 + i);
38            pstmt1.setString(2, "DEPT #" + i);
39            pstmt1.setString(3, "CITY #" + i);
40            pstmt1.executeUpdate();
41
42            // move Smith and Scott to the new department
43            pstmt2.setInt(1, 50 + i);
44            pstmt2.executeUpdate();
45
46            // select the number of departments
47            rs = pstmt3.executeQuery();
48            cnt = rs.next() ? rs.getInt(1) : 0;
49            rs.close();
50          }
51
52        } finally {
53          if (pstmt1 != null) {
54            pstmt1.close();
55          }
56
57          if (pstmt2 != null) {
58            pstmt2.close();
59          }
60
61          if (pstmt3 != null) {
62            pstmt3.close();
63          }
64        }
65
66        // log the time this took
67        time = System.currentTimeMillis() - timestamp;
68    pstmt4 = conn.prepareStatement("insert into measurements (name, x, y)"
69                                 + "values (?, ?, ?)");
70        pstmt4.setString(1, "JDBC with KPRB");
71        pstmt4.setInt(2, count);
72        pstmt4.setLong(3, time);
73        pstmt4.executeUpdate();
```

```
74        pstmt4.close();
75
76        conn.commit();
77   }
78 }
79 /
```

Java created.

We now need to update the PL/SQL call specification and recreate the procedure to execute the tests:

```
SQL> create or replace procedure jdbc_execute(p_count number)
  2  as language java
  3  name 'JdbcTest2.execute(int)';
  4  /
```

Procedure created.

```
SQL> create or replace procedure run_jdbc (
  2      cnt number
  3  )
  4  as
  5  begin
  6    for i in 1..cnt loop
  7      jdbc_execute(1);
  8      jdbc_execute(10);
  9      jdbc_execute(20);
 10      jdbc_execute(30);
 11      jdbc_execute(40);
 12      jdbc_execute(50);
 13    end loop;
 14  end;
 15  /
```

Procedure created.

## PlsqlTest2

Here are the changes to the original `PlSqlTest` class to give our new `PlSqlTest2` class:

```
SQL> create or replace and resolve java source named "PlSqlTest2"
  2  as
  3
  4  import java.sql.*;
  5
  6  public class PlSqlTest2 {
  7
  8    public static void execute(int count) throws SQLException {
  9
 10      CallableStatement cstmt = null;
 11      Connection conn = DriverManager.getConnection("jdbc:oracle:kprb:@");
```

```
12        PreparedStatement pstmt;
13        int cnt;
14
15        // start the measurements
16        long timestamp = System.currentTimeMillis();
17        long time;
18        try {
19
20          // prepare the call
21          cstmt = conn.prepareCall("begin ? := plsql_wrapper(?,?,?); end;");
22          cstmt.registerOutParameter(1, Types.NUMERIC);
23
24          // execute a series of statements
25          for (int i = 0; i < count; i++) {
26            cstmt.setString(2, "DEPT #" + i);
27            cstmt.setString(3, "CITY #" + i);
28            cstmt.setInt(4, 50 + i);
29            cstmt.execute();
30            cnt = cstmt.getInt(1);
31          }
32        } finally {
33          if (cstmt != null) {
34            cstmt.close();
35          }
36        }
37
38        // log the time this took
39        time = System.currentTimeMillis() - timestamp;
40    pstmt = conn.prepareStatement("insert into measurements (name, x, y)"
41                                  + "values (?, ?, ?)");
42      pstmt.setString(1, "PL/SQL with KPRB");
43      pstmt.setInt(2, count);
44      pstmt.setLong(3, time);
45      pstmt.executeUpdate();
46      pstmt.close();
47
48      conn.commit();
49    }
50  }
51  /
```

```
Java created.
```

As with the JdbcTest class, we need to recreate the call spec and the procedure to run the code:

```
SQL> create or replace procedure plsql_execute(p_count number)
  2  as language java
  3  name 'PlSqlTest2.execute(int)';
  4  /

Procedure created.
```

**713**

```
SQL> create or replace procedure run_plsql (
  2      cnt number
  3  )
  4  as
  5  begin
  6      for i in 1..cnt loop
  7          plsql_execute(1);
  8          plsql_execute(10);
  9          plsql_execute(20);
 10          plsql_execute(30);
 11          plsql_execute(40);
 12          plsql_execute(50);
 13      end loop;
 14  end;
 15  /

Procedure created.
```

## Results of Soft Parsing

When we repeat our measurements using the modified classes (after having deleted the existing entries from the MEASUREMENTS table), we get something like the following results:

```
SQL> select x, java, plsql, plsql-java, trunc( (plsql-java)/java*100, 1) pct
  2      from (
  3          select x,
  4              trunc( avg ( decode(name, 'JDBC with KPRB', y, null) ),1) java,
  5              trunc( avg ( decode(name, 'PL/SQL with KPRB', y, null) ),1) plsql
  6          from measurements
  7      group by x
  8  );
```

| X | JAVA | PLSQL | PLSQL-JAVA | PCT |
|---|------|-------|------------|-----|
| 1 | 296,7 | 32,5 | -199,9 | -69,2 |
| 10 | 685,8 | 201,1 | -7,3 | -0,2 |
| 20 | 1589,2 | 350,8 | -48 | -0,5 |
| 30 | 2258,8 | 495,8 | 98,2 | -4,8 |
| 40 | 2698,8 | 671 | 191,7 | 1,9 |
| 50 | 3660,1 | 928,5 | 4,1 | 0,9 |

```
6 rows selected.
```

In most cases, these results are consistent with what we got when we shared statements – except for the case when the statements were executed once (the bolded entry), where using PL/SQL decreased the time it took to execute using JDBC by more than 200 percent! This is consistent with our knowledge of SQL parsing, as we discussed in Chapter 16 *SQL Tuning and Analyzing Queries*. In the case where we executed the statements once, the time taken for soft parsing was such a high proportion of the total execution time that it dramatically affected our results. PL/SQL, on the other hand, caches statements at the *session level*, which means that when we ran our tests for a number of times for the *same* session, the soft parsing overhead was only a small deviation. Also, for an increasing number of statements, the time taken for soft parsing accounted for an increasingly smaller part of the total time, which is why we did not even notice it.

At the beginning of our measurements, we said that we wanted to illustrate the performance of PL/SQL and JDBC for an increasing number of statements. It is of course not common to execute up to 150 statements (3 statements times 50 loops) in a row, in a single method. Figures like one, two, three, or four are probably more common. Thereby, you can see what dramatic impact it has to *share* statements between calls, rather than closing them immediately after use.

To summarize, you should always avoid unnecessarily soft parsing SQL statements, as much as you should avoid hard parsing them. Define your `PreparedStatement` and `CallableStatement` objects on a class level, and close them at the end of a session, rather than at the end of a call.

# The Price of Data Conversion

In our previous benchmarks, we illustrated that for the server-side KPRB JDBC driver, it makes little difference whether you execute a series of SQL statements in a row with JDBC, or whether you group these statements together in a PL/SQL block which you then execute with the `CallableStatement`. In our conclusion for these benchmarks, we noted that those results need not hold for every set of SQL statements you execute. So by now, you might wonder that if this does not apply to *all* SQL statements, then *which* statements does this apply to? Does it relate to the number of statements we execute? If so, at what number of statements should we expect PL/SQL to perform better?

In fact, the throughput of SQL executed through server-side JDBC, either directly or with PL/SQL, should generally not be affected with the number of SQL statements being executed. Not directly, that is. For batch updates it may be though. At the beginning of this chapter, we mentioned some of the overhead of using JDBC for database access. Most notable for the client-side JDBC drivers is the network latency and external calls to the SQL execution engine. We also mentioned that for each statement you execute through Java, there is an inherent cost associated with the conversion of variables from Java data types to SQL data types, and vice versa. For the client-side drivers, this overhead is minimal compared to the network latency. However, for the server-side driver, the cost associated with data type conversion is generally the *predominant* factor of the cost of SQL processing through JDBC. That is because the actual process of SQL execution has been so highly optimized with the KPRB driver, it weighs little compared to the cost of data conversion.

This claim means that for a constant number of identical input to and output from a set of SQL statements you execute through JDBC, there is the same overhead associated with data type conversion, no matter whether you execute the statements in a series or as a single PL/SQL procedure. This explains why the previous benchmarks gave similar results for PL/SQL executed through JDBC as it did for direct JDBC. In these benchmarks, we used the same set of arguments (bind variables) for both the PL/SQL procedures as we did when we combined all of the SQL statements, which gave us the same results.

As before, we would like to provide some tangible evidence to support our claim for the cost of data conversion. In this section, we will guide you through a set of benchmarks set up in order to measure that cost and compare it with the cost of working with data in PL/SQL. As you will see from the results at the end of this section, these benchmarks will demonstrate that the performance of SQL execution from the Java context depends first and foremost on the amount of data passed – and thus amount of data being converted – between the JVM and the SQL engine.

# Benchmark Setup and Preparation

In our data type conversion benchmarks, we will be measuring the time it takes a JDBC program to issue a given SQL query as a function of the number of rows retrieved, and compare those results with the time it takes to execute the query from PL/SQL. The table we will use for our query is illustrated below:

```
SQL> create table data (
  2     x number not null,
  3     y varchar2(500) not null,
  4     constraint pk_data primary key (x)
  5  );

Table created.
```

Now to populate the table with some data:

```
SQL> declare
  2      str varchar2(500);
  3  begin
  4
  5      str := rpad('#', 500, '#');
  6
  7      for i in 1..1000 loop
  8        insert into data
  9        values (i, str);
 10      end loop;
 11      commit;
 12  end;
 13  /

PL/SQL procedure successfully completed.
```

As with the previous JDBC benchmarks, we will log all of our measurements to the MEASUREMENTS database table. However, we ought to TRUNCATE that table before starting these measurements, so that any previous results would not get in our way. Hardware and software setup is identical to the previous benchmarks.

# Using JDBC

To measure the time it takes JDBC to retrieve a given number of rows from the database, we will set up a simple Java class, JdbcResultSetTest, and make it fetch a variable amount of rows from the DATA table. The JdbcResultSetTest contains only a single static method, execute(), which takes for an argument the number of rows to fetch:

```
SQL> create or replace and compile java source named "JdbcResultSetTest"
  2  as
  3
  4  import java.sql.*;
```

```
 5
 6   public class JdbcResultSetTest {
 7
 8     private static Connection conn;
 9     private static PreparedStatement pstmt1;
10     private static PreparedStatement pstmt2;
11
12     public static void execute(int count) throws SQLException {
13
14       // prepare database calls
15       if (conn == null) {
16         conn = DriverManager.getConnection("jdbc:oracle:kprb:@");
17     pstmt1 = conn.prepareStatement("select x, y from data where x < ?");
18         pstmt2 =
19           conn.prepareStatement("insert into measurements (name, x, y) "
20                                 + "values (?, ?, ?)");
21       }
22
23       // start the measurements
24       long timestamp = System.currentTimeMillis();
25       long time;
26       int x;
27       String y;
28       pstmt1.setInt(1, count);
29       ResultSet rs = pstmt1.executeQuery();
30       while (rs.next()) {
31         x = rs.getInt("x");
32         y = rs.getString("y");
33       }
34       rs.close();
35
36       // log the time this took
37       time = System.currentTimeMillis() - timestamp;
38       pstmt2.setString(1, "JDBC Resultset");
39       pstmt2.setInt(2, count);
40       pstmt2.setLong(3, time);
41       pstmt2.executeUpdate();
42       conn.commit();
43     }
44
45     public static void close() throws SQLException {
46       pstmt1.close();
47       pstmt2.close();
48     }
49   }
50   /
```

Java created.

Once the Java class has been created, we define a PL/SQL call spec for its `execute()` and `close()` methods:

```
SQL> create or replace procedure jdbc_rs_execute(
  2    p_count number
  3  )
  4  as language java
  5  name 'JdbcResultSetTest.execute(int)';
  6  /

Procedure created.

SQL> create or replace procedure jdbc_rs_close
  2  as language java
  3  name 'JdbcResultSetTest.close()';
  4  /

Procedure created.
```

We run these measurements for 100 to 1000 rows, as illustrated below:

```
SQL> create or replace procedure run_jdbc_rs (
  2    cnt number
  3  )
  4  as
  5  begin
  6    for i in 1..cnt loop
  7      jdbc_rs_execute(100);
  8      jdbc_rs_execute(200);
  9      jdbc_rs_execute(300);
 10      jdbc_rs_execute(400);
 11      jdbc_rs_execute(500);
 12      jdbc_rs_execute(600);
 13      jdbc_rs_execute(700);
 14      jdbc_rs_execute(800);
 15      jdbc_rs_execute(900);
 16      jdbc_rs_execute(1000);
 17    end loop;
 18    jdbc_rs_close();
 19  end;
 20  /

Procedure created.
```

# Using PL/SQL

To better illustrate the cost of converting variables from Java data types to SQL data types, we will measure the time it would take to fetch the same amount of rows from the DATA table as we did in the JdbcResultSetTest class above, but this time we work entirely with the cursor in a PL/SQL procedure (thereby avoiding data type conversion). By comparing the results of those measurements, we can later evaluate the advantages of avoiding unnecessary passing of data from one language to the other.

To set up our measurements, we define a PL/SQL procedure, JDBC_RS_TEST(), which selects a specified number of rows from the DATA table:

```
SQL> create or replace procedure jdbc_rs_test (cnt number)
  2  as
  3    type rcur is ref cursor;
  4    cur rcur;
  5    num number;
  6    str varchar2(500);
  7  begin
  8
  9    open cur for
 10    select x, y
 11      from data
 12     where x < cnt;
 13
 14    loop
 15      fetch cur into num, str;
 16      exit when cur%notfound;
 17    end loop;
 18    close cur;
 19  end;
 20  /

Procedure created.
```

For a reasonable comparison with the results of executing the JdbcResultSetTest class, we define another Java class, PlsqlResultSetTest which executes the previous JDBC_RS_TEST() procedure. If we instead measure the time it takes to directly execute the JDBC_RS_TEST() procedure from the SQL context (for example, from the SQL*Plus prompt), we would not get an accurate comparison, as we would be omitting the cost of executing a PL/SQL procedure from JDBC. Anyway, it is the intention of this chapter to illustrate issues of SQL access from Java procedures, as we already know that SQL executed from an isolated PL/SQL procedure performs better than SQL executed from JDBC, so by bypassing the Java part, we would not obtain a reasonable comparison.

The PlsqlResultSetTest class is illustrated below:

```
SQL> create or replace and compile java source named "PlsqlResultSetTest"
  2  as
  3
  4  import java.sql.*;
  5
  6  public class PlsqlResultSetTest {
  7
  8    private static Connection conn;
  9    private static CallableStatement cstmt;
 10    private static PreparedStatement pstmt;
 11
 12    public static void execute(int count) throws SQLException {
 13
 14      // start the measurements
```

```
15        long timestamp = System.currentTimeMillis();
16        long time;
17
18        // prepare database calls
19        if (cstmt == null) {
20          conn = DriverManager.getConnection("jdbc:oracle:kprb:@");
21          cstmt = conn.prepareCall("begin jdbc_rs_test(?); end;");
22    pstmt = conn.prepareStatement("insert into measurements (name, x, y)"
23                                      + "values (?, ?, ?)");
24        }
25
26        // execute the statement
27        cstmt.setInt(1, count);
28        cstmt.execute();
29
30        // log the time this took
31        time = System.currentTimeMillis() - timestamp;
32        pstmt.setString(1, "PL/SQL Resultset");
33        pstmt.setInt(2, count);
34        pstmt.setLong(3, time);
35        pstmt.executeUpdate();
36        conn.commit();
37    }
38
39    public static void close() throws SQLException {
40        cstmt.close();
41        pstmt.close();
42    }
43  }
44  /
```

```
Java created.
```

Once the Java class has been created, we define a PL/SQL call spec for its `execute()` and `close()` methods, and a separate procedure for running the tests:

```
SQL> create or replace procedure plsql_rs_execute(
  2     p_count number
  3  )
  4  as language java
  5  name 'PlsqlResultSetTest.execute(int)';
  6  /

Procedure created.

SQL> create or replace procedure plsql_rs_close
  2  as language java
  3  name 'PlsqlResultSetTest.close()';
  4  /

Procedure created.
```

```
SQL> create or replace procedure run_plsql_rs (
  2     cnt number
  3  )
  4  as
  5  begin
  6    for i in 1..cnt loop
  7      plsql_rs_execute(100);
  8      plsql_rs_execute(200);
  9      plsql_rs_execute(300);
 10      plsql_rs_execute(400);
 11      plsql_rs_execute(500);
 12      plsql_rs_execute(600);
 13      plsql_rs_execute(700);
 14      plsql_rs_execute(800);
 15      plsql_rs_execute(900);
 16      plsql_rs_execute(1000);
 17    end loop;
 18    plsql_rs_close();
 19  end;
 20  /

Procedure created.
```

## Results

Once all the Java classes, PL/SQL procedures, and call specs have been created, we can execute the necessary measurements. Once they have been executed a fair number of times, we can gather the average value for each fetch count with the following query:

```
SQL> select x, java, plsql, plsql-java, trunc( (plsql-java)/java*100, 1) pct
  2    from (
  3      select x,
  4        trunc( avg ( decode(name, 'JDBC Resultset', y, null) ),1) java,
  5        trunc( avg ( decode(name, 'PL/SQL Resultset', y, null) ),1) plsql
  6        from measurements
  7        group by x
  8  );

         X       JAVA      PLSQL PLSQL-JAVA        PCT
---------- ---------- ---------- ---------- ----------
       100       37,3       19,5      -17,8      -47,7
       200       48,6       25,3      -23,3      -47,9
       300         59       35,6      -23,4      -39,6
       400         75       47,3      -27,7      -36,9
       500       93,6       61,2      -32,4      -34,6
       600        105       69,3      -35,7        -34
       700        114       79,3      -34,7      -30,4
       800        128       95,5      -32,5      -25,3
       900      141,3      103,3        -38      -26,8
      1000        224        138        -86      -38,3
```

From the results of that query, we can see that passing arguments from the JVM to the SQL execution engine greatly increases the overhead of executing a statement with JDBC. Remember that in both cases we used a Java class to execute a PL/SQL procedure, so the added overhead for the JDBC results only reflects the data type conversion overhead.

To better visualize the results of our benchmarks, let's plot a graph of execution time vs. row count for both measurements. From this graph, we can see the obvious overhead of passing data from JDBC. By adding a trend line to each of the data sets, we can see that they both illustrate a linear relationship between the execution time and the row count.

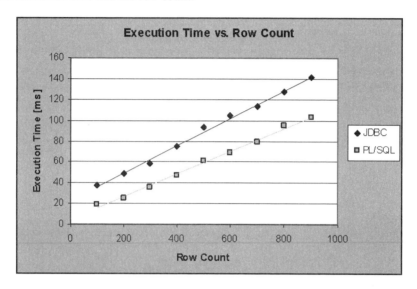

The linear relationship between the execution time and the row count tells us that with an increasing number of arguments, we linearly increase the overhead associated with our JDBC database calls. But what does that tell us?

Firstly, we can deduce that whenever possible, you should avoid passing large amounts of data between your Java classes and the SQL execution engine. This means that if you are working with a set of statements that produce a lot of intermediary results, you should use PL/SQL for database access. That is because otherwise you would need to pass those results to the JVM, which incurs additional overhead. For example, assume that you have to execute a set of statements from a Java class, which generate statistics for a specified date from a set of base tables, and stores them in a summary table. In generating these results, assume that you have to select and work with data from the base tables, outside the boundaries of SQL (you cannot simply INSERT by SELECT). Such data is what we common refer to as intermediary results, since your Java method does not need to handle it directly. By using JDBC to directly generate these statistics, you would have to fetch each relevant row from the base tables, convert the result set to Java data types, work with the data in your Java class, and finally insert the results back to the database, thereby incurring more data conversion overhead. This overhead can be avoided by using a PL/SQL procedure to generate the statistics.

Secondly, if you need to work with a set of SQL statements that do not produce any intermediary results from a Java class, you should evaluate the amount of data being passed, and compare it with the number of statements you have to execute. If the amount of data is little compared with the number of statements – for example, if you can share some of the input variables among multiple statements – you might gain performance by wrapping the statements in PL/SQL. For example, consider the following set of statements:

```
-- bv1 is an integer.
insert into a (x) values (:bv1);
update b set y = :bv1;
delete from c where z =:bv1;
```

In this case, all the statements use the same bind variable, which is an integer. The overhead of data conversion in this case is relatively little, so you might gain performance by wrapping the statements up in a PL/SQL procedure.

On the other hand, consider the following set of statements:

```
-- all bind variables are varchar2(2000)
insert into d (r, s, t) values (:bv1, :bv2, :bv3);

-- bv4 is a varchar2(2000)
update e set u = :bv4;

-- bv5 is a varchar2(2000)
delete from f where v like :bv5;
```

In this case, all the statements accept different bind variables, which can potentially be large strings. Here, the cost of converting the data from Java would be the same whether you issued each statement separately or executed a single PL/SQL procedure, which means that you would not gain any performance by using PL/SQL (however, you might gain maintainability, as we will get to later).

These are the most important points of this chapter. To recap:

❑    Whenever possible, avoid using Java for handling large amounts of data from the database

❑    When you need to work with a set of statements in Java, you must evaluate the cost of data conversion with the number of statements in question, to determine whether PL/SQL would give you any performance gain. For example, if you need to work with intermediary results that need only persist for the duration of the current transaction, you are better off with PL/SQL

## JDBC Performance Updates

In our previous measurements of passing result sets through Java, we made use of the default row prefetch value used by the OracleResultSet. However, as we have discussed in previous chapters, it may increase performance when working with result sets in Java to increase the number of rows that are prefetched. To illustrate what effect that might have on our measurements, we will alter the JdbcResultsSetTest class from above, and have its execute() method take an additional argument – namely the number of rows to prefetch. These changes are highlighted below:

```
SQL> create or replace and compile java source named "JdbcResultSetTest2"
  2  as
  3
  4  import java.sql.*;
  5
  6  public class JdbcResultSetTest2 {
  7
  8    private static Connection conn;
  9    private static PreparedStatement pstmt1;
 10    private static PreparedStatement pstmt2;
 11
 12    public static void execute(int count, int prefetch)
                                     throws SQLException {
 13
 14      // prepare database calls
 15      if (pstmt1 == null) {
 16        conn = DriverManager.getConnection("jdbc:oracle:kprb:@");
 17    pstmt1 = conn.prepareStatement("select x, y from data where x < ?");
 18        pstmt2 =
 19          conn.prepareStatement("insert into measurements (name, x, y) "
 20                                  + "values (?, ?, ?)");
 21      }
 22
 23      // start the measurements
 24      long timestamp = System.currentTimeMillis();
 25      long time;
 26      int x;
 27      String y;
 28      pstmt1.setInt(1, count);
 29      ResultSet rs = pstmt1.executeQuery();
 30      rs.setFetchSize(prefetch);
 31      while (rs.next()) {
 32        x = rs.getInt("x");
 33        y = rs.getString("y");
 34      }
 35      rs.close();
 36
 37      // log the time this took
 38      time = System.currentTimeMillis() - timestamp;
 39      pstmt2.setString(1, "JDBC RS (" + prefetch + ")");
 40      pstmt2.setInt(2, count);
 41      pstmt2.setLong(3, time);
 42      pstmt2.executeUpdate();
 43      conn.commit();
 44    }
 45
 46    public static void close() throws SQLException {
 47      pstmt1.close();
 48      pstmt2.close();
 49      pstmt1 = null;
 50    }
 51  }
 52  /

Java created.
```

Correspondingly, we need to alter our PL/SQL procedures:

```
SQL> create or replace procedure jdbc_rs_execute(
  2    p_count number, p_prefetch number
  3  )
  4  as language java
  5  name 'JdbcResultSetTest2.execute(int,int)';
  6  /

Procedure created.

SQL> create or replace procedure jdbc_rs_close
  2  as language java
  3  name 'JdbcResultSetTest2.close()';
  4  /

Procedure created.

SQL> create or replace procedure run_jdbc_rs (
  2    cnt number,
  3    prefetch number
  4  )
  5  as
  6  begin
  7    for i in 1..cnt loop
  8      jdbc_rs_execute(100, prefetch);
  9      jdbc_rs_execute(200, prefetch);
 10      jdbc_rs_execute(300, prefetch);
 11      jdbc_rs_execute(400, prefetch);
 12      jdbc_rs_execute(500, prefetch);
 13      jdbc_rs_execute(600, prefetch);
 14      jdbc_rs_execute(700, prefetch);
 15      jdbc_rs_execute(800, prefetch);
 16      jdbc_rs_execute(900, prefetch);
 17      jdbc_rs_execute(1000, prefetch);
 18    end loop;
 19    jdbc_rs_close();
 20  end;
 21  /

Procedure created.
```

Now, we can repeat our JDBC tests for different number of prefetches. For example:

```
SQL> call run_jdbc_rs(50,20);

Call completed.

SQL> call run_jdbc_rs(50,30);

Call completed.
```

**725**

```
SQL> call run_jdbc_rs(50,40);

Call completed.

SQL> call run_jdbc_rs(50,50);

Call completed.
```

To determine whether these changes made any difference in terms of performance, we can issue the following query:

```
SQL> select x,
  2     trunc( (plsql-java)/java*100, 1) java_standard,
  3     trunc( (plsql-java_20)/java_20*100, 1) java_20,
  4     trunc( (plsql-java_30)/java_30*100, 1) java_30,
  5     trunc( (plsql-java_40)/java_40*100, 1) java_40,
  6     trunc( (plsql-java_50)/java_50*100, 1) java_50
  7  from (
  8    select x,
  9      trunc( avg ( decode(name, 'PL/SQL Resultset', y, null) ),1) plsql,
 10      trunc( avg ( decode(name, 'JDBC RS', y, null) ),1) java,
 11      trunc( avg ( decode(name, 'JDBC RS (20)', y, null) ),1) java_20,
 12      trunc( avg ( decode(name, 'JDBC RS (30)', y, null) ),1) java_30,
 13      trunc( avg ( decode(name, 'JDBC RS (40)', y, null) ),1) java_40,
 14      trunc( avg ( decode(name, 'JDBC RS (50)', y, null) ),1) java_50
 15    from measurements
 16    group by x
 17  );
```

| X | JAVA_STANDARD | JAVA_20 | JAVA_30 | JAVA_40 | JAVA_50 |
|------|------|------|------|------|------|
| 100 | -47,7 | -15,2 | -10,4 | -18,7 | -11,3 |
| 200 | -47,9 | -32,2 | -25,5 | -39,7 | -43,2 |
| 300 | -39,6 | -30,1 | -38 | -22,6 | -25,8 |
| 400 | -36,9 | -34,3 | -35,6 | -32,4 | -21,1 |
| 500 | -34,6 | -30,4 | -34,5 | -20,8 | -22,8 |
| 600 | -34 | -32,1 | -23 | -23,5 | -18,7 |
| 700 | -30,4 | -29,5 | -23,3 | -30 | -41,3 |
| 800 | -25,3 | -22,3 | -23,2 | -21,2 | -26,8 |
| 900 | -26,8 | -22,5 | -23 | -29,5 | -32,6 |
| 1000 | -38,3 | -12,3 | -4,1 | -16,8 | -20 |

```
10 rows selected.
```

From these results, we can see that for our measurements, increasing the prefetch count does, in some cases, increase performance, although it never beats the performance of using PL/SQL stand-alone (these are all negative values). We can see that using different prefetch values does not always give consistent performance increase or decrease (for example, some times 30 rows prefetch gives better performance than 50 rows, and so on). By observation, it looks like by prefetching 20 rows, we get the best performance. Of course, these results will widely differ between different database setups and server load, but you should always get the same general result; row prefetching in JDBC does increase performance, although not as much as using PL/SQL stand-alone.

**726**

# The Design Factor

From the results of our benchmarks in this chapter, we have deduced that when working with SQL statements from Java stored procedures, you will in most cases gain *similar* performance from using JDBC to issue each and every statement as you would by calling a single stored procedure. The reason for this is that generally the biggest bottleneck in running SQL statements from Java is the cost associated with the translation of Java types to SQL types, and vice versa, as we illustrated in our measurements (assuming that those statements have been optimized, according to our guidelines in Chapter 16 *SQL Tuning and Analyzing Queries*). Consequently, it should be your primary goal when working with Java stored procedures inside the database to limit the amount of data you pass between your Java classes and the SQL engine. This means that you should revert to PL/SQL whenever it helps you reduce data transfer, which is the case when working with intermediary results that need only persist for the duration of the current transaction (for example, you select data from a set of base tables, work with it at the procedural level, and then insert the results into collection tables). Besides performance though, are there other reasons why we should choose one language in favor of the other when working with SQL from our Java stored procedures?

In fact, there is. When working with a complex application, **maintainability** becomes a big factor in design. By using PL/SQL for database access, you separate the database logic from your Java business logic, and thereby make it easier to maintain the database code, in case the structure of tables gets changed. By storing your SQL statements in PL/SQL procedures, you get a better view of the dependencies of your application. If tables get changed or removed, your Java code will fail at run-time, whereas you can immediately deduce what PL/SQL code has become invalid.

You should not conclude from our guidelines that there is no need for using Java in the database. In fact, if you *have* come to that conclusion, it might indicate that you are using Java procedures for the wrong purpose. Do not forget that PL/SQL was designed for database access, while Java is a general programming language, suited for many other purposes than working with Oracle. On terms with our guidelines from other parts of this book, we say that if you can do it in PL/SQL, you should. Java should be your means for extending the functionality of the PL/SQL language – for doing things you either can't do with PL/SQL or is much more simple by using Java. For example, as we have illustrated in other parts of this book, you can use Java to dynamically generate off-screen images from a given input, to work with binary files in the file system, to broadcast notifications via a multicast socket, and much more. Java should not be used for the 'traditional' tasks of PL/SQL – inserting rows from a trigger, gathering statistics, and so on. This should be your general conclusion from this chapter, and this book as a whole, for that part.

So, if we favor PL/SQL for database access, if not in terms of performance then in terms of design, when should we bother to use JDBC to issue SQL? Well, for example, if you do not rely heavily on Java in your database applications, and make use of isolated procedures that infrequently access the database, you can very well use JDBC. Also, when you can make use of the batching capabilities of JDBC, Java may very well be your best choice. For example, in Chapter 14 *Using PL/SQL and Java*, we illustrated an application that will process log files from a remote HTTP server through FTP. As a log file was being transferred, each line in the file was processed and inserted through batches in a results table. For that procedure, PL/SQL would not have made any difference, and Java was the appropriate choice.

# Summary

In this chapter we have evaluated the cost of issuing SQL statements from Java programs inside the Oracle database. This was achieved by comparing the time it takes to execute multiple statements in a row with the time it takes to execute a single PL/SQL procedure that groups together all of the statements in question. We performed this comparison by running a series of benchmarks on different aspects of Java database access. Specifically, we measured:

- ❏ Database access with and without the use of PL/SQL for JDBC outside the database
- ❏ Database access with and without the use of PL/SQL for JDBC inside the database
- ❏ The cost of converting data types from Java to Oracle SQL

From the results of these measurements, we can conclude that when accessing the database from your Java stored procedures, you must evaluate the nature of the SQL in question before you choose whether to use PL/SQL to group together your statements. That is:

- ❏ When dealing with a lot of intermediary results, which are not needed in the invoking Java class, you should use PL/SQL
- ❏ When the amount of input or output for a set of statements is relatively high compared to the number of statements in question, you will probably not gain any performance by using PL/SQL

However, even though Java might give you similar performance as PL/SQL when being run from a Java class, you might still gain better design and maintainability by using PL/SQL in mixture with Java, as we discussed above.

Finally, from the results of this chapter and the previous chapter on SQL tuning, we can conclude on the process of tuning your database application and the choice between PL/SQL and Java:

- ❏ Always start by optimizing your SQL statements before you choose between PL/SQL and Java
- ❏ If you can accomplish what you intend in PL/SQL, you should do that
- ❏ If you need to accomplish a task that is either more limited or impossible to do in PL/SQL, you should use Java
- ❏ If you need to access the database from your Java program, you should evaluate the nature of your SQL by comparing the actual processing with the amount of input and output required, before you determine whether to use PL/SQL with Java for database access.

Oracle 9i Java Programming

# Basic Java Syntax

Oracle 8i and higher versions provide direct support for Java by including the Java Virtual Machine in the database engine. We can write stored functions and procedures in Java. Java is a general purpose object-oriented language, widely used for developing highly reliable and portable applications, which can run securely in the distributed network environments like the Internet. Owing to its security features, and the availability of entire Java runtime classes for use in applications, Java is best suited for writing applications that can be executed inside the database. We can very easily integrate Java and PL/SQL programs. Java programs can be called from PL/SQL programs and the existing PL/SQL procedures or functions can, in turn, be used to call Java programs. There are many things that can be written very easily in Java, which were impossible or difficult to write in PL/SQL like the thread control, opening sockets, sending mails, and so on. Now we can exploit the power and flexibility of Java in our Oracle database applications. We have the choice to use Java or PL/SQL or both for writing procedures, functions, or triggers.

Java provides a clean and efficient implementation of object-oriented concepts and provides the platform to develop object-oriented applications. Java is very simple and is an easy language to learn. The fundamental concepts of the Java language can be learnt very quickly. In this appendix we will cover the fundamental features of Java, operators, variables, data types, and control structure, strings and arrays, and so on. The concepts are compared to PL/SQL concepts wherever appropriate. This section in the book will not cover the object-oriented concepts, classes, objects, access modifiers and so on, which were covered in the opening chapters. These terms are briefly defined, only if they are used here. You shouldn't expect the details of all the Java terminology, but by the end you will be familiar with the basics of the Java language and you will also be able to write simple to moderately complex Java programs.

## Basic Java Program Structure

**Classes** are the building blocks of any Java program. In Java, everything is a class, interface, or a method, except the most basic primitive operations and data types.

A typical Java program looks like the following:

```
package mypackage;
import java.io.*;

class MyClass {

// This is a comment
// Member Variable decrarations
// Member methods definitions

}
```

A **package** is a collection of classes and interfaces.

The package statement in the first line specifies that this class belongs to mypackage, in other words, this class will be put into this package. It should be the first statement in the program, if it is present at all. The syntax is:

```
package <package name>;
```

The import keyword is used to import classes or interfaces to our programs. Import does not mean include. Importing full or partial packages to our program simply instructs the compiler to look in the package for types that it cannot find defined locally in the program at compilation-time. Import doesn't include the imported classes or packages into our program. It is just a way to write shortcuts to the fully qualified names of the classes.

The syntax is:

```
import <package name>.<class name>;
```

If you want to import all the classes in the package then write * in place of <class name>:

```
import <package name>.*
```

A **class** is a template for objects. It specifies the attributes and the behavior of its instances. The class encapsulates the attributes of its instances, called **member variables** or **fields**, and provides the behavior of the instances through methods, which manipulate the attributes.

> *PL/SQL also has a similar feature, but is very less often exploited. In PL/SQL, we can create object types. A class is very similar to a PL/SQL object type. We will explore this in more detail in* Chapter 3 *Using Objects.*

An **object** is an instance of a class. It represents the real world entities having specific attributes and behavior. An object can be thought of as a variable instance of a class definition. In PL/SQL, we define the object types and then create the variables of that type. In the same way, we define classes and then create the objects of those classes in Java.

While it is good to get these fundamental concepts straight right at the start, we are not actually going to delve into the details of defining and using objects in Java just yet (these are discussed in Chapter 2 *Java Classes and Objects* and Chapter 3 *Using Objects*). Our purpose here is to compare and contrast the basic structure and definition of the Java and PL/SQL languages. Let's start by with a side-by-side comparison of the ubiquitous `HelloWorld` program in each language:

Here is the `HelloWorld` program in Java:

```
public class HelloWorld {
  public static void main(String arg[] ) {
    String greeting = "Hello World";
    System.out.println(greeting);
  }
}
```

And the equivalent program in PL/SQL:

```
create or replace package Hello
is
  procedure World;
end;
/

create or replace package body Hello
is
  procedure World
  is
    greeting varchar2(20);
  begin
    greeting := 'Hello World';
    DBMS_OUTPUT.PUT_LINE (greeting);
  end;
end Hello;
/
```

We are all familiar with packages in PL/SQL, the mechanism for grouping related subprograms (procedures and functions), data types, variables, cursors, and so on. PL/SQL functions and procedures are analogous to Java methods (if a method returns some value, then it behaves as a PL/SQL function, otherwise it behaves like a PL/SQL procedure). In Java, we group all related methods, variables and so on, inside a class. In our above Java program, we declared a public class called `HelloWorld`:

```
public class HelloWorld {
```

The Java language also has packages. The Java package is a collection of classes and interfaces. In Java, the related classes and interfaces are generally put in packages. It makes the management and distribution of Java applications easier.

One important thing to note here is that while Oracle PL/SQL is not case sensitive, Java *is* case sensitive. In PL/SQL, we can refer to our class as `HELLOWorld` or `helloworld`, or any other combination of upper and lower case letters. In Java, it must be referred to as `HelloWorld`. Java language doesn't require that the class name should start with a capital letter, but it's a convention. For more on naming conventions see the *Variables in Java* section.

The syntax to define a class is:

```
<access modifier> class <class name>
```

where `<access modifier>` specifies the access control. The `HelloWord` class is `public` so it can be accessed outside the current package. See Chapter 2 *Java Classes and Objects*, for more details on access controls and packages.

Like PL/SQL, Java is also a block-structured language. In Java, a **block** is a collection of statements or sub-blocks enclosed in curly braces { and }, which marks the beginning and end of a block. For example, the class definition as a whole is a block:

```
public class HelloWorld {
   //Body of class goes here
}
```

Within the `HelloWorld` class definition block, we have a single member method called `main` and again, the body of this method is enclosed in braces:

```
public class HelloWorld {
   public static void main( String arg[] ) {
      String greeting = "Hello World";
      System.out.println(greeting);
   }
}
```

Here, the braces are directly analogous to the `BEGIN...END` construct of PL/SQL to denote the beginning and end of a block. An important distinction between PL/SQL and Java is that in PL/SQL we can have standalone anonymous blocks of code. So, we could in fact simplify our PL/SQL program considerably:

```
declare
   greeting varchar2(20);
begin
   greeting := 'Hello World';
   DBMS_OUTPUT.PUT_LINE (greeting);
end;
```

In Java, each method and variable exists only within a class or an object. In Java there is no concept of global functions or variables. In some languages like C and C++ we can define global variables, which can be accessed from different functions and even from different programs, but the global functions functionality can be accomplished in Java, if required, by using `public static` access modifiers.

The execution section of our respective programs look pretty similar, but there are also important differences. In PL/SQL we have a separate declaration section, but in Java there is no declaration section. The variables can be declared anywhere, even after the executable statements, but they have to be declared before their use (we return to the topic of variable scope a little later in the appendix):

```
String greeting = "Hello World";   // variable declaration
System.out.println(greeting);      // executable statement
```

In the case of PL/SQL we declare a variable called `greeting`, of type `varchar2` and assign it a value of `Hello World`. In Java we do the same, except that our variable is of type `String`.

*Of course, if we wished to save the value of a variable of type `String` in the Oracle database table, we would first need to convert it to its equivalent SQL type (in this case, `varchar2`).*

Note also the following:

❑ In PL/SQL, the string literal delimiter is `'`, whereas in Java it is `"`. The single quote is used in Java as `char` delimiter.

❑ In PL/SQL the assignment operator is `:=` whereas in Java it is simply `=`.

`System.out.println()` is the Java counterpart of PL/SQL's `DBMS_OUTPUT.PUT_LINE`. This method prints the `String` object passed to it on the standard output, which is the console by default.

*The `println()` method is defined in the `PrintStream` class. The `out` is a static variable of the `PrintStream` class defined in the `System` class. The `System` and `PrintStream` classes are defined in the Java API.*

Now let's go back and take a look at our `main` method in more detail.

# The main Method

The `main` method is a special method in Java. It is the entry point of every Java application. When you run a program or a class in Java, the first thing it does is to execute the code contained in the `main` method of that class. It is the entry point for the control in a Java application program. In the `main` method we can create objects of the different classes and call other methods that provide the functionality of our program.

The main method should have a *signature* (the combination of the method name, its return type, its parameter names, their data types, and sequence in which they appear) that looks like this:

```
public static void main(String [] args)
```

The description of this method signature is as follows:

❑ As with classes, methods can have access modifiers. The access modifier `public` specifies that this method can be called from outside of this class. The `main` method is a special case and must be declared `public` since this method is automatically called by the JVM. The keyword `public`, along with `private` and `protected`, is part of a system that Java provides to help control access to methods and variables and thus maintain the integrity of the internals of our classes and objects. We achieve a similar thing in PL/SQL by declaring public procedures, types and so on in the package specification and hiding those that are private in the package body. For further details about access modifiers, please refer to Chapter 2 *Java Classes and Objects*.

- ❑ The keyword `static` indicates that the `main` method belongs to the class, not to a particular instance of the class. Static members are shared by all the instances or objects of the class. For further details about static and instance members, again refer to Chapter 2 *Java Classes and Objects*.

- ❑ The keyword `void` means that this method returns nothing. If the method did return a value then, as with a PL/SQL function, we would have to specify the return type.

- ❑ After the method name we can specify the method parameters. The parameter list is contained within parentheses and is a comma-separated list of type and name pairs. A method can accept zero or more parameters. In our case the `main` method accepts only one parameter named `args`, which is an array of `String` objects.

As discussed in Chapter 1, the `main` method is only needed if you wish to make the Java class an executable application. If you wish to execute the Java class methods directly from within Oracle, then we could use the following:

```
public class HelloWorld {
  public static void demo() {
    String greeting = "Hello World";
    System.out.println(greeting);
  }
}
```

# Comments

In the above program, the text enclosed within the `/*` and `*/` is a **comment**, in other words, non-executable text. This is similar to PL/SQL multi-line comments. There are three types of comments in Java, as summarized below:

| Java | PL/SQL |
|---|---|
| `// a single line comment in Java` | `-- a single line comment in PL/SQL` |
| `/*`<br>`  This is a multi-line comment`<br>`in Java.`<br>`  This comment can span more`<br>`than one`<br>`  line.`<br>`*/` | `/*`<br>`  This is a multi-line comment`<br>`  in PL/SQL.`<br>`*/` |
| `/**`<br>`  This comment is similar to`<br>`above, but`<br>`  they have special meaning for`<br>`Java.`<br>`  The text appearing in this`<br>`type of`<br>`  comment is used by the Java`<br>`  documentation tool javadoc.`<br>`*/` | N/A |

# Variables

A **variable** is an identifier to identify a data item stored in memory. It is a name given to the data item. Variables can be of any data type (primitive or class). The data type determines the values it can contain and the operations that can be performed on the data contained in it.

# Naming Variables

A variable or **method identifier** is a string of Unicode characters used to give names to the declared entities like variables, methods, and so on. An identifier must start with a character (Unicode) or an underscore (_) followed by digits or characters again. Symbols other than the underscore are not allowed to be part of an identifier.

> *Unicode is an encoding system, which provides a unique number for every character by assigning a number for each character. Please refer http://unicode.org/ for more details on Unicode.*

Java has special naming conventions for packages, classes, interfaces, methods, and variables. The name of a variable or method should start with a lowercase letter. The name of a class, or an interface should start with a capital letter. The constants are named in all capital letters separated by underscores. Package names are written in lowercase. Examples of good naming conventions are:

```
myVariableName
myMethodName()
MyClassName
MyInterfaceName
MY_CONSTANT_NAME
mypackage
```

The identifiers should be descriptive and easily understandable. Note that there are certain words that have a special, specific meaning in Java. These **reserved words** (or **keywords**) cannot be used by the programmer as identifiers for variables or methods. We have already encountered some examples of Java reserved words, including `class`, `void`, `static`, and `public`.

The Java keywords are listed in following table in ascending order:

| Keyword | Description |
| --- | --- |
| abstract | Declares that a class or method is abstract |
| boolean | Declares a variable or return type of `boolean` data type |
| break | Exit from a loop prematurely |
| byte | Declares a variable or return type of `byte` data type |
| case | A part of the `switch...case` construct in java |
| catch | Specifies the exception-handling block. |

*Table continued on following page*

| Keyword | Description |
|---|---|
| char | Declares a variable or return type of char (character) data type |
| class | Defines a class |
| continue | Returns to the beginning of a loop without executing the statements after it |
| default | Specifies the default action in the switch...case statement |
| do | Specifies the beginning of the do...while loop |
| double | Declares a variable or return type of double data type |
| else | Part of the if...else construct of Java, used to execute operations based on some condition |
| extends | Specifies the parent class of this class |
| final | Declares that a class cannot not be inherited by any other class, a member variable cannot be modified, a method may not be overridden |
| finally | Part of the try...catch...finally construct of Java, which is used to handle abnormal conditions (exceptions) in Java |
| float | Declares a variable or return type of float data type |
| for | Specifies the for loop |
| if | Part of the if...else control structure used to execute statements conditionally. |
| implements | Declares that this class implements the specified interface |
| import | Used to import a class or group of classes or interfaces in a package |
| instanceof | Tests whether an object is an instance of the specified type |
| int | Declares a variable or return type of int data type |
| interface | Defines an interface |
| long | Declares a variable or return type of long data type |
| native | Declares that this method will be implemented in native code |
| new | Create a new instance of the class and allocates memory to it |
| package | Specifies the name of the package in which the classes of this source file will go |
| private | Declares a class, method or member variable to be private, in other words, visible to the members of this class only |
| protected | Declares a class, method or member variable to be protected, in other words, visible only to the members of this class and the classes in this package or the sub-classes |

| Keyword | Description |
|---------|-------------|
| public | Declares a class, method or member variable to be public, in other words, visible in every class |
| return | Returns a value from a method |
| short | Declares a variable or return type of short data type |
| static | Declares that a variable or a method belongs to a class not to a particular instance of the class |
| super | A reference to the superclass of the current class |
| switch | Part of switch...case construct to used to execute statements conditionally |
| synchronized | Specifies a section of code, which requires a lock in order to get executed |
| this | A reference to the current object |
| throw | Throws an object of specified exception class |
| throws | Declares that this method can throw exceptions |
| transient | Specifies that this field will not be serialized |
| try | Part of the try...catch...finally construct, used to mark the block that should be monitored for exceptions |
| void | Declares that this method will not return any value |
| volatile | Specifies that a variable can change asynchronously |
| while | Specifies the beginning of a while loop |

There are some other reserved words, such as const and goto, which are not used in Java, but they are reserved, so it means the programmer cannot use these keywords as identifiers. true and false also cannot be used as identifiers because they are Boolean literals, and neither can null as it is also a literal.

# Declaring Variables

The syntax of declaring variables in Java is:

```
<data type> <variable name1> [,<variable name2>...]
```

If you want to declare and initialize the variable in the same statement then you can use the following syntax:

```
<data type> <variable name1> = <value> [,<variable name2> = <value>...]
```

The following table shows a side by side comparison of initialization and value assignment of a simple character data type:

|  | Java | PL/SQL |
|---|---|---|
| **Declaration** | char myChar; | myChar char(1); |
| **Assigning a Value** | myChar = 'S'; | MyChar := 'S'; |
| **Declaration and Assignment** | char myChar ='S'; | MyChar char(1) := 'S'; |

It is not required to initialize variables at the time of declaration. However they should be initialized before using them. The member variables or fields are initialized by the default values if you don't initialize them. These default values are exposed in the *Primitive Data Types* section. The local variables declared inside the methods are not initialized by default. So, we must initialize local variables before using them otherwise the compiler will generate an error such as the following:

```
variable <variable name> might not have been initialized.
```

The following code is valid in PL/SQL. There will be no compilation error in this code even though its output may not make sense:

```
declare
  varNum1 NUMBER;
  varNum2 NUMBER;
begin
  varNum2 := varNum1 * 20;
  DBMS_OUTPUT.PUT_LINE ( 'varNum2 : ' || varNum2 );
end;
```

However, if we had tried the same in Java, it would have generated a compile-time error because the varNum1 is not initialized before its use in the expression.

In PL/SQL, if we don't initialize a variable, its value by default is NULL. However, in Java we cannot use uninitialized variables. They have to be initialized with some valid values before using in expressions.

If a variable is declared as final then it cannot be modified after its initialization. This is the way to declare constants in Java. For example:

```
final char myChar = 'S';
```

This statement is similar to PL/SQL statement:

```
myChar CONSTANT Char(1) := 'S';
```

After this statement, any attempt to modify the value of myChar variable will fail.

# Scope of Variables

The variable can be accessed only in its **scope**. The scope of the variable is determined by the location of the variable declaration statement. The scope of a variable is from the variable declaration until the end of the block. A variable declared in a block can be accessed inside that block and its sub-blocks or nested blocks, but its not accessible outside the block in which it is declared. It is similar to PL/SQL variable scope rules.

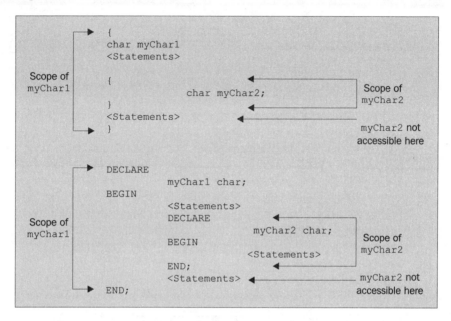

The member variables or fields (the class or instance variables) are accessible to all the member methods of a class. The local variables declared inside the method or a block, are accessible only inside that method or block. The parameters passed to methods or exception handlers are accessible in that method or exception handler block. For details on exception handlers please refer to Chapter 6 *Handling Exceptions*.

# The Primitive Data Types

In the previous section we have been using the Java data type `char`, which holds a single character. This is one of the eight primitive data types available in Java. These eight types fall into three categories:

- ❑ Numeric types – `byte`, `short`, `int`, `long` (integer types) and `float`, `double` (floating-point types)
- ❑ Character type – `char`
- ❑ Boolean type – `boolean`

The following table describes the Java primitive data types:

| Data Type | Description | Allowed values | Default value |
|-----------|-------------|----------------|---------------|
| boolean | true or false | true or false | false |
| char | 16 bit Unicode character | single character | \u0000 |
| byte | 8 bit integer (signed) | -128 to 127 | 0 |
| short | 16 bit integer (signed) | -32768 to +32767 | 0 |
| int | 32 bit integer (signed) | -2147483648 to 2147486347 | 0 |
| long | 64 bit integer (signed) | -9223372036854775808 to 9223372036854775807 | 0 |
| float | 32 bit singleprecision floating-point (conforms to IEEE 754 specifications) | -3.4E38 to +3.4E38 Values are represented with approximately 7 digits accuracy | 0.0f |
| double | 64 bit double precision floating-point (conforms to IEEE 754 specifications) | -1.7E308 to +1.7E308 Values are represented with approximately 17 digits accuracy | 0.0d |

It is interesting to see to which SQL types our primitive Java types would most likely be mapped:

| Java data type | Similar in PL/SQL |
|----------------|-------------------|
| boolean | BOOLEAN |
| char | CHAR(1) |
| byte | RAW(1) |
| short | SHORTINT |
| int | INT or INTEGER |
| long | NUMBER |
| float | REAL |
| double | FLOAT |

It should be noted that Oracle NUMBER types can be mapped to primitive Java types such as long or int, but could suffer from loss of precision. In fact it is safer to map NUMBER types to Java BigDecimal types.

You need to be careful when you use an integer data type other than int. This is because by default an integer literal value, such as 1000000, is assumed to be of type int.

*A value of any kind specified directly in your Java code is referred to as a **literal**; so 10000000, 'a', and "Hello World" are all examples of literals.*

If you want to define a variable of type `long`, and the value you want to assign to the variable is larger than that supported by `int`, you need to append an L to the end of the integer literal. For example, if you wanted to assign the value 10000000000, which is too large for an `int`, to a variable of type `long` you would write:

```
long l = 10000000000L;
```

Just as integer literals were assumed to be of type `int`, floating-point literals, for example 1.234, are assumed to be of type `double` – even if they are within the range of `float`. Therefore, just as you place an L after a literal to store it as a `long`, you place an F after a floating-point literal to store it as a `float`. For example:

```
float f = 1.234F
```

So, we have seen how to declare and initialize integer and floating-point data types and we can change the value stored in the variable, but this isn't much use on its own. What we need now is to discover how we can use these variables in calculations. For this, we need to discuss the operators that are available in Java.

# Operators

Java is an operator-rich language, providing a wide range of **unary**, **binary**, and **ternary operators**. In this section, we will look briefly at the most commonly used operators and their PL/SQL equivalents, if appropriate. A full list of Java operators can be found at http://java.sun.com/docs/books/tutorial/java/nutsandbolts/operators.html.

# Arithmetic Operators

Java provides the usual binary arithmetic operators for addition (+), subtraction (–), multiplication (*), and division (/). Java also provides a modulus operator (%), which calculates the remainder of an integer division. The result of the operation 10%3 would be 1, whereas the result of the integer division 10/3 is 3 (the remainder is discarded).

The following program demonstrates the use of arithmetic operators in Java:

```
public class ArithOperDemo {
   public static void main(String arg[]) {

      // declare local variables
      int a, b, c;

      a = Integer.parseInt(arg[0]);
      b = Integer.parseInt(arg[1]);
```

```
    c = Integer.parseInt(arg[2]);

    // invoke the demo method by passing a, b, c as arguments

    demo(a, b, c);
  }

  public static void demo(int x, int y, int z) {

    // variable declaration and initialization

    int result;

    System.out.println("x = " + x);
    System.out.println("y = " + y);
    System.out.println("z = " + z);

    result = x + y - z;
    System.out.println("Result of x + y - z is: " + result);
    result = x * y - z / x + y;
    System.out.println("Result of x * y - z / x + y is :" + result);
    result = x * y / z;
    System.out.println("Result of x * y / z is: " + result);
    result = x % y + z * (y - x);
    System.out.println("Result of x % y + z * (y - x) is :" + result);
  }
}
```

Here is an example invocation of the program, to which we need to pass three command line arguments:

```
> java ArithOperDemo 10 20 30
x = 10
y = 20
z = 30
Result of x + y - z is: 0
Result of x * y - z / x + y is :217
Result of x * y / z is: 6
Result of x % y + z * (y - x) is :310
```

The result may seem weird to you if you don't know the precedence rules. To understand it properly, you should know the **operator precedence**. The arithmetic operators *, /, % have equal precedence to each other, but they have higher precedence than the + and – operators. So, when an expression is evaluated, it is evaluated according to it precedence. For example, in the above program the expression:

```
result = x * y - z / x + y;
```

is evaluated as:

```
result = ( ( x * y ) - ( z / x) ) + y;
```

The * and / operators will be executed first then and the - and + will be executed. However, you can always override the precedence rules by explicitly putting the expression in parentheses. The arithmetic operators are pretty much similar to their PL/SQL counterparts, with the exception of the modulus operator, which has no counterpart in PL/SQL.

The program takes in the three arguments from the command line and these are passed to the program as an array of String objects. The arg variable, an array of String objects, refers to these parameters. The statement:

```
a = Integer.parseInt(arg[0]);
```

uses a parseInt() method defined in the Java API class Integer. It converts the first element of the arg array to an int, and then assigns it to variable a. It will throw a NumberFormatException if the parameter specified is not parsable.

Notice that the string concatenation operator in Java is +, whereas the equivalent in PL/SQL is ||. For example:

```
DBMS_OUTPUT.PUT_LINE('x = ' || x );
```

## Unary Operators

**Unary operators** are those operators that perform operation on only one operand. In addition to the +, -, and ! operators, which have equivalents in PL/SQL (! is equivalent to NOT), Java provides special operators for incrementing (++) or decrementing (--) the value of a variable by one. Consider the following code snippet:

```
int var1 = 5;
int var2 = 10;
int result;

result = var1++ + ++var2;
System.out.println("result is: " + result );

result = --var1 + var2++;
System.out.println("result is: " + result );
```

The value of result after the first calculation will be 16, since the value of var2 is incremented *before* the expression is evaluated, and the value of var1 is incremented *after* the expression is evaluated. After the second calculation, the value of result will again be 16. These operators are very commonly used in looping constructs:

```
for ( int i = 0; i < 5 ; i++ )
```

## Assignment Operators

We have already used the basic **assignment operator** in Java (=) extensively. It evaluates the expression on its right hand side and assigns the result to the variable on the left hand side. For example:

```
exp1 = exp1 + exp2
```

It is similar to PL/SQL expression:

```
exp1 := exp1 + exp2
```

Java provides a range of assignment operators by combining other operators with the = operator. For example, a shortcut version of the above expression would be:

```
exp1 += exp2
```

There are equivalent assignment operators such as −=, *=, /=, and %=.

## *Arithmetic Promotion*

So far, we have been careful to use the same type of variable in our expressions. However, it is possible to mix the basic types within the same expression. For example:

```
double d = 23.4;
int i = 4;
double result = d + i;
```

This works because the value of the variable i is converted to type double before the expression d + i is executed. This result can then be stored in the variable result, which is of type double.

These conversions follow a simple rule; if either of the operands is of type double, float, or long, the other operand is promoted to the data type of the higher-typed operand before the expression is executed.

In PL/SQL also, the implicit conversion takes place. When the expression has variables of different data types, the PL/SQL performs the implicit type conversion where appropriate. All the numeric types in PL/SQL are the sub-types of the NUMBER data type only. If INT and REAL variables are involved in expression, PL/SQL will automatically promote the expression type to REAL. Before assigning a value to a variable, PL/SQL converts the value from the data type of the source expression to the data type of the target variable if necessary.

> *The implicit type conversion may not work all the time. If the source value is not compatible with the target variable's data type, it may generate a compilation error. Relying on the implicit type conversion is poor programming practice.*

### Casting

If the default conversion of variable type is not what you require, you can explicitly state what type to convert a variable to. This is called **type casting**. For example, if you had the following expression:

```
double result = 2.3 + 3/2;
```

The value of `result` will be 3.3 because the division expression is performed on variables of type `int`. If we wanted the result of 3 divided by 2 to give the result 1.5 we need to cast at least one of the `int` values to type `double`. To do this you write:

```
double result = 2.3 + (double)3/2;
```

Now the value of `result` will be 3.8 because we're dividing the `double` value 3.0 by 2. You can cast any of the basic types to each other, but you need to be careful that you don't lose any information when you do so. Obviously, casting from an `int` to a `double` won't result in any loss of precision but if you cast from a `long` to an `int`, or a `double` to an `int`, there will be some loss of precision.

What happens if the result of an expression on the right hand side is not of the same type as the variable on the left hand side in which the result is to be stored? The answer is that the result is automatically cast into the type of the left hand side variable. This is called an **implicit cast**. For example:

```
long result = 4 + 2;
```

The result of the expression on the right hand side is an `int` with a value of 6. It is automatically cast to a `long` so that it can be stored in the variable `result`, which is of type `long`. This automatic casting occurs so long as we are casting to a type that can hold more information. So you can automatically cast from an `int` to a `double`, but you cannot automatically cast from a `double` to an `int`. If you want to cast the result of an expression to a type that holds less information, you must use an **explicit cast**, for example:

```
int result = (int)(2.3 + 1.2);
```

In PL/SQL, if explicit conversion is needed, we can use the built-in functions. However, if the source and target variables are of convertible data types, then explicit conversion is not needed in PL/SQL, but there may be some information loss. In Java though, if there *is* some precision loss, an explicit cast is needed. Otherwise, there will be a compilation error. If we use the explicit conversion, the results of the expressions will be more predictable and reliable. Using explicit conversion is good programming practice.

# Relational Operators

Again, Java provides the usual **relational operators** for greater than (>), greater than or equal to (>=), and so on. These all have equivalents in PL/SQL. In addition, we also have:

| Operator | Description | Usage Example | PL/SQL Equivalent |
|----------|-------------|---------------|-------------------|
| == | Compares exp1 with exp2 and return true if exp1 is equal to exp2. | exp1 == exp2 | = |
| != | Compares exp1 with exp2 and return true if exp1 is not equal to exp2. | exp1 != exp2 | <>, !=, ~=, ^= |

# Logical Operators

**Logical operators** are used to write complex expressions by combining Boolean expressions. These operators take Boolean expressions as arguments, and yield Boolean values as the result of the operation:

| Operator | Description | Usage Example | PL/SQL equivalent |
|---|---|---|---|
| && | Return `true` if exp1 and exp2 are both true. Evaluates exp2 only if exp1 is true. It is also called a short-circuit AND. | exp1 && exp2 | AND |
| \|\| | Return `true` if any of exp1 and exp2 is true. Evaluates exp2 only if exp1 is false. Its also called short-circuit OR. | exp1 \|\| exp2 | OR |
| & | Return `true` if exp1 and exp2 are both true. Always evaluates both expressions. | exp1 & exp2 | N/A |
| \| | Return `true` if any of exp1 and exp2 is true. Always evaluates both expressions. | exp1 \| exp2 | N/A |
| ^ | Return `true` if exp1 and exp2 are different – that is, if one or the other of the expressions is true, but not both. | exp1 ^ exp2 | N/A |
| ! | Return `true` if exp is false and `false` if it is true. | !exp | N/A |

The following simple program demonstrates the use of logical operators:

```
public class LogicalOperDemo {
  public static void main(String args[]) {
    demo();    // invoke the demo method
  }

  public static void demo() {

    // variable declaration and initialization
    int x = 30;
    int y = 20;
    int z = 20;

    System.out.println("x = " + x);
    System.out.println("y = " + y);
    System.out.println("z = " + z);

    // && demo
    System.out.println("\nAND ( && ) Demo\n");
    System.out.println("(x==y) && (x==z): " + ((x == y) && (x == z)));
```

```
        System.out.println("(x>y)   && (x>z) : " + ((x > y) && (x > z)));
        System.out.println("(x<y)   && (y==z): " + ((x < y) && (y == z)));
        System.out.println("(x!=y)  && (y>z) : " + ((x != y) && (y > z)));

        // & demo
        System.out.println("\nAND ( & ) Demo\n");
        System.out.println("(x==y)  & (x==z) : " + ((x == y) & (x == z)));
        System.out.println("(x>y)   & (x>z)  : " + ((x > y) & (x > z)));
        System.out.println("(x<y)   & (y==z) : " + ((x < y) & (y == z)));
        System.out.println("(x!=y)  & (y>z)  : " + ((x != y) & (y > z)));

        // || demo
        System.out.println("\nOR ( || ) Demo\n");
        System.out.println("(x==y) || (x==z): " + ((x == y) || (x == z)));
        System.out.println("(x>y)  || (x>z) : " + ((x > y) || (x > z)));
        System.out.println("(x<y)  || (y==z): " + ((x < y) || (y == z)));
        System.out.println("(x!=y) || (y>z) : " + ((x != y) || (y > z)));

        // | demo
        System.out.println("\nOR ( | ) Demo\n");
        System.out.println("(x==y) | (x==z) : " + ((x == y) | (x == z)));
        System.out.println("(x>y)  | (x>z)  : " + ((x > y) | (x > z)));
        System.out.println("(x<y)  | (y==z) : " + ((x < y) | (y == z)));
        System.out.println("(x!=y) | (y>z)  : " + ((x != y) | (y > z)));

        // ^ demo
        System.out.println("\nXOR ( ^ ) Demo\n");
        System.out.println("(x==y) ^ (x==z) : " + ((x == y) ^ (x == z)));
        System.out.println("(x>y)  ^ (x>z)  : " + ((x > y) ^ (x > z)));
        System.out.println("(x<y)  ^ (y==z) : " + ((x < y) ^ (y == z)));
        System.out.println("(x!=y) ^ (y>z)  : " + ((x != y) ^ (y > z)));
    }
}
```

When you compile and run this program, you will get the following output:

```
> java LogicalOperDemo
x = 30
y = 20
z = 20

AND ( && ) Demo

(x==y) && (x==z): false
(x>y)  && (x>z) : true
(x<y)  && (y==z): false
(x!=y) && (y>z) : false

AND ( & ) Demo

(x==y) & (x==z) : false
(x>y)  & (x>z)  : true
(x<y)  & (y==z) : false
(x!=y) & (y>z)  : false

OR ( || ) Demo
```

```
(x==y) || (x==z): false
(x>y)  || (x>z) : true
(x<y)  || (y==z): true
(x!=y) || (y>z) : true

OR ( | ) Demo

(x==y) | (x==z) : false
(x>y)  | (x>z)  : true
(x<y)  | (y==z) : true
(x!=y) | (y>z)  : true

XOR ( ^ ) Demo

(x==y) ^ (x==z) : false
(x>y)  ^ (x>z)  : false
(x<y)  ^ (y==z) : true
(x!=y) ^ (y>z)  : true
```

The equivalent `selected` method in PL/SQL will be:

```
SQL> create or replace function selected ( edu NUMBER, exp NUMBER )
  2  return BOOLEAN
  3  is
  4  begin
  5    if ( edu >= 18 AND exp >= 2 ) OR ( edu >= 16 AND exp >= 4 ) then
  6       return true;
  7    else
  8       return false;
  9    end if;
 10  end selected;
 11  /

Function created.
```

Beyond the similarities in the use of logical operators in the two languages, the two programs provide a useful comparison between looping constructs (which we discuss in more detail shortly) and the way in which we specify return values in the two languages.

# Bitwise Operators

Java language provides operators to operate at bit-level. **Bit-level operators** are not available in PL/SQL and are rarely used in Java. For example:

```
exp1>>exp2
```

will shift the bits of `exp1` to the right by `exp2` positions. For a full discussion, please refer to http://java.sun.com/docs/books/tutorial/java/nutsandbolts/bitwise.html.

# Character Data Types

We have already seen the char type in Java, which holds a single character. It is worth noting that we can use the increment operator on a char:

```
char myChar = 'A';
myChar++;
```

The variable myChar will now hold the character B.

It is also worth noting that we can use the +, -, +=, and -= operators on a char to get another char.

# Character Escape Sequences

You may wish to store characters that are not available from within your editor. Fortunately, variables of data type char may also be initialized using their hexadecimal codes. The example below shows a character variable can be initialized to the character A by specifying its four-character hexadecimal code:

```
char myChar = '\u0041';
```

The backslash above is an **escape sequence** character. It means that what follows is a code that corresponds to a particular character. The u after the escape character means that the code is in hexadecimal.

In Java, there are the following escape sequences:

| Escape Sequence | Description |
| --- | --- |
| \n | Line feed (\u000a) |
| \t | Horizontal tab (\u0009) |
| \b | Backspace (\u0008) |
| \f | Form feed (\u000c) |
| \r | Carriage return (\u000d) |
| \" | Double quote (\u0022) |
| \' | Single quote (\u0027) |
| \\ | Backslash (\u005c) |

Of course, most of the time we will want to hold and manipulate a collection of characters, so in Java will find ourselves using the String variable.

# Strings

`String` is not a primitive data type in Java. They are so common that we can hardly see any useful application without them. Java provides built-in support for strings in the form of the `String` class. All string literals in Java programs, such as `"A String"` are treated as instances of this class. The `String` class defines different methods to map the most popular string manipulation operations such as comparison, concatenation, getting individual characters, copying, extracting sub-strings, and so on. In Java `String` objects are immutable; they cannot be modified. When we do some string manipulation the `String` objects are not changed, instead new string objects are created to represent the results of string manipulation and the old ones are garbage collected by the Java garbage collector.

Strings in Java are analogous to the PL/SQL VARCHAR, VARCHAR2, or CHAR data types. We can think of `String` objects as the variables of VARCHAR or CHAR data type. Usage of `String` objects in Java programs is similar to the usage of VARCHAR or CHAR variables. In Java we can create a `String` literal by enclosing the string in double quotes (`" "`). In PL/SQL however, we create string literals by enclosing the string in single quotes (`' '`).

There are many ways to create `String` objects or literals. All the string literals are the objects of `String` class. For example, by specifying the string value in double quotes:

```
String str = "Java"
```

by invoking the constructor of `String` class:

```
String str = new String("Java")
```

or by creating strings from `String` expressions:

```
String str = "Java" + new String(" Language")
```

The last example will create two `String` objects, `"Java"` and `" Language"` in memory, and then these are concatenated, with the resultant `String` being assigned to `str`. The `"Java"` and `" Language"` strings are garbage collected.

Let's write a program to demonstrate the use of strings in Java:

```
class StringDemo {

  public static void main(String[] args) {
    demo();   // invoke the demo method
  }

  public static void demo() {
    String str = "The World ";
    String value = helper(str);   // call helper method
    System.out.println(value);
    value = value.concat("If no why ?");
    System.out.println(value);
```

```
        System.out.println("The length of value: " + value.length());
        System.out.println("The " + str.substring(4, 9)
                        + ", beautiful world !!!!");
        String str4 = "Java";
        String str5 = str4;
        String str6 = new String("Java");
        String str7 = "JAVA";

        System.out.println("str4 : " + str4);
        System.out.println("str5 : " + str4);
        System.out.println("str6 : " + str4);
        System.out.println("str4 == str5 : " + (str4 == str5));
        System.out.println("str4 == str6 : " + (str4 == str6));
        System.out.println("str4.equals(str6): " + (str4.equals(str6)));
        System.out.println("str4.equals(str7): " + (str4.equals(str7)));
        System.out.println("str4.equalsIgnoreCase(str7): "
                        + (str4.equalsIgnoreCase(str6)));
        System.out.println("str4.compareTo(str5): " + (str4.compareTo(str5)));
        System.out.println("str4.compareTo(str7): " + (str4.compareTo(str7)));
        System.out.println("str4.toUpperCase(): " + (str4.toUpperCase()));
        System.out.println("str4.replace( 'a', 'i' ): "
                        + (str4.replace('a', 'i')));
    }

    public static String helper(String str1) {
        String str2 = "is beautiful. ";
        String str3 = str1 + str2 + "Do you like it ? ";
        return str3;
    }
}
```

Most of the statements in the above program are self-explanatory. In this program, some `String` objects are created and some string manipulation operations are performed. There are many more methods provided by the `String` class. For more details see the Java API reference on http://java.sun.com/j2se/1.4/docs/api/index.html.

In string comparisons, the `==` operator doesn't always behave as expected. This operator compares two objects or strings to check whether they are references to the same object or not. So, we should use the `equals()` method of the `String` class to compare two strings for equality. This method compares the actual values of the strings.

There is one more class in the Java API to manipulate strings – `StringBuffer`. The `String` and `StringBuffer` classes are very similar. The `String` class is used to manipulate immutable strings. On the other hand, the `StringBuffer` class is used to manipulate mutable strings. When we write statements like:

```
String str = new String("Hello") + "World" + "!!!!";
```

This statement is converted internally to:

```
String str =
    new StringBuffer("Hello").append("World").append("!!!!").toString();
```

This statement creates an object of the `StringBuffer` class having the value `"Hello"`, and then invokes the `append()` method on it by passing `"World"` as the parameter and then again invokes the `append()` method by passing `"!!!!"` as the parameter. Finally, it invokes the `toString()` method of the `StringBuffer` class, which converts its contents to a `String` class object and then assigns it to the `str` variable on the left. The reason is that instances of the `String` class are immutable and cannot be modified. The instances of the `StringBuffer` class are however mutable and their contents can be modified. See Chapter 15 *Java Application Performance* for more on the performance issues related to the `String` and `StringBuffer` class.

# Control Structures

Simple statements, such as declaration statements, assignment statements, and subroutine calls are the basic building blocks of a program. These simple statements are organized into compound statements to build the more complex structures such as loops and decision-making statements based on the program's logic. We will now move on to discuss these **control structures** in Java, and compare them to their equivalent structure in PL/SQL, where applicable.

Java uses the usual `if...else` structure and loop constructs, the basic loops being `for`, `while`, and `do...while`. It also provides a `switch` statement and three jump statements to extend the looping functionality. These are `break`, `continue`, and `return`.

## The if Statement

The basic `if...else` structure in Java is very similar to the PL/SQL `if...then...else` control structure:

| Java | PL/SQL |
|---|---|
| <pre>if ( <boolean expression> ) {<br>  <statements><br>} else {<br>  <statements><br>}</pre> | <pre>if <boolean expression> then<br>  <statements><br>else<br>  <statements><br>end if;</pre> |

If you want to execute different sets of statements from several mutually exclusive alternatives, you can join another `if` clause to the `else` clause of the previous `if` conditional statement. An `if` statement can have any number of companion `else if` statements but only one `else` at the end. The `if...else` structure in Java is very similar to the PL/SQL `if...elsif...else` control structure:

| Java | PL/SQL |
|---|---|
| <pre>if ( <boolean expression> ) {<br>  <statements><br>} else if ( <boolean expression> ) {<br>  <statements><br>} else if ( <boolean expression> ) {<br>  <statements><br>} else {<br>  <statements><br>}</pre> | <pre>if <boolean expression> then<br>  <statements><br>elsif <boolean expression> then<br>  <statements><br>elsif <boolean expression> then<br>  <statements><br>else<br>  <statements><br>end if;</pre> |

Note that in Java, the Boolean expression must be enclosed in parentheses. The following program demonstrates the use of Java `if...else` control structure. It will take in an argument from the command line and then work out an appropriate discount and final price:

```java
public class Discount {
  public static void main(String[] arg) {
    int sale = 0;
    if (arg.length > 0) {
      sale = Integer.parseInt(arg[0]);
    }

    // invoke calculateDiscount() method by passing sale as parameter
    calculateDiscount(sale);
  }

  public static void calculateDiscount(float sale) {
    float discount;

    if (sale >= 2000) {
      discount = 15;
    } else if (sale >= 1500) {
      discount = 12;
    } else if (sale >= 1000) {
      discount = 10;
    } else {
      discount = 5;
    }

    System.out.println("Sale     : " + sale);
    System.out.println("Discount: " + (sale * discount / 100));
    System.out.println("Amount   : " + (sale - sale * discount / 100));
  }
}
```

The following is the output of the program when executed with a command line argument of 1500:

```
> java Discount 1500
Sale    : 1500.0
Discount: 180.0
Amount   : 1320.0
```

Note that in the `if...else` control structure, only one code block is executed, even though multiple block conditions may be true. In the above program, we have passed a value of 1500 as argument. It satisfies the last two conditions, but only one block satisfying the condition is executed – whichever comes first. Once a condition is satisfied, the appropriate code block is executed and control passes out of the `if` statement without evaluating the remaining conditions.

## Using ?: as a Shortcut to the if Statement

The Java language provides a shortcut to the formal `if` statement via the use of the `?:` ternary operator. For example, the following statement:

```
<boolean expression> ? <expression1> : <expression2>
```

is a shortcut for the following if statement:

```
if ( <boolean expression> ) {
  <expression1>
} else {
  <expression2>
}
```

It is somewhat similar to Oracle's DECODE function:

```
decode(expr, search, expr[, search, expr...] [, default])
```

The DECODE function can have many alternatives and a default expression, but Java's ? : operator have only two alternatives.

The following program demonstrates the use of ? : operator:

```
class TernaryOperDemo {
  public static void main(String arg[]) {
    int num = Integer.parseInt(arg[0]);
    System.out.print("The number is : " + (num % 2 == 0 ? "Even" : "Odd"));
  }
}
```

This program will take in an argument from the command line, process it, and report back whether it is even or odd:

```
> java TernaryOperDemo 5
The number is : Odd
```

PL/SQL doesn't have an equivalent operator, but Oracle's DECODE function is similar in functionality.

# The switch statement

Java supplies a switch statement that transfers control to one of several code blocks depending on the value of an expression. The format of the switch construct is as follows:

```
switch ( <expression> ) {
  case <constant expression1>:
    <statements>
  break;
  case <constant expression2>:
    <statements>
  break;
  default:
    <statements>
  break;
}
```

The expression specified in the `switch` statement is evaluated and its value is compared with the different **case constants**, or **constant expressions**. Whatever case constant matches first with the evaluated value, the statements following that `case` label are executed until the `break` statement or the end of switch block. If no `case` constant matches with the evaluated value then the statements in the following `default` label are executed until the `break` statement or the end of the `switch` block.

There can be as many `case` labels as required, but there can be only one `default` label. The same `case` label cannot be repeated otherwise the compiler will generate an error message. The limitation of a `switch` statement is that the expression must evaluate to a value of `char`, `byte`, `short`, or `int`, otherwise a compile-time error will be generated. The `long`, `float`, `double`, and `boolean` expressions are not allowed in a `switch` statement. Neither can we use the `case` statement with a `String`.

Every constant expression of the `switch` construct must be assignable to the type of the expression specified in the parenthesis followed by the `switch` keyword.

Let's write a program to demonstrate the use of the `switch` construct:

```java
public class AlertDispatcher {
  static final int EMAIL = 1;
  static final int VOICE = 2;
  static final int PAGER = 3;
  static final int SMS = 4;
  static final int WAP = 5;

  public static void main(String[] arg) {
    sendAlert(Integer.parseInt(arg[0]));
  }

  public static void sendAlert(int alertMethod) {
    switch (alertMethod) {
    case EMAIL:
      System.out.println("Sent an email alert");
      break;
    case VOICE:
      System.out.println("Sent a Voice alert");
      break;
    case PAGER:
      System.out.println("Sent a pager alert");
    case SMS:
      System.out.println("Sent an SMS alert");
      break;
    case WAP:
      System.out.println("Sent a WAP alert");
      break;
    default:
      System.out.println("Invalid alert method");
    }
  }
}
```

The output when you run this program will depend on the argument you pass on the command line. The integers from 1 to 5 represent different methods of communication and the `switch` statement returns different output, depending on which constant expressions are satisfied.

Here are a few example invocations:

```
> java AlertDispatcher 1
Sent an email alert

> java AlertDispatcher 3
Sent a pager alert
Sent an SMS alert
```

We got two messages when we passed in 3 as the command line argument because we neglected to place a `break` clause at the end of the `PAGER` case block. In this case, code execution continues until a `break` statement or end of the `switch` construct is encountered.

Also, note that the statements in the different `case` blocks are not enclosed in curly braces. When a `case` constant is matched with the value of the expression, then the statements following that `case` label are executed sequentially, so there is no need for start and end markers.

# The for Loop

The `for` loop is the most widely used looping construct in Java, and is best suited for situations when we know the number of iterations to be performed. It is used extensively in array processing. The format of the `for` loop in Java is:

```
for( <initialization> ; <boolean expression> ; <increment> ) {
  <statements>
}
```

This statement can be compared with the PL/SQL `for` loop:

```
for <variable> IN <lower-bound>..<upper-bound> loop
  <statements>
end loop;
```

However, the Java `for` statement is more powerful and flexible than its PL/SQL counterpart. In Java, a `for` statement has no lower-bound or upper-bound limits. Instead, a Boolean expression controls the number of iterations of the `for` statement. This expression can be arbitrarily complex, but it should evaluate to a value of `boolean` data type.

When the `for` statement is executed:

1. At first, the statements in the initialization section are executed

2. Then the Boolean expression is evaluated

3. If the Boolean expression evaluates to `true` then the statements in the `for` block are executed

4. After that, the statements in the increment section are executed

5. After this, the Boolean expression is evaluated again and so on

The statements in the `for` block are executed iteratively until the Boolean expression evaluates to `false`. The statements in the initialization section are executed only once at the beginning of the loop. They are not executed again and again with each iteration. The initialization section can contain zero or more statements separated by commas. If multiple statements are present, they are executed from left to right. We can also declare a local variable within the initialization section of the `for` statement. The scope of the variable declared inside the initialization section is limited only to the code block of the `for` statement. Its not accessible outside the `for` block.

The Boolean expression is evaluated for each iteration before the start of the iteration. If not present it is assumed to be true. So, if we don't specify the Boolean expression, the `for` statement will become an infinite loop.

The increment section can also contain zero or more statements separated by commas. If multiple statements are present, they are executed from left to right.

Note that all the sections of the `for` statement are optional. The semicolons separating the different sections are mandatory. The following statement is perfectly valid:

```
for ( ; ; ) ;
```

When executed, this statement will create an infinite loop. Its effect is similar to the PL/SQL statements:

```
while true loop
  null
end loop;
```

or:

```
loop
  null
end loop;
```

The following program demonstrates use of the `for` statement in Java. It will take the argument passed to it from the command line and display its factorial:

```java
public class Factorial {
  public static void main(String[] arg) {
    int num = Integer.parseInt(arg[0]);
    factorial(num);    // invoke the factorial method
  }

  public static void factorial(int num) {
    int factorial = 1;

    for (int index = 1; index <= num; index++) {
      factorial = factorial * index;
    }
    System.out.println("Factorial of " + num + " is : " + factorial);
  }
}
```

When you compile and execute this program. It will display the factorial of the given number. For example:

```
> java Factorial 5
Factorial of 5 is : 120
```

The following is the equivalent PL/SQL procedure:

```
SQL> create or replace procedure factorial( num NUMBER )
  2  is
  3     factorial NUMBER := 1;
  4     ndx NUMBER;
  5  begin
  6     for ndx IN 1..num LOOP
  7        factorial := factorial * ndx;
  8     end loop;
  9     DBMS_OUTPUT.PUT_LINE( 'Factorial of ' || num || ' is : ' ||
                                                        factorial );
 10  end;
 11  /

Procedure created.

SQL> exec factorial(5);
Factorial of 5 is : 120

PL/SQL procedure successfully completed.
```

In PL/SQL, the `for` loop is very popular for cursor processing. Java on the other hand, being a general-purpose language, doesn't have any special loop for this purpose. In Java, when we process the `java.sql.ResultSet` (the Java equivalent of a PL/SQL cursor), we generally use the `while` loop instead of `for` loop. You will learn about the `ResultSet` processing in Chapter 5 *Using JDBC*.

The variable defined in the `for` loop is local to the `for` loop *only*; it cannot be used outside the construct. If a variable of the same name exists in the outer scope, the compiler will generate an error.

# The while Loop

The `while` statement is used to create a looping construct to repeatedly execute a set of statements as long as the specified Boolean expression evaluates to `true`. The Boolean expression is the loop's exit condition. When executing the `while` statement, Java evaluates this expression. If it evaluates to `false`, control is transferred to the next statement immediately following the `while` code block, without executing the statements within the block. Otherwise, the statements within the `while` code block are executed. Then, control resumes at the top of the loop and evaluates the expression again. The statements within the `while` code block are executed repeatedly until the expression evaluates to false. The expression is evaluated before each iteration. The `while` loop is also called a **pre-tested loop** because the test condition (the Boolean expression) is evaluated before executing the statements contained in the `while` code block. The format of the `while` construct is:

```
while ( <boolean expression> ) {
  <statements>
}
```

The braces are optional and can be omitted if there is only one statement in the `while` block. If there are multiple statements then they are *required*. It is good programming practice to always use braces to avoid confusion. The `while` statement in Java is similar to `while` statement of PL/SQL:

```
while <Boolean expression> loop
  <statements>
end loop;
```

Let's write a program to demonstrate the use of the `while` statement.

```
public class WhileLoopDemo {
  public static void main(String[] args) {
    demo();    // invoke the demo method
  }

  public static void demo() {
    double varDouble;
    while ((varDouble = Math.random() * 100) > 40) {
      System.out.println(varDouble);
    }
    System.out.println("\nCame out of loop when varDouble was : "
                      + varDouble);
  }
}
```

When you compile and run this program its output will look something like the following:

```
> java WhileLoopDemo
57.047154801069375
96.22942069031109
71.3800225386202
64.64989961519333
53.973160734881006
55.057412590903695
Came out of loop when varDouble was : 22.731742641379647
```

In the above program, `random()` is a static method defined in the `Math` class of `java.lang` package. `Math` is a utility class that defines various methods and constants for the very common mathematical operations. This method returns a random number of type `double` between `0.0` and `1.0`. For more information on the `Math` class see the Java API documentation.

The Boolean expression can be arbitrarily complex. However, it must yield a Boolean value otherwise a compilation error will occur.

When we should choose a `while` loop over a `for` loop is a matter of choice. You can use either loop over the other.

# The do...while Loop

The do...while statement is very similar to the while statement. The only difference is that the Boolean expression in do...while loop is evaluated *after* executing the statements in the do...while block, whereas in the while loop it is evaluated *before* executing the statements in the while block. This ensures that the statements in the do...while loop will be executed at least once, even though the Boolean expression evaluates to false. The do...while loop is also called a **post-tested loop** because the test condition is evaluated after executing the statements, contained in the do...while code block. The general format of do...while statement is:

```
do {
  <statements>
} while( <boolean expression> );
```

Note the ; after the while statement. It is required in the do...while statement, but not required in the while statement. Everything else is exactly the same as the while statement. Braces are again optional if there is only one statement in the loop. PL/SQL doesn't have an exact counterpart, but the same effect can be achieved in PL/SQL by using the following loop:

```
loop
    <statements>
    exit when <boolean expression>;
end loop;
```

If we rewrite the above program using do...while instead of while it will look like the following:

```
public class DoWhileLoopDemo {
  public static void main(String[] args) {
    demo();    // invoke the demo method
  }

  public static void demo() {
    double varDouble;

    do {
      varDouble = Math.random() * 100;
      System.out.println(varDouble);
    } while (varDouble > 40);
    System.out.println("\nCame out of loop when varDouble was : "
                       + varDouble);
  }
}
```

Compiling and running the script will give you similar results to the WhileLoopDemo class.

Note that the code block is executed at least once even if the Boolean expression evaluates to false in the first test only.

# The break statement

The break statement is used to terminate a loop prematurely, or to terminate the case code block in the switch statement. The syntax of a break statement is:

```
break [<label>];
```

The label is optional. If we don't specify the label, a break statement transfers control to the next statement outside the innermost enclosing loop or switch statement. In PL/SQL, we have the exit statement, which is similar to the break statement. Basically, both of them are used for the same purpose; to terminate loops pre-maturely. However, break and exit are different in that you can specify a condition with the exit statement in PL/SQL like this:

```
exit when <boolean expression>;
```

whereas a condition cannot be specified with the break statement in Java. The effect of a break statement is same as the exit statement of PL/SQL when used without condition.

An unlabeled break statement, if written in the case clause of switch statement, terminates the enclosing switch statement, and flow of control is transferred to the statement immediately following the switch block. You have already seen the use of the break statement in the switch construct.

Let's write a program to demonstrate the use of break statement. The following class takes in an argument on from the command line and checks whether it is prime or not:

```java
class PrimeTest {
  public static void main(String[] arg) {
    int number = 0;
    if (arg.length > 0) {
      number = Integer.parseInt(arg[0]);
    }
    testPrime(number);
  }

  public static void testPrime(int number) {
    boolean isPrime = true;
    for (int i = 2; i <= number / 2; i++) {
      if ((number % i) == 0) {
        isPrime = false;
        break;
      }
    }

    if (isPrime) {
      System.out.print(number + " is a prime number");
    } else {
      System.out.println(number + " is not a prime number");
    }
  }
}
```

Compiling and running this program will yield something similar to the following, depending on what you passed to it on the command line:

```
> java PrimeTest 7
7 is a prime number
```

In the above program, the `for` loop will be terminated when the Boolean expression:

```
(number % i) == 0
```

in the `if` condition evaluates to `true`, which means that the Boolean variable `isPrime` is set to `false` and the `break` statement following this statement is executed. This `break` statement causes control to be transferred outside the `for` loop.

The same program if written in PL/SQL will look like the following:

```
SQL> create or replace procedure PrimeTest( num NUMBER )
  2  is
  3     isPrime BOOLEAN := true;
  4     i        NUMBER := 20;
  5  begin
  6     for i IN 2..num/2 LOOP
  7        if MOD( num, i ) = 0 THEN
  8           isPrime := false;
  9           exit;
 10        end if;
 11     end loop;
 12
 13     if isPrime then
 14        DBMS_OUTPUT.PUT_LINE( num || ' is a prime number' );
 15     else
 16        DBMS_OUTPUT.PUT_LINE( num || ' is not a prime number' );
 17     end if;
 18  end PrimeTest;
 19  /

Procedure created.

SQL> exec PrimeTest(7);
7 is a prime number

PL/SQL procedure successfully completed.
```

If the `break` statement is used with a label, then it terminates the loop specified by the label. For example:

```
outer:
for( int i=0 ; i<10 ; i++ ) {
  <statements>
  inner:
  for( int j=0 ; j<5; j++ ) {
```

```
    <statements>

    break outer;

    <statements>
  }
  // if the break is used without label, the control
  // will resume here.
  <statements>
}
// if the break is used with label 'outer', the control
// will resume here
<statements>
```

This is how we can use the labeled break statement to come out of deeply nested loops. Its effect is same as the following PL/SQL code

```
<<outer>>
loop
  <statements>
  <<inner>>
  loop
    <statements>

    EXIT outer;

    <statements>
  end loop inner;
  --  If exit is used without label, control will resume here.
  <statements>
end loop outer;
--  If exit is used with "outer" label, control will resume here.
<statements>
```

The break statement can appear only inside a loop or a switch statement, otherwise a compilation error will occur.

# The continue Statement

The continue statement is used to skip the current iteration of a loop. Whenever a continue statement is encountered in a loop, it makes the control to skip the current iteration of the loop and evaluate the test condition for further iterations. It can be labeled or unlabeled. Its syntax is as follows:

```
continue [<label>];
```

The label is optional. If we don't specify the label, it skips all the remaining statements in the innermost loop's body, jumps back to the beginning of the loop, evaluates the Boolean expression that controls the loop, and continues with the next iteration. In essence, the current iteration is terminated and the next iteration starts with the test condition.

The labeled continue statement skips the current iteration of the loop marked by the label and starts the next iteration with the condition test.

PL/SQL does not have a statement equivalent to the continue statement of Java. The following program demonstrates the use of the continue statement. It will display a list of all the prime numbers up to the number it receives as the command line argument:

```
class PrimeGenerator {
  public static void main(String[] arg) {
    int limit = 50;
    if (arg.length > 0) {
      limit = Integer.parseInt(arg[0]);
    }
    printPrimes(limit);
  }

  public static void printPrimes(int limit) {
    outer:
    for (int i = 1; i < limit; i++) {
      for (int j = 2; j <= i / 2; j++) {
        if (i % j == 0) {
          continue outer;
        }
      }
      System.out.print(i + ", ");
    }
  }
}
```

When you execute this program, you should expect to see output like the following:

```
> java PrimeGenerator 40
1, 2, 3, 5, 7, 11, 13, 17, 19, 23, 29, 31, 37,
```

You can pass any number you want on the command line. The program will generate prime numbers less than the specified number. Whenever the expression:

```
i % j == 0
```

evaluates to true, the continue statement inside the if statement is executed, which skips all the remaining statements in the outer for loop marker by the label outer, and starts the next iteration with the condition test.

The continue statement can appear only inside a loop. Otherwise a compilation error will occur.

# The return statement

We use the return statement to exit from the current method or to return some value. The return statement terminates the current method and the control jumps back to the statement following the method call within the caller method. The syntax of the return statement is:

```
return <expression>;
```

The expression is optional. If the expression is missing, then the method containing the `return` statement must specify `void` as its return type. If the expression is present, its value should be of the same type as specified in the return type of the method, otherwise a compilation error will occur.

The `return` statement of Java is similar to the `return` statement of the PL/SQL and has the same syntax:

```
return <expression>;
```

If a method doesn't return any value, it behaves as a PL/SQL procedure. If it returns a value, then it behaves as a PL/SQL function.

If a method doesn't return a value, then its return type must be `void`. For example:

```
public void someMethod()
```

And in this method we can only use the `return` statement without an expression, like this:

```
return;
```

This statement terminates the current method and returns control to the calling method. A compilation error will occur if we use the `return` statement with an expression in a method that declares its return type to be `void`.

If the method declares a non-void return type, then we must use the `return` statement with an expression. The data type of the expression must be same as the return type of that method. For example if our method is declared as follows:

```
public String getName()
```

we must use the `return` statement with an expression, which evaluates to a `String` object like so:

```
return firstName + lastName;
```

where `firstName` and `lastName` are both `String` objects.

Let's write a program to demonstrate the use of the `return` statement. The `Average` class will print the average of the arguments passed to it from the command line:

```
public class Average {
    public static void main(String[] arg) {
        System.out.println("Average is : " + average(arg));
    }

    public static int average(String array[]) {
        int sum = 0;

        for (int i = 0; i < array.length; i++) {
```

```
      sum += Integer.parseInt(array[i]);
    }

    return sum / array.length;
  }
}
```

Here is an example execution:

```
> java Average 10 20 30 40
Average is : 25
```

Note that the `average()` method specifies `int` as its return type, so the `return` expression must also evaluate to a value of the `int` data type.

There is no `goto` statement in Java, but it is a reserved word. You can get the same functionality by using the `break` and/or `continue` statements with labels.

We have covered all the control structures in this appendix, except the `try...catch` construct, which is covered in detail in Chapter 6 *Handling Exceptions*.

# Arrays

An **array** is a fixed-length linear data structure containing multiple elements of the same type. The elements of the array can be accessed via an **index**, which is the position of the element from the beginning. The beauty of Java arrays is that the bounds checking is done by the runtime environment to ensure that their indices are within the range of the array. You can't access a memory location outside the bounds of the array. If you try to do so, the run-time exception `java.lang.ArrayIndexOutOfBoundsException` is thrown.

Let's write a program to demonstrate the use of arrays. The `Sorter` class will display the values it is passed on the command line in ascending order:

```
public class Sorter {
  public static void main(String[] arg) {
    int[] intArray = new int[arg.length];

    for (int i = 0; i < arg.length; i++) {
      intArray[i] = Integer.parseInt(arg[i]);
    }
    sort(intArray);

    // display the sorted values
    for (int i = 0; i < intArray.length; i++) {
      System.out.print(intArray[i] + ", ");
    }
  }
```

```
public static void sort(int[] array) {
    int temp;
    for (int i = 0; i < array.length; i++) {
        for (int j = i + 1; j < array.length; j++) {
            if (array[i] > array[j]) {
                temp = array[i];
                array[i] = array[j];
                array[j] = temp;
            }
        }
    }
}
```

Compiling and running this program by passing integer values to it will give something like the following:

```
> java Sorter 17 4 34 25 12 34 10 1 6
1, 4, 6, 10, 12, 17, 25, 34, 34,
```

In this program the statement:

```
int[] intArray = new int[arg.length];
```

declares the variable `intArray` to be an array that will contain elements of data type `int` and creates an array object and allocates `arg.length` (the number of parameters passed to it) memory locations, each of which can hold an element of `int` data type. Note that the memory to the array `intArray` is allocated at run-time when this statement is executed. So, we can specify the size of the array by any valid `int` literal or variable. The size of the array will be equal to the number of parameters passed to it, identified by `arg.length`. The empty square brackets `[]` qualify the variable `intArray` to be an array.

The array can also be initialized by directly putting values in it. For example:

```
int[] intArray = {2,4,6};
```

This would create an array of length 3, containing 2,4,6, as the element values. The length will be automatically calculated from the number of elements.

The elements of an array are accessed by specifying the index in square bracket like:

```
var = array[index];
```

or:

```
array[index] = var;
```

where the variable `index` specifies the index of array element that we want to access.

Arrays are treated like objects in Java and they are garbage collected just like objects when they are no longer referenced. The array object has a member field `length` that stores the length (number of elements) of this array, which can be accessed by the dot (.) operator.

The statement:

```
for( int i=0 ; i < intArray.length ; i++ )
```

creates a `for` loop, which is very similar to a `for` loop in PL/SQL. Also, note that the variable `i` is declared inside the `for` construct. This is perfectly valid and is very common in Java programs. Its scope is within the `for` loop block only.

If you don't initialize the elements of an array, they are initialized by the default values.

Also, note that we haven't handled the possible error condition `java.lang.ArrayIndexOutOfBoundsException`. The reason is because this is an unchecked exception. That means the programmer is not required to handle such exceptions. For more information on exceptions, refer to Chapter 6 *Handling Exceptions*.

Oracle 9i Java Programming

# Useful Core Java Classes

The intention is that this appendix will be used as a point of reference for background information on some of the core Java classes used in this book. If, for example, you are examining the file transfer application in Chapter 13, and need to brush up on streams, then hopefully you will find enough information here to get you through. It is not the aim of this appendix to act as a replacement for the extensive Java documentation. There are 50+ classes in the `java.io` package alone, around the same number in `java.lang`, 30+ in the `java.util` package – and this only scratches the surface!

However, the purpose of this appendix is to bring together the objectives of a few key classes that are important to Oracle development, and to provide more of an overview of their collaboration than the API documentation alone can. Once you can see how these classes can be used to supplement and extend the functionality you have available to you in PL/SQL, you will probably find it easier to branch out into using other classes. For the time being, this appendix should give you enough of a grounding for you to appreciate all the Java concepts discussed in this book.

We've tried to cover those classes that you, as an Oracle developer, will find useful time and again. The topics covered here are as follows:

- **Mathematical Operations**
  The primitive types provided by Java to support mathematical operations are more efficient than those provided by PL/SQL, and Java is optimized for CPU-intensive operations. Moving your numeric processing code into Java could immediately make your programs more effective.

- **Formatting Operations**
  Java's support for context-sensitive formatting of data, including internationalization is exceptionally strong, particularly when compared to the limited support offered by Oracle. Although this appendix will not cover internationalization in great detail, it will introduce some of the formatting features that Java provides.

- **The Collections API**
  The life's work of a database developer involves dealing with collections of data organized into result sets. Java provides a rich set of classes for treating collections in different ways, depending on whether they can best be handled as lists, sets, or even maps (data stored against keys, rather like primary keys on database tables). In fact, the set is too rich to be done much justice here, but it will at least be introduced.

❑ **Input and Output**

Java makes working with I/O, or input and output, a fairly painless and easy task, whether you are dealing with network sockets, terminal input, or writing to and reading from files. The latter activity is the one you will probably do the most, and is covered in Chapter 13. This appendix provides an introduction to I/O in Java, so you will easily be able to understand the practical examples in the book.

# Java API Specification

The Java platform includes a complete specification for its core API, which can be found in HTML format both along with the installed software, and online. The documentation for the Java 2, Standard Edition of the Java platform can be found at http://java.sun.com/j2se/.

If you have ever taken a look at the Java 2 API source code, you will have noticed a great deal of comments. Sun has provided a convenient documentation format for learning the API classes. The comments in the Java API source code include special **Javadoc** comments which, when the source code is processed with the Javadoc tool, are used to create formatted HTML documentation.

The HTML documentation makes it easy to find our way around the documentation with the use of frames (showing packages, classes, and interfaces in the currently selected package, and documentation for a specific class) and hypertext links. This documentation is invaluable, and no tutorial or book can serve as a replacement. Once you start writing Java code in earnest, you will probably find yourself using it daily, and it will certainly be useful for explaining the purpose of those hundreds of classes, which this appendix cannot cover.

# Mathematical Operations

It is likely that many of the Oracle applications you work on will involve a large amount of numeric processing. If they do, and if Java is to be incorporated into the applications, then it makes sense to do the processing in the Java code. This is because handling numbers using the SQL data types and operations used by PL/SQL is not nearly as efficient as using the types which are used in Java.

As well as the primitive number types that Java provides, there are also a large number of supporting classes in the Java platform, such as `java.lang.Number` and `java.lang.Math`. These give you the ability to perform complex manipulation of numbers with much more grace and simplicity than is possible in PL/SQL. Therefore, an understanding of how the classes and types work together will allow you to make informed decisions about how you are going to handle the numeric processing your application requires.

# Wrapper Classes

For each primitive data type, a wrapper class exists in the `java.lang` package. For example, `int` has the wrapper class `java.lang.Integer`, and `float` has the wrapper class `java.lang.Float`.

Just to recap, here are the Java primitive types again:

| Primitive | Effective Representation Type | Wrapper Class |
|---|---|---|
| boolean | 1 bit representing true or false | java.lang.Boolean |
| byte | 8 bits representing integral number | java.lang.Byte |
| short | 16 bits representing integral number | java.lang.Short |
| char | 16 bits representing Unicode character | java.lang.Character |
| int | 32 bits representing integral number | java.lang.Integer |
| float | 32 bits representing floating point number | java.lang.Float |
| long | 64 bits representing integral number | java.lang.Long |
| double | 64 bits floating point number | java.lang.Double |

Objects which are instances of wrapper classes contain just a single field of a type relating to the class. So, the field of an object of type java.lang.Integer will be an int, and the field of java.lang.Float will be a float.

The fields of wrapper classes are immutable. For example, if you have an Integer object that represents a value of 6, it is impossible to change the value it represents to 7. To represent the value 7, you need a whole new Integer object.

Given this, it might seem that there is little point in having wrapper classes. It becomes even more confusing if you consider the fact that operations on primitive types will always be quicker than operations on classes. So if you are performing any sort of calculations, it makes more sense to perform them directly on primitive types, rather than have both the overhead of constructing objects to represent them, and of performing operations on those objects.

However, there are three fundamental reasons for using a wrapper class rather than a primitive type:

❏   When you need an actual Java object to represent a value

❏   When you want to convert between strings and primitive types

❏   When you want to record the absence of a value

## Using Objects to Represent Values

Imagine a shopping cart application whereby customers can buy more than one item at a time – they can choose any number of items and will be charged for the total cost at the end.

There are many ways in which such a system might be implemented (and the simplistic solution demonstrated here would probably not be the first choice of many designers!). One such way is to keep a record of the amount of money to be spent by different customers.

The `PaymentRecorder` class does just that. It has a `recordPayment(String name, double payment)` method to record the payment made by a customer. The method takes as parameters the name of the customer, and a `double`, representing the amount they are due to pay. Here's the code for `PaymentRecorder.java`.

```
import java.util.HashMap;

public class PaymentRecorder {

  private HashMap payments;

  public PaymentRecorder() {
    payments = new HashMap();
  }
  public void recordPayment(String name, double payment) {
    Double d = new Double(payment);
    payments.put(name, d);
  }
}
```

The payment needs to be recorded in some way that will make it accessible in the future, and it needs to be recorded against the name of the customer. To do this, a `java.util.HashMap` is used. A hashmap is analogous to an Oracle table that stores data against a primary key: a hashmap stores Java objects against keys, which also must be Java objects.

The two crucial methods of a `HashMap` are `put(Object key, Objectvalue)`, which stores an object using a particular key into the hashmap structure, and `get(Object key)`, which returns the object previously stored under the specified key. Hashmaps will be revisited later in the appendix.

The `recordPayment()` method uses the customer name as the key to store the payment. However, only objects can be stored in hashmaps. If the method reads as follows instead, it would not compile.

```
public void recordPayment(String name, double payment) {
  Double d = new Double(payment);
  payments.put(name, d);
}
```

You would get an error message like:

```
method put(java.lang.String, double) not found in class java.util.HashMap
```

This is where the `Double` wrapper class comes in. By creating a new `Double` object, and passing in the double value, we can store the customer's payment so that it can be retrieved later. Additionally, the method `recordPayment(String name, double payment, boolean add)` allows a new payment for a customer to be added to their old one, if the `add` parameter is true. Since duplicate keys are not allowed in the hash map we do not need to worry that adding a payment for a customer will lead to two entries being stored for the customer.

```
public void recordPayment(String name, double payment, boolean add) {
  if (add) {
    Double d = (Double) payments.get(name);
```

```
      double value = 0;
      if (d != null) {
        value = d.doubleValue();
      }
      payments.put(name, new Double(payment + value));
    } else {
      recordPayment(name, payment);
    }
  }
```

Note also that since we have to use objects as the keys in the hashmap, the wrapper objects would be very useful if we wanted to have a numeric key. It's reasonable to assume that if the key were numeric, there would be times when it would be useful to use it to sort the values in the hash map. However, if we simply used `Strings` to store the keys, then the sorting would not work correctly, since 20 would come before 3. If however we used an `Integer` object instead, the problem would not occur.

All wrapper classes have constructors that take the corresponding primitive type as an argument, which is illustrated in the above example. Also, they all have methods to return their value as the primitive type. This can be seen in the method that returns the payment a particular customer has made, `getPayment()`.

```
  public double getPayment(String name) {
    Double d = (Double) payments.get(name);
    return d.doubleValue();
  }
```

Notice here that the value retrieved from the hash map is being cast to a `Double`. This is because the return type of the `get()` method is simply `java.lang.Object`, since objects of any type can be stored. However, since in this case we know the object will be a `Double`, we tell the compiler to treat it as such.

To see an example of how this code might be used, you can run the class. This will invoke the method which has the signature `public static void main(String[] args)`:

```
  public static void main(String[] args) {
    PaymentRecorder recorder = new PaymentRecorder();
    recorder.recordPayment("Mrs Smith", 23.42);
    recorder.recordPayment("Mr Jones", 99.99);
    recorder.recordPayment("Mrs Smith", 45.95, true);
    System.out.println("Mr Jones's total payments are "
                    + recorder.getPayment("Mr Jones"));
    System.out.println("Mrs Smith's total payments are "
                    + recorder.getPayment("Mrs Smith"));
  }
}
```

In this method we have created a new instance of the `PaymentRecorder` class, since the `main()` method is static. This means that it can only access variables and methods that are also static. None of the methods of the class are in fact static, so the `main()` method cannot access them. However, if we create a new instance that is local to the method, we can call methods on that instance in the normal way.

The method calls that are made produce this output:

```
> java PaymentRecorder
Mr Jones's total payments are 99.99
Mrs Smith's total payments are 69.37
```

This shows how the class keeps a running total of the payments made by a customer.

## Returning Wrapper Class Values As Different Primitive Types

It is possible to return the value of a numeric wrapper class as any numeric type, because the classes all extend java.lang.Number. This is an abstract class, which just contains the six methods:

- ❏ byteValue()
- ❏ doubleValue()
- ❏ floatValue()
- ❏ intValue()
- ❏ longValue()
- ❏ shortValue()

The implementation of these methods, which are found in java.lang.Double and so on, convert the value field of the class to a different primitive type if necessary, and return that. Of course, this may result in loss of data, if truncation has to occur, or if the value is too big for the specified type.

To illustrate this, consider the NumbersDemo1 class:

```
public class NumbersDemo1 {

  public static int i;

  public static void main(String args[]) {
    Double d = new Double(99.99);
    System.out.println(d.doubleValue() + "as an int is " + d.intValue());
    Long l = new Long(1L * 2 * 4 * 8 * 16 * 32 * 64 * 128 * 256);
    System.out.println("big long is " + l + ": int value is "
                        + l.intValue());
  }
}
```

This will produce the output

```
> java NumbersDemo1
99.99 as an int is 99
big long is 68719476736: int value is 0
```

99.99 has to be rounded down to an int value, while only the 32 least significant bits of a long can be used as an int value. This has the effect of chopping off the bits on the left of the long, leaving only the 32 right-most ones. The long's value is actually 68719476736, which represented in binary is 1000000000000000000000000000000000000. Since the 32 least significant bits are all 0, the int value of the long is 0.

## Converting Between Strings and Numbers

Converting a string to a number is something you will probably need to do a great deal. Often, a Java class accepts numeric input will only receive the input in `String` form, and yet needs to treat it as a number. A simple example of this is the `main()` method of a class, whose parameters have to be strings.

Fortunately, the `Integer` class provides the static `parseInt()` method, which will return an int. So you could use the code below to get an `int` type from a `String` passed in on the command line. The method adds up the value of all the numbers passed in and prints it out.

```java
public class StringsAndNumbers {
  public static void main(String[] args) {
    try {
      int total = 0;
      for (int i = 0; i < args.length; i++) {
        total += Integer.parseInt(args[i]);
      }
      System.out.println("Total is " + total);
    } catch (NumberFormatException ex) {
      ex.printStackTrace();
    }
  }
}
```

```
> java StringsAndNumbers 1 2 3
Total is 6
```

If you wanted to get an `Integer` object rather than an `int`, you can use the `Integer.valueOf()` method, or the integer class constructor which takes a `String` as a parameter:

```java
String s = args[i];
Integer i2 = Integer.valueOf(s);
```

or:

```java
String s = args[i];
Integer i2 = new Integer(s);
```

All of the wrapper classes provide similar methods – for example, `Double` has a `parseDouble()` method. These methods will throw the runtime exception `NumberFormatException` if the string supplied cannot be parsed to a number. You will find out more about exceptions in Chapter 6, *Handling Exceptions*.

## Absence Of Values

There is sometimes debate amongst Oracle designers about what NULL in a database table field represents. Some designers insist that it is an actual value encapsulating the fact that a value does not exist for the field, while others would respond that it indicates that the value is not known. Both sides are probably right on different occasions, depending on the design principles which have been followed, and usually developers have more pressing concerns with which to occupy their time but, whatever your feelings on the matter, you will probably be interested in the fact that primitive values in Java make the debate irrelevant.

This is because primitive data types in Java always have values int values which are instance variables. For example are initialized to 0 if the developer does not explicitly assign a value to them, and a double will have an initial value of 0.0. Method variables will not be automatically initialized, but the compiler will force you to assign a value to them, so they will never be valueless either. This may initially not seem to be problematic, but in certain circumstances it can lead to unexpected results.

The ScreenTracker class has been created to illustrate this. This class is supposed to keep track of which screen in an application a user is viewing. It has a list of screens, implemented as a String array:

```
public class ScreenTracker {
    private String[] screens = {"Login", "Catalogue", "Payment"};

    private int selectedScreen;
```

and an int variable to record the index of the screen they are viewing, which can be set through the setSelectedScreen() method.

```
public void setSelectedScreen(int index) {
    selectedScreen = index;
}
```

The getSelectedScreen() method returns the name of the screen that has been selected.

```
public String getSelectedScreen() {
    return screens[selectedScreen];
}
```

When the application is started, and before the index of the selected screen has been set, you might expect no screen to be selected. However, the code shown below will return 'Login' as the selected screen.

```
public static void main(String[] args) {
    ScreenTracker screens = new ScreenTracker();
    System.out.println("Selected screen is " + screens.getSelectedScreen());
}
```

You can verify these results by running ScreenTracker.java:

```
> java ScreenTracker
Selected screen is Login
```

This is because the selectedScreen variable has a value of 0 even if it has not been initialized. So how can you know when no screen has been selected?

The answer is to store the index of the selected screen as an Integer. This way, it will initially be null (and can be set to null, even after having been assigned a value). Then, when the class is asked to return the selected screen, it can return null if it has no index.

```
import java.lang.Integer;

public class ScreenTrackerUsingInteger {
  private String[] screens = {
    "Login", "Catalogue", "Payment"
  };

  private Integer selectedScreenInteger;

  public void setSelectedScreen(Integer index) {
    selectedScreenInteger = index;
  }
  public String getSelectedScreenByInteger() {
    if (selectedScreenInteger != null) {
      return screens[selectedScreenInteger.intValue()];
    }
    return null;
  }

  public static void main(String[] args) {
    ScreenTrackerUsingInteger screens = new ScreenTrackerUsingInteger();
    System.out.println("Selected screen is "
                        + screens.getSelectedScreenByInteger());
  }

}
```

You can verify these results by running `ScreenTrackerUsingInteger.java`:

```
> java ScreenTrackerUsingInteger
Selected screen is null
```

Another situation in which this trick is commonly used is in objects that represent data stored in a database. Quite often, you will initially want to load the object with as little data as possible, because it is quite likely that the end user will only need to access a couple of the object's attributes before discarding it. This is especially true of reference data, which would usually only be used to present the user with a list of values from which to choose.

Occasionally though, you might need to access more information about the object, and it may well be that you design it so that you put off accessing the database for this extra information until the user explicitly requests it. At this point you would need to check whether you already have a value for that piece of information, and go off to the database to get it if you have not.

In this situation, using a primitive to store the value (assuming of course that it is of a type which can be stored in a primitive) is no use. Primitives always have values, so you would have no way of telling whether the data has already been retrieved.

If on the other hand you used a wrapper class, you could leave the object reference set to null until the database has been accessed. In this case, if you checked and found the object reference was null, you would know for certain that its value had not been retrieved, and that going to the database to get it would be a necessary rather than a wasted overhead.

**781**

Of course, if the column in question was *not* constrained to be NOT NULL, then you would probably decide that a null value would be represented by a Number object with a numeric value of 0. In this way you could be sure that the database had been accessed, even if there was no value to be retrieved.

You will probably need to use this feature of the wrapper classes much less than the other two that have been discussed, but it is worth understanding nevertheless.

# java.math.BigDecimal

This class is a subclass of java.lang.Number, and is the only class which can safely be used to store an arbitrary length number obtained from Oracle. It represents a signed number of arbitrary precision, so it is not limited in the way as the Java primitive types and their wrapper classes. It also provides operations for basic arithmetic and scale manipulation, as well as giving you complete control over rounding behavior.

The most common way in which you create a BigDecimal will probably be to retrieve the relevant numeric value (usually from the database), and then pass a string representing this value to the constructor.

```
BigDecimal bd = new BigDecimal("180342.3628");
BigDecimal bd = new BigDecimal("-393.30838729");
```

After that, you can use the various methods of the class to manipulate the numeric value. See the API documentation for more details.

# Arithmetic Errors

The runtime exception java.lang.ArithmeticException is thrown if an error is thrown by integer arithmetic. For example, running NumbersDemo2.java:

```
public class NumbersDemo2 {
  public static void main(String args[]) {
    int j = 2;
    int k = 0;
    try {
      System.out.println("2/0 is " + j / k);
    } catch (ArithmeticException aex) {
      System.out.println("Arithmetic exception: " + aex.getMessage());
    }
  }
}
```

will produce this result:

```
> java NumbersDemo2
Arithmetic exception: / by zero
```

On the other hand, floating point arithmetic does not throw exceptions. If you try to do something using floating point types which would throw an exception were you using integers, the result will still be a `double` or a `float` (depending on the type you were using), but its value will be represented by special constants in the `Float` or `Double` class.

These constants are:

❑   POSITIVE_INFINITY – represents 1.0/0.0

❑   NEGATIVE_INFINITY – represents −1.0/0.0

❑   NaN (Not a Number) – represents 0.0/0.0

You can see an example of these constants by compiling and running `NumbersDemo3.java`:

```
public class NumbersDemo3 {
  public static void main(String args[]) {
    double m = 2;
    double n = 0;
    System.out.println("2/0 is " + m / n);
    System.out.println("Positive infinity: "
                    + (m / n == Double.POSITIVE_INFINITY));
    System.out.println("0/0 is " + n / n);
  }
}
```

This code will return the result:

```
> java NumbersDemo3
2/0 is Infinity
Positive infinity: true
0/0 is NaN
```

Here m/n gives the result `Double.POSITIVE_INFINITY` and n/n gives Not a Number.

There are static methods in the `Float` and `Double` classes to test whether a particular float or double's value is equal to one of these special constants: for instance, `Double.isNaN(double v)` and `Float.isInfinite(float v)` – note that this method does not differentiate between positive and negative infinity. For the other methods, see the API documentation.

# Mathematical Functions

The `java.lang.Math` class provides many mathematical functions. Since its constructor method is private, we cannot instantiate a `Math` object. However, all of the public methods are static, so instead, you use its functions through method calls:

```
public class NumbersDemo4 {
  public static int i;

  public static void main(String args[]) {
    double p = 4.5;
    double q = Math.sqrt(p);
```

```
        System.out.println("The square root of 4.5 is " + q);
    }
}
```

This will assign q the square root of 4.5:

```
> java NumbersDemo4
The square root of 4.5 is 2.1213203435596424
```

The complete list of methods in the `java.lang.Math` class can be found in the API documentation. Many of them are implemented using native code, to make them as efficient as possible.

# Formatting Operations

One of the most useful things to be found in the Java platform, particularly for developers writing software whose users need to be handled gently (pretty much all of us!) is the set of classes which can format program output in many different ways. Java has always been designed to make issues of internationalization as easy as possible to handle, so that the same results can be displayed differently depending on the geographical, political or cultural region of the person viewing them.

This is of great use to Oracle developers, since relational databases by their nature do not naturally support internationalization of the applications which are written using them. Only an application of very narrow scope would never have to concern itself (or, more importantly, its designers) with the needs of users in different countries, or speakers of different languages, and any developer who takes pride in their work will want to make their applications as flexible as possible when addressing such issues.

To that end, we are all familiar with the notion of storing reference data in separate tables, and referencing it through foreign keys, which gives some degree of centralization of the data which might need to change in order to deploy the application to different users. However, there is no easy answer to what happens after that. One solution is to have different sets of data for different sets of users, but this is by no means easy to manage or deploy.

Java, on the other hand, makes internationalization of data much simpler, as we will see in this section.

## java.util.Locale

This class represents a specific region, which could be political, geographical, or cultural. It is used for tasks that require information to be modified according to the region of the user. For example, US and UK-based users expect decimal points to be represented as a full stop or period, while France-based users would expect a comma.

To gain access to a `Locale` object, you can supply a language code and country code to its constructor. These codes are defined by ISO-3166, and can be found at http://www.ics.uci.edu/pub/ietf/http/related/iso639.txt and http://www.chemie.fu-berlin.de/diverse/doc/ISO_31n66.html. However, for our purposes, a simpler way is to use the `Locale` constants provided by the class, such as `Locale.US` and `Locale.FRANCE`.

```
Locale locale = Locale.FRANCE;
```

## java.text.NumberFormat

Once you have a reference to a `Locale` object, you can use it to perform formatting operations. `java.text.NumberFormat` performs formatting on numbers – specifically, on `long`s and `double`s, although this of course means it can implicitly operate on `int`s and `float`s as well.

The class `NumericParser` takes in a `Locale` object as an argument to its constructor.

```
public class NumericParser {
  private Locale locale;

  public NumericParser(Locale locale) {
    this.locale = locale;
  }
```

It then uses the `Locale` object in its methods such as `display()`.

```
public String display(double value) {
  NumberFormat nf = NumberFormat.getNumberInstance(locale);
  return nf.format(value);
}
```

The static `getNumberInstance()` method of the `NumberFormat` class returns a `NumberFormat` instance which uses the `NumericParser`'s `locale` object. It is also possible to call `NumberFormat.getInstance()` without passing in a `Locale` object; in this case, the default locale will be used. The default locale is set by the JVM on startup, and is based on the host environment, but it can be overridden by calling `Locale.setDefault()`.

Once you have a `NumberFormat` object, you can use it to give numbers a format that is sensitive to the user's locale. `NumberFormat.format()` accepts a `long` or a `double`, and returns a `String`. So, for example, the `main()` method of the `NumericParser` class contains the following code:

```
public static void main(String args[]) {
  NumericParser france = new NumericParser(Locale.FRANCE);
  String frenchDisplay = france.display(1000000.66);
  System.out.println("10000000.66 in French is " + frenchDisplay);

  NumericParser usa = new NumericParser(Locale.US);
  String usaDisplay = usa.display(1000000.66);
  System.out.println("10000000.66 in US is " + usaDisplay);
}
```

When run, this returns the result:

```
> java NumericParser
10000000.66 in French is 1 000 000,66
10000000.66 in US is 1,000,000.66
```

The `NumericParser` class also contains the method `displayAsCurrency()`.

```
public String displayAsCurrency(double value) {
  NumberFormat nf = NumberFormat.getCurrencyInstance(locale);
  return nf.format(value);
}
```

This uses the `NumberFormat.getCurrencyInstance()` method, which returns an object capable of formatting currencies. This method can be used in the following way:

```
NumericParser france = new NumericParser(Locale.FRANCE);
String frenchCurrency = france.displayAsCurrency(0.66);
System.out.println("0.66 as currency in French is " + frenchCurrency);

NumericParser usa = new NumericParser(Locale.US);
String usaCurrency = usa.displayAsCurrency(0.66);
System.out.println("0.66 as currency in US is " + usaCurrency);
```

which returns:

```
> java NumericParser
0.66 as currency in French is 0,66 F
0.66 as currency in US is $0.66
```

## Turning Strings Back into Numbers

Since numbers can be displayed as different strings for different regions, it follows that different strings may well represent the same number. Fortunately, `NumberFormat` provides for this eventuality too, with its `parse()` methods. These accept a `String`, and attempt to convert it to a `java.lang.Number` object according to the formatting rules of the locale in use. If it cannot convert the `String`, it throws a `java.text.ParseException`.

The `NumericParser` class therefore contains the method `parseCurrency()`:

```
public Number parseCurrency(String value) throws ParseException {
  NumberFormat nf = NumberFormat.getCurrencyInstance(locale);
  return nf.parse(value);
}
```

The method is called as follows:

```
try {
  NumericParser france = new NumericParser(Locale.FRANCE);
  String frenchCurrency = france.displayAsCurrency(0.66);
  String frenchDisplay = france.display(1000000.66);
  System.out.println("0.66 as currency in French is " + frenchCurrency);
  System.out.println("10000000.66 in French is " + frenchDisplay);
  System.out.println(frenchCurrency + " changed back again is "
                    + france.parseCurrency(frenchCurrency));
```

```
            System.out.println(frenchDisplay + " changed back again is "
                             + france.parse(frenchDisplay));

            NumericParser usa = new NumericParser(Locale.US);
            String usaCurrency = usa.displayAsCurrency(0.66);
            String usaDisplay = usa.display(1000000.66);
            System.out.println("0.66 as currency in US is " + usaCurrency);
            System.out.println("10000000.66 in US is " + usaDisplay);
            System.out.println(usaCurrency  + " changed back again is "
                             + usa.parseCurrency(usaCurrency));
            System.out.println(usaDisplay + " changed back again is "
                             + usa.parse(usaDisplay));
        } catch (ParseException pex) {
            pex.printStackTrace();
        }
```

Running `NumericParser.java`, that contains all of these methods, produces this output:

```
> java NumericParser
0.66 as currency in French is 0,66 F
10000000.66 in French is 1 000 000,66
0,66 F changed back again is 0.66
1 000 000,66 changed back again is 1000000.66
0.66 as currency in US is $0.66
10000000.66 in US is 1,000,000.66
$0.66 changed back again is 0.66
1,000,000.66 changed back again is 1000000.66
```

## Formatting Dates

Dates are clearly more complex than numbers: whereas a number consists purely of digits, some of which are decimal places (and a sign), dates include years, months, days, numbers of the month, a time element, not to mention implicit assumptions about significant historical events from which future dates are measured.

In addition to this inherent complexity, the way that dates are represented in Java can often be a source of confusion amongst Java developers. However this is not because there is anything especially complicated about the way that they are represented, as long as you understand that there are three main classes you need to be concerned with.

These are:

❑   java.util.Date

❑   java.text.DateFormat

❑   java.util.GregorianCalendar

First we'll look at java.util.Date and java.text.DateFormat, since these relate to a similar way to the one we have already seen in Number and NumberFormat.

## Dates and Date Formats

`java.util.Date` represents a moment in time with millisecond precision. To create one, you need to use the class constructor in the normal way. If you supply no parameters, then the `Date` object will represent the moment in time at which it was created. If you want to create an object to represent a different moment in time, you can supply a long value representing the number of milliseconds since January 1st 1970, 00:00:00 GMT. This is of course not the most convenient way of creating a `Date` object, but later on we will look at easier ways of setting the moment in time that it represents. For the time being, we will just use objects representing the current date, created as follows.

```
java.util.Date = new java.util.Date();
```

`java.text.DateFormat` works in a similar way to `java.text.NumberFormat`, with some additional functionality. The `DateParser` class illustrates this.

```
public class DateParser {

  private Locale locale;

  public DateParser(Locale locale) {
    this.locale = locale;
  }
```

This is the constructor of the class. It takes a `Locale` object as a parameter, because dates are locale-specific – the same moment in time would be represented differently to people of different regions.

The `main()` method of the class creates two `DateParser` objects, one for France, and one for the USA:

```
DateParser usa = new DateParser(Locale.US);
DateParser france = new DateParser(Locale.FRANCE);
Date date = new Date();
```

Once the `DateParser` instance has been created, its methods can be called:

```
System.out.println("Short US date is "
                    + usa.format(date, DateFormat.SHORT));

System.out.println("Short French date is "
                    + france.format(date, DateFormat.SHORT));
```

This is almost the same as the way we called methods on the `NumericParser` class, but not quite. In the `NumericParser` class, the code was:

```
NumericParser france = new NumericParser(Locale.FRANCE);
String frenchDisplay = france.display(1000000.66);
```

In the `DateParser` class however, an extra parameter is supplied to the method which formats the date. If we look at the `format()` method, we can see why:

```
public String format(Date date, int style) {
  DateFormat df = DateFormat.getDateInstance(style, locale);
  return df.format(date);
}
```

The getDateInstance() method of java.text.DateFormat, which returns a DateFormat instance, takes an extra parameter as well as the locale. The parameter is an int, and should be one of four constants in the DateFormat class:

❑ DateFormat.SHORT

❑ DateFormat.MEDIUM

❑ DateFormat.LONG

❑ DateFormat.FULL

These constants affect how dates are formatted for display by the DateFormat object. An example can be seen if you run the DateParser class. This will run the code:

```
DateParser usa = new DateParser(Locale.US);
DateParser france = new DateParser(Locale.FRANCE);
Date date = new Date();

System.out.println("Short US date is "
                    + usa.format(date, DateFormat.SHORT));
System.out.println("Medium US date is "
                    + usa.format(date, DateFormat.MEDIUM));
System.out.println("Long US date is "
                    + usa.format(date, DateFormat.LONG));
System.out.println("Full US date is "
                    + usa.format(date, DateFormat.FULL));

System.out.println("Short French date is "
                    + france.format(date, DateFormat.SHORT));
System.out.println("Medium French date is "
                    + france.format(date, DateFormat.MEDIUM));
System.out.println("Long French date is "
                    + france.format(date, DateFormat.LONG));
System.out.println("Full French date is "
                    + france.format(date, DateFormat.FULL));
```

This returns the output:

```
> java DateParser
Short US date is 10/2/01
Medium US date is Oct 2, 2001
Long US date is October 2, 2001
Full US date is Tuesday, October 2, 2001
Short French date is 02/10/01
Medium French date is 2 oct. 01
Long French date is 2 octobre 2001
Full French date is mardi 2 octobre 2001
```

The API documentation gives details of what output you get when using the different styles.

There is another `format()` method in the `DateParser` class:

```
public String formatWithTime(Date date, int style) {
  DateFormat df = DateFormat.getDateTimeInstance(style, style, locale);
  return df.format(date);
}
```

This calls `DateFormat.getDateTimeInstance()`, which returns a `DateFormat` instance capable of formatting the time portion of the date as well as the date portion. A parameter must be supplied to indicate how the time can be formatted; this is again one of the four constants in the `DateFormat` class listed above.

```
System.out.println("Short US date with time is "
                    + usa.formatWithTime(date, DateFormat.SHORT));
System.out.println("Medium US date with time is "
                    + usa.formatWithTime(date, DateFormat.MEDIUM));
System.out.println("Long US date with time is "
                    + usa.formatWithTime(date, DateFormat.LONG));
System.out.println("Full US date with time is "
                    + usa.formatWithTime(date, DateFormat.FULL));

System.out.println("Short French date with time is "
                    + france.formatWithTime(date, DateFormat.SHORT));
System.out.println("Medium French date with time is "
                    + france.formatWithTime(date, DateFormat.MEDIUM));
System.out.println("Long French date with time is "
                    + france.formatWithTime(date, DateFormat.LONG));
System.out.println("Full French date with time is "
                    + france.formatWithTime(date, DateFormat.FULL));
```

This will produce the output:

```
> java DateParser
Short US date with time is 10/2/01 7:45 AM
Medium US date with time is Oct 2, 2001 7:45:22 AM
Long US date with time is October 2, 2001 7:45:22 AM GMT
Full US date with time is Tuesday, October 2, 2001 7:45:22 AM GMT
Short French date with time is 02/10/01 07:45
Medium French date with time is 2 oct. 01 07:45:22
Long French date with time is 2 octobre 2001 07:45:22 GMT+00:00
Full French date with time is mardi 2 octobre 2001 07 h 45 GMT+00:00
```

## Parsing Dates Using Patterns

So far so good, but the formatting we have performed on dates has been restricted to what the `DateFormat` class decides it will do depending on the parameters we supply to it. What if we want to format dates in a particular way? In Oracle it is easy to format a date so that just the month portion is displayed, for example. How can something similar be done in Java?

The easiest way is to use the `java.text.SimpleDateFormat` class, which is a subclass of `DateFormat`. This can be constructed directly, as illustrated in the `formatDateAsMonth()` method – you do not have to use a `getInstance()` method as we did with the other formatting classes.

```
public String formatDateAsMonth(Date date) {
   SimpleDateFormat sdf = new SimpleDateFormat("MMMM", locale);
   return sdf.format(date);
}
```

The first parameter supplied to the constructor is a pattern that tells it how to format the date. The full details of the different possible patterns can be found in the API specification, but here are some of them (copied from the documentation).

| Symbol | Meaning | Presentation | Example |
|--------|---------|--------------|---------|
| G | era | (Text) | AD |
| y | year | (Number) | 1996 |
| M | month in year | (Text & Number) | July & 07 |
| d | day in month | (Number) | 10 |
| h | hour in am/pm (1~12) | (Number) | 12 |
| H | hour in day (0~23) | (Number) | 0 |
| m | minute in hour | (Number) | 30 |
| s | second in minute | (Number) | 55 |

In the above example we are passing in MMMM, – the pattern M four times. This indicates that the full form of the month should be used. If we had passed in the pattern less than four times, for example 'MMM', the shortened form would have been used. For more details about using patterns, see the API documentation.

If the formatDateAsMonth() method is called using the following code

```
System.out.println("Date formatted as US month is "
                  + usa.formatDateAsMonth(date));
System.out.println("Date formatted as French month is "
                  + france.formatDateAsMonth(date));
```

The output is:

```
> java DateParser
Date formatted as US month is October
Date formatted as French month is octobre
```

## Changing the Date an Object Represents

So far we have been dealing with a Date object initialized to represent the time at which the object was created. What if we want to deal with a different date, and don't want to have to work out the number of milliseconds since some arbitrary date over 30 years ago?

In this case we need to use an instance of `java.util.GregorianCalendar` – this is a subclass of `java.util.Calendar`. `Calendar` is an abstract class that provides the facility to change the date, or create an arbitrary date, represented by a `Date` object. Subclasses of it interpret `Date` objects according to the rules of a particular calendar system. `GregorianCalendar` is the only subclass provided by the Java platform, and represents the calendar used by most of the Western world, which divides dates into the two eras BC and AD.

The `setDateToNewYear()` method of the `DateParser` class shows how to use the `GregorianCalendar` class.

```
public String setDateToNewYear(Date date, int style) {
    GregorianCalendar cal = new GregorianCalendar(locale);
    cal.setTime(date);
    cal.set(Calendar.MONTH, Calendar.JANUARY);
    cal.set(Calendar.DATE, 1);
    DateFormat dtf = DateFormat.getDateTimeInstance(style, style, locale);
    return dtf.format(cal.getTime());
}
```

A `GregorianCalendar` object is constructed, passing in a `Locale` object. The `setTime()` method is then called to set the `Date` the `GregorianCalendar` represents.

Then the `set()` method of the `GregorianCalendar` class is called, passing in different parameters. The first parameter is a constant of the `Calendar` class, indicating which field should be set. The second represents what it should be set to – the `Calendar` class also contains constants for some of the possible values.

Once the `set()` method has been called, `GregorianCalendar.getTime()` will return a reference to a new `Date` object that represents a different time. The `setDateToNewYear()` method illustrates this by fully formatting the date. Calling the method:

```
System.out.println("Date as New Years Day is "
            + usa.setDateToNewYear(date, DateFormat.FULL));
```

produces the output:

```
> java DateParser
Date as New Years Day is Monday, January 1, 2001 7:45:22 AM GMT
```

This shows that the date and month have changed, but not the day, year or the time, since we did not change these fields.

The full list of the fields that can be set in a `Calendar` object, and the constants which can be used to set them, can be found in the API documentation.

# String Tokenizers

Before we move on to the next set of classes, there is one last formatting facility that we should know about – the `StringTokenizer` class, in the `java.util` package.

The simple `StringTokenizerDemo` class shows the main facilities provided by the `StringTokenizer` class.

```java
import java.util.StringTokenizer;

public class StringTokenizerDemo {

    public static void main(String[] args) {
        String toParse =
            " fresh basil, buffalo mozzarella, extra virgin olive oil";
        String delim = ",";
        StringTokenizer tk = new StringTokenizer(toParse, delim);
        System.out.println("There are " + tk.countTokens()
                          + " items on the shopping list");
        String returnString = "";
        while (tk.hasMoreTokens()) {
            returnString = returnString + tk.nextToken() + "\n";
        }
        System.out.println(returnString);
    }
}
```

A `StringTokenizer` needs to be constructed with a string to parse, and a string representing the characters to treat as delimiters. Delimiters are characters that are used to break down the string into tokens. In this example, the string to parse is a shopping list, and we are going to break it down every time we encounter a comma ',' character.

❑   `StringTokenizer.countTokens()` returns the number of elements – or tokens – which can be found in the string if it is broken down in the specified way.

❑   `StringTokenizer.nextToken()` will return the portion of the string up until the next delimiter which is encountered.

❑   `StringTokenizer.hasMoreTokens()` will return true if there remain tokens to be parsed.

In this example, we are getting each token in turn, and adding it to a string along with a newline character (\n). The result is:

```
> java StringTokenizerDemo
There are 3 items on the shopping list
 fresh basil
 buffalo mozzarella
 extra virgin olive oil
```

# The Collections API

Working with data structures, collections of data values, is something any database developer has to do a great deal. Result sets returned from the database are the nuts and bolts of virtually every PL/SQL package. However, the facilities Oracle offers for manipulating result sets are not extensive: sorting them once they have been retrieved, for example, cannot be done easily. If you want to format part of the data which is retrieved, concatenating firstnames and surnames with a space in between, perhaps, you can do so as you retrieve it, but your options for reformatting after that are limited.

The **Collections API** in Java, on the other hand provides a great deal of functionality that is not easily available in PL/SQL. If you turn your result sets into some sort of Java collection (which is a whole topic of its own which cannot be covered here), then you will have much more flexibility in the way you can manipulate your result set. So let's look at the `Collections` API and see what it offers.

# The Problem with Arrays

Firstly, we'll just look again at how arrays work in Java, and how they can be used to store and retrieve both objects and primitives.

```
String[] strings = {"one", "two", "three"};
int[] ints = new int[3];
ints[0] = 4;
ints[1] = 5;
ints[2] = 6;
System.out.println("String at position 0 is " + strings[0]);
System.out.println("int at position 1 is " + ints[1]);
```

Arrays can be either initialized with their values when they are created, or initialized with their length. The elements at the position in the array can be set and retrieved, but the size of the array cannot be changed.

This is one of the major restrictions of arrays: there is no way that they can grow. And although indexed access to the elements in the array is very fast, searching through the elements to find a specific one cannot be done efficiently once the array is of any significant size. The fact that only objects (or primitives) of the same type can be stored in the array could also be restrictive in some situations.

# The Solution: Collections

If we need data structures which allow their elements to be searched efficiently, and the number of elements to be increased, then something other than arrays has to be used. This is exactly what the Collections API is designed to address.

The Collections API is a set of interfaces and classes that work together to provide various ways of storing and retrieving elements. The UML diagram below illustrates the key players in the set of classes. Those in bold are the ones on which we will be examining in more detail.

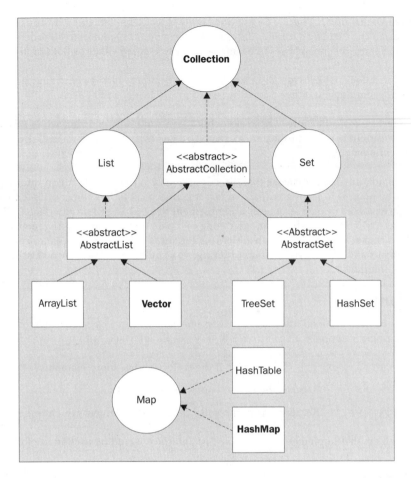

From the diagram, we can see that the `java.util.Collection` interface is the base of the collections classes. Its key methods are:

- ❏ `boolean add(Object o)` – Adds an object to the collection
- ❏ `boolean remove(Object o)` – Removes an element from the collection
- ❏ `boolean contains(Object o)` – Returns true if the collection contains the specified object

Since all of these methods take instances of the type `Object` as their parameters, you cannot store primitives directly in a `Collection`. Instead they must first be encapsulated in one of the wrapper classes mentioned earlier. On the other hand, since every object written in Java is a descendant of `java.lang.Object`, objects of any type can be stored in a `Collection` and there is nothing to prevent the same collection storing objects of different types.

Another important method is `iterator()`, which returns an `Iterator` object reference, but we will return to this in a moment.

You should notice that the Collection interface is not directly implemented by any concrete classes in the Java platform. The Collection interface does not require its elements to be ordered or unique; it leaves it up to its implementing classes to decide whether to enforce either or both of these constraints.

The Java platform does not provide any class that doesn't enforce either constraint; instead, all the classes it provides implement either java.util.List or java.util.Set.

List is an interface for collections whose elements are in some sort of order, while Set is for collections that cannot contain duplicates. ArrayList and Vector implement List, while TreeSet and HashSet implement Set.

Since there are no non-abstract classes that directly implement the Collection interface, you may wonder what the point is in having it at all. In fact it comes back to the object-oriented nature of Java. Since the different types of data structures all implement the Collection interface indirectly, you can refer to them as Collection objects in your code and pass them around in as general a manner as possible, which makes your code very flexible. In addition, if you did want a data structure that allowed duplicate elements and which provided no ordering, you could create your own class that did directly implement the interface.

## The Iterator Interface

As has already been mentioned, the Collection interface has an iterator() method which returns an Iterator object reference. Iterator is a very simple interface, with just three methods.

❏   boolean hasNext() – Returns true if the collection has more elements

❏   Object next() – Returns the next element in the collection

❏   void remove() – Removes from the collection the last element which was returned

Typically, an object that implements the Iterator interface would be used in the following way:

```
Collection c;
Iterator i = c.iterator();
while (i.hasNext()) {
  Object o = i.next();
  // do something with the object
}
```

While an iterator obviously provides only limited functionality, its most obvious restriction being that it only allows its elements to be traversed once, it is a useful way of getting quick access to all the elements of a collection, no matter how the collection is implemented. In other words, it allows developers to learn a single interface, which can be used to access disparate types of collections. Furthermore, each type of collection object can provide its own Iterator implementation, and therefore can use the most efficient means available to step through the collection.

In addition, because it is such a simple interface, it is easy to write your own classes which implement it and which can be used in any custom collections you might want to write.

## java.util.Map

You will probably have noticed that the `Map` interface does not extend the `Collection` interface. Maps work in a slightly different way, in that they map keys to values. This means that they contain two collections: a set of keys, and a collection of values. There can be at most one instance of each key in the map, and each key maps to at most one value.

Although `Map` does not implement the `Collection` interface, it provides three methods that return its contents as collections.

❑   `Set keySet()` – Returns a set of the keys in the map

❑   `Collection values()` – Returns a collection of the values

❑   `Set entrySet()` – Returns a set of the mappings in the map, a mapping being a key-value pair.

There are two main implementations of `Map`: `HashMap` and `Hashtable`. The main difference between these two classes is that `HashMap` allows nulls to be stored as values or keys, while `Hashtable` does not.

`HashMap` and `Hashtable` use hashing to store objects. What this means is that objects in the map are not associated with the identity of their keys, but with the content of their key. A hashing algorithm is performed on the key to retrieve a hash code for it, a hash code being a number that is a function of the data contained in the object. Small changes in the object's data generally generate large differences in the object's hashcode.

This is analogous to Oracle database indexes, where `rowids` are used to associate indexes with particular rows in a table.

An example of generating hash codes can be seen in the `HashCodeDemo` class:

```
public class HashCodeDemo {
  public static void main(String[] args) {
    String stationary = "stationary";
    String stationery = "stationery";
    String practice = "practice";
    String practise = "practise";
    System.out.println("Hash code for " + stationary + " is "
                       + stationary.hashCode());
    System.out.println("Hash code for " + stationery + " is "
                       + stationery.hashCode());
    System.out.println("Hash code for " + practice + " is "
                       + practice.hashCode());
    System.out.println("Hash code for " + practise + " is "
                       + practise.hashCode());
  }
}
```

the output of which is:

```
> javac HashCodeDemo.java
Hash code for stationary is -98468684
Hash code for stationery is -98464840
Hash code for practice is -1405517509
Hash code for practise is -1405517013
```

The upshot of using hashing is that searching a map which uses it can be very quick. However, there needs to be a significant number of elements in the map for the advantages to become apparent, since there is an overhead associated with calculating the hashcodes for the keys.

## Using the Collections Classes

All the classes in the Collections API overcome the limitations of the array's data structure.

❑ Arrays provide fast indexed access, but increasing their size and inserting and removing elements is not supported – instead you have to create an entirely new array. Searching the array is also not easy. Objects or primitives in the array must all be of the same type.

❑ Lists make increasing the size of the store and adding and deleting elements easier, although indexed access is slower than it would be in an array. Objects of any type can be stored in a list.

❑ Maps, particularly hashed maps, do not have particularly fast indexed access to the elements in the collection, but they do provide fast searching. Objects of any type can also be stored in a map.

It may seem that there is such a wealth of data structures to choose from in Java (especially when you consider the fact that it is possible to write your own) that it must be very difficult to decide which to use in any given situation. In fact, most of the time, what you want to do with the collection will make the decision as to which one to use very easy. However, if you want to know more about the advantages of the different types, then *Complete Java 2 Certification*, by Simon Roberts, Philip Heller and Michael Ernest (Sybex), is a great place to start.

### java.util.Vector

A Vector is a list of elements that can be accessed through an index. The size of the vector can grow or shrink as objects are added and removed. Objects can be added to and removed from any position in the list, and objects of different types can be stored in the list.

The code for this section can be found in the CollectionsDemo class.

```java
import java.util.Vector;
import java.util.HashMap;
import java.util.Iterator;

public class CollectionsDemo {

  public void demoVector() {

    Vector v = new Vector();
    v.add("Fargo");
    v.add("Raising Arizona");
    v.add(0, "Blood Simple");
    v.add(1, new Integer(1));
```

```
      Iterator i = v.iterator();
      while (i.hasNext()) {
        System.out.println(i.next());
      }
    }
  }
```

If you do not specify where an object should be added, it will be added at the end:

```
Blood Simple
1
Fargo
Raising Arizona
```

You can check whether a particular element is in the list:

```
System.out.println("Fargo is in list: " + v.contains("Fargo"));
```

```
Fargo is in list: true
```

And you can remove elements from the list:

```
v.remove("Fargo");
System.out.println("Fargo is now in list: " + v.contains("Fargo"));
```

```
Fargo is now in list: false
```

You can also find out where an object is in the list, and get an object at a particular point:

```
int index = v.indexOf("Raising Arizona");
System.out.println(v.get(index));
```

```
Raising Arizona
```

There are of course more things you can do, but, as ever, you should look at the API specification if you are keen to find out more.

### java.util.HashMap

Objects can be added to a HashMap using the put() method. null can also be added to a HashMap instead of an object.

```
HashMap map = new HashMap();
map.put("key1", "The World According to Garp");
map.put("key2", null);
map.put("key3", "The Cider House Rules");
```

```
        Iterator i = map.values().iterator();
        while (i.hasNext()) {
          System.out.println(i.next());
        }
```

```
The Cider House Rules
null
The World According to Garp
```

Notice how this uses the values() method to return the objects in the HashMap. The HashMap values() method returns the objects in an arbitrary order; if you want to retain sorting in a Map, then you should use an implementation of the SortedMap interface.

Objects can also be removed from the HashMap, or replaced. If you call put(), specifying a key which has already been used, then the new value will overwrite the old one at that point. However, the put() method will return the original object which is being replaced or the object itself if it does not replace an object already in the map.

```
    map.put("key4", "The 158-pound marriage");
    Object o = map.put("key1", "The Hotel New Hampshire");
    System.out.println("Removed object is " + o);
    map.remove("key2");

    Iterator i2 = map.values().iterator();
    while (i2.hasNext()) {
      System.out.println(i2.next());
    }
```

```
Removed object is The World According to Garp

The 158-pound marriage
The Cider House Rules
The Hotel New Hampshire
```

The element "The World According to Garp" no longer exists in the HashMap, but it was returned by the second put() method which used its key.

There are more classes available in the API, such as those which implement the functionality associated with mathematical sets (not something which is easily reproducible in PL/SQL!) but there is too much to go into here, and the API documentation does a good job of covering the basics.

# Input and Output

In database programming, as with most other types of programming, there comes a point where our programs have to communicate with other types of devices. At this point, we move away from the (relatively) straightforward manipulation of data within the database, and start having to work with input and output. Some examples are:

❑ Importing information from a file outside the database

❑ Exporting data to a file, perhaps for backup purposes

Java views all input and output (**I/O**) as **streams**, which are ordered sequences of bytes, making up a flow of data. Streams could be used to communicate through sockets, to read or write terminal output, or to read to and write from files. Whatever the type of communication, a stream will be the basis of it.

Working with streams is something that comes up a great deal throughout this book, so it is important that you have a clear understanding of how Java deals with them. Here we will work through sufficient simple examples for you to appreciate how I/O works in Java, and for you to understand how the more complex examples presented elsewhere actually work.

Let's start by looking at a class diagram of some of the key classes:

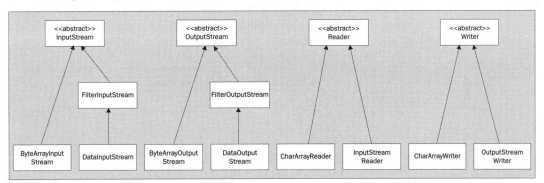

These classes are all in the `java.io` package. The diagram does not show all classes in the package, just some important ones and some we will be looking at.

`InputStream` and `OutputStream` are abstract classes, which are the basis of all other types of streams. Java divides streams into two types:

❑ *Low-level streams* operate on bytes. Input streams read bytes, from an input device or a file. Output streams write bytes to devices. `ByteArrayInputStream` and `ByteArrayOutputStream` are examples of low-level streams: the 'device' on which they operate is simply an array of bytes.

❑ *High-level streams*, or *filter* streams, operate not on bytes, but on other streams. The stream operated on can be a low-level stream, or another high-level stream. The purpose of this is to be able to read and write data in a format other than bytes, which are not the most useful form of information. `DataInputStream` and `DataOutputStream` are examples of filter streams.

❑ *Readers and Writers* are similar to filter streams, but they are specialized for reading and writing Unicode characters. Like streams, they can be either low-level (operating on I/O devices), or high-level (operating on low-level readers and writers). `CharArrayReader` is an example of a low-level reader: it reads from an array of characters. `OutputStreamWriter` is a high-level writer, which writes Unicode characters to an `OutputStream`.

We'll now look at the different types of stream in more detail. All the code for this section can be found in the `StreamsDemo` class.

# Low-Level Streams

The examples we will be looking at are somewhat artificial. Normally files are used as an illustration of I/O, since they make for simple examples, and file processing is one of the most common types of I/O.

In all these examples we will write data to an output stream, and then simulate performing some operations on it to change the data. We will then retrieve the data as an InputStream, and read from it to find out how the data has changed. This is obviously a contrived scenario, as normally the environment would provide both the streams and the operations that are performed on the data contained within the streams. However, using code that is as simple as possible means that you can see exactly what is going on, and that you can run the code without needing to set up anything complicated.

Since InputStream and OutputStream are abstract classes, we cannot instantiate them directly. Instead we have to use one of their subclasses. To start with, we'll be looking at the ByteArrayInputStream and ByteArrayOutputStream, which read from and write to arrays of bytes. Since all streams are essentially a sequence of bytes, they are a nice introduction to how streams work.

It is also easy to construct an array of bytes, to simulate the environment creating a stream of data for us. So, first of all, we'll construct some arrays of bytes which we can operate on.

```
import java.io.DataInputStream;
import java.io.DataOutputStream;
import java.io.FilterInputStream;
import java.io.FilterOutputStream;
import java.io.OutputStream;
import java.io.InputStream;
import java.io.ObjectOutputStream;
import java.io.ObjectInputStream;
import java.io.ByteArrayInputStream;
import java.io.ByteArrayOutputStream;
import java.io.IOException;
import java.util.Vector;
import java.util.Iterator;
import java.io.CharArrayReader;
import java.io.CharArrayWriter;
import java.io.PrintWriter;
import java.io.PrintStream;

public class StreamsDemo {
  public void simpleStreams() throws IOException {
```

This code constructs two arrays, both with five bytes. The first array has bytes representing the numbers 1 to 5, and the second contains the numbers 6 to 10.

```
byte[] bytes = new byte[5];
byte value = 1;
for (byte b = 0; b < 5; b++) {
  bytes[b] = value++;
}
```

```
        byte[] otherBytes = new byte[5];
        byte value2 = 6;
        for (byte b = 0; b < 5; b++) {
          otherBytes[b] = value2++;
        }
```

Next we construct an output stream, and write some data to it.

```
        ByteArrayOutputStream os = new ByteArrayOutputStream();
```

This illustrates the three different ways in which data can be written to the stream. It writes one byte, representing the number 20, to the stream:

```
        os.write(20);
```

writes the `bytes` byte array to the stream:

```
        os.write(bytes);
```

and writes three bytes from the `otherBytes` array, starting with the byte at position 1 in the array.

```
        os.write(otherBytes, 1, 3);
```

Let's look at an illustration of what's happening:

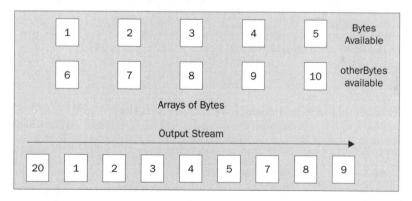

At the top of the figure we see the two arrays of bytes that we constructed. Next we get a reference to an output stream, illustrated as an arrow. Finally, we write some bytes (one which we created directly, and some which we took from our arrays) to the stream.

After we have done this, we can get an input stream, by calling the `simulateSimpleProcess()` method, and passing it the output stream (this is where things become somewhat divorced from reality!). We will return to the `simulateSimpleProcess()` method in a moment.

```
        InputStream is = simulateSimpleProcess(os);
```

To be able to read data from a `ByteArrayInputStream`, we need to construct a new array of bytes into which to read the data. We have already discussed the fact that a major limitation of arrays is the way their size cannot be changed once they have been created. This could cause problems if we are reading from an input stream and have no knowledge of how much data it might contain. Fortunately, the `available()` method of the `InputStream` class returns an `int` representing the number of bytes which can be read from the stream.

```
byte[] newBytes = new byte[is.available()];
is.read(newBytes);
```

This constructs a byte array, initialized to the length of available bytes in the input stream. It then reads from the input stream, into the new array. If we then loop through the elements in this array, we can examine the data:

```
for (int i = 0; i < newBytes.length; i++) {
  System.out.println(newBytes[i]);
}
os.close();
is.close();
```

Finally, we need to close the streams. You should always be careful to close streams after using them, as the resources will not be freed up automatically.

Let's have a look at the `simulateSimpleProcess()` method:

```
public InputStream simulateSimpleProcess(ByteArrayOutputStream bs) {
```

The method calls the `toByteArray()` method of `ByteArrayOutputStream`, which returns the contents of the stream as an array of bytes:

```
byte[] bytes = bs.toByteArray();
```

It then loops through that array and doubles the value of each element in it. Note that the doubled value needs to be cast back to a `byte`, because the compiler will cast `bytes` to `ints` when performing arithmetic operations..

```
for (int i = 0; i < bytes.length; i++) {
  bytes[i] = (byte)(bytes[i] * 2);
}
```

The method then creates a new `ByteArrayInputStream` from the altered array of bytes, which it returns to the calling method: in this case, the `simpleStreams()` method:

```
return new ByteArrayInputStream(bytes);
}
```

If we run this code, it produces the following output:

```
> java StreamsDemo
Simple Streams:
40
2
4
6
8
10
14
16
18
```

We can see that all the values that we wrote to the original output stream have doubled.

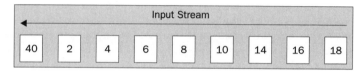

So when the simpleStreams() method reads from the input stream, it accesses the bytes which the simulateSimpleProcess() set in the array.

You may have noticed that the method is declared as throwing an IOException. An IOException signals that some sort of I/O error has occurred. It is thrown by most of the methods that operate on streams, such as methods that read to and write from a stream. For example, a network error when reading from a socket via a stream could cause an IOException to be thrown. In our simple examples, no exceptions should occur, so we are not doing anything special to handle them. In production code, you probably would want to include some code to handle situations like this.

In the real world, the low-level streams that you will probably deal with the most are FileInputStream and FileOutputStream, as covered in Chapter 13.

Let's now move on to filtered streams, which operate on other streams, rather than on raw data.

# Filter Streams

All Java streams are essentially composed of bytes of data, but if we had to retrieve everything from them in the form of bytes, life would be very tedious. If the stream actually represented doubles and booleans, as well it might, then we would have to reconstruct them from the bytes. This is what filter streams exist for: they do exactly that, and therefore do the hard work for us.

The filterStreams() method in the StreamsDemo class shows how to use filter streams. It uses the DataInputStream and DataOutputStream classes, which read and write primitive Java types, such as ints and doubles.

```
public void filterStreams() throws IOException {
```

Filter streams need to be supplied a stream on which to operate, so we start by creating a `ByteArrayOutputStream` as we did before. This can then be passed in to the constructor of the `DataOutputStream` class. This process of supplying one stream to another is called *chaining*. Chains can potentially contain several different streams, each one passed to the next in turn as it is created.

```
ByteArrayOutputStream os = new ByteArrayOutputStream();
DataOutputStream dos = new DataOutputStream(os);
```

Next, three values are written to the stream: a `boolean`, a `double`, and an `int`:

```
dos.writeBoolean(false);
dos.writeDouble(99.99);
dos.writeInt(42);
```

A `DataInputStream` is then retrieved from the `simulateFilterProcess()` method. This actually takes a `DataInputStream` as a parameter, so we need to create one. As with the `DataOutputStream`, it needs to be supplied a stream of its own, so we create a `ByteArrayInputStream` using the contents of our `ByteArrayOutputStream`. Since this is chained to the `DataOutputStream` to which we have written the values, the new data will still be in the original `ByteOutputStream`.

```
DataInputStream dis = simulateFilterProcess(new DataInputStream(
    new ByteArrayInputStream(os.toByteArray())));
```

We then read the values from the stream, in the same order in which we wrote them to the stream, before closing the streams, by closing the last one which was created.

```
System.out.println(dis.readBoolean());
System.out.println(dis.readDouble());
System.out.println(dis.readInt());
dis.close();
}
```

The `simulateFilterProcess()` method, which is called by `filterStreams()`, reads the values from the input stream, in the order they were written to the stream. This of course means the method is making a big assumption about what the input stream contains, and how it can be interpreted, but it is safe to do so in the context of these simple examples. In fact, reading values back in the wrong order will work, and no exceptions will be thrown, but the data read back will be incorrect. For example, reading a `boolean` when we should be reading a wider value (such as an `int`) will throw off all of the data including and following the `boolean`. Therefore, in any streams which are more complex than this example, the developer must be sure that they know and can verify the order of the data.

That aside, the `simulateFilterProcess()` method swaps the value of the `boolean`, and doubles the numeric values. It writes these new values to an output stream, and then returns an input stream that is based on the contents of the output stream:

```
public DataInputStream simulateFilterProcess(DataInputStream dis)
    throws IOException {
boolean b = !dis.readBoolean();
```

```
        double d = dis.readDouble() * 2;
        int i = dis.readInt() * 2;

        ByteArrayOutputStream bytes = new ByteArrayOutputStream();
        DataOutputStream dos = new DataOutputStream(bytes);
        dos.writeBoolean(b);
        dos.writeDouble(d);
        dos.writeInt(i);
        dis.close();
    return new DataInputStream(new ByteArrayInputStream(bytes.toByteArray()));
    }
```

The output from this method is

```
> java StreamsDemo
Filter Streams:
true
199.98
84
```

The boolean value has been swapped, while the numeric values have been doubled.

Passing in between different input and output streams within the same process is of course not likely to happen in the real World, but it is an adequate simulation of how data can be read from and written to streams, and how it might be changed in the process.

Some of the other filter streams that the Java platform provides are:

- ❑ `BufferedInputStream` and `BufferedOutputStream` – These have internal buffers, which means bytes can be read and written in large blocks, to increase efficiency.

- ❑ `PrintStream` – `System.out` and `System.err` are examples of this class. It allows text to be written to the stream. Primitives and objects can also be written to the stream; these will be converted to text.

# Object Streams

Being able to read and write primitive types and text to streams is obviously much more useful than being restricted to bytes. The real power of Java I/O comes from the fact that it is possible to use streams with entire Java objects. Obviously, being able to pass whole objects, with all the data they encapsulate, around your environment, means that you can write some powerful applications, without having to include a large amount of code to deal with the necessary I/O functionality.

We'll look at an example of using objects with streams, and then briefly consider some of the implications of doing so.

## Object Streams Example

The `objectStreams()` method of the `StreamsDemo` class writes a `Vector` to an object stream. It then calls another method to simulate getting an input stream based on the data in the output stream, and examines the input stream to see how the data has changed.

**807**

```
    public void objectStreams() throws IOException {
```

First the `Vector` is created, and objects are added to it. You will remember from earlier that only objects can be added to a `Vector`. This is why the wrapper classes `Boolean`, `Double` and `Integer` are used.

```
    Vector v = new Vector();
    v.add(new Boolean(true));
    v.add(new Double(100.01));
    v.add(new Integer(43));
```

We then create an `ObjectOutputStream`, basing it on a `ByteArrayOutputStream` as before. After the vector has been written to the stream, an `ObjectInputStream` is created, based on the output stream's contents. The input stream is passed to the `simulateObjectProcess()` method, to simulate some system process operating on its contents.

```
    ByteArrayOutputStream os = new ByteArrayOutputStream();
    ObjectOutputStream oos = new ObjectOutputStream(os);
    {
      oos.writeObject(v);
    }
    ObjectInputStream ois = simulateObjectProcess(
      new ObjectInputStream(new ByteArrayInputStream(os.toByteArray())));
    try {
```

Next the `Vector` is read back from the input stream. `ObjectInputStream.readObject()` just returns an `Object` reference, as the objects in the stream could be of any type. So we need to cast the object to a `Vector`, since we know, or at least assume, that that is what it is. If we were wrong, we would get a `ClassCastException` at run-time, but in this little example this will not happen. Once we have the `Vector`, we can loop through its values, using the `iterator()` method which was discussed earlier, and print them out. It is worth noting that even though it was just the `Vector` object which was written to the stream, the objects stored in the `Vector` have been written as well – we didn't have to do anything to get this to happen. This will be revisited in a moment.

```
    v = (Vector)ois.readObject();
    Iterator i = v.iterator();
    while (i.hasNext()) {
      System.out.println(i.next());
    }
  }
```

We need to catch the `ClassNotFoundException`, which would be thrown if the class of the object could not be found.

```
    catch (ClassNotFoundException ex) {
      ex.printStackTrace();
    }
    ois.close();
  }
```

The output of this method is:

```
> java StreamsDemo
Object Streams:
false
200.02
86
```

It seems as if the same thing is happening as before: the `boolean` value is swapped, and the numeric values are doubled. The `simulateObjectProcess()` method confirms this.

It starts by reading the `Vector` from the input stream – which in turn reads the `Boolean`, `Double`, and `Integer` objects from the input stream. Next, the program gets the three elements of the `Vector` (again making large assumptions about what is in the vector, which would probably not be made in normal code!) It changes these values, and sets them back in the `Vector`.

As we discussed earlier, wrapper classes such as `Integer` contain a single immutable value. So, to change the `int` value, which is stored in the `Vector`, we need to create a new `Integer` object, setting its value to be double that of the original `Integer` objects.

```
public ObjectInputStream simulateObjectProcess(ObjectInputStream oos)
   throws IOException {
     try {
       Vector v = (Vector)oos.readObject();
       Boolean b = (Boolean)v.get(0);
       v.set(0, new Boolean(!b.booleanValue()));
       Double d = (Double)v.get(1);
       v.set(1, new Double(d.doubleValue() * 2));
       Integer i = (Integer)v.get(2);
       v.set(2, new Integer(i.intValue() * 2));
```

Once all the values in the `Vector` have been changed, the method writes the `Vector` to an `ObjectOutputStream`, and returns an `ObjectInputStream` based on that output stream's content, in a similar manner to the previous methods. However, what is going on when the object is written to an output stream is slightly more complex than what happens when bytes and other primitives are written.

```
       ByteArrayOutputStream bytes = new ByteArrayOutputStream();
       ObjectOutputStream dos = new ObjectOutputStream(bytes);
       dos.writeObject(v);
       oos.close();
       return new ObjectInputStream(
         new ByteArrayInputStream(bytes.toByteArray()));
     } catch (ClassNotFoundException ex) {
       return null;
     }
   }
```

## Object Serialization

When Java objects are written to output streams, they are **serialized**. Serialization involves using an `ObjectOutputStream` to break down an object's data into a state from which the object can be later reconstituted, or deserialized, using an `ObjectInputStream`.

Not all the data in an object will necessarily be serialized. Static fields, for example, are not serialized, as there is no need for data about them to be saved, since static data is part of the class definition, not the object definition.

On the other hand, if the object being serialized contains references to other objects, then these objects will themselves also be serialized. This was implicitly demonstrated in our example, when the `Boolean`, `Integer` and `Double` objects contained in the `Vector` were still accessible after the `Vector` had been written to the output stream.

Not all objects can be serialized. It would not make sense to serialize output streams themselves, for example. The `FileDescriptor` class, which represents the machine-specific structure of an open file, is another example of class which is not serializable, since deserializing it on another virtual machine would not make sense.

In order for a class to be serializable, it must implement the interface `java.io.Serializable`. This interface does not contain any method declarations: the class must simply declare that it implements it. As a developer, there is nothing else you need to do to be able to write your objects to output streams, and to read them back from input streams. Java takes care of everything for you.

Most core Java classes are serializable, but `Object` itself is not. If it was, then, since every other class ultimately extends it, all classes ever created would be serializable. So the classes you create will not necessarily be serializable, but it is easy to add the capability if you want it, simply by implementing the `Serializable` interface or by extending another `Serializable` class.

From the programmer's point of view then, it would seem that there isn't a great deal to serialization – and indeed there isn't, at least at the initial level. There is of course a lot more which can be said about it, and there are things you can do if you want to override the serialization behavior that Java provides as a default. However, this is not the place to discuss the topic in detail; the API specification is, as always, a good place to start if you want to know more.

However, even at the initial level it is obviously a powerful feature of Java, and very important in network computing. There are two obvious uses for it: one is to pass entire objects across machine boundaries, such as between a client and server, and the other is to save an object's state (to a file, for example) in order that it can be restored later. This means that both data persistence and network communication can be handled by using this simple feature of Java.

# Readers and Writers

It was mentioned earlier that readers and writers are similar to filter streams, and are specialized for reading and writing Unicode. Unicode is a 16-bit character encoding which can represent a huge range of international characters. If the nine most significant bits are all zeros, then the other seven are simply the standard ASCII encoding of the character. If the nine most significant bits are not zeros, then the character is one that is not represented in ASCII.

The `readersAndWriters()` method of the `StreamsDemo` class illustrates how readers and writers can be used.

```
public void readersAndWriters() throws IOException {
```

First, the method creates an array of Unicode chars. It creates a `CharArrayWriter`, which is a low-level writer that writes to a character buffer. It then writes the array to the writer.

```
char[] chars = {'W', 'r', 'o', 'x', ' ', 'P', 'r', 'e', 's', 's'};
CharArrayWriter cw = new CharArrayWriter();
cw.write(chars);
```

The contents of a `CharArrayWriter` can be retrieved using either the `toCharArray()` method, which returns an array of chars, or the `toString()` method, which returns the contents as a `String`. This method gets them as a `String`, and prints them out:

```
System.out.println(cw.toString());
```

The method then creates a `PrintWriter`, passing in the `CharArrayWriter`. The `PrintWriter` class prints representations of text output to a stream, and is an example of a high-level writer – it takes a low-level writer as a parameter in its constructor. The `println()` method writes the system line break to the stream, while the `println()` method with a `String` as a parameter writes the `String` followed by a system line break to the stream. Both these methods are called.

```
PrintWriter pw = new PrintWriter(cw);
pw.println();
pw.println("Arden House");
```

Next the method obtains a reference to a `CharArrayReader` from the `simulateSimpleReader()` method, passing in the `CharArrayWriter`.

```
CharArrayReader cr = simulateSimpleReader(cw);
char[] input = new char[cw.size()];
```

To read from a `CharArrayReader`, you need to supply it with an array of chars. So the method creates one, initialized to the size of the writer. The contents of the `Reader` are read into this new array. The original writer is then cleared of its contents, by calling its `reset()` method. This resets the writer's buffer. The method then writes the new array to the writer, and accesses its contents by calling `toString()`.

```
cr.read(input, 0, cw.size());
cw.reset();
cw.write(input);
System.out.println(cw.toString());
```

Finally, the reader and writer are closed:

```
cw.close();
cr.close();
}
```

The complete output of the method is:

```
> java StreamsDemo
Readers and Writers:
Wrox Press
WROX PRESS
ARDEN HOUSE
```

The first line is the original contents of the writer, after the `char` array has been written to it. The second two lines show the contents of the buffer after an extra line has been added using the `PrintWriter`, and after the `simulateSimpleReader()` method has been called. It appears that the contents of the writer have been changed to upper-case. This is what the `simulateSimpleReader()` method is doing:

```
public CharArrayReader simulateSimpleReader(CharArrayWriter cw) {
    char[] chars = cw.toCharArray();
    for (int i = 0; i < chars.length; i++) {
        chars[i] = Character.toUpperCase(chars[i]);
    }
    return new CharArrayReader(chars);
}
```

It is retrieving the contents of the writer as an array of `chars`, and then simply looping through this and setting all the characters to their uppercase versions.

Although this is not an especially complex or fancy example, it does at least show the basics of how readers and writers work.

Other types of readers and writers that you may encounter are:

❑   `StringReader` and `StringWriter` – A low-level reader and writer which deals with `Strings`

❑   `BufferedReader` and `BufferedWriter` – These are high-level and they have internal buffers to minimize I/O overhead by reading and writing large blocks of data at a time –for example one line at a time – in a similar way to `BufferedInputStream` and `BufferedOutputStream`

❑   `InputStreamReader` and `OutputStreamWriter` – These are also high-level, they convert between bytes and Unicode characters and are used, for example, as a superclass of `FileReader` and `FileWriter` to allow programmers to write text directly to a file

# Sockets

Sockets are low-level communication handles which act as endpoints in a communication between process in a network. Since one of Java's strengths is its support for network computing, and since sockets are the basis for every network protocol used with Java, they are rather a crucial area.

What it is important to understand at this point is that sockets are represented in Java by the `java.net.Socket` class. If you have an instance of this class, then you can use its `getInputStream()` and `getOutputStream()` methods to return a `java.io.InputStream` and `java.io.OutputStream` object respectively.

As we have seen, the more sophisticated filter streams, or readers and writers, can be created using the basic `InputStream` and `OutputStream` objects returned from these methods. This means that the socket's input and output can then be read from and written to using whichever methods from the more sophisticated classes are convenient for and appropriate to the content. So the streams dealt with by a socket can be treated in exactly the same way as you would deal with any other stream.

# Properties

In closing, there is just one class left to look at. This is the `java.util.Properties` class, which ties all the topics covered in this appendix together quite nicely.

`Properties` represent a list of key/value pairs relating information about the environment. These might be things such as the user's region, the location in which files created by the system should be stored, the email address which should be used as the `From` address if any mails are sent by the system, and so on. `Properties` are stored using a string as a key such as `Region`, and a string as the value (for example, `USA`).

`Properties` is a subclass of `Hashtable`, which means that objects of any type can be stored in it. However, it is specialized for storing strings, and therefore provides two new methods to store and retrieve them.

❑ `getProperty(String key)` – Returns the object stored against the specified key or `null` if the property is not found

❑ `setProperty(String key, String value)` – Stores the specified value string against the specified key string

Since `Properties` is a subclass of `Hashtable`, it is perfectly possible to use the `put()` and `get()` methods which store and retrieve objects rather than `Strings`. However, this is strongly discouraged, as the `Properties` object is specifically designed for storing strings, and will not work properly if an attempt is made to store other objects in it. The API documentation gives more details.

`Properties` will usually be stored in files, and so the `Properties` object can be obtained from and written to file streams. Let's look at an example:

```
import java.util.Properties;
import java.io.FileInputStream;
import java.io.FileOutputStream;

public class PropertiesDemo {

  Properties defaults = new Properties();
```

```
   public PropertiesDemo() {
     try {
       FileInputStream props = new FileInputStream("wrox.properties");
       defaults.load(props);
     } catch (java.io.IOException ex) {
       ex.printStackTrace();
     }
   }
```

This class has a `Properties` object as an instance variable. In its constructor, it is populating that object from a file – in this case, the `wrox.properties` file. The class is assuming that the file is in the same place as the class that is looking for it (you will see more about how to access files in different places when File I/O is covered in more detail later on).

The `wrox.properties` file has the following contents:

```
day=Friday
activity.tonight=cinema
activity.tomorrow=restaurant
work.previous=writeChapter
work.next=systemTest(boo)
```

It is conventional to use a dot-separation system in properties files, rather like packages, to group together related properties.

It is also possible to construct an empty `Properties` object, and to write values to it:

```
   public void testProperties() {
     try {
       Properties properties = new Properties(defaults);
       properties.setProperty("day", "Friday");
       properties.setProperty("activity.today", "work");
       properties.setProperty("activity.tomorrow", "rest");

       System.out.println("Activity today is " +
                          properties.getProperty("activity.today"));
     } catch (java.io.IOException ex) {
       ex.printStackTrace();
     }
   }

   public static void main(String[] args) {
     PropertiesDemo demo = new PropertiesDemo();
     demo.testProperties();
   }
```

```
> java PropertiesDemo
Activity today is work
```

Sharp eyes will have spotted that the `Properties` object used here is not actually empty – the `defaults Properties` object, which was constructed earlier, is being passed as a parameter to it. What this does is tell the new `Properties` object to use `defaults` if it cannot find a requested value in itself.

```
System.out.println("Activity tonight is "
                   + properties.getProperty("activity.tonight"));
```

```
> java PropertiesDemo
Activity tonight is cinema
```

This would be useful in situations where you have a core set of properties which are usually used, and a subset of those which need to be overridden for specific users. You can probably see how, together with the internationalization features of Java that we saw in the section of formatting numbers and dates, this makes it easy to write applications in Java that can be switched between users in different regions with no code changes whatsoever.

It is also possible to tell a `Properties` object to return a particular default value, if the requested one does not exist.

```
System.out.println("Activity tomorrow morning is "
                   + properties.getProperty(
                     "activity.tomorrowMorning", "sleep"));
System.out.println("Activity tomorrow is " + properties.getProperty(
                     "activity.tomorrow", "football"));
```

```
> java PropertiesDemo
Activity tomorrow morning is sleep
Activity tomorrow is rest
```

In the first call, the default `sleep` parameter that was passed in is returned, because there is no value for `activity.tomorrowMorning` in either `Properties` object. However, the parameter `football` is not returned, because in the `properties` object the value `rest` is stored for the key `activity.tomorrow`.

As you might imagine, you can save properties to a file as well as loading them from a file. This simply means using a `FileOutputStream` rather than a `FileInputStream`.

```
properties.store(new FileOutputStream("activities.properties"),
                 "Activities");
System.out.println("Properties saved successfully");
```

When the `PropertiesDemo` class runs, it creates a file called `activities.properties`. The file will include the header, was stored as a second parameter, and the time and date at which it was created.

```
#Activities
#Fri Oct 05 09:40:42 GMT 2001
activity.today=work
day=Friday
activity.tomorrow=rest
```

If objects other than strings had been put into the `Properties` object (using the inherited `put()` rather than the `setProperty()` method), storing the object in this way would fail.

As you can probably appreciate, the `Properties` class is a simple one, but can be very effective when it is used in the right way. You will recall that it was mentioned earlier that the storing of reference data in lookup tables on the database, referenced by foreign keys, is not an ideal solution to the problems of internationalization. On the other hand, it is possible to use Java to load different property files depending on a user's locale, and then to extract all the required locale-specific information from the file. The information could be labels to display in the GUI, messages to display to the user, names in different languages for important concepts in your system – the possibilities are endless, and reference data tables become almost redundant. This makes for applications whose power and flexibility is not in proportion with the amount of effort that has to go into making them so!

# Summary

This appendix has given a basic introduction to some of the key areas of functionality provided by the Java platform. We started by considering how often you will use the core Java API classes in everyday programming, and therefore how important it is that you understand how some of the most common ones work. The Java API specification contains a plethora of information, but faced with so many hundreds of classes, it can be difficult sometimes for anyone to know where to start looking for the functionality they require. This appendix has given a few signposts for you to start facing in the right direction.

Firstly we looked at classes that deal with mathematic and numerical functions. Java provides primitive types, which can be processed with maximum efficiency, but sometimes you need to wrap these in Java classes. This might be because you want to use the values with some other object, such as a collection, which only deals with other objects, or because you need to convert between strings and numbers, and back again. Occasionally it might be because you want to encapsulate the absence of a primitive type value, which is not possible using Java primitives since they are always initialized to default values.

We also looked at the different ways in which it is possible to format numbers, and also dates. Both can be formatted in a way that is sensitive to the region of the end user, and the ease with which this can be done is obviously a powerful feature of Java.

We then looked briefly at the `Collections` API, a set of classes that provide more sophisticated data structures than those offered by the simple array. We considered the situations that might make you choose to use one data structure over another, and looked at how to use some of the different types.

Finally, we spent some time examining how I/O is dealt with in Java, using some simple and simulated examples. All I/O is treated as streams of ordered bytes. You have the option of working directly with those bytes (not recommended unless you are overly nostalgic for the days of machine code!), or chaining the basic low-level streams to high-level streams. High-level streams give you a way of dealing with input and output in other forms, such as Java primitives or objects.

We considered some of the implications of using Java objects with streams: namely, that the objects have to be *serialized*. This means that their data is written to a state from which the object can be reconstituted. It also means that any object referenced by the first one must also be serialized. This is obviously a complex and important feature of Java, but fortunately, in most cases, all a developer has to worry about when using it is implementing the interface `java.io.Serializable`.

Finally, we looked at the `java.util.Properties` class, which represents properties used by a system. It ties together the Collections API and I/O operations to form a powerful way of making your applications more flexible.

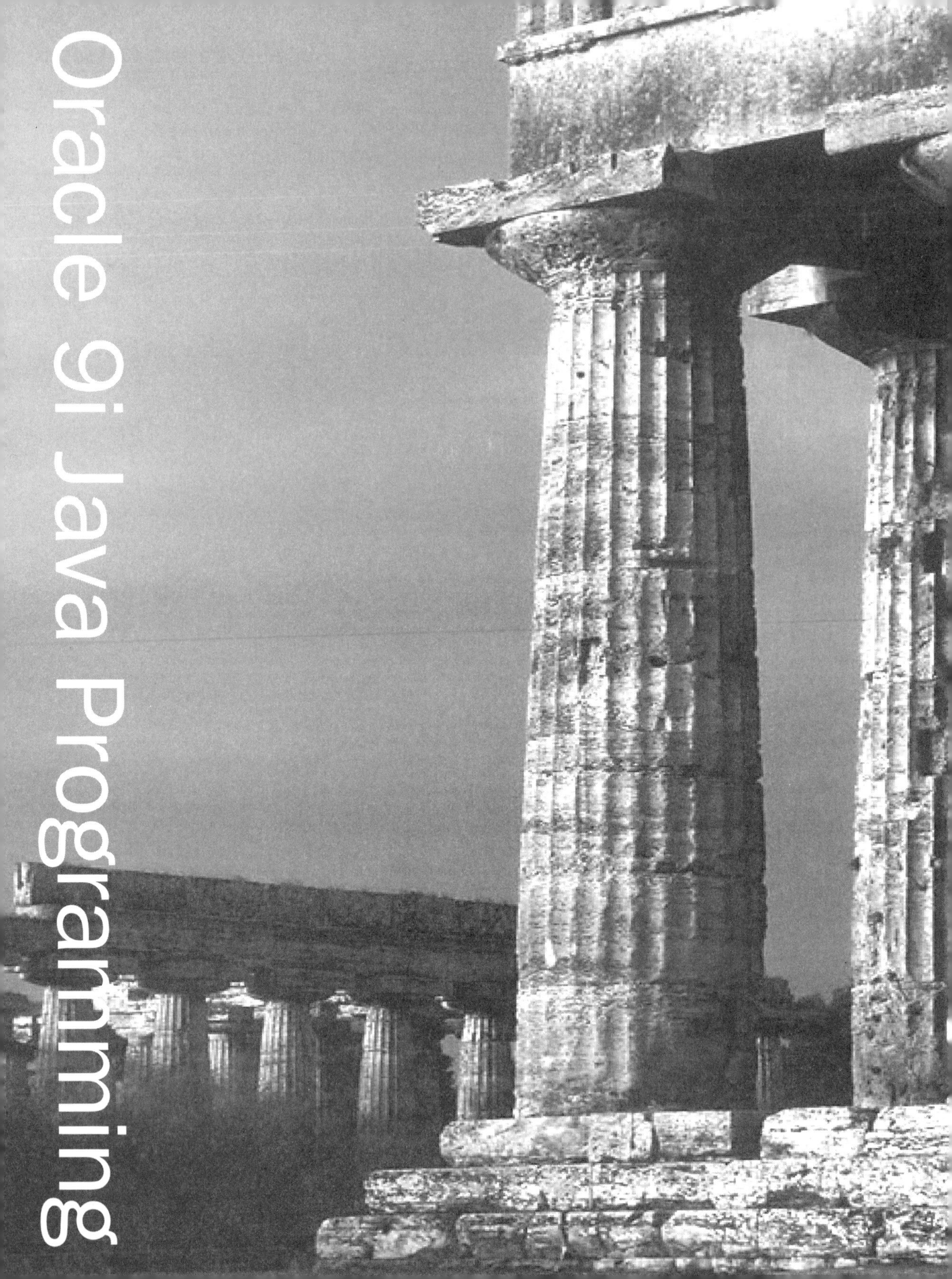
Oracle 9i Java Programming

# The Logging API

If error messages and exceptions are not caught and displayed or logged in some way, then it is quite possible that your program can appear to run successfully when it has actually failed. When working in the database, one way of logging exceptions is to use this **Logging API** that will log down error codes to a database table. The files required for this API are included with the code download for this book.

Basically, the way this class works for debugging and error handling is as follows. If this class was called `Logger`, an application could use it like this:

```
Logger log = Log.getInstance("MyClass");
log.debug("This is debugging information");
log.warning("This is security warning");
log.error("An error occurred!");
log.close();
```

## Setting up the Java Logging API

To set up the Logging API, you must select one schema that should store all the objects. This schema is referred to as `username/password` in the text below. All other users access the logging classes and packages from the specified schema through public synonyms.

Two tables are created, `LOGS` and `LOG_MESSAGES`. For each log you create (each log belonging to a specific application component, for example a Java class), one row is added to the `LOGS` table. Each message you write to the log is added to the `LOG_MESSAGES` table. Only the base user has access to these tables. Other users have access to their own logs through the `MY_LOGS` view. The same rule applies for the actual log messages in the `MY_LOG_MESSAGES` view.

For each application, you can set the log level currently in effect. There are four different log levels available, in the following order (inclusive, so that `INFORMATION` includes both `WARNING` and `ERROR`):

❑   ERROR

❑   WARNING

❑   INFORMATION

❑   DEBUG

Each time you log down a message, you specify the log level associated. The message is actually logged down only if the log level currently in effect is equal to or higher than the specified log level. For example, if the log level is currently set to ERROR, and you specify a DEBUG message, it will not be logged down:

```
Logger lg = LogManager.getInstance().getLogger("My Log");
lg.log("This is a debug message", LogLevel.DEBUG);
```

You can change the log level either through PL/SQL:

```
SQL> call utl_log.set_to_information_level();

Call completed.
```

or Java:

```
LogLevel.setToWarningLevel();
```

You get the current log level with a call to

```
LogLevel.getLogLevel();
```

Now let's run through the set up of the Logging API.

First, you will need to grant the user storing all the objects for the Logging API the abilities to create and drop public synonyms. In this case, we are granting the privileges to a user identified by USERNAME:

```
grant create public synonym to username;
grant drop public synonym to username;
```

Next, create a table to store all the logs:

```
create table logs (
  log_id number not null,
  log_name varchar2(200) not null,
  usr varchar2(200) default user not null,
  constraint pk_logs primary key (log_id)
);
```

On this table, we will need to create a unique index on the username and log name combination. We will be frequently querying for this index:

```
create unique index usr_log_name on logs (usr, log_name);
```

Now we need to create a table to store all the log messages:

```
create table log_messages (
  message_id number not null,
  log_id number not null,
  message_date date default sysdate not null,
  message varchar2(4000) not null,
  log_level varchar2(10) not null,
  usr varchar2(500) default user not null,
  constraint pk_log_messages
    primary key (message_id),
  constraint fk_log_messages_logs
    foreign key (log_id) references logs (log_id)
);
```

and create sequences for the log tables:

```
create sequence log_seq;
create sequence message_seq;
```

We need to create two views now. The first selects all the logs belonging to the current user:

```
create view my_logs as
select * from logs
 where usr = user;
```

and the second selects all the log messages belonging to the current user:

```
create view my_log_messages as
select * from log_messages
 where usr = user;
```

On these views, we need to create public synonyms for them and grant everyone select permissions:

```
create public synonym my_logs for my_logs;
grant select on my_logs to public;
create public synonym my_log_messages for my_log_messages;
grant select on my_log_messages to public;
```

Included in the download for this book is the UTL_LOG PL/SQL package. You now need to create this package as follows:

```
SQL> @utl_log

Package created.


Package body created.
```

On this packages, we need to create public synonyms and grant everyone execute permissions:

```
create public synonym utl_log for utl_log;
grant execute on utl_log to public;
```

We now need to load the Java classes into the database. These should be included as a JAR file and be loaded as follows:

```
> loadjava -user username/password@database -oci8 -resolve -grant PUBLIC -synonym
Logger.jar
```

Once the Java classes have successfully been loaded into the database, you can test whether they work using the following function:

```
SQL> create or replace function log_test
  2  return varchar2
  3  as language java
  4  name 'com.wrox.util.logging.LogTest.test() return java.lang.String';
  5  /

Function created.

SQL> call utl_log.set_to_debug_level();

Call completed.

SQL> call dbms_output.put_line(log_test());
Works fine!

Call completed.

SQL> select count(*) from my_log_messages;

  COUNT(*)
----------
         2
```

If everything works as expected, the last query should return a count of two messages.

You can also SELECT for the log messages in the MY_LOG_MESSAGES table:

```
SQL> column log_name format a15
SQL> column message format a30
SQL> select l.log_name, m.message
  2    from my_logs l, my_log_messages m
  3   where l.log_id = m.log_id;

LOG_NAME        MESSAGE
--------------- ------------------------------
Test            This is an error message
Test            This is debug message
```

Oracle 9i Java Programming

# Index

## A Guide to the Index

The index is arranged hierarchically, in alphabetical order, with symbols preceding the letter A. Most second-level entries and many third-level entries also occur as first-level entries. This is to ensure that users will find the information they require however they choose to search for it.

# P

# S

**wrox**
Programmer to Programmer™

# p2p.wrox.com
## The programmer's resource centre

# A unique free service from Wrox Press
## With the aim of helping programmers to help each other

Wrox Press aims to provide timely and practical information to today's programmer. P2P is a list server offering a host of targeted mailing lists where you can share knowledge with four fellow programmers and find solutions to your problems. Whatever the level of your programming knowledge, and whatever technology you use P2P can provide you with the information you need.

**ASP** Support for beginners and professionals, including a resource page with hundreds of links, and a popular ASP.NET mailing list.

**DATABASES** For database programmers, offering support on SQL Server, mySQL, and Oracle.

**MOBILE** Software development for the mobile market is growing rapidly. We provide lists for the several current standards, including WAP, Windows CE, and Symbian.

**JAVA** A complete set of Java lists, covering beginners, professionals, and server-side programmers (including JSP, servlets and EJBs)

**.NET** Microsoft's new OS platform, covering topics such as ASP.NET, C#, and general .NET discussion.

**VISUAL BASIC** Covers all aspects of VB programming, from programming Office macros to creating components for the .NET platform.

**WEB DESIGN** As web page requirements become more complex, programmer's are taking a more important role in creating web sites. For these programmers, we offer lists covering technologies such as Flash, Coldfusion, and JavaScript.

**XML** Covering all aspects of XML, including XSLT and schemas.

**OPEN SOURCE** Many Open Source topics covered including PHP, Apache, Perl, Linux, Python and more.

**FOREIGN LANGUAGE** Several lists dedicated to Spanish and German speaking programmers, categories include. NET, Java, XML, PHP and XML

How to subscribe
**Simply visit the P2P site, at http://p2p.wrox.com/**